Modern Diffraction and Imaging Techniques in Material Science

Proceedings of the International Summer Course
on Material Science
held at Antwerp, Belgium, 28 July - 8 August 1969
and sponsored by NATO Scientific Affairs Division

Editors:

S. Amelinckx, R. Gevers, G. Remaut, J. Van Landuyt
State University of Antwerp, Belgium

1970

NORTH - HOLLAND PUBLISHING COMPANY • AMSTERDAM - LONDON

Library of Congress Catalog Card Number 70–113747
ISBN North-Holland   7204 0200 x
ISBN American Elsevier 0444 10028 8

Publishers:

NORTH-HOLLAND PUBLISHING COMPANY – AMSTERDAM
NORTH-HOLLAND PUBLISHING COMPANY, LTD. – LONDON

Sole distributors for the U.S.A. and Canada:

AMERICAN ELSEVIER PUBLISHING COMPANY, INC.
52 VANDERBILT AVENUE
NEW YORK, N.Y. 10017

PRINTED IN THE NETHERLANDS

Modern Diffraction
and Imaging Techniques
in Material Science

PREFACE

This book contains the proceedings of a summer school sponsored by NATO and held at the University of Antwerp during the period from July 28th to August 8th, 1969. The objective of the school was to teach at an advanced level the recent developments in "Diffraction and Imaging Techniques" which are increasingly being used in the study of materials.

The school attracted wide interest and a number of applicants had unfortunately to be refused in view of the limited accommodation facilities. It was therefore felt that the proceedings should be published rapidly and in a permanent form making them accessible not only to the participants but also to people which had not been able to attend the course so as to give them an opportunity to benefit from the lectures given by the best experts in their respective fields.

Although the book reflects inevitably the diversity of viewpoints of the different authors, the arrangement of the material is such that it will constitute a consistent treatment requiring a minimum of background knowledge. In most cases this background knowledge is provided in introductory lectures.

The organizing committee is grateful to the different authors for their collaboration in editing this book.

We also gratefully acknowledge the financial help of NATO, and the help of the University of Antwerp in providing the necessary facilities for lecturing and for housing the students.

The Organizing Committee

CONTENTS

...ce only elastic scattering is considered, one has

$$k_o = |\mathbf{k_o}| = |\mathbf{k}| = 1/\lambda \tag{2}$$

λ is the wave length.

...e Bragg law expresses that the scattering amplitudes of the scattering
... by a very large number of scattering centres, arranged at the nodes of
...lar lattice, are perfectly in phase with each other.

...eflection sphere construction

...e Bragg law (1) can be interpreted with the help of the widely used
...d or reflection sphere (see fig. 1). The latter is a sphere with radius $1/\lambda$.
...s its centre and if $\overrightarrow{CO} = \mathbf{k_o}$, then O must be thought to be the origin of
...eciprocal lattice. To any reciprocal lattice node G, defined by the reci-
...l lattice vector $\mathbf{g}$, lying on the reflection sphere, corresponds then a dif-
...ed beam with wave vector $\mathbf{k} = \overrightarrow{CG}$.
...he angle between $\mathbf{k_o}$ and $\mathbf{k}$ is noted as $2\theta_B$, and θ_B is called the Bragg

...Bragg reflection on lattice planes

...n alternative way of interpreting (1) is as follows.
...he reciprocal lattice vector $\mathbf{g}$ can be written as

$$\mathbf{g} = h\mathbf{A} + k\mathbf{B} + l\mathbf{C} \tag{3}$$

...e $\mathbf{A}, \mathbf{B}, \mathbf{C}$ are the base vectors of a unit cell of the reciprocal lattice.

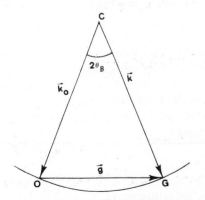

Fig. 1. Reflection sphere construction.

LIST OF CONTRIBUTORS

A.AUTHIER, Minéralogie – Cristallographie, 9, Quai Saint Bernard, Tour 26-O, 2ème étage, Paris (France)

A.BOK, Afdeling Elektronen Optika, T.P.D., T.N.O., Lorentzweg 1, Delft (The Netherlands)

G.BOOKER, Metallurgy Department, Parks Road, Oxford (England)

P.ESTRUP, Physics Department, Brown University, Providence, Rhode Island (U.S.A.)

R.GEVERS, R.U.C.A., Middelheimlaan 1, Antwerp (Belgium)

A.GUINIER, Service de Physique des Solides, Faculté des Sciences, Université de Paris, Orsay (S. & O.) (France)

A.HOWIE, Cavendish Laboratory, Free School Lane, Cambridge (England)

P.HUMBLE, Division of Tribophysics, CSIRO, University of Melbourne, Parkville, N.2, Victoria (Australia)

A.R.LANG, H.H.Wills Physics Laboratory, University of Bristol, Bristol (England)

E.W.MÜLLER, 205, Osmond Laboratory, Pennsylvania State University, University Park, Pennsylvania (U.S.A.)

G.THOMAS, Department of Mineral Technology, University of California, Berkeley, California 94720 (U.S.A.)

C.M.WAYMAN, Department of Mining and Met., University of Illinois, Urbana, Illinois 61801 (U.S.A.)

M.J.WHELAN, Metallurgy Department, University of Oxford, Oxford (England)

M.WILKENS, Max Planck Institut für Metallforschung, 7000 Stuttgart I, Azenbergstrasse 12 (Germany)

KINEMATICAL THEORY OF ELECTRON DIFFRACT

R.GEVERS

1. Introduction

It is well-known that accelerated electrons incident on a sufficie
crystal in a parallel monochromatic beam are not only transmitted
change in direction, but emerge also at the back surface in a numb
crete different directions.

The task of the theory is to calculate the relative number of th
in each of the so-called "diffracted beams".

It is also known that this property is shared by X-ray photons
neutrons, and that the phenomenon is due to the translation syn
crystalline matter. Nevertheless it turns out rapidly that the det:
servations are different for the three types of radiation. This is i
since it allows to gather complementary informations about the
under study by the use of the three different techniques.

1.1. *The Bragg-law*

The common feature of the diffraction of the three differe
particles is the direction of the diffracted beam with respect t
direction and the orientation of the crystal plate. This is rath
is only determined by the translation symmetry of the crysta

The wave vectors $\mathbf{k}_o$ and $\mathbf{k}$ of the incident and the scatte
the well-known Bragg law.

$$\mathbf{k} - \mathbf{k}_o = \mathbf{g}$$

where $\mathbf{g}$ is any reciprocal lattice vector.

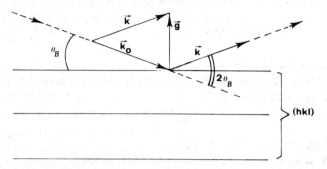

Fig. 2. Schematic representation of the reflection of electrons on a family of lattice planes (hkl). $(\mathbf{g} = h\mathbf{A} + k\mathbf{B} + l\mathbf{C}.)$

The vector $\mathbf{g}$ is then perpendicular to the family of lattice planes with Miller indices (hkl) and its length is a multiple of the reciprocal of its lattice parameter d_{hkl}.

From fig. 2 follows then immediately that (1) expresses that the particles in the beam $\mathbf{k}$ can be considered as obtained by reflection on the lattice planes (hkl). The reflections on the successive planes of the family have to be in perfect phase, and this occurs only if the angle between the incident beam and the lattice plane equals the Bragg angle.

1.4. Condition for diffraction

The Bragg angle is obtained by squaring (1). One finds:

$$k^2 + k_o^2 - 2\mathbf{k} \cdot \mathbf{k}_o = g^2 ,$$

or

$$\frac{1}{\lambda^2}(2 - 2\cos 2\theta_B) = \left(\frac{n}{d_{hkl}}\right)^2 .$$

Finally

$$2d_{hkl} \sin \theta_B = n\lambda , \qquad \sin \theta_B = \frac{n\lambda}{2d_{hkl}} = \frac{g}{2k_o} . \tag{4}$$

One notices immediately that diffraction can only occur if

$$\lambda < 2|d_{hkl}|_{\max} . \tag{5}$$

This condition puts an upper limit to the wave length. There is also a practical lower limit, since the Bragg angles must remain larger than a certain critical value, in order to be observed.

1.5. *Order of magnitude of wave length*

The order of magnitude of λ is of importance for the details of the observations to be expected.

If λ is comparable with $|d_{hkl}|_{max}$ the radius of the reflection sphere and the mesh of the reciprocal lattice have comparable dimensions. This is the case for X-rays and neutrons where wave lengths of the order of magnitude of 1 to 2 Å are used. As a consequence Bragg angles will be not small. For an arbitrary orientation of the crystal with respect to the incident beam, one needs luck to have a reciprocal lattice node on or at least very close to the reflection sphere. One has to imagine methods for bringing reciprocal lattice nodes on this sphere, and only very rarely more than one diffracted beam is observed at the same time. If the diffracted beams are registered, one obtains in general a deformed image of the reciprocal lattice, leading sometimes to indexing problems.

Generally, the incident electrons in electron transmission microscopy have been accelerated by a potential of 100 kV. The corresponding wave length is 37×10^{-3} Å, yielding a value of k_o of about 25 Å^{-1}. This value has to be compared with the mesh of the reciprocal lattice, mostly about hundred times smaller.

A consequence of this relatively small value of λ is that the Bragg angles are small for low index reflections, a few degrees at most. This is an advantageous situation for the electron microscopist, since small deformations in a crystal will lead to local orientation differences of the lattice planes which are not negligibly small as compared to the Bragg angle itself. The induced local and relatively important changes in diffraction conditions make this deformation then visible by a local change in transmitted and diffracted intensity.

Due to the small dimension of the reciprocal lattice as compared to the radius of the reflection sphere, there will always be many reciprocal lattice nodes close to that sphere, giving rise to many diffracted beams at the same time.

In electron transmission microscopy one considers only the Laue case, i.e. all diffracted beams emerge at the back surface of the crystal plate.

Since one has $k_o \cong |\mathbf{k}_o + \mathbf{g}|$ and $k_o \gg g$ for all diffracted beams, all **g**-vectors defining diffracted beams are nearly perpendicular to the incident beam direction. The diffracted beams are obtained by the reflection of electrons on the lattice planes of a same zone, the incident beam being nearly parallel to the zone axis $[uvw]$. If these beams are registered on a photographic plane held normal to the incident beam, one obtains a direct image of this zone of the reciprocal lattice, with negligible deformation since the Bragg angles are small. This zone can be easily indexed, enabling the determination of crystallographic characteristics of the features under observation.

1.6. Strength of the interaction

There is a second possibility for differences to occur for X-ray, neutron- and electron diffraction, namely the different strength of the interaction with the crystalline substance. One must be prepared for significant differences since this interaction is of different nature for the three different types of radiation. Whereas neutrons interact only with the nuclei (if magnetic scattering is not considered), photons only with the electron clouds (the interaction with the heavy nuclei can be neglected), the electrons interact both with the nuclei and with the electron clouds, through strong electrostatic Coulomb forces.

The crystal potential felt by the accelerated electron when passing through the crystal slab, due to the nuclei and the electron clouds, is noted $V(\mathbf{r})$ and it is of course three-dimensionally periodic. It can thus be developed in a Fourier series, following

$$V(\mathbf{r}) = V_o + \sum_{\mathbf{g}} V_{\mathbf{g}} \exp i2\pi \mathbf{g} \cdot \mathbf{r} \tag{6}$$

where the sum runs over all reciprocal lattice vectors. The Fourier coefficients can be computed with the help of the wave functions of the atoms and ions making up the crystal. The mean potential V_o can be estimated to lie mostly in the range of 10–20 V, and it is responsible for the refraction of the incident beam when entering and leaving the crystal. Since V_o is very small as compared to 100 kV (the accelerating potential), this effect is very small and can mostly be neglected.

The fluctuations around this mean potential are described by the further Fourier coefficients $V_{\mathbf{g}}$ which can be estimated to be a few volts for low index $\mathbf{g}$.

Each term of (6) is responsible for a reflection on a family of lattice planes. The coefficient $|V_{\mathbf{g}}|$ is small as compared to the accelerating potential, but there is a very large number of scattering centres. Therefore, for a favourable phase relationship, i.e. if one satisfied nearly (1), one can nevertheless expect strong diffraction. This will be shown in the next sections.

The main consequence is that one has to take dynamical interaction into account. This means that one can mostly not neglect the possibility that an electron is scattered many times, when passing through the crystal. This will be discussed in detail by Professor Whelan.

The electron-crystal interaction is also too strong to overlook the inelastic scattering events by which phonons, plasmons, X-rays a.s.o. are created. This leads to the so-called absorption effect, also to be discussed in other contributions. This effect is responsible for the fact that the crystal plate has to be sufficiently thin, say thinner than 1.000 to 2.000Å for 100 keV-electrons, in order to remain transparent for the electrons.

1.7. *Deviation from the exact Bragg orientation*

Due to the small thickness of the crystal and to the dynamical interactions, the intensities of the different diffracted beams can remain appreciable even if one deviates rather drastically from the condition (1), called the exact condition for Bragg reflection. Therefore, one has to introduce a parameter which describes this deviation adequately. One chooses the distance s_g from the reciprocal lattice point G to the reflection sphere, perpendicular to the entrance

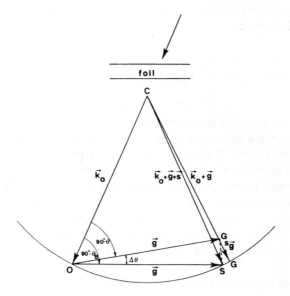

Fig. 3. Reflection sphere construction illustrating the geometrical relationship between s_g, $\mathbf{g}$, and θ, θ_B for the case $s_g > 0$; for $k_0 \gg g \gg s_g$, one has OG $\cong$ OS and CS $\cong$ CG.

surface of the crystal plate, measured in the direction of propagation of the electrons (fig. 3).

This parameter s_g is called the deviation from the exact Bragg orientation, or also the excitation error.

There are two possiblities (1) $s_g > 0$, i.e. the reciprocal lattice node G lies inside the reflection sphere, (2) $s_g < 0$, i.e. it lies outside the sphere. In the first case the angle θ formed by the incident beam and the reflection planes is larger than the Bragg-angle θ_B (fig. 3); in the second case one has $\theta < \theta_B$.

Noting

$$\Delta\theta = \theta - \theta_B \tag{7}$$

one has for small s values, in good approximation

$$\Delta\theta = s_g/g \tag{8}$$

as can be derived from fig. 3.

2. The kinematical approach

2.1. *The kinematical assumptions*

The kinematical treatment is the most simple approach for calculating the amplitudes of the different beams. It involves, however, very daring assumptions, the validity of which must be controlled afterwards. They are:

(1) An electron can only be scattered once;

(2) The depletion of the incident beam when progressing into the crystal can be ignored.

It is clear that one can only hope that these approximations are good, if t! scattering is sufficiently weak. One has only to find out what "sufficiently" means here.

Since one does not allow an electron to be scattered more than once, i.e. one assumes that these events are so rare that they can be ignored, no dynamical interaction between beams are taken into account.

2.2. *Schrödinger equation – Born approximation*

The usual kinematical treatment, as performed in the case of X-rays and neutrons, consist in considering the scattering by each individual scattering centre arranged on a lattice, and by summing up the amplitudes of the events, taking their phase-relationship into account.

However, we prefer to develop for the case of electrons, a different but equivalent method, showing clearly how the extension to the dynamical situation must be made. This method is the Born approximation applied to the Schrödinger equation describing the movement of the accelerated electron in the crystal. For an electron with kinetic energy much higher than the energies of the electrons of the crystal it is a good approximation to consider it as moving in the given crystal potential $V(\mathbf{r})$ defined by (6) (no inelastic scattering is considered). Its wave function ψ satisfies the Schrödinger equation

$$\left[-\frac{h^2}{8\pi^2 m}\Delta - eV(\mathbf{r})\right]\psi = eE\psi \tag{9}$$

where m is the electron mass; $-e$ is the electronic charge $(e>0)$; h is Planck's constant; E is the accelerating potential $(E>0)$. Since the mean interaction is attractive, $-eV_0 < 0$, i.e. V_0 is defined as positive. By putting

$$E' = E + V_0, \qquad eE' = \frac{h^2 k_0^2}{2m}, \qquad (k_0 = 1/\lambda) \tag{10},(11)$$

one can rewrite (9) as follows

$$\Delta\psi + 4\pi^2 k_0^2\,\psi = -\frac{8\pi^2 me}{h^2}\,V'(\mathbf{r})\,\psi \tag{12}$$

with

$$V'(\mathbf{r}) = V(\mathbf{r}) - V_0. \tag{13}$$

The parameter k_0 is the magnitude of the wave vector of the incident wave corrected for refraction. Introducing the further notation

$$U(\mathbf{r}) = \frac{2me}{h^2}\,V'(\mathbf{r}) \tag{14}$$

or

$$U(\mathbf{r}) = \sum_{\mathbf{g}} U_{\mathbf{g}} \exp i2\pi \mathbf{g} \cdot \mathbf{r},$$

$$U_{\mathbf{g}} = \frac{2me}{h^2} U_{\mathbf{g}}, \qquad U_0 = 0 \qquad\qquad (15),(16)$$

one obtains finally the Schrodinger equation in the following form

$$\Delta\psi + 4\pi^2 k_0^2\psi = -4\pi^2 U(\mathbf{r})\,\psi . \qquad\qquad (17)$$

If one ignores the scattering, i.e. one neglects the second member, the integral of (17) is

$$\psi_0 = \exp i2\pi \mathbf{k}_0 \cdot \mathbf{r} \qquad\qquad (18)$$

the wave function describing the incident beam with wave vector $\mathbf{k}_0$ (corrected for refraction).

As well known, the Born approximation consist in replacing ψ in the second member by ψ_0, i.e. the wave function unperturbed by the perturbation potential. It is clear that the term $U\psi_0$ in the second member describes now only electrons scattered out of the incident beam ψ_0, which moreover is not influenced by the scattering. These are nothing else than the kinematical assumptions. One has thus to consider the equation

$$\Delta\psi + 4\pi^2 k_0^2\psi = -4\pi^2 U(\mathbf{r})\,\psi_0 \qquad\qquad (19)$$

or, more explicitely:

$$\Delta\psi + 4\pi^2 k_0^2\psi = -4\pi^2 \sum_{\mathbf{g}} V_{\mathbf{g}} \exp i2\pi(\mathbf{k}_0 + \mathbf{g}) \cdot \mathbf{r} . \qquad\qquad (20)$$

From the theory of linear, unhomogeneous differential equations it follows that the integral of (20) is given by

$$\psi = \psi_0 + \sum_{\mathbf{g}} \psi_{\mathbf{g}}$$

where ψ_g must satisfy the equation

$$\Delta\psi_g + 4\pi^2 k_o^2 \psi_g = -4\pi^2 U_g \exp i2\pi(\mathbf{k}_o+\mathbf{g})\cdot\mathbf{r} \tag{21}$$

with the boundary condition that ψ_g must vanish at the entrance surface.

Each ψ_g represents one of the diffracted beams, the beam **g**, *inside* the crystal. The linear structure of (19) results in the independence of the different beams, as should be in a kinematical treatment.

One can always substitute:

$$\psi_g(\mathbf{r}) = \phi_g(\mathbf{r}) \exp i2\pi(\mathbf{k}_o+\mathbf{g})\cdot\mathbf{r} . \tag{22}$$

Before proceeding to further calculations, we first stress the meaning of (22). One can always write for $\phi_g(\mathbf{r})$.

$$\phi_g(\mathbf{r}) = \int A(\boldsymbol{\sigma}) (\exp i2\pi\boldsymbol{\sigma}\cdot\mathbf{r}) d^3\sigma \tag{23}$$

where $A(\boldsymbol{\sigma})$ in the Fourier transform of $\phi_g(\mathbf{r})$. Introducing (23) into (22) gives

$$\psi_g = \int A(\boldsymbol{\sigma}) [\exp i2\pi(\mathbf{k}_o+\mathbf{g}+\boldsymbol{\sigma})\cdot\mathbf{r}] d^3\sigma . \tag{24}$$

The physical meaning of (24) is straight-forward: the total diffracted beam **g** is obtained by the superposition of different plane waves, with wave vectors $(\mathbf{k}_o+\mathbf{g}+\boldsymbol{\sigma})$ and amplitudes $A(\boldsymbol{\sigma})$. One expects of course that the σ-values for which $|A(\boldsymbol{\sigma})|$ is non zero or non negligible will be small as compared to the dimensions of the reciprocal lattice.

One can now calculate either $A(\boldsymbol{\sigma})$ or $\phi_g(\mathbf{r})$. It will turn out that the calculation of ϕ_g is more easy. Once ψ_g known, $A(\boldsymbol{\sigma})$ can be obtained by Fourier transformation. Since

$$\Delta[\phi_g \exp \exp i2\pi(\mathbf{k}_o+\mathbf{g})\cdot\mathbf{r}] = [\Delta\phi_g] \exp i2\pi(\mathbf{k}_o+\mathbf{g})\cdot\mathbf{r} + 2 \operatorname{grad} \phi_g$$

$$\times \operatorname{grad} [\exp i2\pi(\mathbf{k}_o+\mathbf{g})\cdot\mathbf{r}] + \phi_g[\Delta \exp i2\pi(\mathbf{k}_o+\mathbf{g})\cdot\mathbf{r}]$$

and

$$\operatorname{grad} [\exp i2\pi(\mathbf{k}_o+\mathbf{g})\cdot\mathbf{r}] = i2\pi(\mathbf{k}_o+\mathbf{g}) [\exp i2\pi(\mathbf{k}_o+\mathbf{g})\cdot\mathbf{r}]$$

$$\Delta \exp i2\pi(\mathbf{k}_o+\mathbf{g})\cdot\mathbf{r} = -4\pi^2(\mathbf{k}_o+\mathbf{g})^2 \exp i2\pi(\mathbf{k}_o+\mathbf{g})\cdot\mathbf{r}$$

one has

$$\Delta\phi_g \left[\exp i2\pi(k_o+g)\cdot r\right] = [\Delta\phi_g + i4\pi(k_o+g)$$

$$\text{grad } \phi_g - 4\pi^2(k_o+g)^2\phi_g] \left[\exp i2\pi(k_o+g)\cdot r\right] . \tag{25}$$

Introducing (25) into (21), one obtains, after deviding the two numbers of the equation by $\exp i2\pi(k_o+g)\cdot r$

$$\Delta\phi_g + i4\pi(k_o+g)\cdot \text{grad } \phi_g + 4\pi^2[k_o^2 - (k_o+g)^2]\,\phi_g = -4\pi^2 U_g \tag{26}$$

Let us choose the z-axis along the normal of the entrance surface, in the sense of propagation of the electrons, and the x- and y-axis in the entrance surface. Moreover, we choose the x-axis along the projection of (k_o+g) on the entrance surface. One has then

$$(k_o+g) \cdot \text{grad } \phi_g = [(k_o+g) \cdot e_z]\,\frac{\partial\phi_g}{\partial z} + [(k_o+g)\cdot e_x]\,\frac{\partial\phi_g}{\partial x}$$

or if α in the angle between $k_o + g$ and e_z

$$(k_o+g) \cdot \text{grad } \phi_g = |k_o+g|\left(\cos\alpha\,\frac{\partial\phi_g}{\partial z} + \sin\alpha\,\frac{\partial\phi_g}{\partial x}\right). \tag{27}$$

Next, one introduces a further, but very good, approximation into (26). Since $|k_o+g|$ is very large, it will be very good to neglect the first term with respect to the second one. This approximation will be further discussed in other contributions. In one introduces this approximation into (26), and substitutes then (27) into (26) and devides the two members by $i4\pi|k_o+g|\cos\alpha$, one finds

$$\frac{\partial\phi_g}{\partial z} + \tan\alpha\,\frac{\partial\phi_g}{\partial x} - i2\pi\,\frac{k_o^2-(k_o+g)^2}{2|k_o+g|\cos\alpha}\,\phi_g = i\pi\,\frac{U_g}{|k_o+g|\cos\alpha} . \tag{28}$$

2.3. Discussion of the parameters appearing in the equation

Let us now consider the two parameters showing up in (28). From the reflection sphere construction of fig. 4, it follows that

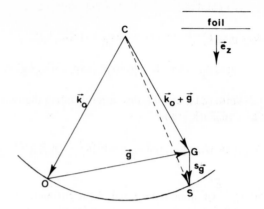

Fig. 4. Construction used for calculating s_g and showing that $|\mathbf{k_o}+\mathbf{g}+s_g\mathbf{e_z}| = k_o$.

$$(\mathbf{k_o}+\mathbf{g}+s_g\mathbf{e_z})^2 = k_o^2 ,$$

or

$$(\mathbf{k_o}+\mathbf{g})^2 - 2s_g|\mathbf{k_o}+\mathbf{g}| \cos\alpha + s_g^2 = k_o^2 .$$

The deviation parameter s_g is smaller than the dimension of the reciprocal lattice, and, a fortiori, very much smallr than $|\mathbf{k_o}+\mathbf{g}| \cong k_o$. Therefore the third term can be neglected with respect to the second one. One finds then

$$s_g = \frac{k_o^2 - (\mathbf{k_o}+\mathbf{g})^2}{2|\mathbf{k_o}+\mathbf{g}| \cos\alpha} . \tag{29}$$

The second parameter has the dimension of a reciprocal length, and one can define

$$\frac{1}{\xi_g} = \frac{|U_g|}{|\mathbf{k_o}+\mathbf{g}| \cos\alpha} . \tag{30}$$

Taking (16) into account one finds explicitly for ξ_g

$$\xi_g = \frac{h^2|\mathbf{k_o}+\mathbf{g}| \cos\alpha}{2me} \frac{1}{|V_g|} . \tag{31}$$

Since $k_0 \gg g$, it is a good approximation to put now

$$|\mathbf{k_0 + g}| \simeq k_0 .$$

Then

$$\xi_g = \frac{h^2 k_0 \cos \alpha}{2me \ |V_g|} . \tag{32}$$

Taking (10),(11) into account, one can also write for ξ_g

$$\xi_g = \frac{1}{k_0} \frac{E' \cos \alpha}{|V_g|} \sim \frac{\lambda E \cos \alpha}{|V_g|} . \tag{33}$$

The parameters ξ_g (for $\cos \alpha \simeq 1$) are called the *extinction distances*.

Whereas the s_g-values describe the illumination conditions, i.e. the orientation of the crystal with respect to the incident beam, the extinction distances depend on the strength of the different reflections.

A strong interaction, i.e. $|V_g|$ is large, corresponds to a small extinction distance, whereas a weak interaction gives rise to a large extinction distance.

The parameters ξ_g depend also on the accelerating potential, they increase with E (like $E^{1/2}$ if relativistic corrections are left out). This corresponds to the classical fact that more accelerated particles are less deflected by the same potential. Bringing into (33) estimated values for $|V_g|$, leads to ξ_g values for low order reflections and for 100 keV-electrons, ranging from about hundred Å to about thousand Å. The extinction distances will be further discussed in other contributions.

2.4. Integration of the equation
Noting further

$$V_g = |V_g| \ \exp i\theta_g \tag{34}$$

one can rewrite (28) as, if one introduces (29) and (30)

$$\frac{\partial \phi_g}{\partial z} + \tan \alpha \ \frac{\partial \phi_g}{\partial x} - i2\pi \ s_g \phi_g = \frac{i\pi}{\xi_g} \exp i\phi_g . \tag{35}$$

If one considers a plate-shaped foil, there is no reason why ϕ_g should depend on x, i.e.

$$\frac{\partial \phi_g}{\partial x} = 0 \quad \text{and} \quad \frac{\partial \phi_g}{\partial z} = \frac{d\phi_g}{dz} .$$

The eq. (35) becomes then

$$\frac{d\phi_g}{dz} - i2\pi \, s_g \phi_g = \frac{i\pi}{\pi_g} \exp i\theta_g . \tag{36}$$

If one substitutes

$$\phi_g = S_g \, (\exp i2\pi \, s_g z) \tag{37}$$

one has finally

$$\frac{dS_g}{dz} = \frac{i\pi}{\xi_g} (\exp i\theta_g)(\exp -i2\pi \, s_g z) . \tag{38}$$

After integration, taking the boundary condition $S_g(0) = 0$ into account, one finds (the entrance surface is at $z=0$)

$$S_g = \frac{i\pi}{\xi_g} (\exp i\theta_g) \int_0^z (\exp -i2\pi \, s_g z) dz .$$

Finally

$$S_g = (\exp i\theta_g)(\exp -i\pi \, s_g z) \frac{i \sin \pi \, s_g z}{s_g \xi_g} \tag{39}$$

or

$$\phi_g = (\exp i\theta_g)(\exp i\pi \, s_g z) \frac{i \sin \pi \, s_g z}{s_g \xi_g} . \tag{40}$$

3. Discussion of the kinematical results

3.1. *Variation of the intensity with crystal thickness*
The intensity

$$I_g = |\phi_g|^2 = \frac{\sin^2 \pi \, s_g z_0}{(s_g \xi_g)^2} \tag{41}$$

(z_0 is crystal thickness), gives the number of electrons leaving the back surface per unit surface and per unit time for unit incident beam (for simplicity we have assumed that $\cos \alpha \simeq 1$). This result can however, only be trusted if $I_g \ll 1$, since one has assumed the depletion of the transmitted beam to be not important.

Let us first suppose that s_g is fixed but that z_0 increases. The diffracted intensity varies then in a period way, the depth-period Δz_0 being given by

$$\Delta z_0 = 1/s_g . \tag{42}$$

For $z_0 = n/s_g$ (n : integer), I_g vanishes, whilst I_g becomes maximal for thicknesses $z_0 = (n+\frac{1}{2})/s_g$ (fig. 5). Furthermore

$$I_g (z_0)_{max} = \frac{1}{(s_g \xi_g)^2} . \tag{43}$$

The fluctuating behaviour of the intensity with crystal thickness is a consequence of the interference of the two plane waves which form inside the crystal the total diffracted beam. From (40) follows that

$$\psi_g = \phi_g \exp i 2\pi (\mathbf{k}_0 + \mathbf{g}) \cdot \mathbf{r} = \frac{\exp i \theta_g}{2 s_g \xi_g} (\exp i 2\pi (\mathbf{k}_0 + \mathbf{g} + s e_z) \cdot \mathbf{r}$$
$$- \exp i 2\pi (\mathbf{k}_0 + \mathbf{g}) \cdot \mathbf{r}] . \tag{44}$$

The two plane waves have wave vectors $(\mathbf{k}_0 + \mathbf{g} + s e_z)$ and $\mathbf{k}_0 + \mathbf{g}$, and opposite amplitudes. The $A(\sigma)$-function from formulae (23) is thus

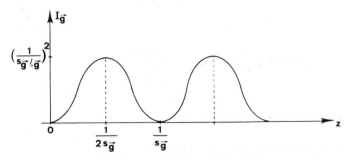

Fig. 5. Periodical variation of the intensity of the diffracted beam I_g as a function of crystal thickness z.

$$A(\sigma) = A\delta(\sigma - se_z) - A\delta(\sigma) \; ,$$

$$A = \frac{\exp i\theta_g}{2s_g\xi_g} \; . \tag{45}$$

For a plate-shaped parallel foil these two plane waves combine again into a single plane wave at the back surface, the diffracted beam outside the foil, with wave vector $k_o + g + se_z$ and amplitude S_g as a consequence of the continuity of the wave function at that surface.

3.2. *Variation of the intensity with crystal orientation*

Next we keep the crystal thickness constant, but increase the deviation from the exact Bragg orientation. Since $I_g(s_g)$ is an even function of s_g we can restrict ourselves to $s_g > 0$, i.e. the scattering angle is larger than $2\theta_B$.

The intensity I_g has its maximum value for $s_g = 0$, i.e. at the exact Bragg orientation and is then given by

$$I_g(s_g = 0) = (\pi z_o/\xi_g)^2 \; . \tag{46}$$

If one leaves the exact orientation, I_g will decrease rapidly and will obtain its absolute minimum value zero for

$$s_g = 1/z_o \; . \tag{47}$$

If s_g increases further, I_g fluctuates, becoming zero for

$$s_g = n/z_o \qquad (n, \text{integer}) \tag{48}$$

and having maxima approximately halfway between two successive minima, i.e. for

$$s_g = (n + \tfrac{3}{2})/z_o \qquad (n = 0,1,2,...) \; . \tag{49}$$

These maxima decrease with k, approximately like

$$I_g(s_g)\big|_{\max} \simeq \frac{1}{(s_g\xi_g)^2} = \left(\frac{z_o}{\xi_g}\frac{1}{n + \tfrac{3}{2}}\right)^2 \; . \tag{50}$$

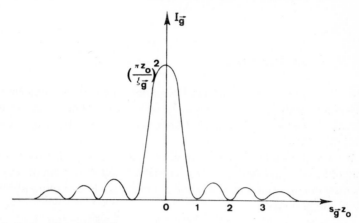

Fig. 6. Schematic graph of the variation of the intensity of the diffracted beam I_g as a function of crystal orientation.

These subsidiary maxima are much smaller than the main maximum at $s_g = 0$, e.g.

$$\frac{I_g(n=0)}{I_g(s_g=0)} = \left(\frac{\tfrac{2}{3}z_0/\xi_g}{\pi z_0/\xi_g}\right)^2 = \frac{4}{9\pi^2} \simeq 0.04 \,.$$

See also fig. 6.

3.3. Validity of the kinematical theory

For the discussion of this section it is better to express the crystal thickness in extinction distances. Let

$$z_0 = y\xi_g \,. \tag{51}$$

The condition for the validity of the kinematical approach is

$$I_g \ll 1 \tag{52}$$

since one must respect the assumption that the depletion of the transmitted beam is not very important. Is it possible that the approximation remains good up to $s_g = 0$? If yes, one must satisfy the condition, following (52), (46), (51)

$$\pi^2 y^2 \ll 1 , \quad \text{or} \quad y \ll 1/\pi$$

say at least

$$y < 1/3\pi \simeq 0.1 .$$

This is in most cases a very stringent condition, and it is only satisfied for very thin crystals of less than about one tenth of an extinction distance. For low order reflections this means thicknesses from a few times $10\,\text{Å}$ to something like $100\,\text{Å}$.

It is possible that a crystal has to be considered as very thin for one reflection, but not for another one. If the crystal is tilted away from the exact Bragg orientation into a position of a subsidiary maxima, the condition is much released and becomes

$$y^2 \ll (n+\tfrac{3}{2})^2 .$$

For a thin crystal, say $y = \frac{1}{2}$, this condition is fairly well satisfied for the first subsidiary maximum ($n=0$). However, for a thick crystal, say $y = 4$, one can only satisfy the condition for very large n-values; the kinematical theory breaks down completely. The kinematical theory can only be accepted as a first approximation

(1) if the crystal is very thin: there are then not enough scattering centres to build up an important diffracted beam.

(2) if the crystal is far from the exact Bragg orientation.

The scattering events with the different scattering centres are so strongly out of phase that the mutual partial annihilation of the scattered wavelets prevents the construction of a strong diffracted beam.

In all other cases an important diffracted beam will already be built up at a depth under the entrance surface still far from the back surface. From (46) follows that one can expect ξ_g to be a measure for this depth.

Electrons which have been scattered from the transmitted beam k_o-direction into the scattered beam (k_o+g)-direction, can later equally be scattered back into the former direction. One can ignore this only if there are only few electrons in the scattered beam. Our discussion learns that this will mostly not be the case. The kinematical theory must be replaced by the more refined dynamical one, taking into account that electrons can be scattered many times between transmitted and scattered beam, and possibly between different scattered beams, before leaving the crystal at the back side. This will be discussed in detail in the lectures by Professor Whelan and by Professor Howie.

3.4. *Relevant features of the kinematical theory*
3.4.1. Introduction

As will be pointed out in the lectures of Professor Whelan, it is possible to realize a so-called "two beam" situation. By this is meant that there is, apart from the transmitted beam, only one strongly diffracted beam **g**. It becomes then a good approximation to neglect the weaker beams.

The results of this dynamical "two-beam" theory must tend asymptotically to those of the kinematical theory if $|s_g|$ becomes large. The qualitative properties predicted by the latter theory, must remain true for small $|s_g|$-values, although important quantitative corrections will become necessary.

3.4.2. Variation with crystal thickness

The kinematical treatment predicted a periodic variation of the intensity of the scattered beam, and thus also of the transmitted beam, with crystal thickness, the depth-period being $|1/s_g|$. The more refined dynamical theory must lead to the same qualitative conclusion: a periodic variation of intensity with thickness. The period will be a function of s_g tending asymptotically to $|1/s_g|$ for large $|s_g|$. For small $|s_g|$ it must deviate strongly from the kinematical result since the latter diverges if s tends to zero. Moreover, one suspects that the period for $s_g = 0$ will be a simple function of ξ_g.

The maxima of I_g, as given by (43) diverge for $s_g \rightarrow 0$. One expects drastic dynamical corrections for small $|s_g|$. It is even plausible that the diffracted beam can become very important at certain thicknesses, resulting in a completely or nearly completely exhausted transmitted beam.

3.4.3. Variation with crystal orientation

The subsidiary maxima of the kinematical expression for the intensity lie approximately on the curve

$$I(s) = 1/(s\xi)^2 . \tag{53}$$

which diverge for $s = 0$. For $s = 0$ itself I equals $(\pi z_0/\xi)^2$. In general this curve will rise very much above one, and $I(s=0) \gg 1$. This can not be, and, consequently, the dynamical treatment must lower this curve very strongly, in order to bring it completely under the value one. However, for large $|s|$ the correct curve must tend to the kinematical one, given by (53). This enables us to estimate roughly the width of this curve, i.e. the interval for the deviation from the exact Bragg position for which the scattered intensity at the positions for maximal scattering is not yet negligible with respect to one. Somewhat arbitrarily we choose $I = 0.1$ as a limit. From (53) follows that $I(s)$ will become smaller than about one tenth of the incident intensity for orientations

$$|s| > \sim 3/\xi . \tag{54}$$

Following (8) this corresponds to a deviation from the exact Bragg angle given by

$$|\Delta\theta| > \sim 3/g\xi = \Delta\theta_o . \tag{55}$$

On the other hand the Bragg angle is given by, following (4)

$$\sin \theta_B = \theta_B = g/2k_o . \tag{56}$$

From (56) and (55) one calculates:

$$\Delta\theta_o/\theta_B \cong \sim 6k_o/g\xi . \tag{57}$$

If one introduces in (57) realistic values for low order reflections, say $k_o = 25 \text{Å}^{-1}, g^2 = 3 \times 10^{-1} \text{Å}^{-2}, \xi = 3 \times 10^2 \text{Å}$, one finds that $\Delta\theta_o/\theta_\Delta$ is of the order of magnitude of one. One concludes thus that the scattered intensity can remain important even for deviations from the Bragg angle comparable with this angle itself. For accelerated electrons one has not to satisfy strictly the Bragg-condition (1), in order to obtain important scattered beams. Stated otherwise: the reciprocal lattices nodes must not lie strictly on the reflection sphere. This, together with the fact that the radius of this sphere is large as compared to the dimensions of the reciprocal lattice, leads to the appearance of many scattered beams of a same zone obtained from the transmitted beam. Moreover, the scattered beams for which $|s_g|$ is small can become very important inside the crystal. Electrons can then be scattered out of these beams into other weaker beams directions. The discussion of this multiple beam effect falls beyond the scope of this lecture and will be treated elsewhere.

The kinematical treatment led to the prediction that the subsidiary maxima were much lower than the main maximum at $s = 0$. This can no longer be expected from a dynamical treatment, since the unreasonable kinematical value of $I(0)$ will be suppressed to a value below one. If $|s|$ increases one expects still that $I(s)$ will fluctuate. However, for thick crystals the values of the maxima will vary rather slowly. Many fluctuations can be expected before the scattered intensity becomes very small. The dynamical treatment will introduce important corrections for the positions of maxima and minima, and for the values of the maxima, for small $|s|$.

3.4.4. Conclusion

The foregoing discussion of the kinematical treatment demonstrates that one can not accept its quantitative results, except if the crystal is very thin, or if the crystal orientation is very far from the exact Bragg orientation.

Nevertheless, its qualitative predictions have to remain true in a more realistic two-beam dynamical treatment: the periodic dependence of the intensity with varying crystal orientation.

One is not also warned that dynamical interaction will be important, but also that multiple beam effects can become important.

We propose to call the kinematical theory, as discussed in these first two lectures, the "one-beam" kinematical theory, since it describes scattering of electrons out of a single beam.

In the last of our lectures we will consider a more general kinematical theory, and which does lead to results which can be realistic, in good approximation.

Before that, we indicate in the next section how the scattered intensities have to be calculated for a deformed crystal, in particular for crystals containing defects.

4. Deformed crystals

Hirsch, Howie and Whelan [1] have first introduced the following elegant way for treating the diffraction by a deformed crystal.

These authors assumed that the deformation could be described by a displacement function $R(r)$, the deviation of an elementary volume element from its normal position at r.

For small R one has then as a good approximation

$$V'(r+R) \equiv V(r) , \quad \text{for all } r$$

where V' is the crystal potential in the deformed crystal, or

$$V'(r) \equiv V(r-R) . \tag{58}$$

If one introduces (6) into (58) one obtains

$$V'(r) = V_0 + \sum_g V_g \exp i2\pi g \cdot (r-R)$$

or

$$V'(\mathbf{r}) = V_0 + \sum_g [V_g \exp -i2\pi\mathbf{g}\cdot\mathbf{R}(\mathbf{r})] \, [\exp i2\pi\mathbf{g}\cdot\mathbf{r}] \, . \tag{59}$$

Strictly speaking, the series (59) is no longer a Fourier series, since the coefficients have become functions of $\mathbf{r}$. This is due to the disturbance of the perfect translation symmetry of the crystal. For small $\mathbf{R}$, however, one can still justify the reasoning of section 2, and one obtains the same result provided one makes the substitution

$$U_g \rightarrow U_g \exp -i2\pi\mathbf{g}\cdot\mathbf{R}(\mathbf{r}) \, . \tag{60}$$

The deformation must be sufficiently small in order to be able to recognize still a lattice, although its dimensions and orientation change slightly which the position in the crystal.

This means mathematically the following. The Fourier transform of the unperturbed potential $V(\mathbf{r})$ is a sum of delta-functions situated at the nodes of the reciprocal lattice. The perturbated potential $V'(\mathbf{r})$ must then have a Fourier transform consisting of peak functions centered around the reciprocal lattice nodes and with *negligible* overlap. For a perfect plate-shaped crystal foil the σ-vectors occurring in (23) has only two values. For a foil containing a defect this will no longer be true: the $A(\sigma)$ function will become a true function with a width still much smaller than the dimension of the reciprocal lattice.

Introducing (60) into (35) leads then to the equation

$$\frac{\partial\phi_g}{\partial z} + \tan\alpha \, \frac{\partial\phi_g}{\partial x} - i2\pi s_g\phi_g = (\exp i\theta_g) \frac{i\pi}{\xi_g}(\exp -i\alpha_g) \tag{61a}$$

if one notices

$$\alpha_g(\mathbf{r}) = 2\pi\mathbf{g}\cdot\mathbf{R}(\mathbf{r}) \, . \tag{61b}$$

For simplicity we consider only the case of an incident beam nearly normal to the foil surface. The angle α is then very small, of the order of magnitude 10^{-2}. As a consequence the second term can be estimated as being very small as compared to the first one, and it becomes a good approximation to neglect this second term. This means that x and y are considered in (61) as parameters and not as integration variables. This is known as the "column approximation". The latter will be discussed in more detail in the other chapters.

The partial differential eq. (61a) simplifies then to the ordinary differential equation

$$\frac{d\phi_g}{dz} - i2\pi s_g \phi_g = (\exp i\theta_g) \frac{i\pi}{\xi_g} (\exp -i\alpha_g) \ . \tag{62}$$

The physical meaning of (62) becomes clearer if one makes the substitution

$$\phi_g = {}_*\phi_g (\exp -i\alpha_g) \ . \tag{63}$$

Bringing (63) into (62), and taking (61b) into account, gives

$$\frac{d_*\phi_g}{dz} - i2\pi \left(s_g + \mathbf{g} \cdot \frac{d\mathbf{R}}{dz} \right) {}_*\phi_g = (\exp i\theta_g) \frac{i\pi}{\xi_g} \tag{64}$$

This equation is the same as the eq. (36) for a perfect crystal provided one substitutes

$$s_g \rightarrow s_g^{(\text{eff.})} = s_g + \mathbf{g} \cdot \frac{d\mathbf{R}}{dz} \ . \tag{65}$$

The deviation parameter s_g, constant for a perfect crystal, has to be replaced by a position dependent parameter which describes the local lattice dimension and lattice orientation. More explicitly: at a position $\mathbf{r}$ one can still recognize the reflecting (hkl)-planes, however, with a lattice parameter d_{hkk} and an orientation which differ slightly from the parameter and the orientation in the non-deformed crystal. At that position one can calculate the local deviation parameter $s_g^{(\text{eff.})}$ and the result is given by (65). Even for a small deformation, the orientation differences can become comparable with the Bragg angle. Taking this fact into account and also the fact that the scattering interval is large, leads one to expect a strong effect,, confirmed by actual calculations. The scattered intensity

$$I_g = |\phi_g|^2 \tag{66}$$

can be observed at the back surface by allowing only this scattered beam to enter the optical system of the electron microscope. This intensity will be a function of x and y, since α_g depends on these parameters,

$$I_g = I_g(x,y) \ . \tag{67}$$

One observes a (dark field) strain contrast image of the deformation associated with the defect in the crystal. Introducing the substitution (37) into (62) gives

$$\frac{dS_g}{dz} = (\exp i\theta_g)\left(\frac{i\pi}{\xi_g}\right)\exp -i(2\pi s_g z + \alpha_g) \ . \tag{68}$$

After integration

$$I_g = |S_g|^2 \ ,$$

$$S_g = (\exp i\theta_g)\left(\frac{i\pi}{\xi_g}\right)\int_0^z \{\exp -i[2\pi s_g z + \alpha_g(\mathbf{r})]\}dz \ . \tag{69}$$

Most images are made in a dynamical situation, and the result (69) is then of no great use and can even lead to errronuous conclusions.

The result (69) can only have some value if one satisfies the kinematical conditions for the perfect foil. Even then one has to check if I_g remains much smaller than one over the entire image. In actual cases this is mostly not the case, the quantitative result (69) can then not be considered as a good approximation over the entire image. Nevertheless, the same arguments as in 3.4.3 lead one to believe that certain qualitative and semi-quantitative properties of the kinematical images must remain true for the dynamical images.

We illustrate this for the images of dislocations for large s_g-values. Except for very small Burgers vector, the kinematical results give unreasonable high values for the scattered intensity near the maximum of the image profile. However, at distances where the kinematical theory predicts a faint contrast, the kinematical result must be a good approximation for the dynamical one. This means that the kinematical theory leads to a fair estimate for the image width, for large $|s_g|$-values.

The kinematical theory learns also that the image centre does not coincide with the dislocation itself and gives a rule for determining the side of the image. Moreover the image profile is skewed. Here also one may believe that these properties will remain true if dynamical corrections are taken into account.

The detailed discussion of the images of defects is beyond the scope of these introductory lectures and will be discussed in other chapters.

5. Multiple beam kinematical theory

5.1. *Introduction*

The "one-beam" kinematical treatment breaks mostly down, since the assumption that an electron is scattered only once is not satisfied. This does not mean that a kinematical approach is unsuitable to calculate, in good approximation, the amplitudes of the weak beams. However, some refinements must then be introduced into the theory.

Suppose that there are n reciprocal lattice nodes close to the reflection sphere with not very large extinction distances. There exist then, apart from the transmitted beam, n strongly scattered beams in the crystal. As a first approximation, one neglects all other weak beams which are also present. One has then to solve a $(n+1)$-multiple beam dynamical problem. The solution in this problem is assumed to be known, i.e. one knows the wave function of the electrons

$$\psi^{(0)}(\mathbf{r}) = \{\phi_0(\mathbf{r}) + \sum_{i=0}^{n} \phi_i(\mathbf{r}) \exp i2\pi\mathbf{g}_i\cdot\mathbf{r}\}\exp i2\pi\mathbf{k}_0\cdot\mathbf{r} \tag{70}$$

inside the crystal.

All other reciprocal lattice nodes lie very far from the reflection sphere or (and) have associated extinction distances which are very large.

The electrons which leave the crystal in one of the weak beam directions can be considered as obtained by scattering out of the $(n+1)$ strong beams. Moreover, the kinematical assumption becomes plausible, i.e. it is a good approximation to neglect the possibility that such an electron will be scattered back into one of the strong beam directions, since the coupling between the system of strong beams and the system of weak beams is small.

An electron is scattered many times between the different strong beams in its way through the crystal plate, always remaining in its wave field. There is a small probability that the electron will be scattered at a certain moment into a weak beam direction. There is little chance that this electron will be scattered back later on into one of the strong beam directions. The kinematical approach neglects this possibility. Moreover, it assumes that one can ignore the depletion of the strong beams for calculating the relative numbers of electrons in the weak beams.

5.2. *(n+1) beam kinematical theory*

This kinematical treatment can be developed in the same way as the one-beam kinematical treatment as a Born approximation.

However, instead of replacing ψ in the second member of the Schrödinger eq. (17) by ψ_0 given by (18) one introduces now the wave function $\psi^{(0)}$ given by (70).

The second member of (20) has then to be replaced by

$$- 4\pi^2 \, U(\mathbf{r}) \, \psi^{(0)}(\mathbf{r}) = - 4\pi^2 \sum_{\mathbf{g}} \left[\sum_{i=0}^{n} U_{\mathbf{g}-\mathbf{g}_i} \phi_i(\mathbf{r}) \right] \exp i2\pi(\mathbf{k}_0+\mathbf{g})\cdot\mathbf{r} \tag{71}$$

leading in the same way as in sect. 2 to the differential equation for $\phi_{\mathbf{g}}$

$$\frac{d\phi_{\mathbf{g}}}{dz} - i2\pi s_{\mathbf{g}}\phi_{\mathbf{g}} = i\pi \sum_{i=0}^{n} \frac{U_{\mathbf{g}-\mathbf{g}_i}}{|\mathbf{k}_0+\mathbf{g}|_\perp} \phi_i(\mathbf{r}) \, ,$$

$$(\mathbf{k}_0+\mathbf{g})_\perp = |\mathbf{k}_0+\mathbf{g}| \cos\alpha \, , \qquad |\mathbf{k}_0+\mathbf{g}|_\perp \cong (\mathbf{k}_0)_\perp \tag{72}$$

which replaces the eq. (36).

As pointed out in other lectures, each beam $\mathbf{g}_i$ is the superposition of $(n+1)$ plane waves with slightly different wave vectors $\mathbf{k}_0 + \mathbf{g}_i + \frac{1}{2}\beta_j\mathbf{e}_z$ $(j=0,1,...,n)$, each plane wave belonging to a Bloch wave numbered by the index j.

Therefore each ϕ_i can be written as

$$\phi_i(z) = \sum_{j=0}^{n} A_{ij} \exp i\pi\beta_j z \, . \tag{73}$$

Introducing (73) into (72) enables us to rewrite the latter equation as follows

$$\frac{d\phi_{\mathbf{g}}}{dz} - i2\pi s_{\mathbf{g}}\phi_{\mathbf{g}} = \sum_{j=0}^{n} \left(\sum_{i=0}^{n} i\pi A_{ij} \frac{U_{\mathbf{g}-\mathbf{g}_i}}{(k_0)_\perp} \right) \exp i\pi\beta_j z \tag{74}$$

or, making the substitution (37)

$$\frac{dS_{\mathbf{g}}}{dz} = i\pi \sum_{j=0}^{n} \left(\sum_{i=0}^{n} A_{ij} \frac{U_{\mathbf{g}-\mathbf{g}_i}}{(k_0)_\perp} \right) \exp -i2\pi(s_{\mathbf{g}}-\tfrac{1}{2}\beta_j)z \, . \tag{75}$$

The eq. (75) suggests us to introduce the following notations

$$\frac{1}{\xi'_{g,j}} = \sum_{i=0}^{n} \frac{U_{g-g_i}}{(k_o)_\perp} A_{ij}$$ (76)

and

$$s_g^{(j)} = s_g - \tfrac{1}{2} \beta_j .$$ (77)

Eq. (75) reads then

$$\frac{dS_g}{dz} = \sum_{j=0}^{n} \frac{i\pi}{\xi'_{g,j}} \exp -i2\pi s_g^{(j)} z .$$ (78)

After integration, one obtains finally

$$S_g = \sum_{j=0}^{n} (\exp -i\pi s_g^{(j)} z) \frac{i \sin \pi s_g^{(j)} z}{s_g^{(j)} \xi'_{g,j}} .$$ (79)

5.3. Discussion and remarks

The structure of eq. (78) shows clearly that the most adequate description consists in considering the kinematical scattering of electrons out of each wave field separately. The term number j of (78) and (79) represents the scattering of electrons out of the jth strong wave field, containing electrons moving in all the strong beam directions, into the weak beam. For this type of scattering one is able to define an effective extinction distance, given by (76), and an effective deviation parameter, given by (77).

The wave vector of each wave field has a direction which differs slightly from the direction of the incident beam (corrected for refraction). The deviation from the exact Bragg orientation must thus be defined with respect to the direction of the wave vector of the wave field under consideration, leading to the introduction of the effective deviation parameter, as given by (77). The directions of the wave vectors of the different wave fields are different with respect to each other and depend on the actual crystal orientation. This is included in the formula (77), since the β_j are orientation dependent.

The reciprocal effective extinction distance, given by (76), is a weighed sum of the reciprocal extinction distances (taking also their phase factors into account) corresponding to the different possible scattering out of one of the strong beam directions, contained in the wave field, into the considered weak beam direction. The weight factors A_{ij} describe how the electrons in a given wave field j are distributed over the different beams g_i in a semi-infinite crystal.

Since an electron cannot be scattered directly from one strong wave field into another strong wave field, and since the kinematical approach neglects the indirect scatterings, strong field → weak beam → strong field, the scattering events between the different wave fields and the weak beam are independent, resulting in the linear structure of eqs. (78) and (79).

The parameters present in (79) depend critically on the illumination conditions.

The terms of (79) represent the kinematical scatterings from a wave field into a given beam, independent with respect to each other. They have in fact the same structure as the one beam kinematical result, provided one uses the adequate definitions of extinction distance and deviation parameter.

The theory as developed here ignores possible dynamical interactions betweeen the weak beams themselves. By using more sophisticated mathematical methods it is, however, also possible to allow for these interactions. They are mostly not important.

5.4. The "two-beam" kinematical treatment

The most simple illumination condition is the two-beam one.

One can now use the wave function (70) calculated in the lecture of Professor Whelan.

Let $\mathbf{G}$ be the dynamical beam, s and ξ the corresponding deviation parameter and extinction distance.

One has then

$$\beta_0 = s + \frac{1}{\xi}(1+\omega^2)^{1/2}, \quad \beta_1 = s - \frac{1}{\xi}(1+\omega^2)^{1/2}, \quad \omega = s\xi \quad (80a,b,c)$$

and

$$A_{00} = \frac{1}{2}\left(1 - \frac{\omega}{\sqrt{1+\omega^2}}\right), \qquad A_{01} = \frac{1}{2}\left(1 + \frac{\omega}{\sqrt{1+\omega^2}}\right) \qquad (81a,b)$$

$$A_{10} = \frac{1}{\sqrt{1+\omega^2}}\exp i\theta_{\mathbf{G}}, \qquad A_{11} = \frac{-1}{\sqrt{1+\omega^2}}\exp i\theta_{\mathbf{G}}. \qquad (81c,d)$$

Introducing (80) and (81) into (76) and (77), gives

$$\frac{1}{\xi'_{g,0}} = \frac{1}{2} \left\{ \left(1 - \frac{\omega}{\sqrt{1+\omega^2}}\right) \frac{U_g}{(k_o)_\perp} + \frac{\exp i\theta_G}{\sqrt{1+\omega^2}} \frac{U_{g-G}}{(k_o)_\perp} \right\} \tag{82a}$$

$$\frac{1}{\xi'_{g,1}} = \frac{1}{2} \left\{ \left(1 + \frac{\omega}{\sqrt{1+\omega^2}}\right) \frac{U_g}{(k_o)_\perp} - \frac{\exp i\theta_G}{\sqrt{1+\omega^2}} \frac{U_{g-G}}{(k_o)_\perp} \right\} \tag{82b}$$

$$s_g^{(0)} = s_g - \frac{1}{2}\left(s + \frac{\sqrt{1+\omega^2}}{\xi}\right), \quad s_g^{(1)} = s_g - \frac{1}{2}\left(s - \frac{\sqrt{1+\omega^2}}{\xi}\right) \tag{83a,b}$$

and for the amplitude of the weak beam, one obtains

$$S_g = (\exp -i\pi s_g^{(0)}z)\frac{i\sin \pi s_g^{(0)}z}{s_g^{(0)}\xi'_{g,0}} + (\exp -i\pi s_g^{(1)}z)\frac{i\sin \pi s_g^{(1)}z}{s_g^{(1)}\xi'_{g,1}}. \tag{84}$$

5.5. *Discussion and observation*

One can rewrite (84) as follows

$$S_g = A^{(0)} + A^{(1)} - A^{(0)}(\exp -i2\pi s_g^{(0)}z) - A^{(1)}$$

$$\times (\exp -i2\pi s_g^{(1)}z) \tag{85}$$

where

$$A^{(0)} = \frac{1}{2}\frac{1}{s_g^{(0)}\xi'_{g,0}}, \quad A^{(1)} = \frac{1}{2}\frac{1}{s_g^{(1)}\xi'_{g,1}} \tag{86}$$

and one is particularly interested in

$$I_g = |S_g|^2 . \tag{87}$$

Let us discuss the variation of I_g with crystal thickness, i.e. the extinction thickness contours to be expected in the weak beam dark-field for a wedge-shaped crystal.

If (85) is brought into (87), one obtains a superposition of terms with different depth-periods, namely (1) the period $1/s_g^{(0)}$, (2) the period $1/s_g^{(1)}$, (3) the period $1/(s_g^{(0)} - s_g^{(1)}) = \xi/\sqrt{1+\omega^2}$.

Since one assumed that

$$|s_g| \gg |s| \, , \; 1/\xi \tag{88}$$

the first and second period differ only slightly. The superposition of the terms with these two periods will still be nearly periodic with a period not deviating very much from $1/s_g$, the usual kinematical period.

The fringe system with depth-period $\approx 1/s_g$ will, however, be modulated by the term with period $\xi/\sqrt{1+\omega^2}$, the latter period being mostly several times the first one. The result is a modulated fringe pattern, the fringe spacing being approximately the kinematical one, whereas the contrast modulation period corresponds to the depth period of the bright and the strong dark field images.

In fig. 7 the dark field image is shown of a wedge-shaped MgO-crystal in the weak kinematical spot $(00\bar{2})$, the dynamical spot being (002), for $s \cong 0$. One observes the expected characteristics of the fringe pattern. Comparison with the bright field image confirms that the modulation period and the bright field fringe spacing are in fact equal. The ratio of the modulation period and the fine spacing is also, in very good approximation, equal to s_g/ξ.

We discuss now a very special prediction of the theory and which can be checked by observation.

For crystals with a centre of symmetry, the Fourier coefficients are all real, if one takes the origin of reciprocal space in such a centre. Moreover for crystals like fcc, bcc metals and NaCl-structures, these coefficients are positive.

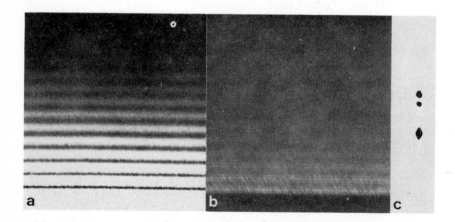

Fig. 7. Extinction contours at a wedge shaped MgO-crystal. a. Bright field image. b. Dark field image in a weak spot. Notice the modulated fringe pattern. c. Enlargement of the spot used for the dark field in b. (Courtesy R.De Ridder.)

In that case, one has

$$\theta_G = 0, \qquad \frac{U_g}{(k_o)_\perp} = \frac{1}{\xi_g}, \qquad \frac{U_{g-G}}{(k_o)_\perp} = \frac{1}{\xi_{g-G}}. \tag{89}$$

From (82) follows then

$$\frac{1}{\xi'_{g,o}} = \tfrac{1}{2}\left[\left(1 - \frac{\omega}{\sqrt{1+\omega^2}}\right)\frac{1}{\xi_g} + \frac{1}{\sqrt{1+\omega^2}}\frac{1}{\xi_{g-G}}\right] \tag{90}$$

$$\frac{1}{\xi'_{g,1}} = \tfrac{1}{2}\left[\left(1 + \frac{\omega}{\sqrt{1+\omega^2}}\right)\frac{1}{\xi_g} - \frac{1}{\sqrt{1+\omega^2}}\frac{1}{\xi_{g-G}}\right]. \tag{91}$$

If one changes the crystal orientation continuously, i.e. if ω varies, the first extinction distance $\xi'_{g,o}$ will always remain finite. On the other hand the second one, $\xi'_{g,1}$ becomes infinite for the orientation

$$\omega = s\xi = \tfrac{1}{2}\left(\frac{\xi_{g-G}}{\xi_g} - \frac{\xi_g}{\xi_{g-G}}\right). \tag{92}$$

Since it follows from (82) that

$$\frac{1}{\xi'_{g,o}} + \frac{1}{\xi'_{g,1}} = \frac{1}{\xi_g} \tag{93}$$

one has for this particular crystal orientation

$$\xi'_{g,o} = \xi_{g,o}, \qquad \xi_{g,1} = \infty. \tag{94}$$

Bringing (94) into (84) gives then, for this particular orientation

$$S_g = (\exp -i2\pi s_g^{(o)}z)\,\frac{i\sin \pi s_g^{(o)}z}{s_g^{(o)}\xi_g}. \tag{95}$$

The physical meaning is as follows.

The scattering amplitudes for the scattering of electrons out of the transmitted and strongly diffracted beam into the weak beam, are in phase for the first wave field,, but in anti-phase for the second wave field. For the first wave field extinction can never occur. For the second wave field, however, there is partial destructive interference. By adjusting the amplitudes of the transmitted and diffracted wave in the second wave field by tilting the crystal plate, one can achieve complete annihilation, i.e. if one satisfies (92). For this situation no electrons in the weak beam come from the second wave.

The intensity for this particular orientation is, from (95)

$$I_g = \frac{\sin^2 \pi s_g^{(o)} z}{(s_g^{(o)} \xi_g)^2} \tag{96}$$

i.e. the same expression as in the one-beam kinematical theory, provided one replaces the deviation parameter by a corrected one.

The formula (96) describes a non-modulated, strictly periodical variation of the intensity with crystal thickness, with depth-period $1/s_g^{(o)}$. The weak dark field image is like the one predicted by the dynamical two-beam theory, indicating that it is a consequence of the scattering of electrons between two entities. However, these are no longer two beams, but a wave field and a beam.

Fig. 8 shows again the weak dark field of a wedge-shaped MgO crystal in the $(00\bar{2})$-spot, the dynamical spot being (002). However, the crystal is now tilted into the orientation (92). One observes now in fact a perfectly non-modulated fringe pattern. The fringe spacing corresponds very well to the value obtained from theory.

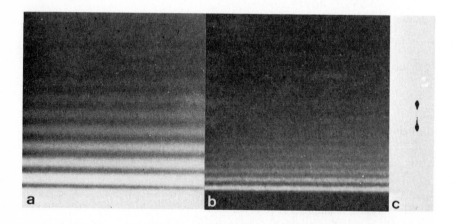

Fig. 8. The same wedge shaped MgO crystal as in fig. 7 slightly changed in orientation. a. Bright field image. b. Dark field image in a weak spot. Notice the different aspect of the fringe pattern and the complete absence of modulation. c. Enlargement of the same weak spot as in 7e used for the dark field in b. (Courtesy R.De Ridder.)

For a very thick crystal, for which absorption becomes very important, the second term of (85) will be exponentially damped, whereas the third term will be exponentially enhanced. This expresses that the electrons are scattered out of a strongly absorbed and a easily transmitted wave field.

For a very thick crystal the third term of (85) becomes much more important than the other two terms. As an approximation one has then

$$I_g \cong \tfrac{1}{4} \left(\exp -2\pi\mu^{(1)}z \right) \frac{1}{|s_g^{(1)}\xi'_{g,1}|^2} \tag{97}$$

where $\mu^{(1)}$ is the (amplitude) absorption coefficient of the easily transmitted wave field.

The expression (97) for I_g becomes a good approximation if the following assumptions are valid: (i) the electrons moving in the strongly absorbed wave field have already all disappeared long before the back surface, (ii) the electrons which are scattered into the weak beam directions at positions still far from the exit surface, do not reach this surface in that direction, due to the uniform absorption.

The expression (97) counts then the number of electrons which have survived first in the easily transmitted wave field up to close to the exit surface, and which are next scattered into the weak beam direction.

Formula (97) describes an exponential decrease of the intensity with respect to the crystal thickness. The approximation leading to (97) is, however, very drastic. Even for a rather thick crystal, the other terms of (95) will contribute somewhat to the intensity, giving rise to small fluctuations of the intensity with respect to the crystal thickness.

References

[1] P.B.Hirsch, A.Howie and M.J.Whelan, Phil. Trans. Roy. Soc. A252 (1960) 499.

DYNAMICAL THEORY OF ELECTRON DIFFRACTION

M.J.WHELAN

1. The dynamical theory of diffraction of fast electrons

By fast electrons we mean electrons in the energy range from a few keV up to several hundred keV, the energy range useful in transmission electron microscopy. The formulation of the theory we are going to present here is similar to the method originally employed by Darwin [1] for the case of X-ray diffraction, and our approach will be to some extent complementary to that which will be given for X-ray diffraction by Authier in this volume. In this chapter we will be concerned with the two-beam theory (fig. 1), where besides the transmitted beam of amplitude ϕ_0, only one strong diffracted beam of amplitude ϕ_g is imagined to be excited in a slab crystal of thickness t. The incident beam amplitude is taken as unity at the top surface of the crystal. This situation is relevant to the calculation of bright-field and dark-field image intensities in electron microscopy, where the corresponding experimental situation is determined by the position of the objective aperture as shown in fig. 1. Generalisation of the theory to cover more than one strong diffracted beam will be given in this volume by Howie.

1.1. *Limitations of the kinematical theory*
Before embarking on the dynamical theory it is useful to consider the range of applicability of the kinematical theory, which has been outlined by Gevers and which gives much qualitative insight into the mechanism of diffraction contrast from defects in transmission electron microscopy. The geometrical conditions are defined in fig. 2. K and λ are the wave vector and wave length ($K=\lambda^{-1}$); g is the reciprocal lattice vector of the operating Bragg reflection; s is the deviation parameter denoting the distance by which the reciprocal lattice point g lies off the Ewald sphere in a direction normal to the

35

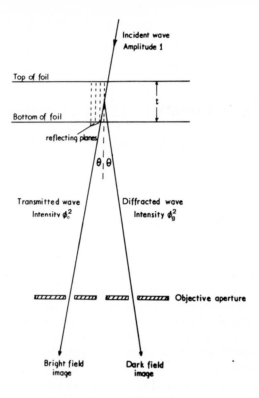

Fig. 1. Illustrating the symmetrical Laue case of transmission electron diffraction through a plate crystal of thickness t. The reflecting planes are perpendicular to the surface. The Bragg angle θ is very small ($\approx 10^{-2}$ rad), so that in practice the symmetrical Laue case is useful for discussing normal incidence.

crystal surface. The kinematical theory leads to the following result for the absolute intensity of the diffracted beam.

$$|\phi_g|^2 = \frac{\pi^2}{\xi_g^2} \frac{\sin^2 \pi t s}{(\pi s)^2} \, . \tag{1}$$

ξ_g is the extinction distance given by

$$\xi_g = \frac{\pi K \Omega \cos \theta}{f(\theta)} = \frac{K \cos \theta}{U_g} \, , \tag{2}$$

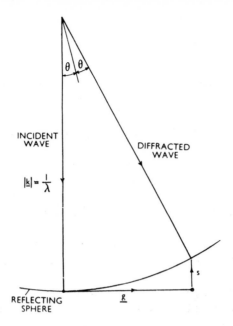

Fig. 2. Ewald sphere construction for determining the direction of the diffracted waves.

Ω is the volume of the unit cell; $f(\theta)$ is the atomic scattering amplitude for electrons; U_g is the Fourier coefficient of a suitably scaled crystal lattice potential experienced by the fast electron. We have assumed that there is only one atom per unit cell. If this is not the case f must be replaced by a structure amplitude of the form $\Sigma_i f_i(\theta) \exp(-2\pi i g \cdot r_i)$, where f_i is the atomic scattering amplitude of atom i at position r_i in the unit cell.

Eq. (1) shows that when $s = 0$

$$|\phi_g|^2 = \pi^2 t^2 / \xi_g^2 . \tag{3}$$

Thus the intensity of the diffracted beam increases quadratically with t, but evidently eq. (3) cannot hold if $\pi^2 t^2 / \xi_g^2 > 1$ (incident intensity), i.e. if $t >$ about $\xi_g/3$. For typical materials with 100 kV electrons ξ_g is in the range 150 to 500 Å for low order reflections. Thus the crystal has to be very thin ($\ll 100$ Å) for kinematical theory to be valid at $s = 0$. We may note here that for X-rays the condition is less stringent since

$$\frac{\xi_{g, \text{X-rays}}}{\xi_{g, \text{electrons}}} \simeq \frac{\lambda_e \, f_e}{\lambda_x \, f_x} \simeq 400 \text{ * or more .} \tag{4}$$

Thus extinction distances for X-rays are typically in the range 10 to 100 μm, and crystals in the micron range of thickness generally behave kinematically for X-ray diffraction.

Breakdown of the kinematical theory is also evident in other aspects, for example the widths of dislocation images derived from this theory and the spacing of thickness fringes (Hirsch et al. [2]) varies as s^{-1}. For $s \to 0$ fringe spacings become infinite, whereas in practice it is known they tend to a finite limit. It is worth noting, however, that for $s \neq 0$, the kinematical theory is a good approximation provided $\xi_g s \gg 1$, even for thick crystals.

1.2. Dynamical equations in the Laue case

By the Laue case is meant the case where the incident beam and diffracted beam enter and leave the crystal slab at opposite surfaces. This is distinguished from the so-called Bragg case, studied by Darwin [1], where incident and diffracted beams enter and leave by the same surface. The solution of the dynamical equations for these two cases are quite different. In particular we shall study the symmetrical Laue case, shown in fig. 1, where the reflecting planes are perpendicular to the surface.

Consider an electron with free-space wave vector χ incident on a slab crystal so that a Bragg reflection $\mathbf{g}$ is excited. Let the amplitude of the transmitted wave as a function of depth z be $\phi_0(z)$ and that of the diffracted wave $\phi_g(z)$. As the wave ϕ_0 propagates into the crystal, its amplitude will be depleted by diffraction and the amplitude ϕ_g will increase, i.e. there is coupling between ϕ_0 and ϕ_g. We can describe the coupling by the following differential equations.

---

* This magnitude can be established by writing

$$f_e(\theta) = \frac{me^2 \lambda^2}{2h^2} \frac{(Z - F(\theta))}{\sin^2 \theta} \text{ (Born approximation) ,}$$

$$f_x(\theta) = \frac{-e^2}{mc^2} F(\theta)$$

where $F(\theta)$ is the atomic scattering factor tabulated in the International Crystallographic Tables. Assuming hydrogen like wave functions, the ratio f_e/f_x may be shown to be approximately $(\hbar c/e^2)^2 = 137^2$ at $\theta = 0$.

$$\frac{d\phi_0}{dz} = \frac{i\pi}{\xi_0} \phi_0 + \frac{i\pi}{\xi_g} \phi_g \exp\left(2\pi i s z\right)$$

$$\frac{d\phi_g}{dz} = \frac{i\pi}{\xi_g} \phi_0 \exp\left(-2\pi i s z\right) + \frac{i\pi}{\xi_0} \phi_g \ . \tag{5}$$

The first of these equations states that the change in ϕ_0 in depth dz is partly due to forward scattering by the atoms in the slice dz, and partly due to scattering from the diffracted beam. A similar interpretation may be given to the second equation. It is to be noted that the coupling constants are proportional to ξ_0^{-1} and ξ_g^{-1} which themselves are proportional to $f(0)$ and $f(\theta)$. Moreover there is a phase change of $\pi/2$ (represented by the factor i) caused by the scattering. Such phase changes arise through the reconstruction of plane wave fronts from waves scattered by single atoms taking due account of phase, and they are well known in problems in physical optics. If in the second of eqs. (5) ϕ_g is small and ϕ_0 is assumed to be approximately unity, the equation may be integrated approximately to give the kinematical result (1) with the correct absolute scaling factor.

A variety of equations like (5) may be obtained by making suitable phase transformations. For example put

$$\phi_0'(z) = \phi_0(z) \exp\left(-i\pi z/\xi_0\right)$$

$$\phi_g'(z) = \phi_g(z) \exp\left(2\pi i s z - \pi i z/\xi_0\right) \ . \tag{6}$$

We find from (5)

$$\frac{d\phi_0'}{dz} = \frac{i\pi}{\xi_g} \phi_g'$$

$$\frac{d\phi_g'}{dz} = \frac{i\pi}{\xi_g} \phi_0' + 2\pi i s \, \phi_g' \ . \tag{7}$$

The solutions of (5) and (7) differ only by phase factors, and therefore, since we are only interested in intensities, both systems of equations will give the same result. The transformation (6) is equivalent to making allowance for the mean refractive index of the crystal, because the directly transmitted wave may be described as

$$\phi_0(z) \exp{(2\pi i \chi \cdot \mathbf{r})} \text{ or as } \phi_0'(z) \exp\left(2\pi i \left(\chi \cdot \mathbf{r} + \frac{z}{2\xi_0}\right)\right) .$$

The argument of the exponential of the latter expression shows that a major part of the z-dependence of ϕ_0 of the former expression is accounted for by a change of wave vector to $\mathbf{K}$, where $K_z = \chi_z + 1/2\xi_0$. $\mathbf{K}$ is the wave vector of the electron wave inside the crystal after allowing for the mean inner potential. It is easy to show that this is equivalent to a mean refractive index

$$\mu = \frac{|\mathbf{K}|}{|\chi|} = 1 + \frac{\lambda \cos\theta}{2\xi_0} = 1 + \frac{\lambda^2}{2\pi} N f(0) \tag{8}$$

where N is the number of atoms per unit volume. μ is slightly greater than unity for electron wave refraction. Typically $\mu - 1 \cong 10^{-4}$ for 100 kV electrons.

1.3. Solution of the dynamical equations for a perfect crystal

We choose to solve the eqs. (7) and (dropping primes) we eliminate ϕ_g by differentiating the first equation with respect to z and by substituting for $d\phi_g/dz$ and ϕ_g from the second and first equations respectively. We obtain

$$\frac{d^2\phi_0}{dz^2} - 2\pi i s \frac{d\phi_0}{dz} + \left(\frac{\pi}{\xi_g}\right)^2 \phi_0 = 0 . \tag{9}$$

By elimination of ϕ_0 it may be shown that ϕ_g satisfies the same equation. We try a solution of (9) of the form $\exp{(2\pi i \gamma z)}$. Substitution in (9) gives

$$\gamma^2 - s\gamma - (1/2\xi_g)^2 = 0 . \tag{10}$$

Eq. (10) is quadratic and has two roots

$$\gamma^{(1)} = \tfrac{1}{2}\left(s - \sqrt{s^2 + \xi_g^{-2}}\right) \tag{11}$$

$$\gamma^{(2)} = \tfrac{1}{2}\left(s + \sqrt{s^2 + \xi_g^{-2}}\right) . \tag{12}$$

Consider first the root $\gamma^{(1)}$. We may then write

$$\phi_0(z) = C_0^{(1)} \exp\left(2\pi i \gamma^{(1)} z\right) \tag{13}$$

$$\phi_g(z) = C_g^{(1)} \exp\left(2\pi i \gamma^{(1)} z\right) \tag{14}$$

where $C_0^{(1)}$ and $C_g^{(1)}$ are constants to be determined by noting that (13) and (14) must satisfy the original coupled differential eqs. (7). Substitution of (13) and (14) in the first of eqs. (7) gives

$$C_g^{(1)}/C_0^{(1)} = 2\xi_g \gamma^{(1)} = \xi_g s - \sqrt{1 + \xi_g^2 s^2} = w - \sqrt{1 + w^2} \tag{15}$$

where $w = \xi_g s$ is a dimensionless parameter which denotes deviation from the Bragg reflecting position, the so-called "deviation parameter" of the dynamical theory of diffraction. It is usual to choose the coefficients C_0, C_g so that $|C_0|^2 + |C_g|^2 = 1$. From (15) we then find

$$C_0^{(1)} = \left\{ \tfrac{1}{2} \left(1 + \frac{w}{\sqrt{1 + w^2}} \right) \right\}^{\frac{1}{2}} \tag{16}$$

$$C_g^{(1)} = - \left\{ \tfrac{1}{2} \left(1 - \frac{w}{\sqrt{1 + w^2}} \right) \right\}^{\frac{1}{2}}. \tag{17}$$

Similarly we may find a solution corresponding to the root $\gamma^{(2)}$

$$C_g^{(2)}/C_0^{(2)} = 2\xi_g \gamma^{(2)} = w + \sqrt{1 + w^2} \tag{18}$$

$$C_0^{(2)} = \left\{ \tfrac{1}{2} \left(1 - \frac{w}{\sqrt{1 + w^2}} \right) \right\}^{\frac{1}{2}} \tag{19}$$

$$C_g^{(2)} = \left\{ \tfrac{1}{2} \left(1 + \frac{w}{\sqrt{1 + w^2}} \right) \right\}^{\frac{1}{2}}. \tag{20}$$

For the root $\gamma^{(i)}$ ($i=1,2$) we can now use the expressions (13) and (14) to write down the wave function propagating in the crystal

$$B^{(i)}(\mathbf{r}) = \phi_0^{(i)} \exp\left(2\pi i \mathbf{K} \cdot \mathbf{r}\right) + \phi_g^{(i)} \exp\left(2\pi i (\mathbf{K}+\mathbf{g}) \cdot \mathbf{r}\right)$$

$$= C_0^{(i)} \exp\left(2\pi i \mathbf{k}_0^{(i)} \cdot \mathbf{r}\right) + C_g^{(i)} \exp\left(2\pi i (\mathbf{k}_0^{(i)}+\mathbf{g}) \cdot \mathbf{r}\right) \tag{21}$$

where

$$(k_o^{(i)})_z = K_z + \gamma^{(i)} . \tag{22}$$

There will be two functions $B^{(1)}$ and $B^{(2)}$ corresponding to the two values of γ. The functions $B^{(i)}$ are two-beam approximations to Bloch functions.

1.4. The dispersion surface

The two Bloch functions have wave vectors $k_o^{(i)}$ given by eq. (22), and we may use this equation to construct a surface which is the locus of the end of the vector $k_o^{(i)}$ as the orientation of the incident beam is varied, i.e. as K varies. There are two branches of this surface corresponding to $i = 1, 2$, as shown in fig. 3. The vector AO represents the incident wave vector K. The reflecting sphere and the distance $s(=s_g)$ are shown. The locus of K is the sphere of radius $|K|$ centred at O. $\gamma^{(i)}$ is the distance of A (parallel to the z direction) from the two branches of the dispersion surface. As A varies over the sphere of radius $|K|$, the wave vectors $k_o^{(i)}$ trace out the two branches of the dispersion

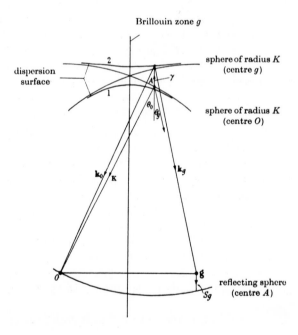

Fig. 3. Illustrating the construction of the dispersion surface.

surface. In practice $|\mathbf{K}| \cong 50 |\mathbf{g}|$, so that the sphere of radius $|\mathbf{K}|$ is practically a plane in the vicinity of the Brillouin zone boundary which bisects the reciprocal lattice vector $\mathbf{g}$. In this case the two branches of the dispersion surface on the two-beam theory are generated by rotation of two branches of a hyperbola about $\mathbf{g}$. The hyperbolic surface is asymptotic to the aforementioned sphere centred at O and to a similar sphere centred at $\mathbf{g}$.

The concept of the dispersion surface is particularly useful as a geometrical aid for describing wave vectors of Bloch functions in the crystal. In general, as we shall see, the incident beam excites two Bloch functions in the Laue case, one on each branch of the dispersion surface. If the dispersion surface is known we can find the crystal wave vectors $\mathbf{k}_0^{(i)}$ simply by constructing a normal to the crystal surface (i.e. along z) through the end of the wave vector $\mathbf{K}$ at A in fig. 3. The intersections of the normal with the branches of the surface give the "wave-points" of the vectors $\mathbf{k}_0^{(i)}$.

The dispersion surface is usually introduced in the wave-mechanical treatment of electron diffraction, following the methods of Bethe [3], MacGillavry [4] and others. In this treatment the dispersion surface enters as a surface of constant energy for crystal wave functions with energy equal to that of the incident electron wave. The construction described above for determining crystal wave vectors arises from the condition of continuity of components of wave vectors parallel to the crystal surface as in problems of wave matching at interfaces in electromagnetic theory. Our method of derivation of the dispersion surface, starting from eqs. (5) or (7), demonstrates that the surface is not a direct consequence of a quantum-mechanical treatment, since the result was obtained from a simple geometrical treatment of scattering. In fact the only point where quantum mechanics needs to be used in our treatment is in calculation of atomic scattering amplitudes (eq. (2)).

The concept of the dispersion surface can be generalised to include the case of more than one strong Bragg reflection. This will be dealt with in a later chapter by Howie, but we should note here that if n-waves are considered, the dispersion surface consists of n-branches asymptotic to spheres of radius $|\mathbf{K}|$ centred at the n reciprocal lattice points.

1.5. Solution in the Laue case

It is useful to introduce a notation due to Takagi for describing deviations from the exact Bragg condition. We introduce a parameter β by the relation

$$w = \cot \beta . \tag{23}$$

In fig. 3, $w = +\infty$ $(\beta=0)$ corresponds to the point A being far to the right of the Brillouin zone boundary. $w = 0$ ($\beta=\pi/2$) occurs when A is at the zone boundary, which is the exact Bragg position. $w = -\infty$ ($\beta=\pi$) occurs when A is far to the left of the zone boundary. It is usual to take s positive if the reciprical lattice point is inside the reflecting sphere and negative in the reverse situation. In terms of β we have

$$C_o^{(1)} = C_g^{(2)} = \cos\tfrac{1}{2}\beta \; ; \qquad C_o^{(2)} = -C_g^{(1)} = \sin\tfrac{1}{2}\beta \; . \qquad (24)$$

Suppose there is only one wave incident on the top surface of the crystal. We write the total crystal wave as

$$\psi(\mathbf{r}) = \psi^{(1)} B^{(1)}(\mathbf{r}) + \psi^{(2)} B^{(2)}(\mathbf{r}) \; . \qquad (25)$$

$\psi^{(1)}$ and $\psi^{(2)}$ represent the amplitude of the two Bloch waves excited in the crystal. Using (21), eq. (25) becomes

$$\psi(\mathbf{r}) = \psi^{(1)} C_o^{(1)} \exp\left(2\pi i k_o^{(1)} \cdot \mathbf{r}\right) + \psi^{(2)} C_o^{(2)} \exp\left(2\pi i k_o^{(2)} \cdot \mathbf{r}\right)$$

$$+ \psi^{(1)} C_g^{(1)} \exp\left(2\pi i (k_o^{(1)}+\mathbf{g}) \cdot \mathbf{r}\right) + \psi^{(2)} C_g^{(2)}$$

$$\times \exp\left(2\pi i (k_o^{(2)}+\mathbf{g}) \cdot \mathbf{r}\right) \; . \qquad (26)$$

The first two terms on the right of (26) represent the directly transmitted wave in the crystal; the second two terms on the right represent the diffracted wave. We choose the origin of coordinates at the top surface of the crystal and equate the amplitude of the directly transmitted wave at the top to unity (the incident beam amplitude), and that of the diffracted wave to zero

$$\psi^{(1)} C_o^{(1)} + \psi^{(2)} C_o^{(2)} = 1 \; ; \qquad \psi^{(1)} C_g^{(1)} + \psi^{(2)} C_g^{(2)} = 0 \; . \quad (27)$$

Using (24), eq. (27) gives

$$\psi^{(1)} = \cos\tfrac{1}{2}\beta \qquad (28)$$

$$\psi^{(2)} = \sin\tfrac{1}{2}\beta \; . \qquad (29)$$

We may now evaluate the amplitudes of the directly transmitted and diffracted waves for a crystal of thickness t. We have

$$\phi_o(t) = \sum_{i=1,2} \psi^{(i)} C_o^{(i)} \exp(2\pi i \gamma^{(i)} t)$$

$$\phi_g(t) = \sum_{i=1,2} \psi^{(i)} C_g^{(i)} \exp(2\pi i \gamma^{(i)} t) \,. \tag{30}$$

Apart from an unimportant phase term, eqs. (30) may be simplified with the aid of eqs. (11), (12), (23), (24), (28) and (29). We obtain the result

$$\phi_o(t) = \cos\left(\frac{\pi t}{\xi_g}\sqrt{1+w^2}\right) - \frac{iw}{\sqrt{1+w^2}} \sin\left(\frac{\pi t}{\xi_g}\sqrt{1+w^2}\right) \tag{31}$$

$$\phi_g(t) = \frac{i\sin\left(\frac{\pi t}{\xi_g}\sqrt{1+w^2}\right)}{\sqrt{1+w^2}}\,. \tag{32}$$

1.6. *Examination of the Laue solution*
From (32) we find that the diffracted beam intensity can be written as

$$|\phi_g|^2 = \frac{\pi^2}{\xi_g^2} \frac{\sin^2 \pi t \bar{s}}{(\pi \bar{s})^2} \tag{33}$$

where $\bar{s}$ is an effective value of s

$$\bar{s} = \sqrt{s^2 + \xi_g^{-2}}\,. \tag{34}$$

Eq. (33) is directly comparable with eq. (1), the kinematical solution. We see that it differs from the kinematical result only by the replacement of s by an effective value $\bar{s}$, which has a minimum value equal to ξ_g^{-1} at the Bragg position. Thus the limitations of the kinematical theory when $s \to 0$ mentioned in sect. 1.1 are effectively removed in the dynamical treatment. The expression (33) is the Bragg reflection "rocking curve" of the crystal obtained from the two-beam dynamical theory. Fig. 4 shows schematic diagrams of rocking curves on (a) the kinematical theory and (b) the dynamical theory. It is worth noting that the width of the central maximum of the rocking curve on the s-scale given by kinematical theory is $2/t$ and decreases with increasing t, a well known result

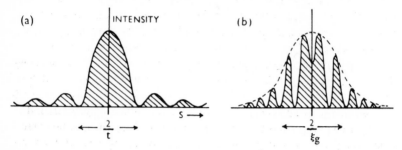

Fig. 4. Schematic diagram of the intensity distribution around a reciprocal lattice point. (a) on the kinematical theory, (b) on the dynamical theory.

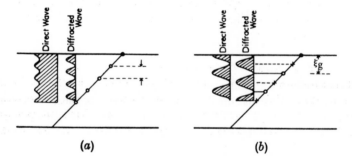

Fig. 5. Schematic diagram of the "Pendellösung" effect, (a) in the kinematical region where the diffracted beam is weak, (b) in the dynamical region where $s = 0$. The depth periodicity of the oscillations of crystal wave intensities is equal to the extinction distance ξ_g.

for particle-size broadening in X-ray diffraction. However, the dynamical rocking curve is more complicated. For $t \ll \xi_g$ the curve approaches the kinematical result. However, for $t > \xi_g$ the behaviour is as illustrated in fig. 4(b). The envelope of the oscillations has a half-width $2/\xi_g$ independent of the crystal thickness.

Fig. 5 illustrates the "Pendellösung" effect for incident and diffracted intensities as given by eqs. (31) and (32). In this diagram we plot schematically the intensities $|\phi_0|^2$ and $|\phi_g|^2$ as a function of depth in the crystal. At the Bragg position the intensities of direct and diffracted waves oscillate with depth as shown in fig. 5(b). The intensity varies between zero and unity with a depth periodicity ξ_g. The coupling of the direct and diffracted intensities is known as "extinction" because in a depth $\frac{1}{2}\xi_g$ the intensity of the direct wave is completely extinguished by scattering into the diffracted beam. Extinction was first noted as an important effect in X-ray diffraction by Darwin [2], particularly for strong X-ray reflections. Extinction effects are even more important in electron diffraction because of the greatly increased atomic scattering amplitude for electron waves. Extinction is responsible for the so-called "thickness extinction contours" observed on bright-field and dark-field electron micrographs of wedge shaped crystals, and they were discussed by Hillier and Baker [5], Heidenreich and Sturkey [6] and others. It is worth noting that "Pendellösung" may be thought of as being due to beating between the wave vectors of Bloch waves on the two branches of the dispersion surface of fig. 3.

Fig. 5(a) illustrates the nature of the kinematical approximation. Away from the Bragg position, the depth periodicity of the crystal waves is reduced to $\xi_g/\sqrt{1 + w^2}$. When w is large this approaches s^{-1}, as given by the kinematical theory. Thus in fig. 5(a) the intensity of the direct wave is close to unity, while the diffracted intensity is small.

1.7. Dynamical equations in the Bragg case

It is instructive to mention this case here in order to emphasise the entirely different nature of the crystal wave. In the symmetrical Bragg case, reflection takes place from planes parallel to the crystal surface. Equations analogous to eq. (7) can be derived. As before z is depth below the surface. The equations are

$$\frac{d\phi_o}{dz} = i\pi s \cot\theta\, \phi_o + \frac{i\pi}{\xi_g} \cot\theta\, \phi_g$$

$$\frac{d\phi_g}{dz} = -\frac{i\pi}{\xi_g} \cot\theta\, \phi_o - i\pi s \cot\theta\, \phi_g\ . \tag{35}$$

It is left as an exercise to the student to show that solutions of the above equation of the form $\exp(-\gamma z)$ exist, where $\gamma = \pi \cot\theta \sqrt{1 - w^2}/\xi_g$.

The ratio ϕ_g/ϕ_o at any depth may be calculated and is found to be

$$\frac{\phi_g}{\phi_o} = \frac{-1}{w + i\sqrt{1 - w^2}}\ . \tag{36}$$

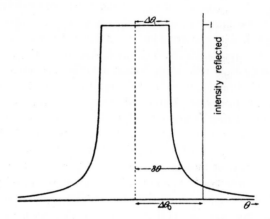

Fig. 6. Rocking curve in the Bragg case. The region where the reflected intensity is unity is given by $|w| \leqslant 1$.

The rocking curve given by (36) is shown in fig. 6. Over the region $|w| < 1$ there is total reflection of the incident wave. The Bragg case was first studied for X-ray diffraction by Darwin [1]. The case is important in the theory of grazing angle electron diffraction. The exponential solution for the crystal waves shows that evanescent waves are excited in the crystal. At the Bragg position ($w=0$), the waves may decay rapidly in a few atomic layers. The crystal wave in this case is not unlike the evanescent wave existing at an interface where total internal reflection of light occurs.

2. Treatment of absorption in the dynamical theory of electron diffraction

The theory as developed in the previous lecture considered the effect of elastic scattering only and led to the idea of the "Pendellösung" solution of the dynamical theory (fig. 5 of sect. 1), where direct and diffracted intensities oscillate with a depth periodicity ξ_g at the Bragg reflection position. It should be noted that for elastic scattering only, this depth oscillation should persist indefinitely, i.e. the visibility of thickness extinction contours on bright-field or dark-field electron micrographs of wedge shaped crystals should be independent of crystal thickness. That this is not the case in practice is evident from micrographs like fig. 7, where it is seen that the intensity of thickness fringes dies away in the thicker regions of the crystal. Only about four or

Fig. 7. Thickness extinction contours in a bright-field image of a wedge crystal of
Cu + 7% Al alloy.

five dark fringes are visible on this micrograph, and ultimately the contrast in
the thick regions is practically uniform, even though there is good transmission
in such regions. Evidently the dynamical theory as developed so far does not
give a sufficiently good description of results. We shall meet other examples in
the next section where the theory including elastic scattering only is at variance
with experiment.

It is well known that a theory treating elastic scattering is a first approximation only. Besides being scattered elastically, the incident electron wave may
also be scattered inelastically by creating various excitations in the crystal, such

as single electron excitations, plasmons, phonons etc. Inelastic scattering phenomena will be discussed in a later chapter by Howie, but we wish to emphasize here that such scattering can give rise to an apparent absorption of the elastically scattered wave by virtue of the fact that the inelastic waves may be scattered outside the aperture of the objective of an electron microscope and hence are prevented from reaching the image. The inelastic scattering appears as a diffuse background between Bragg spots on the electron diffraction pattern.

Yoshioka [7] first showed in a formal quantum-mechanical treatment that the effect of inelastic scattering on the elastic scattering could be represented by the addition of a small imaginary part to the crystal lattice potential, which gives rise to "absorption" of the elastic wave in much the same way as a complex refractive index gives rise to absorption of electromagnetic waves. A similar mechanism had been postulated (Molière [8]) to account for electron diffraction effects in the Bragg case, and a similar theory was also applied in X-ray diffraction by von Laue [9] to explain the experiments of Borrmann [10] (see also Zachariasen [11]).

We intend to give an account of the treatment of absorption due to inelastic scattering in this section, but we wish to emphasize from the start that the theory to be outlined is only a first approximation because the effect of any inelastic scattering which passes through the objective aperture is neglected. Not all the inelastic scattering appears in regions of the diffraction pattern between Bragg spots. Some of the inelastic scattering is concentrated close to the Bragg spots, particularly for single electron and plasmon scattering, and will therefore be included in the electron microscope image for typical aperture sizes. Such scattering can produce image contrast effects which must be added to that due to elastic scattering. Thus the situation can in practice be quite complicated, i.e. the "absorption" itself can be a function of aperture size.

2.1. A uniform absorbing potential

Consider an electron wave with free-space wave vector χ, which enters a crystal with inner potential V_0 volts. If the energy of the electron is E eV, we have

$$E = \frac{h^2}{2me} \chi^2 \tag{37}$$

$$E + V_0 = \frac{h^2}{2me} \mathbf{K}^2 , \tag{38}$$

where $\mathbf{K}$ is the wave vector inside the crystal and e is the electronic charge. To satisfy continuity of the wave function at the plane boundary, we require

$$K_t = \chi_t \tag{39}$$

where these quantities are the tangential components of the wave vectors parallel to the boundary. Hence we find for the refractive index μ

$$\mu = \frac{|\mathbf{K}|}{|\chi|} = \left\{1 + \frac{V_o}{E}\right\}^{\frac{1}{2}} \simeq 1 + \frac{1}{2}\frac{V_o}{E} \tag{40}$$

since $V_o \ll E$. This equation is equivalent to eq. (8) of sect. 1 since V_o is related to $f(0)$ by

$$V_o = \frac{h^2}{2\pi me} N f(0) . \tag{41}$$

Now suppose we add a small imaginary part to V_o, i.e.

$$V_o \rightarrow V_o + i\, V_o' . \tag{42}$$

Then in place of (38) we should write

$$E + V_o + i\, V_o' = \frac{h^2}{2me} (K_t^2 + (K_z + i\delta)^2) \tag{43}$$

where K_z is the perpendicular component of $\mathbf{K}$ in (38), and δ is a small imaginary addition to K_z due to V_o'. The wave in the crystal will now be of the form

$$\exp(2\pi i \mathbf{K}\cdot\mathbf{r}) \exp(-2\pi\delta z) \tag{44}$$

the exponential decay describing absorption.

From (43) we can show (neglecting $O(\delta^2)$) that

$$\delta = \frac{me}{h^2 K_z} V_o' . \tag{45}$$

Hence the absorption coefficient for amplitude, κ, is given by

$$\kappa = 2\pi\delta = \frac{2\pi me}{h^2 K_z} V_o' . \tag{46}$$

Absorption can be described equally well by allowing the atomic scattering amplitude for electron waves to become complex;

$$f(\theta) \rightarrow f(\theta) + if'(\theta) \tag{47}$$

since V_0' will be related to $f'(0)$ by an expression similar to (41). We then find

$$\kappa = \frac{N f'(0)}{K_z} . \tag{48}$$

In keeping with the notation of the previous section, we define "absorption distances", ξ_0', ξ_g' by an expression similar to eq. (2) of sect. 1

$$\xi_g' = \frac{\pi K \Omega \cos\theta}{f'(\theta)} . \tag{49}$$

We then have for a uniform absorbing potential

$$\kappa = \pi / \xi_0' . \tag{50}$$

2.2. Anomalous absorption

We note from above that the effect of a uniform absorbing potential in a crystal lattice would be to attenuate all Bloch waves to the same extent. Thus thickness extinction contours in a wedge crystal should decrease in intensity with increasing thickness t like $\exp(-2\pi t/\xi_0')$. However the visibility of the fringes $((I_{max}-I_{min})/(I_{max}+I_{min}))$ would not depend on thickness. The effect of uniform absorption is simply to decrease the scale of the intensity of fringes in thick regions of the crystal. That this is not the case in practice is evident from micrographs like fig. 7, where even though the fringes fade out, there is still very good transmission in thick regions. We may explain the observations if there is selective absorption of the two Bloch waves in the two-beam theory. The selective absorption is referred to as "anomalous absorption", even though the description "anomalous" is really a misnomer, and the physical explanation of the effect is illustrated in fig. 8. This shows the wave patterns of the two Bloch waves belonging to branches 1 and 2 of the dispersion surface at the Bragg position (w=0). Eqs. (16), (17), (19), (20) and (21) of sect. 1 show that for $w = 0$

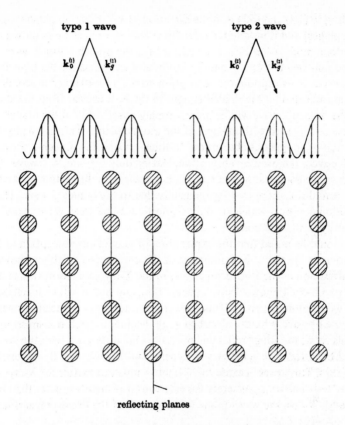

Fig. 8. Schematic diagram illustrating "anomalous absorption" at the Bragg position. The current flow vector is parallel to the reflecting planes. Absorbing regions at atoms are shaded. The type 2 wave is absorbed more than the type 1 wave.

$$B^{(i)}(\mathbf{r}) = \frac{1}{\sqrt{2}} \{\exp{(2\pi i \mathbf{k}_0^{(i)} \cdot \mathbf{r})} + (-1)^i \exp{(2\pi i (\mathbf{k}_0^{(i)} + \mathbf{g}) \cdot \mathbf{r})}\}. \qquad (51)$$

We may express this as

$$B^{(1)}(\mathbf{r}) = -i\sqrt{2} \exp{(2\pi i |\mathbf{k}_0^{(1)} + \tfrac{1}{2}\mathbf{g}|z)} \sin \pi g x \qquad (52)$$

$$B^{(2)}(\mathbf{r}) = \sqrt{2} \exp{(2\pi i |\mathbf{k}_0^{(2)} + \tfrac{1}{2}\mathbf{g}|z)} \cos \pi g x \qquad (53)$$

where x is a coordinate in the surface parallel to $\mathbf{g}$. The current flow corresponding to (52) and (53) is in the direction of $\mathbf{k}_0^{(i)} + \frac{1}{2}\mathbf{g}$ (i.e. parallel to the Bragg planes) and is modulated laterally as $\sin^2 \pi g$ or $\cos^2 \pi g$ as shown in fig. 8. The lateral modulation causes the current for the branch 1 Bloch wave to be located mid-way between planes of atoms and vice versa for the branch 2 Bloch wave. Now suppose the absorption effect is located at the atomic positions as indicated by the shaded regions in fig. 8. It is clear from this diagram that the branch 2 wave will be more strongly absorbed than the branch 1 wave because it is located with maxima at the atomic planes. This is the physical explanation of anomalous absorption. In thick crystals the branch 2 wave will be effectively removed by absorption, leaving only the branch 1 wave. Thus we may have good transmission in thick regions with diffraction contrast effects from dislocations (see fig. 7) mainly due to the branch 1 wave. Thickness extinction contours which are due to interference between waves 1 and 2 will fade away in thick regions.

It should be noted that the explanation of anomalous absorption of electrons given here is the electron counterpart of the corresponding effect known in X-ray diffraction as the Borrmann effect. In the X-ray case absorption is due mainly to K-shell photo-electron production, and hence will be localised very close to the atomic centres. This gives rise to a rather extreme effect whereby one type of wave is hardly absorbed at all, leading to good transmission in thick crystals set at the Bragg reflecting position. One difference with the X-ray case should be noted. The symmetry of types 1 and 2 waves (fig. 8) is interchanged for X-rays. This arises because the refractive index of matter for X-rays is slightly less than unity, whereas for electrons it is slightly greater than unity. Hence for X-rays the wave on the lower branch of the dispersion surface is more strongly absorbed.

The selective absorption of electrons has been referred to as "channelling". Howie will be dealing with this in a later chapter, but we wish to note that channelling effects can be important in situations where multiple Bragg reflections are excited. The channelling properties of all the n Bloch waves excited need to be considered.

2.3. Dynamical equations describing absorption

Absorption may be included in the theory given in the first lecture by allowing the crystal potential to have a small periodic imaginary part or by allowing the atomic scattering amplitude to become complex (eq. (47)). This is equivalent to making the following substitutions in eq. (5) of the previous section

$$\frac{1}{\xi_o} \rightarrow \frac{1}{\xi_o} + \frac{i}{\xi'_o} \tag{54}$$

$$\frac{1}{\xi_g} \rightarrow \frac{1}{\xi_g} + \frac{i}{\xi'_g} . \tag{55}$$

We start with the equations in the form

$$\frac{d\phi_o}{dz} = i \frac{\pi}{\xi_o} \phi_o + i \frac{\pi}{\xi_g} \phi_g$$

$$\frac{d\phi_g}{dz} = i \frac{\pi}{\xi_g} \phi_o + i \left(\frac{\pi}{\xi_o} + 2\pi s \right) \phi_g \tag{56}$$

which can be derived from (5) of section 1 by putting $\phi'_g = \phi_g \exp(2\pi i s z)$. In eqs. (56) we must make the substitutions (54) and (55).

We put

$$\phi'_o = \phi_o \exp\left(-i\pi z \left(\frac{1}{\xi_o} + \frac{i}{\xi'_o} \right) \right)$$

$$\phi'_g = \phi_g \exp\left(-i\pi z \left(\frac{1}{\xi_o} + \frac{i}{\xi'_o} \right) \right) \tag{57}$$

in (56), and note that besides accounting for mean refraction by the term in ξ_o^{-1} as before, these equations now contain a mean absorption term $\exp(\pi z/\xi'_o)$. We then find

$$\frac{d\phi'_o}{dz} = i\pi \left\{ \frac{1}{\xi_g} + \frac{i}{\xi'_g} \right\} \phi'_g$$

$$\frac{d\phi'_g}{dz} = i\pi \left\{ \frac{1}{\xi_g} + \frac{i}{\xi'_g} \right\} \phi'_o + 2\pi i s \, \phi'_g \tag{58}$$

which are eqs. (7) of section 1 in the case of absorption. Proceeding as before we find that ϕ'_o and ϕ'_g both satisfy the differential equation

$$\frac{d^2\phi'_o}{dz^2} - 2\pi i s \frac{d\phi'_o}{dz} + \pi^2 \left\{ \frac{1}{\xi_g^2} - \frac{1}{\xi'^2_g} + \frac{2i}{\xi_g \xi'_g} \right\} \phi'_o = 0 . \tag{59}$$

We try a solution of (59) of the form $\exp(2\pi i \gamma z)$ and find

$$\gamma^{(1)} = \tfrac{1}{2}\left(s - \frac{1}{\xi_g}\sqrt{1 + w^2} + 2i\frac{\xi_g}{\xi'_g} \right)$$

$$\hat{=} \tfrac{1}{2}\left(s - \frac{1}{\xi_g}\sqrt{1 + w^2} - \frac{i}{\xi'_g \sqrt{1 + w^2}} \right)$$

$$= \frac{1}{2\xi_g}(w - \sqrt{1+w^2}) - \frac{i}{2\xi'_g \sqrt{1 + w^2}} \;. \tag{60}$$

We have neglected ξ'^{-2}_g and assumed that ξ_g/ξ'_g is small compared with unity. Similarly we find for $\gamma^{(2)}$

$$\gamma^{(2)} = \frac{1}{2\xi_g}(w + \sqrt{1+w^2}) + \frac{i}{2\xi'_g \sqrt{1 + w^2}} \;. \tag{61}$$

We note that eqs. (60) and (61) differ from (11) and (12) of sect. 1 only by the appearance of a small imaginary part describing absorption. To obtain the actual absorption coefficient we must take account of the mean absorption term in (57). We find that the amplitude absorption coefficients for the two Bloch waves are

$$\kappa^{(1)} = \pi\left(\frac{1}{\xi'_0} - \frac{i}{\xi'_g \sqrt{1 + w^2}} \right)$$

$$\kappa^{(2)} = \pi\left(\frac{1}{\xi'_0} + \frac{i}{\xi'_g \sqrt{1 + w^2}} \right). \tag{62}$$

The wave on branch 1 of the dispersion surface has a lower absorption co-efficient than that of the branch 2 wave. At the reflecting position ($w=0$), the difference between the two absorption coefficients is a maximum, and the effect is most extreme when $\xi'_g = \xi'_0$. In this case the wave on branch 1 has zero absorption coefficient, while that on branch 2 has twice the average absorption coefficient. The conditions $\xi'_g = \xi'_0$ implies through eq. (49) that $f'(\theta) = f'(0)$, i.e. the absorptive power is distributed in the crystal lattice like δ-functions at the atomic positions in fig. 8. For X-ray diffraction $f'(\theta)$ is very nearly equal to $f'(0)$ because the absorption is due to K-shell photoelectric processes concentrated close to the atomic centres. For electrons it has often been assumed that $\xi'_0 = \xi'_g$ and that $\xi'_g \cong 10\xi_g$ in calculations of diffraction contrast. Absorption parameter have been estimated by Hashimoto [12] and by Metherell and Whelan [13] using experimental profiles of thickness extinction contours. For aluminium ξ_0'/ξ_g' is about 30. Thus the rough estimates mentioned above may not be very reliable. Calculations of ξ_g'/ξ_g for various elements as a function of temperature and g have been made by Humphreys and Hirsch [14] on the basis of single electron and phonon scattering.

2.4. The Laue solution with absorption

Having estimated the amplitude absorption coefficients (62) for the two crystal Bloch waves, we can proceed as in sect. 1.4 to evaluate direct and diffracted waves from a crystal of thickness t. In place of (25) of sect. 1 we have

$$\psi(\mathbf{r}) = \psi^{(1)} B^{(1)}(\mathbf{r}) \exp(-\kappa^{(1)}z) + \psi^{(2)} B^{(2)}(\mathbf{r}) \exp(-\kappa^{(2)}z) . \tag{63}$$

The boundary conditions at the top surface of the crystal are applied in the same way. We find the same values for the excitation amplitudes $\psi^{(1)}$ and $\psi^{(2)}$. Eventually we obtain

$$\phi_0(t) = \exp(-\pi t/\xi_0') \left\{ \cos X - \frac{iw}{\sqrt{1+w^2}} \sin X \right\} \tag{64}$$

$$\phi_g(t) = \exp(-\pi t/\xi_0') \frac{i \sin X}{\sqrt{1+w^2}} \tag{65}$$

where

$$X = \frac{\pi t}{\xi_g} \sqrt{1+w^2} + \frac{i\pi t}{\xi_g' \sqrt{1+w^2}} . \tag{66}$$

We see that the solution including absorption is formally similar to that without absorption (eqs. (31), (32) of sect. 1).

Absorption is included simply by allowing the arguments of the sines and cosines to become complex according to (66) and by multiplying by the term $\exp(-\pi t/\xi_0')$ which represents the average absorption.

2.5. Examination of the Laue solution with absorption

Figs. 9 and 10 show examples of "rocking curves" computed from eqs. (64) and (65). Fig. 9 shows the effect of increasing absorption for a crystal of constant thickness ($t=4\xi_g$). Fig. 9a is for the case of no absorption and we see that the bright-field (full curve) and dark-field (broken curve) rocking curves are

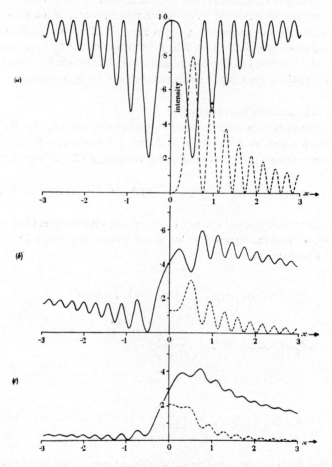

Fig. 9. "Rocking curves" computed from the two-beam theory for $t = 4\xi_g$. Full curves refer to bright field; broken curves refer to dark field.(a) No absorption, (b) $\xi_g/\xi_g' = 0.05$, (c) $\xi_g/\xi_g' = 0.10$. $\xi_0' = \xi_g'$.

complementary, as expected for no absorption. With increasing absorption, i.e. increasing ξ_g/ξ_g', the bright-field curve becomes asymmetrical about $w = 0$. The dark-field curve remains symmetrical. Note also that the amplitude of the oscillations of the curves decreases with increasing absorption and increasing thickness (fig. 10). In fig. 10 oscillations are visible for $t = 1.5\xi_g$ but are no longer visible when $t = 10\xi_g$. The decrease in amplitude of the oscillations is a direct consequence of the preferential absorption of the branch 2 wave.

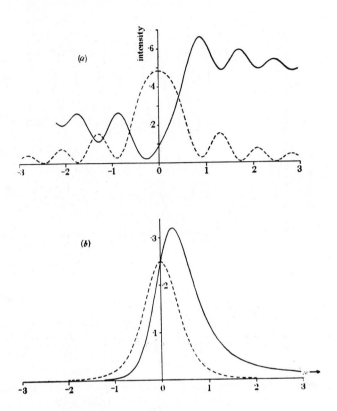

Fig. 10. "Rocking curves" computed from the two-beam theory. Full curves refer to bright field; broken curves refer to dark field. $\xi_g/\xi'_g = 0.10$, $\xi'_0 = \xi'_g$. (a) $t = 1.5\xi_g$, (b) $t = 10\xi_g$.

Fig. 11 shows the effect of absorption on thickness extinction contours at the Bragg position. In fig. 11a Pendellösung fringes persist indefinitely in the thick regions, whereas in figs. 11b and c they are seen to fade out more rapidly with increasing absorption.

Figs. 7, 12 show examples of extinction contours in various materials illustrating the effects predicted by the theory. We have already discussed the significance of the fading-out of fringes in fig. 7 and we can understand this in terms of the theory of Pendellösung fringes including anomalous absorption (figs. 11b and c). Fig. 12 is an example of a bend extinction contour in an aluminium foil whose thickness increases over the field of view. The contour

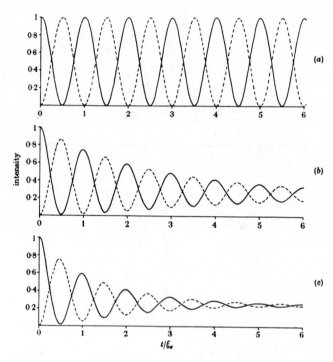

Fig. 11. Profile of Pendellösung fringes computed from the two-beam theory. $\xi'_0 = \xi'_g$. (a)
No absorption, (b) $\xi_g/\xi'_g = 0.05$ (c) $\xi_g/\xi'_g = 0.10$.

is due to a pair of Bragg reflections, 111 and $\overline{1}\overline{1}\overline{1}$. Because of the smallness of
the Bragg angle, a region of the foil where the 111 reflections is strongly ex-
cited will only be separated by a small distance from the adjacent region
where $\overline{1}\overline{1}\overline{1}$ is excited for moderate bending of the foil. These contours are
therefore due to pairs of Bragg reflections like 111 and $\overline{1}\overline{1}\overline{1}$, each edge of the
contour producing one or other of these reflections. Thus the form of the
bright-field image of the contour is qualitatively described by a pair of curves
like figs. 9 and 10 arranged back to back, joining up in the region of negative
w (shown as x on these figures) where the bright field intensity is low. In thin
regions a trace across the contour shows intensity oscillations as predicted in
figs. 8 and 10. In thicker regions the intensity oscillations fade out as predicted in fig. 10b, so that in such regions the bend extinction contour looks
like a dark band. The regions on either side of this dark band show good trans-

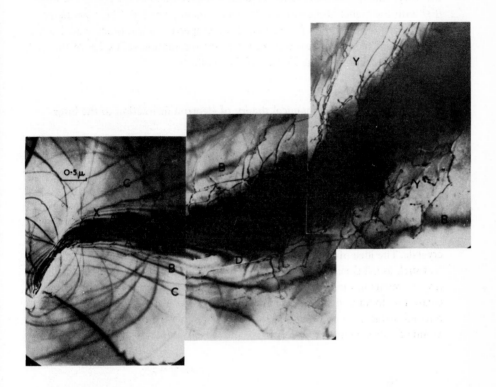

Fig. 12. Bright-field image of a bend extinction contour in a region of varying thickness of an aluminium foil. Note the reduced intensity inside the contour compared with the outside especially in thick regions. Note also the disappearance of subsidiary oscillations in thick regions.

mission corresponding to the maximum in the intensity profile for $w > 0$ in figs. 9 and 10.

We conclude by pointing out the physical reason for the asymmetry about $w = 0$ of bright-field images of bend extinction contours. We refer to eqs. (28) and (29) of sect. 1 which give the amplitudes $\psi^{(1)}$ and $\psi^{(2)}$ describing the excitation of the two Bloch waves on the two branches of the dispersion surface. We see from these equations that at $w = 0$ ($\beta = \pi/2$), both Bloch waves are excited to the same extent. However for $w > 0$ ($\beta < \pi/2$) $\psi^{(1)}$ is greater than $\psi^{(2)}$ and vice-versa for $w < 0$ ($\beta > \pi/2$). Thus for $w > 0$ the Bloch wave $B^{(1)}$, with the lower absorption coefficient is mainly excited, whereas for $w < 0$ the wave $B^{(2)}$ with the higher absorption coefficient is mainly excited. The asymmetry is therefore a result both of the channelling properties of the Bloch waves and of the extent to which these are excited as the orientation varies, i.e. of the boundary conditions at the surface of the crystal.

3. Applications of the dynamical theory of electron diffraction to the interpretation of contrast effects at crystal defects

We saw in the previous two sections how the theory could be developed in a simple manner and we have applied it to explain the details of extinction contours in perfect crystals. We now intend to apply the theory to crystals containing defects such as dislocations, faults, etc. The application of the theory is based on the use of the so-called "column approximation", which enables us to calculate the diffracted intensities from continuously deformed crystals. The idea of the column approximation is illustrated in fig. 13. A defect such as a dislocation line is located at O and it is assumed that the atomic displacements in the foil due to the defect are known. It is required to calculate the direct and diffracted amplitudes ϕ_o and ϕ_g at a point B on the bottom surface. We consider a narrow column of crystal AB in which the atomic displacement function is $\mathbf{R}(z)$, and we calculate the amplitudes ϕ_o and

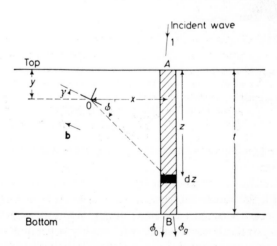

Fig. 13. Illustrating the coordinates used to describe a dislocation in a foil. r is a radial coordinate measured from O.

ϕ_g for this column as if it were of great lateral extent, i.e. we calculate for a crystal in which the displacement function $R(z)$ is independent of the lateral coordinate. Such a crystal may be thought of as made up of a number of slabs, each perfect but displaced relative to each other according to $R(z)$. The column approximation is a good approximation for electron diffraction, mainly because the Bragg angles are very small. Thus the fan included by direct and diffracted rays emanating from a point A on the top surface is very slender, and such rays essentially sample the strain field along a line in the crystal. For X-rays however the Bragg angle is much larger and the fan mentioned above may be quite wide. In this case account must also be taken of the variation of R with a lateral coordinate [15−17]. The significance of the column approximation is that it enables us to forget about the lateral dependence of displacements R when calculating contrast, and hence a system of coupled partial differential equations is reduced to a system of coupled ordinary differential equations. The contrast near the defect is obtained by varying the position x of the column, when, of course, the displacement field $R(z)$ in the column will vary. The column approximation was first used in the treatment of contrast effects at stacking faults [18,19] where it was noted that the method led to the same result as a more detailed wave matching calculation at an inclined fault. Subsequently the approximation was used in the kinematical treatment of contrast at dislocations [20] and in the dynamical treatment [21,22]. A critical discussion of the column approximation has been given by Basinski and Howie [17].

3.1. Dynamical equations in a deformed crystal

If the displacement at depth z in the column is $R(z)$, the equations corresponding to (5) of the first section are

$$\frac{d\phi_o}{dz} = i\frac{\pi}{\xi_o}\phi_o + i\frac{\pi}{\xi_g}\phi_g \exp\left(2\pi i s z + 2\pi i \mathbf{g}\cdot\mathbf{R}\right)$$

$$\frac{d\phi_g}{dz} = i\frac{\pi}{\xi_g}\phi_o \exp\left(-2\pi i s z - 2\pi i \mathbf{g}\cdot\mathbf{R}\right) + i\frac{\pi}{\xi_g}\phi_g. \tag{67}$$

In this form the atomic displacements appear in the arguments of the exponentials in much the same way as they appear in the kinematical theory. We can see this by noting from eq. (2) of sect. 1 that ξ_g^{-1} is proportional to $f(\theta)$. If an atom is displaced by $\mathbf{R}$, the phase of the scattered wave is changed by $\exp(-2\pi i \mathbf{g}\cdot\mathbf{R})$. Thus in the first of eqs. (67) above a phase change of $\exp(+2\pi i \mathbf{g}\cdot\mathbf{R})$ should be introduced because the term describes scattering from the diffracted to the direct wave. Similarly in the second of eqs. (67) the phase change is $\exp(-2\pi i\mathbf{g}\cdot\mathbf{R})$ because the scattering is from the direct to the diffracted wave. If eqs. (67) are integrated down a column for a crystal of thickness t we obtain the amplitudes of direct and diffracted waves at the lower surface.

3.2. Stacking fault

The situation is illustrated in fig. 14. We have a stacking fault characterised by a displacement vector $\mathbf{R}$ at depth t_1. The displacement function is

$$R(z) = 0, \quad 0 \leqslant z \leqslant t_1 ; \quad R(z) = \mathbf{R}, \quad t_1 \leqslant z \leqslant t . \qquad (68)$$

For the upper portion 1 of the crystal, the waves $\phi_o(t_1)$ and $\phi_g(t_1)$ incident on the fault are the same as for a perfect crystal of thickness t_1, the solution of which we have already obtained, (cf. eqs. (24), (27) and (30) of sect. 1). We may write this in matrix form

$$\begin{pmatrix}\phi_o(t_1)\\ \phi_g(t_1)\end{pmatrix} = \begin{pmatrix}\cos\frac{1}{2}\beta & \sin\frac{1}{2}\beta\\ -\sin\frac{1}{2}\beta & \cos\frac{1}{2}\beta\end{pmatrix}\begin{pmatrix}\exp(2\pi i\gamma^{(1)}t_1) & 0\\ 0 & \exp(2\pi i\gamma^{(2)}t_1)\end{pmatrix}$$
$$\times \begin{pmatrix}\cos\frac{1}{2}\beta & -\sin\frac{1}{2}\beta\\ \sin\frac{1}{2}\beta & \cos\frac{1}{2}\beta\end{pmatrix}\begin{pmatrix}\phi_o(0)\\ \phi_g(0)\end{pmatrix}. \qquad (69)$$

We have allowed for the possibility that $\phi_g(0)$ has a non-zero value at the top surface. In a similar manner eqs. (67) may be integrated in the lower crystal and obviously the solution must be like that of a perfect crystal of thickness t_2, except that we must now allow for the displacement $\mathbf{R}$. We put $\alpha = 2\pi\mathbf{g}\cdot\mathbf{R}$; α is called the phase angle of the fault. The constant displacement $\mathbf{R}$ causes the terms $C_g^{(i)}$ in eq. (30) of sect. 1 to become $C_g^{(i)}\exp(-i\alpha)$. Thus for the lower portion z of the crystal we have

$$\begin{pmatrix}\phi_o(t)\\ \phi_g(t)\end{pmatrix} = \begin{pmatrix}\cos\frac{1}{2}\beta & \sin\frac{1}{2}\beta\\ -\sin\frac{1}{2}\beta\exp(-i\alpha) & \cos\frac{1}{2}\beta\exp(-i\alpha)\end{pmatrix}\begin{pmatrix}\exp(2\pi i\gamma^{(1)}t_2) & 0\\ 0 & \exp(2\pi i\gamma^{(2)}t_2)\end{pmatrix}$$
$$\times \begin{pmatrix}\cos\frac{1}{2}\beta & -\sin\frac{1}{2}\beta\exp(i\alpha)\\ \sin\frac{1}{2}\beta & \cos\frac{1}{2}\beta\exp(i\alpha)\end{pmatrix}\begin{pmatrix}\phi_o(t_1)\\ \phi_g(t_1)\end{pmatrix} \qquad (70)$$

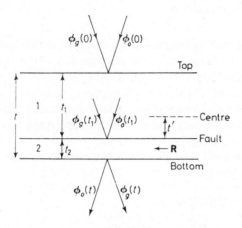

Fig. 14. Schematic diagram illustrating the parameters used to describe a stacking fault parallel to the surface. For an inclined fault t' varies across the fault.

For the column vector at the right of (70) we use the expression (69), and the solution for the faulted crystal becomes the products of several matrices. Putting $\phi_o(0) = 1$, $\phi_g(0) = 0$, corresponding to having only an incident wave at the top, we find after some algebra (omitting an unimportant phase term $\exp(\pi i(\gamma^{(1)}+\gamma^{(2)})t))$,

$$\phi_o(t) = \cos(\pi\Delta kt) - i \cos\beta \sin(\pi\Delta kt)$$

$$+ \tfrac{1}{2} \sin^2\beta \, (\exp(i\alpha)-1) \cos(\pi\Delta kt)$$

$$- \tfrac{1}{2} \sin^2\beta \, (\exp(i\alpha)-1) \cos(2\pi\Delta kt') \tag{71}$$

$$\phi_g(t) = i \sin\beta \sin(\pi\Delta kt)$$

$$+ \tfrac{1}{2} \sin\beta \, (1-\exp(-i\alpha)) \, [\cos\beta \cos(\pi\Delta kt) - i \sin(\pi\Delta kt)]$$

$$- \tfrac{1}{2} \sin\beta \, (1-\exp(-i\alpha)) \, [\cos\beta \cos(2\pi\Delta kt') - i \sin(2\pi\Delta kt')] \tag{72}$$

where $t' = t_1 - \tfrac{1}{2}t$ is the distance of the fault from the centre of the crystal (fig. 14), and where

$$\Delta k = (1+w^2)^{\frac{1}{2}}/\xi_g \tag{73}$$

For an inclined fault running across the crystal, t' in (71) and (72) will vary. Thus there will be fringes due to the third terms in (71) and (72). The depth periodicity of the fringes will in general be $\xi_g/\sqrt{1 + w^2}$. If $\alpha = 0$, or $2n\pi$ we note that (71) and (72) reduce to the perfect crystal expression of the first section, as expected. Moreover, even when α is non zero, the solutions (71) and (72) join continuously to that of the perfect crystal at the top and bottom surfaces ($t'=-\frac{1}{2}t$ and $t'=+\frac{1}{2}t$).

We note also that (71) and (72) are applicable to the case of an absorbing crystal provided we put

$$\Delta k = \frac{\sqrt{1 + w^2}}{\xi_g} + \frac{i}{\xi_g' \sqrt{1 + w^2}} \tag{74}$$

and multiply ϕ_0 and ϕ_g by $\exp(-\pi t/\xi_0')$ to include mean absorption.

3.3. Dislocations, inclusions etc.

Each problem encountered under this heading usually has to be studied individually. The first step is to try to find a satisfactory model for describing the displacement field **R** around the defect. Usually simple models based on isotropic continuum elasticity theory are employed for want of more exact models. Effects such as the nature of relaxation of the strain field due to the free surface of a foil or to the presence of oxide films are usually neglected, or crudely approximated. We wish to stress, therefore, that there may be difficulties involved in expressing the displacement field **R** accurately, before proceeding with the computation of contrast from eq. (67).

It is useful to transform eqs. (67) by putting

$$\phi_0' = \phi_0 \exp(-i\pi z/\xi_0) \tag{75}$$

$$\phi_g' = \phi_g \exp\left(-i\pi \frac{z}{\xi_0} + 2\pi isz + 2\pi ig\cdot R\right). \tag{76}$$

Making the substitutions (54) and (55) of sect. 2, we obtain

$$\frac{d\phi'_0}{dz} = -\frac{\pi}{\xi'_0}\phi'_0 + \pi\left(\frac{i}{\xi_g} - \frac{1}{\xi'_g}\right)\phi'_g$$

$$\frac{d\phi'_g}{dz} = \pi\left(\frac{i}{\xi_g} - \frac{1}{\xi'_g}\right)\phi'_0 + \left(-\frac{\pi}{\xi'_0} + 2\pi i(s+\beta')\right)\phi'_g \tag{77}$$

where

$$\beta' = \frac{1}{2\pi}\frac{d\alpha}{dz} = \frac{d}{dz}(\mathbf{g}\cdot\mathbf{R}(z)). \tag{78}$$

The transformations (75) and (76) do not affect intensities, and in practice the eqs. (77) are simpler to use than eqs. (67), since calculation of an exponential at every step of the integration by numerical methods is undesirable. Moreover, eqs. (77) now contain only the derivative of the displacement, β', and in some cases it is easier to calculate the derivative than the displacement itself. The eqs. (77) also demonstrate that strain contrast essentially arises from local bending of the lattice planes causing Bragg reflection. The tilting of these planes is proportional to β', and the equations show that this tilt simply increases the deviation parameter s locally.

3.4. Examples of the application of the theory to contrast problems
3.4.1. Stacking faults $|\alpha| = 2\pi/3$

The image of a stacking fault is characterised by the value of $\alpha = 2\pi\mathbf{g}\cdot\mathbf{R}$ in eqs. (71) and (72). In face centred cubic materials stacking faults may be produced on $\{111\}$ planes by a shear of type $\frac{1}{6}\langle 112\rangle$, or by removal or insertion of a plane of atoms as happens when vacancies or interstitial atoms condense on close packed planes. The nature of the faults produced by shear or by condensation of point defects is the same. The only difference lies in the type of partial dislocation bounding the fault. Faults formed by shear are bounded by glissile Shockley partials, whereas those formed by condensation of point defects are bounded by sessile Frank partials. Experimentally stacking faults may be produced in a variety of ways, by deformation (by movement of Shockley partial dislocations), by accidents during crystal growth (e.g. vapour deposition or electrodeposition of thin films) or by experiments involving condensation of point defects (e.g. in quenching or radiation damage). In face centred cubic materials faults are generally classified as intrinsic or extrinsic. An intrinsic fault is caused by motion of a single Shockley partial (involving shear on one plane only), or by condensation of vacancies (i.e. by removal of a plane of atoms). An extrinsic fault is caused by motion of a Shockley partial involving shear on two adjacent planes, or by condensation of interstitial atoms (i.e. by insertion of a close packed plane of atoms). The net shear of an extrinsic fault is opposite to that of an intrinsic fault. Therefore if an intrinsic fault is characterised by a certain value of α in a particular situation, an extrinsic fault in the same situation will be characterised by the negative of that value.

We may take an intrinsic fault on (111) in the fcc lattice with shear vector $\mathbf{R} = \frac{1}{6}[1\bar{2}1]$. For the reflection $\mathbf{g} = (h,k,l)$, $\alpha = 2\pi\mathbf{g}\cdot\mathbf{R}$ is then given by

$$\alpha = \tfrac{1}{3}\pi\,(h-2k+l)\,. \tag{79}$$

In the fcc lattice, h,k,l are either all odd or all even, thus α turns out to be $2n\pi/3$, where $n = 0, \pm1, \pm2$ etc., depending on the indices of the Bragg reflection. It is customary to refer to α modulo 2π ($-\pi<\alpha\leqslant+\pi$). The possible values of α are $0, \pm2\pi/3$ modulo 2π. For $\alpha = 0$ the fault will be invisible. This vanishing criterion can be used to determine the direction of $\mathbf{R}$ by examining the visibility of a fault in a number of reflections. The method can be used to determine the phase angle of a fault, e.g. to distinguish between π-faults and $2\pi/3$-faults (Drum [23], Van Landuyt et al. [24]).

The contrast from $2\pi/3$-faults computed from eqs. (71) and (72) is shown in fig. 15 for the case of no absorption (Whelan and Hirsch [18]). The abscissa

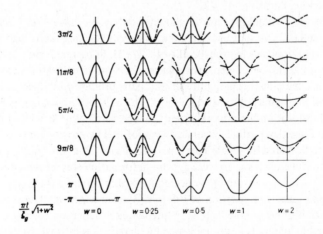

Fig. 15. Computed profiles of stacking fault fringes for the case of no absorption. Broken curves refer to negative values of w.

on each graph is $2\pi t' \sqrt{1 + w^2}/\xi_g$. It is seen that when $w = 0$ the fringes have a depth periodicity $\Delta t' = \frac{1}{2}\xi_g$, i.e. half that of the corresponding wedge fringes which would be observed if one half of the faulted crystal were removed. Away from the Bragg position, fringes are alternately strong and weak and the depth periodicity is $\Delta t' = \xi_g/\sqrt{1 + w^2}$. Without absorption the fringe profile across the fault is uniform. Fig. 16a and b illustrates schematically the appearance of fringes in a wedge crystal and in a bent crystal. It is seen that the fringes show a branching behaviour near where they cross extinction contours in the foil.

Fringes at stacking faults are well known experimentally. Figs. 17 and 18 show examples from a Cu + 7% Al alloy and fcc cobalt (due to Heidenreich). Fig. 17a is a bright-field image; fig. 17b is the corresponding dark-field image. We notice immediately a discrepancy between the theoretical profiles without absorption and the experimental images. While the image in fig. 17a is symmetrical about the centre of the foil, the fringe profile is not uniform across the fault. The visibility of the fringes is greater near the edges of the fault, i.e. near where the fault intersects top and bottom surfaces. Moreover, the dark-field image is asymmetrical about the centre. One edge has a dark fringe while the other has a light fringe. This behaviour which is not explained by the curves of fig. 15, is a result of absorption. Fig. 18 shows the branching of fringes near thickness extinction contours. It is clear from this picture that the branching occurs near the centre of the fault, the edge fringe being continuous. This

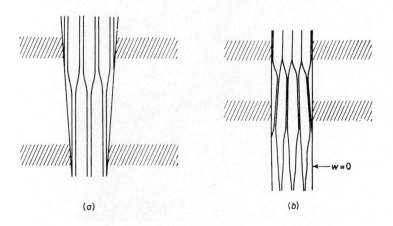

(a) (b)

Fig. 16. Schematic diagram of branching of fringes at stacking fault images for no absorption. (a) fixed w, t varying; (b) fixed t, w varying.

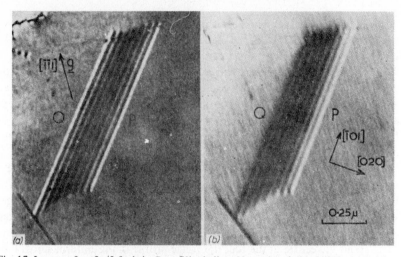

Fig. 17. Images of a $+2\pi/3$-fault in Cu + 7% Al alloy. Normal to foil is [101]. (a) Bright-field image; (b) dark-field image. Compare with fig. 19.

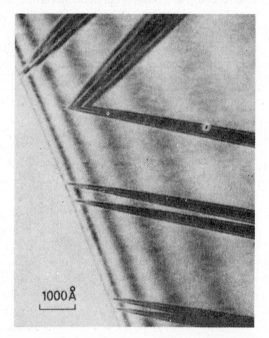

Fig. 18. The behaviour of fringes at stacking faults near thickness extinction contours in cobalt foil. Note that the branching of fringes occurs near the centre of the fault. The micrograph is due to R.D.Heidenreich.

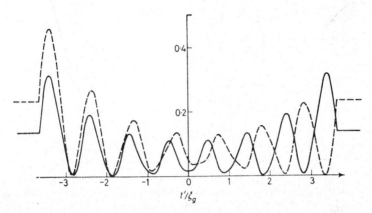

Fig. 19. Computed profile of stacking fault fringes in fig. 17. Full line is bright-field image; broken line is dark-field image. $a = +2\pi/3$; $t/\xi_g = 7.25$; $\xi_0' = \xi_g'$; $\xi_g/\xi_g' = 0.075$; $w = -0.2$.

again is in disagreement with the theory without absorption, where branching should occur uniformly across the fault and in particular at the edges (fig. 16).

In fig. 19 we show a computed profile of stacking fault fringes calculated to match the images in fig. 17. Account has been taken of anomalous absorption by the method mentioned at the end of sect. 3.2. We notice that the bright-field image is symmetrical while the dark-field image is asymmetrical, as observed experimentally. Also the visibility of the fringes is lower near the centre of the foil. A detailed study of the fringes in wedge shaped or bent crystals also shows that the branching of the fringes occurs near the middle of the foil only, the edge fringes being continuous, as observed in fig. 18 [25,26]. Thus these special contrast effects at faults provide further evidence for the correctness of the theory of electron diffraction including absorption.

3.4.2. Determination of the type of stacking fault

Fig. 19 also illustrates a further important point from which interesting deductions can be made. The edge fringes in the bright-field image are seen to be bright for the chosen case $\alpha = +2\pi/3$. If α had been chosen to be $-2\pi/3$, the edge fringes would have been a dark fringe. Thus the sense of the edge fringe is determined simply by the sign of the phase angle α. The result holds for reasonably thick crystals in the presence of anomalous absorption. From fig. 19 we also see that bright-field and dark-field images are similar at the top surface ($t'=-\frac{1}{2}t$, where the electron beam enters) and are pseudo-complementary near the bottom surface ($t'=+\frac{1}{2}t$). We can therefore say that P is the top

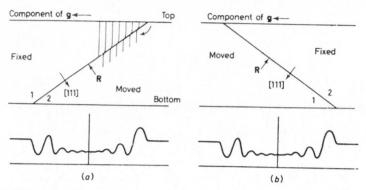

Fig. 20. Illustrating the two possible senses of inclination of a stacking fault. The bright field images would differ. In (a) $\alpha = +2\pi/3$ and the edge fringe of the bright-field image would be light; in (b) $\alpha = -2\pi/3$ and the edge fringe of the bright-field image would be dark. The dark field images of both cases are the same as illustrated.

surface and Q is the bottom surface for the fault in fig. 17a and b. Thus by taking bright-field and dark-field micrographs we can distinguish between the two possible senses of inclination of the fault, as shown in fig. 20. Since we know the sign of α from the edge fringe of the bright-field image, we have the information necessary to determine the sense of **R**, the displacement of crystal 2 with respect to crystal 1 in fig. 14. The method was first given by Hashimoto et al. [27]. The sense of **R** enables us to say whether the fault is intrinsic or extrinsic.

The method has been elaborated by Gevers et al. [26], who pointed out that the type of the fault can be determined from the dark-field image alone, the sense of inclination not being required. This is understandable in terms of fig. 20, where we note that although (for the same type of fault) the sign of α will be different in the two situations illustrated, the dark-field image will be the same. Gevers et al. [26] have given a rule, illustrated in fig. 21, which enables the type of fault to be determined with little geometrical consideration. The diffraction vector g is drawn as an arrow with its origin at the centre of the dark-field image. g is arranged to point towards the right as in fig. 21. Fig. 21 then lists the sense of the edge fringes bordering the fault for two possible inclinations of the fault and the two possible types of fault. B denotes a a bright-fringe while D denotes a dark fringe. Full lines denote the top surface fringe; broken lines denote the bottom surface fringe. A and B denote two classes of Bragg reflections. A includes {200}, {222}, {440}; B includes {111}, {220}, {400}. For a given class (A or B), the dark-field image (with

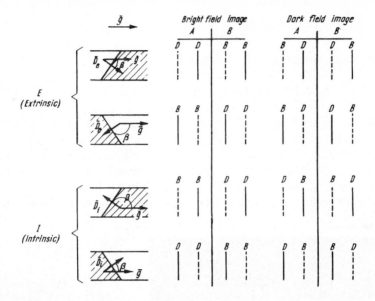

Fig. 21. Schematic diagram illustrating the nature of the edge fringes at $\pm 2\pi/3$-faults for various cases (after Gevers et al. [26]).

$\mathbf{g}$ inscribed as above) enables the type of fault to be determined by inspection of fig. 21. For example in fig. 17b, $\mathbf{g}$ points towards the dark fringe. The reflection is of class B (111), and therefore the fault is intrinsic by comparison with column B for intrinsic faults.

3.4.3. Stacking faults $|\alpha| = \pi$

In certain crystal structures stacking faults or anti-phase domain boundaries with phase angle π may occur. π-anti-phase boundaries in ordered alloys, produced by slip of imperfect dislocations or by thermal treatment are well known (Pashley and Presland [28]), Fisher and Marcinkowski [29]). More recently examples of π-faults in inorganic crystal structures such as hexagonal AlN (Drum and Whelan [30]) and tetragonal TiO_2 (rutile) (van Landuyt et al. [24]) have been studied. Eqs. (71) and (72) can be applied to the case $\alpha = \pi$ [30,24]. An exhaustive discussion is given by van Landuyt et al. [24]. Here we give only a brief survey of the main points of interest.

We consider the case of $\alpha = \pi$ with no absorption. At the reflecting position ($\beta=\pi/2$) the intensity derived from eq. (71) is

$$I_0(t',t) = \cos^2\left(2\pi t'/\xi_g\right) . \tag{80}$$

The corresponding equation for a $2\pi/3$-fault is

$$I_0(t',t) = \tfrac{1}{4}\cos^2\left(\pi t/\xi_g\right) + \tfrac{3}{4}\cos^2\left(2\pi t'/\xi_g\right) . \tag{81}$$

We notice immediately that the fringe profile across a π-fault with no absorption should be independent of the thickness fringes visible in a wedge crystal because (80) does not contain t. On the other hand, for a $2\pi/3$-fault eq. (81) shows that the fringe profile is dependent on t through the term $\cos^2\left(\pi t/\xi_g\right)$. Examples of this behaviour are given in figs. 22a and b. Fig. 22 refers to a $2\pi/3$-fault in AlN, while fig. 22b refers to a π-fault in the same material.

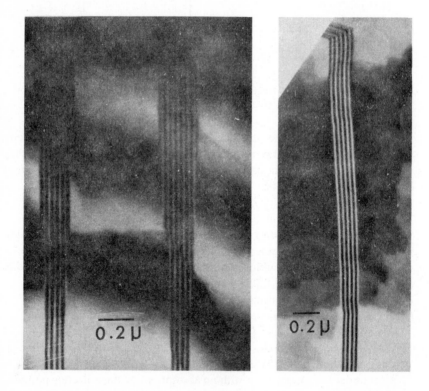

Fig. 22a, b. Illustrating the behaviour of fault fringes in AlN. (a) $a = 2\pi/3$, basal fault; (b) $a = \pi$, $(\bar{1}2\bar{1}0)$ fault.

Fig. 22b demonstrates the uniformity in the fringe profile, even though the thickness varies from about $3\xi_g$ to $2\xi_g$ along the fault. Figs. 23a and b illustrate another difference in the behaviour of $2\pi/3$-faults and π-faults for the case where stacking fault bends are observed. Fig. 23a refers to a triangular stacking fault defect in silicon (Booker and Stickler [31]) for which $\alpha = 2\pi/3$, while fig. 23b refers to bent and intersecting stacking faults in magnetite (Fe_3O_4 with a spinel structure). Fig. 23b is due to G.S.Baker (unpublished work) who has shown that these faults are on {110}planes with $\frac{1}{4}\langle 112 \rangle$ shear vectors and that $|\alpha| = \pi$. In fig. 23a the operating Bragg reflection is $20\bar{2}$ and the fault parallel to $\mathbf{g}$ is "out of contrast". Thus only two faults of the triangular defect are visible, and for one of these $\alpha = +2\pi/3$, giving rise to bright edge fringes, while for the other $\alpha = -2\pi/3$ giving rise to dark edge fringes. As a result, at the stacking fault bend the fringes are discontinuous, bright fringes

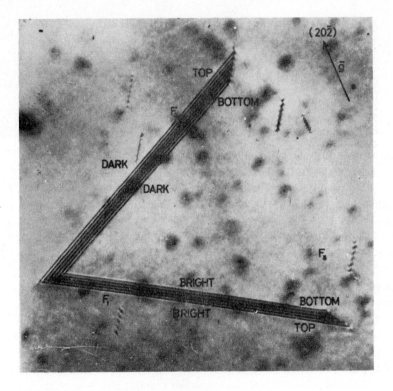

Fig. 23a. Illustrating the behaviour of fault bends. $\alpha = 2\pi/3$, faults at triangular defects in silicon.

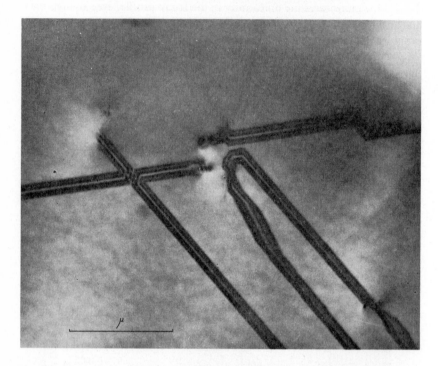

Fig. 23b. Illustrating the behaviour of fault bends. $\alpha = \pi$ faults in magnetite, Fe_3O_4.
The faults are on {110}planes with shear vectors $\frac{1}{4}\langle 112\rangle$. See text for discussion.

joining to dark fringes. This behaviour is commonly observed at bends in $2\pi/3$-faults. In the fcc structure it is also possible to have bent faults for which α has the same sign for both faults. In this case the fringes are continuous across the bend [24]. However when $\alpha = \pi$, there is no difference between these two situations, since a fault with phase angle π has the same profile as one with phase angles $-\pi$. Thus in fig. 23b the fringes are continuous across the fault bends in all cases.

Another interesting effect occurs at the intersection of faults. A column of crystal passing through the intersection will have a net phase angle equal to the sum of the phase angles of the individual faults. For $2\pi/3$-faults either the sum may be zero for values of α with opposite sign, or the sum may be non-zero for values of α with the same sign. For example if $\alpha_1 = \alpha_2 = 2\pi/3$, the sum is $4\pi/3$, which is equivalent modulo 2π to a value $-2\pi/3$. However, if $\alpha_1 = -\alpha_2 = 2\pi/3$, the sum is zero, and the contrast from a column through the point of intersection will be the same as that for a perfect crystal, i.e. there will be no contrast at the line of intersection of the faults. Thus for $2\pi/3$-faults there may either be contrast or no contrast at the intersection depending on the values of α_1 and α_2. However, for π-faults the intersection will always show no contrast. An example of this is visible in fig. 23b.

A further property of fringes at π-faults is that the bright-field and dark-field images are both symmetrical about the centre of the fault, and they are pseudo-complementary, even when absorption occurs [24]. This can be understood physically in terms of the offset of the Bragg reflecting planes. For a π-fault the offset of the planes above and below the fault is half the interplanar spacing. The fringes at faults are essentially due to interference between the two Bloch waves on each branch of the dispersion surface (fig. 3, sect. 1) after redistribution of amplitudes of the Bloch waves has occurred at the fault. A fuller discussion of this so-called interband and intraband scattering is given by Hirsch et al. [32]. Reference to fig. 8 of sect. 2 will make clear the fact that when the offset is half the interplanar spacing, the type 1 Bloch wave in the upper crystal propagates into the lower crystal as the type 2 Bloch wave, and similarly the type 2 Bloch wave propagates as the type 1 wave in the lower crystal. Thus the two Bloch waves switch branches of the dispersion surface on propagating through a π-fault, i.e. the scattering is entirely interband. It therefore makes no difference in which order the two crystals are encountered. The same waves emerge whether they encounter the crystal of thickness t_1 first and that of thickness t_2 second, or vice-versa. The bright-field and dark-field profiles are therefore symmetrical about the centre for π-faults even with absorption, contrary to the situation for $2\pi/3$-faults.

3.4.4. Overlapping stacking faults

Configurations of faults are often observed with consist of two or more stacking faults on closely spaced parallel planes. The fringe profile will depend on the separation and nature of the faults, and a particular situation can always be dealt with by the scattering matrix method outlined in sect. 3.2. We consider here the case where the faults are closely spaced so that propagation phase factors due to the separation of the faults can be ignored. Fig. 24 shows an example of overlapping faults in austenitic (fcc) stainless steel. Here we have a configuration of faults which might be produced by the twinning mechanism involving a spiral source of partial dislocation rotating round a pole dislocation. It is well known that this mechanism produces a thin lamellar region of twin by generating stacking faults on adjacent close-packed planes, the number of overlapping faults increasing from the edge of the lamella. If the phase angle α is $2\pi/3$ for a single fault, the net phase angle for n overlapping

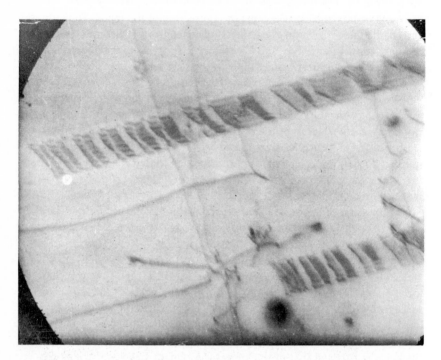

Fig. 24. Sequence of overlapping stacking faults in stainless steel. The number of overlapping faults increases from one at the leading fault. Every third overlap produces no contrast.

faults will be $2n\pi/3$. Thus for two intrinsic faults α is $4\pi/3$, or $-2\pi/3$ (modulo 2π). The sign of α changes, and as a result a reversal of fringe contrast occurs [19]. For three overlapping faults α is zero (modulo 2π). We therefore see a characteristic set of fringes where every third fault shows no contrast. Such a sequence of fault fringes is visible in fig. 24.

Defects resembling stacking faults in silicon are shown in fig. 25 (Booker and Howie [33]). The micrograph is a bright-field image, and we note that, contrary to the situation for single faults, the image is asymmetric about the centre, one edge of the faults having a bright fringe (B) while the other has a dark fringe (D). These contrast effects may be explained by assuming that the defects are intrinsic-extrinsic fault pairs separated by distances of about 50 to 100Å. For this separation phase factors corresponding to propagation between faults are not negligible, and therefore fringes are visible even though no fringes would be expected simply by adding the α values of each individual

'LINE' DEFECTS

BRIGHT FIELD IMAGE

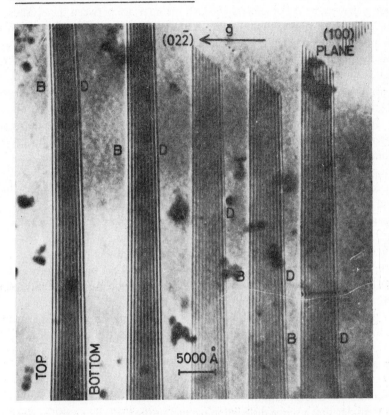

Fig. 25. Fringes at defects in silicon. The defects are believed to be pairs of intrinsic and extrinsic faults separated by small distances. Note that one edge fringe is bright and the other dark in the bright-field image.

fault. The asymmetric image can be explained by attributing one edge fringe to the intrinsic fault and the other to the extrinsic fault.

3.4.5. Moiré fringes; δ-fringes

In a number of papers [34–39] Gevers and his coworkers have considered contrast effects at more general planar defects. The theoretical basis of the investigations is again eqs. (67), but now we allow the possibility that g and s may be slightly different for two overlapping crystals.

The situation where $s_1 \cong s_2$, but $g_1 \neq g_2$, due to some small rotation or lattice parameter difference, gives rise to the case of moiré patterns. In this case g changes by Δg on passing through the interface between the crystals. Δg is generally parallel to the interface. It may be shown [34] that the profile of moiré fringes is given by the fault eqs. (71) and (72) provided $\alpha = -2\pi \Delta g \cdot r_s$, where r_s is a coordinate in the interface. α is therefore a linear function of r_s and is constant along lines perpendicular to Δg. Thus we obtain fringes of constant α, i.e. moiré fringes, perpendicular to Δg. The spacing of the fringes is given by $|\Delta g|^{-1}$. These are well known properties of moiré fringes.

In a more general situation both g and s may change on passing through an interface, and the resulting situation has applications to contrast effects at domain boundaries [38]. The fringes have been referred to as δ-fringes, and they resemble stacking fault fringes but they are not regularly spaced. In the dark-field image the first fringe at the top and bottom of the foil is the same and is bright if $s_1 > s_2$, and is dark if $s_1 < s_2$. Bright-field and dark-field images are similar near the top surface and pseudo-complementary near the bottom surface. The theory is able to predict the nature of fringes at ferroelectric domain boundaries in barium titanate [38], where the crystal structure is actually tetragonal and the domain boundaries are twin boundaries. Similar domain boundaries formed by twinning have been observed in V_3Si at low temperatures (Goringe and Valdrè [40]).

More complicated boundaries having a fault component as well as a lattice misorientation may also be treated with the theory. Such boundaries are referred to as $\alpha-\delta$ boundaries and the student is referred to Gevers et al. [35] for a full discussion.

3.4.6. Images of dislocations

Consider first a screw dislocation parallel to the surface of a foil at depth y (fig. 13). The image of an inclined dislocation may be calculated by allowing y to vary and by including an inclination factor which affects the image width [20]. We will generally ignore inclination factors. The atomic displacements around the screw are given by isotropic elasticity theory,

$$R = \frac{b}{2\pi} \tan^{-1} \{(z-y)/x\}. \tag{82}$$

Thus α to be inserted in eqs. (78) is

$$\alpha = n \tan^{-1} \{(z-y)/x\} \tag{83}$$

where $n = \mathbf{g \cdot b}$ is an integer which may take values 0, ±1, ±2 etc. If $n = 0$, i.e. if the Burgers vector $\mathbf{b}$ lies in the Bragg reflecting planes, the dislocation will be invisible. The eqs. (77) may be integrated by numerical methods with a computer. Image profiles for $n = 1$ and 2 are shown in figs. 26 and 27. For $n = 1$ near $w = 0$ (fig. 26) the image profile consists of a single dark peak of similar shape for both the bright-field and the dark-field images. This is a result of anomalous absorption for thick crystals. For $n = 2$ the image profile consists of a pair of dark peaks, the region at the dislocation core having background intensity. The reason for this is that a column passing through the core will have a displacement function equal to a lattice vector below the core when $\mathbf{g \cdot b} = 2$. When the dislocation is inclined, the image profile may vary as y varies (particularly for regions near the surfaces) giving rise to special contrast effects. Examples of such contrast effects at inclined dislocations are visible in fig. 1 of sect. 1. The dislocations may appear like a zig-zag line or as a string of dark blobs depending on the total thickness of the foil [22].

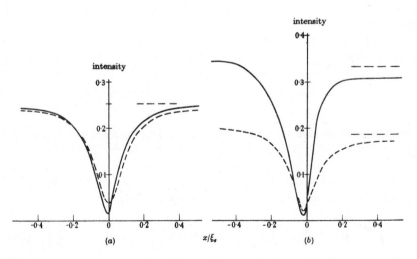

Fig. 26. Computed images of screw dislocation in the middle of a foil with $t = 8\xi_g$. $\mathbf{g \cdot b} = 1$, $\xi_0' = \xi_g'$, $\xi_g/\xi_g' = 0.1$. In (a) $w = 0$; in (b) $w = 0.3$. Full curves are bright-field images; broken curves are dark-field images.

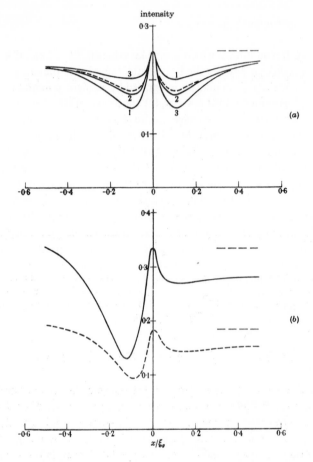

Fig. 27. Computed images of a screw dislocation for $g \cdot b = 2$, $t = 8\xi_g$. (a) $w = 0$, (b) $w = 0.3$. Curves (1), (2) and (3) in (a) refer to $y/\xi_g = 4$, 4.25 and 4.5 respectively.

For a general dislocation parallel to the surface in fig. 13 we may use the atomic displacements given by isotropic elasticity theory

$$R = \frac{1}{2\pi} \left\{ b\Phi + b_e \frac{\sin 2\Phi}{4(1-\nu)} + b \times u \left(\frac{(1-2\nu)}{2(1-\nu)} \ln |r| + \frac{\cos 2\Phi}{4(1-\nu)} \right) \right\} \quad (84)$$

where ν is Poisson's ratio, $\Phi = \phi - \gamma$, b is total Burgers vector, b_e is the edge component of b, and u is a unit vector along the dislocation line. If g lies in the foil plane $g \cdot (b \times u) = g \cdot b_e \tan \gamma$ and the expression for α becomes

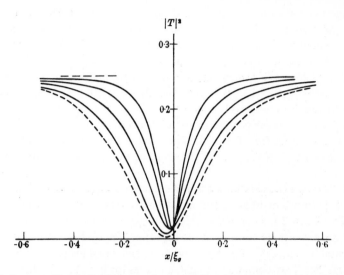

Fig. 28. Computed bright-field images of mixed dislocations shown as a function of p (see text). $\mathbf{g \cdot b} = 1$, $t/\xi_g = 8$, $y/\xi_g = 4$, $w = 0$, $\xi'_0 = \xi_g$, $\xi_g/\xi'_g = 0.1$. In order of increasing width the images are for $p = -0.5$, 0, 0.5 and 1.0. The broken curve is for $p = 1$, $\tan \gamma = 1$.

$$\alpha = \mathbf{g \cdot b} \phi + \mathbf{g \cdot b}_e \left\{ \tfrac{3}{8} \sin 2\phi + \tan \gamma \left(\tfrac{1}{4} \ln |r| - \tfrac{3}{8} \cos 2\phi \right) \right\} \qquad (85)$$

where we have put $\nu = \tfrac{1}{3}$. When $\mathbf{g \cdot b}_e = 0$ the image of the mixed dislocation is the same as that of a pure screw dislocation. Images calculated for general dislocations in terms of the parameter $p = \mathbf{g \cdot b}_e / \mathbf{g \cdot b}$ are shown in fig. 28. The curve for $p = 0$ is that for a pure screw; $p = 1$ is that for a pure edge. All curves in fig. 28 except the broken curve refer to $\gamma = 0$. It is seen that the image of an edge dislocation is wider than that of a screw dislocation. The broken curve in fig. 28 shows the effect of tilting an edge dislocation so that $\gamma = 45°$.

3.4.7. Computer simulation of images

Recently [41] a very useful technique has been developed for displaying computed images of dislocations and stacking faults directly on computer output paper by arranging for the output printer to produce a "scale of grey" by over-printing type symbols. The numbers giving the intensities as solutions of eqs. (77) may then be displayed as a "dot" of a certain density, and the image may be constructed by a two-dimensional array of "dots". Head [42] has also shown that if surface relaxation effects are neglected, eqs. (77) need not

be integrated every time the depth of the defect is changed. The equations are
linear, and therefore only two independent solutions need be found to satisfy
the initial boundary conditions for the defect at any depth. The equations are
integrated for a column with the defect at the centre of a foil of thickness
$2t$, and the solutions ϕ_0 and ϕ_g at 128 points spaced $t/64$ apart are found for
the conditions $\phi_0(0) = 1$, $\phi_g(0) = 0$ and $\phi_0(0) = 0$, $\phi_g(0) = 1$. A linear combination of these solutions is easily found for which $\phi_0 = 1$, $\phi_g = 0$ at any of the
chosen points. Thus the column of length $2t$ needs only two integrations to
obtain the solutions for a foil of thickness t with the defect at 64 different
depths. A considerable increase in the speed of the calculation is thereby obtained.

Fig. 29 is an example of the method applied to dislocations in ordered β-
brass [41]. In this material elastic anisotropy is important. This leads to the
result that screw dislocations for which $\mathbf{g} \cdot \mathbf{b} = 0$ are visible as a pair of closely
spaced images with no contrast at the core (fig. 29a, b). Fig. 29 a–d show experimental images. Fig. 29 e–h are computer simulated images for $\mathbf{b} = [\bar{1}11]$,
while fig. 29 i–l are computer simulated images for $\mathbf{b} = \frac{1}{2}[\bar{1}11]$. Direct comparison shows that the Burgers vector $\mathbf{b} = [\bar{1}11]$ provides the closest correspondence with the observed images. This example illustrates how it has become possible to determine not only the direction of the Burgers vector but
also its magnitude by comparison with computer simulated images. Further
applications of the method have been given by Head et al. [42], by Humble
[43] and by Head [44].

The technique has been refined by Bullough, Maher and Perrin (unpublished
work), who have used a cathode ray tube curve plotter to produce simulated
images of dislocation loops, which are almost indistinguishable in quality from
experimental images. Fig. 30 (due to Bullough et al.) shows the simulated image
of a loop in the centre of a (001) foil of Nb of thickness $5\xi_{110}$. The loop lies
on (111), has a radius ξ_{110}, and has Burgers vector $\mathbf{b} = \frac{1}{2}[\bar{1}\bar{1}\bar{1}]$. The two pictures show the change in size of the image with n. In one picture $n = \mathbf{g} \cdot \mathbf{b} = +1$
while in the other $n = -1$. For comparison purposes we show experimental
micrographs of loops in α-irradiated aluminium (Mazey et al. [45]). This demonstrates the change in size of the image with tilting. The simulated pictures
and the micrographs are not directly comparable since the parameters are different. However, the simulated images do show how well the theory accounts
for the details observed in experimental images.

Undoubtedly the computer simulation technique will be widely used in the
future.

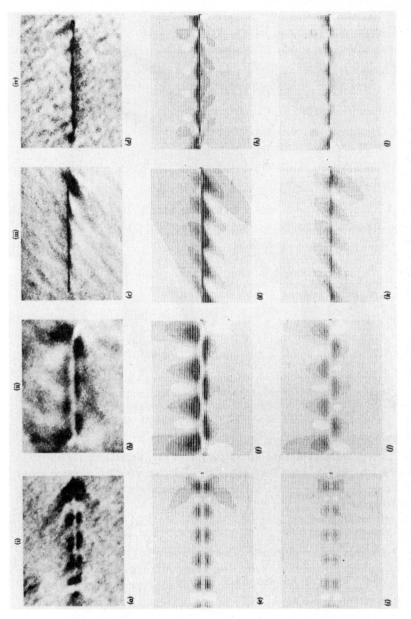

Fig. 29. Comparison of experimental and computer simulated images in β-brass. (a)–(d) experimental images for reflections indicated. (e)–(h) computer simulated images for $\mathbf{b} = [\bar{1}11]$. (i)–(l) computer simulated images for $\mathbf{b} = \frac{1}{2}[\bar{1}11]$. (After Head [41]).

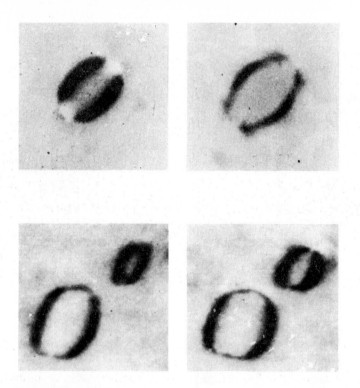

Fig. 30. Experimental images (lower pair) and computer simulated images (upper pair) of dislocation loops. Upper pair is due to Bullough, Maher and Perrin (unpublished). The lower pair is due to Mazey et al. [45]. (See text for discussion.)

3.4.8. Determination of Burgers vectors

Electron microscope image contrast provides a very useful technique for obtaining information about Burgers vectors of dislocations. Information about the direction of the Burgers vector, its magnitude, and also its sense can be obtained from suitable images.

The direction of the Burgers vector is usually obtained from tilting experiments in which one endeavours to make the dislocation vanish. We have seen (sect. 3.4.6) that a screw dislocation vanishes when $g \cdot b = 0$, i.e. when the Burgers vector is parallel to the reflecting planes. Although this criterion does not strictly hold for a mixed dislocation, very often it approximately holds (except in certain special cases), and weak residual contrast visible at a mixed dislocation when $g \cdot b = 0$ is often referred to as an "effective invisibility". The $g \cdot b = 0$ criterion for invisibility is illustrated in fig. 31. The material is quenched

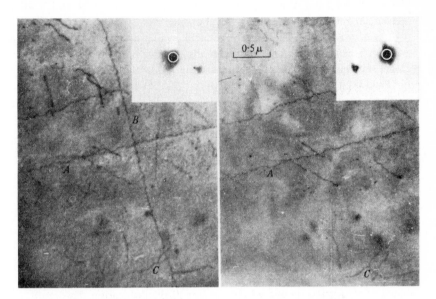

Fig. 31. Illustrating the vanishing of dislocations when $\mathbf{g} \cdot \mathbf{b} = 0$.

Al + 4% Cu alloy. It is known that this material contains long screw dislocation which have become helical by vacancy climb [46]. Thus the helical dislocations A and B in fig. 31 have Burgers vectors along the axes of the helices.
The diffraction patterns inset show the operating Bragg reflections. It is clear
that in fig. 31a with the 020 reflection $\mathbf{g} \cdot \mathbf{b} = 1$ for dislocations A and B and
both are visible. However, in fig. 31b the foil has been tilted to bring in the
$2\bar{2}0$ reflection. For this reflection the Burgers vector of B lies in the reflecting
planes and the dislocation B vanishes while A is still visible.

In using this method it is important to have available a specimen stage with
good goniometer facilities for tilting the specimen to various Bragg positions.
Kikuchi lines and bands are often used as an aid for tilting to a required reflection. If a dislocation can be made to vanish in two different reflections, the
direction of $\mathbf{b}$ is uniquely defined.

Care should be exercised in using the vanishing criterion to determine
Burgers vectors as evidenced by the experiences of Dingley and Hale [47], who
used large $\mathbf{g}$ vectors in dark-field to determine Burgers vectors in iron and steel.
Vanishing evidence suggested there were appreciable numbers of $\langle 100 \rangle$ and
$\langle 110 \rangle$ Burgers vectors in addition to the expected Burgers vector $\frac{1}{2}\langle 111 \rangle$. It
turns out, however, that "effective invisibility" may be obtained, even when

$\mathbf{g \cdot b} \neq 0$, when dislocations are observed with large $\mathbf{g}$ vectors such as $321, 013$, and 222 in a deviated condition $s \neq 0$. For the large $\mathbf{g}$ vectors employed, $w = \xi_g s$ may be in the range 4 to 6 for small angular deviations from the Bragg position because of the large extinction distance for high order reflections. Under such conditions calculations show that "effective invisibility" may be obtained even though $\mathbf{g \cdot b} \neq 0$ [48–50].

The magnitude of the Burgers vector can be obtained by comparison of the images observed with theoretically expected images. An example of this was given for β-brass in the previous section (fig. 29). Even in fig. 31 for which accurate comparisons have not been made, it is possible to surmise that $|\mathbf{g \cdot b}| = 1$ in fig. 31a and that $|\mathbf{g \cdot b}| = 2$ for A in fig. 31b from the appearance of the images, and hence that $b = \frac{1}{2}\langle 110\rangle$. Near the Bragg position the image for $|\mathbf{g \cdot b}| = 2$ may be double while that for $|\mathbf{g \cdot b}| = 1$ is always single (figs. 26,27). The image in fig. 31b is typical of a $|\mathbf{g \cdot b}| = 2$ case in a deviated condition. Fig. 27b shows that the image in this case is characterised by a rather sharp edge on one side and a tail on the other, as is visible in fig. 31b.

The sense of the Burgers vector of a dislocation may be obtained by using the fact that even for $n = \mathbf{g \cdot b} = 1$ the image of a dislocation observed in a deviated condition lies on one side of the core of the dislocation. This result may be obtained by the kinematical theory of contrast [20], and calculations also show that the result follows from dynamical theory [22,32]. The behaviour of the image as s varies in a bent foil is indicated schematically in fig. 32. The FS/RH-perfect crystal convention is used to define the Burgers

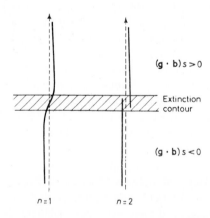

Fig. 32. Behaviour of a dislocation image at an extinction contour as seen by an observer looking from below the foil as in a normal positive photographic point.

vector. The side on which the image lies is determined by the sign of $(\mathbf{g \cdot b})s$. It is clear that if $\mathbf{g}$ is known and the sign of s is known, the sense of the Burgers vector may be obtained from the image displacement. The sign of s can be obtained from the position of Kikuchi lines. Often when using low order reflections, the specimen is observed with w or s positive ($w \cong 1$) corresponding to the regions of good transmission in the perfect crystal rocking curve (figs. 9 and 12 of sect. 2). In this case the movement of the image may be observed by tilting the crystal so that the sign of $\mathbf{g}$ is changed. This is done by tilting so that a dark bend contour (as in fig. 12 of sect. 2) sweeps across the dislocation. In carrying out the analysis it is important to allow for an inversion of the diffraction vector $\mathbf{g}$ with respect to the image which occurs in the electron optical imaging process in electron microscopes employing three magnifying lenses [51].

Numerous determinations have been made of the sense of Burgers vectors of dislocation loops produced by various methods such as quenching, radiation damage or fatigue. It is important to find $\mathbf{b}$ in order to establish whether such loops are of the vacancy or interstitial type. The image of a loop will lie entirely inside or entirely outside the core of the dislocation depending on the sign of $(\mathbf{g \cdot b})s$ (figs. 30 and 33). The formal analysis outlined above may of course be used, but the situation is made much clearer by a diagram like fig. 34 (Groves and Kelly [52]), where it can easily be seen on what side the image lies from the sense of bending of lattice planes. This diagram also shows that two loops of opposite sense inclined in different ways will give the same image contrast. Hence it is necessary to distinguish the sense of inclination of the loop. This may be done by tilting the specimen in a known sense through a large angle and noting the change in shape of the loop. Loops in MgO crystals have been studied by Groves and Kelly [52]. The loops were found to be vacancy type. Loops in α-irradiated aluminium have been studied by Mazey et al. [45] (see fig. 30) and were found to be of interstitial type. A simple method

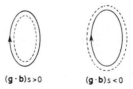

$(\mathbf{g \cdot b})s > 0$ $(\mathbf{g \cdot b})s < 0$

Fig. 33. Relative positions of a dislocation loop (continuous line) and its image (broken line) for $(\mathbf{g \cdot b})s$ positive and negative as viewed from below the specimen.

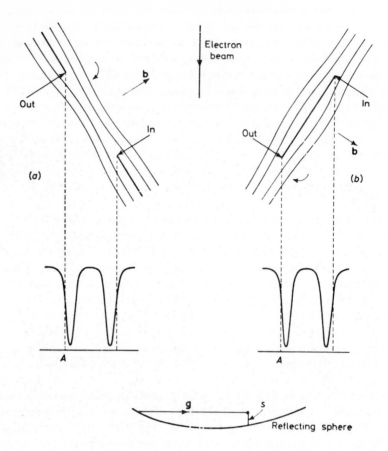

Fig. 34. Schematic diagram illustrating the influence of both the nature (i.e. interstitial or vacancy) of a loop and its sense of inclination in the foil on the size of the image. With a change in either of these quantities the loop image would lie outside the loop. s is assumed to be positive and the arrows indicate local lattice rotation.

of determining the nature of loops from the appearance of images on tilting through an extinction contour has been given by Edmondson and Williamson [53].

3.4.9. Partial dislocations

A partial dislocation has a Burgers vector which is not a lattice translation vector, and therefore the parameter $n = \mathbf{g} \cdot \mathbf{b}$ need not necessarily be an integer

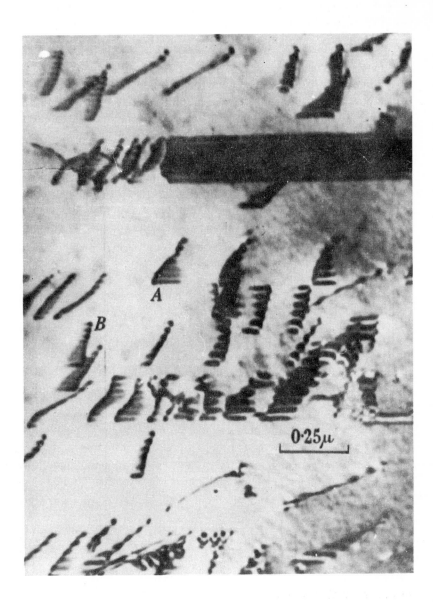

Fig. 35. Extended dislocations in Cu + 7% wt Al alloy. Note that for the dislocations A, B and others, one partial dislocation is visible as a dark line, while the other is invisible.

as for a whole dislocation. Also the partial dislocation must have a stacking fault on one side. For both Shockley and Frank partials in the fcc lattice n takes values $0, \pm\frac{1}{3}, \pm\frac{2}{3}, \pm 1$ etc. Howie and Whelan [22] have considered the images of screw Shockley partials for various values of $\mathbf{g}\cdot\mathbf{b}$ and have shown that there is an effective invisibility when $\mathbf{g}\cdot\mathbf{b} = \pm\frac{1}{3}$, as well as the real invisibility when $\mathbf{g}\cdot\mathbf{b} = 0$. On the other hand partials for which $\mathbf{g}\cdot\mathbf{b} = \pm\frac{2}{3}$ are visible as dark lines. Fig. 35 shows an example of this behaviour where extended dislocations with stacking fault fringes are visible. Only one partial bounding the fault shows up as a dark line. Silcock and Tunstall [54] have studied the images of partials at precipitates of NbC in stainless steel. They were able to show that the precipitation occurred at extrinsic faults formed from a whole dislocation by dissociation into a sessile Frank partial and a Shockley partial. Further applications to faults and partial dislocations have been given by Booker and Tunstall [55], and to double faults and partial dislocations at loops in quenched aluminium by Tunstall and Goodhew [56].

3.4.10. Inclusions and vacancy clusters

The situation illustrated in fig. 36 refers to the case of a coherent precipitate or inclusion embedded in a matrix. The lattice parameter of the inclusion is different from that of the matrix and a strain field is set up in the matrix and precipitate which gives rise to diffraction contrast. The contrast was studied the Cu + Co system using kinematical diffraction theory by Phillips and

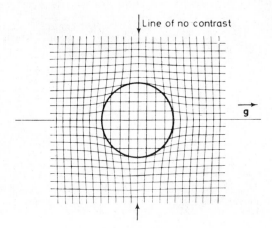

Fig. 36. Illustrating the strain field of a coherent spherical precipitate of Co in Cu + Co alloy.

Livingstone [57], and using dynamical theory by Ashby and Brown [58].
The displacement $\mathbf{R}$ to be inserted in eq. (78) for the dynamical calculation of
contrast is

$$\mathbf{R} = \frac{\epsilon r_0^3}{r^3}\,\mathbf{r}, \qquad |\mathbf{r}| \geqslant r_0$$

$$\mathbf{R} = \epsilon\mathbf{r}, \qquad |\mathbf{r}| \leqslant r_0 \tag{86}$$

where ϵ is a parameter called the "constrained strain". For isotropic elasticity
theory, where inclusion and matrix have the same elastic contants, $\epsilon = \frac{2}{3}\delta$,
where δ is the misfit parameter of inclusion and matrix lattices. For small precipitates of cobalt in copper the lattice distortion is as illustrated in fig. 36
and the misfit parameter δ is about 0.018.

In eq. (86), $\mathbf{r}$ is the radius vector from the centre of the inclusion; r_0 is the
radius of the inclusion. We see immediately that   there will be a line of no

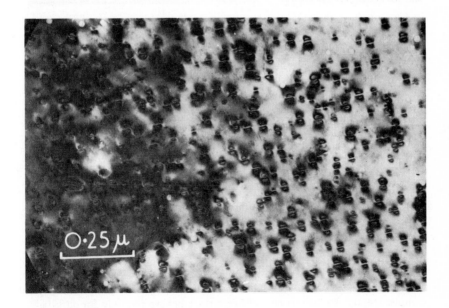

Fig. 37. Bright-field image of coherent Co precipitates in Cu + Co alloy. 311 reflection.
(After Ashby and Brown [58]).

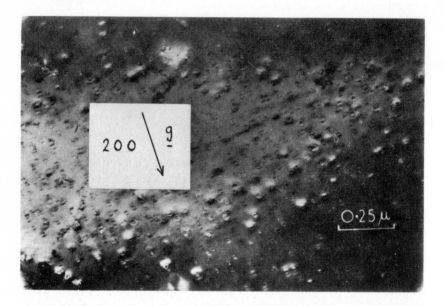

Fig. 38. Dark-field image of coherent Co precipitates in Cu + Co alloy. 200 reflection.
(After Ashby and Brown [58].)

contrast on the image perpendicular to the g vector, since the displacements
are radial (fig. 36). Examples of this behaviour are shown in figs. 37 and 38,
due to Ashby and Brown. Fig. 37 is a bright field image taken with a 311 reflection, while fig. 38 is a dark field image taken with a 200 reflection. The
image of a spherical inclusion consists of a pair of lobes of strain contrast
separated by the line of no contrast. Ashby and Brown [58] have studied the
profiles and widths of the images and have given graphs from which it is possible to estimate ϵ from the observed width.

It is also possible to determine the nature of the inclusion from the appearance of the dark-field image, i.e. to determine the sign of ϵ. A rule similar to
that for the dark-field image of an intrinsic stacking fault with a class B reflection holds (sect. 3.4.2. and fig. 21). For inclusions near the top foil surface,
bright-field and dark-field images are similar for thick crystals with anomalous
absorption, while for inclusions near the bottom surface the images are pseudo-
complementary. Inclusions near either surface behave similarly for dark-field
images, and the contrast is in the form of a pair of lobes, one dark and the
other bright (fig. 38). For an interstitial type inclusion (ϵ positive) the g vector

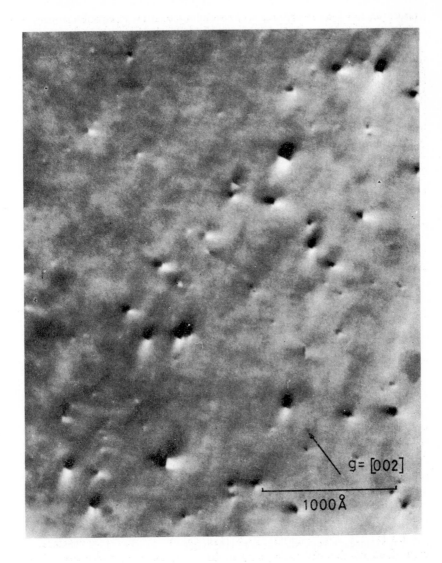

Fig. 39. Bright-field image of point defect clusters produced by irradiating thin copper foils with Cu$^+$ ions of energy 30 keV. Analysis shows that the clusters are Frank vacancy type loops on {111} planes of diameter ≈50 A. (After Wilson [61].)

points towards the dark lobe, and vice-versa for a vacancy type inclusion (ϵ negative). For further discussion of precipitate contrast effects the student should refer to Hirsch et al. [32].

Finally, reference should be made to the problem of determining the nature of very small point defect clusters in irradiated metals (Rühle et al. [59], McIntyre [60].) Usually the observed defects are very small (≈ 70 Å diameter) so that a distinct loop of dislocation is not resolved. Instead the clusters often appear as very small regions of strain contrast, similar in appearance to the contrast of inclusions mentioned above. It is thought that the defects represent small dislocation loops. The plane of the loop may be inclined to the foil surface, and the line of no contrast is not always perpendicular to $\mathbf{g}$. In attempting to determine the nature of these loops, a rule similar to the one outlined above for inclusions is expected to hold, at least for Frank sessile loops perpendicular to the surface, and very close to the surface, observed with a $\mathbf{g}$ vector perpendicular to the plane of the loop. Complications occur for very small loops since the contrast is found to reverse with increasing depth. Clusters in neutron irradiated metals will be distributed throughout the foil thickness, so that it becomes necessary to determine the depth of the clusters by stereo techniques. The work of Rühle et al. [59] suggests that loops in neutron irradiated copper are of vacancy type, while that of McIntyre [60] suggests that they are of interstitial type. Fig. 39 shows point defect clusters in copper foils which have been irradiated with copper ions of energy 30 keV. The penetration of the ions is small so that the clusters are located within about 100 Å from the surface. Analysis shows that the clusters are of vacancy type (Wilson [61]).

References

[1] C.G.Darwin, Phil. Mag. 27 (1914) 315, 675.
[2] P.B.Hirsch, A.Howie and M.J.Whelan, Phil. Trans. Roy. Soc. 252 (1960) 499.
[3] H.A.Bethe, Ann. Phys., Lpz. 87 (1928) 55.
[4] C.H.McGillavry, Physica 7 (1940) 329.
[5] J.Hillier and R.F.Baker, Phys. Rev. 61 (1942) 722.
[6] R.D.Heidenreich and L.Sturkey, J. Appl. Phys. 16 (1945) 97.
[7] H.Yoshioka, J. Phys. Soc. Japan 12 (1957) 628.
[8] K.Molière, Ann. Phys. Lpz. 34 (1939) 461.
[9] M.von Laue, Acta Cryst. 2 (1949) 106.
[10] G.Borrmann, Phys. Zeitschrift 42 (1941) 157.
[11] W.H.Zachariasen, Theory of X-ray diffraction in Crystals, 1945 (Dover, 1967).
[12] H.Hashimoto, J. Appl. Phys. 35 (1964) 277.
[13] A.J.F.Metherell and M.J.Whelan, Phil. Mag. 15 (1967) 755.

[14] C.J.Humphreys and P.B.Hirsch, Phil. Mag. 18 (1968) 115.
[15] S.Takagi, Acta Cryst. 15 (1962) 1311.
[16] B.Jouffrey and D.Taupin, Phil. Mag 16 (1967) 703;
    D.Taupin, Acta Cryst. 23 (1967) 25.
[17] A.Howie and Z.S.Basinski, Phil. Mag. 17 (1968) 1039.
[18] M.J.Whelan and P.B.Hirsch, Phil. Mag. 2 (1957) 1121.
[19] M.J.Whelan and P.B.Hirsch, Phil. Mag. 2 (1957) 1303.
[20] P.B.Hirsch, A.Howie and M.J.Whelan, Phil. Trans. Roy. Soc. A252 (1960) 499.
[21] A.Howie and M.J.Whelan, Proc. Roy. Soc. A263 (1961) 217.
[22] A.Howie and M.J.Whelan, Proc. Roy. Soc. A267 (1962) 206.
[23] C.M.Drum, Phil. Mag. 11 (1965) 313.
[24] J.van Landuyt, R.Gevers and S.Amelinckx, Phys. Stat. Sol. 7 (1964) 519.
[25] H.Hashimoto and M.J.Whelan, J. Phys. Soc. Japan 18 (1963) 1706.
[26] R.Gevers, A.Art and S.Amelinckx, Phys. Stat. Sol. 3 (1963) 1563.
[27] H.Hashimoto, A.Howie and M.J.Whelan, Proc. Roy. Soc. A269 (1962) 80.
[28] D.W.Pashley and A.E.B.Presland, J.Inst. Metals 87 (1959) 419.
[29] R.M.Fisher and M.J.Marcinkowski, Phil. Mag. 6 (1961) 1385.
[30] C.M.Drum and M.J.Whelan, Phil. Mag. 11 (1965) 205.
[31] G.R.Booker and R.Stickler, Brit. J. Appl. Phys. 13 (1962) 446; 33 (1962) 3281.
[32] P.B.Hirsch, A.Howie, R.B.Nicholson, D.W.Pashley and M.J.Whelan, Electron Micro-
    scopy of Thin Crystals (Butterworths, 1965).
[33] G.R.Booker and A.Howie, Appl. Phys. Letters 3 (1963) 156;
    G.R.Booker, Disc. Faraday Soc. No. 38 (1964) 298.
[34] R.Gevers, Phil. Mag. 7 (1962) 1681.
[35] R.Gevers, P.Delavignette, H.Blank and S.Amelinckx, Phys. Stat. Sol. 4 (1964) 383.
[36] R.Gevers, Phys. Stat. Sol. 3 (1963) 1672.
[37] R.Gevers, J.Van Landuyt and S.Amelinckx, Phys. Stat. Sol. 11 (1965) 689.
[38] R.Gevers, P.Delavignette, H.Blank, J.Van Landuyt and S.Amelinckx, Phys. Stat.
    Sol. 5 (1964) 595.
[39] R.Gevers, J.Van Landuyt and S.Amelinckx, Phys. Stat. Sol. 18 (1966) 325.
[40] M.J.Goringe and U.Valdrè, Proc. Roy. Soc. A295 (1966) 192.
[41] A.K.Head, Australian J. of Phys. 20 (1967) 557.
[42] A.K.Head, M.H.Loretto and P.Humble, Phys. Stat. Sol. 20 (1967) 505.
[43] P.Humble, Australian J. of Phys. 21 (1968) 325.
[44] A.K.Head, Australian J. of Phys. 22 (1969) 43.
[45] D.J.Mazey, R.S.Barnes and A.Howie, Phil. Mag. 7 (1962) 1861.
[46] G.Thomas and M.J.Whelan, Phil. Mag. 4 (1959) 511.
[47] D.J.Dingley and K.F.Hale, Proc. Roy. Soc. A295 (1966) 55.
[48] K.F.Hale and M.Henderson Brown, Proc. Fourth Eur. Regional Conf. on Electron
    Microscopy, Rome Vol. 1 (1968) p. 409;
    K.F.Hale and M.Henderson Brown, Proc. Roy. Soc. A310 (1969) 479.
[49] L.K.France and M.H.Loretto, Proc. Fourth Eur. Regional Conf. on Electron Micro-
    scopy, Rome Vol. 1 (1968) p. 301.
[50] D.J.Dingley, Proc. Fourth Eur. Regional Conf. on Electron Microscopy, Rome Vol.
    1 (1968) p. 303.
[51] G.W.Groves and M.J.Whelan, Phil. Mag. 7 (1962) 1603.
[52] G.W.Groves and A.Kelly, Phil. Mag. 6 (1961) 1527; 7 (1962) 892.

[53] B.Edmondson and G.K.Williamson, Phil. Mag. 9 (1964) 277.

[54] J.M.Silcock and W.J.Tunstall, Phil. Mag. 10 (1964) 361.

[55] G.R.Booker and W.J.Tunstall, Phil. Mag. 13 (1966) 71.

[56] W.J.Tunstall and P.J.Goodhew, Phil. Mag. 13 (1966) 1259.

[57] V.A.Phillips and J.D.Livingston, Phil. Mag. 7 (1962) 969.

[58] M.F.Ashby and L.M.Brown, Phil. Mag. 8 (1963) 1083, 1649.

[59] M.Rühle, M.Wilkens and U.Essmann, Phys. Stat. Sol. 11 (1965) 819.

[60] K.G.McIntyre, Phil. Mag. 15 (1967) 205.

[61] M.M.Wilson, Proc. Fourth Eur. Regional Conf. on Electron Microscopy, Rome Vol. 1 (1968) p. 365;
     M.M.Wilson, Radiation Effects 1 (1969) 207.

COMPUTED ELECTRON MICROGRAPHS AND THEIR USE IN DEFECT IDENTIFICATION

P.HUMBLE

*Commonwealth Scientific and Industrial Research Organization,
Division of Tribophysics, University of Melbourne,
Victoria, Australia*

1. Introduction

An important advance in the quantitative electron microscopy of defects in crystals occurred with the introduction of the two-beam dynamical theory of electron diffraction by Howie and Whelan in 1961 [1]. Since that time, the theory has been used increasingly in the detailed identification of defects, especially in relation to dislocations and various forms of stacking fault. Most of the deductions and calculations using the theory have referred to defects in elastically isotropic crystals and have been mainly concerned with establishing general rules for the behaviour of the images of defects under different diffracting conditions. The simple invisibility rules ($\mathbf{g} \cdot \mathbf{b} = 0$ for a screw dislocation, for example) and the symmetry properties of stacking faults can be deduced directly from the Howie and Whelan equations, but many of the more sophisticated rules (for example, those concerning the contrast of dislocations bordering a stacking fault) require extensive numerical calculation.

What I want to describe in the first part of this lecture is a method of doing the numerical contrast calculations for linear and planar defects which is much more efficient than previous methods. As a consequence, the results of the calculations have been employed in a way which was not possible with previous calculations. One of the main inovations has been to use the calculated intensities to form a complete two-dimensional image — a theoretical or computed micrograph. This method of presentation has the advantage that it is displayed in the same form as the experimental image and it is thus much easier for an observer to make a comparison between the theoretical and experimental situations. Previously, the theoretical results were presented in the

99

form of intensity profiles: that is, as a plot of the variation of the intensity along a line traversing the defect. In this case, the observer has to mentally reconstruct a two-dimensional image from several of these profiles before making the comparison. In addition to the micrograph form of presentation, another innovation is the use of anisotropic elasticity to calculate the displacement fields around dislocations. Thus, although we use the same Howie and Whelan equations, the intensity calculations are more representative of dislocations in real crystals than previous calculations.

A short section of this lecture will concern some general rules for image contrast from various defects. It should be pointed out at this stage, however, that partly as a result of the use of anisotropic elasticity, but mainly because this fast method of computing has enabled us to examine many more cases than previously possible, it has become clear that there are, indeed, very few general rules of image contrast behaviour. This unfortunate situation is redeemed, however, by the speed of the method itself because it is this which allows us to produce, if we wish, a theoretical micrograph corresponding to each specific experimental micrograph. In many uses this makes the need for general rules largely redundant. On the other hand, general rules do have an important role to play in the prediction of image behaviour leading to quick recognition of broad classes of defect. One or two such rules will be illustrated.

Calculation of the contrast from defects for specific cases has led to a technique of defect identification which, because of the aspects of speed and presentation emphasised above, is both quick and easy to use. The technique consists of computing theoretical micrographs corresponding to a series of experimental micrographs of the unknown defect. The theoretical micrographs have the same diffracting conditions etc. as the experimental ones, but are scanned over all probable types of defect. The unknown defect is then identified as that defect for which a particular set of theoretical micrographs matches the experimental set. The last part of this lecture will describe several instances of this use of the theoretical micrographs. Most of the examples are particular applications which have occurred in recent work carried out at the Division of Tribophysics, but they illustrate the general types of problem which can be attempted with the technique of image matching.

2. The computer programmes

The aim of this section of the talk is to describe the principles of the programmes and to provide such additional information which, together with the information in the original references, will enable the reader to set up and run a programme of this sort. In this way it is hoped that he may have immediate access to the theoretical micrographs which suit his own particular needs.

Head [2] has described the general principles for producing the information necessary for a picture quickly, and has shown how it may be assembled into a half-tone micrograph using the computer line printer. Humble [3] has extended the ideas of Head to handle more complicated defects under situations which are met with in routine microscopy. The theoretical micrographs are produced in about one minute by a CDC 3600 computer, most of this time being spent in the numerical integration of the Howie and Whelan differential equations. The programmes we have evolved will reproduce all the conditions met with in two-beam experimental electron microscopy (tilted foils, different exposure times, different magnifications etc.) and all the characteristics of the material (appropriate elastic constants, anomalous absorption, crystallography etc.). Thus in every case a direct comparison may be made between computed and experimental micrographs.

Most of what follows refers specifically to dislocations and stacking faults, but in fact the descriptions hold good for any straight line or planar defect. Also the description is limited to two-beam calculations in foils of constant thickness. However, the principles also apply to multi-beam diffraction conditions and to cases where the foil tapers uniformly.

2.1. *The two basic principles*

The information necessary to compile a picture is essentially that contained in a large number of profiles across the dislocation image. The fact that makes computer pictures of dislocations a practical proposition is that about 65 profiles, which is sufficient for one picture, can be computed in essentially the same time as 4 profiles using older methods. The reason for this lies in the simple form of the elastic displacements around a straight defect and the linearity of the Howie-Whelan differential equations.

The equations of Howie and Whelan that describe the interaction of beam and displacement field are a pair of first-order linear differential equations for T and S, the amplitudes of the transmitted and scattered beams. The equations are:

$$\frac{dT}{dZ} = -RT + QS$$

$$\frac{dS}{dZ} = QT + (-R+2iw+2\pi i\beta')S$$

where R = normal absorption, $Q = (i - \text{anomalous absorption})$, $\beta' = \text{d}/\text{d}z(\mathbf{g}\cdot\mathbf{R})$
where $\mathbf{R}$ is the displacement field, w = dimensionless deviation from the
Bragg condition and the units in the beam direction (Z) are π/ξ_g, ξ_g being the
extinction distance corresponding to the diffracting vector, $\mathbf{g}$.

There can be only two independent solutions of these equations and if these
are known, then all other solutions can be obtained by taking linear combinations of them. The programmes are designed to find the two solutions by inte-
grating two independent beams (each of which splits into two beams of the
two-beam approximation) concurrently through the crystal.

If we consider configurations consisting only of parallel straight dislocations (defects) with or without faults connecting them, and if no surface relaxations are allowed, then the elastic displacement field of the dislocations is
constant along any line parallel to them. (This is true in either isotropic or
anisotropic elasticity; as stated above, the programmes we have developed use
anisotropic elasticity.) Under these conditions it is possible to reduce the
problem to one in two dimensions by projection along the line of the dislocations, $\mathbf{u}$, onto a plane containing the electron beam direction, $\mathbf{B}$, which intersects the dislocations. For convenience, the plane we have chosen is normal
to the vector defined by $(\mathbf{u}\times\mathbf{B}) \times \mathbf{B}$. On this plane, called the generalised
cross-section, all the displacements due to the presence of the dislocations are
unique and single valued. By moving a pair of lines of constant separation
(equal to the foil thickness) across this plane, it is possible to sample the displacement field through which the electron beam passes during the formation of the entire micrograph. The linear combination of solutions referred to
above are taken on the lower of this pair of lines in such a way that the
boundary condition at the upper line is that for an electron beam entering the
crystal from a vacuum.

2.2. *Application of the principles to the case of a single dislocation in an untilted foil*

Fig. 1a shows a dislocation sloping through an untilted foil. The dislocation
enters the bottom surface of the foil on the line HG and leaves the top surface
on the line LM. The vertical lines in fig. 1a are parallel to the beam direction.
The generalised cross-section for this configuration is obtained by projection
in a direction parallel to the dislocation onto the plane LMNO. This generalised
cross-section is shown in fig. 1b. The dislocation is coming out of the paper
but is not normal to it. The dashed letters in fig. 1b correspond to the un-
dashed letters in fig. 1a. Note that the line HG projects into H'G', which is
coincident with L'M', the projection of LM. Lines E'F' and H'G' represent the
top and bottom surfaces of the foil respectively for the profile in which the

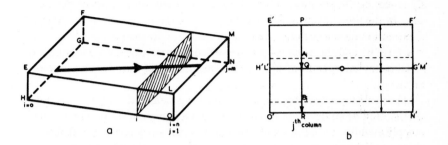

Fig. 1. The geometry and the generalised cross-section for a single dislocation in an untilted foil.

dislocation is just entering the bottom of the foil; L'M' and O'N' represent the top and bottom surface of the foil for the profile in which the dislocation is just leaving the top of the foil. Intermediate profiles on, for example, the shaded plane shown in fig. 1a, are obtained by taking the portion of the displacement field between the two dashed lines on the generalised cross-section in fig. 1b.

The amplitudes T and S are integrated down columns in the cross-section parallel to the beam direction. An equal number of columns on either side of the dislocation is considered, care being taken not to integrate down a column that is within a small distance of the dislocation core. If columns close to the dislocation core are considered, the programme takes an excessive amount of time to integrate through the rapidly changing strain field.

Consider the jth column from the dislocation as shown in fig. 1b. The integration down this column is done in two main parts, the first part (A) from P to Q and the second part (B) from Q to R. Each part is divided into n steps of equal size. Two beams, with independent initial amplitudes at the top of the cross-section are integrated down the column simultaneously, and the amplitudes (corresponding to the four beams) at the end of each step stored in the computer memory. The intensity of the image for the surfaces of the foil in the positions shown by the dashed lines in fig. 1b is obtained by combining the two solutions for the position B_i linearly and in such a manner as to give the correct boundary conditions for the top surface of the foil; that is, $T = 1$ and $S = 0$ at A_i.

By allowing i to run from 0 to n, we obtain $n + 1$ values of the intensity for the jth column in successive profiles running from the plane EFGH to the plane LMNO in fig. 1a. Thus we have $n + 1$ intensity values to establish the points on one row of the theoretical micrograph parallel to the dislocation line. By repeating the procedure for $j = 1$ to m, we obtain the m rows of the picture. In the present case, $n = 128$ and $m = 60$. In fact, for foils of the order of 5 extinction distances thick, the time to compute the micrographs is optimised if $n + 1 = 65$ and the other 64 points needed for each row of the picture are obtained by interpolation [2]. This has been found to introduce no serious error.

The geometry of projection, both onto the generalised cross-section and in the electron beam direction to produce the micrograph itself becomes more complicated for tilted foils containing more than one defect [3], but the theoretical micrographs are obtained using the same principles as outlined above.

In addition to simulating tilted foils and obtaining images of more complicated configurations, an important feature which it is necessary to be able to reproduce is that of variable magnification. This is important so that direct comparisons can be made with experimental images. In fact, the human eye seems to be much more sensitive to small differences in magnification when making a comparison than it is to the somewhat large differences in overall darkness which can occur between the theoretical and experimental micrographs. Magnification is obtained by restricting the range of integration to some fraction of PQ and the same, corresponding fraction of QR whilst still dividing these smaller ranges into 128 steps. Reduction, on the other hand, is obtained by using multiples of PQ and QR divided into 128 steps. Because the resolution in a computed micrograph is limited by the spacing between the rows (or columns), the magnification facility is also important when increased resolution is required. For example, figs. 2a and b show micrographs

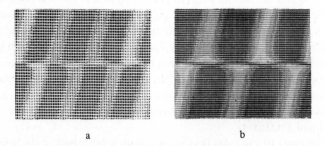

a   b

Fig. 2. Theoretical micrographs of a stepped Frank dislocation loop taken under identical conditions illustrating the increased resolution available at increased magnification.

of the same defect (a complex Frank dislocation loop) under identical diffraction conditions imaged at two different magnifications. In fig. 2b a fine dark line can be seen running along the centre of the micrograph.This is not resolved in fig. 2a which is at about half the magnification of fig. 2b.

After taking the linear combinations of the amplitudes for given levels, either the bright-field or dark-field intensities can be obtained by multiplying the appropriate amplitudes by their complex conjugates. Thus, one may obtain the dark-field micrograph at the same time as the bright-field one with the expenditure of only a few seconds spent in multiplication and printing the picture. All the micrographs shown here are bright-field micrographs.

2.3. The production of the half-tone micrograph

It was decided to use the line printer to produce the half-tone pictures because this is the piece of equipment most commonly used for computer output and so lends itself to easy routine use. More sophisticated ways of half-tone reproduction can be used (for instance, a television type display used with some form of photography [4]), but in most cases this increases the cycle time to produce a picture from the order of 1 min to the order of 5 min, is not in routine use in most computer networks and so increases the turn-round time and only a little more detail is available in the image.

A typical line printer picture of a dislocation is shown in fig. 3 together with the grey scale used. In order to get the blackest symbols it was found necessary to use over-printing. All combinations of printing and overprinting of the available symbols were examined and 11 different shades of grey could be distinguished, one of which was blank paper. The composition of the 10 printed shades chosen is shown in the grey scale. There are six lines of each symbol, the first and second columns being the individual characters and the third being the result when the first column is overprinted by the second. Most of the characters used are, of necessity, punctuation marks and other special symbols, since it is a characteristic of a good type face that letters and numerals do not have large differences in apparent blackness.

The standard picture size used is 60 lines of 129 symbols, which in the original form is 10 by 13 in. It is usually reduced by about a factor of 10 for journal reproduction so that the individual characters lose their identity. The dislocation runs from left to right, intersecting the bottom surface of the foil at the left-hand margin of the picture and the top surface at the right margin. The line of the dislocation is located midway between the rows of the picture indicated by the letters D on the right-hand margin. Due account is taken of the different spacings of characters along a line and between lines so that angles are true and linear scales are equal in all directions. The actual scale

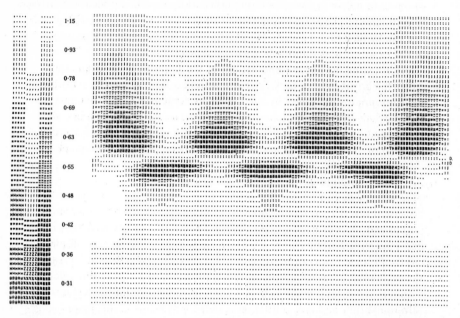

Fig. 3. Large magnification of a computed micrograph of a dislocation. The third column of characters at the left-hand side depicts the grey scale together with the intensity values (referred to background intensity) at which they begin to operate. The characters are obtained by overprinting column one with column two.

of the picture will depend on the foil thickness and the angle at which the dislocation slopes through the foil as well as the chosen range of integration.

The correspondence between value of intensity and shade of grey was determined by photometric measurements of the reflectivity R of large areas of the 11 shades. The corresponding intensity values I are then given by

$$\log I = \gamma^{-1} \log (R/E) ,$$

where the chosen values of the constants E and γ correspond to the photographic variables of exposure and contrast. Unless otherwise stated, the 10 boundary values indicated on the grey scale in fig. 3 were used for all of the present pictures. These values are not intensities as such but are the ratios of intensity to background. This means that all the pictures have the same contrast but each exposure is adjusted so that the background is always the first shade of grey. This appears a suitable choice for bright-field pictures of dislocations, for which most of the information is in the regions darker than background and one shade, full white, is sufficient to represent those areas that are significantly lighter than background. The contrast was chosen so that the values at which the background symbol changes (0.93 and 1.15) are approximately the experimental visibility limits for deviations from background.

Different choices for the exposure and contrast are necessary for dark-field pictures, for defects which produce very faint images or when comparisons are being made with unusually exposed experimental micrographs. The computer programmes which we have been using contain nine calibrations of the grey scale representing the combinations of three values of exposure with three values of contrast. In practice, however, the calibration of the grey scale shown in fig. 3 is the one which has been most used; two or three others have been used occasionally.

2.4. The parameters needed to run the programme and their evaluation

The quantities needed to produce a theoretical micrograph of a single dislocation are: the elastic stiffnesses (for cubic crystals, C_{11}, C_{12}, C_{44}); the anomalous absorption constant* (this may be measured using the image matching technique itself [5] : for most cases, this has been taken as 0.1); the Burgers vector, b (this is usually the quantity to be determined); the direction of the dislocation line, u; the reflecting vector, g; the electron beam direction, B; the foil normal, FN; the dimensionless deviation from the Bragg condition, w; and the thickness of the foil, t, in units of the extinction distance.

The elastic constants for many materials may be found in standard references on anisotropic elasticity (e.g. Huntington [6]), and u may be obtained by stereographic analysis of three or more micrographs taken when the differences in the foil tilt are large. g can be found by indexing the diffraction patterns, and B, FN and w can all be evaluated using Kikuchi line patterns. These are standard techniques, which, together with methods for measuring t, may be found in [7].

Providing due account is taken of the rotations of the image when going to the diffraction pattern, g can be determined exactly, but the evaluation of the other quantities is subject to experimental error. Moreover, it has been our experience that in a certain small number of cases the images of defects are sensitive to the values of these quantities. For instance, at small values of any one of anomalous absorption, w or t, the images are often sensitive to small varia-

---

* Since intensities are normalised to background intensity, the other absorption constant which appears in the equations, the real absorption constant, divides out and its precise value is never needed.

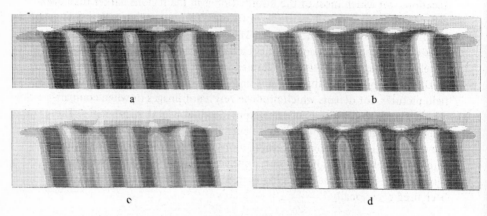

Fig. 4. Examples of the change in image character of an intrinsic stacking fault on (111) together with its bounding Shockley dislocation ($\mathbf{b}=\frac{1}{6}[11\bar{2}]$) for small changes in foil thickness. The reflecting vector is $\bar{1}11$, the value of w is 0.15 and in (a) and (b) the anomalous absorption is 0.07 and in (c) and (d) 0.05. t/ξ_g is 3.1 for (a), 3.2 for (b), 3.0 for (c) and 3.15 for (d).

tions in the values of the other two. Fig. 4 shows the images of a Shockley dislocation ($\mathbf{b}=\frac{1}{6}[11\bar{2}]$), bordering an intrinsic stacking fault (on (111)) taken with $\mathbf{g} = \bar{1}11$ at a w of 0.15. Figs. 4a and b have a value of anomalous absorption of 0.07; t is 3.1 ξ_g for fig. 4a and 3.2 ξ_g for fig. 4b. Although this represents a change in thickness of only 25 Å the difference in the fringe number and contrast is obvious. Figs. 4c and d have an anomalous absorption constant of 0.05 and t for fig. 4c is 3.0 ξ_g and for fig. 4d is 3.15 ξ_g. This change of thickness of about 36 Å produces a change in the dislocation contrast which is so marked that the dislocation could be said to be "out of contrast" in fig. 4c but "in contrast" in fig. 4d. For this particular example similar image sensitivity has been observed to occur at other combinations of w, t and anomalous absorption.

The "shearing" effect on an image of a dislocation due to the non-coincidence of $\mathbf{FN}$ and $\mathbf{B}$ has been discussed elsewhere [3], but in general large differences in $\mathbf{FN}$ and $\mathbf{B}$ are necessary before the change in the image becomes large. The angle which fault fringes make to the line of the terminating dislocation, on the other hand, can be extremely sensitive to the value of $\mathbf{FN}$ under certain circumstances, and the images of composite defects which have interacting displacement fields are often sensitive to the electron beam direction, $\mathbf{B}$. Fig. 5 shows an example of this last effect. It contains two micro-

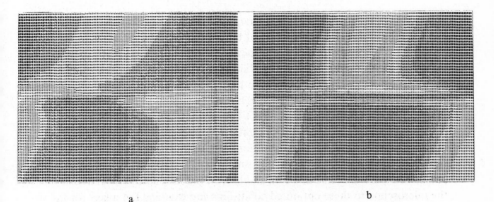

a   b

Fig. 5. Theoretical micrographs of a step in a complex Frank dislocation loop taken under identical diffraction conditions but with slightly different beam directions. The beam direction is [011] in (a) and [057] in (b).

graphs of a region of a complex Frank loop [8] where two dislocations and three stacking faults are in close proximity. The narrow stacking fault (180 Å wide) separating the two dislocations is vertical, and the dislocations are on top of each other in fig. 5a ($B=[011]$), but this is not the case in fig. 5b ($B=[057]$). In going from $B = [011]$ to a B of [057] (a rotation of $9\frac{1}{2}°$) a strong dark line has appeared in the image. A rotation of $9\frac{1}{2}°$ in the opposite sense from [011], however, produces virtually no change in the image shown in fig. 5a. [057] is typical of the sort of beam direction it is necessary to use in the vicinity of [011] in order to get good two-beam conditions, and in examples of the type described above, therefore, it is necessary to use the exact beam direction and not the nearest low index direction.

Unfortunately, it is usually impossible to predict if large variations in the image will result from small variations in the parameters. Commonly, therefore, for the purpose of image matching to be described later, each parameter is varied over two or three values within the experimentally determined error range to see if the images are sensitive. It is largely because of this unpredictable degree of sensitivity that it is extremely difficult to formulate any meaningful rules for image behaviour.

3. Illustrations of the use of computed micrographs

Since the introduction of the programmes, we have used the theoretical micrographs in three ways. The first of these concerns computations to distinguish quickly between different types of defect without resort to specific and detailed computing. The aim has been the compilation of a few simple properties of several types of defect so that an observer may rapidly select the defects of interest from the images he sees in situ on the microscope screen. This use is equivalent to that of the general rules established previously. The second way in which the theoretical micrographs have been used is to establish a range of diffraction conditions in which images are most characteristic or most suitable for detecting small changes in a particular defect parameter. With such information, an observer may set up the specimen in the microscope to these optimised conditions and examine the image for the features of interest. The third way in which the computed micrographs have been employed is in the detailed image matching of experimental images in order that defects may be identified. The sequence of events in this case is that the observer takes experimental micrographs of the defect to be identified under as many different diffracting conditions as possible. Theoretical micrographs are then computed for each of the experimental images, the Burgers vector or the fault shear (for example) being scanned until a matching set of computed micrographs is obtained. The defect is then identified.

3.1. The symmetry properties of images and the classificiation of defects

As an example of the first type of use, consider the symmetry properties of three defects: a dislocation, a line of dilation and a dislocation dipole. The basic types of symmetry of a dislocation image are well known (see [7]). The image of a dislocation may have no symmetry (fig. 6a), may be symmetrical on either side of a line along its length (fig. 6b), or symmetrical on either side of a line about mid-foil (fig. 6c). It can be shown, however [9], that the image of a dislocation has a centre of inversion symmetry when w is zero and anomalous absorption is zero (fig. 7). Since this is the only known case, the images of dislocations in real materials probably never have such symmetry. However, there are two defects whose images always possess such symmetry and this may be used as a test to distinguish them from dislocations. One of these defects is a dislocation dipole [10,11] and the other is a line of dilation [12]. Figs. 8 and 9 show the experimental and theoretical micrographs of a dislocation dipole taken under five different reflecting conditions and fig. 10 shows the theoretical micrographs of a line of dilation. (The displacements around the line of dilation are calculated on isotropic elasticity.)

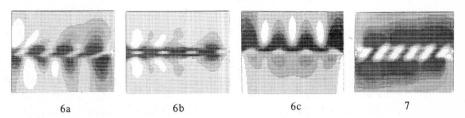

6a   6b   6c   7

Fig. 6. Computed micrographs of dislocations illustrating the three possible types of symmetry this defect may possess for non-zero values of anomalous absorption.

Fig. 7. Illustrating the centre of inversion symmetry of a dislocation image when anomalous absorption and w are both zero.

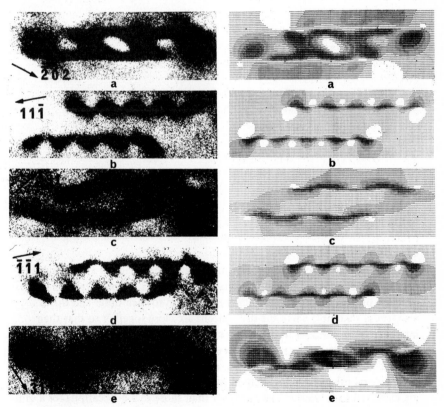

Fig. 8. Experimental micrographs showing the images of a dislocation dipole in nickel taken under five different diffracting conditions.

Fig. 9. Theoretical micrographs of a dislocation dipole in nickel which match the experimental micrographs in fig. 8. Note that the micrographs all have centre of inversion symmetry.

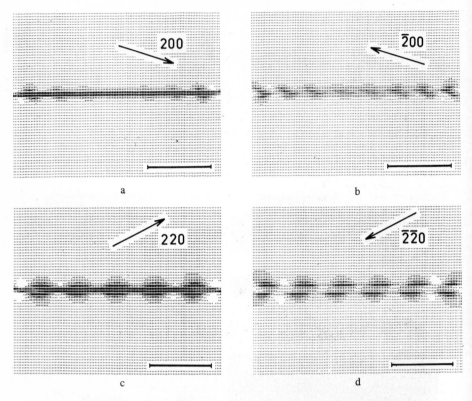

Fig. 10. Four images of a line of dilation. Note that they also have centre of inversion symmetry and that there is no relation between images taken with ± **g**.

On reversing the reflecting vector, the bright-field image of a dislocation becomes the 180° rotation of the original image. In general, however, the images of a line of dilation taken on ± **g** bear no relation to each other and this is also true for a dipole when the dislocations are close together so that their images overlap. Thus, although it is easy to instantly distinguish a dislocation from the other two defects, it is not easy to find a way to distinguish between a line of dilation and a dislocation dipole and to the author's knowledge there is no general rule which can be invoked. However, images of a line of dilation are expected to be weaker and narrower than those of a dislocation (for a similar displacement at the cores of the two defects [12]), and this may enable a distinction to be made. Also a reflecting vector along the line of the defect will produce a weak image for a line of dilation (no image at all in isotropic elasticity) but would produce a weak image in the case of a dipole only if the dislocations were of edge character.

3.2. *Pre-computation to determine favourable experimental conditions*

The recent work of Clarebrough and Morton [13,14] contains examples of the use of computed micrographs in determining the optimum conditions for observing a given defect. They were interested in trying to detect the separation of two dislocations at the edge of a Frank dislocation loop. Figs. 11 and 12 consist of computed micrographs of this defect taken on $02\bar{2}$ and $0\bar{2}0$ reflect-

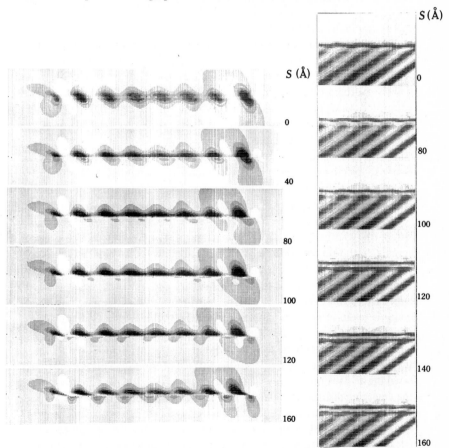

Fig. 11. Six computed micrographs of a Frank dislocation dissociated into a Shockley and a stair-rod dislocation separated by a distance S. The reflecting vector is $02\bar{2}$ so that the stacking fault is out of contrast. Note that the images change most rapidly for values of S in the range 0 to 40 Å.

Fig. 12. Seven computed micrographs of the same defect as in fig. 11 but with a **g** of $0\bar{2}0$. The images in this set change most rapidly for values of S in the range 80 to 120 Å.

ing vectors respectively for various separations, S (in Å) of the Shockley and stair-rod dislocations. It is apparent from fig. 11 that the diffracting conditions chosen for these micrographs are suitable for identifying separations in the range 0 to 40Å since there is a marked change of image in this range. However, there is little change in the images for separations in the range 80 to 160Å. On the other hand, it can be seen from the differences in the images for values of S from 80 to 120Å in fig. 12, that these diffraction conditions would be suitable for detecting dissociations of this magnitude.

3.3. *Image matching and defect identification*

Whilst theoretical micrographs prove useful in many cases for predicting the type of experimental image to be expected, the problems have usually been approached the other way round. Commonly, one already has a set of experimental micrographs of a defect of interest and theoretical micrographs are computed which correspond to the conditions of the experiment. The sets of theoretical images are then compared with the experimental set of micrographs until a match is obtained.

Before describing several cases of such identification, it is perhaps necessary to define what is meant by a "match" in this context and what criteria are used in comparing the computed and experimental micrographs. In general it is only the topology of the images which is compared and not their absolute intensities. First, the broad features of the image are noted and compared, e.g. whether it is double or single, dotted or continuous, one-sided or symmetrical, fine or wide and so on. In many cases these broad features are sufficient to enable a match to be made, but in some cases one has to take note of finer detail such as the shape of a dark dot, the occurrence of small light areas or the slight offset of prominent features etc. Although no account is taken of absolute intensities, in general, use is sometimes made of the fact that one image is much fainter than another. When we first began to use the image matching technique, we placed little reliance on features of the image which occurred close to the surface of the foil. This is because the programme does not allow for surface relaxations in the neighbourhood of the emerging dislocations which presumably occur in practice. However, experience with the technique has shown that the detail in the image close to a surface is remarkably well reproduced and since distinctive images usually occur at these places, we have often used this detail when making comparisons.

The process of matching a set of computed micrographs to an experimental set usually begins as one of rejection. The experimental image with the most character* is selected first and the images of all the probable defects computed for this case. The gross mis-matches, judged on the criteria outlined above, are immediately rejected. The next most characteristic experimental image is then compared with the theoretical micrographs computed for the remaining possibilities. After comparison with two or three experimental micrographs in this way one is usually left with two or three likely defects. At this stage, theoretical micrographs for these defects are computed corresponding to the diffraction conditions of all the available experimental micrographs. A process of selection and rejection then ensues until the final match is chosen.

As a specific example of image matching, consider the four images of an unknown dislocation in beta-brass shown in fig. 13. Because of the large elastic anistropy of this material, the $\mathbf{g} \cdot \mathbf{b} = 0$ type of rule for the invisibility of dislocations does not apply in general and it is necessary to devise some other method of Burgers vector determination [15,16]. Fig. 14 shows the theoretical micrographs corresponding to the image in fig. 13a for all the $\frac{1}{2} \langle 111 \rangle$, $\langle 111 \rangle$, $\langle 100 \rangle$ and $\langle 110 \rangle$ Burgers vectors possible in beta-brass. The image in fig. 13a may be characterised as being double, dotted, having a region at background intensity along the centre of the image, an "arrow head" at one end and a light area at the other. Scanning through the micrographs shown in fig. 14 the reader may choose figs. 14a, c, e, g and i as being possible matches to the experimental image. Some are obviously better matches than others, but it may be agreed that all the images rejected are gross mis-matches. Fig. 15 shows the micrographs computed for the dislocations depicted in figs. 14a, c, e, g and i but with diffracting conditions appropriate to fig. 13b. The image in fig. 13b may be characterised as being double and dotted, the dots being much larger on one side of the line than the other. It also has a region at background intensity along the centre. Only the theoretical micrographs in figs. 15a and c match this description, the others are mis-matches. Distinction between the possiblities represented by these two micrographs may be made by comparing fig. 13c with figs. 16a and b. The image in fig. 16a is not sufficiently one-sided and it is therefore concluded that fig. 16b is the match in this case. Further confirmation may be obtained by computing the theoretical micrograph for the dislocation in fig. 16b but for the diffraction conditions of fig. 13d. This is shown in fig. 17.

---

* By "the image with most character" we usually mean (at least in the case of a dislocation image) one which differs most from a featureless straight line. Images of "good character" (and thus most suitable for the image matching technique) may often be obtained by setting a small value of the deviation parameter, w.

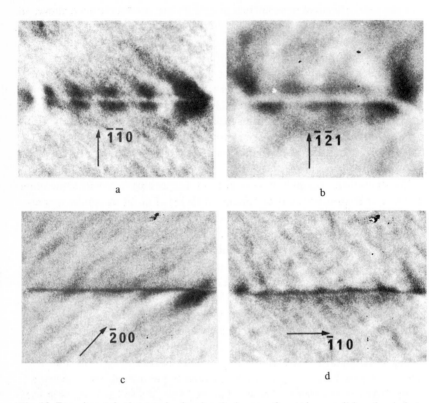

Fig. 13. Experimental micrographs showing the images of an unknown dislocation in beta-brass taken under four different reflecting vectors which are marked. The dislocation line direction, **u**, is close to $[\bar{1}11]$ and **FN** is close to [001]. **B** is close to [001] for (a), (c) and (d) and to [113] for (b). w is about 0.5 for (a), (c) and (d) and 0.7 for (b). The foil thickness is about 5.0 ξ_{110}.

In summary, the theoretical micrographs which match the experimental images in figs. 13a–d are figs. 14e, 15c, 16b and 17 respectively. The Burgers vector for these micrographs is $[\bar{1}11]$ and since the dislocation line is also along $[\bar{1}11]$ the dislocation in question is identified as being a pure screw superlattice dislocation of Burgers vector $[\bar{1}11]$. It is noteworthy that figs. 13a and b which have **g·b** = 0 show more contrast than figs. 13c and d which have **g·b** = 2. Although this is an exaggerated example, since the elastic anisotropy of beta-brass is unusually large, similar effects also occur in materials of lesser

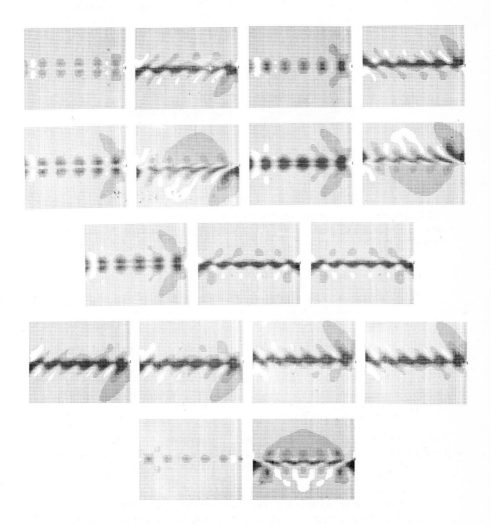

Fig. 14. Theoretical micrographs computed for the diffraction conditions of fig. 13a for dislocations of all Burgers vectors probable in beta-brass. Reading from a to q the Burgers vectors are: $\frac{1}{2}[\bar{1}11]$, $\frac{1}{2}[111]$, $\frac{1}{2}[1\bar{1}1]$, $\frac{1}{2}[\bar{1}\bar{1}1]$, $[\bar{1}11]$, $[111]$, $[1\bar{1}1]$, $[\bar{1}\bar{1}1]$, $[001]$, $[010]$, $[100]$, $[011]$, $[101]$, $[0\bar{1}1]$. $[\bar{1}01]$. $[\bar{1}10]$ and $[110]$.

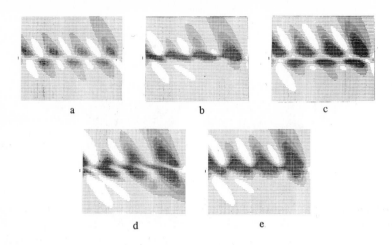

Fig. 15. Theoretical micrographs computed for the diffraction conditions of fig. 13b for the remaining possible Burgers vectors after comparing fig. 13a with fig. 14. Reading from a to e the Burgers vectors are $\frac{1}{2}$ [$\bar{1}$11], $\frac{1}{2}$ [1$\bar{1}$1], [$\bar{1}$11], [1$\bar{1}$1] and [001].

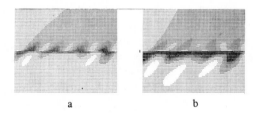

Fig. 16. Theoretical micrographs computed for the diffraction conditions of fig. 13c for the remaining possible Burgers vectors after comparing figs. 13a and 14 and figs. 13b and 15. The Burgers vector for a is $\frac{1}{2}$ [$\bar{1}$11] and for b is [$\bar{1}$11].

anisotropy. In many cases it is known that true invisibility cannot occur, but the extent of the contrast can only be determined by computation. This is an instance, therefore, in which a previously established rule breaks down. It can be re-established only on a very restricted basis for pure edge or pure screw dislocations which lie normal to mirror planes in the crystal [16,17].

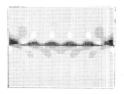

Fig. 17. A theoretical micrograph computed for the diffraction conditions of fig. 13d with a Burgers vector of [$\bar{1}$11].

Before leaving this particular example, consider the sets of intensity profiles shown in figs. 18a–d. These are computed for the same conditions as the micrographs in figs. 14e, 15c, 16b and 17 and correspond to about every third column of the micrographs, starting at the right-hand side. It will be noted that although they contain the same information as the theoretical micrographs they are much more difficult to compare with the experimental images and such features as the "arrow head" in fig. 14e tend to be missed in the profiles (fig. 18a).

Another case in which an established approximation was shown to be inaccurate by the use of theoretical micrographs was that of the contrast from three overlapping stacking faults [18]. In low stacking fault energy materials, the glide dislocations are widely split into Shockley partial dislocations connected by ribbons of stacking fault. Since slip often takes place on closely spaced planes in the crystal, there are usually many regions of overlapping stacking faults. An example which is believed to be one such region is shown in fig. 19. This is an electron micrograph of a thin foil of a Cu-8 at% Si alloy which has been deformed about 1%. It was taken under two-beam conditions and the reflecting vector 0$\bar{2}$0 is indicated. If the fault fringes at A are assumed to be due to a single stacking fault, then it can be shown that the fault is intrinsic. The fringes at B are apparently those typical of an extrinsic fault. However, following the interpretation of Whelan and Hirsch [19,20] the contrast from this area is probably due to the presence of a second closely overlapping intrinsic fault. In region C faint fringe contrast may be seen. It was proposed that in this area a third intrinsic fault is present, and the faint fringe contrast is due to three overlapping intrinsic stacking faults. Another separate and fainter example of this type of contrast can be seen running from D to E.

It can be seen from fig. 19 that the set of fringes at C is asymmetrical about mid-foil and that at DE symmetrical. The fringes at C are more intense than those at DE. Microdensitometer traces across the fringes showed that the maximum intensity of the fringes at C is about 18% below background intensity and the fringes at DE are only about 5% below background intensity.

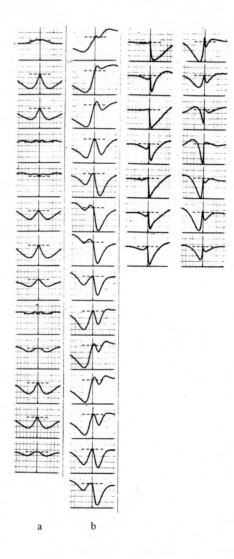

a   b

Fig. 18. Sets of profiles computed for the diffraction conditions of fig. 13 with a Burgers vector of [$\bar{1}11$].

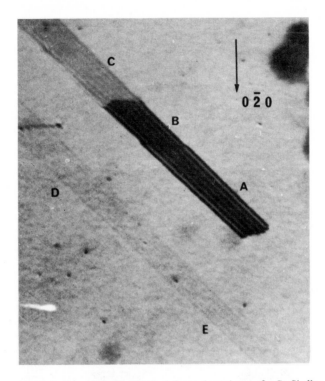

Fig. 19. Experimental micrograph of a lightly deformed specimen of a Cu-Si alloy showing faint fringe contrast at C and at DE.

Figs. 20 and 21 contain theoretical micrographs showing the contrast to be
expected from three overlapping stacking faults for several spacings of the
faults. The spacing of the faulted planes, x and y, in units of the slip plane
spacing are

		a	b	c	d	e	f
for fig. 20	x	1	1	2	1	2	3
	y	1	2	1	3	2	1

		a	b	c	d	e
for fig. 21	x	1	2	3	4	5
	y	5	4	3	2	1

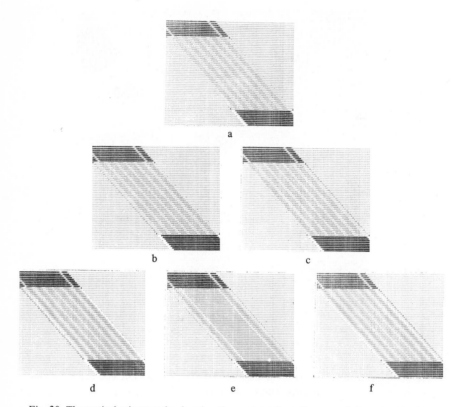

Fig. 20. Theoretical micrographs showing the contrast from three parallel overlapping in-trinsic stacking faults computed for the diffraction conditions of fig. 19 and for the separations given in the text.

Since the contrast from these defects is everywhere weak, this is one case where a special calibration of the grey scale has been used when printing the theoretical micrographs. In fact, the visibility limits for these micrographs are 5% above background intensity and 2% below background intensity rather than the commonly used ones of 15% above and 7% below. Moreover, this is one case where the absolute intensity of the images had to be taken into account when image matching.

It can be seen from these theoretical micrographs that whenever $x = y$ a set of fringes which is symmetrical about mid-foil results. When $x \neq y$ the fringes are asymmetrical about mid-foil. It is also apparent that the set of fringes for

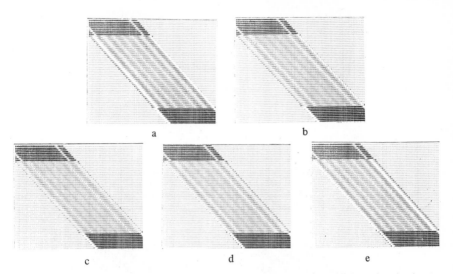

Fig. 21. Theoretical micrographs showing the contrast from three parallel overlapping intrinsic stacking faults computed for the diffraction conditions of fig. 19 and for the separations given in the text.

$x = n$, $y = m$ (where n and m are integers) become the set of fringes for $x = m$, $y = n$ by a 180° rotation. The fringes increase in intensity as the sum $(x+y)$ increases.

By noting both the symmetry and the intensity, it is possible to choose the theoretical micrograph in fig. 20a as the only one which will match the contrast at DE in the experimental micrograph. Thus the defect giving rise to this contrast may be identified as three overlapping intrinsic stacking faults on neighbouring slip planes (spaced about 2.1 Å apart). Similarly, the contrast at C may be identified as that due to three overlapping faults spaced 1 and 5 slip planes apart (fig. 21a).

It should be mentioned that since (to a good approximation) stacking faults do not have any strain field associated with them, elasticity theory plays no part in the image forming process, so that the success of the image matching technique in this case is independent of isotropic or anisotropic elasticity.

A more recent problem in which image matching has been used is that of identifying the precise nature of large faulted Frank loops formed on quenching low stacking fault energy materials (Ag and CuAl alloys [8,13,14]). When metals are quenched rapidly from close to the melting point down to ≈0°C the large supersaturation of vacancies trapped in the lattice can aggregate

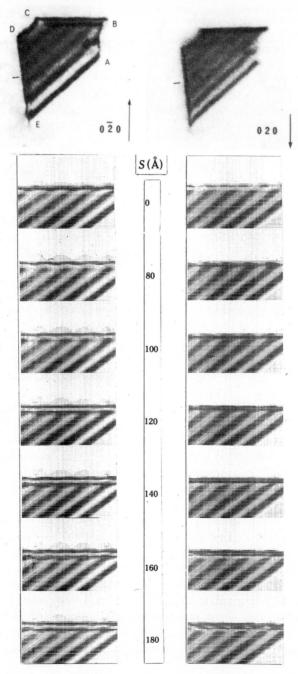

Fig. 22. Two images of a Frank dislocation loop together with the corresponding theoretical micrographs computed for the edge CB with various separations, S, of the Shockley and stair-rod dislocations.

either as planar defects (dislocation loops) or as three dimensional defects (voids or stacking fault tetrahedra). In low stacking fault energy materials, however, many of the Frank loops which are formed have features which run across the plane of the loop. In some well developed examples, it could be seen that this feature was, in fact, a step in the plane of the fault. It was thought that the explanation of this might lie in the fact that the Frank dislocations bounding the loop are dissociated (into Shockley and stair-rod dislocations connected by a ribbon of stacking fault), so that during growth vacancies cannot add on at the edge of the loop but have to add on to the plane of the loop. In order to test this it was necessary to determine if Frank dislocations are dissociated in these materials and whether the steps in the loop are consistent with the fault climb mechanism.

Fig. 22 shows two experimental images of a Frank loop in a quenched Cu 15.6% Al alloy and the corresponding theoretical images for edge CB of this loop (which lies along [$\bar{1}01$]) computed for various separations of the Shockley and stair-rod dislocations. It may be seen by inspection that the best match between theory and experiment occurs at a separation of 160Å. This is in agreement with the stacking fault energy of this alloy measured by other methods. It should be noted that the edges DC and BA which do not lie along a ⟨110⟩ direction and, therefore, cannot be dissociated, have images which are matched by the computed micrographs for zero separation.

For the alloys examined [13,14] the width of the dissociation varied from about 80Å to 160Å. Because the separation is so small, and because the {111} plane of dissociation was often shallowly inclined to the electron beam, the two dislocations and the ribbon of stacking fault could not be resolved as separate entities. Image matching, however, left no doubt as to the actual physical situation.

The problem of identifying the nature of the step was also one in which the dislocations and the stacking fault could rarely be separately resolved [3]. The quantities to be determined were the Burgers vectors of the two dislocations at the step, their relative orientation, whether the plane of the step was faulted and if so, intrinsically or extrinsically, and the height of the step. Fig. 23 shows an image of a stepped (complex) loop in Cu 9.4% Al, together with theoretical micrographs for 6 of the 36 probable physical configurations for this case. Although many other experimental micrographs were taken and compared with their corresponding theoretical micrographs, it happens that in this case this one $\bar{2}00$ image was sufficient to distinguish unambiguously between all 36 probabilities. By inspection of the fine detail in the images close to the step, it is possible to select the image in fig. 23b as the match to the experimental image. The step is, therefore, identified as consisting of low energy stair-rod disloca-

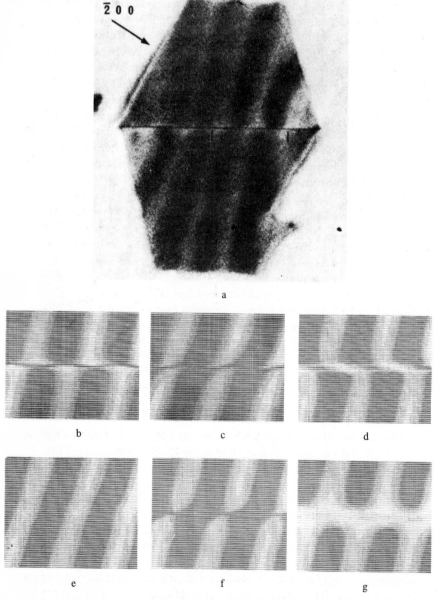

Fig. 23. The image of a complex Frank dislocation loop in a quenched Cu 9.4% Al alloy with theoretical micrographs for 6 of the 36 probable configurations which could give rise to the contrast at the step.

tions of Burgers vector $\pm \frac{1}{6}$ [101] bounding a region of intrinsic fault on the {111} plane acutely inclined to the main plane of the loop. The step height is close to 180Å.

With information of this type obtained for many such loops, together with the information on the dissociation of Frank dislocations lying along ⟨110⟩ it was possible to show that fault climb by vacancy addition was the only way in which the occurrence of complex loops could be explained [8].

The last example of the image matching technique which will be given here concerns the detailed identification of the Burgers vectors and geometry of dislocation dipoles in nickel [10,11]. Although nickel is not very elastically anisotropic, calculation shows that the anisotropy is sufficient to affect the position of stable equilibrium (measured by the angle ϕ from the slip plane) of oppositely signed $\frac{1}{2}$ ⟨110⟩ dislocations.

Fig. 8 shows five experimental images of a dislocation dipole lying along the [$\bar{1}\bar{1}2$] direction in a nickel specimen, and fig. 9 shows the corresponding theoretical micrographs computed for dislocations of Burgers vector $\pm \frac{1}{2}$ [$\bar{1}01$] and $\phi = 60°$. It can be seen that these images match the experimental ones. The value of $\phi = 60°$ was obtained from anisotropic elasticity theory using the known elastic constants for nickel: using isotropic elasticity, such dislocations, being only 30° from screw orientation, would have an equilibrium position directly above each other, $\phi = 90°$. In several of the cases examined so far, it has been possible to determine ϕ to $\pm 5°$ and within this error, agreement between theory and experiment has been obtained in every case. In fact the image shown in fig. 9e is particularly sensitive to changes in ϕ and fig. 24 shows five images computed for this particular diffracting vector with ϕ running between 55° and 65° in steps of 2.5°. Inspection of these shows that mismatches are obtained for the two extreme values so that $\phi = 60° \pm 2.5°$. Thus in this example it was possible to illustrate a new type of interaction and stability for dislocations in moderately anisotropic materials.

4. Future developments in defect identification using electron microscopy

In the preceding examples of defect identification using theoretical micrographs, one is involved in computing all the probable physical situations and comparing them with experiment. Whilst this is sufficiently convenient and successful to be employed as a routine method, it is not the most direct or general way of defect identification. Head has recently shown [9,21] that the possibility exists, at least in principle and under certain conditions, of taking the intensity information present in the experimental micrographs and using it to

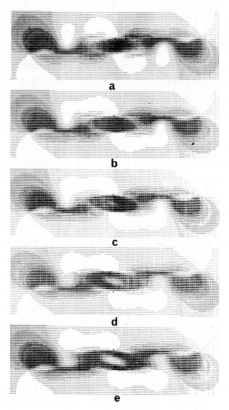

Fig. 24. Computed micrographs of a dislocation dipole in nickel corresponding to the diffraction conditions of fig. 8e. From a to e the equilibrium angle ϕ varies from $65°$ to $55°$.

reconstruct the displacement field of the defect producing the images. It is perhaps worthwhile, therefore, to spend a little time considering the principles behind this method of defect identification.

For two-beam diffraction conditions and for objects along which there is a direction in which the displacements are constant, Head has shown that the reconstruction may be done uniquely, even though all the phase information in the electron beams forming the image has been lost. Put another way, this theorem states that different defects produce different sets of electron diffraction images. This, of course, has been implicitly assumed in the "compute and match" method of defect identification discussed previously. Moreover, it follows from this theorem that a set of images from a defect will be unique to that defect for any degree of elastic anisotropy. Thus, a set of images from a dislocation (for example) even in an isotropic material will have detail in their topology etc. which will distinguish it from all other dislocations and defects.

The reconstruction method essentially rests on the fact that for defects for which there is a direction along which the displacements are constant, the displacements in one column (in the electron beam direction) in the crystal (at y) are related to those in the neighbouring column (at $y+\delta y$) by the addition and subtraction of the derivatives of the displacements $\beta'(y)$ and $\beta'(y-t)$ in small elements of material at the top and bottom surfaces of the foil. It follows that the scattering matrices for these columns are closely related. In fact, Head has shown that the scattering matrix for the column at y is related to the derivatives of the displacements in the small elements ($\beta'(y)$ and $\beta'(y-t)$) for a column at $y+\delta y$ through the second derivative of the intensity, I'', for the column at $y+\delta y$. By starting the reconstruction in undistorted crystal, where the scattering matrix is known and $I'' = 0$, it is possible to proceed along the direction in the image which is the projection of the line of constant displacement and determine either $\beta'(y)$ or $\beta'(y-t)$. For one direction of reconstruction, only one of these is unknown on moving to a neighbouring column (the other will have been determined for a column earlier in the reconstruction) and so by moving from undistorted crystal past the defect and back into undistorted crystal again one complete component (in the **g** direction) of the displacement field will be reconstructed. Thus, intensity information from three micrographs taken with non-coplanar diffracting vectors is sufficient to completely define the vector displacement field and hence identify the defect.

Obviously, this method of defect identification, if it is practically realized and put into routine use, is much to be preferred over the present one and would give the electron microscope an even greater role in the identification of defects in crystalline materials.

In compiling the material for this lecture, the author has relied heavily on the work of a number of his colleagues: L.M.Clarebrough, C.T.Forwood, A.K.Head, M.H.Loretto and A.J.Morton. In some cases their arguments have been followed closely, but in others the lack of space has restricted the discussion to only a brief summary of the work and thus does not do it full justice. The author would like to thank these colleagues for permission to discuss their work in this way and for much helpful criticism in preparing this manuscript.

References

[1] A.Howie and M.J.Whelan, Proc. Roy. Soc. A263 (1961) 217.

[2] A.K.Head, Aust. J. Phys. 20 (1967) 557.

[3] P.Humble, ibid. 21 (1968) 325.

[4] R.Bullough, D.M.Maher and R.C.Perrin, Nature 224 (1969) 364.

[5] L.M.Clarebrough, Aust. J. Phys., in press.

[6] H.B.Huntington, Solid State Phys. 7 (1958) 213.

[7] P.B.Hirsch, A.Howie, R.B.Nicholson, D.W.Pashley and M.J.Whelan, Electron Micro-
    scopy of Thin Crystals (Butterworths, London, 1966).

[8] A.J.Morton and L.M.Clarebrough, Aust. J. Phys. 22 (1969) 393.

[9] A.K.Head, ibid. 22 (1969) 43.

[10] C.T.Forwood and P.Humble, ibid., to be published.

[11] A.T.Morton and C.T.Forwood, unpublished work.

[12] P.Humble, ibid. 22 (1969) 51.

[13] L.M.Clarebrough and A.J.Morton, ibid. 22 (1969) 351.

[14] L.M.Clarebrough and A.J.Morton, ibid. 22 (1969) 371.

[15] A.K.Head, M.H.Loretto and P.Humble, Phys. Stat. Sol. 20 (1967) 505.

[16] A.K.Head, M.H.Loretto and P.Humble, ibid. 20 (1967) 521.

[17] A.N.Stroh, Phil. Mag. 3 (1958) 625.

[18] P.Humble, Phys. Stat. Sol. 30 (1968) 183.

[19] M.J.Whelan and P.B.Hirsch, Phil. Mag. 2 (1957) 1121.

[20] M.J.Whelan and P.B.Hirsch, ibid. 2 (1957) 1303.

[21] A.K.Head, Aust. J. Phys. 22 (1969) 345.

SOME APPLICATIONS OF TRANSMISSION ELECTRON MICROSCOPY TO PHASE TRANSITIONS

G.THOMAS

Inorganic Materials Research Division, Lawrence Radiation Laboratory,
Department of Materials Science and Engineering, College of Engineering,
University of California, Berkeley, California, USA

1. Introduction

The most important advantage of transmission electron microscopy in materials science is its ability to provide almost all the data needed to characterize completely the microstructure of materials [1,2] as indicated by the scheme shown in fig. 1. Today it is possible to resolve substructural details down to ≈20Å (discrete particles) and atomic plane spacings ≈1Å can be

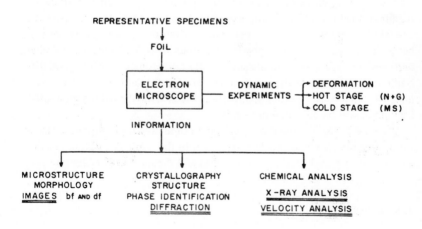

Fig. 1. Scheme illustrating the main functions of the electron microscope.

imaged. The new technique of velocity analysis (e.g. refs. [3–5]) has considereable promise for obtaining information regarding the chemistry of the specimen down to the resolution limits of the instrument.

The applications of the technique are almost unlimited [1,2] and it is obviously impossible to describe all of them here. However, some general methods of identification are discussed as applied to two or more phase systems resulting from phase transformations, excluding martensites.

Most commercially useful alloys contain two or more phases as a result of thermal or more complex thermal-mechanical processing. It is important to characterize the structure in terms of alloy composition and treatment as this approach is a necessary part of efforts to control alloy performance through control of structure. This chapter is not intended to be comprehensive, but is representative of some typical research work in materials science and engineering at Berkeley.

In the analysis of structure equal attention must be given to the diffraction pattern, corresponding bright and dark field images, and how these change upon tilting. As indicated in fig. 2 of the chapter on Kikuchi diffraction, only two orientations are necessary for the analysis of microstructure, namely (a) the symmetrical orientation, to provide accurate crystallographic information, e.g. orientation relations, identification of phases by utilizing the camera constant equation, and so on, and (b) the systematic two beam orientation so that contrast effects can be investigated in terms of various $g \cdot R$ conditions.

The interpretation of the image and the diffraction pattern is of course facilitated by careful selected area diffraction analysis, together with dark field investigations of the features present. It is important to emphasize that several photographs of a given area under various controlled conditions is far better than random photography of numerous areas. When the second phase particles are large enough or are sufficiently numerous to provide good diffraction patterns the analysis is generally straightforward except that care must be taken to isolate diffraction phenomena resulting from double diffraction as will be indicated in sect. 3.

Before discussing some typical examples of analysis of multiphase structures some points will be made with regard to the two basic techniques of identification viz selected area diffraction and the dark field technique.

2. Basic techniques

2.1. *Selected area diffraction*

This technique [1,2] provides a means for selecting various features of the

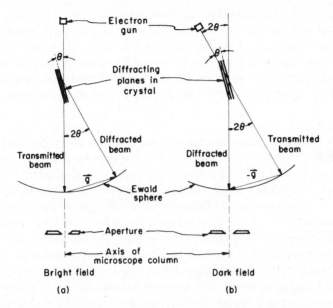

Fig. 2. Sketches showing that for maximum contrast gun tilt the dark field image must be formed of the negative diffraction vector corresponding to the bright field image; thus the sign of **g** is reversed from bright to dark field. The specimen is not tilted.

image for examination by diffraction and dark-field imaging. In order to distinguish between several different regions of the specimen it is necessary to be able to select the smallest possible area e.g. in diffraction analysis of small and different particles [1]. The minimum selected area (ΔA) contributing to the diffraction pattern is limited chiefly by the spherical aberration $\{C_s\}$ of the objective lens as follows:

$$(\Delta A) \cong C_s\theta_B^3 = C_s(\lambda/d)^3$$

where θ_B is the Bragg angle of a set of reflecting planes spacing d for incident wavelength λ.

Since C_s is roughly proportional to λ^{-1}, then $\Delta A \approx \lambda^2$ and decreases rapidly with increasing accelerating voltage (decreasing λ). Thus, there are advantages in high voltage microscopy for identifying small particles by selected area diffraction, e.g., at 100 kV $\Delta A \approx 2 \, \mu$m, while at 1 meV $\Delta A \approx 0.02 \, \mu$m.

The procedures which must be observed to eliminate errors and misinterpretation in carrying out selected area diffraction (SAD) are discussed in detail in ref. [2] . It must be remembered that when correlating the SAD pattern to the image, all rotations (optical and magnetic) must be accounted for and pre-calibration is essential. For example, in microscopes of lens sequence objective, intermediate, projector there is an optical rotation of 180° between image and pattern. For alignment fix the image and rotate the SAD pattern (both plates emulsion up) 180° plus the magnetic rotation, clockwise.

2.2. Dark field

High resolution images are obtained only when the diffracted beam to be utilized for the dark field image is tilted so that is passes down the optical axis of the microscope. This is necessary in order to minimize errors such as chromatic aberration and spherical aberration, but objective aperture images of off axis beams can be used for preliminary investigations since these can be obtained very quickly. The important point is that in order to obtain the dark-field image of maximum intensity by tilting the illumination and without tilting the specimen, it is necessary to tilt the optical system in a direction which translates the origin to the point occupied by the Bragg spot responsible for bright field contrast [6] . This operation reverses the sign of g as shown in fig. 2. This procedure applies whether manual or electrical tilting systems are to be used. The advantages of the electrical system include ease and speed of operation and fast switching from bright to dark field and vice-versa.

The advantages of dark field imaging are many as some of the illustrations indicate. Also the images of defects near either the top or bottom surfaces can be selectively brought into contrast by dark field imaging at $s < 0$ and $s > 0$, respectively [7] e.g. fig. 5a. As an example of the combined use of diffraction pattern and dark field imaging consider fig. 3 which is of a commercial aluminium alloy designed for cryogenic applications*. The two beam bright field image at $s \approx 0$ of the 200 reflection (fig. 3a) shows strain contrast from plate shaped particles. No strain contrast images are seen for $g \cdot R = 0$. For fig. 3 the plates on (100) are visible, and so R is normal to (100). The orientation is [011] (fig. 3b) and the inclined plates on (010) and (001) are not in suitable orientation for strain contrast since they (and hence R) are inclined at 45° to the foil plane normal. In order to obtain strain contrast $g \cdot R$ must be a maximum i.e., R should lie in the foil plane. Thus plates must be oriented to be nearly parallel to the incident beam. In fig. 1c a dark field image is obtained of the streak near the 200 spot. No strain contrast is observed, only "structure factor contrast". In order to utilize such dark field images small objective apertures are required so that only one diffraction

* I'am grateful to Dr. D.Rowcliffe of Lockheed, Palo Alto, for providing this specimen.

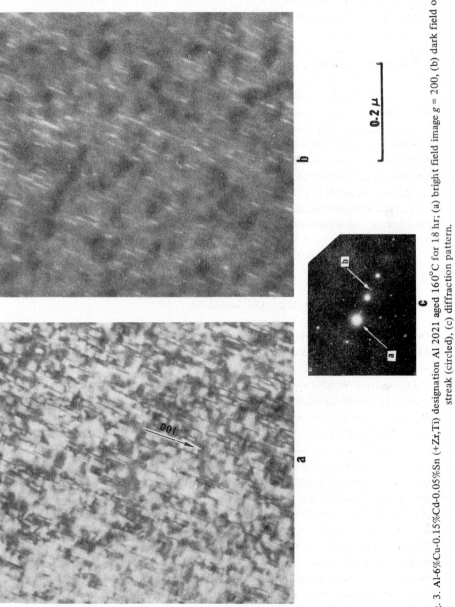

Fig. 3. Al-6%Cu-0.15%Cd-0.05%Sn (+Zr,Ti) designation Al 2021 aged 160°C for 18 hr; (a) bright field image $g = 200$, (b) dark field of streak (circled), (c) diffraction pattern.

phenomenon is to be imaged at a time. This is not always possible of course, when reflections are close together.

3. Double diffraction

The complexities of a diffraction pattern are most easily solved with the aid of dark field analysis of the various features present. In this way the maximum information can be obtained with minimum errors of identification. In two phase structures it is essential to recognize special effects due to double diffraction in order to correctly identify the phases which are present. This is also effected by dark field experiments.

In single phase BCC or FCC structures, double diffraction does not produce reflections of zero structure factor in the pattern since multiple reflections yield only allowed positions, e.g., in $[1\bar{1}0]$ BCC orientations

$$002 \pm 110 \leftrightharpoons 112 \text{ or } \bar{1}\bar{1}2$$

or

$$110 \pm 112 \leftrightharpoons 222 \text{ or } 00\bar{2} \text{ and so on.}$$

Twinning in these systems can however produce double diffraction [2], and it also occurs in less symmetrical structures such as diamond cubic or HCP, e.g., 200 (DC) and (0001) HCP.

In situations where two (or more) phases can exist, then double diffraction becomes more probable and care must be taken to identify spots which are due to this phenomenon. A spot which is present as a result of double diffraction, when used to form a dark field image will simultaneously reverse contrast in the corresponding diffraction regions of the phases responsible.

As an example consider fig. 4 taken from a Fe-Ni-Co maraging alloy which consists of a Widmanstatten pattern of austenite plates in martensite [8,9] (for review see ref. [10]). The SAD pattern consists of a mixture of the basic BCC $[0\bar{1}1]$ orientation (martensite) on which is superimposed several FCC orientations (austenite) in $\langle 111 \rangle$. For example, spot C is a 220 austenite reflection which in the dark field image (fig. 3c) reverses contrast only at those austenite plates that have this particular orientation. Spot d is a double diffraction spot produced by interactions of BCC and FCC reflections as shown by its dark field image in fig. 3d; similarly for spot b. Thus, the "quartets" of spots along $\langle 112 \rangle$ BCC in the pattern are mixtures of FCC reflections and

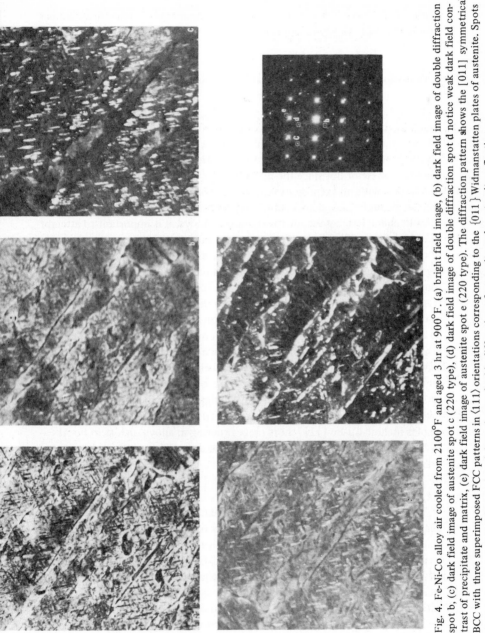

Fig. 4. Fe-Ni-Co alloy air cooled from 2100°F and aged 3 hr at 900°F. (a) bright field image, (b) dark field image of double diffraction spot b, (c) dark field image of austenite spot c (220 type), (d) dark field image of double diffraction spot d notice weak dark field contrast of precipitate and matrix, (e) dark field image of austenite spot e (220 type). The diffraction pattern shows the [011] symmetrical BCC with three superimposed FCC patterns in ⟨111⟩ orientations corresponding to the {011} Widmanstatten plates of austenite. Spots such as at b and d are due to double diffraction of austenite and martensite reflections.

double diffraction. They are not due to any intermetallic compounds. Similar arguments apply to any multiphase structure.

4. Detection and identification of small coherent particles

When second phase particles are large enough to give diffraction effects which are recognizable from those due to the matrix, their contrast can be reversed by dark field imaging and detection is not difficult. However situations can arise when it is not easy to be certain that the microstructure is indeed two-phase or not since the diffraction pattern may remain single crystal orientation with no extra spots visible and other diffraction effects due to second phases (strain, shape factor) may be too diffuse to be easily detected. Thus in characterizing the microstructure of alloys, it is important to attempt to utilize all possible pieces of information which may be present — observable or otherwise. This requires painstaking work in bright and dark field, obtaining high resolution, well exposed diffraction patterns, and ensuring that no spurious effects due to foil preparation (e.g. rough surfaces) do not confuse the issue. As will be illustrated in sect. 4.2, even though individual particles may not be resolvable, evidence for decomposition into two (or more) phases can be obtained by considering various possible contrast effects. Thus it is convenient to consider two general cases (a) when individual particles can be resolved and (b) when they cannot. Case (b) seems to be characterized by systems in which small, very coherent particles form in very large densities ($> 10^{17}$ cm^{-3}) so that any strain fields overlap and strain contrast images reveal net matrix strains rather than individual particle strain contrast. Examples include Cu-Be [11], short range ordering in alloys such as in Fe-Al [12], Fe-Si [13], Cu-Al [13], Ni-Mo [14] and possibly in interstitially ordered alloys such as Ta-C [15].

4.1. *Resolvable particles*
The visibility of precipitate particles depends on one or more different contrast mechanisms as discussed in detail in ref. [2], e.g., (a) diffraction contrast due to coherency strain fields, resulting from the matrix deforming locally to accommodate the precipitate, e.g., fig. 3a, (b) contrast due to the differences in structure factor between the phases present e.g. fig. 3b, (c) interface contrast in the form of fringes due to misorientation, phase contrast (as with stacking faults or antiphase boundaries) or geometrical effects such as at wedges, (d) Moiré contrast due to overlapping reflecting planes diffracting simultaneously in matrix and precipitate, (e) contrast due to the matrix being

in diffracting orientation when the particle is not (or vice versa), (f) thickness differences due to preferential thinning of the one phase with respect to its neighbor when preparing foils, (g) interface dislocation contrast when phases are partially coherent (e.g. figs. 14, 15).

When the precipitate particles are coherent, of similar lattice spacings, and are small with respect to the extinction distance ($\approx 100 \text{Å}$ or less) only the first two contrast mechanisms are significant. Such cases of precipitation occur generally in alloys which undergo decomposition from supersaturated solid solutions such as age-hardening alloys (see e.g. ref. [16] for review).

In the early stages of precipitation when large numbers of small particles can be formed several factors influence the microstructure and observed contrast, e.g., (a) coherency strains, (b) volume fraction, (c) elastic anisotropy, represented by the ratio of the shear moduli G $\langle 110 \rangle$: G $\langle 100 \rangle$.

In aluminum alloys where the anisotropy is ≈ 1, the shapes of particles are determined by the atom size factor. Spherical (as in Al-Ag), needle-like (Al-Mg_2Si) and plate-like (Al-Cu) particles have all been identified [16]. Needles and plates are most easily distinguished in the early aging stages when particles are very small by analysis of the SAD pattern since this is modified by the shape factor. Needles give rise to rel-sheets of intensity perpendicular to their axes while plates give rise to rel-rods, normal to the plane of the plate [1,2]. Fig. 5 shows examples of needles in Al-Mg_2Si and the diffraction pattern shows the curved streaks which are produced when the reflecting sphere intersects the sheets of intensity which are normal to $\langle 100 \rangle$ for all needles which do not lie normal to the beam. By comparison to fig. 5b the straight streaks in fig. 6 are due to small plates (GP zones) on $\{001\}$. Thus, the [110] orientation immediately distinguishes between plates and rods in these alloys. Shape factor effects can be understood geometrically by the superposition of all respective reciprocal lattices [17].

If the volume fraction of the particles is not too large so that individual small particles can be resolved by diffraction contrast, and the strain fields do not overlap to a considerable extent, qualitative information can be obtained as to the direction and magnitude of strain and the shape and dimensions of the particles by utilizing the strain contrast rules to dark-field images first developed by Ashby and Brown [18]. These rules can be summarized by reference to fig. 7 which shows the type of strain contrast images expected for different (simple) defects under conditions where $\mathbf{g} \cdot \mathbf{R} \neq 0$ (where $\mathbf{R}$ is the displacement vector). These images show dark contrast to the same side as $\mathbf{g}$ when the strain field is interstitial in nature and white when the strain field is of the vacancy type, provided that exactly $s = 0$ condition applies to the area being considered [18]. In principle, therefore, the sense of the image

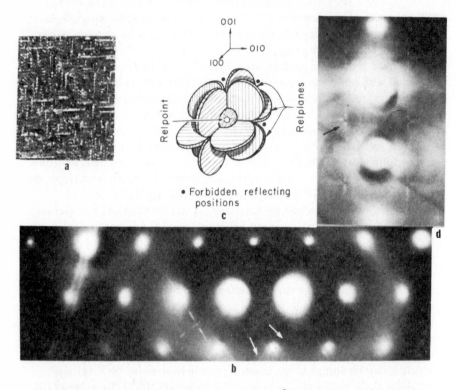

Fig. 5. a, foils of Al-Mg$_2$Si quenched and aged 5 hr 220°C; dark-field at $s < 0$, only precipitates near top surface are in good contrast. The needles along [100] and [010] inclined at 45° exhibit extinction contrast and strain contrast. The strain contrast indicates interstitial strain fields. b SAD pattern of a, notice parabolic streaks spread
about [002] due to the [100] and [010] needles, and straight streaks along [220] due to
the [001] needles. c. Schematic representation of the intensity sheet distribution about
rel-points. d. Diffraction pattern ($\approx$[103]) of needles showing cancellation of intensity at
nonallowed reflecting positions (cf-c).

contrast with respect to the direction of g can be used to determine the sense
of the strain fields. However, due to the periodic intensity oscillations with
depth in the foil as illustrated in fig. 8, it is essential that the position of the
particle in the foil be accurately known when the size of the particle is smaller
than the extinction distance before this rule can be applied. Details of this type
of analysis are described in the chapter by Wilkins. If precipitation has in fact
occurred in the bulk of the material and not on the surfaces then roughly half

Fig. 6. [110] orientation of Al-Cu aged to form GP zones on {100} the streaks along
[001] show that plates and not needles are present (compare to fig. 5b).

the particles have white contrast and half have dark contrast on the same side
as the direction of **g** (fig. 9). Also, if the particle size is large (of same order as
the extinction distance) there is no problem in defining the sense of displacement from the image e.g. the larger θ' plates in fig. 9, all have their white
images on the same side while the GP zone images have mixed contrast.

4.2. Alloys containing very large volume fractions of small particles

The illustrations of figs. 3, 8 and 9 show that strain contrast images are
determined by **g · R** where *g* is a matrix reflection and **R** represents the dis-
placement(s) around the precipitate. If the precipitate reflection is used to

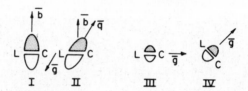

Fig. 7. Scheme illustrating strain contrast images expected from individual precipitates
I plate shaped particle displacement vector **b** normal to habit plane or rods viewed with
axes normal to the beam. II As I but displacement vector inclined to habit plane. III
Similar to a screw dislocation end-on. IV Spherical particle or rod viewed end-on. In I and
II the image (line of dividing contrast LC) is independent of **g**; in III LC is parallel to **g**,
in IV LC is normal to **g**. These predictions may be modified when the volume fraction of
particles is very large so that strain fields overlap and interact, and for more complex
shaped particles.

form a dark field image, e.g., the streak in fig. 3, only structure factor contrast is observed. Such images thus may provide more accurate information
regarding true particle size and shape than the strain contrast image.

Difficulties in resolving particles may be encountered when the volume
fraction is very large and the particles are very small (<100Å) so that the
strain fields overlap. The image contrast can then be determined by *net strains*
rather than by individual particles and it is convenient to refer to this effect
as net strain contrast. The simplest example is found in the Cu-Be precipitation hardening system [11] in which only ⟨110⟩ strain "striations" (also
called tweed patterns) can be observed during the initial stages of aging (see
fig. 10a). Tanner [11] in a detailed investigation concluded that the strain
patterns were due to small plates on {100}, but with strain fields in ⟨110⟩.
This result was inferred from a series of **g · R** experiments. However, in Cu-2%
Be additional helpful information can be gained from the diffraction patterns,
for example in fig. 10b streaks are observed in ⟨100⟩ from rel-point to rel-point
proving that small plates with {001} habit must be present. The interpretation
of strain fields in ⟨110⟩ is confirmed by the short ⟨110⟩ diffuse streaks observed in the pattern. The reason for {001}⟨110⟩ strains may be related to the
anisotropy factor > 1*. When the volume fraction is high, fig. 7 is no longer

---

* The anisotropy factor is also important when coherency is lost; e.g. partially coherent
  dislocations are generated with minimum energy expenditure so that dislocations with
  b = ⟨110⟩ rather than ⟨100⟩ may exist (cf. figs. 14, 15).

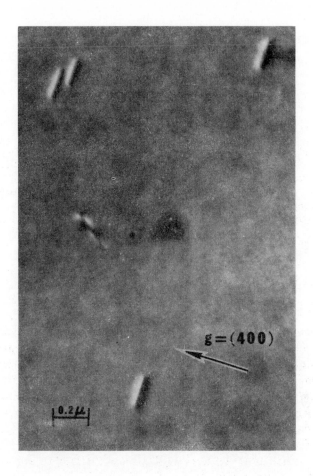

Fig. 8. Rods of precipitate formed in silicon doped with phosphorus strain contrast images; the rods lying normal to the beam indicate vacancy contrast (cf. fig. 7-I) but the inclined rod shows oscillatory contrast due to the depth dependence of the intensity.

an accurate guide to interpretation but the zones in Cu-Be if resolved should appear as in fig. 7 II with $b = [100]$ and $q = [110]$.

Similar but not identical results occur in short range ordered alloys. For example, fig. 11 shows a series of $g \cdot R$ experiments on Ni-20%Mo which indicate that R is principally along $\langle 110 \rangle$ but no individual particles can be resolved until aging is prolonged sufficiently so that superlattice spots can be

Fig. 9. Al-4% Cu dark field strain contrast image showing heterogeneously precipitated
θ' (large plates) and GP zones. Compare to figs. 3 and 7 I. Displacement **R** parallel to
g = 200. Foil orientation [001], plates on (010) are not visible since **g · R** is zero for these.

seen. In this case the dark field image of a superlattice spot reverses contrast
for particles of that particular orientation (fig. 11f). However, unless diffuse
or superlattice spots are present the net strain contrast image may be the only
indication that precipitation has occurred. If the individual particles cannot be
resolved and shape factor and/or strain diffuse streaks cannot be seen or dis-

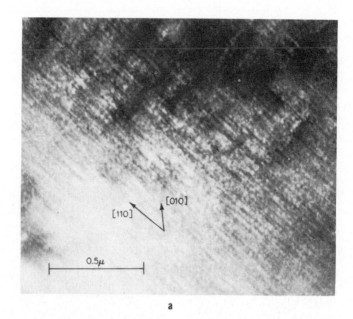

a

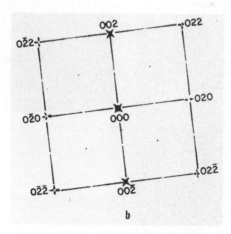

b

Fig. 10. Cu-2% Be aged to form GP zones (a) bright field image g = [220], (b) sketch of
SAD pattern to show ⟨110⟩ strain diffuse streaks and ⟨100⟩ form factor streaks.

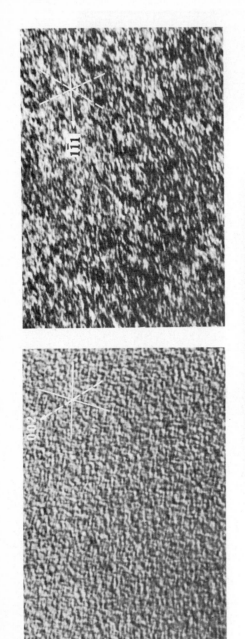

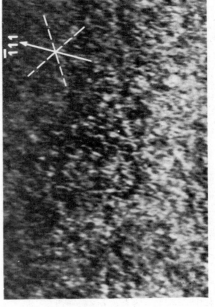

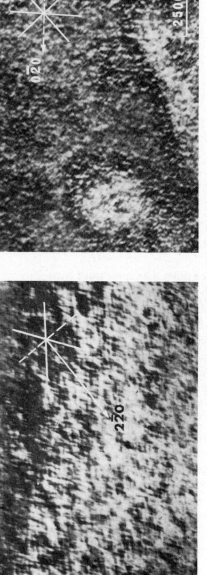

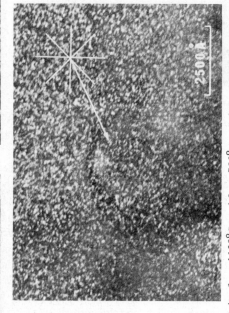

Fig. 11. Ni$_4$Mo quenched to ice brine from 1100°C aged 5 sec 750° (a–d) foil near [110]. Courtesy P.R.Okamoto. (a) bright field two beam g = 002 (b) bright field two beam g = 1̄11̄ (c) bright field two beam g = 111 (d) bright field two beam g = 220. Solid and dashed lines show traces of {110} planes. Strain contrast in ⟨110⟩ is parallel to solid lines. (e) bright field g = 02̄0 after tilting to near [001] zone. (f) dark field of superlattice reflection showing one of the six orientational variants possible for ordered Ni$_4$Mo particles.

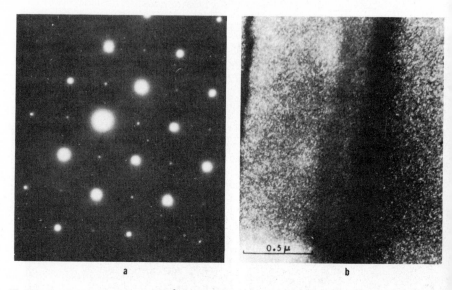

Fig. 12. Fe-19% Al aged 1 week 300°C, (a) diffraction pattern (b) dark field image of "superlattice spot", showing two-phase nature of the alloy.

tinguished, there is little more to be concluded other than some small parti-cles, of undefined shape and associated strain vector are present. Considerable effort is currently being devoted to this problem in order to better define physically the meaning of short range order. For example fig. 12 shows a SAD pattern of Fe-19% Al after aging one week at 300°C [12]. This pattern may be interpreted to be single phase, single crystal, but ordered with super-lattice spots at $\{h00\}$ and equivalent positions. However, a dark-field image of a "superlattice" spot, fig. 12b, clearly reveals small particles. The microstruc-ture may thus be characterized as two phase with small ordered particles in a disordered matrix, and the pattern in (a) can be regarded as consisting of two superposed ordered and disordered patterns of the same [001] orientation and almost identical lattice parameter since no doubling of the spots is seen. Thus the two phases in (b) must be almost ideally coherent. This characteriza-tion seems to indicate that short range ordered alloys consist of small ordered particles in a disordered matrix. It should be emphasized that it is difficult to prove that two phases exist when the contrast is very weak and no obvious ef-fects are to be seen in the SAD patterns. Other techniques such as field ion microscopy may then be combined to advantage [14].

5. Spinodal decomposition

In spinodal decomposition, periodic fluctuations in composition occur along the elastically soft directions (generally $\langle 001 \rangle$ in metals) [19]. The consequence of this on the diffraction pattern is to produce "side-bands", i.e., satellite reflections alongside the main reflections in a direction parallel to the direction of modulation. The important feature of the sidebands is that their spacing dpeends only on the wavelength of the compositional fluctuation. For cubic phases the wavelength can be calculated from [20]

$$\lambda = \frac{h(d_{h'k'l'}) \tan \theta}{(h^2+k^2+l^2)\Delta\theta}$$

where $h'k'l'$ is direction of fluctuation and $\Delta\theta$ the angular separation between spot and satellite. For high energy electrons and for fluctuations along $[h00]$ this reduces to

$$\lambda = \frac{ha}{(h^2+k^2+l^2)} \left(\frac{g}{\Delta g} \right)$$

where a is the lattice parameter, and $g : \Delta g$ is given by the ratio of the distances from 000 and satellite to the hkl spot. Similar equations apply to the $0k0$, $00l$ directions of fluctuation. The wavelengths obtained from fig. 13 increase from $60\,\text{Å}$ (b) to $160\,\text{Å}$ (e) [21]. This method of measuring λ is more convenient than direct measurements of the image for two main reasons viz., (a) because the sideband spacing is independent of magnification and (b) because mean values are immediately obtained for all distributions of λ contributing to thepattern (i.e., within the selected area). When the phases are coherent with small strains involved the images do not show strong strain contrast. For Cu-Fe-Ni the strain is $< 0.6\%$ (fig. 17b). Interface fringes (δ-fringes [22]) typical of coherent boundaries can be observed when the interface plane is inclined to the incident beam. Many examples of δ-fringes have now been given, e.g. at domain interfaces [22–24]. The characteristic of these fringes is that their contrast is the opposite to that of stacking fault contrast in FCC systems. Delta fringes show asymmetry at the top and bottom of the foil in bright field, and are symmetrical in dark field. These fringe patterns occur due to the slight mismatch in lattice spacing at the interface giving rise to a Δg (and Δs) mismatch in the reciprocal lattice. In such cases splitting of the diffraction spots and Kikuchi lines may be resolved particularly at large 2θ values [25]. From measurements of the Kikuchi patterns the axial ratios

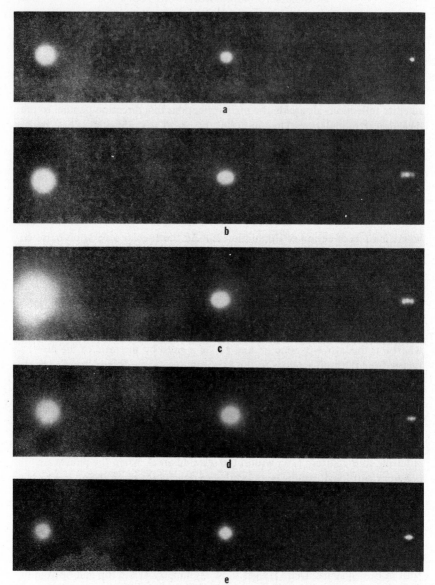

Fig. 13. 51.5 Cu-33.5Ni-15 Fe alloy quenched and aged at $625°C$ showing development of side-bands due to spinodal decomposition along {100}. (a) fast quenched (no decomposition), (b) 1 min, (c) 5 min, (d) 15 min, (e) 60 min. Notice decrease in satellite spacing at 400 reflection as aging increases (λ increases).

of non-cubic structures may be measured quite accurately [23]. It should be noted that satellites from modulated (side-band) structure can be distinguished from Δg splitting since the spacing of the former depends only on spinodal wavelength whereas the latter increases with $|g|$.

6. Partially coherent phases

When the misfit between two phases exceeds that which can be tolerated by elastic distortion (visible as strain contrast), coherency breaks down and interfacial dislocations can be generated. Mechanisms to account for loss of coherency have been investigated in several alloy systems by Weatherly and Nicholson [26]. In Al-4% Cu coherency between θ' plates and the matrix is lost by the generation of prismatic pure edge-dislocation loops inside the plates with the loop lying parallel to the habit plane {001}. The contrast from these loops is directly analogous to the contrast from large edge-loops in quenched or irradiated crystals. For a plate viewed with its normal parallel to the incident beam $g \cdot b = 0$ but the resolved components of the displacement normal to b, i.e., $b \times u$ where u is a vector normal to b are only normal to g where g is tangent to the loop ($g \cdot b \times u = 0$). This is the only condition when $g \cdot b = 0$, and $g \cdot b \times u = 0$ is simultaneously satisfied. The image has maximum contrast when g and $b \times u$ are parallel. Thus, the image consists of double arcs normal to g and the images are complementary on opposite sides since $g \cdot b \times u$ changes sign about a line through the center of the plate. An example is shown in fig. 14. The doublets and triplets in the images are due to the effect of foil thickness on image contrast. Triple images occur for loops near the bottom surface of the foil.

For precipitates, such as θ' in Al-Cu, which form on cube planes, the misfit dislocations are expected to have their Burgers vectors along ⟨100⟩ in the interface, i.e., be pure edge. However, this is not a universal rule and interesting differences occur in the Cu-Fe-Ni spinodal system when the wavelength > 1000Å and coherency is lost [21].

Fig. 15a,b shows the interface structure. Only one set of interface dislocations has been generated and these have b of the $\frac{1}{2} a$ [110] type. The mismatch $\delta = |b|/d$, where d is the spacing, is ≈0.6%. The corresponding diffraction pattern (fig. 16) shows a splitting in the [010] but not in the [100] direction, (e.g., the 440 spot). The mismatch in fig. 16 ≈ 0.7%. This result shows that as coherency is lost the structure must change from cubic to tetragonal. At later stages when a second set of dislocations has been generated so that all grains are relieved at the interface, the structure becomes cubic again [21].

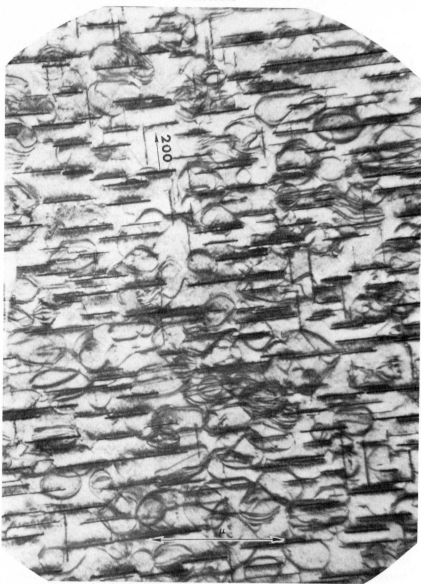

Fig. 14. Showing interfacial pure edge prismatic loops around partially coherent θ' plates in Al-4% Cu. Foil in [001]. Notice that $\mathbf{g} \cdot \mathbf{b}$ is zero for one set of edge-on plates and $\mathbf{g} \cdot \mathbf{b} \times \mathbf{u}$ and $\mathbf{g} \cdot \mathbf{b}$ is zero simultaneously for parts of loops with $b = [001]$ normal to the foil plane. Compare to strain contrast images of θ' in fig. 9.

Fig. 15. Interfacial dislocations in spinodal Cu-Fe-Ni alloy aged 200 hr 700°C visible for $g = 11\bar{1}$ in (a), but invisible for **g** = $1\bar{1}1$ in (b). The dislocations lie in [100]; their most probable Burgers vector is along [011].

Fig. 16. Diffraction pattern corresponding to area similar to that in fig. 15. Zone is [001].
The resolvable doublet at 440 is parallel to the interface normal. Notice that there is no
splitting along [100]. The structure is thus tetragonal.

The contrast experiments illustrated by fig. 15 prove that the Burgers vectors of these interface dislocations are parallel to $\langle 110 \rangle$ directions with the dislocations lines along $\langle 100 \rangle$. Thus roughly twice as many dislocation are required to relieve the mismatch than if dislocations of $\mathbf{b} = \mathbf{a} \langle 100 \rangle$ were formed. It is possible that nucleation of dislocations with $\frac{1}{2} a \langle 110 \rangle$ Burgers vectors is more favorable energetically than $a[100]$ type in this system and in view of the high anisotropy ratio.

7. Note on grain boundaries

Phase transformations from supersaturated solutions occur neither by nucleation and growth (N and G), homogeneously as in the spinodal, or martensitically. The latter case will not be discussed here. Homogeneous and heterogeneous decomposition can be distinguished morphologically since in the latter case nucleation is favored at defects such as dislocations, boundaries, faults, point defects, etc. Noticeable differences occur at and near grain boundaries as illustrated in fig. 17. Fig. 17a shows a grain boundary microstructure in Al-Zn-Mg alloy showing typical N + G conditions with precipitation along the boundary, precipitate free zones adjacent to boundaries (PFZ) [27] and a decrease in number (but increase in size) of particles in the matrix adjacent to the PFZ. The homogeneous microstructure resulting from spinodal decomposition of Cu-Fe-Ni on the other hand (fig. 17b) shows none of these features. Although it is easy to distinguish such heterogeneous and homogeneous transformations, it is not recommended as a general principle to use microstructure to define the type of transformation since this is determined by kinetic and thermodynamic principles, and usually the experimentalist never really "sees" the nucleation (or lack of) stage in the process, even when direct observations are possible.

Fig. 17 . a. Heterogeneous precipitation in Al-Zn-Mg. b. Homogeneous precipitation in Cu-Fe-Ni spinodal.

8. Dynamic studies of phase transformations

As indicated in fig. 1 it is possible to obtain direct observations of dynamic events, e.g., deformation, precipitation, recovery, etc., with the use of appropriate specimen stages and ciné techniques (see ref. [28] for review). The high voltage microscope may be useful in this regard since it will be possible to work with thicker specimens and possibly have fewer problems due to surface effects. Some examples have already been given by Fujita et al. [29].

This work was done under the auspices of the United State Atomic Energy Commission. I also acknowledge helpful discussions with Dr. Paul Butler and my graduate students.

References

[1] G.Thomas, Transmission Electron Microscopy of Metals (John Wiley and Sons, New York, 1962).
[2] P.B.Hirsch et al., Electron Microscopy of Thin Crystals (Butterworths, London, 1965).
[3] A.J.F.Metherell and M.J.Whelan, J. Appl. Phys. 37 (1966) 1737.
[4] Electron Microscopy, Kyoto, ed. R.Uyeda (Maruzen Company, Tokyo, 1968) pp. 85–99.
[5] S.L.Cundy and P.J.Grundy, Phil. Mag. 14 (1966) 1233.
[6] W.L.Bell, D.M.Maher and G.Thomas, Lattice Defects in Quenched Metals (Academic Press, New York, 1965) p. 739.
[7] W.L.Bell and G.Thomas, Phys. Stat. Sol. 12 (1965) 843.
[8] G.Thomas, I-Lin Cheng and J.R.Mihalisin, Trans. ASM, in press.
[9] I-Lin Cheng and G.Thomas, ibid. 61 (1968) 14.
[10] S.Floreen, Met. Rev. (1968) p. 115.
[11] L.E.Tanner, Phil. Mag. 14 (1966) 111.
[12] H.Warlimont and G.Thomas, J. Mat. Sci. (in press) (UCRL-18610).
[13] H.Warlimont (private communication).
[14] P.R.Okamoto and G.Thomas, to be published.
[15] P.Rao and G.Thomas, to be published.
[16] A.Kelly and R.B.Nicholson, Prog. Mat. Sci. 10 (1963) 151.
[17] G.Thomas, W.L.Bell and H.M.Otte, Phys. Stat Sol. 12 (1965) 353.
[18] M.F.Ashby and L.M.Brown, Phil. Mag. 8 (1963) 1083, 1649.
[19] J.W.Cah, Trans. TMS-AIME 242 (1968) 166.
[20] V.Daniel and H.Lipson, Proc. Roy. Soc. 182 (1943) 378.
[21] E.P.Butler and G.Thomas, Acta Met. (in press) (UCRL-18840).
[22] R.Gevers, J.van Landuyt and S.Amelinckx, Phys. Stat. Sol. 11 (1965) 689; G.Gemant et al.Phys. Stat. Sol. 13 (1966) 125.
[23] R.E.Villagrana and G.Thomas, Phys. Stat. Sol. 9 (1965) 499.

[24] E.P.Butler and P.M.Kelly, Trans. TMS-AIME 242 (1968) 2107.
[25] G.Thomas, Trans. TMS-AIME 233 (1965) 1608.
[26] G.C.Weatherly and R.B.Nicholson, Phil. Mag. 17 (1968) 801.
[27] G.Thomas and J.Nutting, J. Inst. Metals 88 (1959-60) 81.
[28] G.Thomas, High Temperature High Resolution Metallography (Gordon and Breach, 1967) p. 217.
[29] J.Fujita, Y.Kawasaki, E.Furubayashi, S.Kajiwara and T.Taoka, Jap. J. Appl. Phys. 6 (1967) 214.

KIKUCHI ELECTRON DIFFRACTION AND APPLICATIONS

G.THOMAS

Inorganic Materials Research Division, Lawrence Radiation Laboratory,
Department of Materials Science and Engineering, College of Engineering,
University of California, Berkeley, California, USA

1. Geometry and orientations

1.1. *Geometry of formation*

The name Kikuchi electron diffraction is given to the patterns of lines that are observed from fairly thick crystals after their discovery in 1934 by Kikuchi [1]. The mechanism of formation is as follows: The electron beam, on entering a specimen, suffers inelastic and incoherent scattering by interaction with the atoms. These electrons can be subsequently rescattered coherently when Bragg's law is satisfied at a suitable set of reflecting planes.

Cones of radiation are emitted and if the incident waves are symmetrically impinging on the plane AB, cones of equal intensity are scattered, with semi-vertex angles of $(90-\theta)$ (fig. 1a), to each side and bisecting the reflecting plane AB. If, however, the waves impinge on an inclined reference plane AB (fig. 1b), then most of the electrons are initially scattered into the direction K_1 and relatively few into the forward direction K_2. Under normal conditions and on a positive print, one then observes a bright line corresponding to K_1 near the Bragg spot and a dark line corresponding to K_2 near the origin. Since for most applications a knowledge of the geometry is sufficient, a discussion of the dynamical behavior [2] and intensities of the Kikuchi lines [3] will not be given here.

The intersection of the cones of Kikuchi radiation with the reflecting sphere produces slightly hyperbolic lines due to the small angles θ and large radius of the sphere for fast electrons. These lines are actually straight on the photographic plate for the usual angles recorded in a pattern ($\approx 9°$ at 100 kV for

159

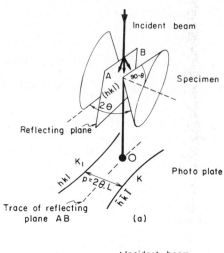

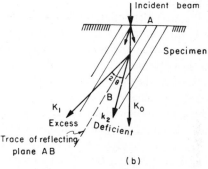

Fig. 1. Geometry of formation of Kikuchi lines. a. Incident beam is inelastically scattered; inelastic electrons are then rescattered coherently by plane AB to produce cones of radiation which intersect the reflecting sphere as slightly curved lines, which bisect the reflecting plane. Each Kikuchi pair corresponds to a unique reflecting plane. b. Diffraction representation for crystal oriented for Bragg diffraction. In this case, more electrons are scattered into the diffracting direction so that the Kikuchi lines K_1 are bright, and K_2 dark.

and *hkl* whose respective intensities depend principally upon the orientation, perfection, and thickness of the crystal. Figs. 2a, b show the geometry for crystals oriented symmetrically and at the exact Bragg condition. These are really the only two orientations that are needed during electron microscopy applications; case (b) should be used when crystallographic data is needed and case (a) is the two-beam situation necessary for contrast analysis.

It should be noted that in the case of rescattering of inelastic beams, the specimen acts as a monochromator, i.e., the planes (hkl) reflect electrons which are satisfied by Bragg's law for the wavelengths involved: $2d \sin(\theta)' = n\lambda'$. Since typically the characteristic energy losses are of the order of tens of volts, then $\lambda' \approx \lambda$ (incident), and the same reflecting sphere-reciprocal lattice construction describing the spot pattern can be used for the Kikuchi pattern (figs. 2a, b).

Kikuchi patterns are always produced even in thin crystals, but the specimen must be thick enough in order that a sufficiently intense Kikuchi cone to be observed on the photo plate is produced. Furthermore, the specimen should be relatively free from long range internal strains (e.g., elastic buckling, a high dislocation density), otherwise, the Kikuchi cones will be incoherently scattered and may become too diffuse to be observed. The absence of observable Kikuchi lines or the appearance of very broad diffuse lines from heavily dislocated structures, e.g., ferrous martensite, is due to incoherent scattering. As the thickness of the foil increases, the diffraction pattern changes from spots, to Kikuchi lines and spots, to Kikuchi lines or bands, until finally complete absorption within the foil occurs. The thickness limits for these events increase with increasing voltage, due to enhanced penetration.

It can be seen from fig. 2a, b, that on tilting the specimen in one sense, the Kikuchi lines sweep across the pattern in the opposite sense. In fig. 2a the crystal has been tilted by θ_{hkl} anti-clockwise so as to excite the first order (hkl) relfection. The Kikuchi origin is fixed in the crystal so that as the crystal is tilted, the cones sweep across the pattern as if rigidly "fixed" to the specimen. Thus, the Kikuchi pattern is extremely useful in determining the precise orientation, as well as for calibrating tilt angles, etc. Since each Kikuchi line in a pair bisects the reflecting plane, then the angle subtended by each pair is always 2θ independently of crystal orientation*. Furthermore, the Kikuchi pattern represents the traces of all reflecting planes in the crystal and can thus be directly compared to the appropriate stereographic projection. The Kikuchi lines are also parallel to the Bragg extinction contours. Applying Bragg's law and the appropriate structure factor rules enables one to plot the complete Kikuchi pattern. Fig. 3 is derived to scale for the first order Kikuchi reflections for Al at 100 kV. This can be compared to the actual patterns shown in figs. 9–11, and the Bragg contour pattern of a bent foil in fig. 4. Further applications are described in sect. 1.4.

---

* Special situations arise when this rule is not strictly correct; and is important for large angle reflections (see Tan et al., ref. [3]).

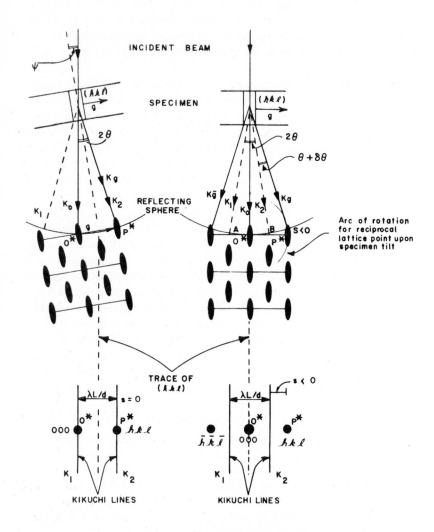

Fig. 2. Reciprocal lattice – reflecting sphere construction showing relation of Kikuchi pattern to spot pattern for, (a) exact Bragg two-beam orientation, and (b) the symmetrical orientation. The spacing of Kikuchi lines is independent of crystal orientation. (Courtesy of Physica Stat. Solidi).

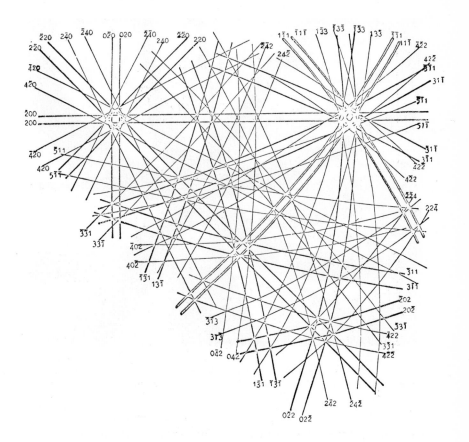

Fig. 3. Stereographic projection of first order Bragg contours (and Kikuchi pairs) drawn to scale for 100 kV electrons in aluminum up to $(h^2+k^2+l^2) = 27$. (After K.Ashbee and J.Heavens, University of California, UCRL Report No. 17614.).

Tilting the crystal tilts the reciprocal lattice in the same sense and magnitude. The spot pattern thus translates only slightly on tilting since each spot rotates on tilting about an arc of radius |g| centered at the origin (fig. 2b). The Kikuchi pattern, however, shifts in an easily observable manner (≈ 1 cm per $1°$ tilt for $\lambda L \approx 2$ Å cm).

The Kikuchi lines associated with a particular reflection *hkl* always lie perpendicular to g(*hkl*), i.e., on a line through the origin and normal to the Kikuchi pair.

Fig. 4. a. Bragg extinction contours in copper foil symmetrically deformed about [011].
Compare to [011] region of figs. 3 and 11. (Courtesy W.L.Bell.)

The centers of symmetry of the spot pattern and Kikuchi pattern thus coincide only in symmetrically oriented foils. For accurate determinations of orientation relationships the foil can be tilted until the symmetrical situation appears on the screen.

1.2. *Relation to spot pattern and determination of deviation parameter*

The Bragg deviation parameter s is important in contrast analysis. Both the sign and magnitude of s can be readily obtained by noting the orientation of the Kikuchi pattern to that of the spot pattern [4].

Since by definition $s > 0$ occurs when the reciprocal lattice point lies inside the reflecting sphere, then the Kikuchi line lies outside its corresponding diffraction spot (fig. 2). Thus, in a symmetrical orientation, $s < 0$ (fig. 2a). The sense of tilt of a foil is thus immediately apparent from the relation between the Kikuchi and spot patterns.

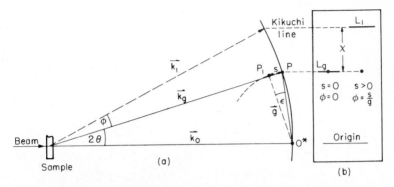

Fig. 5. Sketch showing shift in Kikuchi lines produced by a tilt ϵ. Position of Kikuchi lines at L_g and L_1 correspond to the cases $s = 0$, $s > 0$, respectively. The tilt ϵ moves the Kikuchi line through **a** and the spot through distance s about the radius O*P. (Courtesy J. Appl. Phys., ref. [4]).

In fig. 5 is shown the effect of tilting the foil to produce an $s > 0$ orientation (such as is required for maximum bright-field contrast in absorbing crystals). As the foil is tilted from the exact Bragg condition by an angle ϵ the Kikuchi lines move outwards a distance χ along g_{hkl} whereas the spot moves inside the sphere on the arc $O*PP_1$. In the pattern the Kikuchi line now lies outside the corresponding spot as shown in (b).

Since the Bragg angles are small, we can write

$$\phi = \chi/L = \chi\lambda/rd$$

where L is the camera length.

Since χ can be measured on the plate and since r and d are known from the indexed pattern, ϕ is calculated. Also

$$\phi = s/g \ .$$

Hence

$$s = \chi g/L = \chi/Ld$$

for a given Kikuchi band of separation p_1, $2\theta_1 \cong p_1/L = \lambda/d_1$ hence

$$s = \chi/Ld = \chi\lambda/d(p_1d_1) \ .$$

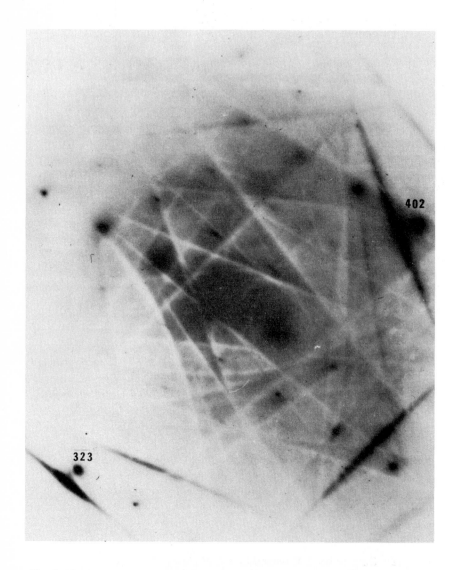

Fig. 6. Kikuchi pattern from molybdenum. For the 402 $s < 0$ and for $\overline{3}2\overline{3}$ $s > 0$. The orientation is $0.3°$ from $[\overline{3}\overline{3}5]$. (Courtesy, J. Appl. Phys., ref. [4]).

For example, for the 402 reflection in fig. 6, s is negative and has the value $0.0073(\text{Å})^{-1}$.

1.3. *The precise determination of orientations*

The general method of solving a Kikuchi pattern and determining the precise foil orientation is similar to the method for solving spot patterns. Since the spacing of each Kikuchi pair is proportional to 2θ (fig. 1a), then we have for different sets of Kikuchi pairs of spacings, p_1p_2, etc.,

$$p_1 = K2\theta_1 , \qquad p_2 = K2\theta_2 , \qquad p_n = K2\theta_n$$

where K is the effective camera length L.

Thus if the reflections $h_1k_1l_1 \text{ --- } h_nk_nl_n$ are identified, the pattern can be calibrated in terms of distances on the plate and corresponding angles.

The identification of the Kikuchi reflections is done as follows. Suppose in fig. 7 there are three sets of intersecting Kikuchi lines at angles α, β, γ, the points of intersection A, B, C are zone axes (Kikuchi poles). If the crystal is cubic, then since $p_1 \propto 1/d_{h_1k_1l_1}$, etc., we have $p_1d_1 = \lambda L, p_2d_2 = \lambda L \text{ --- } p_nd_n = \lambda L$, or

$$\frac{p_1}{p_2} = \frac{\sqrt{h_1^2 + k_1^2 + l_1^2}}{\sqrt{h_2^2 + k_2^2 + l_2^2}} \qquad \text{and} \qquad \frac{p_1}{p_3} = \frac{\sqrt{h_1^2 + k_1^2 + l_1^2}}{\sqrt{h_3^2 + k_3^2 + l_3^2}}$$

and so on.

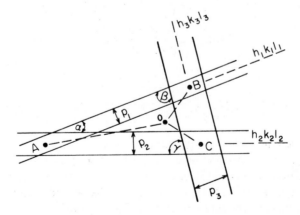

Fig. 7. Sketch to illustrate indexing of any Kikuchi pattern. If the poles A, B, C do not appear on the plate, use tracing paper to extend the Kikuchi lines through points of intersection.

Measure the spacings $p_1 p_2 p_3$, take their ratios and then, by using either tables of d-spacing ratios or a slide rule, the tentative indices $h_1 k_1 l_1$, etc., are assigned. The correctness of the assignment is then made by measuring the angles α, β, γ, and comparing them to the calculated values based on $h_1 k_1 l_1$, $h_2 k_2 l_2$, etc.

$$(\cos \alpha = (h_1 h_3 + k_1 k_3 + l_1 l_3)/(\sqrt{h_1^2 + k_1^2 + l_1^2} \cdot \sqrt{h_3^2 + k_3^2 + l_3^2}).$$

This process can be time consuming, as it is often a question of trial and error in order to obtain the correct solution. The results can be checked by measuring other Kikuchi lines in the pattern.

Once the lines are indexed, the poles A, B, C are obtained by taking the respective cross products, e.g. $A = [h_1 k_1 l_1] \times [h_2 k_2 l_2]$. Let these poles be $p_1 q_1 r_1, p_2 q_2 r_2$ and $p_3 q_3 r_3$. The indices of the direction of the beam through the crystal (i.e., where the transmitted beam intersects the pattern at O) can be found either by calculation or by stereographic analysis. Both require measurement of the angles $\hat{OA}$, $\hat{OB}$, $\hat{OC}$ (fig. 7). Measure the distances OA, OB and convert to angles using either the calibration $p_1 = K2\theta$, or by measuring the distances AB-BC-CA and converting into angles since the angles $\hat{AB}$, $\hat{AC}$, $\hat{BC}$ can be calculated once, A, B, C are indexed*. Let $[uvw]$ be the axis O, then if $\theta_1 \theta_2 \theta_3$ are the angles $\hat{OA}$, $\hat{OB}$, $\hat{OC}$

$$\cos \theta_1 = \frac{u p_1 + v q_1 + w r_1}{\sqrt{u^2 + v^2 + w^2} \cdot \sqrt{p_1^2 + q_1^2 + r_1^2}}$$

$$\cos \theta_2 = \frac{u p_2 + v q_2 + w r_2}{\sqrt{u^2 + v^2 + w^2} \cdot \sqrt{p_2^2 + q_2^2 + r_2^2}}$$

$$\cos \theta_3 = \frac{u p_3 + v q_3 + w r_3}{\sqrt{u^2 + v^2 + w^2} \cdot \sqrt{p_3^2 + q_3^2 + r_3^2}}$$

and uvw is determined by solving these equations.

The solution can also be found by use of stereographic projection as described in detail elsewhere [5]. The reader can use these methods to check that the orientation of fig. 8 is [419] which can also be verified from the Kikuchi map of fig. 9, at A. The solution can be found in ref. [6].

* E.g. for the Siemens Elmiskop 1 at 100 kV and projector pole piece 3, 1 cm $\equiv 1°$.

Fig. 8. Symmetrical orientation of a Kikuchi pattern from silicon corresponding to point A of fig. 9. (Courtesy of J. Appl. Phys., ref. [6]).

For patterns containing one Kikuchi pole or none the solution can only be obtained by reference to the appropriate Kikuchi map.

1.4. *Kikuchi maps*

The solution of a Kikuchi pattern when there are no Kikuchi poles present can be obtained by comparing an unknown pattern with standard Kikuchi projections, called Kikuchi Maps [6,7]. The most usual case when no Kikuchi poles occur is when one works in two-beam orientations. However, in general the Kikuchi map is suitable and convenient for solving any unknown pattern

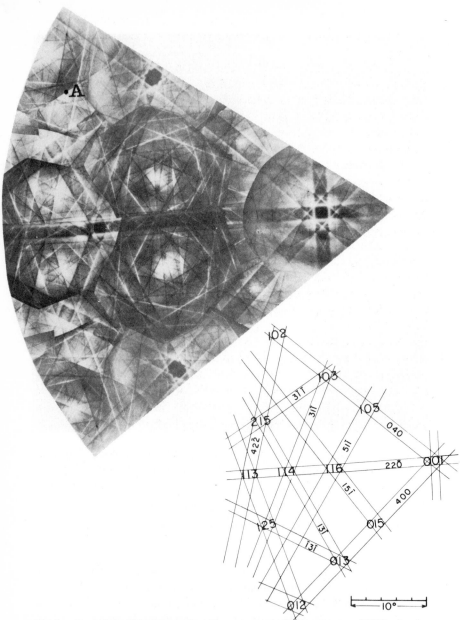

Fig. 9. a. Part of the Kikuchi map for silicon corresponding to area near [001] of reciprocal space. b. Indexing of (a) together with scale factor. (Courtesy J. Appl. Phys. ref. [6]).

since the maps eliminate the three-pole (or two-pole) solutions described above. The maps also eliminate the usual trial and error procedures involved in indexing.

If one is working with a particular crystal system all one needs is a Kikuchi map of that system. The maps are obtained so as to cover completely the standard triangle of the appropriate stereographic projection. In order to do this either single crystals or large randomly oriented polycrystalline specimens should be used. The specimen is then tilted into a symmetrical low index orientation, and by tilting outwards successively along principal Kikuchi lines, successive photographs are obtained so that some overlap of the pattern occurs from one plate to the next. After all the plates are printed, they can be glued onto a board so that successive photographs are matched. It is necessary to completely cover the area of reciprocal space in order to complete the map. If a complete [001] - [011] - [111] map is plotted, the curvature of the Kikuchi lines causes some distortion of the map. The distortion is not noticeable if one works with regions of about 20° around a principal pole. Further details are to be found in refs. [6] and [7].

Maps can also be obtained by utilizing the stereographic projection to obtain traces of reflecting planes, as is shown in fig. 3 to scale for aluminum at 100 kV.

Figs. 9—13 show composite maps for diamond cubic, BCC and HCP crystals. Figs. 9—11 can also be used for FCC crystals (compare to fig. 3) by allowing for the differences in structure factor (e.g., 200 is normally missing in diamond cubic). However, both the DC and HCP maps include reflections of zero structure factor which appear due to double diffraction [7]. In general, for non-cubic crystals separate maps need to be used for each material so that axial ratios and angles are identical.

Many difficulties can be avoided in the case of hexagonal crystals if the four index notation is used as described in detail by Okamoto and Thomas [8]. For example, any pole is determined from intersection of two Kikuchi bands $(h_1 k_1 i_1 l_1)(h_2 k_2 i_2 l_2)$ from the equation,

$$uvtw = \left[\begin{vmatrix} l_1 k_1 i_1 \\ l_2 k_2 i_2 \\ 0\ 1\ 1 \end{vmatrix}, \begin{vmatrix} h_1 l_1 i_1 \\ h_2 l_2 i_2 \\ 1\ 0\ 1 \end{vmatrix}, \begin{vmatrix} h_1 k_1 l_1 \\ h_2 k_2 l_2 \\ 1\ 1\ 0 \end{vmatrix}, \begin{vmatrix} h_1 k_1 i_1 \\ h_2 k_2 i_2 \\ 1\ 1\ 1 \end{vmatrix} \right].$$

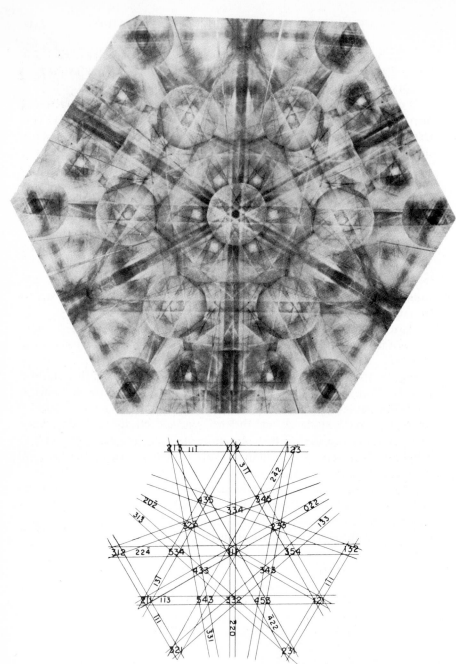

Fig. 10. a, b as fig. 9 for [111] region. (Courtesy J. Appl. Phys., ref. [6].)

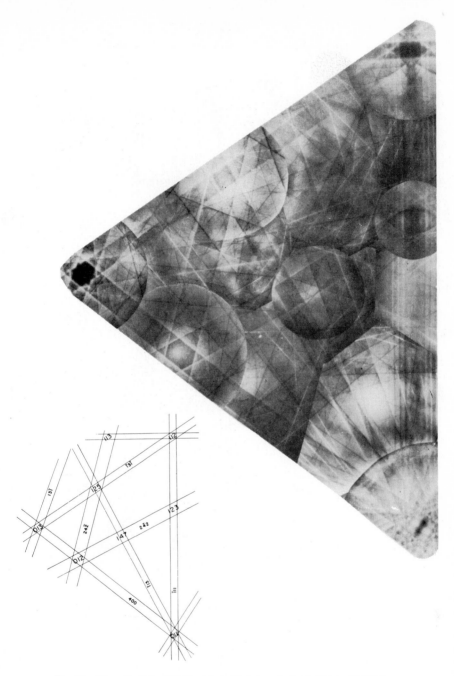

Fig. 11. a, b as fig. 9 for [110] region. (Courtesy J. Appl. Phys. ref. [6].)

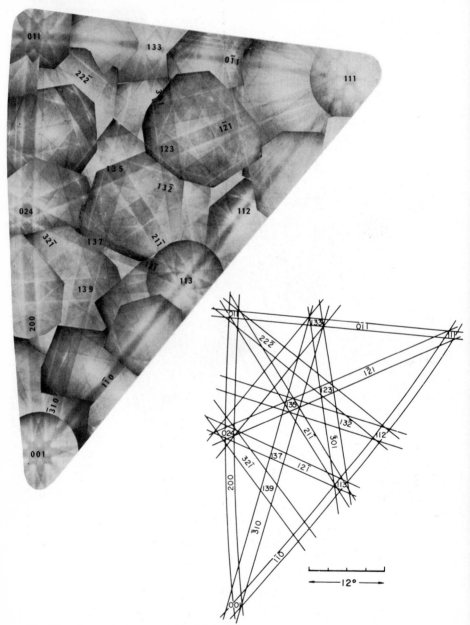

Fig. 12. a. Composite Kikuchi map for bcc crystal, b. indexing and scale factor. (Courtesy
J. Appl. Phys. ref. [7].)

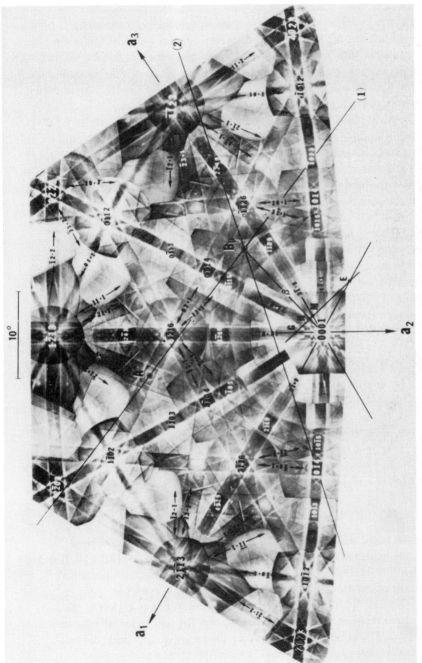

Fig. 13. Composite Kikuchi map for hcp crystals centered about [0001] pole. All poles are given in directional indices. The scale factor shown corresponds to a c/a ratio of 1.588 (e.g., Ag₂Al, Ti). (Courtesy Phys. Stat. Sol., ref. [8].)

As a rule, the more useful working orientations coincide with one of the prominent poles of the Kikuchi map. However, in cases when the foil orientation coincides with one of the less prominent poles, such as A in fig. 13 its indices $[u_A v_A t_A w_A]$ can be obtained immediately. Since A is the intersection of several Kikuchi bands, any two such as the $[02\bar{2}1]$ and $[\bar{3}121]$ may be used to obtain $[u_A v_A t_A w_A] = [5,\bar{7},2,18]$ from the above equation.

In the worst possible situation corresponding to a completely arbitrary foil orientation, a simple solution is still possible provided the center of the unknown diffraction pattern lies at the intersection of two lines passing through pairs of poles which are or can be indexed. In view of the large numbers of such poles, the probability of finding two suitable lines is large. For example, suppose the unknown diffraction pattern is compared with the map and its center found to lie at B_p in fig. 13. We find it lies at the intersection of lines (1) and (2) where line (1) passes through poles A and $[\bar{1}013]$, and line (2) through poles $[10\bar{1}4]$ and $[\bar{2}\bar{2}49]$. But these lines are themselves parallel to Kikuchi bands and if they can be indexed, the orientation of pole B_p can be determined as before.

Since $\mathbf{g} \cdot \mathbf{r} = 0$ for any Kikuchi band passing through the zone axis of $\mathbf{r}$, any two such zones $\mathbf{r}_1 = [u_1 v_1 t_1 w_1]$ and $\mathbf{r}_2 = [u_2 v_2 t_2 w_2]$ will suffice for the determination of its indices. They are the solution to the system of equations

$$\mathbf{g} \cdot \mathbf{r}_1 = hu_1 + kv_1 + it_1 + lw_1 = 0 ,$$

$$\mathbf{g} \cdot \mathbf{r}_2 = hu_2 + kv_2 + it_2 + lw_2 = 0 ,$$

$$h + k + i = 0 .$$

Therefore, the indices of the unknown Kikuchi band can be written

$$(hkil) = \left(\begin{vmatrix} \bar{w}_1 v_1 t_1 \\ \bar{w}_2 v_2 t_2 \\ 0 \;\; 1 \;\; 1 \end{vmatrix} , \begin{vmatrix} u_1 \bar{w}_1 t_1 \\ u_2 \bar{w}_2 t_2 \\ 1 \;\; 0 \;\; 1 \end{vmatrix} , \begin{vmatrix} u_1 v_1 \bar{w}_1 \\ u_2 v_2 \bar{w}_2 \\ 1 \;\; 1 \;\; 0 \end{vmatrix} , \begin{vmatrix} u_1 v_1 t_1 \\ u_2 v_2 t_2 \\ 1 \;\; 1 \;\; 1 \end{vmatrix} \right) .$$

For our particular problem, using the orientation of pole A calculated earlier, the indices of lines of lines (1) and (2) are $(h_1 k_1 i_1 l_1) = (3,\bar{15},18,\bar{7})$ and $(h_2 k_2 i_2 k_2) = (11,\bar{14},3,\bar{2})$ respectively. When these indices are substituted into eq. (4), the orientation of pole B_p is found to be $[u_B v_B t_B w_B] = [\bar{1},\bar{1}.\bar{85},2.85,11.7]$. It should be pointed out, however, that in view of the large angular range covered by the Kikuchi map, Kikuchi bands are actually curved lines. Therefore, in order to justify the use of straight lines, the two pairs of poles defining lines (1) and (2) should be chosen as close together as possible.

2. Some applications of Kikuchi patterns

2.1. *Introduction*

In the foregoing we have shown how Kikuchi patterns facilitate obtaining the precise orientation of the foil. If the Kikuchi pattern is sharp, the orientation may be obtained to within one hundredth of a degree and without the 180° ambiguity inherent in spot patterns. Thus the Kikuchi pattern is obviously very useful for obtaining crystallographic data, such as orientations, orientation relationships, trace analysis and habit planes, lattice parameters and axial ratios, identification of phases, detection of deviations from random solid solutions, etc. Kikuchi patterns also greatly simplify contrast analysis by facilitating selection of particular reflections and control of orientation and for obtaining stereoscopic images quickly and accurately. In addition, the Kikuchi pattern provides the most accurate method for calibrations, such as image rotation, electron wavelength, foil thickness, etc., and can provide information on non-isotropic elastic strains, and the angular misorientation across subgrains and dislocation walls.

Since space is limited, a comprehensive survey will not be attempted, but included in the following are representative examples of some of these applications. The details are to be found in the references listed.

2.2. *Some general applications of Kikuchi maps*

(a) Structure analysis. Since the Kikuchi patterns map out reciprocal space very accurately, they provide very useful means for structure analysis by electron diffraction. Examples have been described previously [11]. The maps can be constructed as described in the previous section. The main advantage of the Kikuchi pattern over the spot pattern is that the symmetry of the Kikuchi pattern is precisely that of the crystal giving rise to the pattern. This is not true of spot patterns at least if they are in symmetrical orientation or confined to a single Laue zone. This can be illustrated by fig. 14 which compares the symmetrical dc and hcp patterns from silicon and magnesium. Although both spot patterns show sixfold symmetry, the Kikuchi pattern of [111] silicon is threefold, but the [0001] pattern of Mg is sixfold. This ia particularly clear upon examining the high order lines near the center of the patterns

(b) Contrast work. The Kikuchi map can be utilized in a similar way to a road map when one is operating the microscope. Examination of a low index pattern on the screen and comparison to the appropriate map (which can be placed in front of the operator) immediately locates the orientation. Once this is established suitable diffraction vectors via the shortest tilting paths can be quickly chosen to examine the contrast behavior of defects, e.g., determination

Fig. 14a. Symmetrical [111] silicon diffraction pattern.

Fig. 14b. Symmetrical [0001] magnesium diffraction.pattern. Notice 6 fold symmetry of spot pattern in cases but in (a) the Kikuchi symmetry is three-fold.

of Burgers vectors [6,7]. The map is particularly useful for studies of dislocations in non-cubic crystals where spot patterns are often difficult to analyse
by inspection at the microscope. Examples of the use of hexagonal maps have
been given for the system Ag-Al [10]. Contrast theory predicts that under
two-beam conditions and $s \approx 0$, a defect characterized by a displacement vector
$\mathbf{R}$ is invisible (or weakest) when $\mathbf{g} \cdot \mathbf{R} = 0$. Thus, any Kikuchi pair ($\mathbf{g}$) which
converges at a pole $\mathbf{R}$ satisfies $\mathbf{g} \cdot \mathbf{R} = 0$ and the Kikuchi map indicates the sense
and amount of tilt needed to obtain that two-beam orientation (fig. 2a). For
example, fig. 12 is the appropriate map for bcc crystals; dislocations whose
Burgers vector are along [111] will thus be invisible for all reflections (Kikichi
lines) which pass through the [111] pole, e.g., $0\bar{1}1$, $1\bar{2}1$, $1\bar{1}0$ (fig. 6b). Similar
arguments apply to strain contrast images in general.

Fig. 15 illustrates an example where the map has been used to prove that
the loops in the slip bands in prismatically oriented Ag_2Al (hcp) have Burgers
vectors of the $\frac{1}{3} a [1\bar{2}10]$ type [10].

Such applications enable the somewhat tedious process of contrast analysis
to be done at the microscope in the minimum of time.

(c) Stereomicroscopy. The electron microscope image is a two dimensional
projection of the volume of the specimen being examined. The true three
dimensional image of the specimen can be obtained, however, by taking stereo
pairs (two pictures) of the same area without changing $\mathbf{g}$ (or s) by simply tilting along the Kikuchi band corresponding to $\mathbf{g}$ by about $10°$. Examples may
be found in refs. [13,14]. The Kikuchi map greatly simplifies and facilitates
this process, e.g., suppose one wanted a stereo image near the 0001 zone of a
hcp crystal, using $g = [0\bar{1}10]$. Reference to fig. 13 shows that a tilt from [0001]
to [$2\bar{1}\bar{1}9$] left along the $0\bar{1}10$ Kikuchi band shifts the viewing angle by about
$13°$ which is ample for stereo images. Although the scale factor for hcp (and
non-cubic in general) maps will depend on c/a, the tilt angle is not critical
merely for obtaining three dimensional information. Sometimes the tilt angle
does need to be known accurately, e.g., for accurate thickness measurements
or depth determinations such as in the analysis of small defects after irradiation [15]. The tilt angle is accurately measured by taking two diffraction patterns, one before and one after tilting, and after locating these on the map, the
tilt angle can be measured directly from the map using the appropriate scale
factor (figs. 9–13).

(d) Measurements from intensity distributions. Normally, diffraction patterns are obtained using a defocused condenser lens system in which the illumination is nearly parallel. When a fully focussed condenser lens system is
employed, a divergent beam pattern is obtained for the diffraction "spot" exhibiting the intensity fluctuations ("rocking curve") across the image of the

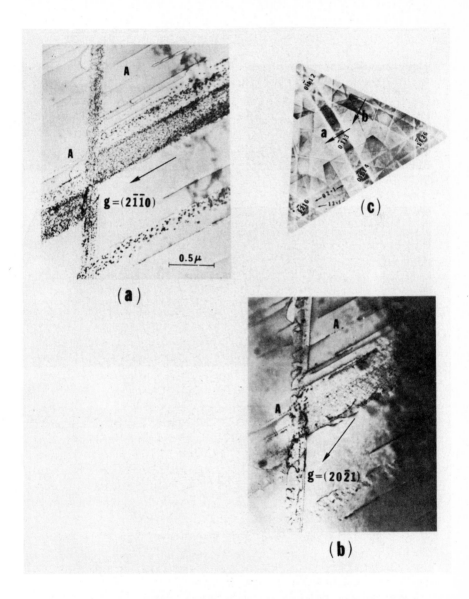

Fig. 15. a, b. Contrast experiment utilizing pre-determined **g** vectors with the aid of part of the map shown in (c). The prismatic loops in (a) go out of contrast in (b) showing that Burgers vector is $\frac{1}{3} a [\bar{1}2\bar{1}0]$.

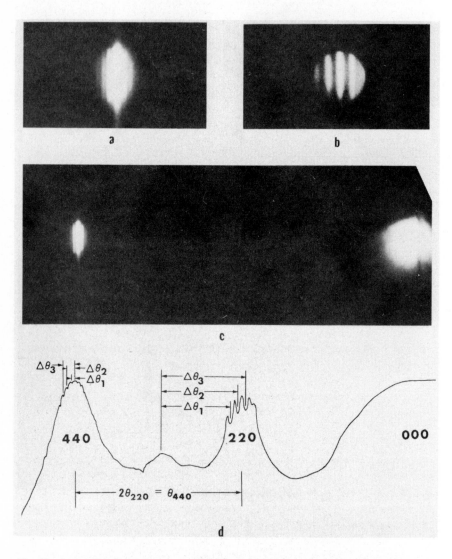

Fig. 16 a–c. Diverging beam photograph of the diffraction pattern of the 000, 220 and
440 maxima in silicon, (a), (b) are enlargements of the 220 and 440 reflections in (c).
d. Microphotometer trace of (c).

condenser aperture. The control of orientation and unique indexing of the diffraction spot used for intensity measurements is facilitated by utilizing the Kikuchi pattern. For example, fig. 16 a–c shows a divergent beam pattern for the 440, 220, and 000 reflections in silicon. The microphotometer traces corresponding to these are shown in fig. 16d.

Amelinckx's relation between foil thickness and intensity distribution is [12p

$$t = 2^{\frac{1}{2}} \{ s_1^2 - 2s_2^2 + s_3^2 \}^{-\frac{1}{2}}$$

where s_1, s_2, s_3 are the deviation parameters of three successive darkfield intensity minima in the dynamical intensity distributions.

For small angles this equation can be rewritten [16] as

$$t = \frac{2^{\frac{1}{2}} d^2}{\lambda} \left\{ \left[\frac{\Delta\theta_1}{2\theta_B} \right]^2 - 2 \left[\frac{\Delta\theta_2}{2\theta_B} \right]^2 + \left[\frac{\Delta\theta_3}{2\theta_B} \right]^2 \right\}^{-\frac{1}{2}}$$

where θ_B is the Bragg angle and $2\theta_B$ is the angle between diffraction "spots". Thus, $\Delta\theta_1$, $\Delta\theta_2$, $\Delta\theta_3$, $2\theta_B$ can be measured in any convenient units, and is independent of magnification. For fig. 16, the foil thickness is 2380Å using either the 220 or the 440 reflections.

Further applications of this method include determination of extinction distances [3] and magnification calibrations.

(e) Calibration of electron wavelength (and accelerating voltage). The wavelength of electrons is related to the magnification of the diffraction pattern through the camera constant equation

$$\lambda L = pd$$

where p is the measured width of the Kikuchi band in the pattern (fig. 7). In order to find λ it is necessary to known the value of L. This can be done by using the Kikuchi pattern as first indicated by Uyeda et al. [17]. Actually, by utilizing a known pattern which has been accurately calibrated as to the angle-distance scale factor (figs. 9–13), a simple method of analysis can be followed.

Suppose on a given Kikuchi pattern two poles, A and B, have been uniquely indexed e.g. by comparing to the appropriate map. Since the angle ϕ between these poles can easily be calculated or obtained from tables of angles, and the distance y between poles measured on the actual pattern, the scale factor is ϕ/y (rad. cm^{-1}). Now take any known low index (hkl) Kikuchi band of spacing p then since by Bragg's Law

$$2d \sin \theta = \lambda$$

or

$$\lambda \cong 2\theta/d \quad \text{(for small angles)}$$

then

$$\lambda = (\phi/y)\ (p/d)$$

which for cubic crystals is written

$$\lambda = \frac{\phi a p}{y \sqrt{h^2 + k^2 + l^2}}\ .$$

Hence, λ can be found without a knowledge of the plate-specimen distance L. For the Kikuchi map of silicon in fig. 9, $a = 5.142\text{Å}$, the scale factor is $2°\ \text{cm}^{-1}$ so for the 400 reflection near [001] p is measured to be 0.8 cm, hence $\lambda = 0.0376\text{Å}$. The voltage is thus actually 97.2 kV and not 100 kV.

This map may be used as a standard to calibrate other voltage e.g. for high voltage microscopes. If λ_1 is the true wavelength determined for a given map for a single crystal pattern of identical orientation to a part of a map, the unknown

$$\lambda_2 = \lambda_1 \left(\frac{p_2}{p_1} \times \frac{y_1}{y_2} \right)$$

where p_1, y_1 and p_2, y_2 are measured on the map and pattern, respectively.

(f) Applications in studies of phase transformation. The Kikuchi pattern is helpful in identifying changes in microstructure produced by phase transformations, e.g., detecting modulations in composition (and/or structure) due to ordering, clustering and spinodal reactions. Two types of approach can be utilized, viz., (a) analysis of symmetrical patterns and (b) overlapping patterns in which line pairing from reflections of identical indices but different d spacings are examined [18]. Examples have been given in ref. [11], (see also ref. [19]). Also, since Kikuchi patterns enable orientations to be obtained very accurately, the Kikuchi pattern should always be used where possible for determining orientation relationships between phases and for measurements of orientation changes across boundaries.

The continued support of the United States Atomic Energy Commission through the Inorganic Materials Research Division of the Lawrence Radiation Laboratory is gratefully acknowledged. I am delighted to acknowledge the research efforts of my students who have been involved in the development of many of the applications described here. I would particularly like to acknowledge the contributions of Dr. W.L.Bell.

References

[1] S.Kikuchi, Japan J. Phys. 5 (1928) 83.
[2] G.Thomas and W.L.Bell, Proc. Rome Eur. Electron Microscopy Congress, 1968, p. 283.
[3] Y.Kainuma, Acta Cryst. 8 (1955) 247;
    T.Tan, W.L.Bell and G.Thomas (to be published) UCRL-19020.
[4] M.Von Heimendahl, W.L.Bell and G.Thomas, J. Appl. Phys. 35 (1964) 361.
[5] O.Johari and G.Thomas, The Stereographic Projection and Applications (J. Wiley and Sons, New York, 1969).
[6] E.Levine, W.L.Bell and G.Thomas, J. Appl. Phys. 37 (1966) 2141.
[7] P.R.Okamoto, E.Levine and G.Thomas, J. Appl. Phys. 38 (1967) 289.
[8] P.R.Okamoto and G.Thomas, Phys. Stat. Sol. 25 (1968) 81.
[9] P.B.Hirsch et al., Electron Microscopy of Thin Crystals (Butterworths, London, 1965).
[10] P.R.Okamoto and G.Thomas, Acta Met. 15 (1967) 1325.
[11] G.Thomas, Trans. AIME 233 (1965) 1608.
[12] S.Amelinckx, Direct Observation of Dislocations (Academic Press, 1964) p. 193.
[13] Z.S.Basinski, Proc. Fifth Int. Congress Electron Mic., Vol. 1, B13 (Academic Press, New York, 1962).
[14] E.Levine, G.Thomas, J.Washburn, J. Appl. Phys. 38 (1967) 81, 87.
[15] M.Wilkens, These Proceedings.
[16] W.L.Bell and G.Thomas, EMSA (1969) St. Paul, Minn. Claitor's Publishers La., p. 158.
[17] R.Uyeda, M.Nomoyma and M.Kogiso, J. Elect. Mic. (Japan) 14 (1965) 296.
[18] R.E.Villagrana and G.Thomas, Phys. Stat. Sol. 9 (1965) 499.
[19] G.Thomas, These Proceedings.

MARTENSITIC TRANSFORMATIONS

C.M.WAYMAN*

The University of Cambridge, Cambridge, England

1. Introduction

Martensitic or "shear" transformations occur in numerous materials as a kind of solid state reaction. When a parent phase transforms into a product phase martensitically, the product is known as "martensite". The nomenclature is independent of the material involved, and is based on certain common geometrical characteristics in all cases. Some years ago the name martensite was used solely to describe the microconstituent (product phase) in steels hardened by quenching, but now it is known that many materials undergo martensitic transformations. Metals such as Fe, Co, Hg and Li, alloys of Fe (i.e., Fe-Mn, Fe-Ni, Fe-C) and commercial steels (Fe-C-X, where X = Mn, Cr, Mo, etc.), non-ferrous alloys (Au-Cd, In-Tl, Cu-Al, Cu-Sn, Cu-Zn), and compounds and intermetallics of recent interest such as $BaTiO_3$, V_3Si, Nb_3Sn undergo martensitic transformations. The present status of martensitic transformations has been summarized recently by Christian [1] for metals and alloys in general, and by the author [2] for alloys of iron. Both of these treatments emphasize the crystallographic characteristics of martensitic transformations, but the former review also includes topics such as nucleation, the effects of pressure, etc.

Martensitic transformations have received widespread study by means of transmission electron microscopy and diffraction in the past few years. There are a number of reasons why this is so:

(1) Investigators have attempted to confirm by means of electron microscopy the predictions of the phenomenological crystallographic theories of martensite formation.

(2) The important and prototype of all martensitic transformations occurs

* Professor of Metallurgy, University of Illinois, Urbana, Illinois, 61801, USA.

in quenched steels, and the long-standing (actually age-old) question of the source of strength in quenched steels has been studied by electron microscopy – a new research tool. Thus far other techniques have failed to produce a completely satisfactory elucidation.

(3) In many cases the martensite crystals which form are too small for conventional studies – for example determining the lattice orientation relationship between the parent and product (martensite) phases by X-ray diffraction. Thin foil selected area electron diffraction techniques have been employed to overcome this difficulty.

(4) Electron microscopy is a very convenient technique for studying martensite formation in situ in thin films within the electron microscope or transformations which have occurred in thin films per se.

(5) And finally, thermodynamic theories of martensitic transformations require Angstron scale although finite sized nuclei (or embryos), which perpetuate into full grown units of the product phase. Considering the expected small size of such embryos the electron microscope has been and will be employed to search for these.

To varying degrees (2)–(4) above are related to (1), the crystallographic theory of martensitic transformations, and in particular the theoretically predicted substructure (or inhomogeneous nature) in martensite. The nucleation aspect of martensitic transformations has received comparatively less attention, although this is probably one of the most important and least understood aspects of martensite.

The plan of the present paper lends itself conveniently into division into two parts: A survey of the crystallographic information and theory pertaining to martensitic transformations (Part I), followed by a description of different electron microscopic investigations which have been aimed at elucidating various aspects (Part II). Specific examples as cases in point will be considered in II, whereas the treatment in I is essentially an academic review.

2. The crystallography of martensitic transformations

A martensitic transformation involves a change from one crystal structure to another (i.e., fcc to bcc) and the most fundamental characteristic of these transformations is the nature of the change in shape of the region which has undergone transformation [3]. The idealized macroscopic change in shape is shown in fig. 1. Since a volume change usually occurs upon transformation, the shape change is not simply a shear, but rather is an invariant plane strain, the direction of displacement generally not lying in the invariant plane as shown

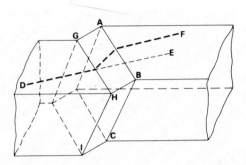

Fig. 1. Idealized representation of the kind of change in shape produced by a martensitic transformation. The initially straight reference scratch DE becomes DF. The habit (or interface) planes ABC and GHI are invariant) i.e. undistorted and unrotated) [2].

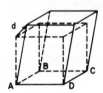

Fig. 2. General description of invariant plane (ABCD) strain. All points are displaced in the common direction **d**, and the magnitude of the displacement |**d**| is proportional to the distance from the invariant plane ABCD [2].

in fig. 2. Interferometry and analysis of reference scratch displacements verify that the plane ABC (or GHI) in fig. 1 is macroscopically unrotated and undistorted at the scale of observation of the light microscope. Since the shape change is *approximately* a shear, phases which form martensitically usually take the form of plates, like mechanical twins, as shown in fig. 3, except in a few special cases where single interface transformations [4] have occurred. The lens shaped nature for both twins and martensite plates arises because of accommodation stresses set up in the matrix [15].

There have been numerous recent determinations of the martensite shape strain now that reliable experimental techniques have been developed [6–9]. The results of such investigations yield the (habit) invariant plane, **p**, the

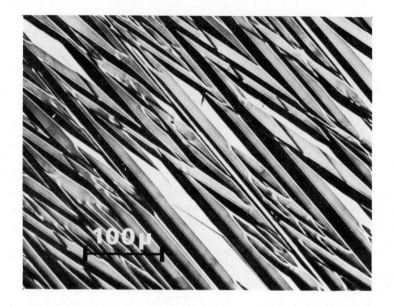

Fig. 3. Surface relief produced by a martensitic transformation in a Cu-39% Zn alloy, cooled to −40°C after quenching from 850°C to room temperature to retain the parent phase in a metastable condition [44].

direction of displacement, **d**, and the magnitude, m, of the displacement vector. The shape strain is then determined as the (3×3) matrix,

$$\mathbf{P} = \mathbf{I} + m\mathbf{d}\mathbf{p}'$$

$$= \begin{pmatrix} 1 & 0 & 0 \\ 0 & 1 & 0 \\ 0 & 0 & 1 \end{pmatrix} + m[d_1 d_2 d_3](p_1 p_2 p_3)$$

$$= \begin{pmatrix} 1 + md_1p_1 & md_1p_2 & md_1p_3 \\ md_2p_1 & 1 + md_2p_2 & md_2p_3 \\ md_3p_1 & md_3p_2 & 1 + md_3p_3 \end{pmatrix} \tag{1}$$

where $\mathbf{p}'$ (prime meaning transpose) being a plane normal with covariant components is written a row matrix, in contrast to $\mathbf{d}$, a lattice vector with contravariant components, which is written as a column matrix.

It was both a triumph and disappointment for investigators [10] to realize that the measured shape strain, $\mathbf{P}$, when applied to the parent lattice did not generate the known product lattice, and this is the case in general.

Another characteristic of martensitic transformations is the experimental fact that the martensite-parent interface or habit plane (usually referred to the parent phase) is not one of simple Miller indices as is often the case for solid state reactions, i.e. precipitation from solid solution. Various materials exhibit different habit planes, as shown in fig. 4 for several iron alloys. The scatter in habit plane indices for a given material is considered to be greater than that arising from experimental error [2]. In addition to the martensite habit plane being generally irrational, experiments have shown that the lattice orientation relationship is not a simple one. Important low-index planes and directions in the parent and product phases are usually non-parallel.

It has been observed that ordered phases will transform into other ordered phases (with a change in structure) martensitically and there is no evidence that diffusion occurs in martensitic transformations. Thus martensitic transformations are often called diffusionless transformations. In some cases, i.e.,

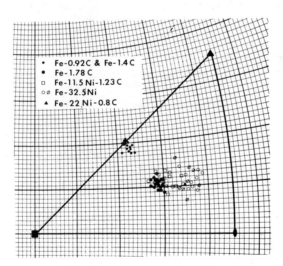

Fig. 4. Experimental results of martensite habit plane determinations for a number of iron alloys [2].

steels, high speed experimental techniques [11] have established that an individual plate of martensite can form in less than a microsecond. Some other martensitic transformations are considerably slower although the evolution of a plate in these cases may consist of a number of intermittently delayed rapid sequences.

The rapidity of martensite formation in steels led Bain to propose his well-known model shown in fig. 5 for the fcc to bcc (or bct) martensitic transformations, according to which the delineated bct cell is simply upset to the proper dimensions [12]. This homogeneous distortion is a mode of atomic shift requiring minimum atomic motion and involves a *correspondence* which specifies a unique relation between lattice points in the parent and product lattices. There are other possible fcc–bcc correspondences and hence homogeneous strains but it has been shown that the one proposed by Bain involves minimum atomic displacements [13]. For some transformations, for example the $\beta \to \alpha$ martensitic transformation in uranium, the choice of the likely correspondence is not obvious. That martensitic transformations exhibit an invariant plane strain shape change implies that a lattice correspondence exists because of the coordinated or "military" like atomic movements which must occur [14]. In a way

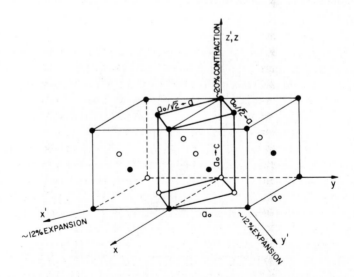

Fig. 5. Correspondence and distortion for the fcc to bcc (bct) transformation proposed by Bain [12]. The delineated bct unit cell is simply "upset" to the proper dimensions. The magnitudes of the principal distortions shown are typical of those for the martensite transformation in iron alloys [2].

of speaking, a correspondence means that each atom in the parent has a "pre-destined" position in the product [15].

According to the Bain correspondence shown in fig. 5, the pure distortion which generates martensite from the fcc parent is

$$\mathbf{B} = \begin{pmatrix} \sqrt{2}a/a_0 & 0 & 0 \\ 0 & \sqrt{2}a/a_0 & 0 \\ 0 & 0 & c/a_0 \end{pmatrix} \qquad (2)$$

expressed with respect to the orthogonal axes defining the fcc unit cell. The principal axes are parallel to the delineated bct unit cell. For the fcc—bct (or bcc) transformation in iron alloys, when typical lattice parameters results are substituated for a_0, a, and c representative numerical values are

$$\mathbf{B} = \begin{pmatrix} 1.12 & 0 & 0 \\ 0 & 1.12 & 0 \\ 0 & 0 & 0.8 \end{pmatrix}. \qquad (3)$$

Apart from its merits, the distortion proposed by Bain is inconsistent with a fundamental piece of evidence — that the habit plane is invariant, i.e., undistorted and unrotated. This is readily seen from the numerical values of the principal distortions η_i in eq. (3). As such the Bain distortion would provide only cones of unextended lines centered about the z axis. It is readily shown that for a pure distortion to leave a plane invariant, the necessary and sufficient condition is that $\eta_1 > 1$, $\eta_2 < 1$ and $\eta_3 = 1$. That is, one of the principal distortions must be unity, and the other two must be respectively greater and less than unity [16,17]. There are no correspondences in known martensitic transformations which enable this condition to be fulfilled by the implied distortion, and thus pure distortions such as the one proposed by Bain for iron alloys are not in themselves a proper description of martensitic transformations.

The present martensite crystallography theories [16,18—20] retain the notion of a correspondence and Bain-type homogeneous strain but also incorporate an additional distortion to meet the requirement that the habit plane be undistorted. Since the necessary lattice change is brought about by the Bain distortion, any additional distortion is restricted to a shear, such as slip or twinning. It can be shown mathematically that a simple shear coupled with a homogeneous distortion such as the Bain strain provides for an undistorted plane, provided that the plane, direction, and magnitude of the simple shear are unique [17].

It is useful here to introduce an analogy to clarify the previous points. Considering for example the fcc to bct transformation as in iron alloys, a hypothetical unit sphere of the parent phase is transformed into an ellipsoid of revolution as a result of the Bain distortion (eq. (2)). An undistorted contact plane between the hypothetical sphere and ellipsoid does not exist because of the relative magnitude of the principal distortions, as already pointed out. If now the simple shear is properly chosen, as a result of its occurrence the ellipsoid can be sheared into tangency with the initial sphere, the diametrically opposed points of tangency defining a net principal distortion of value unity. Thus the necessary conditions for an undistorted contact plane (habit plane) can be met as a consequence of the *two* distortions. A two dimensional analogy is given in fig. 6, showing the undistorted planes AC and BD. Note that these planes although undistorted are rotated relative to their original positions, i.e. BD came from B'D', and are thus not invariant planes, since invariant planes are undistorted *and* unrotated. Therefore in addition to the

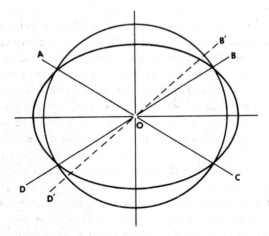

Fig. 6. Two dimensional example showing that even if a homogeneous distortion results in undistorted planes AOC and BOD, these planes are not invariant (undistorted and unrotated) unless a rigid body rotation is employed to restore, for example, BOD to its initial position B'O'D' [2].

Bain distortion and simple shear, a rigid body rotation must be incorporated into an overall theoretical description.

The basic equation of the crystallography theories is

$$P_1 = R\overline{P}B \tag{4}$$

where B is the Bain distortion, $\overline{P}$ is a simple shear which is taken in the mathematical sense to occur after the Bain distortion, R is a rigid body rotation, and P_1 is the invariant plane strain shape change. P_1, R, $\overline{P}$ and B are (3×3) matrices, and the rotation R rotates the plane left undistorted by $\overline{P}B$ to its initial position. Thus $P_1 = R\overline{P}B$ is an invariant plane strain.

Although different in the physical sense, the same mathematical result can be produced by slip and twinning [16], as shown in fig. 7. The same matrix describes both of these situations which are effectively simple shears, the shear angle being γ. Furthermore the same mathematical results are obtained by taking the shear to occur in the parent phase. There are certain computational simplifications when the simple shear is taken to precede the Bain distortion in which case the basic equation becomes

$$P_1 = RBP . \tag{5}$$

Since P is a simple shear and is of the form $(I+m\mathbf{dp'})$, its inverse $P^{-1} = I - m\mathbf{dp'}$ represents a simple shear of the same magnitude on the same plane, but in the opposite direction [18]. Both P and P^{-1} are invariant plane strains.

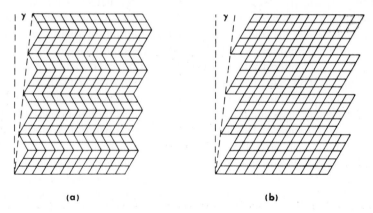

(a)　　　　　　　　　　(b)

Fig. 7. Schematic representation of the mathematical equivalence of twinning (a) and slip (b). The same effective shear angle, γ, is involved in each case [2].

It is convenient to rewrite (5) in the form

$$P_1P_2 = RB \tag{6}$$

where $P_2 = P^{-1}$. Since both P_1 and P_2 are invariant plane strains, their product, RB, is an invariant line strain, S, defined by the planes which are invariant to P_1 and P_2 [18]. Once S is known, all the crystallographic features of a given transformation can be predicted [18–20]. The Bain correspondence and distortion are known from the lattice parameters of the two phases and R can be determined once the plane (p_2') and direction (d_2) of P_2 are assumed. It is beyond the scope of the present account to go into the details of the invariant line strain analysis [18,19]. The important results are stated without proof after noting that the shape strain is $P_1 = I + m_1 d_1 p_1'$ and the simple shear (preceding the Bain distortion) is $P_2 = I + m_2 d_2 p_2'$. In the previous the magnitudes, directions, and planes of the component invariant plane strains are given by m, d, and p. The relevant equations are [2]

$$d_1 = [Sy_2 - y_2]/p_1'y_2 \tag{7}$$

$$p_1 = (q_2' - q_2'S^{-1})/q_2'S^{-1}d_1 \tag{8}$$

where y_2 is any vector lying in p_2' except the invariant line, x, and q_2' is any normal other than n' (the row unit eigenvector of S^{-1}, i.e., $n'S^{-1} = n'$) to a plane containing d_2. The normalization factor for d_1 in (7) is $1/m_1$, and thus P_1, m_1, d_1 and p_1' are determined. The matrix R is determined from the condition that x and n' which are displaced by the Bain distortion must be invariant. R defines the orientation relationship (within any small region of the martensite plate not involving P_2) [18–20]. Thus the assumed correspondence and lattice parameters fix B; the assumption of p_2' and d_2 allows R to be determined; $RB = S$ defines the elements of P_1 from (5) and (1), and therefore the complete transformation crystallography is predictable in closed form.

The previous description parallels the theoretical formulation given by Bowles and Mackenzie [18–20]; however, the treatments of Wechsler et al. [16] and Bullough and Bilby [21] are entirely equivalent.

According to the previous discussion, martensite plates are expected to be inhomogeneous on a sub-microscopic scale, although the macroscopic shape change is homogeneous only on a larger scale. This is schematically shown in fig. 8.

The martensite transformation crystallography can also be viewed from the surface dislocation approach [21] when the simple shear of the theories cor-

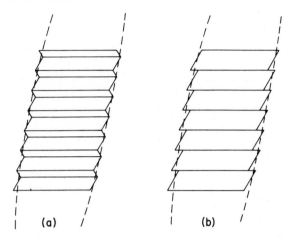

Fig. 8. Idealized representation of internally twinned (a) and slipped (b) martensite plates. These deformations ensure that the interface plane is macroscopically undistorted [2].

corresponds to a slip process. In this case the interface contains a set of parallel dislocations. If these dislocations have a Burgers vector defined in either lattice or are pure screw, the parent-product interface will be glissile [5]. The movement of these dislocations accomplishes the simple shear or lattice invariant deformation. If the transformation inhomogeneity is twinning, interfacial dislocations are not expected. Fig. 9 is an idealized example of these two types of interface.

The theory just described may be justifiably confronted with two demands: (1) a consistent explanation of the transformation crystallography for a given material, and (2) the ability to account for various habit planes and other crystallographic features as in iron alloys.

For the fcc to bct transformation in Fe-22%Ni-0.8%C and the fcc to bcc transformation in Fe-32%Ni the theoretical predictions [16,20] are in excellent agreement with the experimental habit plane and orientation relationship. By assuming that the martensite is internally twinned on a $(112)_m$ plane (twinning direction $[\bar{1}\bar{1}1]$) or equivalently that the simple shear occurs on $(101)\,[\bar{1}01]_p$ in the parent phase* the predicted habit plane comes very close to the experimental mean value $(3,10,15)_p$ as shown in fig. 10. The orientation relationship predictions are equally good, and more recent work [9] veri-

---

* Subscripts p and m refer to the parent and martensitic phases respectively.

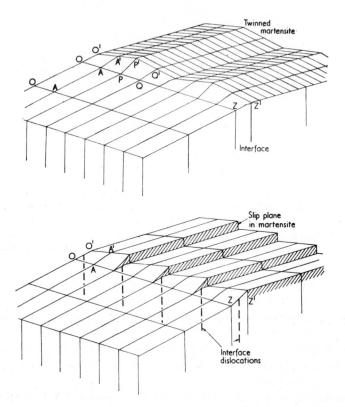

Fig. 9. (Top) Idealized description of the parent-martensite interface for internally twinned martensite. OA and O′A′ are corresponding lattice vectors in the parent and one product (twin) orientation. PQ and P′Q′ are corresponding vectors in the parent and other product orientation. (Bottom) Idealized description of the formation of internally slipped (single crystal) martensite. OA and O′A′ are corresponding lattice vectors, and OZ and O′Z′ are identical habit plane vectors. If the interface dislocations have a Burgers vector defined in either lattice or are pure screw the interface will be glissile [5] and the movement of these dislocations accomplishes the simple shear (lattice invariant deformation of the crystallographic theory [65]).

fies that the theoretical and experimental magnitudes and directions of the shape strain are in good agreement. And finally, the predicted substructure consisting of $(112)_m$ twins is observed by transmission electron microscopy [22,31]. The unique variants of $\{112\}_m$ and $\{3,10,15\}_p$ go together as the

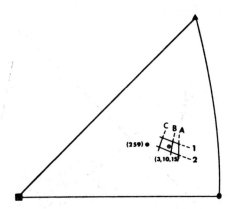

Fig. 10. The habit plane pole (3,10,15) is the mean result obtained by Greninger and Troiano [10] for an Fe-22% Ni-0.8%C alloy. The lines near (3,10,15) correspond to the theoretical predictions of Wechsler et al. obtained by assuming that the bct martensite is internally twinned on (112) [$\bar{1}\bar{1}1$]. Lines A, B and C represent different assumptions for the transformation volume change ratio (1.03, 1.04 and 1.05, respectively) and lines 1 and 2 are lines of constant axial ratio, being respectively 1.00 and 1.08. All predictions are near the observed habit plane pole [2].

theory requires. That is, a particular variant of $\{112\}_m$ predicts a particular variant of $\{3,10,15\}_p$, etc.

Within the theoretical framework there have been two approaches to account for varying crystallographic features. These have most immediate bearing on iron alloys where the habit plane variation is considerable, although the principles involved are general. The explanation offered by Wechsler et al. [23,24] is that different habit planes and orientation relationships, etc., may be explained by varying the plane and direction of P_2 (eq. (6)). On the other hand Bowles and Mackenzie [18–20] contended that (for iron alloys) p_2' and d_2 were always the $\{112\} \langle \bar{1}\bar{1}1 \rangle_m$ twinning elements but that the interface (habit) plane may depart from the exact invariant plane strain condition for certain transformation. The degree of departure was given by a dilatation parameter δ, which varied from 1.000 (in which case the interface plane is invariant) to ≈ 1.015. According to their formulation

$$P_1 P_2 = \delta RB \qquad\qquad (9)$$

and the scalar parameter δ represents a uniform expansion or contraction. The Bowles-Mackenzie predictions are given in fig. 11. A continuous variation of

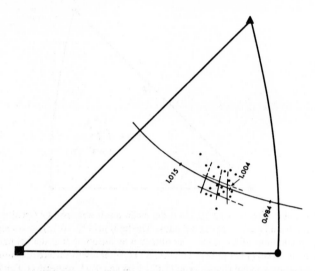

Fig. 11. Experimentally determined habit planes for Fe-32.5% Ni (see fig. 3) with the mean result ≈(3,10,15). The predictions of the Bowles-MacKenzie theory [20] (see text) as a function of the dilatation parameter δ, follow the curved line [2]. The gridwork is the same as described for fig. 10.

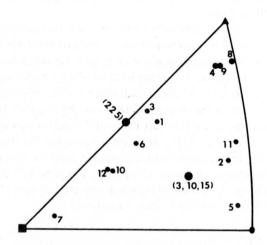

Fig. 12. Habit plane predictons for iron alloys [4] obtained by assuming that the martensite is internally slipped on (011) or equivalently that the parent phase undergoes slip on (111) [2].

the habit plane occurs as δ increases and for $\delta = 1.000$ the predicted habit plane is $(3,10,15)_p$ as with the analysis of Wechsler et al.

The habit plane predictions of Wechsler et al. [24] taking the simple shear to occur on $\{110\}_m$ (equivalent to $\{111\}_p$) rather than $\{112\}_m$ are shown in fig. 12. More extensive calculations involving many different planes and directions for P_2 have been carried out more recently [25].

Considering recent experimental information [7] it appears that neither the dilatation approach nor the one of varying elements of P_2 produces satisfactory agreement between theory and experiment. In addition experiments [9] have shown that δ cannot be as large as 1.015. It thus appears that the transformation crystallography is yet unsolved for habit planes in iron alloys away from $(3,10,15)_p$; this is particularly so for the $\{225\}_p$ habit plane found in a number of alloys.

More recent modifications of the basic theory (eq. (5)) have been made. For example, Bowles and Dunne [9] have suggested that P is no longer a simple shear. Instead P is decomposed into a multiple deformation $(\overline{\overline{C^{-1}}})$ involving two planes with a common direction plus another strain $(\overline{\overline{P}})$ consisting of two additional invariant plane strains. Acton and Bevis [26] have explored the possibilities of factoring P (eq. (5)) into two simple shears. However, in both of these recent cases a comparison between theory and experimental results reveals some discrepancies and it still appears that for those habit planes in iron alloys away from $\{3,10,15\}_p$ there is as yet no satisfactory crystallography theory.

3. Applications of electron microscopy to various transformations

3.1. *The fcc to bct transformation in Fe-Ni-C alloys*

The excellent agreement between theory and experiment for the $\{3,10,15\}_p$ transformation in Fe-22 Ni-0.8%C and Fe- $\approx$32%Ni has been pointed out. The same crystallographic features, i.e. habit plane, orientation relationship, etc. are exhibited by a number of Fe-Ni-C alloys having M_s (transformation start) temperatures below room temperature. As representative of these alloys we may consider Fe-30% Ni-0.4%C which has been extensively studied by electron microscopy [22]. Fig. 13a is a transmission electron micrograph of a martensite plate in this alloy showing numerous parallel striations within the plate which are identified as transformation twins. Fig. 13a should be compared to the idealized example of an internally twinned martensite plate (fig. 8) given earlier. Diffraction pattern analysis verifies two twin orientations within the plate. The particular twin plane variant is $(112)_m$ and the

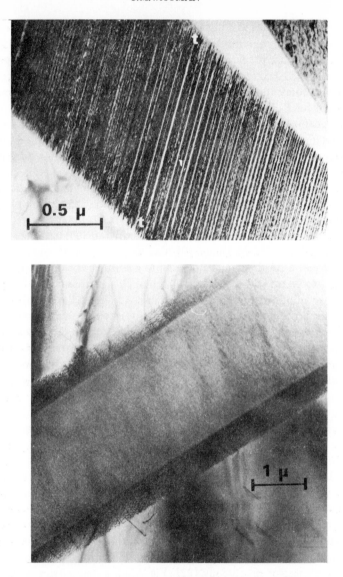

Fig. 13a. Transmission electron micrograph of martensite plate in Fe-30% Ni-0.4%C showing (112) transformation twins [22] parallel to t-t. Compare to the idealized example,
fig. 8a. 13b. Same material as for fig. 13a except that transformation twins are not in contrast [27]. Details of the parent-martensite interface can be seen, i.e. the transformation
twin tips.

habit plane variant is $(3,10,15)_p$. These two variants are theoretically consistent and thus the success of the phenomenological theory for the $\{3,10,15\}_p$ transformation is also borne out by electron microscopy.

A transmission electron micrograph [27] of another martensite plate in Fe-30% Ni-0.4%C is shown in fig. 13b, and serves to illustrate an important point. The plate shows virtually no internal substructure since the twins are not in Bragg contrast orientation in this case. In other words, the $g \cdot r = 0$ invisibility criterion applies. This point may be overlooked by investigators and emphasizes the need for using a goniometer stage to tilt specimens to obtain the proper contrast conditions. Fig. 13b is a very good example of the parent-martensite interface. The tips of the transformation twins as they meet the interface are in contrast and the stepped nature of the interface on the scale of a few Angstoms is to be compared to fig. 9.

3.2. *The fcc to bcc transformation in Fe₃Pt*

Another $\{3,10,15\}_p$ transformation occurs in Fe-Pt alloys of approximate composition Fe$_3$Pt [8]. The transformation can occur from either a disordered or ordered (Cu$_3$Au type) parent. The crystallography of this transformation has been studied in detail, and the theoretical predictions, assuming the martensite is internally twinned on $\{112\}_m$, are in excellent agreement with the observed habit plane, orientation relationship, and shape strain [8]. At the time electron microscopy was not employed. More recently Tadaki and Shimizu [28] have studied the transformation from the ordered parent to martensite (ordered) and have verified that the habit plane and orientation relationship are no different, compared to the disordered-parent to martensite transformation. By electron diffraction they were able to verify that the martensite formed by the Bain distortion from the Cu$_3$Au type superlattice of the parent, as shown in figs. 14a and 14b, in which case the expected and observed diffraction patterns may be compared. Fig. 15 is a transmission electron micrograph of an ordered martensite plate showing internal $\{112\}_m$ twins of the particular variant (112), and from trace analyses the habit plane variant is $(3,10,15)_p$ which is thoroughly consistent. The fine transformation twins extend completely across the martensite plates as would be ideally expected.

3.3. *The fcc to bcc transformation in Fe-Ni alloys*

As with the Fe-Ni-C and Fe-Pt alloys, Fe-Ni alloys (bcc martensite) containing 29-33% Ni exhibit a habit plane near $\{3,10,15\}_p$, although the habit plane is slightly composition dependent [29]. As in the previous two cases, the theory predicts the observed habit plane, etc. Fe-Ni martensites do, however, serve nicely to illustrate a variety of complications as well as interesting features.

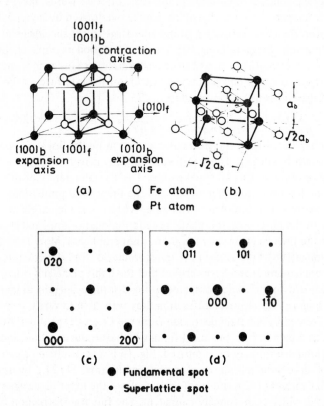

Fig. 14a. Bain distortion for the fcc to bcc transformation (a), bcc superlattice formed by Bain distortion of Cu₃Au type matrix (b), and reciprocal lattices sections expected from bcc superlattice as seen in (001) and (111) orientations (c and d) [28].

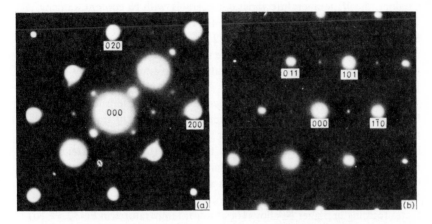

Fig. 14b. Electron diffraction patterns of ordered Fe₃Pt martensite which correspond to (001) and (111) reciprocal lattice planes. Compare with fig. 14a at c and d [28].

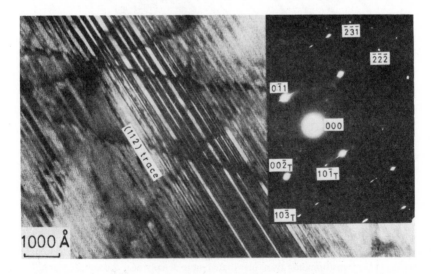

Fig. 15. Transmission electron micrograph and selected area diffraction pattern of ordered Fe₃Pt martensite plate. The fine striations are (112) transformation twins and from trace analysis the habit plane variant is (3,15,10) [28].

Although the habit plane in Fe-Ni alloys is not strongly composition dependent, the M_s temperature varies considerably with Ni content, ranging from approximately room temperature for Fe-29% Ni to $\approx -196°C$ for Fe-34% Ni [30,31]. The extent of $\{112\}_m$ internal transformation twinning in these alloys parallels the temperature dependence of the M_s temperature, the plates forming at the lower temperature being more completely twinned [30,31].

Fig. 16 is a transmission electron micrograph of a martensite plate in an Fe-32.5% Ni alloy ($M_s \approx -110°C$) showing a high density of transformation twins (parallel to the single arrow) near the central or midrib region (dashed line) of the plate. The twinning density falls off as the parent-martensite interface i-i is approached and there are large volumes of untwinned material between the twins. Note that the twins appear to be shaped as parallelograms. The direction parallel to the double arrow is the $\langle 111 \rangle_m$ twinning direction. Plates forming in higher Ni alloys (or at lower temperatures in Fe-32.5% Ni) tend to be more fully twinned as with the Fe-Ni-C alloy shown in fig. 13a. However, for lower Ni contents, the twins are concentrated to the near vicinity

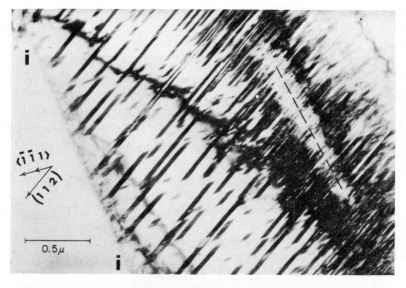

Fig. 16. Transmission electron micrograph of martensite (bcc) plate in Fe-32.5 wt% Ni showing (112) transformation twins distributed more densely near the midrib region (dashed line) and less densely as the martensite-parent interface i-i is approached. The twins are bounded by [$\bar{1}\bar{1}1$] directions and appear as parallelograms [30,31].

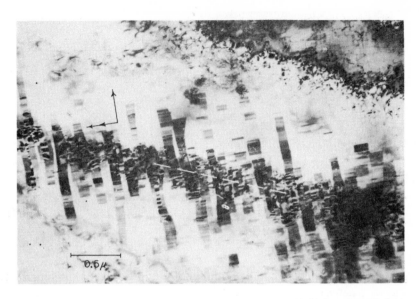

Fig. 17. Transmission electron micrograph of martensite plate in Fe-29.8 wt% Ni showing high transformation twin density near midrib region (dashed line), steps in twins, and moiré effects from twin overlap. The single and double arrows are defined in fig. 16 [31].

of the midrib region as shown in fig. 17 for an Fe-29.8% Ni alloy ($M_s \approx -20°$C), and the balance of the plate is untwinned. The striations appearing within the twins and moiré-like fringes (parallel to the double arrow) result from steps (i.e. twinning dislocations) in the twin boundary and is an effect similar to that observed from overlapping stacking faults [31]. Fig. 18, also for Fe-29.8% Ni, shows the appearance of the $\{112\}_m$ transformation twins under a different Bragg condition as well as a fringe shift (from black to white) at a step, marked A.

In the previous cases where the martensite plates in Fe-Ni alloys are not completely twinned, the untwinned regions are found to consist of arrays of screw dislocations with $\langle 111 \rangle_m$ Burgers vectors, as shown in fig. 19 for an Fe-29.8% Ni alloy. All four sets of $\langle 111 \rangle$ screws are present in equal density as verified by tilting [31].

Although seemingly complicated, the previous results for Fo-Ni alloys may be rationalized [31]. It appears that the mode (i.e. slip versus twinning) of lattice invariant shear in Fe-Ni alloys is strongly temperature dependent. Those plates forming at low temperatures are essentially completely twinned, whereas those in the more dilute alloys forming at higher temperatures exhibit twins

Fig. 18. Transformation twins in Fe-29.8 wt% Ni showing interference fringes and fringe shifts (for example at A) due to twin overlap causing a phase change of $\pm 2\pi/3$. The single and double arrows are defined in fig. 16 [31].

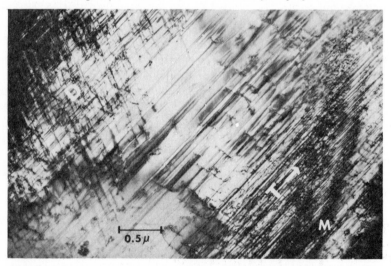

Fig. 19. Transmission electron micrograph showing both twinned (T) and untwinned (D) regions in a martensite plate in Fe-29.8 wt% Ni. The midrib region of the plate is M-M, and in the dislocated region (D) four sets of screw dislocations with $\langle 111 \rangle$ Burgers vectors are present (although only two sets are in contrast) [31].

and dislocations. Furthermore, the width of the densely twinned region in-creases as the M_s temperature is decreased. It is thought that the release of the latent heat of transformation, ΔH, in essentially an adiabatic way at the in-terface of a thin plate will cause a transition from twinning to slip because of the localized temperature rise ($\approx 40°C$). This phenomenon would be of less importance at low temperatures, and explains the profuse internal twinning in the higher Ni alloys with lower M_s temperature. Thus it appears that some martensite plates involve both slip and twinning modes for the lattice in-variant shear; apparently the plates begin thickening by a twinning mechanism which is "damped out" because of the temperature effect. However, since the habit plane is the same whether slip, twinning, or both are involved, the slip thickening stage must involve the twinning elements, i.e. $\{112\}\langle 111\rangle_m$.

For plates which have at least partially thickened by an internal slip process, it is probable that the dislocations observed in the untwinned regions are not those which effect the lattice invariant shear because in principle these dis-locations should appear only at the interface (see fig. 9). It may therefore be concluded that the observed arrays of screw dislocations with $\langle 111\rangle_m$ Burgers vectors result from accommodation distortion of the plate caused by con-straints exerted by the parent phase matrix.

An extensive study of deformation in Fe-Ni (bcc) and Fe-Ni-C (bct) marten-site has been made by Bevis and co-workers [32,33] who have discovered twinning modes other than the usual $\{112\}\langle 111\rangle_m$ mode. Additional twinning planes from theoretical analysis were found to be $\{011\}_m$, $\{154\}_m$, $\{5,11,8\}_m$ and $\{013\}_m$. Although these modes may be unimportant as transformation twinning modes, there is evidence that some of them are operative during de-formation by compression (and perhaps also as a means of accommodation distortion). A detailed analysis of the interaction of deformation and trans-formation twins has been made. The most likely deformation twinning ele-ments involve those twins which are able to penetrate the common $\{112\}_m$ transformation twins without being deviated.

Fig. 20a is a transmission electron micrograph of a region of a martensite plate in Fe-32% Ni showing $(121)_m$ transformation twins plus deformation twins on $(\overline{1}21)_m$ and $(4\overline{1}5)_m$. These latter two have a common orientation relationship (rotation of 180° about $[\overline{1}11]_m$) as evidenced by the dark field micrograph, fig. 20b. Fig. 21 is an example of a deformation twin in Fe-32% Ni martensite which has penetrated and displaced the $\{112\}_m$ transformation twins although itself is undeviated. The "retwinned" transformation twins have been termed secondary twins. $\{5,8,11\}$ deformation twins in several alloys have been confirmed by two-surface analysis and optical metallography [33].

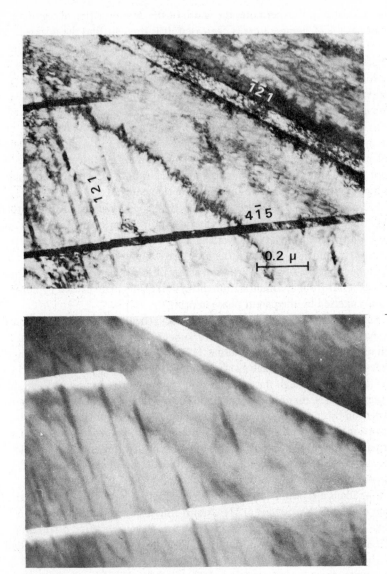

Fig. 20a. Transmission electron micrograph of martensite plate in Fe-32 wt% Ni showing (121) transformation twins and ($\bar{1}2$1) and (4$\bar{1}$5) deformation twins induced by compression [66]. 20b. Dark field micrograph of fig. 20a showing that the ($\bar{1}2$1) and (4$\bar{1}$5) deformation twins have a common orientation relationship (rotation of π about [$\bar{1}$11]) [66].

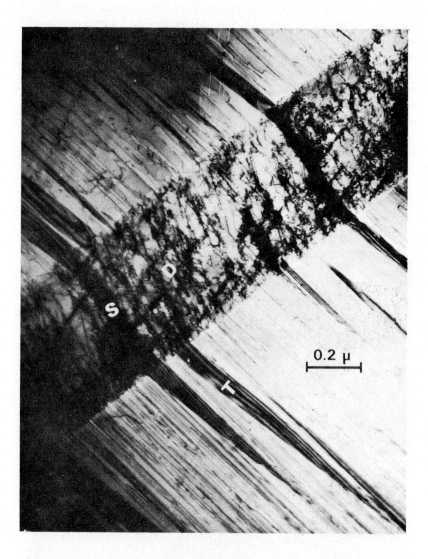

Fig. 21. Transmission electron micrograph showing deformation twin (D) − transformation twin (T) interaction in Fe-32% Ni martensite. The deformation twin readily penetrates the transformation twins without deviation; however the transformation twins are
reoriented forming secondary twins (S) [66].

3.4. *Studies of some other martensitic transformations in other alloys*

Electron microscopy has been employed to study the substructure of martensite plates in iron alloys which do not exhibit the theoretically "well-behaved" $\{3,10,15\}_p$ habit plane. The objective of these investigations has been to attempt to correlate the observed substructure with the assumptions and predictions of the crystallographic theories. The $\{225\}_p$ transformation has been of particular interest since the theory of Wechsler et al. [24] predicts a habit plane near $\{225\}_p$ by assuming the inhomogeneous shear occurs on $\{110\}$ of the martensite ($\{111\}$ of the parent); on the other hand Bowles and Mackenzie [20] contended that the same (as for the $\{3,10,15\}_p$ transformation) $\{112\}\langle111\rangle$ twinning elements are involved, and that the habit plane shift from $\{3,10,15\}_p$ to $\{225\}_p$ is due to a dilation (fig. 11).

The classical $\{225\}_p$ transformation occurs in carbon steels containing from $0.9 - 1.4\%$C [2], and the overall crystallographic analysis is made dif-

Fig. 22. Transmission electron micrograph of $\{225\}$ martensite plate in Fe-1.28 wt% C showing $\{112\}$ transformation twins [34].

ficult by the fact that the M_s temperatures for these alloys are considerably above room temperature, and at room temperature, where observations are usually made, virtually complete transformation of the parent phase has occurred. A study of martensite plates in Fe-1.3% C [34] has revealed the primary substructural inhomogeneity to be $\{112\}_m$ twinning as shown in fig. 22. The particular variant of the $\{112\}_m$ twin plane is consistent with the particular variant of the habit plane predicted by the Bowles-Mackenzie analysis, but there is also substantial evidence [34] that more than a single $\{112\}_m$ inhomogeneity is involved. Whether or not the additional $\{112\}_m$ inhomogeneities are due to accommodation effects is not clearly established yet. However, as pointed out earlier, the assumption of the (single) usual $\{112\}_m$ twin inhomogeneity and dilatation predicts an orientation relationship contrary to that which is observed, and in addition, recent work has established that a dilatation of the required magnitude $\approx 1.5\%$, is improbable [9] . As fig. 22 shows, a careful analysis of the substructure in Fe-1.3%C is hampered by numerous bend contours, contrast reversal, etc., in addition to the generally nondescript appearance of the substructure.

By suitable additions of substitutional elements such as Mn and/or Cr to Fe-C alloys, the M_s temperature can be depressed to room temperature or below although the martensite habit plane is still $\{225\}_p$. Studies of the substructure in such alloys by electron microscopy have also been made [7,35–36], but unfortunately the results thus far obtained have not particularly enlightened the understanding of the $\{225\}$ transformation. Fig. 23 is a transmission electron micrograph of a martensite plate in Fe-8%Cr-1.1%C. Two sets of internal striations in the plate are seen. In this case the particular habit plane variant is $(252)_p$ and trace 1 corresponds to the usual variant of the $(112)_m$ transformation twins; trace 2 is identified with the variant (011) which is approximately parallel to the (111) faulting plane of the parent phase and is in fact derived from $(111)_p$ according to the Bain correspondence. The significance of the often observed $\{011\}_m$ inhomogeneity is difficult to assess because in binary Fe-C alloys the crystallographic features (i.e. habit plane, orientation relationship, and shape strain) are virtually identical, yet $\{011\}_m$ planar defects have not been observed [34] , and it must be questioned if these are of general significance.

To further complicate matters $\{225\}$ plates in Fe-8%Cr-1.1%C are frequently found which exhibit no $\{011\}_m$ planar defects, but rather the usual $\{112\}_m$ transformation twins in an irregular manner. Fig. 24 shows a $\{225\}_p$ plate with $\{112\}_m$ transformation twins appearing on only one side of the plate [2] . Yet the habit plane is equally planar and identical on both sides, and in light

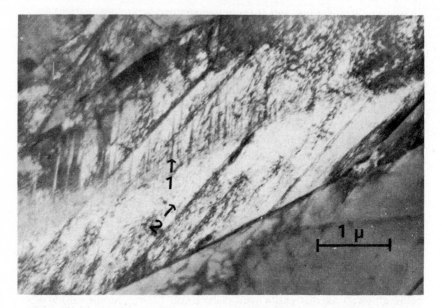

Fig. 23. Transmission electron micrograph of {225} martensite plate in Fe-8%Cr-1.1%C
showing {112} transformation twins (1) and {011} planar defects (2) [7].

of this it appears valid to question if the observed $\{112\}_m$ twins are at all
related to the transformation process.

Another alloy, Fe-3%Mn-3%Cr-1%C, also exhibits the {225} habit and
other crystallographic features found in the previous two alloys and has been
the subject of recent research [37]. The findings thus far partly parallel
those of previous works on the $\{225\}_p$ transformation, but some additional
results are of interest. Fig. 25 is a transmission electron micrograph of a martensite plate in this material showing internal $\{112\}_m$ twins of the usual
variant. However, the twins although extending (as ideally) completely across
the plate appear in patches along the plate length, and there are wide untwinned gaps between the transformation twins. Since the habit plane is
everywhere identical and there are no twins in the gapped regions it would
appear that the transformation inhomogeneity in these areas must be slip involving the same twinning elements.

Studies have also been made of an Fe-1.8%C steel [34] which transforms
into martensite with a habit plane near $\{259\}_p$. As this habit plane is on the
$\{225\}_p$ side of $\{3,10,15\}_p$ this transformation as with the {225} case is not

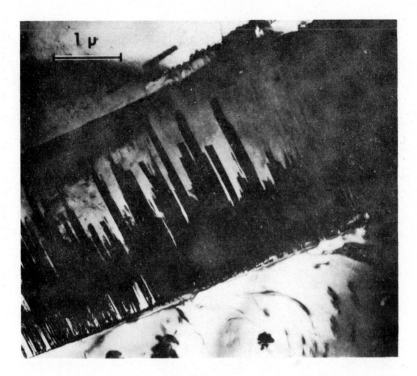

Fig. 24. Transmission electron micrograph of {225} martensite plate in Fe-8%Cr-1.1%C showing transformation twins on only one side of the plate [2].

understood theoretically. In addition to the usual $\{112\}_m$ transformation twins. $\{011\}_m$ twins have also been observed [38], and it has been argued [37] that these are related to accommodation effects becuase $\{011\}_m$ twins (derived from $\{111\}$ in the parent) do not have equivalent correspondences. In other words the Bain contraction axes are not symmetrically disposed relative to the twin plane [19]. It is possible that the $\{011\}_m$ planar defects observed in Fe-8%Cr-1.1%C and Fe-3%Mn-3%Cr-1%C which exhibit the $\{225\}_p$ transformation are also $\{011\}_m$ twins, but in these cases the martensite tetragonality is lower ($c/a \approx 1.04$ compared to 1.08 for Fe-1.8%C) and the separation of twinned reciprocal lattice points if so is more difficult to detect.

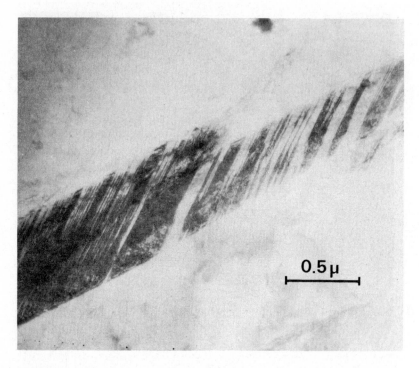

Fig. 25. Transmission electron micrograph of {225}martensite plate in Fe-3%Mn-3%Cr-1%C showing untwinned gaps between transformation twins of variable width [37].

3.5. *The martensite transformation in more dilute iron alloys*

In numerous iron alloys of low solute content relative to cases considered thus far the martensite takes the form of laths rather than lenticular plates [39]. Whereas the lenticular plates in iron alloys are usually at least partially internally twinned, transformation twins have not been observed in the laths. An example of lath martensite in an Fe-4%Ni-0.05%C alloy is shown in the transmission electron micrograph, fig. 26. Since the M_s temperature in dilute alloys is relatively high, complete transformation of the parent phase occurs during quenching, so the entire field of view in fig. 26 consists of a number of more or less parallel laths which have impinged during growth. The laths contain numerous dislocations, and often the interfaces are irregular. Irregular

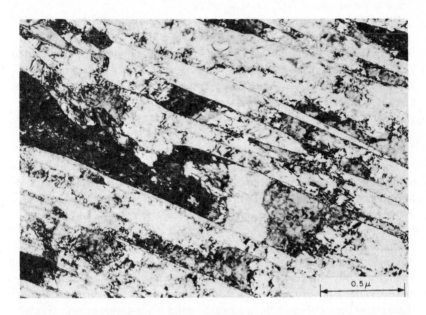

Fig. 26. Transmission electron micrograph showing typical appearance of lath martensite.
See text for discussion [39].

interfaces are also found in plate-like martensite in Fe-Ni (29–32%) alloys [31]
in which case the final stage of thickening is due to a slip mechanism, and it
may be that irregular interfaces are characteristic of martensite when the lattice invariant shear is slip. As mentioned in the discussion of Fe-Ni alloys the
dislocations observed within the lath martensite are probably formed by constraints and are not likely to be transformation dislocations.

Because of virtually complete transformation of the parent phase in cases
where lath martensite forms, crystallographic analysis of the transformation
has proved difficult. A further complication arises in that sub-boundaries
within the laths may be interpreted as lath boundaries, and apparent habit
plane results deduced from selected area electron diffraction and trace analysis
are not consistent. Results reported thus far are in the vicinity of $\{111\}_p$
(working backwards through the Bain correspondence) but a scatter in results as high as $19°$ is found [39].

There is as yet no satisfactory explanation for the lath morphology as opposed to lenticular plates which are usually observed in martensitic transformations.

3.6. The formation of TaO_y in oxidized Ta

When Ta is oxidized in an oxygen atmosphere at 400–500°C an orthorhombic suboxide phase in the form of plates occurs [40]. These plates form from a supersaturated solid solution consisting of O_2 interstitially dissolved in Ta and their habit plane is irrational, $\approx \{320\}$ relative to the parent phase. This transformation has all the characteristics of a martensitic transformation. Once the cubic Ta lattice dissolves a certain amount of oxygen it become unstable and transforms in a diffusionless manner (interstitial O_2 atoms remaining in phase) to a new orthorhombic phase TaO_y. It is not to be implied that TaO_y formation is an oxidation reaction in the usual sense.

The crystallography of this bcc (oxygen saturated Ta) to bco (TaO_y) transformation has been studied in considerable detail [41]. The predicted crystallographic features (habit plane, orientation relationship, shape deformation, etc.) assuming that martensite crystallography analysis applies and that the lattice invariant shear is twinning on $\{110\}_m$ in the product phase are in outstanding agreement with those determined experimentally. Fig. 27a is a transmission electron micrograph showing four TaO_y plates in an O_2-saturated Ta matrix. Only two crystallographically different habit plane variants are involved. Plates 1 are of the same variant, and plates 2 are of a different variant; these plates have impinged along a pseudo-habit plane during growth. Transmission electron diffraction analysis confirmed that the fine striations within the plates are in fact $\{110\}_m$ twins of the theoretical variant consistent with the measured habit plane [41].

In the crystallographic analysis, the correspondence between the two phases is given by the identity matrix, i.e. the bcc cube axes become the **a**, **b** and **c** axes of the orthorhombic unit cell. From the measured lattice parameters of the two phases the principal distortions are 0.985, 0.964 and 1.087. The first of these is almost unity and the other two are of opposite sign; their magnitudes are such that the Bain distortion for this transformation is itself *nearly* an invariant plane. Thus, the magnitude of the simple shear of the theory to effect an undistorted plane need not be large, and for the case of $\{110\}_m$ internal twinning is 0.0191. The relative volumes of the two twin orientations, taking into account the inclination of the transformation twins with respect to the foil surface, were found to be on the average 10:1. This corresponds to a simple shear of magnitude $m_2 = 0.0196$, in excellent agreement with theory (0.0191). Thus in all respects the formation of TaO_y is consistent with the martensite crystallographic theory [41].

Fig. 27b is a selected area diffraction pattern from the double plates shown in fig. 27a. The enlargement to the right is an interesting example of Frauen-

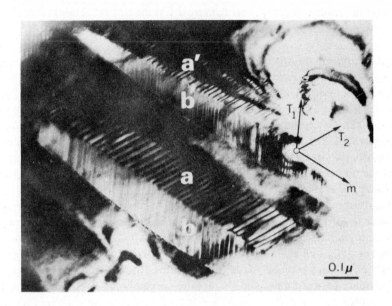

Fig. 27a. Transmission electron micrograph showing two pairs of orthorhombic TaO$_y$ plates joined along a pseudo-habit plane m. Plates a and a' are of the same habit plane variant whereas plates b and b' are also of the same variant (but different from a and a'). The traces T$_1$ and T$_2$ correspond to {110} microtwins in the TaO$_y$ [40].

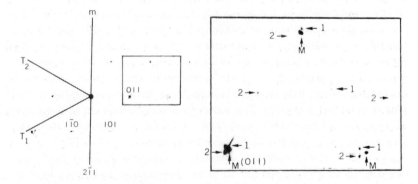

Fig. 27b. Selected area diffraction pattern from region shown in fig. 27a. The traces of the two sets of twins (T$_1$,T$_2$) and the midrib (m) are indicated. The enlargement to the right shows matrix spots (M), spots due to plate orientation b and b' (1) and spots due to plate orientation a and a' (2). Frauenhofer splitting of the diffraction maxima can be seen near the (011) reflection at the arrow 1 [40].

hofer diffraction [42,43] (near the arrow 1 at the 011 reflection) caused by the thin twins acting as slits as in the light optical case.

3.7. Martensite transformations in Cu and Au alloys

Alloys in the systems Cu-Zn, Cu-Ga, Cu-Sn, Cu-Al, Au-Cd, Cu-Zn-Al, Cu-Zn-Ga, Au-Cd-Cu, for example, undergo martensitic transformations [44]. In these cases the composition of the parent phase is such that the electron/atom ratio is approximately 3/2 and such (parent) phases are known as "β" phases which are bcc in the disordered state and B2 (CsCl) or DO_3 (Fe_3Al) in the ordered state. It is interesting that in these systems the crystal structure of the martensite can vary with rather small composition changes in the parent phase. For example in Au-Cd alloys, at 47.5 at% Cd the parent phase (B2) transforms into an orthorhombic martensite, whereas at 50.0% Cd the parent phase transforms into a martensite whose structure is different (and recently a controversial matter [45]). Similarly, in β Cu-Al alloys, over the composition range 23–26 at% Al, a β' orthorhombic martensite forms, whereas from 27–28% Al an hexagonal martensite, γ, forms. It is difficult to rationalize the difference between the β' and γ structures on purely the electronic structure basis [46].

The cubic-orthorhombic transformation in Au-47.5 at% Cd has been widely studied from the crystallography theory point of view and the predictions of the theory, assuming the product phase to be twinned on $\{111\}_m$, are in good agreement with the observed habit plane, orientation relationship, shape deformation, etc. [4]. In bulk crystals, the transformation twins are large enough ($\approx 2 \mu m$) to be visible by the optical microscope, and it has been verified that the habit plane and twin plane variants are consistent [4]. In this transformation, plates of martensite are not formed. Rather, the transformation proceeds by the movement of a single interface which generates a twinned single crystal product from a single crystal parent; or, several of these interfaces are nucleated at the same time resulting in domains of martensite bounded by impinged single interfaces. Fig. 28 is a dark field transmission electron micrograph of the orthorhombic martensite in Au-47.5 at% Cd. The regions A are twin related to regions B, and no interface is seen in the field of view. The thin stacking faults visible in twins of orientation B are not related to the theory and result from accommodation distortion. It is interesting to note that for this transformation, although the *relative* widths of the transformation twins A and B are approximately constant, the absolute width appears markedly dependent on the size of the crystal or region undergoing transformation. Fig. 28 applies to a transformation which has occurred in a 0.5 mm sheet, whereas in large single crystals ≈ 5 mm diameter, the transformation twins are an order of

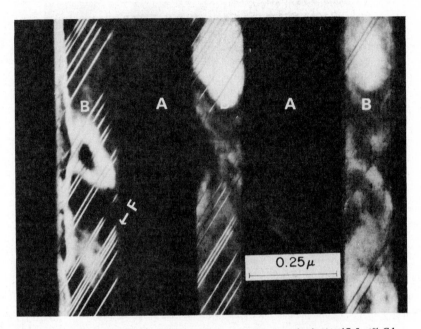

Fig. 28. Dark field transmission electron micrograph of martensite in Au-47.5 at% Cd showing transformation twins A and B and stacking faults F within twins of orientation B [52].

magnitude larger in absolute width. In any case, however, one would not expect the twins to be as thin as those observed in Fe-alloy martensites because for Au-47.5% Cd. The principal distortions are smaller.

In the Cu-Al system the martensites which form are designated β', β'_1 and γ. The essential difference between the first two of these is in ordering; β' forms from a disordered parent (bcc) whereas β'_1 forms from an ordered (DO_3) parent. These martensites have been the subject of numerous electron microscopy and X-ray investigations and the reported results particularly as to the structures of β' and β'_1 are conflicting [47]. The internally twinned γ martensite appears to be hexagonal and there is no controversy here.

A typical transmission electron micrograph of β'_1 martensite in Cu-24 at% Al is shown in fig. 29a in which case numerous parallel sided martensite plates

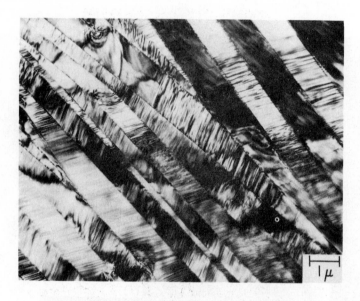

Fig. 29a. Transmission electron micrograph of β'_1 martensite in Cu-25 at% Al showing thin parallel-sided plates with internal striations [48].

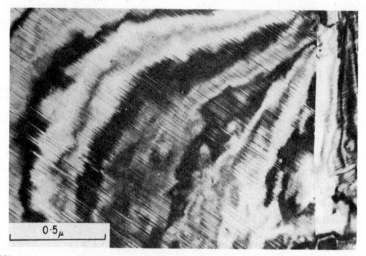

Fig. 29b. Higher magnification photograph showing substructure (stacking faults) in two impinged martensite plates in Cu-25 at% Al [48].

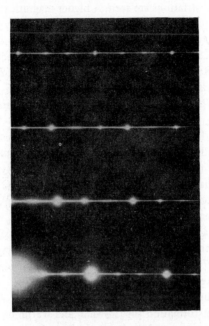

Fig. 29c. A quadrant of the selected area diffraction pattern taken from fig. 29b. Note the extensive streaking caused by relaxation of the Laue conditions in the direction perpendicular to the fault plane [48].

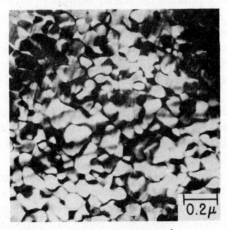

Fig. 29d. Dark field transmission electron micrograph of β_1' martensite showing anti-phase domain boundaries due to ordering of the parent phase prior to the formation of martensite [48].

exhibiting internal striations are seen. A higher magnification transmission electron micrograph of β_1' martensite in the same alloy is given in fig. 29b which shows clearly the fineness of the internal striae which cause extensive relaxation of the Laue conditions in a perpendicular direction as shown in fig. 29c, a selected area diffraction pattern taken from the encircled area of fig. 29b. Fig. 29d is a dark field electron micrograph of β_1' martensite showing antiphase domain boundaries due to ordering of the parent phase prior to transformation.

Swann and Warlimont [48] were the first to make an extensive electron microscopy and diffraction investigation of Cu-Al martensites and they tentatively identified the β' martensite as having an internally faulted fcc structure, and the β_1' martensite as having an internally faulted tetragonal structure. Follow-ups on their proposals were made by Wilkens and Warlimont [49], Nishiyama and Kajiwara [47], and Kajiwara [50], for example. It now appears that a suitable description of the β_1' martensite structure is that of an ordered orthorhombic lattice consisting of 18 close-packed layers along the c-direction [47]. However, such a structure is equivalent to an fcc structure which is faulted on every third $\{111\}_m$ plane [50].

Basically the parent to β' or β_1' transformations in Cu-Al alloys can be viewed as a bcc to fcc transformation [44]. Swann and Warlimont [48] analyzed the crystallography this way, and the habit plane predictions were in quite good agreement with those observed assuming that the inhomogeneous shear occurs on $\{111\}$ of the product. From lattice parameters and the assumed bcc–fcc correspondence, the principal distortions are $\eta_1 = \eta_2 = 0.89$, and $\eta_3 = 1.26$. These values are large and are such that the Bain distortion is even farther from an invariant plane strain than for iron alloys, in which case the principal distortions are acknowledged to be quite large. From Swann and Warlimont's calculations the theoretical magnitude of the lattice invariant shear is 0.251 which corresponds approximately to slip of a vector difference $a/6 \langle 112 \rangle$ on every third plane of the fcc lattice generated from the bcc parent by the Bain distortion. It is thus not surprising that differences in crystal structure interpretation and semantic difficulties in definition arise because of the theoretically required and observed high density of stacking faults in the product phase which cause shifts in diffraction maxima, streaking, etc.

Although the β_1' martensite structure can be explained as orthorhombic with a c-direction containing 18 close packed layers, it is to be recalled that this structure can be produced from an fcc structure by faulting on every third plane, and thus there is no reason not to regard the transformation as *basically* a bcc to fcc one. However, since the simple shear of the theory occurs by faulting it is not lattice invariant in this case and the fcc structure produced by the

Bain distortion loses its simple identity. It is also to be noted that one fault
every third fcc plane is theoretically consistent.

One of the difficulties in studying the Cu-Al martensites is that the observed stacking fault probability varies from martensite plate to plate within
a given specimen. This was attributed by Nishiyama et al. [51] to varying
constraints being operative.

Toth and Sato [52] have also studied the β_1' martensite crystal structure
in Cu-23.5 at% Al by electron microscopy and concluded it to be of the 3R
type (using their notation). This is equivalent to the 18 layer orthorhombic
structural unit posposed by Nishiyama and Kajiwara [47]. Fig. 30 is a dark
field electron micrograph of region of a β_1' martensite plate showing a 6.5 Å
substructure resolved which agrees very favorably with the theoretical value,
6.37 Å for a fault on every third plane. In addition to the regular faulting,
random faulting can also be seen in fig. 30.

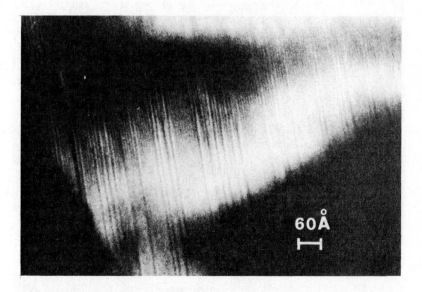

Fig. 30. Direct lattice lattice resolution electron micrograph (obtained by placing the objective aperture around two (hkl) maxima) of β_1' martensite in Cu-23.5 at% Al showing a
resolved periodicity of 6.5 Å, corresponding to a stacking fault on every third plane of the
martensite. Random faults can also be seen [52].

3.8. *The martensite transformation on thin foils*

Since martensitic reactions are shear phenomena one might expect some
effect upon the removal of certain constraints, i.e. by allowing the transformation to occur in a "two-dimensional" thin foil. Pitsch [53] studied martensite formed in thin foils in a number of ferrous alloys and found the morphology to be quite different, compared to martensite formed in the bulk.
Fig. 31 from his work is a transmission electron micrograph of martensite in
Fe-1.5 wt% N showing "patches" of internally twinned martensite which do
not appear to be bounded by particular crystallographic planes. By contrast
martensite forming in bulk Fe-1.5% N takes the form of internally twinned
lenticular plates [54]. The same behaviour was found for Fe-Ni alloys.

Kajiwara made an extensive study of the martensite formed in thin foils
in Cu-24 at% Al and his results show that constraints (i.e., foil thickness)
have a marked effect on the β_1' martensite stacking fault density [50]. Fig. 32
is an example of the shift in diffraction maxima as a consequence of a variation
in fault density from plate to plate formed in thin foils. The intensity distri-

Fig. 31. Transmission electron micrograph of martensite in Fe-1.5 wt% N alloy formed in
a thin foil [53].

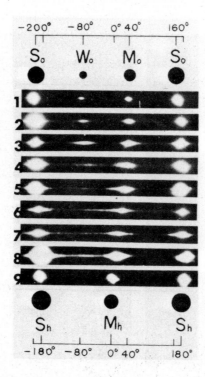

Fig. 32. Intensity distributions along the c^* direction for β_1' martensite in Cu-24 at% Al formed in thin foils in various specimens. Numbers 1-9 apply to different martensite crystals and the patterns are arbitrarily arranged in order of increasing stacking fault probability. The pattern at the top S_o, W_o, M_o, S_o corresponds to one fault per three fcc planes, while the lower pattern S_h, M_h, S_h corresponds to one fault on every other fcc plane (i.e., hcp) [50].

butions along the c^* reciprocal lattice direction are shown for nine different martensite specimens arranged in ordering of increasing fault density. The higher fault densities (fig. 32, bottom) correspond to martensite approaching an hcp structure and are not observed in specimens of the same composition transformed in the bulk and then thinned.

Fig. 33 is an interesting example of a martensite plate formed in a wedge shaped crystal (taken at 500 kV). The diffraction patterns, a, b, c (zone axes $[1\bar{1}0]$) correspond to the framed areas indicated. The spots by the arrows in b are due to twin reflections, and an increased shift in maxima with decreasing

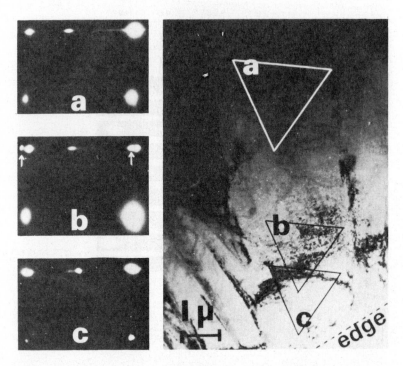

Fig. 33. Transmission electron micrograph and diffraction patterns (500 kV) taken from martensite formed in a wedge-shaped crystal in Cu-24 at% Al. Patterns *a, b,* and *c* were taken from the indicated framed areas, and the effect of foil thickness on the shifts of diffraction spots can be seen. The spots indicated at the arrows (b) are due to twinning [50].

foil thickness is noted. The martensite formed in the thinnest regions has more of a tendency to approach the hexagonal structure, rather than the orthorhombic. Sato, Toth and Warlimont [46] have used this observation to argue that β_1' martensite (rather than γ) is formed mainly because of the constraint of the surroundings during the transformation, and suggested the importance of this effect in general, in addition to electronic effects.

In other cases it is known that martensite will form at room temperature during the electrothinning of foils of certain materials although the bulk M_s temperature is considerably below room temperature [55]. Thus removal of matrix constraints by thinning raises the M_s temperature in some materials.

3.9. *The nucleation of martensite*

For various reasons (i.e., martensite plates will frequently nucleate at identical places during cyclic transformations) it has been thought for some time that structural imperfections may be nucleating sites for martensitic transformations. For the fcc to bcc transformation, Zener [56] pointed out that a half-faulted fcc lattice is in a near bcc configuration, which suggests the importance of stacking faults as nuclei. Venables [57] claimed the bcc martensite in stainless steels is readily formed when two {111} stacking faults in the parent fcc phase intersect.

The present thermodynamic ideas on martensite formation [58] require the existence of "embryos", oblate-spheroidal in shape with a semicoherent interface and size ≈ 200Å. Attempts to observe embryos by electron microscopy have been either unsuccessful or misinterpreted [59]. Recently Pati and Cohen [60] have pointed out, on the basis of thermodynamic theory, that the probability of observing such an embryo by transmission electron microscopy

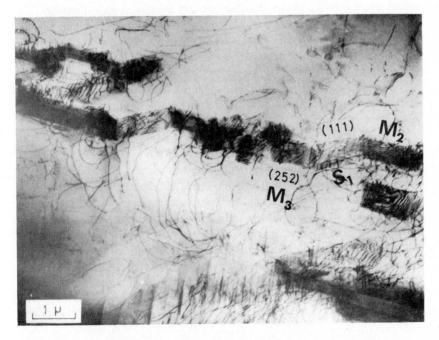

Fig. 34. Transmission electron micrograph showing thin (252) martensite plates and (111) "associated" stacking faults in Fe-8%Cr-1.1% C. It is inferred for example that faults S_1 are produced by plate M_2 but in turn can act to nucleate plate M_3, etc. [61].

is 2 in 10^5 which is consistent with past difficulties in detecting embryos. On the other hand other work [36,61] indicates the possible importance of stacking fault nuclei (or embryos) in which case the probable density is much larger than 2 in 10^5. Fig. 34 shows numerous thin martensite plates in Fe-8%Cr-1.1%C of habit plane variant (252) and associated stacking faults of the particular variant (111). Indications are that faults can nucleate martensite, particularly those which have been formed by accommodation due to prior formed plates. The details of this work will be published soon [61].

3.10. *The hardness of martensite in quenched steels*

The explanation for the strength of quenched steels has long been sought. One of the first transmission electron microscope investigations to attempt to shed some light on the problem was carried out by Kelly and Nutting [62]. They observed that in low carbon steels both internally twinned plates and untwinned laths of martensite formed, and that the percentage of plates increased with carbon content. It was argued that the increased number of plates would give rise to the observed higher strength because in such internally twinned plates the number of available deformation systems is reduced as only slip systems compatible with both twinned orientations would likely operate. At the time, this explanation seemed plausible. However, later work [63] seems to suggest that the twinned substructure does not exert a profound strengthening effect. Most recently it has been estimated that twinned martensite is approximately 15% stronger than untwinned martensite, for a given composition [64].

This discussion was prepared while the author was a Visiting Professor in the Metallurgy Department at the University of Cambridge and Fellow of Churchill College and the John Simon Guggenheim Memorial Foundation. I am much indebted to these groups for their kindness and sponsorship. Some of the research work from my own laboratory which has been described herein was made possible by the continued interest in phase transformations and support by the US Army Research Office (Durham) and the US Atomic Energy Commission. I would particularly like to thank many friends and colleagues for providing photographs and information from both published and unpublished work.

References

[1] J.W.Christian, in: The Mechanism of Phase Transformations in Crystalline Solids No. 33 (Institute of Metals Monography, London, 1969). p. 129.

[2] C.M.Wayman, The Crystallography of Martensitic Transformations in Alloys of Iron, Vol. III, Advances in Materials Research, ed. H.Herman (Interscience Publishers, New York, 1968) p. 147.

[3] B.A.Bilby and J.W.Christian, Inst. Met. Monograph 18 (1956) 121.

[4] D.S.Lieberman, M.S.Wechsler and T.A.Read, J. Appl. Phys. 26 (1955) 473.

[5] J.W.Christian, The Theory of Transformations in Metals and Alloys (Pergamon Press, Oxford, 1965).

[6] J.S.Bowles and A.J.Morton, Acta Met. 12 (1964) 629.

[7] A.J.Morton and C.M.Wayman, Acta Met. 14 (1966) 1567.

[8] E.J.Efsic and C.M.Wayman, Trans. AIME 239 (1967) 873.

[9] J.S.Bowles and D.P.Dunne, Acta Met. 17 (1969) 201, 677.

[10] A.B.Greninger and A.R.Troiano, Trans. AIME 185 (1949) 590.

[11] R.F.Bunshah and R.F.Mehl, Trans. AIME 197 (1953) 1251.

[12] E.C.Bain, Trans. AIME 70 (1924) 25.

[13] M.A.Jaswon and J.A.Wheeler, Acta Cryst. 1 (1948) 216.

[14] J.W.Christian, Iron and Steel Inst. Spec. Rept. 93 (1965) 1.

[15] C.Laird and H.I.Aaronson, Acta Met. 15 (1967) 73.

[16] M.S.Wechsler, D.S.Lieberman and T.A.Read, Trans. AIME 197 (1953) 1503.

[17] J.W.Christian, J. Inst. Met. 84 (1956) 386.

[18] J.S.Bowles and J.K.Mackenzie, Acta Met. 2 (1954) 129.

[19] J.K.Mackenzie and J.S.Bowles, Acta Met. 2 (1954) 138.

[20] J.S.Bowles and J.K.Mackenzie, Acta Met. 2 (1954) 224.

[21] R.Bullough and B.A.Bilby, Proc. Phys. Soc. B 69 (1956) 1276.

[22] I.Tamura et al., Trans. Japan Inst. Metals 5 (1964) 47.

[23] M.S.Wechsler and T.A.Read, On the Formation of Martensite in Low and Medium Carbon Steels, unpublished report Contract AF18(600)-951, Columbia University, 1954.

[24] M.S.Wechsler, T.A.Read and D.S.Lieberman, Trans. AIME 218 (1960) 202.

[25] A.G.Crocker and B.A.Bilby, Acta Met. 9 (1961) 678.

[26] A.F.Acton and M.Bevis, to be published.

[27] I.Tamura, private communication.

[28] T.Tadaki and K.Shimizu, Trans. Japan Inst. Met., to be published.

[29] R.P.Reed, U.S. Department of Commerce, National Bureau of Standards, Report No. 9256 (August 22, 1966).

[30] R.L.Patterson and C.M.Wayman, Acta Met. 12 (1964) 1306.

[31] R.L.Patterson and C.M.Wayman, Acta Met. 14 (1966) 347.

[32] M.Bevis, P.C.Rowlands and A.F.Acton, Trans. AIME 242 (1968) 1555.

[33] P.C.Rowlands, E.O.Fearon and M.Bevis, Trans. AIME 242 (1968) 1559.

[34] M.Oka and C.M.Wayman, Trans. ASM, 62 (1969) 370.

[35] K.Shimizu and C.M.Wayman, Acta Met. 14 (1966) 1390.

[36] K.Shimizu and C.M.Wayman, Electron Microscopy 1966 (The Maruzen Company, Tokyo, 1966) p. 459.

[37] S.Jana and C.M.Wayman, to be published.

[38] M.Oka and C.M.Wayman, Trans. AIME 242 (1968) 337.

[39] J.M.Chilton, C.J.Barton and G.R.Speich, JISI, to be published.

[40] J.Van Landuyt and C.M.Wayman, Acta Met. 16 (1968) 803.

[41] C.M.Wayman and J.Van Landuyt, Acta. Met. 16 (1968) 815.

[42] A.G.Fitzgerald and M.Mannami, Proc. Roy. Soc. 293 (1966) 343.

[43] R.Gevers, J.Van Landuyt and S.Amelinckx, Phys. Stat. Sol. 18 (1966) 343.

[44] J.W.Christian, T.A.Read and C.M.Wayman, in: Intermetallic Compounds, ed. J.H.Westbrook (John Wiley and Sons, Inc., New York, 1967(p. 428.

[45] H.M.Ledbetter and C.M.Wayman, to be published.

[46] H.Sato, R.S.Toth and H.Warlimont, to be published.

[47] Z.Nishiyama and S.Kajiwara, Japan J. Appl. Phys. 2 (1963) 478.

[48] P.R.Swann and H.Warlimont, Acta Met. 11 (1963) 511.

[49] M.Wilkins and H.Warlimont, Acta Met. 11 (1963) 1099.

[50] S.Kajiwara, J. Phys. Soc. Japan 22 (1967) 795.

[51] Z.Nishiyama, J.Kakinoki and S.Kajiwara, J. Phys. Soc. Japan 20 (1965) 1192.

[52] R.S.Toth and H.Sato, Acta Met. 15 (1967) 1397; 16 (1968) 413.

[53] W.Pitsch, J. Inst. Metals 87 (1958) 444; also Phil. Mag. 4, No. 41 (1959) 577.

[54] T.Bell, private communication.

[55] J.F.Breedis, in: Thin Films, American Society for Metals, Metals Park, Ohio (1964) p. 295.

[56] C.M.Zener, Elasticity and Anelasticity of Metals (The University of Chicago Press, 1948).

[57] J.A.Venables, Phil. Mag. 7 (1962) 35.

[58] L.Kaufman and M.Cohen, Prog. Metal. Phys. 7 (1958) 165.

[59] M.H.Richman, M.Cohen and H.G.F.Wilsdorf, Acta Met. 7 (1959) 819.

[60] S.R.Pati and M.Cohen, Acta Met. 17 (1969) 189.

[61] K.Shimizu, M.Oka and C.M.Wayman, to be published.

[62] P.M.Kelly and J.Nutting, Proc. Roy. Soc. A259 (1960) 45.

[63] P.G.Winchell and M.Cohen, Trans. ASM 55 (1962) 347.

[64] P.M.Kelly, private communication.

[65] J.W.Christian, to be published.

[66] M.Bevis et al., to be published.

IDENTIFICATION OF SMALL DEFECT CLUSTERS IN PARTICLE-IRRADIATED CRYSTALS BY MEANS OF TRANSMISSION ELECTRON MICROSCOPY

M.WILKENS

Max-Planck-Institut für Metallforschung, Institut für Physik,
Stuttgart, Germany

1. Introduction

For about ten years it has been known that particle irradiation causes damage in crystals which appears on the transmission micrographs in general as "black dots" or "black spots" with diameters $d \lesssim 100\text{Å}$, i.e. small compared with the extinction length ξ_g of the operating diffraction vector $\mathbf{g}$. Consequently the geometrical structure of the lattice defects, giving rise to the black dot contrast, is in general not resolvable. As examples we mention the early work of Pashley and Presland [1], who observed black dots in gold foils which were irradiated with O^- ions inside the microscope.

At about the same time Makin and coworkers [2,3] studied neutron-irradiated copper. They found a small number of large, well resolved dislocation loops with perfect Burgers vector $\mathbf{b} = \frac{1}{2} \langle 110 \rangle$ and, apart from these, a high density of black, unresolved dots. In the present paper we will deal only with the nature and the analysis of the small black dots. The large, well resolved loops, which were found also in other irradiation-damaged metals, for instance in neutron-irradiated platinum by Ruedl, Delavignette and Amelinckx [4,5], will not be treated in this contribution.

In the above mentioned papers the black dots were inspected mainly under so-called kinematical image conditions resulting in contrast figures of rather unspecific shape (fig. 1). Therefore the crystallographic nature of the irradiation-induced lattice defects could not be derived from the micrographs.

A certain progress was made when Essmann and Wilkens [6] detected that the black dots in neutron-irradiated copper reveal a characteristic black-white structure, if the foils are imaged under two-beam dynamical contrast conditions

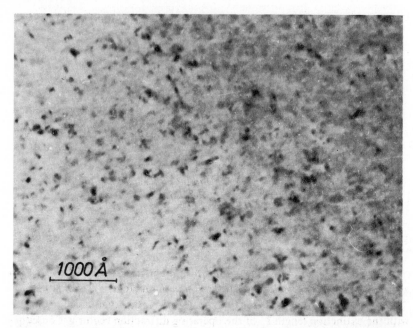

Fig. 1. Small Frank dislocation loops in copper, irradiated at $\approx 80°C$ with 6×10^{17} fast neutrons/cm^2. Foil plane $\approx (001)$, bright field, black dots revealed under kinematical contrast conditions.

(excitation error $s \cong 0$) (figs. 2 and 3). These black-white contrast figures resembled to some extent the black-white contrast from spherical inclusions which was studied rather extensively a little earlier by Ashby and Brown [7]. From the observed crystallographic orientation of the black-white contrast streaks (figs. 2 and 3), Essmann and Wilkens [6] concluded that the lattice defects giving rise to the black dot or to the black-white dot contrast (depending on the image conditions) are small Frank dislocation loops, i.e. dislocation loops with habit planes parallel to a (closed-packed) $\{111\}$-plane and with Burgers vectors $\mathbf{b} = \frac{1}{3} \langle 111 \rangle$ perpendicular to the loop habit plane (such a loop will be called an "edge loop"). However, the fundamental question whether these loops were due to agglomeration of (irradiation-produced) vacancies or interstitials could not be answered. It was in fact concluded that the diffraction contrast theory for small elastic strain centres, as published at that time mainly by Ashby and Brown [7,8], was insufficient to resolve this problem.

Stimulated by this lack in theoretical background, Rühle, Wilkens and

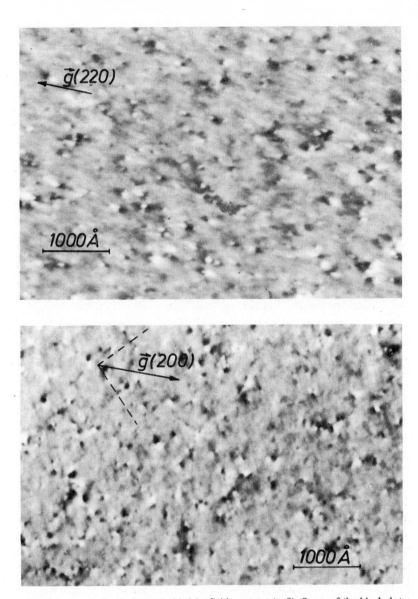

Fig. 2. The same as fig. 1, dynamical bright field contrast ($s=0$). Some of the black dots of fig. 1 appear now as black-white dots. The black-white vectors l are mainly parallel or antiparallel to g in fig. 2a and at $45°$ or $135°$ to g in fig. 2b as expected for b parallel to $\langle 111 \rangle$.

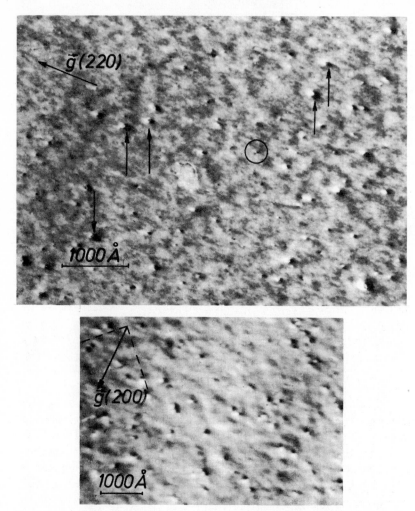

Fig. 3. Black-white contrast figures from Frank loops of vacancy type in copper foils ir-radiated with 100 keV O⁻ ions, foil plane ≈ (001), bright field. All the black-white dots reveal the same sign of $(\mathbf{g} \cdot \mathbf{l})$. With respect to the direction of $\mathbf{l}$ see fig. 2. Notice the fine structure of the black-white separation line of the indicated loops. The black-white con-trast figure enclosed by a circle was explained by Rühle [11] as due to a Frank loop of special diameter with its centre just between the layers L1 and L2. In fig. 3a a thin gold layer was evaporated on the ion-irradiated foil surface for the stereo measurements.

Essmann [9] and Rühle [10,11] made an extensive theoretical study of the diffraction contrast from small Frank dislocation loops, which was later confirmed and in some points extended by McIntyre and Brown [12,13]. On the basis of these calculations Diepers and Diehl [14,15] and Rühle [10,11] developed experimental methods designed to differentiate between vacancy and interstitial type loops. In the mean time these methods have been applied by different workers to various kinds of point defect agglomerates in irradiation-damaged crystals,(sect. 6).

So far, mainly the comparatively simple damage structure in fcc metals was studied. It was in fact found that in fcc metals the overwhelming majority of the small point defect clusters created by particle irradiation are Frank loops. However, during a recent investigation of the neutron-irradiation damage in niobium [16] it was concluded that the contrast calculations for edge loops are presumably not sufficient for an analysis of the black dots in bcc metals. From a theoretical point of view it is expected that in bcc metals the irradiation-induced small dislocation loops may have a large shear component implying that the Burgers vector may be inclined to the loop normal. This shear component of the Burgers vector can modify to some extent the results of the contrast calculations valid for pure edge loops. The present paper summarizes the state of our present knowledge.

In this paper we restrict ourselves mainly to the analysis of the contrast from small dislocation loops, where the term "small" means "small compared with the extinction length ξ_g". With respect to the problems connected with the identification of other defect configurations, as for instance large dislocation loops (which are resolved as loops on the micrographs), voids, tracks from fission fragments, and stacking fault tetrahedra, we refer to the recent survey papers of Wilkens [17] and Rühle [18]. Sect. 2 contains the main results of the contrast calculations for small edge loops. Some preliminary results for loops with shear components are discussed in sect. 3. The results of sects. 2 and 3 are, as usually, obtained by numerical integrations of the differential equations which describe the electron diffraction in a distorted lattice. In order to obtain a quicker qualitative understanding of the type of black-white contrast which is expected for a given type of elastic strain centre it is expedient to solve the differential equations approximately in an analytical way. This is outlined in sect. 4. In sect. 5 the experimental procedures for the application of the theoretical contrast calculations are described. Sect. 6 presents a short review of those experimental results which confirm the applicability of the theoretical results and experimental methods as outlined in the foregoing sections.

A more complete review of the experimental results on the structure of the radiation damage in crystals is given in the survey papers of [17,18].

2. Theoretical results of the contrast calculations for small dislocation loops of edge type

For a proper description of the black-white contrast figures on the micrographs we define a vector **l** which points from the centre of the black part to the centre of the white part of the contrast figure ("black" and "white" on positive prints). It is expedient to discern between the direction of **l**, irrespective of the sign, and the sign of **l** as determined by the sign of the product (**g·l**). The following contrast properties for edge loops have been derived [9–11].

(1) A loop oriented with (**g·b**) $\neq$ 0 (**b** is the loop's Burgers vector) and with its centre close to one of the foil surfaces reveals under dynamical image conditions ($s \cong 0$) a black-white contrast. The orientation of the black-white vector **l** is independent of the direction of **g** and lies parallel (or antiparallel) to the Burgers vector **b** or to its projection onto the image plane (= plane perpendicular to the electron beam). Small, but insignificant deviations from this direction are expected for large angles between **b** and **g**.

(2) The sign of (**g·l**) depends on the actual depth position of the loop centre and on whether the loop is of vacancy or interstitial type. The results for a vacancy loop are schematically shown in fig. 4. For interstitial loops the direction **g** in fig. 4 must be reversed. The regions near the foil surfaces are divided into the layers L1, L2, ... The sign of (**g·l**) changes if the loop centre changes from one layer to the adjacent layer, thus leading to "depth oscillations" of the black-white contrast. The thickness of layer L1 amounts to about 0.3 ξ_g, depending slightly on the loop size, whereas the inner boundaries of the subsequent layers L2, L3 ... correspond to distances of $\frac{3}{4} \xi_g$, $\frac{5}{4} \xi_g$ ... to the adjacent foil surface. The sign of (**g·l**) for loops in layer L1 is the same as was predicted by Ashby and Brown [7] for (large) spherical inclusions, which do not show the depth oscillations of the sign in the subsequent layers (see point (8)).

(3) Due to the anomalous absorption the black-white contrast is damped with increasing distance of the loop centre from the adjacent foil surface. For the frequently used value $\xi'_g/\xi_g = 0.1$ (ξ'_g = anomalous absorption length) [19–21,7,10] the black-white contrast is expected to be observable only in the first two or three layers. For smaller values of ξ'_g/ξ_g the observable depth oscillations extend deeper into the foil.

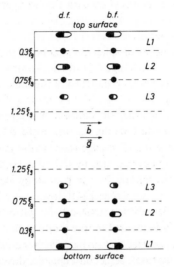

Fig. 4. Schematic plot of the depth oscillation of the black-white contrast figures from small dislocation loops of vacancy type; the contrast figures are drawn at those depth positions at which the loop centres were assumed. d.f. = dark field, b.f. = bright field. For loops of interstitial type the direction of **g** must be reversed.

Actually, the boundaries between L1 and L2, and between L2 and L3 etc. have a finite thickness of about 0.1 ξ_g which means that for loops whose centres are within these intermediate layers the black-white contrast is too weak to be observable. Consequently these loops reveal only a black-dot contrast.

(4) For loops in the middle region of the foil, i.e. outside the region of observable black-white contrast, the contrast consists of a black dot of unspecific shape.

(5) Loops oriented with $(\mathbf{g}\cdot\mathbf{b}) = 0$ show only a very weak contrast which is due to the displacement field transverse to **b** (residual contrast, Querkontrast). Therefore, the well-known $(\mathbf{g}\cdot\mathbf{b}) = 0$ extinction rule for the determination of **b** may be applied, provided care is exercised.

(6) For large excitation errors $s(|s|\cdot\xi_g \gg 1)$, which corresponds approximately to kinematical diffraction, only a black contrast remains for all loop positions. The black dot diameter, measured for instance at the 20% image width (for definition see ref. [7]) corresponds within 10% to the projected loop width. Therefore measurements on the size distribution functions of the radiation

damage should be performed under kinematical image conditions. For $|s| \cdot \xi_g \lesssim 1$ the black-white contrast on dark-field images depends in a critical manner upon whether the loops are located close to the top or the bottom surface respectively, for details see refs. [22,23,10].

(7) For small strain centres of spherical symmetry most of the above summarized properties remain unchanged. However, contrary to point (1) the black-white vector l turns always parallel (or antiparallel) to g [7] for spherical strain centres.

(8) The question as to whether the depth oscillations of the black-white contrast depend on the amount of the volume misfit ΔV of the strain centre demands a separate discussion. (For edge loops with diameter d and Burgers vector b the volume misfit corresponds to $\Delta V = \frac{1}{4} \pi d^2 b$.) This question has been studied especially for spherical strain centres by McIntyre and Brown [12] and by Chik, Wilkens and Rühle [24]. It was found that the sign of (g·l) oscillates with depth only for strain centres with a sufficiently small volume misfit ΔV. This is explained by the modification of the strain field due to the adjacent traction-free foil surface. With increasing ΔV, the width of the contrast profile increases. As a consequence, the contrast profile is influenced more by the modification of the strain field, resulting in an increase of the thickness of the layer L1 at the expense of the layer L2.

If ΔV exceeds a critical value $\Delta V_c = \pi \cdot \xi_g^2 / g$, the layer L2 for which the sign of (g·l) is reversed as compared with L1 and L3 is completely suppressed. Since for reasonable values of the anomalous absorption parameter ξ_g' / ξ_g the black-white contrast in the layer L4 is hard to observe, the depth oscillations of the sign of (g·l) are practically suppressed for $\Delta V \gtrsim \Delta V_c$. Thus on dark field images (g·l) assumes a unique sign, which depends upon whether the strain centre is of vacancy type ((g·l) > 0) or of interstitial type ((g·l) < 0). In the first paper, dealing with the properties of the black-white contrast, Ashby and Brown [7] treated only this special case, occasionally referred to as "Ashby-Brown rule".

In principle, the same influence of the traction-free surface on the strain field and, consequently, on the thicknesses of the layers L1 and L2 exists for dislocation loops. However, using the "infinitesimally small loop approximation" for the correction of the strain field as due to the adjacent traction-free surface, McIntyre and Brown [12] have shown that, for low order reflexions g and for b in the order of the lattice spacing, the critical misfit volume for suppressing the depth oscillations is reached only for loops with diameters d in the order of, or larger than, the extinction length ξ_g. However, loops with $d \gtrsim \xi_g$ are in general resolvable on the micrographs. Consequently, a decision as to whether they are of vacancy or interstitial type may be obtained by means of "conventional" methods based on the properties of the dislocation contrast. We conclude that for loops, too small to be resolved, i.e. $d \lesssim \xi_g/3$, the sign of $(\mathbf{g} \cdot \mathbf{l})$ oscillates with depth. The thickness of the critical layer L2 in this size region is not expected to be very sensitive to the loop size. On the other hand some uncertainties remain concerning the black-white contrast from loops with diameters d between $\xi_g/3$ and ξ_g. For loops of this size the infinitesimal loop approximation, which has been used so far for the contrast calculations [12], fails to give reliable results for the surface corrections of the loop strain field. For some properties of the contrast from loops of this size region we refer to [25].

3. Contrast from small loops containing a shear component of the Burgers vector

Using the theoretical prediction of the direction of the black-white vector $\mathbf{l}$ as an indicator, several authors have found that small point defect agglomerates in radiation-damaged fcc metals are mainly of Frank type. Thus, for a differentiation between vacancy and interstitial loops it was justified to use the above summarized properties of the black-white contrast from edge loops. However, the formal application of these theoretically predicted properties to point defect clusters in bcc metals may give rise to complications: Tucker and Ohr [26] and Huber, Rühle and Wilkens [27,16] concluded from the observed directions of the black-white vector $\mathbf{l}$ in neutron irradiated niobium that the small point defect agglomerates may be interpreted as small dislocation loops with Burgers vectors $\mathbf{b}$ parallel to the directions $\langle 111 \rangle$, $\langle 110 \rangle$ or $\langle 100 \rangle$. Assuming that all these loops have been nucleated by agglomeration of single point defects on closed packed $\{110\}$ planes, one must expect that the Burgers vector of those loops with $\mathbf{b}$ parallel to $\langle 111 \rangle$ or $\langle 100 \rangle$ has an appreciable shear component $\mathbf{b}_s$ ($\mathbf{b} = \mathbf{b}_e + \mathbf{b}_s$, $\mathbf{b}_e$ = edge component). If a loop of this kind is oriented with respect to $\mathbf{g}$ in such way that $|\mathbf{g} \cdot \mathbf{b}_s|$ is small compared with $|\mathbf{g} \cdot \mathbf{b}_e|$ one may assume that the properties of the black-white contrast remain practically the same as calculated for pure edge loops. In fact, for configurations so far treated, the direction of $\mathbf{l}$ coincides, as was found for pure edge loops, with the direction of $\mathbf{b}$ (or its projection onto the image plane), thus justifying the Burgers vector determination of [26,27] in niobium. If, however, $|\mathbf{g} \cdot \mathbf{b}_e|$ is small compared with $|\mathbf{g} \cdot \mathbf{b}_s|$, one must be aware of essentially different properties of the black white contrast. This is confirmed by preliminary results of corresponding contrast calculations. It is interesting to note that for special configurations of loops, containing an appreciable shear component, not only the thickness of the most important layer L1 is changed, but that in some cases also the sign of (g·l) within the layer L1 is reversed. Extended calculations on this rather complicated problem which is important for the analysis of the structure of radiation damage in bcc metals are under way [28].

4. Some remarks on the analytical calculations

Let us assume that the primary electron beam is represented by a plane wave

$$\psi_o = \exp(2\pi i k_o \cdot r) \,,$$

which penetrates the top surface of the transmission foil exactly under the Bragg angle (excitation error = 0). Inside the crystal foil the electrons propagate in the form of two Bloch waves $\psi^{(1)}$ and $\psi^{(2)}$ (notation similar as in [22])

$$\psi = \varphi^{(1)} \cdot \psi^{(1)} + \varphi^{(2)} \cdot \psi^{(2)}$$

with

$$\psi^{(1)} = \frac{1}{\sqrt{2}} \exp -\pi(\tau_o + \tau_g)z \cdot \exp 2\pi i(k_o \cdot r + \tfrac{1}{2}\sigma z) \cdot [1 + \exp 2\pi i(g \cdot r)] \,,$$
$$(1a)$$

$$\psi^{(2)} = \frac{1}{\sqrt{2}} \exp -\pi(\tau_o - \tau_g)z \cdot \exp 2\pi i(k_o \cdot r - \tfrac{1}{2}\sigma z) \cdot [1 - \exp 2\pi i(g \cdot r)] \,;$$
$$(1b)$$

$\tau_o^{-1} = \xi_o' =$ normal absorption length, $\tau_g^{-1} = \xi_g' =$ anomalous absorption length, $\sigma^{-1} = \xi_g =$ extinction length. z-axis parallel to the electron beam (column approximation), origin at the top surface. $g =$ diffraction vector of the two-beam reflexion.

In a perfect crystal foil and under the assumed condition $s = 0$, the two Bloch wave amplitudes $\varphi^{(1)}$ and $\varphi^{(2)}$ are given by

$$\varphi^{(1)} = 1/\sqrt{2}\,, \qquad \varphi^{(2)} = -1/\sqrt{2}\,.$$

At the exit surface at $z = t_o$ the Bloch waves split into the transmitted (ψ_t) and reflected (ψ_g) plane waves respectively,

$$\psi_t = \frac{1}{\sqrt{2}} \exp\left[-\pi\tau_0 t_0\right] \{\varphi^{(1)} \cdot \exp\left[-\pi\tau_g t_0\right] \cdot \exp\left[\pi i\sigma t_0\right]$$

$$+ \varphi^{(2)} \cdot \exp\left[+\pi\tau_g t_0\right] \cdot \exp\left[-\pi i\sigma t_0\right]\} \exp\left[2\pi i(\mathbf{k}_0 \cdot \mathbf{r})\right], \quad (2a)$$

$$\psi_g = \frac{1}{\sqrt{2}} \exp\left[-\pi\tau_0 t_0\right] \{\varphi^{(1)} \cdot \exp\left[-\pi\tau_g t_0\right] \cdot \exp\left[\pi i\sigma t_0\right]$$

$$- \varphi^{(2)} \cdot \exp\left[+\pi\tau_g t_0\right] \cdot \exp\left[-\pi i\sigma t_0\right\} \exp\left[2\pi i(\mathbf{k}_0 + \mathbf{g} \cdot \mathbf{r})\right]. \quad (2b)$$

In a distorted lattice the bending of the reflecting planes is described by the displacement component $u(z)$ parallel to the diffraction vector $\mathbf{g}$. If the derivative $du/dz = u_z \neq 0$, a scattering between the two Bloch waves is induced which is controlled by the differential eqs. [22]

$$\frac{d\varphi^{(1)}}{dz} = i\pi u_z \exp\left(2\pi\tau_g z\right) \exp\left(-2\pi i\sigma z\right) \cdot \varphi^{(2)}(z), \quad (3a)$$

$$\frac{d\varphi^{(2)}}{dz} = i\pi u_z \exp\left(-2\pi\tau_g z\right) \exp\left(+2\pi i\sigma z\right) \cdot \varphi^{(1)}(z), \quad (3b)$$

with the boundary conditions $\varphi^{(1)}(0) = 1/\sqrt{2}$, $\varphi^{(2)}(0) = -1/\sqrt{2}$. The radiation-induced defects, which are of interest to us, are small compared with the extinction length ξ_g. Consequently, u_z will essentially be $\neq 0$ only in an interval $\ll \xi_g$. The centre of the defect lies in the depth position z_0. Then eq. (3) can be integrated in a Born first approximation. For this purpose we set on the right hand sides of eq. (3) $\varphi^{(1)}(z) = \varphi^{(1)}(0)$ and $\varphi^{(2)}(z) = \varphi^{(2)}(0)$. Furthermore the absorption factors $\exp\left(\pm 2\pi\tau_g \cdot z\right)$ can be considered as slowly varying functions over that region, in which u_z is essentially $\neq 0$. We obtain as the first approximation

$$\varphi^{(1)}(t_0) = \frac{1}{\sqrt{2}} - \frac{\pi}{\sqrt{2}} \exp\left(2\pi\tau_g z_0\right) [S + iC], \quad (4a)$$

$$\varphi^{(2)}(t_0) = -\frac{1}{\sqrt{2}} - \frac{\pi}{\sqrt{2}} \exp\left(-2\pi\tau_g z_0\right) [S - iC], \quad (4b)$$

$$S = \int_{0}^{t_0} u_z(z) \sin 2\pi\sigma z\, dz \,, \qquad C = \int_{0}^{t_0} u_z(z) \cos 2\pi\sigma z\, dz \,. \quad (5)$$

In the "thick foil approximation", it is assumed that the foil is thick enough to suppress the Bloch wave $\psi^{(1)}$ which is weakened much more strongly by anomalous absorption than the Bloch wave $\psi^{(2)}$, consequently we assume

$$\exp(-\pi\tau_g t_0) \ll 1, \qquad \exp(+\pi\tau_g t_0) \gg 1 \,.$$

Let us first consider a strain centre close to the top surface which corresponds to $\exp(\pm 2\pi\tau_g \cdot z_0) \approx 1$. Then the bright field contrast $|\psi_t|^2$ and the dark field contrast $|\psi_g|^2$ are given by

$$|\psi_t|^2 \cong |\psi_g|^2 \cong |\varphi^{(2)}(t_0)|^2 \cdot \exp[-2\pi(\tau_0 - \tau_g)t_0]\,.$$

Therefore, in "linear approximation" (linear in u_z) the contrast is essentially given by

$$|\psi_t|^2 \cong |\psi_g|^2 \propto \tfrac{1}{2}[1 + 2\pi \cdot \exp(-2\pi\tau_g z_0) \cdot S] \,. \qquad (6)$$

If the defect lies close to the exit surface (bottom surface) we have to assume that

$$\exp[\pm 2\pi\tau_g(z_0 - t_0)] \approx 1 \,.$$

One obtains with eqs. (2)–(4) after some simple rearrangement in the linear approximation

$$|\psi_t|^2 = \tfrac{1}{2}\{1 - 2\pi \exp[-2\pi\tau_g(t_0 - z_0)] \cdot S'\} \exp[-2\pi(\tau_0 - \tau_g)t_0] \,, \tag{7a}$$

$$|\psi_g|^2 = \tfrac{1}{2}\{1 + 2\pi \exp[-2\pi\tau_g(t_0 - z_0)] \cdot S'\} \exp[-2\pi(\tau_0 - \tau_g)t_0] \,, \tag{7b}$$

$$S' = \int_{0}^{t_0} u_z(z) \sin 2\pi\sigma(z - t_0)\, dz \,. \qquad (8)$$

The linear approximation is valid only for the tails of the contrast profiles. This, however, is sufficient to determine the essential properties of the black-white contrast. In [22] the analytic calculation was extended to a quadratic approximation (proportional to S^2 and C^2). For thick foils the quadratic terms, which will not be considered here, result in a reduction of both, $\varphi^{(1)}$ and $\varphi^{(2)}$.

We state that our approximation, i.e. eqs. (6) and (7), obeys the well-known symmetry properties of diffraction contrast: the contrast from defects close to the top surface are similar in bright and dark field; the contrast from defects close to the bottom surface are complementary in bright and dark field. Hence, in the following it is sufficient to consider defects close to the top surface, although the same considerations can be applied in a similar way to defects close to the bottom surface.

Now let us consider as the simplest case a Frank loop (which may be of interstitial type) with **b** parallel to **g**, as shown in fig. 5a. The corrections of the strain field due to the traction-free surfaces are neglected. Then, the dis-

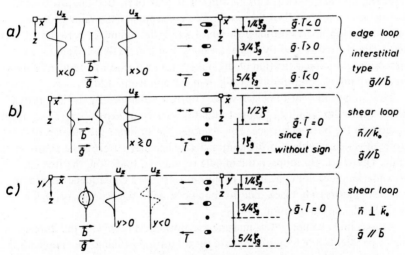

Fig. 5. First order calculation of the black-white contrast from small dislocation loops with g ‖ b, schematically. (a) edge loop of interstitial type. (b) and (c) shear loop, n= loop normal. In (c) the full lines represent the bent lattice planes and the function u_z for $y > 0$ (above the drawing plane). The dotted lines refer to $y < 0$ (below the drawing plane).

placement derivative u_z may be idealized by an antisymmetric double-peak function with the depth position z_0 of the loop centre between the two peaks. As shown in fig. 5a u_z changes its sign when changing from one side of the loop to the other. As a consequence, a positive sign of S on the one side (bright contrast tail) corresponds to a negative sign of S on the other side (dark contrast tail). Thus, the black-white contrast is explained in our linear approximation as a consequence of the symmetry of the loop strain field. From the antisymmetry of $u_z(z)$, it follows directly that S vanishes, if z_0 coincides with the extrema of $\sin 2\pi oz$, i.e. $S = 0$ for $z_0 = \frac{1}{4}\xi_g + \frac{1}{2}n\xi_g$, n is an integer. These depth positions determine the boundaries of the layers L1, L2, ... Loops with their centres such that $S = 0$, i.e. just between the layers, reveal only a comparatively narrow black dot contrast, which follows from the quadratic approximation [22] which is not treated here.

For z_0 within the layers the sign of $S \neq 0$ is the same for layers with odd and with even numbers respectively. Consequently S changes its sign when z_0 changes from one layer to the adjacent layer (depth oscillations). Due to the antisymmetric shape of u_z, S assumes maximum values for those values of z_0 for which $\sin 2\pi o z_0$ vanishes, i.e. for $z_0 = n \cdot \xi_g/2$. Loops within the first layer require an additional consideration. The adjacent foil surface must be assumed to be traction-free. This modifies that peak of u_z that lies just beneath the surface more than the other peak. As a consequence the value of S is enhanced and the first vanishing position of S (i.e. the boundary between L1 and L2) is shifted to slightly higher z-values. For a more detailed analytical discussion of the modification of the black-white contrast as a result of the elastic boundary conditions see Chik, Wilkens and Rühle [24].

The "amplitude" of the black-white contrast is damped by the absorption factor $\exp(-2\pi\tau_g z_0)$ for z_0 close to the top surface or $\exp(-2\pi\tau_g(t_0-z_0))$ for z_0 close to the bottom surface. This damping factor limits the number of layers in which the black-white contrast is sufficiently strong to be observable. Therefore, for loops in the middle region of a thick foil, the first approximation does not contribute to the contrast. As a consequence the loop contrast appears only black, due to the above mentioned property of the second order approximation.

As a second example let us imagine a hypothetical loop with the Burgers vector parallel to the loop plane (pure shear loop). Assuming, for simplicity, **b** parallel to **g**, there are two essentially different configurations as shown in fig. 5b and c. In the case of fig. 5b the strain parameter $u_z(z)$ is the same on either side of the loop. Consequently the tails of the contrast figure are expected to be either black or white on both sides, depending on the actual depth position of the loop centre. Since u_z is a symmetric function of $z-z_0$

the first order perturbation integral S vanishes for $z_0 = \frac{1}{2}n\,\xi_g$, i.e. in comparison to fig. 5a the thickness of the first layer of the depth oscillations is changed to $\frac{1}{2}\,\xi_g$. In the case of fig. 5c, the strain parameter u_z changes its sign when changing from one side to the other side of the loop. Therefore the contrast is of the black-white type. Furthermore, due to the antisymmetry of u_z as a function of $(z-z_0)$ the depth oscillations obey the same periodicity as has been found for pure edge loops.

The sign of the $(\mathbf{g}\cdot\mathbf{l})$ product of the contrast figure from edge loops depends upon the actual loop position, z_0, and upon whether the loop is of vacancy or interstitial type. For a shear loop in the position of fig. 5b the contrast is symmetric, so that a vector $\mathbf{l}$ cannot be defined, whereas in fig. 5c $\mathbf{l}$ points perpendicularly to $\mathbf{g}$. Consequently we may say that $(\mathbf{g}\cdot\mathbf{l}) = 0$ for both cases. This appears satisfactory, since shear loops are neither of vacancy nor of interstitial type.

5. Experimental methods

For an understanding of the mechanisms of the radiation damage in crystals the following points are of considerable interest:

(i)   Identification of the symmetry of the lattice defects;

(ii)   Determination of the Burgers vector of small dislocation loops;

(iii) Differentiation between strain centres of vacancy and interstitial type.

(iv) Determination of volume density and of the size distribution of the lattice defects.

(i) In order to decide as to whether a small point defect agglomerate has a strain field of spherical or non-spherical symmetry, the transmission foils must be imaged under dynamical two-beam conditions with different (non-parallel) diffraction vectors $\mathbf{g}$ [6–10]. If a defect, giving rise to a black-white contrast, turns its black-white vector $\mathbf{l}$ always parallel (or antiparallel) to $\mathbf{g}$, the strain field is, at least approximately, of spherical symmetry.

In this context we mention the experiments of Chik [29] on stacking fault tetrahedra in quenched and subsequently annealed gold. When the tetrahedra revealed a black-white contrast, the direction of $\mathbf{l}$ turned always parallel to $\mathbf{g}$, thus indicating that, with respect to the direction of $\mathbf{l}$, a tetrahedron may be considered as a strain centre of spherical symmetry.

(ii) If, for different dynamical images, obtained with different $\mathbf{g}$, the direction of $\mathbf{l}$ remains unaltered irrespective of the direction of $\mathbf{g}$, one may conclude that the defect consists of a dislocation loop with its Burgers vector $\mathbf{b}$, or with the projection of $\mathbf{b}$ onto the image plane, parallel to $\mathbf{l}$. Thus, by observing the directions of l for different g and for different foil orientations, the loop Burgers vectors may be determined rather definitely.

That line on the micrograph, along which the black and the white dot of the black-white contrast figure meet each other, is sometimes called "line of no contrast". Some authors [30–32] have tried to use the line of no contrast as an indicator for the identification of the loop Burgers vector or the loop habit plane. In these papers it was assumed that the line of no contrast, which is really defined only for spherical inclusions [7], extends always perpendicular to the loop Burgers vector or to its projection onto the image plane. However, this method is not justified by the theoretical contrast calculations. On the contrary, the line of no contrast displays in some cases a peculiar fine-structure (compare [11] and fig. 3a), which is not yet understood and which in the future may allow further conclusions to be drawn on details of the structure of the loops.

(iii) In order to discriminate between loops of vacancy and interstitial type, it is necessary to observe the sign of $(g \cdot l)$ on dynamical images and to determine the depth position of the loop centres with respect to the adjacent foil surface. For the latter several methods have been proposed which are based on the following idea: If one takes micrographs of the same foil area with different extinction lengths (i.e. by changing from g_1 to g_2 with $\xi_{g_1} \neq \xi_{g_2}$, by varying the acceleration voltage or by changing the excitation error s) some of the loops may change their "black-white" layers, resulting in a reversal of the sign of their $(g \cdot l)$ products. Then, by more or less reliable statistical considerations, these sign reversals may allow a decision as to whether the loops are of vacancy or interstitial type. This method have been applied by several authors [33,34,11], however, the results were not very convincing.

So far, the best technique for the determination of the depth position appears to be the method of stereo microscopy in the form as developed by Diepers and Diehl [14,15] and by Rühle [10]. For this technique two micrographs of the transmission foil must be taken, one with a tilting angle $+\beta$ (in the order of $10°$) and the other with a tilting angle $-\beta$, both measured with respect to the foil orientation perpendicular to the electron beam as the reference orientation and with the operating diffraction vector g as the tilting axis. In order to achieve the necessary accuracy of the depth measurements the two tilting angles must be measured with high accuracy (using Kikuchi patterns). To obtain comparable images of the defects on the two stereo micrographs, it is necessary to perform the stereo micrographs under kinematical contrast conditions ($|s| \cdot \xi_g \gg 1$) for the following reasons: according to the contrast calculations the shape of the contrast figures from small dislocation loops depends for $|s| \cdot \xi_g \gg 1$ only insensitively on the actual image conditions, i.e. the black dot contrast coincides rather well with the position of the loop.

However, under dynamical contrast conditions ($|s| \cdot \xi_g \lesssim 1$), the structure of the contrast figures of those loops, which give rise to a black-white contrast, is rather sensitive to the image conditions. Thus, for $|s| \cdot \xi_g \lesssim 1$, it is difficult to obtain an equivalent pair of stereo micrographs.

Since the distance of the defects from the adjacent foil surface must be measured (for instance by an optical stereo device), it is necessary to mark the position of the foil surface. In the case of copper and niobium foils the following procedure has been applied with success: after obtaining the dynamical images for the determination of the signs of ($\mathbf{g} \cdot \mathbf{l}$) of the individual defects, a small amount of gold is evaporated onto one side of the foil, condensing on the foil surface in the form of small islands of about 50 Å diameter and less than 10 Å thickness. Then the kinematical stereo micrographs are performed. The small gold islands are easily observed in the optical stereo viewer, thus defining the reference mark for the depth measurements. However, special care must be taken to avoid any amorphous layer on the foil surface, as produced before the gold evaporation, for instance by a non-appropriate electro polishing method or by carbon contamination inside the microscope. After the gold evaporation such a layer simulates a wrong position of the real specimen surface.

A critical discussion of the error sources involved in the stereo measurements indicates that an accuracy of about ± 20 Å is achievable. Since the thickness of the critical first layer of the black-white contrast, L1, ranges in the order of 50–100 Å, this accuracy should be just enough to discern between the loop depth positions in the most important layers L1 and L2.

(iv) We add some remarks on the accuracy of the loop size measurements. Although the contrast calculations may give predictions of the relation between the true loop size and the contrast width as defined by a given percentage deviation from the background intensity level, the experimental methods for measuring the diameter of the small unresolved black dots are rather uncertain. This is due to different reasons: (i) everyone has his own peculiarities in measuring the black dot diameter, (ii) within each of these individual techniques there exists a rather large uncertainty especially for dots with diameters smaller than ≈ 50 Å, (iii) the apparent dot sizes on the kinematical micrographs depend in a critical way, which is difficult to control in practice, on the film exposure, the film processing and the positive printing procedures. Consequently, size distribution functions obtained on the same subject but by different research groups are difficult to compare quantitatively. Deviations in the order of ± 30% may easily occur. With respect to further details of the experimental procedure we refer to [18].

6. Experimental results

Before the calculations of the black-white contrast from small dislocation loops were performed, the most striking feature was observed and interpreted intuitively in a correct sense by Essmann and Wilkens [6] : Studying the damage in neutron-irradiated copper, they found that the direction of the black-white vector l of individual black-white dots remains fixed, when the same foil area is dynamically imaged with different diffraction vectors **g**. In the mean time this property has been used by various authors to determine the Burgers vector of defect agglomerates in crystals damaged by irradiation with fast neutrons, ions or high-energy electrons, compare [17,18]. It appears that in pure fcc metals small point defect agglomerates occur mainly in the form of Frank loops with **b** parallel to ⟨111⟩. In most of the fcc metals only a small fraction of perfect loops with **b** parallel to ⟨110⟩ have been found [6,10]. As an interesting exception, not yet understood, we mention neutron-irradiated platinum [35,17,18], where the number of loops with **b** parallel to ⟨110⟩ was comparable with the number of Frank loops. In neutron-irradiated copper a high fraction of ⟨110⟩ loops has been found only after the specimens (irradiated at 80°C or at 4°K) had been annealed at 300°C [35,17,18].

In bcc metals, so far only the black-white contrast in neutron-irradiated niobium has been studied in detail (Tucker and Ohr [26], Huber, Rühle and Wilkens [27, 16]. As already mentioned in sect. 3, loops with Burgers vectors **b** parallel to the directions ⟨111⟩, ⟨110⟩ and ⟨100⟩ have been identified. All three kinds of loops were found with about the same frequency.

Strain centres whose black-white vector l turns parallel to **g** for all directions of **g** have been observed by Bourret and Dautreppe [36] in neutron-irradiated nickel and by Rühle et al. [35,17,18] in neutron-irradiated platinum.

In the case of nickel it was concluded from the geometrical shape of the contrast figures on kinematical images that the lattice defect has tetrahedral symmetry. Consequently the authors interpreted these defects as being tetrahedral voids or stacking fault tetrahedra. In platinum, even on well focussed kinematical images, no geometrical structure of these "spherical" strain centres (diameter in the order of 50Å) could be detected. Perhaps these defects may be identified as the zones of extremely high concentration of point defects that have been observed in neutron-irradiated platinum by means of field ion microscopy [37].

The first attempts to apply the method of stereo microscopy to the discrimination between vacancy and interstitial loops have been published by Diepers and Diehl [14,15]. The authors found by stereo microscopy that the damage produced by the impact of 5 keV argon ions on the surface of copper foils consists of small Frank loops located at a rather sharply defined distance of about $100 - 200$Å (depending on the irradiation conditions) below the irradiated surface. From the mean depth of the loops in connection with the predominantly observed sign of the $(g \cdot l)$ products, the authors concluded that the loops are mainly of interstitial type.

A more rigorous analysis of the vacancy or interstitial nature of small loops was performed by Rühle [10,11] and Rühle and Wilkens [38]. More than 200 loops were registrated with respect to the sign of their $(g \cdot l)$ product and their depth position inside the foil as determined by stereo microscopy. In fig. 6 the numbers of loops found in a certain depth interval were plotted above the abscissa for $(g \cdot l) > 0$ and below the abscissa for $(g \cdot l) < 0$. The plot displays just that change in the sign of $(g \cdot l)$ and at that depth position expected from theory for vacancy loops. Thus, it is indicated that the depth measurement by means of stereo microscopy is sufficient to discriminate between the different layers of the black-white depth oscillations. With respect to further results mentioned below it must be said that in this work [10,11,38] only loops with diameters between 30 and 50Å were stereo-analysed since experience shows that the stereo technique is most easily applied in this size range. This restriction in size was not stated in the original papers.

In the following time the stereo experiments of Rühle on neutron-irradiated copper were repeated by several authors, who found only vacancy loops (Crump III [39]) or only interstitial loops (McIntyre [40]) or either vacancy or interstitial loops depending on the atmospheric environment of the copper specimens during the neutron-irradiation (Bourret and Dautreppe [41]). In order to clarify these striking discrepancies Rühle et al. [35] repeated the measurements under careful control of the conditions for specimen preparation and irradiation. Furthermore, in contrast to the former work, loops with diameters between about 15 and 150Å were analysed. Similarly as in fig. 6 black-white dots belonging to the two first layers L1 and L2 of the depth oscillations were found. The results are plotted in the diagram of fig. 7.

At a certain variance with the earlier results it was found that small loops with diameters $d \lesssim 75$Å are predominantly of vacancy type, whereas the loops with $d \gtrsim 75$Å are mainly of interstitial type. This separation in size may account for the above mentioned discrepancies. Presumably different authors stereo-measured different size groups. Furthermore, the critical size, at which vacancy and interstitial loops are separated, may depend on details of the irradiation conditions.

In addition to the already mentioned work on neutron-irradiated and 5 keV Ar$^+$ ion-irradiated copper we refer to some further results.

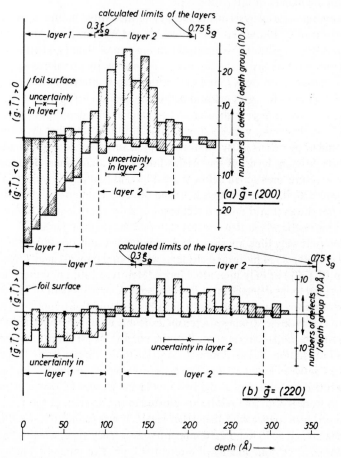

Fig. 6. Results of the stereo analysis of the black-white contrast figures from Frank loops with diameter d between 30 and 50Å in neutron-irradiated copper [10,11,38]. The number of black-white dots with $(g \cdot l) > 0$ and $(g \cdot l) < 0$ are plotted against the distance of the defect centre from the bottom surface of the transmission foil (bright field, positive prints). The depth oscillations of the sign of $(g \cdot l)$ are clearly demonstrated. Thus, according to fig. 4, the loops are mainly of vacancy type. The extinction length ξ_g used in the figure is corrected for many-beam effects.

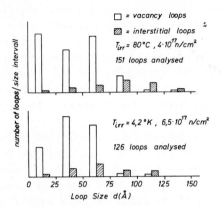

Fig. 7. Vacancy and interstitial loops in neutron-irradiated copper as a function of the loop diameter [27,35].

Neutron-irradiation: In nickel, Bourret and Dautreppe [36] found only interstitial loops. However, since only loops with $d > 40$Å were analysed, the nature of the high number of loops with $d < 40$Å remain, up to now, undetermined. In analogy to copper, the smaller loops may be predominantly of vacancy type [17]. Brimhal and Mastel [42] studied the damage in rhenium (hcp). From the direction of l they determined the Burgers vector to be parallel to $\langle 11\bar{2}0 \rangle$. The depth measurements of the loops with d between 40 and 100Å, which revealed the sign change of $(g \cdot l)$ from layer L1 to layer L2, resulted in mainly interstitial loops. In platinum, Rühle, Häussermann, Rapp and Wilkens [35,17] identified the small loops as being mainly of vacancy type, which holds also for the already mentioned "spherical" strain centres. Vacancy loops were found also in gold by Eades [43].

The damage structure in niobium was studied by Huber, Rühle and Wilkens [16,27]. Under the assumption that the signs of $(g \cdot l)$ and the thicknesses of the layers L1, L2, ..., as calculated for pure edge loops, are valid also for the loops with shear components occurring in particle irradiated bcc metals, the authors found about $\frac{2}{3}$ of the small loops to be of interstitial type and $\frac{1}{3}$ of vacancy type. However, since there were some indications for a large shear component of the loop Burgers vectors, it is just this assumption which must be confirmed by further contrast calculations.

Ion-irradiation: If the energy of heavy ions, irradiated on fcc specimens, are high enough (energies transferred to the lattice atoms higher than about 10 keV) the damage consists of small Frank loops close to the irradiated specimen surface. By stereo technique these loops have been identified as vacancy loops (Rühle and Wilkens [44,11], Norris [45]). These loops are presumably produced by displacement cascades or depleted zones. In the case of extremely low ion energies (too low to produce depleted zones) only "half loops" of interstitial type are produced, which are intersected by the irradiated surface.(Bowden and Brandon [46]; Thomas and Balluffi [47]). However, compared with the vacancy loops, as produced by high energy ions, these interstitial loops require a much higher irradiation dose for their formation.

Electron-irradiation: Bourret and Dautreppe [36] irradiated nickel below the annealing stage III ($\approx 100°$C). Only interstitial loops were found. As an interesting result of annealing experiments, it came out that the total number of interstitials, agglomerated in the loops, increased by about a factor of 2, when the specimens were annealed at $100°$C (i.e. within stage III). In copper, irradiated at $120°$K and inspected in the electron microscope at room temperature (several weeks after irradiation) a mixture of about the same number of vacancy and interstitial loops was found (Häussermann et al. [48]).

Finally, we mention a significant difference between the damage, as visible on the micrographs, due to neutron or electron irradiation and the damage by heavy ions respectively.

For fast neutron and high energy electron irradiation the damage must be expected to be homogeneously distributed over the entire depth of the transmission foil. Thus, even on dark field images and even for defects of either only vacancy or only interstitial type, due to the depth oscillations, both signs of $(g·l)$ occur on the micrographs.

On the other hand, the penetration depth of heavy ions, falling onto specimens which are prepared for transmission microscopy before irradiation, is extremely small. Consequently one expects that the damage is produced within a thin surface layer. In fact, several authors [11,34,44,49,51] have found that the damage consists of small Frank loops, all of which reveal the same sign of $(g·l)$. As an example we refer to fig. 3 which shows micrographs from copper foils irradiated with 100 keV O⁻ ions. Under the assumption that all the loops lie within the first layer L1 of the depth oscillations, it was concluded from the observed sign of $(g·l)$ that the loops are of vacancy type. (Apart from this rather indirect conclusion, the vacancy nature of the loops have now been confirmed also by the stereo technique, see above.)

Acknowledgement

The author thanks his colleagues Dr. M.Rühle and Dipt. Phys. F.Häussermann for their helpful and stimulating discussions.

References

[1] D.W.Pashley and A.E.B.Presland, Phil. Mag. 6 (1961) 1003.

[2] M.J.Makin, A.D.Whapham and F.J.Minter, Phil. Mag 6 (1961) 465; 7 (1962) 285.

[3] M.J.Makin and S.A.Manthorpe, Phil. Mag. 8 (1963) 1725.

[4] E.Ruedl, P.Delavignette and S.Amelinckx, Radiation Damage in Solids (Vienna, 1962) p. 363.

[5] E.Ruedl and S.Amelinckx, J. Phys. Soc. Japan 18, Supp. III (1963) 195.

[6] U.Essmann and M.Wilkens, Phys. Stat. Sol. 4 (1964) K53.

[7] M.F.Ashby and L.M.Brown, Phil. Mag. 8 (1963) 1083.

[8] M.F.Ashby and L.M.Brown, Phil. Mag. 8 (1963) 1649.

[9] M.Rühle, M.Wilkens and U.Essmann, Phys. Stat. Sol. 11 (1965) 819.

[10] M.Rühle, Phys. Stat. Sol. 19 (1967) 263.

[11] M.Rühle, Phys. Stat. Sol. 19 (1967) 279.

[12] K.G.McIntyre and L.M.Brown, J. Phys. Radium 27 (1966) C3-178.

[13] K.G.McIntyre and L.M.Brown, Symposium on the Nature of Small Defect Clusters, Harwell, AERE Report R 5269 (1966) p. 351.

[14] H.Diepers and J.Diehl, Phys. Stat. Sol. 16 (1966) K109.

[15] H.Diepers, Phys. Stat. Sol. 24 (1967) 235, 623.

[16] P.Huber, M.Rühle and M.Wilkens, to be published.

[17] M.Wilkens, Studies of Point Defect Clusters by Transmission Electron Microscopy, in: Vacancies and Interstitials in Metals, eds. Seeger et al. (North-Holland, Amsterdam, 1970) p. 485.

[18] M.Rühle, Proc. of the Symposium on Radiation Damage in Reactor Materials Vol. 1 (Vienna, 1969) p. 113.

[19] N.Hashimote, A.Howie and M.J.Whelan, Phil. Mag. 5 (1960) 967.

[20] F.Häussermann and M.Wilkens, Phys. Stat. Sol. 18 (1966) 609.

[21] J.W.Steeds, Phil. Mag. 16 (1967) 785.

[22] M.Wilkens, Phys. Stat. Sol. 6 (1964) 939.

[23] W.L.Bell and G.Thomas, Phys. Stat. Sol. 12 (1965) 843.

[24] K.P.Chik, M.Wilkens and M.Rühle, Phys. Stat. Sol. 23 (1967) 113.

[25] W.L.Bell and G.Thomas, Phil. Mag. 13 (1966) 395.

[26] R.P.Tucker and S.M.Ohr, Phil. Mag. 16 (1967) 643.

[27] M.Rühle, F.Häussermann, P.Huber and M.Wilkens, Proc. 4th European Reg. Conf. of Electron Microscopy, Vol. I (Rome, 1968) p. 397.

[28] M.Rühle and M.Wilkens, to be published.

[29] K.P.Chik, Phys. Stat. Sol. 16 (1966) 685.

[30] W.L.Bell, D.M.Maher and G.Thomas, Lattice Defects in Quenched Metals (Academic Press, New York, London, 1965) p. 739.

[31] L.M.Howe, J.F.McGurn and R.W.Gilbert, Acta Met. 14 (1966) 801.

[32] P.Rao and G.Thomas, Acta Met. 15 (1967) 1153.

[33] J.L.Brimhal, H.E.Kissinger and B.Mastel, J. Appl. Phys. 37 (1966) 3317.

[34] W.L.Bell, D.M.Maher and G.Thomas, Symposium on the Nature of Small Defect Clusters, Harwell AERE Report R 5269 (1966) p. 314.

[35] M.Rühle, F.Häussermann, M.Rapp and M.Wilkens, to be published.

[36] A.Bourret and D.Dautreppe, Phys. Stat. Sol. 29 (1968) 283.

[37] M.J.Attardo and J.M.Galligan, Phys. Rev. 161 (1967) 558.

[38] M.Rühle and M.Wilkens, Phil. Mag. 15 (1967) 1075.
[39] J.C.Crump III, Bull. Am. Phys. Soc. 13 (1968) 462.
[40] K.G.McIntyre, Phil. Mag. 15 (1967) 205.
[41] A.Bourret and D.Dautreppe, Phys. Stat. Sol. 24 (1967) K174.
[42] J.L.Brimhall and B.Mastel, Phys. Stat. Sol. 27 (1968) K89.
[43] J.A.Eades, Phil. Mag. 19 (1969) 47.
[44] M.Rühle and M.Wilkens, Proc. 6th Intern. Conf. for Electron Microscopy, Vol. I
     (Kyoto, 1966) p. 379.
[45] D.I.Norris, Phil. Mag. 19 (1969) 527.
[46] P.B.Bowden and D.G.Brandon, Phil. Mag. 8 (1963) 935.
[47] L.E.Thomas and R.W.Balluffi, Phil. Mag. 15 (1967) 1117.
[48] F.Häussermann, M.Rühle, G.P.Scheidler and G.Roth, Phys. Stat. Sol. 32 (1969)
     K103.
[49] K.L.Merkle, L.R.Singer and R.K.Hart, J. Appl. Phys. 34 (1963) 2800.
[50] K.L.Merkle, Phys. Stat. Sol. 18 (1966) 173.
[51] R.V.Hesketh and G.K.Richards, Phil. Mag. 13 (1966) 1069.

THE STUDY OF PLANAR INTERFACES
BY MEANS OF ELECTRON MICROSCOPY

S.AMELINCKX

*Studiecentrum voor Kernenergie, S.C.K./C.E.N. Mol
and Rijksuniversitair Centrum, Antwerpen*

1. Introduction

"Single crystals" in the common sense of the word are often fragmented into domains. The origin of the fragmentation is usually connected with the creation of order of some kind, accompanied by a decrease in symmetry.

One can distinguish domains due to: (i) chemical order, i.e. ordering of atoms according to their chemical nature; (ii) magnetic ordering, i.e. ordering of magnetic moments either in the ferromagnetic or in the anti-ferromagnetic mode; (iii) electric order, i.e. ordering of electric dipoles either according to the ferroelectric or to the anti-ferroelectric mode.

The structures within the different domains are of course identical; however, the structures within different domains can be geometrically related in various ways. The structure in one domain may be derived from that in another domain by a pure translation characterized by a constant displacement vector $\mathbf{R}$. The boundary between two such domains will be called either a stacking fault (SF), or an anti-phase boundary (APB) (fig. 1a).

In some cases the lattice or the structure in one domain can be derived from that in another domain by taking the mirror image with respect to some common lattice plane. Such domains are twin related. If the contact plane coincides with the mirror plane we shall call the boundary a *coherent domain boundary*. Twins are characterized by a displacement field rather than by a constant displacement vector. The displacement vector now increases linearly in length with the distance from the coherent twin plane (fig. 1b). In the case of interest here, the twinning vector $\mathbf{\Delta}$ (fig. 1b) is very small.

Crystals containing such interfaces can conveniently be described as consisting of two perfect crystal parts. The one first met by the electrons is called part I, part II, in the case of a stacking fault has suffered a parallel displacement.

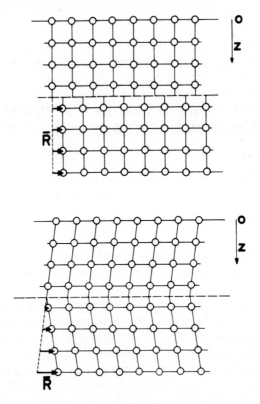

Fig. 1a. Geometry of lattice planes along a stacking fault or anti-phase boundary. The displacement field consists of a constant vector **R**. 1b. Geometry of lattice planes along a coherent twin boundary. The displacement field consists of parallel vectors of which the magnitude is proportional to the distance from the interface.

In the case of domain boundaries the second part is deformed by the displacement field represented in fig. 1b.

In our lectures we shall discuss the images produced in the electron microscope by the different types of interfaces using a method which is different from that used in the lectures by Prof. Whelan and which is based on refs. [2–4].

2. Basic equations for the perfect crystal

We shall systematically make the following assumptions: (i) the dynamical theory for the symmetrical Laue case applies; (ii) a two-beam situation is realized; (iii) the column approximation applies; (iv) anomalous absorption is adequately taken into account by making the extinction distance complex; (v) normal absorption is systematically neglected unless otherwise stated.

The meaning and validity of these assumptions have been discussed in other lectures.

Under the given conditions the following set of equations describes the diffraction of electrons by a perfect crystal [1]:

$$\frac{d\psi_o}{dz} = \frac{\pi i}{t_{-g}} \psi_g \tag{1a}$$

$$\frac{d\psi_g}{dz} = \frac{\pi i}{t_g} \psi_o + 2\pi i s \psi_g \tag{1b}$$

ψ_o and ψ_g are the amplitudes of transmitted and scattered waves respectively; t_g and t_{-g} are the extinction distances corresponding to the reflections g and $-g$ respectively. In the centro-symmetrical case one has in general $t_g = t_{-g}$ (Friedel's law). The extinction distance t_g is inversely proportional to the coefficient having the same index g, in the Fourier expansion of the lattice potential:

$$V(\mathbf{r}) = \sum_g V_g \exp(2\pi i g \cdot \mathbf{r}) \tag{2}$$

V_g is in turn proportional to the structure amplitude F_g; s is a parameter describing the deviation from the Bragg orientation. The z-axis is perpendicular to the entrance face of the foil; its positive sense coincides with the sense of propagation of the electrons.

Anomalous absorption will be taken into account by means of the substitution [5]:

$$\frac{1}{t_g} \rightarrow \frac{1}{t_g} + \frac{i}{\tau_g}$$

where τ_g is called the absorption length. This substitution can be performed in the final solution of the system of eqs. (1).

For a perfect crystal and with as boundary conditions $\psi_0 = 1$ and $\psi_g = 0$ at the entrance face, one finds the following solution:

$$\psi_0 = (\cos \pi\sigma z - i\frac{s}{\sigma} \sin \pi\sigma z) \exp(\pi i s z) \tag{3a}$$

$$\psi_g = \frac{i}{\sigma t_g} \sin \pi\sigma z \, \exp(\pi i s z) \tag{3b}$$

where

$$\sigma = \frac{1}{t_g}\sqrt{1 + (st_g)^2} \; .$$

If anomalous absorption is taken into account σ becomes complex $\sigma = \sigma_r + i\sigma_i$. To a good approximation one has

$$\sigma_r = \frac{1}{t_g}\sqrt{1 + (st_g)^2} \tag{4a}$$

$$\sigma_i = \frac{1}{\tau_g \sqrt{1 + (st_g)^2}} \; . \tag{4b}$$

It is further a good approximation to substitute σ_r for σ in the coefficients but of course not in the exponentials or goniometric functions, leading to the following expressions:

$$\psi_0 = [\cos \pi(\sigma_r + i\sigma_i)z - \frac{s}{\sigma_r} \sin \pi(\sigma_r + i\sigma_i)z] \, \exp(\pi i s z) \tag{5a}$$

$$\psi_g = \frac{i}{\sigma_r t_g} \sin [\pi(\sigma_r + i\sigma_i)z] \, \exp(\pi i s z) \; . \tag{5b}$$

These expressions describe adequately the variation of

$$I_T = \psi_0\psi_0^* \quad \text{and} \quad I_S = \psi_g\psi_g^*$$

with the crystal thickness (z) and with the deviation parameter (s).

The system of eqs. (1) can be written in a more symmetrical way by means of the substitution

$$\psi_o = T \exp(\pi isz) \qquad \psi_g = S \exp(\pi isz) \tag{6}$$

it now reduces to the following system:

$$\frac{dT}{dz} + \pi is\, T = \frac{\pi i}{t_{-g}} S$$

$$\frac{dS}{dz} - \pi is\, S = \frac{\pi i}{t_g} T \tag{7}$$

of which the solution with the initial values $T = 1$, $S = 0$ for $z = 0$ is clearly:

$$T(z,s) = \cos \pi \sigma z - i\frac{s}{\sigma_r} \sin \pi \sigma z$$

$$S(z,s) = \frac{i}{\sigma_r t_g} \sin \pi \sigma z \; . \tag{8}$$

The solution of the same system of equations but for the initial values $T = 0$, $S = 1$ at $z = 0$ is on the other hand

$$T = S(z,-s) \equiv S^-$$

$$S = T(z,-s) \equiv T^- \; . \tag{9}$$

This can be deduced by noting that the initial values

$$\begin{pmatrix} T \\ S \end{pmatrix} = \begin{pmatrix} 1 \\ 0 \end{pmatrix} \text{ reduce to the initial values } \begin{pmatrix} T \\ S \end{pmatrix} = \begin{pmatrix} 0 \\ 1 \end{pmatrix}$$

if one interchanges T and S. If one performs the same interchange in the set of equations, and simultaneously interchanges s into $-s$ the set of equations remains unchanged. We can therefore obtain the solution by performing the same changes in the expressions (8). This immediately leads to (9). We can now write down the solution under matrix form for arbitrary initial values as follows:

$$\begin{pmatrix} T \\ S \end{pmatrix}_{out} = \begin{pmatrix} T & S^- \\ S & T^- \end{pmatrix} \begin{pmatrix} T \\ S \end{pmatrix}_{in} \tag{10}$$

where $\begin{pmatrix} T \\ S \end{pmatrix}_{in}$ represents the amplitudes of the incoming waves and $\begin{pmatrix} T \\ S \end{pmatrix}_{out}$ the

amplitudes of the outgoing waves.

The matrix

$$\mathcal{M}(z,s) = \begin{pmatrix} T & S^- \\ S & T^- \end{pmatrix} \tag{11}$$

is called the *transmission matrix* for a slab of perfect crystal. This matrix describes the response of the crystal slab to the incoming waves. It is sufficient to have this matrix operate to the left of the column vector representing the amplitudes of the incoming waves (in transmitted and scattered directions) in order to obtain the amplitudes of the waves leaving the crystal in these two directions.

For instance

$$\begin{pmatrix} T \\ S \end{pmatrix} = \mathcal{M}(z,s) \begin{pmatrix} 1 \\ 0 \end{pmatrix} \tag{12}$$

represents clearly the amplitudes T and S leaving a crystal of thickness z per unit amplitude of the incident beam.

Evidently the matrix $\mathcal{M}$ must have the property

$$\mathcal{M}(z_1+z_2+z_3+...z_n,s) = \mathcal{M}(z_n,s) \ldots \mathcal{M}(z_2,s)\mathcal{M}(z_1,s) \tag{13}$$

which is easy to verify. This property is physically evident. The matrix product on the right hand side would represent transmission and scattering through different lamella of the same single crystal. The relation expresses the fact that it should be immaterial whether or not the perfect crystal is thought to be divided into a number of lamella by imagining interfaces parallel to the foil surfaces.

3. Equations for the faulted crystal

The deformation is described by the vector field $\mathbf{R}(\mathbf{r})$ which means that the atom which in the perfect crystal would be at the position $\mathbf{r}$ is to be found at the position $\mathbf{r} + \mathbf{R}(\mathbf{r})$ in the deformed crystal. In particular the lattice potential $V(\mathbf{r})$ at the point $\mathbf{r}$ will in the deformed crystal be found at $V(\mathbf{r}+\mathbf{R})$, conversely we shall have the relation

$$V(\mathbf{r})_{\text{deformed crystal}} = V(\mathbf{r}-\mathbf{R})_{\text{perfect crystal}} \cdot \tag{14}$$

The series expansion of the lattice potential in the deformed crystal thus becomes:

$$V(\mathbf{r}) = \sum_{g} V_g \exp\left[2\pi i g \cdot (\mathbf{r}-\mathbf{R})\right] = \sum_{g} [V_g \exp(-i\alpha_g)]$$

$$\times \exp(2\pi i g \cdot \mathbf{r}) \tag{15}$$

where $\alpha = 2\pi \mathbf{g} \cdot \mathbf{R}$. The deformation can thus be taken into account by replacing the Fourier coefficient V_g relative to the perfect crystal by $V_g \exp(-i\alpha_g)$. Since the extinction distance t_g is inversely proportional to V_g this substitution implies the following one:

$$\frac{1}{t_g} \to \frac{1}{t_g} \exp(-i\alpha_g) \tag{16}$$

and since $\alpha_{-g} = -\alpha_g$ we also have

$$\frac{1}{t_{-g}} \to \frac{1}{t_{-g}} \exp(i\alpha_g) . \tag{17}$$

The set of differential eqs. (7) can therefore easily be generalized to deformed crystals; one obtains

$$\frac{dT}{dz} + \pi i s\, T = \frac{\pi i}{t_{-g}} S\, \exp(i\alpha)$$

$$\frac{dS}{dz} - \pi i s\, S = \frac{\pi i}{t_g} T \exp(-i\alpha) \tag{18}$$

where for brevity we have noted $\alpha_g \equiv \alpha$.

The substitution

$$T = T' \exp(\pi i \alpha') \qquad\qquad S = S' \exp(-\pi i \alpha') \qquad\qquad (19)$$

reduces this set of equations to the following one:

$$\frac{dT'}{dz} + \pi i \left(s + \frac{d\alpha'}{dz} \right) T' = \frac{\pi i}{t_{-g}} S'$$

$$\frac{dS'}{dz} - \pi i \left(s + \frac{d\alpha'}{dz} \right) S' = \frac{\pi i}{t_g} T' \qquad\qquad (20)$$

where $\alpha' = \alpha/2\pi$. The effect of the deformation is clearly to replace s by some effective s-value $s + d\alpha'/dz$ which varies with z.

For a stacking fault α = constant and this set of equations reduces to that for a perfect crystal. Physically this means that the amplitudes T and S do not vary in magnitude (only in phase) for a parallel displacement of the crystal. It is therefore inconvenient to use the set of eqs. (20) in order to describe the waves scattered by a crystal which has suffered a parallel displacements.

For a domain boundary on the other hand, since $\alpha' = \mathbf{g} \cdot \mathbf{R}$ and since $\mathbf{R}$ increases linearly in length with z, $d\alpha'/dz$ is a constant. The system of eqs. (20) now shows that such a deformation field simply causes s to adopt a different value in part II: $s_2 = s_1 + k$, where s_1 is the s-value in part I of the crystal.

4. Transmission matrix for a crystal containing a planar interface

We shall now derive the transmission matrix for a crystal consisting of two parts. The second part has suffered a displacement leading to a phase shift α; moreover this part has undergone a twin shear which we shall describe by assuming different s-values s_1 and s_2 in the two crystal parts.

The transmission matrix for the first part is clearly $\mathcal{M}(z_1, s_1)$. The transmitted and scattered beams emerging from this part are now incident on the second part. Let the transmission matrix for this second part be represented by

$$\begin{pmatrix} X & U \\ Y & V \end{pmatrix} \qquad\qquad (21)$$

then we must determine the different elements of (21) using eq. (18) with $s = s_2$.

We first note that this system of equations reduces to that for a perfect crystal by means of the following substitution:

$$T' = T \qquad\qquad S' = S \exp(i\alpha) \qquad\qquad (22)$$

which does not affect the initial values. The solution for the initial values

$$\begin{pmatrix} T' \\ S' \end{pmatrix} = \begin{pmatrix} 1 \\ 0 \end{pmatrix}$$

is therefore

$$T' = T(z_2, s_2) \qquad\qquad S' = S(z_2, s_2). \qquad\qquad (23)$$

For the original system of eqs. (18) the solutions are

$$T = T(z_2, s_2) \qquad\qquad S = S(z_2, s_2) \exp(-i\alpha). \qquad\qquad (24)$$

The elements X and Y of the matrix therefore become

$$X = T(z_2, s_2) \qquad\qquad Y = S(z_2, s_2) \exp(-i\alpha). \qquad\qquad (25)$$

In order to determine U and V we look for the solution of (18) for the initial values

$$\begin{pmatrix} T \\ S \end{pmatrix}_{z=0} = \begin{pmatrix} 0 \\ 1 \end{pmatrix}.$$

We note that these initial values reduce to the previous ones if one interchanges T and S. On the other hand if one interchanges T and S and make simultaneously the substitution $\alpha \to -\alpha$ and $s \to -s$, the system of eqs. (18) remains invariant. As a result we obtain for the solution:

$$U = S(z_2, -s_2) \exp(i\alpha) \qquad\qquad V = T(z_2, -s_2). \qquad\qquad (26)$$

The complete scattering matrix therefore becomes

$$\begin{pmatrix} T_2 & S_2^{(-)} \exp(i\alpha) \\ S_2 \exp(-i\alpha) & T_2^{(-)} \end{pmatrix} \tag{27}$$

where we have introduced the following abbreviations:

$$T_2 = T(z_2, s_2) ; \quad S_2 = S(z_2, s_2) ; \quad T_2^{(-)} = T(z_2, -s_2) ; \quad S_2^{(-)} = S(z_2, -s_2) .$$

This last matrix can be written as the product of three matrices:

$$\begin{pmatrix} 1 & 0 \\ 0 & \exp(-i\alpha) \end{pmatrix} \begin{pmatrix} T_2 & S_2^{(-)} \\ S_2 & T_2^{(-)} \end{pmatrix} \begin{pmatrix} 1 & 0 \\ 0 & \exp(i\alpha) \end{pmatrix} . \tag{28}$$

If we introduce as a shorthand notation

$$\mathcal{S}(\alpha) \equiv \begin{pmatrix} 1 & 0 \\ 0 & \exp(i\alpha) \end{pmatrix} \tag{29}$$

and

$$\mathcal{M}_j \equiv \begin{pmatrix} T_j & S_j^{(-)} \\ S_j & T_j^{(-)} \end{pmatrix} \tag{30}$$

the final result can be written as:

$$\begin{pmatrix} T \\ S \end{pmatrix} = \mathcal{S}(-\alpha)\mathcal{M}_2 \, \mathcal{S}(\alpha)\mathcal{M}_1 \begin{pmatrix} 1 \\ 0 \end{pmatrix} . \tag{31}$$

It is now easy to see how this formulism can be generalized if several over-lapping interfaces are present. Let the phase angles introduced by the different interfaces and *all referred to the front part of the crystal* (part I) be repre-sented by α_j', and let the s-values in the successive parts be s_j, then we can write

$$\left(\begin{array}{c}T\\S\end{array}\right) = ...\delta(-\alpha_2')\mathcal{M}_3\,\delta(+\alpha_2')\delta(-\alpha_1')\mathcal{M}_2\,\delta(\alpha_1')\mathcal{M}_1\left(\begin{array}{c}1\\0\end{array}\right).\tag{32}$$

Noting that $\delta(\alpha_1)\delta(\alpha_2) = \delta(\alpha_1+\alpha_2)$ and introducing the angles $\alpha_j = \alpha_j' - \alpha_{j-1}'$ $(\alpha_0'=0)$ we can rewrite this as

$$\left(\begin{array}{c}T\\S\end{array}\right) = ..\mathcal{M}_3\,\delta(\alpha_2)\,\mathcal{M}_2\,\delta(\alpha_1)\mathcal{M}_1\left(\begin{array}{c}1\\0\end{array}\right)\tag{33}$$

where now the α_j represent the phase angles resulting from the *relative* displacement of two successive lamella; each lamella is always considered to be displaced with respect to the previous one.

5. The interpretation of formulae (31)

The expressions for T and S, in the case of a single interface can be given a simple physical interpretation which is represented in fig. 2. The explicit expressions are:

$$T = T_1 T_2 + S_1 S_2^{(-)} \exp{(i\alpha)}\tag{34a}$$

$$S = T_1 S_2 \exp{(-i\alpha)} + S_1 T_2^{(-)}.\tag{34b}$$

According to the first of these expressions the amplitude of the transmitted beam can be considered as resulting from the interference between the doubly transmitted beam $(T_1 T_2)$ and the doubly scattered beam $(S_1 S_2^{(-)} \exp{(i\alpha)})$. For this last beam one has to remember that for the second scattering event the beam is incident on part II in the scattered direction; this is accounted for by using $-s$ for the deviation parameter (fig. 3b). Furthermore the wave scattered by the second part suffers a phase change α as a result of the stacking fault; this introduces the factor $\exp{(i\alpha)}$.

A similar interpretation can be given to the expression for S. The two interfering beams are now (i) the beam scattered by part I and subsequently transmitted (in the scattered direction) $ST_2^{(-)}$ and (ii) the beam transmitted by part I and subsequently scattered by part II. For this last term the scattered beam

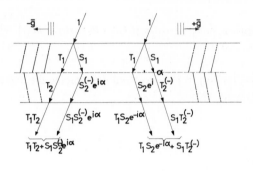

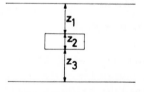

Fig. 2. Interpretation of formulae (31). The transmitted beam results from the interference between the doubly transmitted and the doubly scattered beams. The scattered beams result similarly from the interference between two beams (i) the beam scattered by part I and subsequently transmitted; (ii) the beam transmitted by part I and subsequently scattered by part II.

Fig. 3. Cavity in crystal.

suffers a phase change $-\alpha$ because scattering by part II now occurs from the other side as compared to the term $S_1 S_2^{(-)} \exp(i\alpha)$ in T.

This type of interpretation can of course be extended to the case of overlapping interfaces; the number of beams to be considered becomes rapidly large however.

6. The vacuum matrix [6]

In order to take into account the presence of certain crystal parts which are very far from a reflecting position, like e.g. in the case of a microtwin in an fcc crystal, we also need the transmission matrix for a *vacuum layer*. In such a non-reflecting part the extinction distance becomes infinite since no diffraction out of the incident, or scattered beams occurs. It is therefore sufficient to put $t_g = \infty$ in the set of eq. (7). They then become

$$\frac{dT}{dz} + \pi is\, T = 0 \; ; \qquad \frac{dS}{dz} - \pi is\, S = 0 \,. \qquad (35)$$

The two equations are now uncoupled, which simply translates the physical fact that also the two beams are uncoupled. One obtains after integration

$$T = T_0 \exp(-\pi isz) \; ; \qquad S = S_0 \exp(+\pi isz) \qquad (36)$$

where T_0 and S_0 are the amplitudes of the beams incident on the vaccum layer respectively in the transmitted and the scattered directions and s the deviation parameter in the layer preceding the vacuum layer. This relation can be written in matrix form as

$$\begin{pmatrix} T \\ S \end{pmatrix}_{\text{out}} = \begin{pmatrix} \exp(-\pi isz) & 0 \\ 0 & \exp(+\pi isz) \end{pmatrix} \begin{pmatrix} T \\ S \end{pmatrix}_{\text{in}} \qquad (37)$$

or

$$\begin{pmatrix} T \\ S \end{pmatrix}_{\text{out}} = V(z,s) \begin{pmatrix} T \\ S \end{pmatrix}_{\text{in}} \qquad (38)$$

where $V(z,s)$ is the vacuum matrix.

7. Some applications of the transmission matrix method

We shall now demonstrate how problems concerning the contrast at planar interfaces can be solved formally. A detailed analytical discussion of the fringe pattern may be difficult but at least one can write down the formal solution and in some cases one can obtain information concerning the fringe pattern without working out the details.

7.1. *Cavity* [7]

The contrast at a cavity can be treated in a straightforward manner. Let the geometry be as presented in fig. 3. The transmitted and scattered amplitudes are then given by:

$$\begin{pmatrix} T \\ S \end{pmatrix} = \mathcal{M}_3 \ V(z_2; s_1) \mathcal{M}_1 \begin{pmatrix} 1 \\ 0 \end{pmatrix}. \tag{39}$$

Since a cavity causes no normal absorption it is clear that the influence of normal absorption on the contrast must now be taken into account also. A detailed discussion is given in ref. [7]. Fig. 4 demonstrates clearly that the

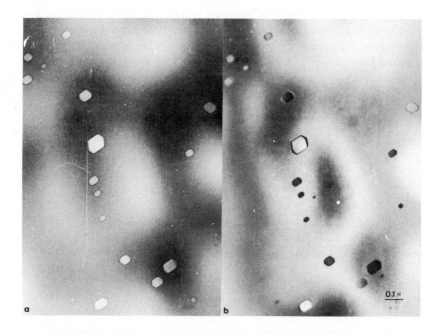

Fig. 4. Two images of the same cavity under different contrast conditions demonstrating that the contrast must, at least partly, be diffraction contrast (ref. [7]).

contrast cannot be normal absorption contrast only. This figure shows the same area for two different s-values; certain cavities show up brighter than the background in one photograph and darker in the other, which must obviously be due to diffraction contrast.

7.2. Overlapping π-faults

Using the matrix method we shall demonstrate a simple property of the fringes due to the overlap of the two stacking faults which both case a phase shift π; in other words $\alpha_1 = \alpha_2 = \pi$ [8]. We shall prove that for $s = 0$ the region of overlap always has a uniform shade, whatever the distance between the faults. We first note that quite generally $S^{(-)} = S$ and that moreover for $s = 0$, $T^{(-)} = T$. The transmitted and scattered amplitudes are then given by:

$$\begin{pmatrix} T \\ S \end{pmatrix} = \begin{pmatrix} T_3 & S_3 \\ S_3 & T_3 \end{pmatrix} \begin{pmatrix} 1 & 0 \\ 0 & \exp(i\pi) \end{pmatrix} \begin{pmatrix} T_2 & S_2 \\ S_2 & T_2 \end{pmatrix} \begin{pmatrix} 1 & 0 \\ 0 & \exp(i\pi) \end{pmatrix}$$

$$\begin{pmatrix} T_1 & S_1 \\ S_1 & T_1 \end{pmatrix} \begin{pmatrix} 1 \\ 0 \end{pmatrix} = \begin{pmatrix} T_3 & S_3 \\ S_3 & T_3 \end{pmatrix} \begin{pmatrix} T_2 & -S_2 \\ -S_2 & T_2 \end{pmatrix} \begin{pmatrix} T_1 & S_1 \\ S_1 & T_1 \end{pmatrix} \begin{pmatrix} 1 \\ 0 \end{pmatrix}$$

$$= \mathcal{M}(z_3,0)\mathcal{M}(-z_2,0)\mathcal{M}(z_1,0) \begin{pmatrix} 1 \\ 0 \end{pmatrix} = \mathcal{M}(z_1+z_3-z_2,0) \begin{pmatrix} 1 \\ 0 \end{pmatrix}$$

$$= \mathcal{M}(z_0-2z_2,0) \begin{pmatrix} 1 \\ 0 \end{pmatrix} \tag{40}$$

where the total thickness $z_0 = z_1 + z_2 + z_3$. Since z_0 and z_1 are constants, the difference $z_0 - 2z_1$ is constant too and therefore the amplitudes will not depend on the variables z_1 (or z_3), i.e. the contrast is uniform in the regions of overlap. The intensity is in fact the same as that due to a perfect crystal of thickness $z_0 - 2z_2$ (and for $s = 0$). Fig. 5 shows an example of overlapping π-faults in titanium dioxide.

7.3. Overlapping domain boundaries [9,10]

The fringe pattern due to a single domain wall shall be discussed below in some detail. However, it is easy to see that the pattern must be asymmetrical in the BF. This is obvious if one notes that

Fig. 5. Overlapping system of π fringes; note that there is no fringe contrast in the region of overlap (ref. [8]).

$$T = T_1 T_2 + S_1 S_2^{(-)}$$

is not invariant with respect to an interchange of the indices 1 and 2 (note that $s_1 \neq s_2$!).

On the other hand we shall now show that overlapping domain walls, limiting one domain within a second one (fig. 6), i.e. such that $s_1 = s_3 \neq s_2$, produce a symmetrical BF fringe pattern in the region of overlap.

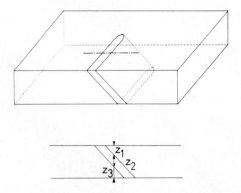

Fig. 6. Geometry of overlapping domain walls due to a single domain completely surrounded by a larger domain (a) in space, (b) in cross section.

We have essentially to show that the expression for T is invariant with respect to the substitution $z_1 \rightleftharpoons z_3$. We have

$$\begin{pmatrix} T \\ S \end{pmatrix} = \mathcal{M}_3 \mathcal{M}_2 \mathcal{M}_1 \begin{pmatrix} 1 \\ 0 \end{pmatrix} \tag{41}$$

or explicitely

$$T = T_1 T_2 T_3 + S_1 S_{\bar{2}} S_3 + S_2 S_{\bar{3}} T_1 + S_1 S_{\bar{3}} T_{\bar{2}} . \tag{42}$$

Noting that $S = S^-$ it is clear that interchanging the indices 1 and 3 does not change T; this operation does change S however; S has the property

$$S(z_1, z_3, s_1, s_2, s_3) = S(z_3, z_1, -s_1, -s_2, -s_3) .$$

Fig. 7 shows overlapping domain walls in barium titanate.

7.4. Microtwin in a fcc crystal [11]

For an fcc crystal twin and matrix are either simultaneously in a reflecting position with the same s-value, or one crystal part reflects, the other being far from any reflecting position. Only the latter situation is of interest and will be discussed. The geometry is shown in fig. 8; both crystal parts on either side of the twin lamella reflect, but the twin lamella itself is far from any reflecting

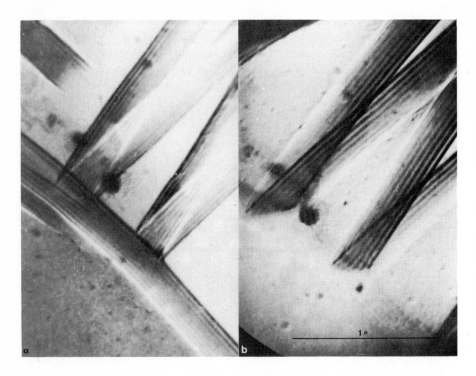

Fig. 7. Overlapping domain walls in barium titanate. One of the domain walls is out of contrast in (b). Note that the region of overlap is bright in (a) and dark in (b) (ref. [11]).

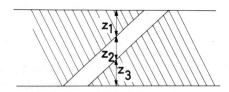

Fig. 8. Geometry of a microtwin in an fcc crystal. The cross-hatched parts are in reflecting position.

position. Depending on the exact number of close packed (111) planes within the twin lamella, the phase difference introduced by the twin lamella may be either 0, or $\pm 2\pi/3$. Furthermore, the layer of vertical thickness z_2 constitutes a vacuum layer. The amplitudes of transmitted and scattered beams can therefore be found by the following matrix multiplication

$$\begin{pmatrix} T \\ S \exp(i\alpha) \end{pmatrix} = \mathcal{M}_2 \, V(z_2) \mathcal{S} \mathcal{M}_1 \begin{pmatrix} 1 \\ 0 \end{pmatrix} \tag{43}$$

where the order of multiplication of V and $\mathcal{S}$ may be interchanged since it is not determined unambigeously by the physical situation; the multiplication of diagonal matrices is commutative anyway. V and $\mathcal{S}$ are explicitly given by

$$V = \begin{pmatrix} \exp(-\pi i s z_2) & 0 \\ 0 & \exp(+\pi i s z_2) \end{pmatrix} \quad \mathcal{S} = \begin{pmatrix} 1 & 0 \\ 0 & \exp(i\alpha) \end{pmatrix}. \tag{44}$$

On multiplying out $V\mathcal{S}$ (43) can be written as

$$\begin{pmatrix} T \\ S \end{pmatrix} = \mathcal{M}_2 \begin{pmatrix} 1 & 0 \\ 0 & \exp(i\beta) \end{pmatrix} \mathcal{M}_1 \begin{pmatrix} 1 \\ 0 \end{pmatrix} \tag{45}$$

with $\beta = \alpha + 2\pi i s z_2$ (we have left out a phase factor which does not influence the intensities). It thus becomes clear that the contrast will be the same as that due to a stacking fault, except that now the phase angle (β) becomes s-dependent.

Furthermore it should be noted that the thickness which matters for anomalous absorption is $z_1 + z_3$ whereas the thickness that causes normal absorption is $z_1 + z_2 + z_3 = z_0$.

Fig. 9 shows the contrast effects at a twin in TiO_2; the same area is shown under different contrast situations [12].

Similar contrast effects occur at thin lamella of one phase included within a second phase in such a way that one of the phases only is reflecting. An example is shown in fig. 10 which represents a thin lamella of wurtzite within a sphalerite matrix. The overlap region exhibits stacking fault like fringes [13].

7.5. Moiré pattern due to a vacuum wedge

Consider the transmission through two plane parallel plate-like crystals

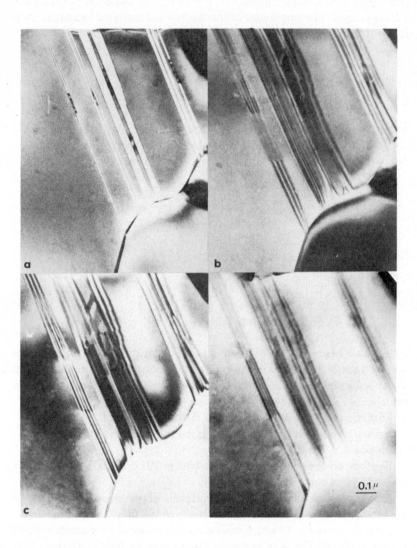

Fig. 9. Contrast effects at twins in TiO_2; the same area is shown under different contrast conditions. Note the strong orientation dependence of the fringe pattern (see ref. [12]).

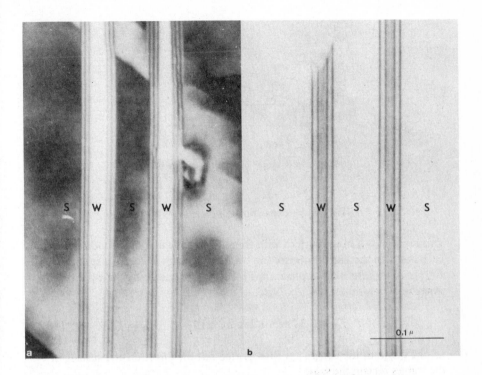

Fig. 10. Fringes due to a thin lamella of wurtzite within a sphalerite matrix. (a) non-overlapping, (b) overlapping (see ref. [20]).

which are slightly inclined one with respect to the other, so as to leave a vacuum gap of vertical thickness $z_2 = x$ tg α where x is measured along the normal to the line of intersection of the two plates (fig. 11). One now finds:

$$
\begin{pmatrix} T \\ S \end{pmatrix} = \mathcal{M}_2 \begin{pmatrix} \exp(-\pi i s_1 z_2) & 0 \\ 0 & \exp(\pi i s_1 z_2) \end{pmatrix} \mathcal{M}_1 \begin{pmatrix} 1 \\ 0 \end{pmatrix}
$$

$$
= \exp(-\pi i s_1 z_2) \mathcal{M}_2 \begin{pmatrix} 1 & 0 \\ 0 & \exp(2\pi i s_1 z_2) \end{pmatrix} \mathcal{M}_1 \begin{pmatrix} 1 \\ 0 \end{pmatrix} \quad (46)
$$

or explicitly, leaving out a phase factor which does not affect the intensity:

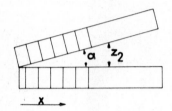

Fig. 11. Vacuum wedge producing a moiré pattern.

$$T = T_1 T_2 + S_1 S_2 \exp(2\pi i s_1 ax) \; ; \qquad a = \mathrm{tg}\,\alpha . \qquad (47)$$

This represents a fringe pattern with fringes perpendicular to the x-direction, i.e. parallel to the line of intersection of the two plates and with a spacing $x = 1/s_1 a$. If there is also a phase shift for waves diffracted by the two crystal plates one obtains:

$$T = T_1 T_2 + S_1 S_2 \exp[i(2\pi s_1 ax + \varphi)] \qquad (48)$$

i.e. the origin of the fringes has been shifted but the direction and spacing of the fringes remain the same.

8. Fringe profiles [14]

The relations (34) are in fact expressions for the amplitudes T and S. The intensities are of course obtained by multiplying with the complex conjugate

$$I_T = TT^* \; ; \qquad I_S = SS^* .$$

These expressions are rather complicated and cannot easily be discussed analytically, especially since σ is complex as a result of anomalous absorption. An analytical discussion for the general case has nevertheless been given in ref. [14].

In these notes we shall limit ourselves to summarizing the results for the two extreme cases:

(i) $\alpha \neq 0$; $s_1 = s_2$ (i.e. $\delta = 0$)

(ii) $\alpha = 0$; $s_1 t_{1g} - s_2 t_{2g} \equiv \delta \neq 0$.

The fringe patterns are characteristically different in these two cases; this allows sometimes to derive geometrical features of the interfaces responsible for the fringe pattern.

8.1. α-fringes

This name is given to fringes for which $\alpha \neq 0$ but $s_1 = s_2$. Stacking faults and anti-phase boundaries are for instance imaged as α-fringes [15] .

The symmetry properties can be derived without a detailed calculation. The expressions for T being invariant when interchanging the indices 1 and 2 (i.e. z_1 and z_2) one can conclude that the BF pattern must be symmetrical with respect to the foil centre. The dark field (DF) image, described by S, has the following property

$$I_S(z_1, z_2, s, \alpha) = I_S(z_2, z_1, -s, -\alpha) \ . \tag{49}$$

This can easily be verified on the expression (34b).

We shall limit our analytical discussion to the simple case $s = 0$. The transmitted and scattered intensities can then be written (ref. [14]) as the sum of three terms

$$I_{T,S} = I_{T,S}^{(1)} + I_{T,S}^{(2)} + I_{T,S}^{(3)}$$

with

$$I_{T,S}^{(1)} = \tfrac{1}{2} \cos^2 (\alpha/2) \ [\cosh 2\pi\sigma_i z_0 \pm \cos 2\pi\sigma_r z_0]$$

$$I_{T,S}^{(2)} = \tfrac{1}{2} \sin^2 (\alpha/2) \ [\cosh 4\pi\sigma_i u \pm \cos 4\pi\sigma_r u]$$

$$I_{T,S}^{(3)} = \tfrac{1}{2} \sin \alpha \ [\sin (2\pi\sigma_r z_1) \sinh 2\pi\sigma_i z_2 \pm \sin 2\pi\sigma_r z_2 \sinh 2\pi\sigma_i z_1] \ . $$

$$\tag{50}$$

The upper sign corresponds to I_T, the lower to I_S. z_0 is the total thickness, whereas $2u = z_1 - z_2$ (i.e. u represents the distance of the interface from the foil centre).

The first terms $I_{T,S}^{(1)}$ only depend on the sum $z_0 = z_1 + z_2$; therefore they cannot represent the stacking fault fringes. They contain a steadily increasing term and a periodic part. For $\alpha = 0$ the first terms are the only remaining ones. They represent therefore a property of the perfect crystal; they describe the extinction contours of the perfect crystal.

The second terms contain an aperiodic part and a periodic part with depth period $\frac{1}{2}\, t_g$. The aperiodic part represents the background which is a minimum in the centre of the foil ($u=0$). The periodic term represents fringes of which the position is determined by u; these fringes are therefore parallel to the central line (fig. 12, top). The relative importance of this contribution will be largest for $\alpha = \pi$; since then $\sin\alpha/2 = 1$. In the BF image the central fringe is bright, whereas it is dark in the DF image.

To contributions $I_{T,S}^{(3)}$ each consist of two terms:

$$\sinh 2\pi\sigma_i z_2 \,\sin 2\pi\sigma_r z_1$$

and

$$\sinh 2\pi\sigma_i z_1 \,\sin 2\pi\sigma_r z_2 \;.$$

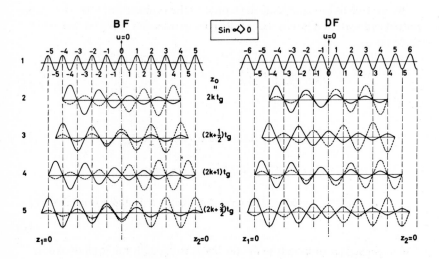

Fig. 12. Schematic representation of the contributions due to the terms $I_{T,S}^{(2)}$ and $I_{T,S}^{(3)}$ for different thicknesses in the case of pure a-fringes ($\sin a > 0$).

The first term is large at the entrance face where z_2 has its maximum value z_0. It is represented by a damped sinusoid which disappears at the back surface where $z_2 = 0$ (fig. 12). The second term on the other hand is largest at the back surface where z_1 is largest; it is also represented by a damped sinusoid which now becomes zero at the front surface (fig. 12).

The terms represent fringes parallel to the closest surface; the depth period is t_g. The general shape of the fringe system will adequately be described by this third contribution alone under the condition that

$$\sin \alpha \sinh 2\pi\sigma_i z_0 \gg \sin^2 \alpha/2$$

i.e. if the following inequality is satisfied

$$2 \sinh 2\pi\sigma_i z_0 \gg \operatorname{tg} \alpha/2 .$$

A foil which has a thickness z_0 such as to satisfy this inequality will be called thick. We conclude that in *thick* foils the fringe pattern is adequately described by $I_{T,S}^{(3)}$. It is clear that this "ad hoc" definition leads to a lower limit for thick foils depending on α; in particular if $\alpha = \pi$ a foil can never be thick. The case $\alpha = \pi$ is therefore a singular one which has to be treated seperately.

In thick foils (for $\alpha \neq \pi$) the fringe characteristics can now easily be deduced since the only term to be discussed is $I_{T,S}^{(3)}$. It is represented schematically in fig. 12 for the case $\sin \alpha > 0$; it is clear that in the BF image represented by I_T the two outer fringes are bright whereas in the DF image, represented by I_S the first fringe is bright and the last one is dark. The fringes are opposite in nature for $\sin \alpha < 0$. The results for thick foils are summarized in table 1.

Table 1

	BF		DF	
	F	L	F	L
$\sin \alpha > 0$	B	B	B	D
$\sin \alpha < 0$	D	D	D	B

Close to the foil centre the two parts of the contribution $I^{(3)}_{T,S}$ may either reinforce one another, or they may partly cancel one another depending on the exact thickness. For z_0 equal to an integer number of extinction distances the two terms cancel partly (fig. 12) and now the contributions for $I^{(2)}_{T,S}$ may lead to visible effects. This means that in the central part fringes with a depth spacing of $t_g/2$ may become visible. This is unlikely to be the case if the total thickness is an integral number $\pm\, t_g/2$ thick (fig. 12).

The superposition of the two terms $I^{(2)}_{T,S}$ and $I^{(3)}_{T,S}$ may thus lead to complications in the central part of the fringe pattern (fig. 14).

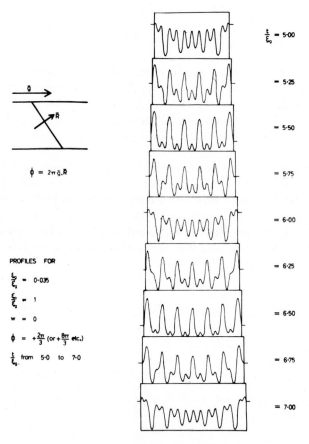

Fig. 13. (a) Fringe profiles for stacking faults with varying thickness (s=0). (After Booker.)

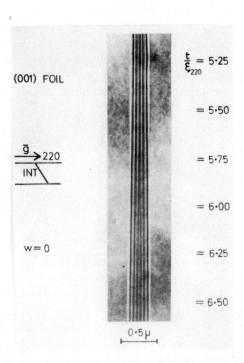

(001) FOIL

$\dfrac{t}{\xi_{220}}$ = 5·25

= 5·50

$\overline{g}$ →220

INT

= 5·75

= 6·00

w = 0

= 6·25

= 6·50

0·5 μ

Fig. 13. (b) Stacking fault fringes in silicon which can be compared with (a) (after Booker).

Fig. 13a shows fringe systems due to a stacking fault with $\alpha = 3\pi/2$ which can be compared directly with the photograph of fig. 13b. The experimental fringe patterns are adequately described by the theory. Fig. 14 shows that in a thick foil the outer fringes are consistently of the same type independently of the thickness.

For $\alpha = \pi$ ($s=0$) the pattern is completely described by $I^{(2)}_{T,S}$, i.e.

$$I_{T,S} = \tfrac{1}{2}\left(\cosh 4\pi\sigma_i u \pm \cos 4\pi\sigma_r u\right) \tag{51}$$

with $\sigma_r = 1/t_g$. From this expression one can deduce the following properties of π-fringes:

(i) Bright and dark field images are complementary with respect to the background given by

$$\tfrac{1}{2}\cosh 4\pi\sigma_i u .$$

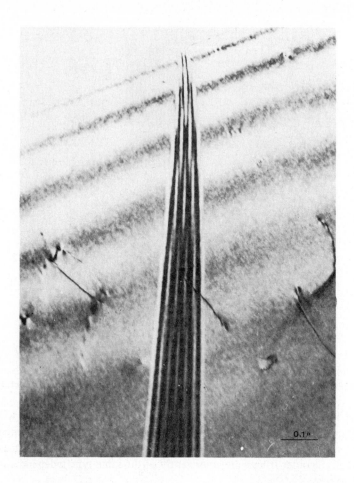

Fig. 14. Stacking fault fringes in foils with varying thickness and for which $a = 2\pi/3$.
Note that for a sufficient large thickness the outer fringes are consistently bright.

(ii) The central fringe is bright in the BF image and dark in the DF image.
(iii) The fringes are parallel to the foil centre; their depth spacing is $t_g/2$.
(iv) In foils of increasing thickness new fringes are generated at the surfaces.
For every thickness extinction contour two new fringes are generated.

Fig. 15, 16 and 17 show these features which allow to identify fringes due
to $\alpha = \pi$; such an identification may help in determining the displacement
vector **R** of the interface.

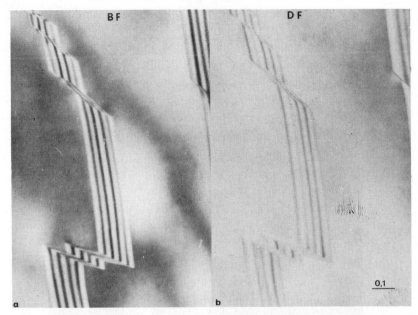

Fig. 15. Illustrating the characteristic features of fringes for which $a = \pi$. (a) BF, the central fringe is bright. (b) DF; the central fringe is dark. BF and DF are complementary (ref. [8]).

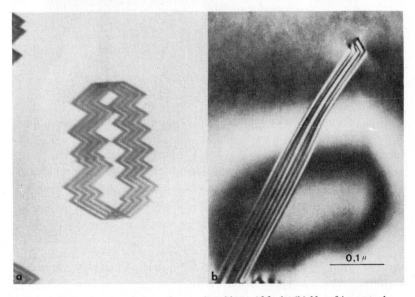

Fig. 16. (a) Fringes are continuous along a closed loop of fault; (b) New fringes are born at the surface with varying thickness (ref. [8]).

Fig. 17. With every thickness fringe two stacking fault fringes are born (ref. [8]).

8.2. *Use of the fringe patterns*

The displacement vector $\mathbf{R}$ may be determined by looking for reflections for which the fringes disappear, i.e. for which α is equal to zero or to an integral number of 2π. This leads to a set of equations of the form

$$h_i u + k_i v + l_i w = \text{integer}$$

where $(a^{-1})[h_i k_i l_i]$ represents $\mathbf{g}$ whereas $\mathbf{R} = a[uvw]$. Usually the system of equations has not a unique solution [16].

Extrinsic and intrinsic stacking faults in fcc crystals have displacement

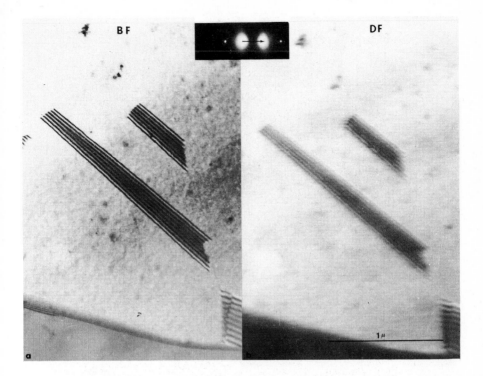

Fig. 18. Intrinsic stacking fault in alloy with low stacking fault energy. Bright and dark field images (ref. [18]).

vectors of the type $\pm \frac{1}{3} a$ [111] and of opposite sign and therefore they give rise, for the same sense of inclination of the fault plane, to outer fringes of opposite nature. It is therefore in principle possible to distinguish between intrinsic and extrinsic stacking faults from a study of the nature of the outer fringes [17,18]. A practical method was worked out in ref. [18]. The procedure is summarized in the contribution of Prof. Whelan and will therefore not be discussed here. Only a dark field image is required. From fig. 18 can for instance be deduced that the fault is intrinsic.

In hcp crystals single and double faults can be distinguished by means of the following rule [19]. Make two images using reflections with $h + k$ values of the same type, i.e. both with $h + k = 3n$, $h + k = 3n + 1$ or $h + k = 3n - 1$, but with l values of different parity, i.e. one with l = even and the other with l = odd. If the nature of the outer fringes is different in the two images the fault is single; if it is the same the fault is double. An example is shown in fig. 19, which refers to wurtzite [20].

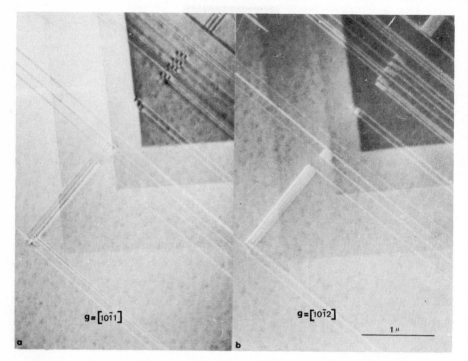

Fig. 19. Two different images of faults in wurtzite. From the change of the nature of the outer fringes as l changes from odd to even we can conclude that the faults are single.(ref. [20]).

8.3. δ-fringes [21–23]

Again we shall only consider a specially simple case, the general one is treated in ref. [14]. We shall assume that $s_1 = -s_2 = s$ this is the so-called *symmetrical* orientation. We shall furthermore assume that the foil is sufficiently thick so that the general aspect of the fringe system is adequately described by the terms $I_{T,S}^{(3)}$ which are now:

$$w^4 I_T^{(3)} = -\tfrac{1}{2} \delta \ \{\cos 2u_{1r} \sinh [2(u_{2i}-\phi) - \cos 2u_{2r} \sinh [2(u_{1i}+\phi)] \}$$
(52a)

$$w^4 I_S^{(3)} = -\tfrac{1}{2} \delta \ \{\cos 2u_{1r} \sinh [2(u_{2i}+\phi) + \cos 2u_{2r} \sinh [2(u_{1i}+\phi)] \}$$
(52b)

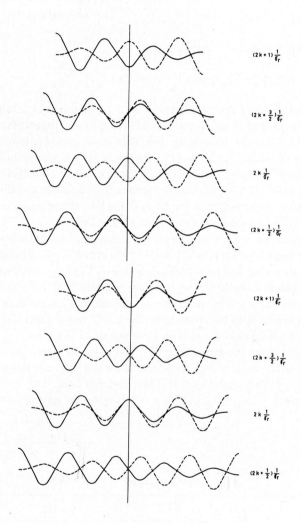

Fig. 20. Intensity profiles of δ-fringes in thick foils (a) BF; (b) DF.

where

$$u_{1r} = \pi\sigma_{1r}z_1 ; \qquad u_{2r} = \pi\sigma_{2r}z_2 ; \qquad 2\phi = \text{argsinh}\,(st_g) ;$$

$$u_{1i} = \pi\sigma_{1i}z_1 \qquad u_{2i} = \pi\sigma_{2i}z_2 ;$$

$$\delta = s_1 t_{g1} - s_2 t_{g2} ; \qquad w^2 = 1 + (st_g)^2 .$$

The general aspect of the fringe pattern for $\delta > 0$ is represented in fig. 20. The fringes are parallel to the closest surface. Close to the front surface the first terms of $I_{T,S}^{(3)}$ are the dominating ones; their depth period is $1/\sigma_{1r}$. The two terms are "in phase" in $I_T^{(3)}$ and $I_S^{(3)}$ the fringe pattern is therefore similar close to the front surface and the nature of the first fringe is therefore the same in BF and DF. If $\delta > 0$ the first extremum is a maximum and therefore the first fringe is bright as well in the BF as in the DF. The opposite is true if $\delta < 0$; the first fringes are therefore dark in BF and DF.

Close to the surface the second terms of $I_T^{(3)}$ dominate the behaviour of the fringes; their pseudo-period is now $1/\sigma_{2i}$. For the symmetrical orientation $\sigma_{1r} = \sigma_{2r}$. Since the second terms differ in sign in $I_T^{(3)}$ and $I_S^{(3)}$ the fringe patterns will be pseudo-complementary in bright and dark field. If $\delta > 0$ the last fringe in the BF image will be dark, whereas the last fringe in the dark field image will be bright. Also the character of the last fringes changes if $\delta < 0$. The main characteristics of the pattern are summarized in table 2.

It is also clear from the expression (52a) that in the BF image the contrast will be better at the back surface for $\phi > 0$, whereas it will be better at the front surface for $\phi < 0$. This results from that fact that sinh $[2(u_{2i}-\phi)] <$ $< \sinh [2(u_{1i}+\phi)]$ for $u_{1i} = u_{2i}$ and for $\phi > 0$; whereas the reverse is true for $\phi < 0$.

Table 2
Nature of fringes.

	BF		DF	
	F	L	F	L
$\delta > 0$	B	D	B	B
$\delta < 0$	D	B	D	D

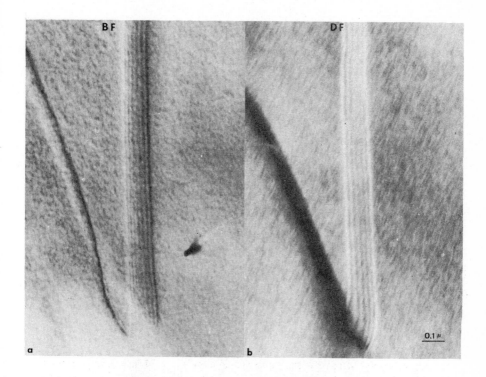

Fig. 21. δ-fringes observed at domain boundaries in niobium suboxide. Note the nature
of the outer fringes in BF and DF (ref. [23]).

Fig. 21 represents fringes observed at domain walls in niobium suboxide
[24]. The characteristics of the bright and dark field images can clearly be
verified. Fig. 22 shows ferroelectric domain walls in barium titanate [25]
whereas fig. 23 represents antiferromagnetic domain walls in nickel oxide
[26].

δ-type fringes can also be produced at the interface between matrix and
precipitate [27] as well as at the interface between two different phases, e.g.
cubic and hexagonal within the same matrix [28].

The extinction criterion for δ-fringe patterns is that $\Delta g \equiv g_2 - g_1 = 0$. For
such a reflection $\Delta s = s_1 - s_2$, which is the component of $\overline{\Delta g}$ in the beam
direction, disappears. For a coherent twin extinction occurs for diffraction

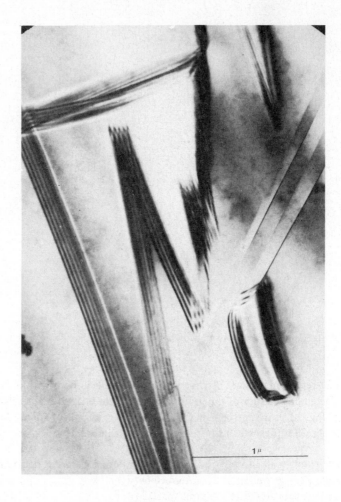

Fig. 22. Fringe patterns due to ferroelectric domain walls in barium titanate (ref. [23]).

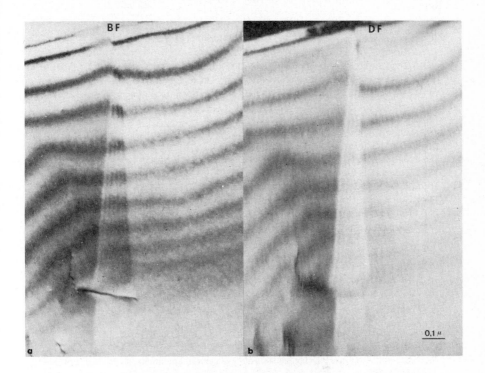

Fig. 23. Fringe patterns due to antiferromagnetic domain walls in nickeloxide (ref. [23]).

against lattice planes which are either parallel or common in both parts of the twin. Since the displacement field now consists of parallel vectors this can also be expressed by means of the condition $\mathbf{g} \cdot \mathbf{R} = 0$.

At certain interfaces as well α and δ differ from zero; one then observes fringes which have characteristics intermediate between those of pure α and pure δ fringes [14].

I wish to thank Drs. Delavignette, Van Landuyt, Remaut, Booker, Blank, Secco d'Aragona and Art for the use of photographs.

References

[1] A.Howie and M.J.Whelan, Proc. Roy. Soc. A263 (1961) 217; A267 (1962) 206.
[2] R.Gevers, Phys. Stat. Sol. 3 (1963) 1672.
[3] R.Gevers, in: The interaction of radiation with solids, eds. R.Strumane, J.Nihoul,
     R.Gevers and S.Amelinckx (North-Holland, Amsterdam, 1964) p. 471.
[4] S.Amelinckx, International Conference on Electron Diffraction and Crystal Defects
     (Melbourne, 1965) p. J-1.
[5] H.Yoshioka, J. Phys. Soc. Japan 12 (1957) 618.
[6] R.Gevers, Phys. Stat. Sol. 9 (1965) 135.
[7] J.Van Landuyt, R.Gevers and S.Amelinckx, Phys. Stat. Sol. 10 (1965) 319.
[8] J.Van Landuyt, R.Gevers and S.Amelinckx, Phys. Stat. Sol. 7 (1964) 519.
[9] G.Remaut, R.Gevers, A.Lagasse and S.Amelinckx, Phys. Stat. Sol. 10 (1965) 121.
[10] G.Remaut, A.Lagasse and S.Amelinckx, Phys. Stat. Sol. 7 (1964) 497.
[11] G.Remaut, R.Gevers, A.Lagasse and S.Amelinckx, Phys. Stat. Sol. 13 (1966) 125.
[12] J.Van Landuyt, R.Gevers and S.Amelinckx, Phys. Stat. Sol. 9 (1965) 135.
[13] F.Secco d'Aragona, P.Delavignette, R.Gevers and S.Amelinckx, Phys. Stat. Sol. 31
     (1969) 739.
[14] R.Gevers, J.Van Landuyt and S.Amelinckx, Phys. Stat. Sol. 11 (1965) 689.
[15] S.Amelinckx, Proc. International Conference on Electron Diffraction and Crystal
     Defects (Melbourne, 1965) p. J-1.
[16] J.Van Landuyt, Phys. Stat. Sol. 16 (1966) 585.
[17] H.Hashimoto, A.Howie and M.J.Whelan, Proc. Roy. Soc. A269 (1962) 80.
[18] A.Art, R.Gevers and S.Amelinckx, Phys. Stat. Sol. 3 (1963) 697;
     R.Gevers, A.Art and S.Amelinckx, Phys. Stat. Sol. 3 (1963) 1563.
[19] H.Blank, P.Delavignette, R.Gevers and S.Amelinckx, Phys. Stat. Sol. 7 (1964) 774.
[20] F.Secco d'Aragona, P.Delavignette, R.Gevers and S.Amelinckx, Phys. Stat. Sol. 31
     (1969) 739.
[21] R.Gevers, P.Delavignette, H.Blank and S.Amelinckx, Phys. Stat. Sol. 4 (1964) 383.
[22] R.Gevers, P.Delavignette, H.Blank, J.Van Landuyt and S.Amelinckx, Phys. Stat.
     Sol. 5 (1964) 595.
[23] J.Van Landuyt, R.Gevers and S.Amelinckx, Phys. Stat. Sol. 9 (1965) 135.
[24] J.Van Landuyt, R.Gevers and S.Amelinckx, Phys. Stat. Sol. 13 (1966) 467.
[25] H.Blank and S.Amelinckx, Appl. Phys. Letters 2 (1963) 140.
[26] P.Delavignette and S.Amelinckx, Appl. Phys. Letters 2 (1963) 236;
     P.Delavignette, R.Gevers and S.Amelinckx, Electron Microscopy 1964, Proc. 3rd
     European Regional Conference on Electron Microscopy, ed. M.Titlbach (Publishing
     House of the Czechoslovak Academy of Sciences, Prague, 1964) p. 259.
[27] A.J.Ardell, Phil. Mag. 16 (1967) 147.
[28] A.Fourdeux, R.Gevers and S.Amelinckx, Phys. Stat. Sol. 24 (1967) 195.

THE THEORY OF
HIGH ENERGY ELECTRON DIFFRACTION

A. HOWIE

Cavendish Laboratory, Cambridge, UK

1. Introduction

The dynamical theory of diffraction of high energy electrons in crystals can be developed in a number of ways. In earlier lectures Dr. Whelan showed how the two beam dynamical theory could be built up by considering single Bragg reflection events in successive slices of the crystal. This approach is quite similar to the first formulation of dynamical diffraction in the X-ray case due to Darwin [1] and has the advantage that the physical processes involved are made clear together with the relationship between the dynamical theory and the kinematical theory. In the following lectures an alternative, rather more formal approach, will be followed which is better suited to the problem of extending the theory to take account of several simultaneous Bragg reflections and also of the effects of inelastic scattering. This approach, which is based on the solutions of the Schrödinger wave equation in a periodic potential, was first employed in electron diffraction by Bethe [2] but bears some resemblance to the X-ray dynamical theories of Ewald and of Laue. It is also closely related to the so-called almost free electron approximation which has been extensively used to describe the properties of conduction electrons in metals. Before any of these applications arose however a good deal of the basic mathematics had already been worked out by nineteenth century mathematicians notably Floquet.

2. Dynamical diffraction in perfect crystals

2.1. *Derivation of the basic equations of dynamical theory*
We start from the Schrödinger wave equation which describes the steady state wave function $\psi(\mathbf{r})$ of an electron of energy eE moving in a potential $V(\mathbf{r})$.

$$\nabla^2 \psi(\mathbf{r}) + (8\pi^2 me/h^2)\{E + V(\mathbf{r})\}\psi(\mathbf{r}) = 0 . \tag{1}$$

This equation can be used to describe the diffraction of fast electrons in crystals provided that E and m are related to the accelerating potential E_0 and electron rest mass m_0 by the relativistic equations

$$m = \frac{m_0}{\sqrt{1 - v^2/c^2}} = m_0 (1 + eE_0/m_0 c^2) \tag{2}$$

$$E = E_0 \frac{1 + \frac{1}{2} eE_0/m_0 c^2}{1 + eE_0/m_0 c^2} . \tag{3}$$

The term $(eE_0)/(m_0 c^2)$ has the value $1.9576 \times 10^{-6} E_0$ when E_0 is measured in volts so that the corrections are important only for accelerating potentials above 100 keV.

Using the result

$$\nabla^2 \exp(2\pi i \boldsymbol{\chi} \cdot \mathbf{r}) = -4\pi^2 \chi^2 \exp(2\pi i \boldsymbol{\chi} \cdot \mathbf{r}) \tag{4}$$

we see that in the case of propagation in a vacuum ($V(\mathbf{r}) = 0$) eq. (1) has plane wave solutions with a wavelength λ given by

$$\lambda = \chi^{-1} = \frac{h}{\{2m_0 eE_0 (1 + eE_0/2m_0 c^2)\}^{1/2}} . \tag{5}$$

The variation of these and some other parameters of interest in electron diffraction is given for various accelerating voltages E_0 in table 1.

A suitable expression for the periodic potential $V(\mathbf{r})$ can be taken in the form

$$V(\mathbf{r}) = \frac{h^2}{2me} \sum_g U_g \exp(2\pi i \mathbf{g} \cdot \mathbf{r}) = \sum_g V_g \exp(2\pi i \mathbf{g} \cdot \mathbf{r}) . \tag{6}$$

Table 1

Variation of electron mass m_0, wavelength λ, velocity v and related quantities as a function of accelerating voltage E_0.

E_0 (kV)	λ (Å)	$\chi = \lambda^{-1}$ (Å^{-1})	$\dfrac{m}{m_0}$	$\dfrac{m_{100}}{m}$	$\dfrac{v}{c}$	$\dfrac{v}{v_{100}}$	$\left(\dfrac{v}{c}\right)^2$
20	0.0859	11.64	1.0391	1.151	0.2719	0.4959	0.07391
40	0.0602	16.62	1.0783	1.109	0.3741	0.6823	0.1399
60	0.0487	20.55	1.1174	1.070	0.4462	0.8139	0.1991
80	0.0418	23.95	1.1566	1.034	0.5024	0.9164	0.2524
100	0.0370	27.02	1.1957	1.000	0.5482	1.000	0.3005
200	0.0251	39.87	1.3914	0.8594	0.6953	1.268	0.4835
300	0.0197	50.80	1.5871	0.7534	0.7765	1.416	0.6030
500	0.0142	70.36	1.9785	0.6044	0.8629	1.574	0.7445
700	0.0113	88.56	2.3698	0.5045	0.9066	1.654	0.8219
1000	0.0087	114.7	2.9569	0.4044	0.9411	1.717	0.8856
2000	0.0050	198.3	4.9138	0.2433	0.9791	1.786	0.9586

This is a perfectly general way of expressing a periodic potential in terms of a summation over all the vectors of the reciprocal lattice which we will label throughout as $\mathbf{g}$ or $\mathbf{g}'$. The detailed form of the potential is specified by the constants U_g or V_g (usually quoted in Å^{-2} or eV respectively). In general these are complex, but since the potential is real, $V(\mathbf{r}) = V^*(\mathbf{r})$, we have the relation

$$U_g = U_{-g}^* . \tag{7}$$

In addition, if the crystal has a centre of symmetry at the origin so that $V(\mathbf{r}) = V(-\mathbf{r})$ we can also write

$$U_g = U_{-g} = U_g^* . \tag{8}$$

Frequently where such a centre of symmetry exists this coincides with the centre of an atom where the potential energy is a minimum. In terms of the sign convention used here (with e a positive constant) the quantities U_g would then be real and usually positive.

For a crystal whose unit cell has volume V_c and contains l atoms the jth of which has position $\mathbf{r}_j$ and electron scattering amplitude

$$f_j\left(\frac{\sin\theta}{\lambda}\right)$$

the general expression for U_g is

$$U_g = \frac{m}{m_0} \frac{\exp(-M_g)}{\pi V_c} \sum_{j=1}^{l} \exp(-2\pi i g \cdot r) f_j \left(\frac{\sin\theta}{\lambda}\right) . \tag{9}$$

U_g thus increases with electron energy because of the factor (m/m_0). f_j is the atomic scattering amplitude for electrons calculated on the Born approximation and is tabulated as a function of $(\sin\theta)/\lambda = g/2$, see for instance the data due to Ibers and Vainshtein [3] (also reproduced by Thomas [4] and by Hirsch et al. [5]). More recent tables have been given by Doyle and Turner [6]. The remaining term $\exp(-M_g)$ is the well known Debye-Waller factor which takes account of the thermal vibrations of the crystal (see sect. 4.3.3). For low-order values of g this usually results in a reduction of U_g by a few percent. It must therefore be included if accurate results are required particularly when high order reflections are involved since M_g increases proportionately with g^2. Values of M_g can be found in the "international tables for X-ray crystallography".

Guided by the idea of Bragg reflection we are led to attempt to find a solution ψ for eq. (1) in the presence of the crystal potential in the form

$$\psi(r) = \sum_g C_g \exp[2\pi i(k+g)\cdot r] . \tag{10}$$

Comparison with eq. (6) for the periodic potential shows that this expression for $\psi(r)$ has the form $\exp(2\pi i k \cdot r) u_k(r)$ where $u_k(r)$ has the periodicity of the lattice. All wave functions in crystals must have this Bloch form and are therefore known as Bloch wave functions.

We now substitute our expressions (6) and (10) for $V(r)$ and $\psi(r)$ in eq. (1), using eq. (4) to evaluate the effect of ∇^2 on each separate term. We also note the result

$$V(r)\,\psi(r) = \frac{h^2}{2me} \sum_g U_g \sum_{g'} C_{g'} \exp[2\pi i(k+g+g')\cdot r]$$

$$= \frac{h^2}{2me} \sum_g \exp[2\pi i(k+g)\cdot r] \left(U_0 C_g + \sum_{g'}' U_{g'} C_{g-g'}\right) \tag{11}$$

obtained by rearranging terms in the double summation. The prime on the final summation serves to indicate that the term $g' = 0$ is excluded since it has been extracted and written explicitly. We thus obtain the result

$$\sum_g \exp\left[2\pi i(\mathbf{k}+\mathbf{g})\cdot\mathbf{r}\right]\left[(\chi^2+U_0-(\mathbf{k}+\mathbf{g})^2)\,C_g + {\sum_{g'}}'\,U_{g'}C_{g-g'}\right] = 0 .$$

(12)

Since the exponential terms associated with different reciprocal lattice vectors are independent, their coefficients can be individually equated to zero to give a set of equations (one for each reciprocal lattice vector $\mathbf{g}$).

$$[K^2 - (\mathbf{k}+\mathbf{g})^2]\,C_g + {\sum_{g'}}'\,U_{g'}C_{g-g'} = 0$$

(13)

where K^2, a constant depending essentially on the electron energy, is given by

$$K^2 = \chi^2 + U_0 .$$

(14)

The set of eqs. (13) are the basic equations of the dynamical theory. Strictly speaking they constitute an infinite set of equations in an infinite number of unknown quantities C_g (the wave amplitudes), however in practice it is usually possible to describe the wave function using a reasonable number N ($N \lesssim 100$ say) of plane wave components. We then have N simultaneous equations in N unknown quantities C_g. The condition for a non-zero solution is that the $N \times N$ determinant formed from the coefficients in the simultaneous equations (the quantities $K^2 - (\mathbf{k}+\mathbf{g})^2$, U_g, etc.) should vanish. This leads to an equation defining the so-called dispersion surface in $\mathbf{k}$ space (previously discussed by Dr. Whelan). The wave vector $\mathbf{k}$ of the Bloch wave must lie on the dispersion surface if it is to propagate in the crystal. The significance of these rather general statements about the solution of the dynamical equations will become clearer when we examine some of the simple methods of solution in the next section.

2.2. *Solution of the equations of the dynamical theory*

The dynamical eqs. (13) can be solved only if the number of beams employed is restricted to a finite number N and even then it is usually possible to obtain only a numerical solution from a computer. Before discussing the numerical method of solution however we will describe some of the analytical solutions which can be obtained in particularly simple situations.

2.2.1. Free electron theory

In this lowest approximation only one wave amplitude, C_0 say, is considered to be appreciable. The terms $U_{g'}C_{g-g'}$ occurring in eq. (13) are then regarded as second order and negligible unless $g' = g$. The equation for $g = 0$ thus reads

$$(K^2 - k^2)\, C_0 = 0\,. \tag{15}$$

The condition for a non-zero solution for C_0 thus yields the dispersion equation

$$k^2 = K^2 = \chi^2 + U_0\,. \tag{16}$$

This condition can be represented by a surface in k space, the dispersion surface, which in this case is a sphere with radius K centred on the origin. We would obtain a similar sphere centred on the reciprocal lattice point g if we took C_g to be the large term. The magnitude of k differs from the value χ which would occur in vacuo because of the mean potential term U_0 which expresses the refractive index effect of the crystal in changing the wavelength of the electron (see eq. (8) of Dr. Whelan's chapter in this volume).

A slightly improved solution incorporating the weak Bragg reflected beams can be obtained by substituting for K^2 in eq. (13) using the result (16). For $g \neq 0$ the largest term in the summation is $U_g C_0$ and in comparison the others can be ignored (provided all the other wave amplitudes remain small). We thus obtain the result

$$C_g = \frac{U_g C_0}{(\mathbf{k+g})^2 - k^2}\,. \tag{17}$$

For self consistency in the approximation we require $|C_g| \ll |C_0|$ i.e. $|(\mathbf{k+g})^2 - k^2| \gg |U_g|$. This restriction breaks down completely when $k^2 = (\mathbf{k+g})^2$ which is the condition for Bragg reflection (refer to the Ewald sphere construction). The critical condition $k^2 = (\mathbf{k+g})^2$ can be rewritten as

$$\mathbf{k \cdot g} = -g^2/2\,. \tag{18}$$

This again is a condition on the wave vector $\mathbf{k}$ which can be represented graphically by surfaces in $\mathbf{k}$ space. In this case the surface are planes called Brillouin zone boundaries and associated with each reciprocal lattice vector $\mathbf{g}$ there is a Brillouin zone boundary normal to $\mathbf{g}$ and passing mid-way between the origin and the reciprocal lattice point **g**. The exact Bragg reflection occurs where the dispersion surface cuts the zone boundary but appreciable Bragg reflection can occur for wave vectors on the dispersion surface at some distance from the boundary if U_g is large since eq. (17) shows that C_g may then no longer be negligible. In these situations an improved approximation is necessary.

2.2.2. The two-beam approximation

In this approximation it is assumed that the Bragg reflection **g** is strongly excited so that two wave amplitudes C_o and C_g are of importance. The dynamical equations for 0 and g can then be written out as

$$(K^2 - k^2)\, C_o + U_{-g} C_g = 0$$

$$U_g C_o + (K^2 - (\mathbf{k+g})^2)\, C_g = 0 . \tag{19}$$

The dispersion equation now becomes

$$\begin{vmatrix} K^2 - k^2 & U_{-g} \\ U_g & K^2 - (\mathbf{k+g})^2 \end{vmatrix} = 0 . \tag{20}$$

Once again this can be represented by a dispersion surface (shown in fig. 1). It can be seen from eq. (20) that as $U_g \to 0$ the surface degenerates into two spheres of radius K centred on 0 and **g**. We are interested in the region of Bragg reflection i.e. near the Brillouin zone boundary where the two spheres intersect. In this vicinity the effect of the Bragg reflection (represented by the U_g terms in eq. (20) causes the surface to split into the form shown in fig. 1 with two branches (1) and (2). Since in practice $K^2/|U_g| \approx 10^4$, $K^2 - k^2$ and $K^2 - (\mathbf{k+g})^2$ are very small in comparison with K^2 and eq. (20) can be rewritten as

$$(k-K)\,(|\mathbf{k+g}| - K) = U_g U_{-g}/4K^2 = |U_g|^2/4K^2 . \tag{21}$$

This shows that the dispersion surface has an approximately hyperbolic form near the zone boundary with the spheres as asymptotes. Any point D on the dispersion surface then represents a possible Bloch wave in the crystal at the energy concerned, the lines DO and DG representing the wave vectors **k** and **k + g** of the two plane wave components involved. It is customary to label these vectors with a superscript to denote the branch of the dispersion surface on which they lie viz $\mathbf{k}^{(1)}$, $\mathbf{k}^{(2)}$. Fig. 1 shows for instance that in the plane of

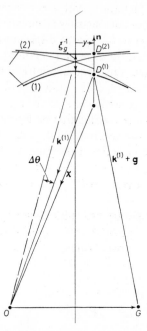

Fig. 1. The dispersion surface for high energy electrons in the two-beam approximation. χ is the incident wave vector and the waves excited in the crystal correspond to the points $D^{(1)}$ and $D^{(2)}$ with wave vectors $k^{(1)}$ and $k^{(2)}$ respectively. The minimum separation between the two wave points occurs at the reflecting position (when $y=0$ and $\Delta\theta=0$) and is equal to the reciprocal of the extinction distance ξ_g. The drawing is not to scale since in practice for 100 keV electrons, $\chi \approx 50\ g$ and $g \approx 100\ \xi_g^{-1}$. (Courtesy Royal Society [69].)

the diagram shown there will be two wave points $k^{(1)}$ and $k^{(2)}$ at any particular distance y from the zone boundary and that these differ in their z components parallel to the zone boundary. At the zone boundary itself where the difference Δk between the wave vectors is a minimum and the exact Bragg condition is fulfilled we have using eq. (21)

$$\Delta k = K \cos\theta_B / |U_g| = 1/\xi_g \tag{22}$$

where ξ_g is the extinction distance introduced by Dr. Whelan. As pointed out by him, the mechanism of the pendellösung effect in transmission diffraction can be understood in terms of an interference effect between the Bloch waves (with different wave vector components in the z direction) which are excited by the incident wave. These waves have the same components of wave vector tangential to the entrance surface as the incident wave vector χ and are found from the intersections with the dispersion surface of a line drawn through the end of the wave vector χ and in the direction $\mathbf{n}$ of the normal to the entrance surface of the crystal (see fig. 1).

The values of the wave amplitudes C_0 and C_g can be found for any wave vector $\mathbf{k}^{(j)}$ on the dispersion surface by substituting for $\mathbf{k}^{(j)}$ in either of the two eqs. (19). In particular at the Bragg reflecting position where $K^2 - k^2 = \pm |U_g|$, it can be seen that, for real and positive values of U_g, $C_0^{(2)} = C_g^{(2)}$ and $C_0^{(1)} = - C_g^{(1)}$ in agreement with the results quoted by Dr. Whelan. As an exercise it may be shown that the results of both methods for the wave amplitudes and wave vectors are in agreement for all conditions of Bragg reflection.

As in the case of the free electron approximation, the two-beam approximation can be improved somewhat by using eqs. (13) to obtain approximate expressions for the weak beams $C_{g''} \neq 0, \mathbf{g}$. We have

$$[K^2 - (\mathbf{k}+\mathbf{g}'')^2] \, C_{g''} = - \sideset{}{'}\sum_{\mathbf{g}'} U_{g'} \, C_{g''-g'}$$

$$\approx - U_{g''} \, C_0 - U_{g''-g} \, C_g \qquad (23)$$

This expression for the weak beams $C_{g''}$ in terms of the strong beams C_0 and C_g can then be used in eq. (13) to obtain improved two-beam equations.

$$(K^2 - k^2 + U_{00}) \, C_0 + U_{go} C_g = 0$$

$$U_{og} C_0 + (K^2 - (\mathbf{k}+\mathbf{g})^2 + U_{gg}) \, C_g = 0 \qquad (24)$$

where the so-called Bethe [2] potentials are given by

$$U_{00} = - \sideset{}{''}\sum_{g''} \frac{U_{g''} U_{-g''}}{K^2 - (\mathbf{K}+\mathbf{g}'')^2}$$

$$U_{gg} = - \sideset{}{''}\sum_{g''} \frac{U_{g-g''} U_{g''-g}}{K^2 - (\mathbf{K}+\mathbf{g}'')^2}$$

$$U_{og} = U_{go} = U_{-g} - \sideset{}{''}\sum_{g''} \frac{U_{g''} U_{g''-g}}{K^2 - (\mathbf{K}+\mathbf{g}'')^2} \, . \qquad (25)$$

The double prime on the summation signs indicates that the terms $g'' = 0$, g are excluded. Evidently these potentials will lead to a corrected value of the extinction distance

$$(\xi_g)_{\text{Bethe}} = K \cos \theta_{\text{B}} / |U_{og}| .$$ (26)

For the usual case when the potentials U_g are all positive it can be seen from eqs. (25) that the effect of a given weak beam is to increase or decrease the extinction distance depending on whether the associated reciprocal lattice point g'' lies inside or outside the reflecting sphere. These results have some qualitative value in assessing some of the many-beam effects which arise in practice.

2.2.3. Many-beam dynamical theory

As remarked previously, it is in general necessary to resort to numerical methods to solve the eqs. (13) of the dynamical theory. This is a fairly straight-forward process in the case of fast electrons since the reciprocal lattice vectors involved will then usually all lie in a single plane of the reciprocal lattice (the x,y plane) thus constituting a cross grating pattern. In terms of the quantities $\gamma = k_z - K_z$ used by Dr. Whelan we can then write

$$K^2 - k^2 \cong 2K(K-k) \approx -2K\gamma$$

$$K^2 - (k+g)^2 \cong 2K(K-|k+g|) \cong -2K(\gamma-s_g)$$ (27)

where as usual s_g denotes the distance in the z direction of the reciprocal lattice point g from the Ewald sphere (regarded as positive when the point lies inside the sphere). Some factors like $\cos \theta_{\text{B}}$ which are negligibly different from unity have been ignored here. Dividing throughout by $2K$ we can then recast eqs. (13) in a simple matrix form Sturkey [7], Niehrs [8], Fujimoto [9]

$$
\begin{pmatrix}
A_{oo} & A_{og} & A_{og'} & A_{og''} & \cdots \\
A_{go} & A_{gg} & A_{gg'} & A_{gg''} & \cdots \\
A_{g'o} & A_{g'g} & A_{g'g'} & A_{g'g''} & \cdots \\
A_{g''o} & A_{g''g} & A_{g''g'} & A_{g''g''} & \cdots \\
\vdots & \vdots & \vdots & \vdots
\end{pmatrix}
\begin{pmatrix}
C_o \\
C_g \\
C_{g'} \\
C_{g''} \\
\vdots
\end{pmatrix}
= \gamma
\begin{pmatrix}
C_o \\
C_g \\
C_{g'} \\
C_{g''} \\
\vdots
\end{pmatrix}
$$ (28)

where $A_{oo} = 0, A_{gg} = s_g, A_{gg'} = A_{g'g} = U_{g-g'}/2K$.

The advantage of this change is that the basic equations are now in a standard eigen value and eigen vector form. Given the matrix A whose off diagonal elements depend on the crystal potential and whose diagonal elements depend on the orientation of the incident beam, computer programmes are readily available which will calculate the N eigen values $\gamma^{(j)}$ ($j=1,2,...N$) and the associated eigen vectors ($C_o^{(j)}, C_g^{(j)}, C_{g'}^{(j)}, C_{g''}^{(j)}$ ...). These correspond to the Bloch waves excited on a dispersion surface of N sheets. By carrying out this matrix diagonalisation procedure for a series of values χ_x, χ_y of the tangential components of the incident wave vector, it is thus possible to determine the shape of the dispersion surface and the form of the Bloch wave $B(\mathbf{r})$ associated with each point on it. The generalisation of the relations used by Dr. Whelan for the Bloch waves and the total wave function $\psi(\mathbf{r})$ are thus

$$B^{(j)}(\mathbf{r}) = \sum_g C_g^{(j)} \exp\left(2\pi i(\mathbf{k}^{(j)}+\mathbf{g})\cdot\mathbf{r}\right) \tag{29}$$

$$\psi(\mathbf{r}) = \sum_g \phi_g(z) \exp\left(2\pi i(\mathbf{K}+\mathbf{g})\cdot\mathbf{r}\right) \tag{30}$$

$$= \sum_{j=1}^{N} \psi^{(j)} B^{(j)}(\mathbf{r}) . \tag{31}$$

The excitation amplitudes $\psi^{(j)}$ of the Bloch waves are determined by the boundary condition $\phi_o = 1, \phi_g = \phi_{g'} = \phi_{g''} ... = 0$ at the entrance surface $z = 0$. Using some orthogonality relations obeyed by the Bloch wave elements

$$\sum_g C_g^{(j)} C_g^{(i)} = \delta_{ij} \tag{32}$$

$$\sum_{j=1}^{N} C_g^{(j)} C_{g'}^{(j)} = \delta_{gg'} \tag{33}$$

it is easily seen that

$$\psi^{(j)} = C_o^{(j)} . \tag{34}$$

Using eqs. (29), (30) and (31) we then find

$$\phi_g(z) = \sum_{j=1}^{N} C_0^{(j)} C_g^{(j)} \exp\left(2\pi i \gamma^{(j)} z\right) . \qquad (35)$$

Hence the intensity I_g of the Bragg beam $\mathbf{g}$ is given by

$$I_g(z) = \sum_{j,j'} C_0^{(j)} C_g^{(j)} C_0^{(j')*} C_g^{(j')*} \exp\left[2\pi i (\gamma^{(j)} - \gamma^{(j')}) z\right] . \qquad (36)$$

This equation gives the intensity in usual bright-field ($\mathbf{g}=0$) or dark field ($\mathbf{g}\neq 0$) image and demonstrates the more complicated pendellösung effect which may be expected in the many-beam case due to interference between the N different Bloch waves excited.

When it is desired to observe the crystal lattice directly by electron microscopy an objective aperture which admits two or more Bragg beams must be used. The intensity of this image is then given by the expression

$$|\psi|^2 = \sum_{\mathbf{g},\mathbf{g}'} \exp\left[2\pi i(\mathbf{g}-\mathbf{g}')\cdot\mathbf{r}\right] \sum_{j,j'} C_0^{(j)} C_0^{(j')*} C_g^{(j)} C_{g'}^{(j')*}$$

$$\times \exp\left[2\pi i(\gamma^{(j)} - \gamma^{(j')}) z\right] . \qquad (37)$$

Any reciprocal lattice vectors $\mathbf{g}$ and $\mathbf{g}'$ corresponding to beams admitted by the aperture should be included in the summation. This equation shows how several different sets of lattice planes may be resolved simultaneously but the contrast and position of the fringes will depend on crystal thickness.

2.2.4. Solutions under conditions of symmetry

In orientations of particular symmetry the dynamical eqs. (13) or (28) sometimes simplify considerably so that an analytical solution can be obtained even when several Bragg reflections are excited strongly. Although these solutions are of rather restricted practical value, they give some additional insight into the operation of the general formalism just described.

As an example consider the case when the Ewald sphere passes exactly through the four reciprocal lattice points $\mathbf{g}_0 = (0,0,0)$; $\mathbf{g}_1 = (2,0,0)$, $\mathbf{g}_2 = (2,2,0)$, $\mathbf{g}_3 = (0,2,0)$. This four-beam problem is of some interest for direct lattice resolution work using tilted illumination and only two Fourier components of lattice potential are of importance $U_1 = U_{200} = U_{020}$ and $U_2 = U_{220} = U_{2\bar{2}0}$. The higher-order reflections which will certainly occur to some extent are ignored here. Using an obvious notation the dynamical eqs. (13) become

$$\begin{vmatrix} K^2-k^2 & U_1 & U_2 & U_1 \\ U_1 & K^2-k^2 & U_1 & U_2 \\ U_2 & U_1 & K^2-k^2 & U_1 \\ U_1 & U_2 & U_1 & K^2-k^2 \end{vmatrix} \begin{pmatrix} C_o \\ C_1 \\ C_2 \\ C_3 \end{pmatrix} = 0 . \tag{38}$$

The symmetry manifests itself in the equality of all the diagonal elements. Solutions for the wave elements can either simply be guessed or can be obtained by noting that the problem is invariant under a 90° rotation. This rotation must therefore multiply the Bloch wave elements only by a phase factor $\exp(i\delta)$ and can be written as

$$\begin{pmatrix} C_o \\ C_1 \\ C_2 \\ C_3 \end{pmatrix} \rightarrow \begin{pmatrix} C_1 \\ C_2 \\ C_3 \\ C_o \end{pmatrix} = \exp(i\delta) \begin{pmatrix} C_o \\ C_1 \\ C_2 \\ C_3 \end{pmatrix} . \tag{39}$$

Since application of this procedure four times restores the starting position we must have $\exp(4i\delta) = 1$ hence $\exp(i\delta) = 1, -1, \pm i$ occur as distinct cases. Normalised eigenvectors corresponding to these cases can then be written

$$\begin{pmatrix} \tfrac{1}{2} \\ \tfrac{1}{2} \\ \tfrac{1}{2} \\ \tfrac{1}{2} \end{pmatrix} \begin{pmatrix} \tfrac{1}{2} \\ -\tfrac{1}{2} \\ \tfrac{1}{2} \\ -\tfrac{1}{2} \end{pmatrix} \begin{pmatrix} \tfrac{1}{2} \\ \tfrac{1}{2}i \\ -\tfrac{1}{2} \\ -\tfrac{1}{2}i \end{pmatrix} \begin{pmatrix} \tfrac{1}{2} \\ -\tfrac{1}{2}i \\ -\tfrac{1}{2} \\ \tfrac{1}{2}i \end{pmatrix}$$

$$\exp(i\delta) = 1, \qquad -1, \qquad i \qquad -i$$
$$k^2-K^2 = U_2+2U_1, \ U_2-2U_1, \ -U_2, \ -U_2 . \tag{40}$$

The third and fourth of these Bloch waves are degenerate i.e. have the same value of k_z and new linear combinations of the sum and difference of the two can be taken yielding in the latter case a wave which is not excited by the incident beam since $C_0 = 0$ (see eq. (34)). The intensity oscillations with depth z in the crystal, given by eq. (36), will be due to interference between the remaining three Bloch waves. If desired it would also be possible, by substituting the values of $C_0^{(j)}$, $C_g^{(j)}$, $\gamma^{(j)}$ in eq. (37), to compute the position and intensity of the lattice image formed from the four sets of crystal planes as a function of crystal thickness.

The foregoing calculation could evidently be easily adapted to cover cases where different numbers of simultaneous reflections are present such as three or six-beam cases which can occur in cross grating patterns with six-fold symmetry. It is also possible by the same methods to treat cases where the incident beam lies parallel to some symmetry axis or plane in the crystal so that a number of reciprocal lattice points lie at equal distances from the Ewald sphere. For the three beam (0, $\pm g$ reflections), five-beam ([100] incident beam direction) and seven-beam ([111] incident beam direction) details have been given by Hirsch et al. [5]. In these three cases, using the number of beams noted, only two of the possible N Bloch waves are actually excited so that the thickness fringes have a simple structure.

Furthermore, using the same method it is possible to make some corrections to the two-beam theory at the exact Bragg reflecting position by including the effect of nearby Bragg reflections. Thus for the Bragg reflection g exactly satisfied, a four-beam calculation, taking into account the reflections $-g$ and $2g$, yields a revised estimate [10] for the splitting Δk of the dispersion surface and hence a corrected extinction distance $\xi_g = (\Delta k)^{-1}$.

$$2K\Delta k = U_1 + U_3 + [(g^2 + (U_1 - U_3)/2)^2 + (U_1 + U_2)^2]^{1/2}$$

$$- [(g^2 - (U_1 - U_3)/2)^2 + (U_1 - U_2)^2]^{1/2}. \tag{41}$$

A similar correction may easily be calcualted for the second order reflection $2g$ at the Bragg position taking into account the reflection g. Using the same notation as before, the dynamical eqs. (13) become

$$\begin{pmatrix} K^2 - k_z^2 - g^2 & U_1 & U_2 \\ U_1 & K^2 - k_z^2 & U_1 \\ U_2 & U_1 & K^2 - k_z^2 - g^2 \end{pmatrix} \begin{pmatrix} C_0 \\ C_1 \\ C_2 \end{pmatrix} = 0. \tag{42}$$

By using our symmetry arguments, or simply by inspection, we see that there are two Bloch waves in which $C_0 = C_2$, $C_1 \neq 0$; and one Bloch wave with $C_0 = -C_2$, $C_1 = 0$. The values of $K^2 - k_z^2$ for these three waves can then be evaluated. We then select the pair which are associated with the spheres centred on 0 and $2g$ by the fact that the splitting, Δk, between them should reduce to the two-beam value, U_2/K, as $U_1 \rightarrow 0$. The corrected splitting is then found to be given by

$$K\Delta k = U_2 - (\tfrac{1}{4}) \; \{((g^2 - U_2)^2 + 8U_1^2)^{1/2} - (g^2 - U_2)\}. \tag{43}$$

As noted in the discussion of the Bethe potentials, (eq. (25)), the effect of the reciprocal lattice point inside the Ewald sphere is to reduce Δk. In fact it may be noted that Δk will in fact vanish provided

$$U_2^2 + U_2 g^2 = U_1^2 \; . \tag{44}$$

Finally it should be repeated that, although the analytical solutions outlined in this section have some instructive value in illustrating some of the basic effects of many-beam theory, it is usually essential, if accurate results are to be obtained, to include larger numbers of beams. Numerical solution of the general equations is then the only alternative.

2.3. Phemenological treatment of anomalous absorption effects

As pointed out by Dr. Whelan, there are a number of experimental observations such as disappearance of thickness fringes in thick crystals and asymmetries of the bright field intensity at low-order bend controus which indicate that the amplitudes of the various Bloch waves are attenuated at different rates as they propagate into the crystal. These anomalous absorption effects are due to scattering of electrons outside the aperture of the instrument by processes not already considered in the theory, and, as was first shown by Yoshioka [11], can be taken into account by adding a periodic imaginary potential $iV'(\mathbf{r})$ to the crystal potential $V(\mathbf{r})$. In principle a small correction should also be applied to the real part of the crystal potential but experimental evidence on this point is lacking and it is usually ignored. Yoshioka's original calculation referred to inelastic scattering due to ionisation processes but later calculations [12–14] have indicated that a more important contribution to $V'(\mathbf{r})$ usually comes from thermal diffuse scattering processes. There is also a small contribution due to the effect of weak Bragg reflections not included in the dynamical theory [15,16]. Inelastic scattering effects will be considered in more detail later (see sect. 4.3). At present we merely discuss the consequences

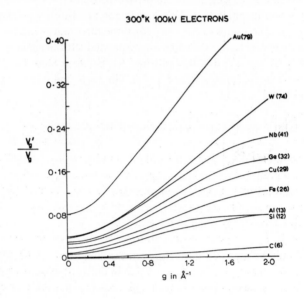

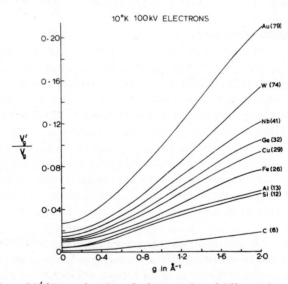

Fig. 2. Values of V'_g/V_g as a function of g for a number of different elements at room temperature and at $10°K$. (Courtesy Phil. Mag. [17]).

of adding the extra imaginary part $iV'(\mathbf{r})$ to the periodic potential. $V'(\mathbf{r})$ is expanded in a Fourier series in the same way as $V(\mathbf{r})$ in eq. (6)

$$V'(\mathbf{r}) = \frac{h^2}{2me} \sum_g U'_g \exp(2\pi i g \cdot \mathbf{r}) = \sum_g V'_g \exp(2\pi i g \cdot \mathbf{r}) . \qquad (45)$$

The ratio $(V'_g/V_g) = (U'_g/U_g)$ is always small (often less than 0.1) but depends on g and on temperature. Fig. 2 due to Humphreys and Hirsch [17] shows values of (V'_g/V_g) calculated as a function of g for a number of different elements at $300°$K and $10°$K. The Debye-Waller factor (see eq. (9)) is already included in both V_g and V'_g in these calculations which refer to 100 keV electrons. The ratio $(V'_g/V_g) = (U'_g/U_g)$ is in fact energy dependent and can be converted to other energies by multiplying by the factor (v_{100}/v). This ratio of electron velocities is provided in table 1.

If necessary the imaginary terms iU'_g could be added to the elements of the dynamical matrix A_{gh} in eq. (28) and the eigenfunctions and eigenvalues γ (which will now be complex quantities) found by matrix diagonalisation. However since the imaginary potential is small it is usually sufficient to treat it by perturbation theory. We may use the standard first order calculation for the change in energy ΔeE which in our case may be related to a change $\Delta k_z^{(j)}$ in the z components of the wave vectors $k_z^{(j)}$ given by $\Delta k_z^{(j)} = iq^{(j)}$ $= - me\Delta E/h^2 K$. We then obtain

$$q^{(j)} = \frac{me}{h^2 K} \int |B^{(j)}(\mathbf{r})|^2 \, V'(\mathbf{r}) \, d\tau . \qquad (46)$$

$B^{(j)}(\mathbf{r})$ is a normalised Bloch wave whose *amplitude* will now decay as $\exp(-2\pi q^{(j)}z)$. Substituting for $B^{(j)}$ from eq. (29) and for V' from eq. (45) we obtain

$$q^{(j)} = \frac{1}{2K} \sum_{g,g'} C_g^{(j)*} C_{g'}^{(j)} U'_{g-g'} . \qquad (47)$$

This equation, which can easily be shown to give the result quoted by Dr. Whelan for the two-beam case, is quite convenient for numerical computation since it can be cast into matrix multiplication form. However eq. (46) is also quite useful since it shows the relationship between the Bloch wave intensity $|B^{(j)}(\mathbf{r})|^2$ and the imaginary potential $V'(\mathbf{r})$ which determines the distribution of the absorbing regions (near the atoms) in the crystal. Bloch's theorem shows that $|B^{(j)}(\mathbf{r})|^2$ has the same periodicity as the crystal and it is sometimes of interest to plot this function out for various Bloch waves. Dr. Whelan already illustrated the mechanism of anomalous absorption in the two-beam case by showing the intensity distributions of the two Bloch waves at the Bragg reflecting position. When higher order systematic reflections (those with recprical lattice vectors parallel to $\mathbf{g}$ i.e. $2\mathbf{g}, 3\mathbf{g}, -\mathbf{g}, -2\mathbf{g}$ etc.) are taken into account these intensity distributions become somewhat modified [10] and are shown in fig. 3 for the four most important Bloch waves which are excited at the Bragg reflecting position $\mathbf{g}$. At higher energies these modifications evidently become more significant because of the increasing importance of many-beam effects which results because the Ewald sphere becomes larger and the values of U_g greater due to the factor m/m_o in eq. (9).

When account is taken of other (non-systematic) Bragg reflections with reciprocal lattice vectors lying in a plane rather than in a line, the Bloch wave intensities are localised in two dimensions so that anomalous absorption and transmission effects can be still more extreme. Waves which are concentrated in the channels between the atoms will be well transmitted while those which are concentrated at the rows of atoms are heavily absorbed. Contour plots of such wave field intensities have been given for the seven beam case of the incident beam parallel to a [111] axis by Hirsch et al. [5]. It is suggested that the reader should calculate and construct similar plots for the intensities of the Bloch waves in the four-beam case of simultaneous reflections given by eqs. (39) and (40) above.

2.4. *Summary of perfect crystal dynamical theory computations and observations*

Although these lectures are intended to be primarily theoretical in nature it may not be inappropriate at this point to indicate, if only in brief outline, the ways in which the perfect crystal theory just described has been applied in practice and the extent to which it agrees with observation.

Transmission electron micrographs of bent crystals such as that shown in fig. 4 (due to M.S.Spring) are effectively two-dimensional rocking curves which evidently contain a great deal of information and allow the many-beam theory to be tested in a detailed way. However although it is clear that a qualitative explanation of many of the observations of this kind can be given, quantitative agreement is quite difficult to achieve since many of the results are quite sensitive to the values of U_g and U_g' which are used (for a general discussion see Cowley [18]). The same remarks can be made about the two dimensional patterns obtained by the convergent beam technique [19] which,

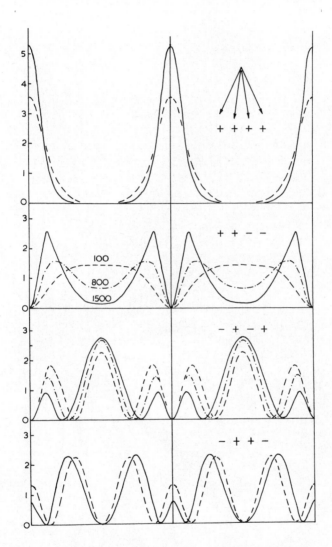

Fig. 3. Ten-beam calculations of the current distribution in the four most important Bloch waves in copper at the 111 reflecting position. Vertical lines denote the positions of the atomic planes. Note the change in channelling properties with voltage shown by the broken curve (100 keV), continuous curve (1500 keV), third curve (800 keV). (Courtesy Phil. Mag. [10].)

Fig. 4. Transmission electron micrograph near [100] orientation in a tungsten crystal at
750 keV. (Courtesy M.S. Spring.)

with a single exposure, is a more convenient way of obtaining a rocking curve of a flat crystal than more conventional tilting methods [20].

In the interests of simplicity therefore attention has so far largely been directed to crystal orientations where only the systematic reflections (along a line) are near to the Ewald sphere. It should be appreciated that if one wishes to operate near the Bragg reflection g, the effects of these other systematic reflections ng cannot be avoided. Computations of transmitted and diffracted intensities as a function of orientation in this situation are shown for electrons and positrons in figs. 5a and b. Curves like that shown in fig. 5a can be fitted in detail to experimental observations [21]. Analysis of convergent beam patterns involving the systematic reflections [22] has for instance enabled accurate values of U_{200} to be deduced for MgO. Sometimes in these cases only two Bloch waves are strongly excited and the observations are qualitatively similar to the two-beam theory predictions but a number of quantitative changes may occur due to the influence of the other reflections. The effective extinction distances (thickness fringe separations) of the lowest order reflections are often substantially reduced [21,5,22,23]. For illustration, some values of the extinction distance $\xi_g^{(c)}$ corrected for systematic reflections at 100 keV are compared with the two-beam values in table 2. Although experimental evidence for these changes exists only in a few cases [23,24] there is no doubt that they occur. They can also be estimated roughly using the Bethe potentials eq. (25) or the four-beam result eq. (43). The former equation also shows that the fractional correction will increase with accelerating voltage because of the dependence of U_g on m/m_0 (eq. (91)). As a consequence, the extinction distance is not exactly proportional to electron velocity v as the two-beam theory (see eqs. (2), (5), (9), (14) and (22)) would suggest but increases rather more slowly than this, particularly at high energies. Observations of this effect in MgO [25] have been explained with reasonable success [26].

Related changes, in some ways more striking, occur for the extinction distances of higher-order Bragg reflections. These were first noticed in terms of a disappearance of the Kikuchi lines associated with second order Bragg reflections 2g at particular voltages [27,28]. However the effect also occurs as a disappearance of the relevant extinction contour on electron micrographs. Many-beam calculations have shown [28–30] that the spacing between the two branches of the dispersion surface (those associated with the spheres centred on 0 and 2g) decreases to zero at the critical accelerating voltage and then increases again. Again an approximate estimate of the critical voltage can be obtained from the Bethe potential [27] eq. (25) or from the three beam condition given by eq. (44). No doubt a great many effects of this kind will be found to occur for higher-order Bragg reflections. Evidently, depending on the

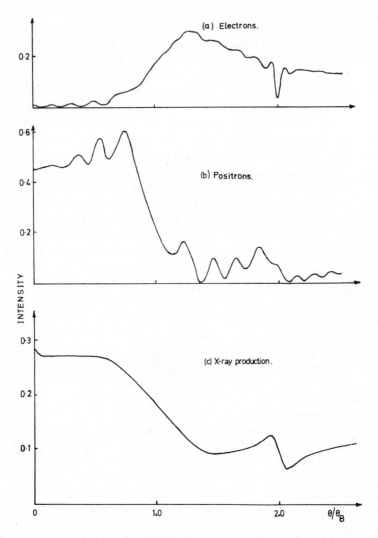

Fig. 5. Calculated angular dependence of (a) electron transmission and (b) positron transmission for channelling between (111) planes in Al at 100 keV. (c) is the calculated K-
shell X-ray production [36] for 100 keV electrons channelling between the (200) planes
in Ni.

Table 2

Reflection	111		200		220		311	
Element								
Al	556	503	673	630	1058	1036	1300	1285
Ni	236	199	275	245	409	393	499	488
Cu	243	203	283	251	418	402	508	496
Ag	224	175	255	214	363	342	433	417
Pt	146	108	166	132	231	211	274	260
Au	159	116	179	141	248	227	293	277

Reflection	110		200		211		310	
Element								
Fe	270	231	395	375	503	409	712	705
Nb	261	210	367	339	458	439	619	609
Mo	232	187	329	303	411	394	561	552
W	161	121	222	196	272	255	365	355

point of view, they provide a rather nice test of the dynamical theory, a means of determining precise values of low order constants U_g in terms of U_{2g}, U_{3g} etc. which are usually more accurately known, or a method of determining the accelerating voltage. Inclusion of the Debye-Waller factor in the expression for U_g (eq. (9)) is vital in these calculations and its presence has been confirmed directly in other measurements [31]). The influence of non-systematic reflections could be of importance in some of these effects however. Calculations [23] for the extinction distances of the 111, 200 and 220 reflections showed that the non-systematic reflections become of increasing importance with the larger values of g.

These increasing many-beam effects due to the increase in U_g and in χ, the radius of the Ewald sphere, at high energies result in considerable changes in the channelling properties and excitations of the various Bloch waves. Examples of the changes in the wave fields are shown in fig. 3 and have been calculated by a number of authors [10,29]. On the two-beam theory the penetration of the Bloch waves, $(q^{(j)})^{-1}$, is expected to be proportional to v^2 but could evidently be significantly modified by many-beam effects of this kind. So far no really striking instances of this effect have been observed although at high energies in Au and Pb anomalous transmission begins to occur at the symmetry position between the (111) and $(\bar{1}\bar{1}\bar{1})$ reflections because of the in-

creasing excitation of a higher order Bloch wave which is favourably transmitted [33].

Bloch waves with large intensities near the atomic cores in the crystal are
expected to cause anomalously high rates of ionisation and X-ray production
[34] and also to be more strongly scattered through large angles than waves
which avoid the atoms. Duncumb [35] first observed such anomalies in back
scattering and X-ray production; the latter effect was later studied in more detail by Hall [36] (see fig. 5c). This back scattering effect gives rise to the selected area channelling patterns observed in the scanning electron microscope
[37] discussed in Dr. Booker's lectures) and depends on the sensitivity of the
back scattering to the orientation of the incident beam [38]. A similar sensitivity is however expected with respect to the emergent angular distribution of
the back scattered beam. This follows from an application of the principle of
reciprocity (or reversibility) originally used by von Laue to explain X-ray
Kossel line patterns. The principle states that in the presence of some scatterer
the amplitude at a point B of a wave coming from a point A is equal to the
amplitude at A due to the same source placed at B. Taking the point B on an
atom in the crystal and the point A at infinity in a direction θ, the principle
then shows the equivalence of the incident angle and the emergence angle in
back scattering experiments of this kind. Observations [39] of Kikuchi lines
and bands at high angles of scattering demonstrated the importance of the
emergence angle in determining the back scattered intensity several years ago.
More recent studies of the angular distribution of electrons or positrons
emitted from lattice sites in activated crystals illustrate the same point [40–
42].

In the last few years a very large number of experiments have been done
showing that protons and other heavy ions exhibit in crystals many of the effects just discussed for electrons, such as anomalous transmission or channelling for certain incident directions, anomalous back-scattering effects and X-ray
or γ-ray production efficiencies again depending on the incident beam angle,
and related angular effects in the spectrum of particles emitted from activated
crystals (for references see [43,44]). Apart from their relevance to radiation
damage and ion implantation techniques, many of these experiments are capable of giving valuable information about the defect structure of the crystal, in
particular about the crystallographic sites occupied by various impurity atoms.
Although these experiments can all be interpreted quite satisfactorily on the
basis of a particle model of channelling [45] it is evident that the same phenomenon is involved as occurs in electron diffraction theory. All positively
charged particles such as protons or positrons (see fig. 5b) show anomalous
transmission for incident directions parallel to a symmetry axis or plane in

the crystal. The classical oscillations of the particle in the channel can be related directly to the extinction distance in the wave theory [46,47]. The success of the particle model in the case of the proton experiments is because the Bragg angle for these particles (typically $\approx 10^{-4}$ rad at the energies involved) is much less than the divergence of the incident beam. Uncertainty principle arguments then show [46,48] that the particle can be definitely located in a channel in the crystal. At the same time of course a good deal of the angular structure specifically associated with Bragg interference effects is averaged out leaving only the channelling effect.

3. Dynamical diffraction in imperfect crystals

The extension to the case of imperfect crystals of the dynamical theory just described would be a prohibitively complex task were it necessary for us to to follow up all the important applications and detailed ramifications. Fortunately however for many practical purposes, such as the identification of various lattice defects, the two-beam theory discussed by Dr. Whelan or even the kinematical theory given by Dr. Gevers are perfectly adequate. After demonstrating therefore the way in which the general approach based on the Schrödinger equation leads to the formulation used in these earlier lectures, we can concentrate on the more formal questions for which it is better suited such as the identification and critical examination of the various approximations used with a view to their subsequent improvement in cases where this seems necessary. To a considerable extent the treatment given here follows that of Howie and Basinski [23].

3.1. Derivation of the equations of dynamical theory in an imperfect crystal

We start once more with the Schrödinger equation in a potential $V(\mathbf{r})$

$$\nabla^2 \psi(\mathbf{r}) + (8\pi^2 me/h^2) \, [E + V(\mathbf{r})] \, \psi(\mathbf{r}) = 0 . \tag{48}$$

Although the potential is no longer periodic it can be written in the form

$$V(\mathbf{r}) = h^2/2me) \sum_{\mathbf{g}} u_g(\mathbf{r}) \exp(2\pi i \mathbf{g} \cdot \mathbf{r}) \tag{49}$$

and the wave function $\psi(\mathbf{r})$ may be written as

$$\psi(\mathbf{r}) = \sum_g \phi_g(\mathbf{r}) \exp\left(2\pi i(\chi+\mathbf{g}+\mathbf{s}_g)\cdot\mathbf{r}\right) \tag{50}$$

where, as before, χ is the wave vector of the incident wave outside the crystal and s_g is the usual Bragg deviation parameter (drawn in the z direction) so that $\chi^2 = (\chi+\mathbf{g}+\mathbf{s}_g)^2$. These equations assume nothing about the form of $V(\mathbf{r})$ or $\psi(\mathbf{r})$. Even the choice of reciprocal lattice appears rather arbitrary at this stage since although in most cases this would be the reciprocal lattice of the perfect crystal from which the imperfect crystal is "derived" such a perfect crystal may not always be easy to define. Inspection of the equations shows that we can in fact always ensure that $u_g(\mathbf{r})$ and $\phi_g(\mathbf{r})$ have no Fourier components corresponding to wave vectors $\mathbf{q}$ lying outside the first Brillouin zone. We therefore assume this to be done and in cases of severe imperfection where the choice of a reciprocal lattice is not automatic we suggest that this should be chosen in such a way that the Fourier components of the terms $u_g(\mathbf{r})$ corresponding to $\mathbf{q}$ vectors in the outer parts of the Brillouin zone be as small as possible. Physically this means roughly speaking that we choose our reciprocal lattice to coincide with as many of the maxima in the kinematical diffraction pattern as possible.

Following the same procedures as were used in the perfect crystal case we obtain from these equations the result

$$\sum_g \exp\left(2\pi i \mathbf{g}\cdot\mathbf{r}\right)\left[\nabla^2\phi_g(\mathbf{r}) + 4\pi i(\chi+\mathbf{g}+\mathbf{s}_g)\cdot\nabla\phi_g(\mathbf{r}) + 4\pi^2 \sum_{g'} u_{g-g'}\phi_{g'}(\mathbf{r})\right.$$

$$\left. \times \exp\{2\pi i(s_{g'}-s_g)z\}\right] . \tag{51}$$

Assuming that the coefficient of each exponential, i.e. the expression in square brackets, can be equated to zero we obtain a set of equations

$$(\chi+\mathbf{g}+\mathbf{s}_g)_z \frac{\partial\phi_g}{\partial z} = \sum_{g'} \pi i u_{g-g'}(\mathbf{r})\phi_{g'}(\mathbf{r}) \exp\{2\pi i(s_{g'}-s_g)z\}$$

$$-(\chi+\mathbf{g})_x \frac{\partial\phi_g}{\partial x} - (\chi+\mathbf{g})_y \frac{\partial\phi_g}{\partial y} + \frac{i}{4\pi} \nabla^2\phi_g . \tag{52}$$

These equations only follow from the previous eq. (51) if all the terms in the square bracket are sufficiently slowly varying so that terms from one reciprocal lattice cell do not spread over to another. We have already seen that the terms in $u_g(\mathbf{r})$ and $\phi_g(\mathbf{r})$ can be chosen to meet this condition but in severe cases it may evidently be violated by the product term $u_{g-g'}(\mathbf{r})\phi_{g'}(\mathbf{r})$. Physically this corresponds to a situation where the deformation of the crystal varies so rapidly with position that diffuse scattering is visible in the regions mid-way between the Bragg spots in the diffraction pattern.

Frequently, since χ_z greatly exceeds χ_x or χ_y or g, the last three terms of eq. (51) are small in comparison with the term on the left hand side and may be neglected. This constitutes the column approximation [49,5] which converts the equation from a partial differential equation to an ordinary differential equation to be solved in each individual column x, y. The approximation has already been discussed by Dr. Whelan but some further remarks are made in sect. 3.6.

When the displacement of the ions at the point $\mathbf{r}$ in the crystal is $\mathbf{R}(\mathbf{r})$ the potential in the imperfect crystal at this point is the same as in the perfect crystal at the point $\mathbf{r} - \mathbf{R}(\mathbf{r})$. This is the *deformable ion approximation,* valid when the displacement $\mathbf{R}(\mathbf{r})$ is slowly varying, and leads with the aid of eqs. (6) and (49) to the result

$$u_g(\mathbf{r}) = U_g \exp\{-2\pi i g \cdot \mathbf{R}(\mathbf{r})\}. \tag{53}$$

Making the column approximation in eq. (52) then yields the result

$$\frac{d\phi_g}{dz} = \sum_{g'} \frac{\pi i}{\xi_{g-g'}} \phi_{g'} \exp\{2\pi i(s_{g'}-s_g)z + 2\pi i(g'-g)\cdot\mathbf{R}\} \tag{54}$$

where, ignoring as usual the small differences between $(\chi+g+s_g)_z$ and K_z, ξ_g is given by eq. (22). This set of equations is the generalisation of one of the various equivalent forms used (see Dr. Whelan's chapters) in the two-beam dynamical theory of imperfect crystals. Evidently the extension to cover the case of absorption by the introduction of the imaginary potential $iV'(\mathbf{r})$ will simply result in the change $1/\xi_g \to 1/\xi_g + i/\xi_g'$, in these equations provided we assume that $V'(\mathbf{r})$ depends on deformation $\mathbf{R}$ in the same way as $V(\mathbf{r})$. The method of derivation followed here is based on an approach due to Takagi [50] and has the advantage that the various mathematical approximations made at each stage can be clearly stated.

3.2. *Two beam approximation*

Although the numerical integration of eqs. (54) for a given displacement function $\mathbf{R}$ presents no difficulty in principle it can become rather time-consuming if large numbers of beams are included. In particular the presence of weak beams with rather large values of s_g can lead to integration errors unless a rather small step length (proportional to $1/s_g$) is taken.

So far therefore very few calculations have in fact been done in other than the two-beam approximation. Humphreys et al. [24] gave fringe profiles for stacking faults in Si using up to 36 beams and obtained reasonable agreement with experiment but this problem is a special case of matching perfect crystal Bloch waves at the fault interface rather than integration of eqs. (54). Calculations have been done however to confirm the existence of double images from dislocations in the presence of simultaneous Bragg reflections [51] and to illustrate the extended appearance of the images of unextended dislocation nodes [52] in similar Bragg reflection conditions. In the case of systematic reflections only, it can be seen that many of the qualitative results of kinematical theory or two-beam dynamical theory such as the identification of faults by the condition $\mathbf{g} \cdot \mathbf{R} =$ integer or of dislocations from the condition $\mathbf{g} \cdot \mathbf{b} = 0$, will be unaffected since these conditions would hold for all the systematic reflections if they hold for the one of lowest order. For more quantitative work, such as the measurement of coherency strain fields, precise calculations are necessary. In the case of spherically symmetric strain fields it has been shown [23] using four-beam theory for instance that the image width is appreciably different than the two-beam theory prediction [53] and that the correction cannot be made simply by using a corrected extinction distance in the two-beam theory.

As remarked before, all of these many-beam effects, tend to become more serious with increasing electron energy. Detailed analysis of defect images may therefore become a task of increasing complexity with the development of high voltage microscopy. It may of course prove possible to find orientations where only the systematic interactions are excited, thus simplifying the problem. On the other hand perhaps the possibility of using an incident beam divergence greater than the Bragg angle should be examined. It might then be possible to make use of a rather simpler analysis of defect images in electron micrographs using the classical theory of particle channelling [45] mentioned above.

3.3. Symmetry properties of defect images

The effect of the column approximation leading to eqs. (54) is to reduce the imperfect crystal to a succession of parallel perfect crystal slices displaced by varying amounts with respect to one another. A formal matrix solution can thus be given [54,5] by successive application of the matrix methods described in sect. 2.2.3. By studying the formal result of this calculation, whose derivation is not reproduced here, certain useful symmetry relations can be deduced about the defect images in the case of perfect centro-symmetric crystals.

The most useful result of this kind can be expressed in the form "the bright field images from two columns of a crystal of thickness t where the displacement functions are $\mathbf{R}(z)$ and $\mathbf{R_o} - \mathbf{R}(t-z)$ will be identical". $\mathbf{R_o}$ is an arbitrary constant displacement. A number of examples where this result applies are shown in fig. 6. These predictions, which hold in the presence of absorption, have been confirmed in a wide variety of cases.

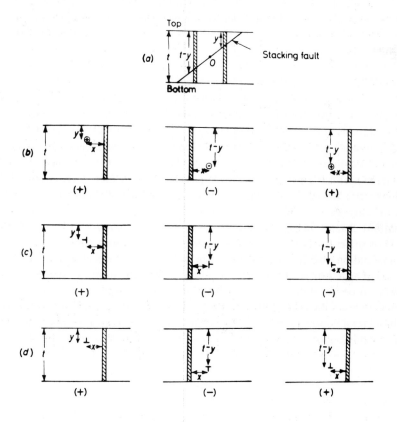

Fig. 6. Symmetry properties of defect images. The displacement functions in each of the two columns in (a) and in each of the three columns in (b), (c) and (d) are related by the rule $\mathbf{R_1}(z) = \mathbf{R_o} - \mathbf{R}_z(t-z)$. (Courtesy Royal Society [54].)

A further symmetry principle governing the dark field image holds only at the exact Bragg condition and was first proved for the two-beam case by Ball [55] but recently extended to the case of systematic interactions by Pogany and Turner [56] using the reciprocity theorem. This principle states that at the exact Bragg position identical dark field images will be obtained from columns of crystal in which the displacement functions are $R(z)$ and $R_o + R(t-z)$. The so-called δ boundaries (small angle tilt boundaries) considered by Gevers et al. [57] are a case to which this principle applies. It also explains the symmetrical form of the dark field rocking curve of a perfect crystal or of a crystal in the presence of a magnetic field [58].

The symmetry principles are probably mainly of use in situations where the observed image is due to a defect of a relatively unknown kind. Various possibilities can then be rapidly eliminated if they are inconsistent with any observed symmetry.

3.4. *The potential in the imperfect crystal*

A number of criticisms can be made of the deformable ion type of imperfect crystal potential which is most commonly used in diffraction contrast calculations in the form defined by eqs. (49) and (53). Firstly, it can be seen from the second of these equations that in highly strained regions of crystal the functions $u_g(\mathbf{r})$ may no longer be slowly varying in the sense required for eq. (51). This is especially true for large values of g. A more serious criticism however is that this potential includes only the effect of *strain contrast* (i.e. local changes in the Bragg reflection conditions due to rotation, shear or dilatation). Dilatation can also give rise to *structure factor contrast* [59] however which arises because of the dependence of U_g on V_c the volume of the unit cell (and on $\sin\theta/\lambda$ (eq. (9)). Structure factor contrast will also arise in the case of aggregates of vacancies, interstitials or foreign atoms. In special cases when it occurs alone it can be treated directly by regarding it as a local change in extinction distance [59]. Frequently, however, strain contrast and structure factor contrast are present together and cannot be treated independently. It would then be better to use the *rigid ion approximation* for $V(\mathbf{r})$

$$V(\mathbf{r}) = \sum_n v_n \{\mathbf{r} - \mathbf{r}_n - \mathbf{R}(\mathbf{r}_n)\} \tag{55}$$

where v_n is the potential of the nth ion in the crystal. To a first approximation a similar equation could possibly be used for $V'(\mathbf{r})$, the imaginary part of the potential. A potential of this type will still be useful even when the vacancies, interstitials or foreign atoms are isolated or arranged in aggregates which are too small to give visible individual images. In such cases their presence may still be detected by accurate measurements of the average extinction distance or of the absorption parameters [60] obtained from electron micrographs of thickness fringes. In addition, particularly in the case of order-disorder effects in alloys, diffuse maxima may be visible in the diffraction pattern. In all of these cases a dynamical theory based on a potential of the type given by eq. (55) is required. Unfortunately it may be rather laborious in practical cases to convert this potential into the form specified by eq. (49) which is needed for use in the theory as developed so far. It is however possible to make use of more general imperfect crystal potentials in a slightly different formation of the theory which we now outline since it has some additional conceptual value.

3.5. Scattering of Bloch waves in imperfect crystals

While eqs. (52) and in some cases eqs. (54) are adequate in general for computations of scattering of fast electrons in strained crystals, there are situations (involving strains which are very small, or very slowly varying or localised within a small region) when a simpler physical picture can be given in terms of the behaviour of Bloch waves in the imperfect crystal.

Instead of expressing the wave function $\psi(\mathbf{r})$ as a sum of plane waves with spatially varying amplitudes (eq. (50)) we now describe it in terms of the perfect crystal Bloch waves $B^{(j)}$ with wave vectors $\mathbf{k}^{(j)}$ (which will be complex in the presence of absorption)

$$\psi(\mathbf{r}) = \sum_j \psi^{(j)}(z)\, B^{(j)}(\mathbf{r}) .$$

The summation should extend over all states $\mathbf{k}^{(j)}$ on the branches of the dispersion surface which are considered. In a perfect crystal the amplitudes $\psi^{(j)}$ of these Bloch waves would be constant but in the imperfect crystal changes occur because of scattering from a state $\mathbf{k}^{(l)}$ to a state $\mathbf{k}^{(j)}$ as a result of the imperfection. At the entrance surface only one state on each branch (defined by the matching condition given in fig. 1) would usually be excited but deeper in the crystal there will be a distribution of excited states on the various branches of the dispersion surface as shown in fig. 7.

Differential equations for the varying amplitudes $\psi^{(j)}(z)$ have been given [5] for the case when the imperfect crystal potential is described by eqs. (49) and (53). A more sophisticated method using modified Bloch waves which are particularly suitable for the case of slowly varying strains was introduced by

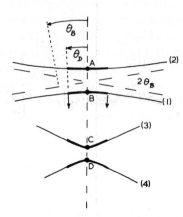

Fig. 7. Dispersion surfaces in the four-beam case showing the relation between θ_B and θ_D (the current divergence angle) for a given lateral spread of excited waves. (Courtesy Phil. Mag. [23].)

Wilkens [61]. Both of these formulations make use of the column approximation which in this context involves restricting the Bloch waves used in eq. (56) to those with tangential components of wave vector equal to those of the incident beam. For our purposes however it is preferable to describe the Bloch wave scattering by a potential $V_p(\mathbf{r})$ equal to the difference between the potentials in the imperfect crystal and in the perfect crystal. We then find on substituting into the Schrödinger eq. (48) and using the orthogonality relations for different Bloch waves, the equations

$$\frac{d\psi^{(j)}_{(z)}}{dz} = \frac{2\pi i m e}{h^2 k^{(j)}_z} \sum_l \psi^{(l)}(z) \iint B^{(j)*}(\mathbf{r}) \, V_p(\mathbf{r}) \, B^{(l)}(\mathbf{r}) \, dx dy . \quad (57)$$

The second derivative of $\psi^{(j)}$ has been ignored but otherwise the equations are exact. This approach is particularly useful when the scattering is weak so that $\psi^{(l)}(z)$ is to a first approximation constant. We then have

$$\psi^{(j)}(z) = \psi^{(j)}(o) + \frac{2\pi i m e}{h^2 k^{(j)}_z} \sum_l \psi^{(l)}(o)$$

$$\times \int_o^z dz \iint B^{(j)*}(\mathbf{r}) V_p(\mathbf{r}) B^{(l)}(\mathbf{r}) \, dx dy . \quad (58)$$

We see here the usual quantum mechanical result that the transitions from the state $\mathbf{k}^{(l)}$ to the state $\mathbf{k}^{(j)}$ are controlled by the matrix element of V_p between the two Bloch wave states — the quantity given by the integral in eq. (57). Using eq. (29) for the Bloch waves it can be seen that this matrix element depends on the various Fourier components of $V_p(\mathbf{r})$.

$$\psi^{(j)}(z) = \psi^{(j)}(o) + \frac{2\pi i m e}{h^2 k_z^{(j)}} \sum_l \psi^{(l)}(o) \sum_{g,g'} C_{g'}^{(j)*} C_{g'-g}^{(l)}$$

$$\times \int_0^z dz \iint V_p(\mathbf{r}) \exp\left(2\pi i (\mathbf{k}^{(l)} - \mathbf{k}^{(j)} - \mathbf{g}) \cdot \mathbf{r}\right) dx dy . \quad (59)$$

The transitions involved can be conveniently separated into intraband transitions ($j=l$) and interband transitions ($j \neq l$). When $V_p(\mathbf{r})$ varies relatively slowly in the x, y directions the scattering is confined to waves with closely similar k_x and k_y components i.e. the column approximation is valid. In this situation, which holds for most defect images observed by electron microscopy, it can be seen that diffraction contrast is mainly associated with the transitions of the interband type and the intraband transitions are relatively ineffective since the Bloch wave elements $C_g^{(j)}$, $C_g^{(l)}$ are then nearly equal with the result that the wave amplitudes ϕ_0 and ϕ_g are more or less unaffected. Such interband transitions will only occur however if $V_p(r)$ has an appreciable Fourier component in the z direction at an argument $k_z^{(l)} - k_z^{(j)}$, the relevant wave vector change involved. In cases of strain contrast this means that the wavelength of the strain in the z direction must be of the order of the relevant extinction distance. For a dislocation this rate of change of strain occurs at the order of an extinction distance from the dislocation. We thus see how the present theory leads to a simple explanation of the widths of defect images. These ideas can be made more quantitative and in the case of coherency strain fields round spherical particles for instance, where the interband transition matrix element can be evaluated analytically [61,23], the results deduced from the perturbation theory of eq. (59) for the image width as a function of particle size and misfit are in quite good agreement with the computed data.

Although it is likely that in many cases a full-scale dynamical calculation will be necessary to provide all the quantitative data which may be required, the perturbation theory outlined can often be very helpful since it has a number of advantages.

(a) It can be used with any potential $V_p(\mathbf{r})$ so that for instance structure factor contrast and strain contrast can be included together.

(b) The relationship between $V_p(\mathbf{r})$ and the image contrast is simpler than in the dynamical theory so that in the case of an unknown defect it is easier to work back from the observed image to deduce the structure of the defect.

(c) For a given scattering potential $V_p(\mathbf{r})$ the important interband or intraband scattering processes can be identified even in a many-beam situation where a large number of Bloch waves may be involved. Considerations of this kind often indicate that the visibility of small defects would be best in dark field pictures taken not too close to the Bragg reflecting position. In symmetry situations some of the transition matrix elements may vanish because of the symmetry properties of the Bloch wave matrix elements.

(d) The theory can also be used in the case of defects which are too small to be resolved e.g. individual vacancies or interstitials and in some order-disorder problems. In these cases the most noticeable effects usually occur in the diffraction pattern where the intensity is very directly related to the distribution of scattered Bloch waves on the dispersion surface. Some of the symmetry properties of the diffusely scattered intensity and its occasional systematic absence near certain Bragg spots despite strong dynamical effects can be explained [62] in terms of eq. (59). As mentioned previously, accurate measurements of thickness fringes have shown [60] that the presence of point defects can also be detected as a change in the absorption properties of the Bloch waves. Evidently, for instance, the anomalous transmission effect will be reduced by the presence of interstitial atoms in the channels of the crystal. The change in the $q_z^{(j)}$ can be computed from eq. (46) using some expression $V_p'(\mathbf{r})$ for the change in the imaginary potential due to the defects in place of $V'(\mathbf{r})$ in the integral. In general there will be contribution to this effect not only from the point defects themselves but also from the strains round them [60]. A change in the extinction distance is also expected to occur for the same reasons.

3.6. *The column approximation*

Empirically there is no doubt that the dynamical theory with the column approximation is very successful in high energy electron diffraction. It might be expected that the images of small defects would be somewhat wider or more diffuse when they are near the entrance surface of the crystal. Although a "top-bottom effect" of this kind has been reported [63] it seems to be due to the beam divergence resulting from inelastic scattering rather from an elastic scattering effect. At any rate there is no sign of the systematic increase in image width with distance of the defect from the exit surface which is observed in the X-ray case. The manifest failure of the column approximation in the X-ray case stimulated some calculations which did not use it [64,65]. Somewhat similar calculations were made independently for the electron diffraction case [23] by integration of eqs. (52). A large number of columns have to be considered together and the x and y derivates of ϕ_0 and ϕ_g computed from an interpolation formula. These calculations were quite laborious but showed that the effect of the column approximation is only noticeable for the very smallest defect images and is quite undetectable for dislocations. It was also shown that the approximation, whereby the effect of a magnetic field on diffraction contrast is simulated by applying the theory to a crystal bent to a radius of curvature equal and opposite to the cyclotron radius of the fast electron in the field [66,67], is a good one and can be used even in the vicinity of a Bloch wall where the magnetic field varies quite rapidly.

As discussed in the previous section, the validity of the column approximation is related to the lateral distribution on the dispersion surface of Bloch waves excited as a result of scattering by the defect in question. The column approximation is valid when all of the scattered waves are closely concentrated in the neighbourhood of the unscattered waves (e.g. near the points A, B, C, D of fig. 7). For very small defects the scattered waves will have a wider spread Δk_x, Δk_y of wave vector components and a range of values of wave amplitudes C_0, C_g etc. These scattered Bloch waves will also travel in slightly different directions since their velocity is along the direction of the normal to the dispersion surface. Reference to fig. 7 shows however that the resulting divergence angle θ_D of the current flow in the crystal will usually be much less than θ_B the Bragg angle. This is probably the main reason for the slightly surprising success of the column approximation in electron diffraction.

4. Inelastic scattering of electrons in crystals

4.1. Effects of inelastic scattering in electron microscopy

The presence of inelastically scattered electrons in electron microscope pictures is probably most noticeable in the diffraction pattern. In the case of crystals thinner than 100 or 200Å for instance elastic scattering i.e. Bragg reflection, predominates and the corresponding spots in the diffraction pattern are sharp. The momentum transfer from the fast electron is then delivered to the crystal as a whole and the energy transfer is negligible. With a thicker, but still perfect crystal the spots in the diffraction pattern become more diffuse as a result of small-angle inelastic scattering and at the same time a faint background intensity due to inelastic scattering through larger angles may be apparent. Kikuchi lines may also be observed as a result of the subsequent Bragg reflection of these inelastically scattered electrons.

In electron micrographs the presence of inelastic scattering is most easily noticeable as a result of "absorption" effects. As a result of the scattering into the background of the diffraction pattern the total intensity of the Bragg spots is reduced. In particular we find that in situations where the two-beam theory is roughly valid, the bright-field and dark-field images are not complementary to one another. As already noted in sect. 2.3, these absorption effects due to inelastic scattering outside the aperture of the instrument can be described by the use of a complex potential. Some inelastically scattered electrons will however pass through the objective aperture and make a positive contribution to the image contrast. So far we have not considered these electrons in the theory of diffraction contrast — a rather serious omission since in thick crystals almost all of the electrons contributing to the image have been inelastically scattered. It is therefore at first sight rather surprising that the theory described so far should be very successful at all, however the experiments of Kamiya and Uyeda [68] in which the aperture was placed to receive the inelastically scattered electrons but reject elastically scattered electrons (see position 2 in fig. 8) showed that the former produce image effects similar to those obtained with the elastically scattered electrons. These experiments suggest therefore that the success of dynamical theory in describing diffraction contrast effects depends to a considerable extent on some mechanism which results in the preservation of contrast after inelastic scattering [69]. The existence of this effect has now been confirmed in much more detail using energy selecting [70] or energy analysing electron microscopes

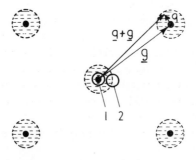

Fig. 8. Diffuse intensity round each spot in a cross grating pattern can arise by momentum transfer $h\mathbf{q}$ (intraband process) or by $h(\mathbf{q}+\mathbf{g})$ (interband process). Normally elastic and inelastic scattered electrons contribute to the image (aperture position (1)) but the displaced aperture position (2) only inelastically scattered electrons contribute.

[71] by means of which the contrast due to the elastically scattered (no loss) electrons and the contrast due to the inelastically scattered electrons can be directly observed and compared.

In the next few sections in which various selected aspects of the theory of inelastic scattering are described the aim has been to concentrate on the general principles and results which are of direct relevance to electron microscopy and to avoid mathematical detail as much as possible.

4.2. General principles of inelastic scattering in crystals

After inelastic scattering and energy loss the electron will in general be travelling in a different direction in the crystal but will still be subject to the Bragg reflection and anomalous absorption effects already discussed. This is confirmed by the observation of Kikuchi lines and bands in the inelastically scattered background of the diffraction pattern. This means that in general the inelastically scattered electrons should be described by Bloch waves associated with a dispersion surface for the appropriate energy. In practice the most important inelastic scattering processes involve relatively small energy losses ($\Delta E \lesssim 50$ eV) so that the change in electron wavelength and Bragg angle can be ignored to a very good approximation. If the angle of inelastic scattering is not too large the dispersion surface for inelastically scattered electrons of energy eE' is identical to that of the elastically scattered electrons of energy eE and velocity v but translated in the k_z direction by an amount

$$\Delta k_z = \Delta E/hv .$$

This is shown in fig. 9 for the two-beam case (for simplicity). The result still holds for the many-beam case and the dispersion surface so obtained will be adequate for the inelastically scattered electrons provided enough beams are taken so that any new Bragg reflections excited as a result of the change in direction of the inelastically scattered electron will still be included. In many cases the angle of scattering is quite small so that it is not necessary to increase the number of beams considered to cover the inelastic scattering. For losses of the order of 10 eV the displacement Δk_z between the two dispersion surfaces is of the same order as the separation of the various branches in each surface.

With the aid of a diagram like fig. 9, the various possible transitions from a point P on one of the branches of the dispersion surface of energy eE can be conveniently classified. Elastic transitions to other points on the same energy surface may occur because of the presence of lattice defects. As mentioned previously, these may be classified as intraband or interband transitions de-

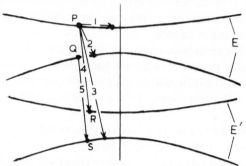

Fig. 9. Two-beam dispersion surfaces for elastically scattered electrons of energy eE and inelastically scattered electrons of energy eE'. Transitions 1, 2 and 3 are elastic intraband, elastic interband and inelastic interband respectively. Transitions 4 and 5 are inelastic intraband and preserve contrast effects.

pending on whether the electron stays on the same branch of the dispersion surface or not. For small angle scattering, diffraction contrast is mainly associated with the interband type of transition. Evidently the inelastic scattering transitions can also be classified as interband or intraband transitions. We can look at this in another way using fig. 8. The diffuse scattering in the vicinity of any diffraction spot g can arise either by inelastic scattering with a small momentum change hq from the nearest spot (intraband process) or else by a larger momentum transfer $h(q+g)$ from some other spot (interband scattering). Evidently processes of the second kind are more likely to contribute to anomalous absorption and produce contrast effects. The way in which diffraction contrast effects may actually be preserved after inelastic scattering can only be seen in terms of fig. 9 however. Since the two different dispersion surfaces are related by a simple displacement Δk_z it can be seen [69] that the two small angle inelastic intraband transitions (4) and (5) will involve the same change in wave vector q. This means that the same crystal excitation (plasma oscillation, phonon etc.) will be involved in both cases. Consequently the phase relation between the Bloch waves P and Q responsible for diffraction contrast effects will be preserved between the waves R and S after inelastic scattering so that any diffraction contrast effect due to interference between these waves will still occur. Preservation of contrast will not occur when the same crystal excitation cannot operate simultaneously for all the branches of the dispersion surface since the phase relations between different crystal excitations are quite arbitrary in general. It can also be seen that interband transitions PS or QR in fig. 9 will tend to destroy the contrast. It can be seen therefore that contrast preservation will occur if most of the inelastically scattered electrons accepted by the aperture have suffered small-angle intraband scattering.

As remarked above interband inelastic scattering involving large reciprocal lattice vectors can be discussed in terms of many-beam generalisations of fig. 9. In these cases the initial Bloch wave of energy eE will be strongly excited so that $\psi^{(j)} = C_0^{(j)}$ is large. The inelastically scattered wave of energy eE would usually have a small value of C_0 so that few of the electrons would pass through the aperture and the process would mainly contribute to anomalous absorption. It should be noted that in all cases the wave vector change q can be taken to lie in the first Brillouin zone.

The mathematical formulation of these principles has been given by Howie [69] based on an extension of Yoshioka's original treatment [11]. However it is not necessary to reproduce the details here since the physical principles are quite clear. Detailed calculations and experiments have to be carrier out for any particular inelastic scattering process of course to determine whether the scattering will be predominantly of the intraband or interband type. The results are summarised in the next section for the more important inelastic scattering mechanisms.

4.3. Inelastic scattering processes
4.3.1. Plasmon excitation

The Coulomb interaction between the fast electron and the electrons of the crystal is a long-range one so that, in addition to having inelastic collisions with individual electrons of the crystal, the fast electron can excite collective oscillations of the whole valence electron gas. These long wave density oscillations of the electron gas are called plasma oscillations or plasmons and have a characteristic frequency ω_p and corresponding excitation energy $\hbar\omega_p$ usually in the range 3 eV to 30 eV. They are basically an excitation of the crystal not related in any way to excitations which may occur in the inelastic scattering of electrons by isolated atoms. For further details reference should be made to Pines [72]. Strong evidence for the existence of these plasmons is provided by the energy loss spectra of many materials which show a series of fairly sharp peaks corresponding to energy losses of 0, $\hbar\omega_p$, $2\hbar\omega_p$ ... etc. The probability $P_n(t)$ of the nth loss is given by the Poisson formula

$$P_n(t) = (t/\lambda_p) \exp(-t/\lambda_p)/n! \tag{60}$$

where t is the thickness of the crystal and λ_p the mean free path for plasmon excitation. Typical values for λ_p for 100 keV electrons lie in the range 1000 to 5000Å so that in many cases almost all of the electrons emerging from the crystal have lost energy. The plasmon wavelength is long compared with the lattice spacing (i.e. the wave vector $q \ll g$) and it is not expected that Bragg reflection would occur during plasmon excitation. Only small angle intraband transitions of the fast electron are involved therefore so that, although most of the inelastically scattered electrons still pass through the objective aperture, the diffraction contrast is preserved and there is no contribution to anomalous absorption. The bright field and dark field image contributions of the nth energy loss electrons are therefore $|\phi_0|^2 P_n(t)$ and $|\phi_g|^2 P_n(t)$ respectively where $|\phi_0|^2$ and $|\phi_g|^2$ are calculated by the methods of the usual dynamical theory with absorption. Since $\Sigma_{\kappa=0}^{\infty} P_n(t) = 1$ the total intensities are correctly given by the usual theory. These results have been qualitatively confirmed in considerable detail using energy selecting [70] or energy analysing [71] electron microscopes. Recently however more quantitative studies in Al have shown [73] that a small loss in contrast occurs after plasmon excitation not because of any interband transitions but because of the finite range of scattering angles involved.

Finally it should be noted that the use of energy selecting or energy analysing electron microscopes allows many detailed measurements of plasmon frequency ω_p and excitation mean free path λ_p to be made in very small crystals or precipitates [74—77] or in local regions of inhomogeneous alloys [78,79] to yield important information about band structure effects or segregation effects in solid solutions. These developments however lie outside the scope of the present lectures.

4.3.2. Single electron excitation

As remarked above, the long-range part of the Coulomb interaction between the fast electron and the electrons of the crystal excites plasmons and is effectively screened by them. The residual interaction is then of a more local character and mainly involves collisions with individual electrons. For the electrons of the atomic core the cross section for these processes is roughly proportional to the area of the orbit. Consequently the ionisation of inner shells, detectable by means of the characteristic X-rays subsequently emitted, is relatively unimportant from the point of view of image contrast despite the fact that, as noted previously, it depends strongly on the Bloch wave nature of the incident electron. An appreciable contribution to V_0', the average part of the imaginary potential, comes from less tightly bound electrons but the contribution to V_g' is rather small since the orbits of these electrons are less tightly localised in the atomic core region [11,14]. After excitation of an individual valence electron the fast electron may still pass through the aperture and make some contribution to image contrast (although the process is usually much less probable than plasmon excitation). At present it appears that this single electron excitation process also preserves diffraction contrast and some progress has been made in explaining this theoretically [80,73]. More experiments are needed however and a more complete theory of the excitation of valence electrons in crystals taking into account the role of plasma oscillations and single electrons excitations simultaneously is still lacking.

4.3.3. Thermal diffuse scattering

Thermal diffuse scattering involves very small changes in energy ($\Delta E \cong kT = 0.025$ eV at room temperature) but the scattered intensity is greatest at moderate angles of the order of $10°$. The inelastic transitions of the fast electron are thus mainly of the interband type and fairly large reciprocal lattice vectors can be involved [13]. Despite this there is some evidence [70] that a certain amount of contrast preservation can occur after thermal diffuse scattering, particularly in thin crystals. However this does not appear to hold for defect images in general [73]. Only a very small fraction (usually a few percent) of the electrons passing through the aperture have been subjected to thermal diffuse scattering so that the point is not of great practical importance in any case.

The contribution of thermal diffuse scattering to the anomalous absorption effect is however very important and at the present time the latest calculations [17] quoted earlier (which also take into account the small contribution from single electron scattering) seem to be capable of explaining the observed values of the imaginary potential parameters. The calculations are also in reasonable agreement with the observations which have been made so far on the temperature dependence of anomalous transmission effects [81,33]. Typically on going from room temperature to liquid helium temperatures the penetration (measured by the reciprocals of the imaginary part $q_z^{(j)}$ of the Bloch wave vector) increases by a factor of about two or three. Attenuation of the waves still occurs at low temperatures because of the temperature independent electronic contribution to V_0' and because of the residual thermal diffuse scattering due to the zero point vibrations of the crystal. Above room temperature the penetration decreases but, because few of the electrons pass through the aperture after thermal diffuse scattering, the image contrast does not appear to deteriorate [73].

4.4. *Energy-dependence of inelastic scattering and diffraction contrast effects*

The recent development of electron microscopes operating at voltages substantially above 100 keV and their increasing use in the study of defects in thick aperture specimens has made necessary a reliable theory of the factors which control the maximum usable specimen thickness t_m at a given voltage. Uyeda and Nonoyama [82] have identified loss of intensity due to increasing absorption as a result of large-angle inelastic scattering, loss of contrast due to small-angle inelastic scattering and loss of resolution due to increasing energy spread leading to chromatic aberration as the possible controlling mechanisms.

Howie [83] pointed out that the penetration distance should be roughly proportional to v^2 where v is the electron velocity. On this basis it can be seen from table 1 that the improvement in penetration for accelerating voltage above 100 keV is limited to a factor of about three and that most of this factor is achieved by going to 300 keV. More strictly we expect that if t_m is controlled by loss of intensity it should be proportional to the mean free path Λ of the inelastic scattering process mainly involved. Usually due to relativistic retardation effects Λ increases slightly slower than v^2 and may actually decrease for energies above 1 or 2 MeV [84,85]. Account should also be taken of the change in channelling properties of individual Bloch waves which as stated previously takes place because of increasing many-beam effects [10,33].

If t_m is controlled by loss of contrast due for instance to multiple plasmon excitation, eq. (60) suggests that t_m will be proportional to λ_p, the mean free path for plasmon excitation, and would to a first approximation be proportional to v^2 in this case also. Again however we may expect a correction due to relativistic retardation and changing many-beam effects as the energy is raised. Loss of contrast would appear to present a more fundamental limit to the study of thick crystals than loss of intensity since the latter can, at least in principle, be compensated by increased exposure.

In the remaining case of chromatic aberration the resolution r_c is given by

$$r_c = 2\alpha C_c \sqrt{1 - v^2/c^2}\ \Delta E/m_0 v^2 \tag{61}$$

where C_c is the aberration constant, α is the objective aperture angle and ΔE the energy spread of the beam. Apparently ΔE varies with $(t/\Lambda)^\nu$ where ν lies between $\frac{1}{2}$ (the value expected for a Poisson distribution, eq. (60)) and 1. Hence for a constant value of r_c, t_m increreases faster than $v^2/(\alpha\sqrt{1-v^2/c^2})$. This is a good deal faster than usually observed and at present it is thought [85] that loss of resolution cannot be the factor controlling t_m at high voltages (except possibly in rather low atomic number materials).

At high energies a number of other inelastic scattering processes become of importance. These include the emission of Cerenkov radiation by the crystal and the emission of Bremmstrahlung radiation by the fast electron. The latter process in particular becomes an important mechanism of energy loss at high energies and would be expected to contribute to anomalous absorption effects since large angles of scattering are involved. Extensive studies of the Bremmstrahlung process in crystals have been carried out for very high energy electrons in nuclear accelerators [36] and show a strong dependence on crystal orientation.

For electrons of energy greater than a few hundred keV the momentum transfer in a large angle collision becomes enough to knock an atom out of its site in most crystals. Damage of this kind has been observed by Makin [87] in the Cambridge high voltage electron microscope. From the electron back scattering results noted previously one would expect that this damage process would also depend strongly on the Bloch wave nature of the incident electron beam.

References

[1] C.G.Darwin, Phil. Mag. 27 (1914) 315, 675.
[2] H.A.Bethe, Ann. Phys. Lpz. 87 (1928) 55.
[3] J.A.Ibers and B.K.Vainshtein, Int. Crystallographic Tables III (1962).
[4] G.Thomas, Transmission Electron Microscopy of Metals (Wiley, New York, 1962).
[5] P.B.Hirsch, A.Howie, R.B.Nicholson, D.W.Pashley and M.J.Whelan, Electron Microscopy of Thin Crystals (Butterworths, London, 1965).
[6] P.A.Doyle and P.S.Turner, Acta Cryst. A24 (1968) 390.
[7] L.Sturkey, Acta Cryst. 10 (1957) 858.
[8] H.Niehrs, Z. Naturf. 14a (1959) 504.
[9] F.Fujimoto, J. Phys. Soc. Japan 14 (1959) 1558.
[10] A.Howie, Phil. Mag. 14 (1966) 223.
[11] H.Yoshioka, J. Phys. Soc. Japan 12 (1957) 618.
[12] H.Yoshioka and Y.Kainuma, J. Phys. Soc. Japan 17 (1962) 134.
[13] C.R.Hall and P.B.Hirsch, Proc. Roy. Soc. A286 (1965) 158.
[14] M.J.Whelan, J. Appl. Phys. 36 (1965) 2099, 2103.
[15] J.Gjønnes, Acta Cryst. 15 (1962) 703.
[16] C.R.Hall and P.B.Hirsch, Phil. Mag. 12 (1965) 539.
[17] C.J.Humphreys and P.B.Hirsch, Phil. Mag. 18 (1968) 115.
[18] J.M.Cowley, Acta Cryst. A25 (1969) 129.
[19] P.Goodman and G.Lempfuhl, Z. Naturf. 19a (1964) 818.
[20] M.Horstmann and G.Meyer, Z. Phys. 159 (1960) 563.
[21] A.Howie and M.J.Whelan, Proc. Eur. Regional Conf. on Electron Microscopy, Delft, 1960, Vol. 1 (1960) p. 181.
[22] P.Goodman and G.Lempfuhl, Acta Cryst. 22 (1967) 14.
[23] A.Howie and Z.S.Basinski, Phil. Mag. 17 (1968) 1039.
[24] C.J.Humphreys, A.Howie and G.R.Booker, Phil. Mag. 15 (1967) 507.
[25] G.Dupouy, F.Perrier, R.Uyeda, R.Ayroles and A.Mazel, J. Microsc. 4 (1965) 429.

[26] M.J.Goringe, A.Howie and M.J.Whelan, Phil. Mag. 14 (1966) 217.

[27] D.Watanabe, R.Uyeda and M.Kogiso, Acta Cryst. A24 (1968) 249.

[28] D.Watanabe, R.Uyeda and A.Fukuhara, Acta Cryst. A25 (1969) 138.

[29] A.J.F. Metherell and R.M.Fisher, Phys. Stat. Sol. 32 (1969) 551.

[30] M.S.Spring and J.W.Steeds, Phys. Stat. Sol. 37 (1970) 303.

[31] M.Horstmann and G.Meyer, Phys. Kondens. Materie 1 (1963) 208.

[32] A.Howie and U.Valdrè, Phil. Mag. 15 (1967) 777.

[33] J.W.Steeds and U.Valdrè, Proc. Eur. Conf. on Electron Microscopy, Rome Vol. 1 (1968) p. 43.

[34] P.B.Hirsch, A.Howie and M.J.Whelan, Phil. Mag. 7 (1962) 2095.

[35] P.Duncumb, Phil. Mag. 7 (1962) 2101.

[36] C.R.Hall, Proc. Roy. Soc. A295 (1966) 140.

[37] D.G.Coates, Phil. Mag. 16 (1967) 1179.

[38] G.R.Booker, A.M.B.Shaw, M.J.Whelan and P.B.Hirsch, Phil. Mag. 16 (1967) 1185.

[39] N.Alam, M.Blackman and D.W.Pashley, Proc. Roy. Soc. A221 (1954) 224.

[40] G.Astner,, I.Bergström, B.Domeij, L.Eriksson and A.Persson, Phys. Letters 14 (1965) 308.

[41] E.Uggerhøj, Phys. Letters 22 (1966) 382.

[42] P.N.Tomlinson and A.Howie, Phys. Letters 27A (1968) 491.

[43] Atomic Collisision and Penetration Studies, Can. J. Phys. 46 (1968) 449–782.

[44] M.W.Thompson, Contemp. Phys. 9 (1968) 375.

[45] J.Lindhard, Mat. Fys. Medd. Dan. Vid. Selsk. 34 (1965) 14.

[46] A.Howie, Brookhaven National Laboratory Report 50083 (Solid State Physics with Accelerators) (1967) 15.

[47] L.T.Chadderton, Phil. Mag. 18 (1968) 1017.

[48] J.M.Cowley, Phys. Letters 26A (1968) 623.

[49] P.B.Hirsch, A.Howie and M.J.Whelan, Phil. Trans. A252 (1960) 499.

[50] S.Takagi, Acta Cryst. 15 (1962) 1311.

[51] A.Howie and M.J.Whelan, Proc. Roy. Soc. A267 (1962) 206.

[52] A.M.B.Shaw and L.M.Brown, Phil. Mag. 15 (1967) 797.

[53] M.F.Ashby and L.M.Brown, Phil. Mag. 8 (1963) 1083.

[54] A.Howie and M.J.Whelan, Proc. Roy. Soc. A263 (1961) 217.

[55] C.J.Ball, Phil. Mag. 9 (1964) 541.

[56] A.P.Pogany and P.S.Turner, Acta Cryst. A24 (1968) 103.

[57] R.Gevers, J.van Landuyt and S.Amelinckx, Phys. Stat. Sol. 11 (1965) 689.

[58] P.B.Hirsch, A.Howie and J.P.Jakubovics, Proc. Melbourne Electron Diffraction Conference (Australian Academy of Sciences, 1965) IB-5.

[59] M.F.Ashby and L.M.Brown, Phil. Mag. 8 (1963) 1649.

[60] C.R.Hall, P.B.Hirsch and G.R.Booker, Phil. Mag. 14 (1966) 979.

[61] M.Wilkens, Phys. Stat. Sol. 6 (1964) 939.

[62] F.Fujimoto and A.Howie, Phil. Mag. 13 (1966) 1131.

[63] H.Hashimoto, Proc. AMU-ANL workshop on high voltage electron microscopy (1966) 68.

[64] D.Taupin, Acta Cryst. 23 (1967) 25.

[65] B.Jouffrey and D.Taupin, Phil. Mag. 16 (1967) 703.

[66] M.F.Wilkens, Phys. Stat. Sol. 9 (1965) 255.

[67] J.P.Jakubovics, Phil. Mag. 13 (1966) 85

[68] Y.Kamiya and R.Uyeda, J. Phys. Soc. Japan 16 (1961) 1361.
[69] A.Howie, Proc. Roy. Soc. A271 (1963) 268.
[70] R.Castaing, Ali El. Hili and L.Henry, Comptes Rendus 262 (1966) 169, 1051.
[71] S.L.Cundy, A.J.F.Metherell and M.J.Whelan, Phil. Mag. 15 (1967) 623.
[72] D.Pines, Elementary Excitations in Solids (Benjamin, New York, 1963).
[73] S.L.Cundy, A.Howie and U.Valdrè, Phil. Mag. 20 (1969) 147.
[74] S.L.Cundy, A.J.F.Metherell and M.J.Whelan, Proc. VI International E.M.Conf.,
     Kyoto, 1966, p. 87.
[75] S.L.Cundy, A.J.F.Metherell and M.J.Whelan, Phil. Mag. 17 (1968) 141.
[76] D.R.Spalding and A.J.F.Metherell, Phil. Mag. 18 (1968) 41.
[77] W.Y.Liang and S.L.Cundy, Phil. Mag. 19 (1969) 1031.
[78] S.L.Cundy, A.J.F.Metherell, M.J.Whelan, P.N.T.Unwin and R.B.Nicholson, Proc.
     Roy. Soc. A307 (1968) 267.
[79] D.R.Spalding, R.E.Villagrana and G.A.Chadwick, Proc. IV Eur. E.M. Conf., Rome,
     1968, p. 347.
[80] C.J.Humphreys and M.J.Whelan, Phil. Mag.20 (1969) 164.
[81] A.Howie and U.Valdrè, Proc. IIIrd European E.M. Conf. 1, Prague, 1964, p. 377.
[82] R.Uyeda and M.Nonoyama, J. J. Appl. Phys. Japan 7 (1968) 200.
[83] A.Howie (quoted in discussion by M.J.Whelan and P.B.Hirsch), J. Phys. Soc.,
     Japan 17 (1962) 118.
[84] L.D.Landau and E.M.Lifshitz, Electrodynamics of Continuous Media (Pergamon,
     1960) pp. 349–359.
[85] P.B.Hirsch and C.J.Humphreys, Proc. IVth European E.M. Conf. Rome, 1968, Vol.
     1, p. 49.
[86] G.D.Palazzi, Rev. Mod. Phys. 40 (1968) 611.
[87] M.J.Makin, Phil. Mag. 18 (1968) 637.

RECENT PROGRESS IN HIGH VOLTAGE
ELECTRON MICROSCOPY

V.E.COSSLETT

Cavendish Laboratory, Cambridge, England

1. Technical features of high voltage electron microscopes

1.1. *Introduction*

Standard commercially available electron microscopes have high resolution but limited specimen penetration: in Al at most 1 μm (in optimum orientation), in heavy metals such as tungsten or uranium less than 0.1 μm (1000Å). Specimen thickness for given image brightness, or on a criterion of constant chromatic aberration, increases with beam voltage at a rate which depends on the atomic number (or density) of the specimen and on the angular aperture of the objective. Between 100 kV and 1 MV the increase in observable thickness is about three times in the worst case but 8 to 10 times in optimum conditions (light element and large aperture).

So the chief reason for high voltage microscopy is greater specimen penetration, enabling thicknesses a little nearer to that of bulk samples to be examined. Other advantages are:

(a) lower specimen-damage in most working conditions;

(b) higher practical resolution from specimens just observable at 100 kV;

(c) higher potential resolution on very thin specimens;

(d) greater beam brightness (which further aids visibility through thick specimens).

Disadvantages are few, but not unimportant:

(a) greater radiation damage in some conditions (displacement of atoms);

(b) lower contrast in specimens of given thickness;

(c) poorer response of viewing screens and photographic emulsions;

(d) greater danger from X-radiation;

(e) higher cost, roughly in proportion to the maximum operating voltage.

The prospective benefits of greater penetration and improved resolution have been sufficiently attractive to encourage the construction in recent years of several microscopes for operation up to 1 MV. A 3 MV microscope is now being built at Toulouse [1].

1.2. *Historical*

Several attempts were made during and just after the War to design and construct electron microscopes for voltages up to 3 or 4 times that of the standard instrument. Results were actually published from only one project (van Dorsten, Oosterkamp and Le Poole [2]). They obtained clear micrographs of yeast cells and of aluminium oxide films at voltages up to 350 kV. Their paper throughly discusses the advantages and problems of high voltage microscopy, including that of protection from X-rays. AEI in Great Britain and RCA in USA also got some way with similar projects and obtained high voltage micrographs.

No further developments took place, partly because of cost but also because biologists about that time found how to cut sections of tissues thin enough to examine at 100 kV and less. A little later metallurgists developed techniques for thinning their specimens also to the order of a few hundred Ångstrom units thick. It was the consequent outburst of activity in metal physics, and the growing realisation of the importance of dislocations, which brought back an interest in higher voltages for looking at thicker specimens. Microscopes operating up to 350 kV were built in Japan in the 1950's with these practical applications in mind (Maruse et al. [3]; Kobayashi et al. [4]), and led later to production models from the Hitachi (1 MV) and the Shimadzu (500 kV) companies. The Japan Electron Optics Laboratories followed later, also with a 1 MV instrument. Pioneering projects in Britain (Coupland [5]) and USSR (Popov [6]) did not produce further developments.

A quite independent line was followed by Dupouy in France, from a desire to observe wet (and, if possible, living) material. A microscope for 1.5 MV was designed and built at Toulouse (Dupouy and Perrier [7]). The first results published were of bacteria (Dupouy et al. [8]), but since then most of the applications have been in metal physics there also (for a review see Dupouy [9]).

In the past decade several other high voltage microscopes have been built. The Cavendish Laboratory, Cambridge, 750 kV instrument (Smith, Considine and Cosslett [10]) has been developed into a 1 MV commercial version (EM 7) by AEI Ltd., and RCA have built a 650 kV and a 1 MV microscope in the USA. Publication of the results of work done by all these instruments is now growing, in the polymer and biological fields as well as in metal physics (for reviews see Cosslett [11,12]).

1.3. *Special design and operational considerations*

Compared with a standard 100 kV microscope, high voltage microscopes have certain extra or altered features which can be classified as follows:

(a) High voltage supply.

(b) Electron gun design.

(c) Electron gun brightness.

(d) Accelerator design and operation.

(e) Lens design.

(f) Viewing screen response.

(g) Photographic emulsion sensitivity.

(h) X-radiation protection.

(i) Remote viewing and image intensification.

(a) High voltage supply. Although attempts have been made to utilise a van de Graaff belt generator, the preferred source of high voltage is a Cockcroft-Walton (or Greinacher) rectifier-capacitor circuit coupled to a separate accelerator column. The system may be either air-insulated or confined in a tank filled with an insulating gas (freeon, nitrogen, SF_6) under pressure. When air-insulated a large room is required or even a separate building, to provide adequate clearance against spark-over. Pressurised sets require almost as much space, however, since height must be enough to lift off the upper half of the tank and ground area enough to park it. The minimum size of a high voltage microscope hall is about 10 m × 10 m × 10 m, but a greater length (up to 15 m) is desirable for accommodating auxiliary apparatus. Some systems have both generator and accelerator in a common tank (Watanabe et al. [13]; Katagiri et al. [21]), others use two tanks to minimise electrical interaction and facilitate servicing.

Electrical stability is ensured by the usual double feed-back circuitry, with a slow loop to control drift and a fast loop for ripple. Stabilities of 1 in 10^5 or better are specified. An extra difficulty, not encountered at 100 kV and below, is corona discharge in the generating stack and/or in the accelerator. To minimise this it is becoming usual to employ multi-stage systems, with only a moderate voltage across each stage (50–90 kV). The earlier HT sets (Toulouse, Cavendish) had fewer stages with up to 150 kV per stage, requiring higher vacuum in the accelerator and greater attention to cleanliness of insulators and corona shields to avoid flash-over.

(b) Electron gun design. If the voltage range of the microscope is limited (2 to 1, or at most 3 to 1), the electron gun can be identical with that fitted to 100 kV instruments. But if a wide working range is desired, as in the AEI model (100 kV to 1 MV), then it is not possible to get a compromise design with adequate performance over the whole range. Two solutions are available.

First, the anode-Wehnelt cylinder separation can be adjusted to the value
giving optimum gun efficiency as the voltage is varied. Alternatively, as in the
Cavendish microscope, the gun can be operated at constant voltage from a
separate supply in the HT terminal, independent of the overall voltage. This
mode has the advantage of constant output current, otherwise the beam current will increase with operating voltage (unless special circuitry is provided).

(c) Electron gun brightness. The brightness β_s of the beam delivered on the
specimen is defined as the current per unit area per unit solid angle. It is related directly to the brightness of the emitting cathode β_E and the accelerating
voltage V_A

$$\beta_s = I_s/\pi^2 r_s^2 \alpha_c^2 = \beta_E(V_A/V_E) \, . \tag{1}$$

Here I_s is the current into a spot of radius r_s on the specimen, α_c is the semi-
aperture angle of the beam leaving the second condenser and V_E is the effective
emission voltage of the electrons leaving the cathode. For $V_A = 100\,\text{kV}$, the
value of β_s may be as high as 10^5 A/cm^2/sr if the cathode is operated at about
2700°K, emitting about 1 A/cm^2. This theoretical value can only be attained in
practice if the cathode tip is correctly positioned in the aperture of the Wehnelt
cylinder and the correct bias voltage is applied to the cylinder. If these optimum conditions can be maintained, the beam brightness will increase in proportion to the operating voltage. So the available illuminating brightness is
higher in the high voltage microscope than at 100 kV. This is so, however, only
so long as the beam completely fills the second condenser aperture, which can
be ensured by proper design and operation of the accelerator and first condenser lens. The increase is in fact greater than indicated by eq. (1), because of
relativistic effects. For instance, between 100 kV and 1 MV the factor will
be 18 instead of 10 times.

(d) Accelerator design and operation. It is essential to couple the electron
gun efficiently to the accelerator. For convenience in operating the microscope, the input beam to the condenser system should not vary greatly as
overall voltage is changed. In particular the position of the crossover of the
beam leaving the accelerator — the virtual electron source for the microscope
— should not move appreciably along the axis. To ensure this, the input conditions of the accelerator must be appropriately varied with working voltage.
Either a magnetic electron lens of variable strength is fitted between gun and
accelerator, as in the Cavendish and the original Toulouse microscopes, or a
variable voltage is applied to the first stage of the accelerator (which is effectively a strong electrostatic lens for the beam), as in most of the production
models. The design of the accelerator itself is still to some extent a matter of

rule of thumb practice. Our experience and that of one of the Japanese teams (Watanabe et al. [13]) is that the focussing action of the accelerator proves to be considerably stronger than predicted by the theoretical relationships.

In operation an accelerator is more temperamental than the simple electron gun of a 100 kV microscope. It is liable to microdischarges from the internal electrodes or even to flash-over between them in poor vacuum. To meet this difficulty it is necessary to "condition" the accelerator before commencing normal microscopy, by raising the applied voltage in steps to a final value that is 50 kV or 100 kV above the desired running voltage. After several hours at running voltage the procedure should be repeated. Each type of accelerator has its special conditioning drill, as laid down by the makers. In general little trouble is encountered at running voltages below 500 kV, but at very high voltage the recommended procedure must be carefully followed, as a major breakdown might seriously damage the accelerator or the HT supply circuits.

(e) Lens design. Electron lenses for focussing high voltage beams have to be larger and carry greater excitation (ampere-turns) than those for 100 kV. The focussing properties of a magnetic lens may be expressed in terms of a parameter k^2

$$k^2 = \frac{Kl^2B_0^2}{V_r} \tag{2}$$

where B_0 is the maximum value of the magnetic induction between the polepieces, l is a length characteristic of the lens, K is a numerical factor incorporating the charge and mass of the electron and V_r is the relativistically corrected value of the beam voltage. If V_A is in megavolts

$$V_r = V_A (1+0.98V_A) . \tag{3}$$

The length l is sometimes taken as the half-width of the axial magnetic field distribution (Glaser [14]) or more practically as the polepiece gap S or the radius R of the hole through the polepieces (Liebmann [15]).

The objective lens has to be strong, to minimise aberrations. There is no unique solution, as recent work has confirmed (Mulvey and Wallington [16]; Kamminga et al. [17]). Broadly speaking, B_0 must be kept as high as possible without saturating the soft iron polepieces, whilst l is kept small in order to keep the lens compact and the whole microscope column reasonably short. However if k^2 is to be maintained constant as beam voltage is raised, with B_0 fixed, l would have to be increased in proportion to $(V_r)^{1/2}$, i.e. by a factor of 4.2 between 100 kV and 1 MV. In practice some increase in B_0 is obtained over the value used at 100 kV, with the result that the polepiece gap and focal length of an objective is about 3 times greater at 1 MV. With 12 000 to 15 000 amp-turns excitation, requiring water-cooling of the lens, the focal length can be kept to about 5 or 6 mm.

All other dimensions of the lens have to be increased, roughly in the same degree, so that the outer diameter becomes 45–50 cm compared with the 15–20 cm of a standard electron microscope. The weight escalates correspondingly, and even more so if massive X-ray protection is built in. The Cavendish lenses were designed to electron optical limits and none weighs more than 150 kg, so that a fork-lift truck can handle them. In some of the production models a lens may weigh half a ton, assembly or dismantling requiring a major effort with the aid of a crane.

The first condenser and final projector lenses have to be of short focal length and are similar in design to the objective. The second condenser and the other projector lenses may be much weaker, but still proportionately stronger than for 100 kV operation. The result is that the microscope column has an overall height of 3 m or more. Aperture drives and specimen airlock are then difficult to reach, so that a ladder must be used unless remote control devices are provided.

(f) Viewing screen. The response of a fluorescent screen of standard thickness decreases with increasing voltage. The range of 100 kV electrons is about equal to the mass-thickness of the coating usually provided (5–10 mg cm^{-2}). Range increases approximately as $V_A^{1.5}$, so that at 1 MV it is about 250 mg cm^{-2} and most electrons pass right through the screen. Also the energy lost per unit path length decreases with rise in beam voltage. So thicker screens must be used. On the other hand the lateral spread of the beam then increases, blurring the fluorescent image. Little accurate measurement of these effects has so far been made, although different laboratories have clearly tried to find an acceptable compromise thickness of phosphor, giving adquate brightness without undue loss of resolution (Fisher and Lally [18] ; Iwanaga et al. [19]). We have found a ZnS layer of 15–20 mg cm^{-2} suitable for most conditions, but for fine focussing we use a thinner layer on a transparent plastic membrane to avoid the backscatter of electrons which occurs from a solid substrate.

(g) Photography. The response of photographic emulsions falls for the same reasons as that of the fluorescent screen, requiring a longer exposure at given current density of the electron image. The effect is not so drastic as had been predicted, however. Measurements made by two Japanese teams (Iwanaga et al. [19] ; Katagiri et al. [20,21]) on a variety of emulsions showed a decrease in sensitivity (for an optical density of unity) of about 4 times between

100 kV and 500 kV. We use mainly cut film, for which the factor is only 1.5 between 60 kV and 600 kV, as confirmed by careful measurements made in accurately controlled conditions of exposure and processing (Jones, unpublished). The effect of back-scattered electrons in increasing the intensity of the photographic image is readily demonstrated by exposing a film with and without a metal backing plate. It should be noted that the plate or film magazine must be properly shielded from X-radiation, to ensure that the emulsion is not fogged whilst in store before or after exposure.

(h) X-radiation protection. The column of a high voltage microscope is an X-ray tube of high power, radiation being emitted from apertures, liners and any other surface that is struck by the electron beam. In most operating conditions, with a total beam current of a few μA, adequate shielding is provided by the amount of copper and iron in the lenses and it is only necessary for the designer to ensure that other units (such as the specimen chamber and camera) have thick enough walls. But for examining very thick specimens, and even more so when irradiating them in situ to study radiation damage, very much bigger beam currents may be required. To meet this need some of the experimental installations (Toulouse, Cavendish) include a radiation wall from behind which the microscope can be remotely operated. Other instruments (US Steel, AEI) have detachable control desks, which can be wheeled away to a safe operating distance for heavy beam experiments.

Regular monitoring of a high voltage microscope is essential, even when safety devices are installed, and especially if auxiliary apparatus such as an energy analyser is being used. An appreciable X-ray output can be produced by scattered electrons in areas not struck by the direct beam, and also by secondary X-ray production. So any modification to the original structure of the microscope must be made with such possibilities in mind. The tolerance level of X-radiation internationally accepted is 2.5 mR/hr for personnel receiving regular medical checks and working for not more than 40 hr per week in a radiation zone. Much higher levels are permissible over short periods, however, under the control of the radiation protection officer. For ordinary laboratory personnel the permitted dose rate is 0.75 mR/hr, but most high voltage microscope manufacturers seem to aim at reducing the level in all accessible areas to that set for the general public, 0.25 mR/hr.

(i) Remote viewing and image intensification. Radiation hazards for the operator can obviously be reduced by remote viewing via a closed link TV chain. A still greater convenience is to use an image intensifier, placed directly below the camera, which is then retracted. It is possible with a good modern unit (Philips, AEI-English Electric) to observe very much fainter electron images than can be seen on the viewing screen of the microscope. High aperture optical coupling is desirable, or a fibre optics connection, between a transmission fluorescent screen and the photocathode of the intensifier. In our experience it is not easy to find a good enough cathode ray tube for the displayed image. It is best to have a dual system, with an ordinary tube for focussing purposes and a storage tube for photography.

1.4. *Summary*

Most of the special features of a high voltage microscope are matters requiring careful attention in design and construction. In operation the instrument differs little from a standard 100 kV microscope. The chief new requirement is the conditioning procedure for the accelerator column, and the consequent need to keep an eye on vacuum and imaging fluctuations for signs that re-conditioning is necessary. The layout and operation of the controls are very similar to normal practice, except that more are automated. Filament changing is more difficult, but filament life is liable to be longer since there is ample gun brightness available. The image at 1 MV is hard to distinguish from one at 100 kV, although it is likely to look rather sharper in dark-field. Electron diffraction patterns are smaller than usual, due to the smaller Bragg angles corresponding to the shorter wavelength, but this can be corrected if the lens arrangements allow very long camera length operation.

2. Energy loss, resolution and penetration in high voltage microscopy

2.1. *Introduction*

High voltage microscopes are used primarily to gain penetration, rather than image resolution. So we consider first the transmission of electrons through matter, which is accompanied by both elastic and inelastic scattering. Elastic scattering chiefly affects the angular spread of a beam, whereas inelastic scattering broadens the energy distribution so that the beam is no longer monochromatic. The image resolution suffers correspondingly, because of the severe chromatic aberration of electron lenses. The theoretical position will be discussed first, followed by a survey of recent experimental evidence for the increase in penetration with voltage.

Theory can deal effectively with only two simplified and extreme cases: a completely ordered arrangement of atoms (the perfect crystal) and a completely random collection of isolated atoms (the perfect gas). The treatment of electron propagation in thin crystals has been discussed earlier by Howie (Ch. 00). It will be referred to later in the present context where we discuss the difficulty of its extension to relatively thick crystals. The alternative approach, starting from scattering at single atoms, will now be outlined. It proves to be applicable, to first order at least, to amorphous materials and almost equally well to polycrystalline specimens also. Even where the quantitative fit is not exact, the variation with voltage is closely predicted and this is so for thicknesses up to the limit for imaging in the electron microscope.

2.2. Electron transmission as limited by elastic and inelastic scattering

(a) Single scattering. To treat scattering by isolated atoms requires first a model of the potential distribution around the atom, from which an expression for the angular distribution of the scattered beam is obtained via the differential cross-sections for elastic and inelastic processes. In electron microscopy we are concerned with scattering at very small angles, since the objective aperture is in the order of 10^{-3} to 10^{-2} radian. The only successful attempts to deal with this situation, for scattering layers more than one mean free path thick (i.e. for plural as well as single scattering), are those due to Lenz [22] and to Burge and Smith [23] (also Smith and Burge [24]). The theory due to Lenz will be outlined here, since it fits better the experimental results: Burge and Smith start from the atomic scattering factors of atoms, as deduced theoretically, and attempt to fit analytical functions to them which can then be integrated. Lenz takes a fairly simple analytical model of the atom (Wentzel [25]), the potential $V(r)$ at distance r from the centre in a screened Coulomb field being given by

$$V(r) = \frac{Ze}{r} \exp(-r/R) \qquad (4)$$

where Z is the atomic number of the atom, R is its "mean" radius and e is the electronic charge. From this he obtains, in the first Born approximation, the differential cross-section for elastic scattering

$$\frac{d\sigma_e}{d\Omega} = \frac{4}{a_H^2 q^4} \frac{Z^2}{(1+q^{-2}R^{-2})^2} \qquad (5)$$

where $d\sigma_e/d\Omega$ is a measure of the probability of the electron being scattered into solid angle $d\Omega$ through the angle ϕ, which is related to q by

$$q = \frac{4\pi \sin(\phi/2)}{\lambda} = \frac{2\pi\phi}{\lambda} \qquad (6)$$

in small angle approximation; λ is the wavelength of the electron beam and

a_H is the Bohr radius of the hydrogen atom, relativistically expressed. The value of R for a particular atom may be taken from the approximate relation

$$R = a_H Z^{-\frac{1}{3}} .$$

Alternatively it may be deduced from calculations of the electron density around the atom, or from measurements of the diamagnetic susceptibility.

Elastic scattering arises from the interaction of incident electrons with the field due to the core of an atom. In such a "collision" between a very light and a massive particle very little energy is transferred, but deflections may be through any angle, including 180°. Electrons incident on the outer regions of an atom, on the other hand, effectively suffer collisions with individual electrons in which up to half the initial energy can be transferred, resulting in deflections of up to 90°. Inelastic scattering is more difficult to deal with, as it should involve a summation over all energy loss processes. At present we do not know in sufficient detail the relative probabilities of all these processes and their angular distribution. By a simpler approach Lenz [22] arrives at an expression for the differential cross-section for inelastic scattering, analogous to eq. (5) for elastic scattering

$$\frac{d\sigma_i}{d\Omega} = \frac{4Z}{a_H^2 q_i^4} \left(1 - \frac{1}{(1+q_i^2 R^2)^2} \right) \tag{7}$$

where q_i differs from q of eq. (6) by the inclusion of an energy loss term. In small angle approximation, with ϕ in place of $\sin \phi$, the form of q_i is

$$q_i = \frac{2\pi}{\lambda} \left(\phi^2 + \left(\frac{\Delta E}{2E_o} \right)^2 \right)^{\frac{1}{2}} . \tag{8}$$

As a first approximation Lenz took ΔE as half the primary ionisation energy, in effect limiting discussion to small energy loss processes; E_o is the incident electron energy.

Eqs. (5) and (7) enable us to calculate the variation of elastic and inelastic scattering with angle and by integration to find the fraction of the incident beam scattered within an angular aperture of given size. But this is only valid for single scattering conditions, i.e. for specimens so thin that the chance of an electron suffering more than one collision in it is negligible. As the mean free path for scattering is no more than a few hundred Ångstrom units at 100 kV even in light elements, and proportionately less in high - Z elements, such an integration is of use only for relatively thin specimens in electron microscopy. For thicker specimens plural scattering theory must be used.

It follows from a comparison of eq. (5) and eq. (7) that the elastic and in-elastic cross-sections are of the same order of magnitude. In Lenz's treatment the ratio of the total cross-sections σ_e and σ_i, the probabilities of elastic and inelastic scattering into any angle greater than zero, is given by

$$\frac{\sigma_i}{\sigma_e} = \frac{4}{Z} \log_n \frac{1}{\overline{q}R} \tag{9}$$

where $\overline{q}$ is the smallest possible value of q_i (from eq. (8) with $\phi=0$). At 50 kV this ratio falls from about 4 for carbon to about 0.36 for gold, although experiment shows a value of about 2.6 for carbon and 0.20 for gold (Lippert [26]). From eq. (9) the ratio varies with voltage, because $\overline{q}$ involves λ.

(b) Plural scattering. The fraction of the incident beam that falls within the objective aperture after passing through a specimen of mass-thickness ρt, obeys an absorption law of the usual form

$$I/I_o = \exp(-S_1 \rho t) \tag{10}$$

where S_1 may be regarded as a mass absorption coefficient, in $(g\ cm^{-2})^{-1}$. In single scattering conditions S_1 is simply related to the total scattering cross-section per atom σ_T by

$$S_1 = N\sigma_T/A \tag{11}$$

if N is Avogadro's number, A the atomic number of the scatterer and $\sigma_T = \sigma_e + \sigma_i$. S_1 depends on the angular size of the aperture as well as on the beam voltage and the nature of the scatterer.

As the specimen thickness increases there is an increasing probability that subsequent scattering acts will deflect an initially scattered electron back into the aperture. So the effective value of S_1 falls below the single value given by eq. (11) to some new value S_p, where the suffix p indicates plural scattering. The thickness of the scatterer is usually given in terms of the number of mean free paths for elastic scattering, p_e, where

$$p_e = \frac{N}{A} \rho t \sigma_e . \tag{12}$$

As an example, the single-scattering thickness for aluminium at 100 kV is about 1100 Å and for gold about 100 Å from the Lenz theory.

To calculate the angular distribution in plural scattering conditions, the single scattering differential cross-section has to be folded with itself the appropriate number of times. This has been done by Lenz [22], with some simplifying assumptions. He presents the results as a set of universal curves for each of three typical elements, carbon, chromium and gold, from which graphical integration gives the fraction of the beam falling within an aperture of given angular subtension. His main simplification was to take q_i in the inelastic scattering equation to be equal to q as defined in eq. (6), which slightly overweights the inelastic contribution in the imaging beam.

A great deal of experimental work has largely confirmed Lenz's predicted values of S_p in the voltage range $10 - 100$ kV and for a variety of elements (for a review, see Reimer [27]), to much better than an order of magnitude. Closer agreement can be obtained if a second parameter θ_o is allowed to vary, in addition to R, in eqs. (5) and (7). (Lippert and Frese [28]). θ_o is a screening factor, or cut-off angle, preventing the cross-section going to infinity as $\phi \to 0$, and taken by Lenz as

$$\theta_o = \lambda/2\pi R . \tag{13}$$

It is doubtful whether the Lippert and Friese procedure has anything other than a limited practical value, as it seems difficult to obtain a perfect fit for all apertures and all voltages. The reasonably good fit of Lenz's calculations with experiment already relies on a suitable choice of R, since this parameter cannot be uniquely computed.

Lenz's equations in relativistic form have the advantage of giving correctly the variation in electron transmission up to very high voltages. For experimental convenience transmission is not discussed in terms of S_p (or $1/S_p$), since the value of the effective absorption coefficient changes with specimen thickness, but in terms of a transmission factor T, defined by

$$T = [\log_e (I_o/I)]^{-1} . \tag{14}$$

The variation in T with beam voltage will depend on the aperture used, as does S_p, as well as on the nature of the specimen. Recent work by Curtis [29] (also Curtis et al. [30]) gave results for T at voltages up to 700 kV for carbon and gold, with apertures of 1.1×10^{-3} and 5.5×10^{-3}. In figs. 1 and 2, T is graphed against voltage for a specimen of *given thickness,* of carbon and gold respectively. Single scattering conditions are approached only at top voltage. At lower voltages there is a great deal of plural scattering, which lifts the curve at that end and tends to obscure the true increase in transmission with voltage. The effect of the plural contribution can be seen by comparing the theo-

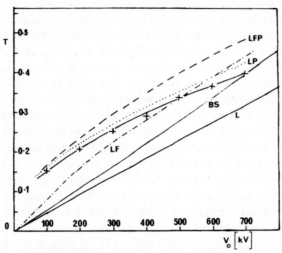

Fig. 1. Electron transmission T through a carbon film of mass-thickness 260 μg cm^{-2} in function of accelerating voltage V_0, for $a_0 = 5 \times 10^{-3}$, calculated from the single scattering theories of Lenz (L), Burge and Smith (BS) and Lippert and Friese (LP), and the plural scattering theories of Lenz (LP) and Lippert and Friese (LFP). Crosses = experimental points of Curtis [25] for $a_0 = 5.5 \times 10^{-3}$.

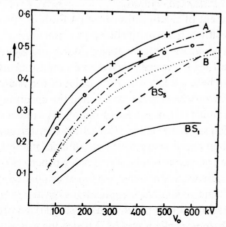

Fig. 2. Electron transmission T through a gold film of thickness 450Å in function of accelerating voltage V_0, calculated from the plural scattering theories of Lenz (A,B) and Burge and Smith (BS_5, BS_1) for $a_0 = 5 \times 10^{-3}$ and 1×10^{-3} in each case, compared with the experimental points of Curtis [29] for $a_0 = 5.5 \times 10^{-3}$ (crosses) and 1.1×10^{-3} (circles).

retical curves of Lenz for single and plural scattering (L and LP) in fig. 1. These results agree with Lenz's theory very closely for carbon and mederately so for gold, over the whole range of voltage. The Burge and Smith calculations give a poorer fit, and differ from Lenz (and experiment) in showing a much greater variation with aperture (curves BS_1 and BS_5 in fig. 2). The empirical expression of Lippert and Friese, fitted at low voltage, runs too high as voltage increases, even when corrected for plural scattering (curve LFP in fig. 1).

Reimer and Sommer [31] have also published results for several elements at voltages up to 1200 kV, but they are mostly in single scattering conditions. They find rather greater discrepancy from Lenz's predictions, and discuss how far agreement can be improved by taking account of next neighbour interactions by a method due to Raith [32].

It is more informative to plot results for transmission at a given degree of plural scattering, instead of for given specimen thickness; that is, to plot the thickness which corresponds to a given transmission against voltage. In effect this gives curves of constant (I/I_o) ratio, which are nearer to the subjective estimate a microscope operator will make of the increase in usable specimen thickness as voltage increases. We discuss transmission from this point of view in sect. 3, when describing experimental results on specimen penetration at high voltages.

2.3. *Electron transmission in crystals.*

The wave treatment of electron transmission through crystals has been fully described by Howie in earlier lectures. For thin crystals it gives good agreement with experiment at high voltages (Mazel and Ayroles [33]; Goringe, Howie and Whelan [34]), especially when corrected for many-beam effects. By "thin" we mean here a thickness of the order of the reciprocal of the effective absorption coefficient, sometimes called the absorption distance, which is the thickness in which (I/I_o) is reduced to e^{-1}. At present the theory cannot deal with the much greater thicknesses for which transmission approaches the lower limit of visibility, and hence which are of chief interest to high voltage microscopists. The equivalent of plural scattering processes on the one hand, and energy loss processes on the other, make the evaluation of the angular distribution of the imaging beam too complicated a matter. It is significant that in very thick crystals the difference in transmission at and off the Bragg reflecting position disappears (Ichimiya [35]); also the energy distributions for these two orientations differ only slightly (Uyeda [36]). An empirical theory has been proposed by Ichimiya to account for these observations, but at present it lacks any firm physical foundation. It may turn out that a working solution will be more readily found along the lines of channelling theory than by the wave treatment.

2.4. *Energy loss*

As regards energy loss, the situation in a thin perfect crystal is again well understood but is impossible to evaluate in most specimens of practical interest in high voltage microscopy. A few metals have a simple energy loss spectrum, the angular distribution and mean free path for which are known. In aluminium, for instance, the main plasmon loss is 15 eV, the mean free path for it is about 1000 Å at 100 kV, and the cut-off angle is so small that all the loss electrons pass through the objective aperture in the imaging beam. Most other metals suffer a more or less complicated set of free electron losses, the spectra of which are sometimes known but not the respective mean free paths nor the angular distributions.

The only element which has been studied in adequate detail is carbon, for which spectra were obtained through apertures of various sizes (Misell [37]; Misell and Crick [38]). In this case it is possible by fairly straightforward folding procedure to calculate the angular and energy distributions of an imaging beam in typical conditions of electron microscopy. But even this procedure is not accurate enough for thick films, unless loss spectra have been measured out to high enough values to include the lower energy X-ray lines. In carbon, for instance, the K-excitation energy is about 280 eV, whereas the main discrete loss (of a plasmon nature) has a peak at about 25 eV. Since the mean free path for the latter is about 800 Å at 100 kV, the X-ray loss will make an appreciable contribution to the energy loss peak for a specimen 5000 Å thick or more. It should be remarked that the cross-section for K-level excitation in carbon is relatively high, although most of the energy appears as Auger electrons, not as X-quanta.

The situation is even more difficult to evaluate in an amorphous or polycrystalline specimen, where elastic scattering is convoluted with the angular displacements occurring in the inelastic processes. Even if we had all the data about energy loss spectra, mean free paths and angular distributions for each loss process, it would be a difficult matter to compute for a thick specimen the final angular distribution in the imaging beam and the energy loss distribution, the parameters of which are the position of the peak (E_p) and the half-width of the peak at half-height (ΔE_w). In the absence of such detailed knowledge we have to appeal to one or other of the more general theories of energy loss, which do not depend on knowing the component loss mechanisms. The Bethe energy loss relation gives only the mean energy of the transmitted beam, which is always at lower energy than the most probable or peak value because of the weighting effect of the higher energy losses. The Landau [39] treatment, however, gives expressions for both E_p and the half-width ΔE_w

$$E_0 - E_p = \Delta E_p = \frac{2\pi Ne^4 Z\rho t}{m_0 v^2 A} \left(\log_n \frac{4\pi Ne^4 Z\rho t}{J^2 A(1-\beta^2)} - \beta^2 + 0.37 \right) \quad (15)$$

$$= \frac{15.3 \times 10^4 \rho t}{\beta^2} \frac{Z}{A} \left(\log_n \frac{15.6 \times 10^{10} Z\rho t}{J^2 A(1-\beta^2)} \right.$$

$$\left. - \beta^2 + 0.37 \right) \quad (16)$$

$$\Delta E_w = 4 \times \frac{15.3 \times 10^4 \rho t}{\beta^2} \frac{Z}{A}. \quad (17)$$

Here m_0 is the electron rest mass, v its velocity, $\beta = v/c$ where c is the velocity of light and J is the mean ionisation energy (frequently taken to be given by $J = 11.5Z$); the remaining symbols have already been defined.

The calculated values for a 1 μm thickness of carbon and of gold at several values of incident electron energy E_0 are then as follows

Table 1

Energy loss parameters for 1 μm thickness of carbon and gold at different beam voltages E_0.

E_0 (keV)	Carbon		Gold	
	ΔE_p (eV)	ΔE_w (eV)	ΔE_p (eV)	ΔE_w (eV)
100	430	205	2310	1550
200	275	125	1460	960
500	180	82	1015	625
1000	165	69	945	520

After certain corrections Landau's equations agree fairly well with experiment at both low and high energies for films of medium thickness, although in general the predicted value of ΔE_p is too high and that of ΔE_w too small (see Birkhoff [40]). The theory fails seriously for very thin films, the peak becoming asymmetrical, because of the lesser occurrence of the higher energy losses. The value of the width falls less rapidly than the shift of the peak, however, so that ΔE_p may become less than ΔE_w for extremely thin films.

Knop et al. [41] have made extensive measurements at 1 MV on several elements over a wide thickness range to study this change in shape of the energy distribution. They show that results can be quantitatively explained by subtracting from the Landau treatment, which includes all possible electron excitations, the less frequent inner shell excitations. The K, L, M, etc. contributions are omitted in succession as the film thickness is decreased. Good agreement, however, was not obtained for very thin films ($<$ 1 mg cm^{-2}), possibly because the losses to be measured were then smaller than the resolution of the energy analyser they used.

The theory (and the experiments of Knop et al.) are not directly comparable with the conditions of electron microscopy, where we are interested only in the energy losses in a narrow forward cone. Experiments in these conditions are only now beginning to be made, by fitting an energy analyser into the electron microscope. Results of Kamiya for magnesium oxide, as reported by Uyeda [36], apparently agree in trend with the Landau theory but not quantitatively. The values for ΔE_w at 200 and 500 kV were 50 to 60% greater than predicted by eq. (17), whereas ΔE_p was 20 to 30% smaller than given by eq. (16). In fact ΔE_p was about the same as ΔE_w instead of being about twice as great. In the 200 Bragg diffracting orientation, as expected, anomalous transmission (or "channelling") reduced the energy loss so that ΔE_p was less by 33% in a specimen 1 μm thick. But the difference decreased with thickness and was only 12% in a 4 μm thickness. The width of the distribution was less affected, ΔE_w being only about 15% less than in the non-diffracting position. Our own preliminary measurements, using the Ichinokawa [42] type of energy analyser, support Kamiya's results (Considine [43]). In aluminium 3 μm thick, for instance, we find that at both 200 kV and 500 kV the width is as predicted by Landau, but that ΔE_p is about one-third his theoretical value. When compared with the plasmon theory, ΔE_w is much greater than predicted but ΔE_p agrees closely with the values calculated from the mean free path for the 15.3 eV loss at 200 kV and 500 kV as computed relativistically by Hirsch and Humphreys [44].

2.5. Chromatic Aberration

The significance of energy loss for electron microscopy is that it is the chief cause of poor resolution in most imaging conditions, for all except the very thinnest specimens. The chromatic aberration of the objective lens is such that a point object is imaged as a disc of confusion, the radius δ_c of which is directly proportional to the fractional energy loss in the imaging beam

$$\delta_c = C_c \alpha_o (\Delta V/V)_{rel.} . \tag{18}$$

Here α_o is the semi-angular aperture of the objective and C_c is the chromatic constant of that lens. The energy loss factor is in relativistic form

$$\frac{\Delta V}{V}\bigg|_{\text{rel.}} = \frac{\Delta V}{V_A} \frac{1 + 1.96\ V_A}{1 + 0.98\ V_A} \tag{19}$$

where voltage is expressed in MV.

In high voltage microscopes the product $C_c\alpha_o$ is usually kept constant as voltage is varied, so the chromatic aberration changes in proportion to $(\Delta V/V)_{\text{rel.}}$. The value of this factor falls rapidly as V_A is increased, because ΔV falls and V_A rises. Hence a great reduction in chromatic aberration occurs in the image of a specimen just visible at 100 kV, as the voltage goes up. Between 100 kV and 1 MV the resolution, as measured by δ_c, may improve by as much as 15 to 20 times in a specimen of constant thickness.

The exact degree of improvement depends on whether δ_c is determined by the position or the width of the energy peak. For very thin specimens we must set $\Delta V = \Delta E_p$, so long as the imaging beam contains an appreciable proportion of no-loss electrons. Assuming a Poisson distribution for the energy loss, a specimen one mean free path thick will transmit a beam such that e^{-1} of the electron intensity has suggered no loss, e^{-1} has a single loss, and the remainder have multiple losses. As the mean free path for the first plasmon loss in aluminium is about 1000 Å at 100 kV, rising to about 2800 Å at 1 MV (Hirsch and Humphreys [44]), ΔE_p is the determining parameter for chromatic aberration only relatively thin specimens.

For thicker specimens, the fraction of no-loss electrons is negligibly small and we are concerned only with the width of the energy distribution. δ_c is then determined by ΔE_w, or more exactly by $\pm \Delta E_w/2$. The disc of least confusion is defined by electrons of maximum and minimum energy, not by those of no-loss and minimum energy as for a very thin film. In these circumstances, and with the skew distribution of the energy peak produced by specimens of intermediate thickness, graphical construction shows that the effective disc of least confusion has a radius about half the value given by eq. (18) (Cosslett [45]). Taking the values of ΔE_w from table 1 for carbon and gold, and Kamiya's values (in non-diffracting conditions) for magnesium oxide, the image resolution through a thickness of 1 μm of each element will then be as shown in table 2.

The actual image resolution is unlikely to be as good as predicted for carbon and gold, since we have neglected other sources of energy loss (such as thermal diffuse scattering) and instrumental instabilities, but the table should be a good indication of the degree of improvement attainable in high voltage microscopy (see also Sahashi [46]. Accurate measurements of resolution on specimens of known thickness are difficult to make, to check these predictions.

Table 2

Image resolution from eq. (18) (with $\Delta V = \Delta E_W/2$) for $t = 1$ μm, $C_c = 2$ mm, $a_0 = 5 \times 10^{-3}$.

E_0 (kv)	Carbon (Å)	Gold (Å)	MgO (Å)
100	112	865	315*
200	36.5	280	108
500	11.0	83	36
1000	5.2	39	15*

* Extrapolated values.

Some results of a preliminary nature were recently reported by Koike [47] on magnesium oxide, which showed a resolution at 100 kV and 200 kV even better than that in table 2, but he may have been imaging in a diffracting orientation.

For practical microscopy it is more interesting to discuss the increase in thickness of specimen that can be imaged with a given chromatic aberration as working voltage is raised. If ΔE_W from eq. (17) is inserted as the value of ΔV in eq. (18), it follows that the limiting thickness for given δ_c would be directly proportional to V_{rel}, provided that C_c and α_0 remained constant. Taking the relativistic correction into account, a specimen can be about 7 times as thick at 1 MV as at 100 kV so long as resolution is determined by chromatic aberration. This factor of increased penetration is independent of the size of the aperture employed, although the absolute thickness for a given chromatic aberration depends directly on α_0 (figs. 3 and 4 in sect. 3).

2.6. Ultimate resolution

For extremely thin specimens, such that chromatic aberration is negligibly small, the ultimate resolution of an electron microscope is determined by diffraction and spherical aberration. The radius of the disc of least confusion due to spherical aberration δ_s is given by

$$\delta_S = \tfrac{1}{4} C_S \alpha_0^3 . \tag{20}$$

and that of the corresponding disc due to diffraction δ_D by

$$\delta_D = 0.61 \, \lambda/\alpha_0 \tag{21}$$

in small angle approximation. C_S is the spherical aberration constant of the objective lens. Their combined effect is assumed not to enlarge either disc appreciably, so that the minimum value of resolving power δ_T is taken as

$$\delta_T = \delta_S = \delta_D \tag{22}$$

corresponding to an optimum aperture

$$\alpha_o^* = 1.41 \, (\lambda/C_S)^{\frac{1}{4}} . \tag{23}$$

In these terms the ultimate resolving power of an electron microscope, as limited by electron optical factors, is

$$\delta_T = 0.43 \, C_S^{\frac{1}{4}} \, \lambda^{\frac{3}{4}} . \tag{24}$$

If C_S could be held constant as V_A is increased, resolving power would improve in proportion to $\lambda^{3/4}$ and so to $V_r^{-3/8}$. In practice, if we operate an objective to give minimum C_S at 100 kV by exciting maximum field B_o, then C_S is bound to increase as voltage is raised. From eq. (2) the excitation parameter k^2 can only be kept constant if the product $l^2 B_o^2$ increases in proportion to V_r, since $k^2 = K l^2 B_o^2 / V_r$. So, for fixed B_o, l must increase in proportion to $V_r^{1/2}$, and focal-length and C_S increase in the same ratio. Hence the ultimate resolution increases only as

$$\delta_T \propto V_r^{-1/4} . \tag{25}$$

Between 100 kV and 1 MV the gain in resolving power would be a factor of about 2.1, other things being equal, but in fact the technical problems of stabilising the HT supply become increasingly difficult.

The net result is that high voltage microscopy does not give any gain in the actual resolution achieved, even with very thin specimens, and this is offset by the fall in contrast. There is someting to be said in favour of going to a slightly higher voltage than 100 kV, say to 200 or 300 kV, to achieve some gain in resolution without running into too many technical difficulties, but nothing in favour of very high voltage operation.

3. Recent work on penetration and on applications of high voltage microscopy

3.1. *Introduction*

The usual way of operating a high voltage electron microscope is to maintain the focal length constant at all voltages, using maximum B_o at maximum voltage and a lower field strength at low voltages. The objective lens dimensions are normally optimised for the top working voltage, and so performance is rather poorer at all other voltages than if the lens could be adjusted to optimum dimensions and field each time. The operator will not as a rule keep all other important experimental factors constant, so that comparison between theory and published results is frequently impossible. A meaningful comparison would require him to keep constant the incident illumination at the specimen I_o, the objective aperture size, the image magnification and the brightness of the image judged to be just visible as specimen thickness was increased. Comparison of the predicted increase in usable specimen thickness with voltage would then be possible. Alternatively, he could work to a constant value of image resolution and check whether the corresponding specimen thickness increased approximately linearly with voltage.

Most results of high voltage microscopy so far published have been obtained in poorly controlled conditions, allowing a semi-quantitative analysis at best and usually only a qualitative assessment. The theoretical basis provided by the previous lectures will first be set out, and compared with the available evidence for the increase in usable specimen thickness with voltage. Some more practical applications of high voltage microscopy in metallurgy, polymer science and biology will then be outlined.

3.2. *Specimen penetration at constant fractional transmission*

Electron transmission through a specimen of mass thickness ρt obeys an absorption law

$$I/I_o = \exp(-S\rho t) . \tag{26}$$

So effective penetration can be measured in terms of the specimen thickness which causes a given attenuation of intensity, I/I_o. The wave theory of electron propagation in a perfect crystal takes e^{-1} as the reference attenuation, but for discussing maximum usable thickness we must take a much smaller value. For present purposes we take e^{-4}, corresponding to an imaging beam intensity of about $0.02\,I_o$, i.e. 2% transmission into the objective aperture. It should be noted that the *total* transmission through the specimen is then something like 95%, measured over the whole forward hemisphere.

The thickness of specimen needed to attenuate the beam to e^{-4} will depend on the size of the objective aperture α_o, as well as on the nature of the specimen and the beam voltage. From the plural scattering theory of Lenz described earlier, we may calculate the required mass-thickness of a given element in function of voltage for different values of α_o. The predicted curves for carbon and gold are graphed in figs. 3 and 4, for three values of α_o in each case. When α_o is vanishingly small (curves A are drawn for $\alpha_o = 10^{-5}$), the increase in thickness with voltage approximates to the β^2 curve of single scattering theory, but as α_o is enlarged the effect of plural scattering makes itself felt in an increasing steepness of the curve (see previous lecture). In carbon

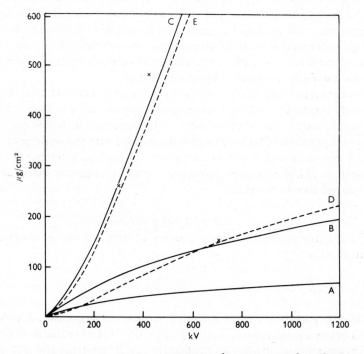

Fig. 3. Carbon: A, B, C = mass-thickness for $I/I_0 = e^{-4}$ when $a_0 = 10^{-5}$, 10^{-3} and 5×10^{-3} respectively, calculated from Lenz [22]. D, E = mass-thickness for a chromatically limited resolution δ_c of 10A when $a_0 = 10^{-3}$ calculated from the most probable energy loss (D), and for $\delta_c = 100$A when $a_0 = 5 \times 10^{-3}$ calculated from the width of the energy distribution (E). x = experimental points of Curtis [29] for $a_0 = 1.1 \times 10^{-3}$ and 5.5×10^{-3} (reproduced from Quarterly Reviews of Biophysics, with permission).

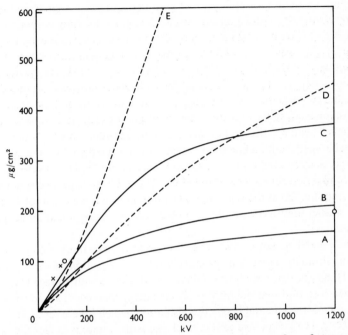

Fig. 4. Gold: A, B, C = mass-thickness for $I/I_0 = e^{-4}$ when $a_0 = 10^{-5}$, 10^{-3} and 10^{-2} respectively, calculated from Lenz [22]. D, E = mass-thickness for a chromatically limited
resolution δ_C of 10A when $a_0 = 10^{-3}$ calculated from the most probable energy loss (D)
and for $\delta_C = 100A$ when $a_0 = 5 \times 10^{-3}$ calculated from the width of the energy distribution (E). x = experimental points of Curtis [29] for $a_0 = 5.5 \times 10^{-3}$; o = experimental
points of Reimer and Sommer [31] for $a_0 = 1.5 \times 10^{-3}$ (reproduced from Quarterly Reviews of Biophysics, with permission).

the effect is very marked, because of the large amount of small-angle inelastic
scattering, so that for $\alpha_0 = 5 \times 10^{-3}$ the curve (C in fig. 3) is almost linear.
The greater elastic scattering in gold is spread over wider angles, so plural
scattering contributes less; even for $\alpha_0 = 10^{-2}$ the curve (C in fig. 4) turns
over sharply beyond 400 kV.

   The few available experimental data are also plotted in figs. 3 and 4, from
Curtis [29] and Reimer and Sommer [31]. Measurements of transmission are
unfortunately only occasionally carried as far as an attenuation of e^{-4}. These
few points show good agreement with Lenz's predictions, within experimental
error; the plural treatment of Smith and Burge [24] predicts much lower
values.

Even greater observable specimen thicknesses are possible at a greater attenuation, which can indeed be achieved at very high voltages. At 100 kV, the maximum incident intensity I_o at the specimen is about 1 A cm^{-2} and the minimum intensity needed on the viewing screen for focusing is about 10^{-11} A cm^{-2}. With an attenuation of e^{-4} the imaging beam leaving the objective has intensity 2.10^{-2} A/cm^2, so that the maximum magnification that can be tolerated is $(2.10^9)^{1/2}$, or 44,000 X, which is adequate for photographing an image with a resolution of 20Å or worse. If the beam voltage is raised to 1 MV, the gun brightness should be at least an order of magnitude greater, as earlier explained, so that for the same conditions of imaging an attenuation of between e^{-6} and e^{-7} should be allowable, corresponding to a 50% increase in observable specimen thickness over and above that predicted by the appropriate curve calculated for a constant attenuation of e^{-4}. Thus a very great increase in observable thickness could be obtained in an experiment in which the current falling on the specimen was not monitored to a constant value. A rather smaller improvement might be obtained by making use of an image intensifier.

Figs. 3 and 4 also show the curves for specimen mass-thickness at a constant value of chromatic aberration, calculated from the equations given in sect. 2.5. Curve D in each figure shows the increase in thickness with voltage when the specimen is so thin that the most probable energy loss (eq. (15)) governs the chromatic aberration, and hence the resolution, which is here set at 10Å (with $\alpha_o = 10^{-3}$). The percentage gain in thickness with voltage is in fact the same for both elements but appears to be more marked in gold than carbon, because the energy loss per unit mass-thickness is relatively greater in elements of low atomic number. Curves E, on the other hand, show the constant chromatic aberration result for a relatively thick specimen, for which the width of the energy distribution (eq. (17)) is the determining factor; δ_c is taken as 100Å and α_o as 5×10^{-3}.

These curves of thickness versus voltage for constant attenuation and for constant chromatic aberration are of interest because they may be compared with the practical microscopist's estimates of the gain in usable specimen thickness at high voltages. The basis of his judgement is likely to be "image quality", which primarily involves resolution (but also contrast). From figs. 3 and 4 we expect the gain with voltage to be greater for carbon than for gold, so long as image visibility is the criterion in the observer's mind (approximating to a constant attenuation factor), the gain becoming almost linear for an aperture of 5×10^{-3}. But if images of the same resolution are the criterion, then the improvement in thickness with voltage should be much the same for both light and heavy elements. When a high resolution is taken as reference datum, using relatively thin specimens, it can happen that intensity becomes the limiting factor on observable thickness as voltage rises, as indicated by the intersection of curve D with curve E in both figs. 3 and 4. The upper parts of curves D are then inaccessible to observation unless a lower level of visibility can be accepted, or the incident beam brightness can be increased (Cosslett [48]).

It must be borne in mind that these conclusions are based on a theory which strictly applies only to amorphous materials. Experiments have shown, however, that good agreement is obtained for polycrystalline materials as well (Reimer [27]), for which the complicating effects of crystalline orientation are averaged out. But since the basic scattering cross-sections enter into the theory of electron transmission through perfect crystals also (Heidenreich [49]), the general trend of the variation of penetration with voltage can be expected to be much the same for a single crystal as for an amorphous specimen. To the extent that the same energy loss processes are effective in limiting the resolution of the image, the same should be true for penetration limited by chromatic aberration.

3.3. *Experimental results for specimen penetration*

The rate of increase in observable specimen thickness with voltage has been confirmed semi-quantitatively by direct observations on a number of elements and some compounds, such as aluminium, copper, iron, tungsten, uranium, MgO, MoS_2 (Fujita et al. [50]; Makin and Sharp [51]). Unfortunately most of the experiments have been done in poorly controlled conditions and with largely qualitative judgement of image definition, so that comparison between the results of different authors and with theoretical predictions is difficult.

Taking an "average" quality of image as criterion, Hale and Henderson Brown [52] obtained the curves shown in fig. 5 for cement and glass at voltages up to 750 kV, and for iron to 1000 kV. When plotted in terms of mass-thickness, the curves for cement and iron coincide, within experimental error. The observable thickness increased by a factor of 4 for cement and glass, but 5 for iron, between 100 and 750 kV. The experiments were made in normal operating conditions of aperture size and image visibility. The general shape of the curves is in agreement with the theoretical form shown in figs. 3 and 4.

Thomas [53] took a more exact criterion in his study of silicon and stainless steel foils: the visibility of stacking fault fringes. The beam voltage was reduced on a foil of known thickness until the fringes were at the limit of visibility. His results, for an aperture of 3×10^{-3}, fall almost on a straight line for silicon, but for stainless steel they are closer to a $(v/c)^2$ form (fig. 6). When plotted as mass-thickness against voltage, the silicon curve still lies above that

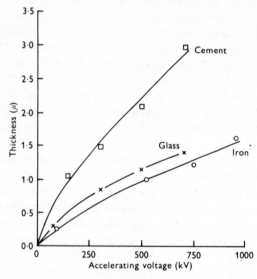

Fig. 5. Thickness of specimens giving good average penetration in high voltage electron microscopy, by Hale and Henderson Brown [52].

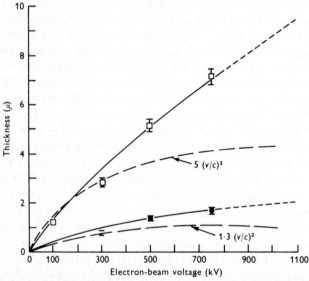

Fig. 6. Maximum thickness of specimen through which stacking-fault fringes could be imaged at different voltages by Thomas [53]. □ = silicon; ○ = stainless steel.

for steel as expected for the lighter element (from figs. 3 and 4). The increase in thickness between 100 and 750 kV is 4 times for steel but 6 for silicon. The visibility of fringes is a complicated matter, involving the coherence of the imaging beam as well as contrast and resolution, and does not necessarily have the same thickness limit as ordinary image details for which amplitude contrast is predominant. Uyeda and Nonoyama [54] by using very long exposures, found that dislocations were still clearly resolved in molybdenite at thicknesses greater than the visibility limit for fringes. So it seems probable that Thomas's results were limited by intensity rather than by chromatic aberration.

Uyeda and Nonoyama [54,55] have carried out the most comprehensive investigations so far published on limiting thickness. They took the image obtained through 5 μm of molybdenite at 1000 kV as the reference standard for definition, and then found the thickness that gave a comparable image at other voltages from 50 to 1200 kV. There is an appreciable spread in the results, especially at high voltage (fig. 7), but the mean curve is only a little higher than a $(v/c)^2$ curve. The thickness increased by a factor of 3 between 100 and 1000 kV. This was a resolution limited experiment, but it is difficult to compare with theory because the aperture was not kept constant, being 10^{-2} at low voltages and 4×10^{-3} at high voltages, to allow enough intensity to keep exposures short at 50 and 100 kV. But the tendency to a $(v/c)^2$ form is in keeping with the general deduction from figs. 3 and 4 that this should be so for elements of higher atomic number. A higher and steeper curve (broken curve in fig. 7) for images of low contrast, where intensity limitations would play a greater role, shows an increase in thickness nearer to 4 times between 100 kV and 1000 kV, in closer agreement with the results obtained for iron by Thomas and by Hale and Henderson Brown.

All such experiments, however, are open to a serious source of error known as the "top and bottom" effect. A detail on the lower side of a specimen some microns thick will be imaged much more sharply than a similar detail situated on the upper side of the specimen. The observer is likely to select the best image at any given voltage, without being sure whether it is on the top or the bottom of the specimen. So experiments can only give valid results for comparison with theory if a marker is used, such as magnesium oxide or latex particles, or if a large number of observations are made on randomly selected image details.

In summary, experiments on a number of metals and compounds have confirmed the general trend of increase with voltage in the thickness that gives an image of acceptable quality, judged by one standard or another. The factor of increase depends on the objective aperture used and on the nature of the spec-

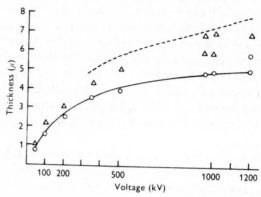

Fig. 7. Maximum usable thickness of molybdenite, as judged from images of dislocation networks by Uyeda and Nonoyama [55]. ○ = images of the same quality as the reference standard (5 μm specimen at 1000 kV). Δ = images of low contrast.

imen: atomic number, density, crystalline or amorphous. With a low atomic number specimen and an aperture of average size $(3-5 \times 10^{-3})$ the usable thickness increases by a factor of 5 or more between 100 kV and 1 MV. A gain of this magnitude is supported by theory, either on the assumption that the fractional transmission (I/I_o) is kept constant or that the resolution as limited by chromatic aberration is constant.

3.4. Applications of high voltage microscopy

Detailed studies in electron microscopy at high voltages have only recently begun to appear in the literature. Most of the earlier work was of an exploratory nature (for reviews of the subject see Dupouy [9]; Cosslett [11,12]). Research into problems of metal physics and metallurgy has predominated, but some observations have been made on polymers, and biological applications are also now being actively investigated.

3.5. Metallurgy and materials science

The greater penetration provided by very high voltages makes it possible to investigate the variation in the density and behaviour of dislocations in thin and thick foils of metals and other crystalline specimens. The limiting effect of the surface becomes progressively less effective as thickness is increased. Foils thin enough to examine at 100 kV may be dominated by surface conditions, quite apart from the probability that the dislocation arrangements may be modified by the preparation procedure.

Fujita and his team [56,50] have carried out careful studies to discover at what thickness a foil begins to show the properties of the bulk metal, in appearance and also in dynamic behaviour. They found that the "threshold" thickness differed for different types of phenomena, as well as from one metal to another. For instance, the bulk value for dislocation density was not reached until a thickness of 0.8 μm in aluminium, compared with 0.1 μm in iron. But in respect of recrystallisation, the critical thickness was about 1 μm in both metals. Further, when aluminium was strained the motion of dislocations did not show bulk behaviour until a thickness of 1.5 μm in respect of cell formation and 3 μm for three-dimensional structure. Fujita states that the maximum observable thickness at 500 kV was 4 μm for aluminium and 1 μm for iron in normal viewing conditions, but about twice these values for photography of dim images with long exposures.

Some studies have also been made of elements of high density, such as tungsten and uranium, which have to be thinned to below 1000 Å for observation at 100 kV, and even then the results are poor. At 500 kV we have been able to get clear images of dislocation networks in both metals through a thickness of about 0.5 μm. Similar results have been obtained from lead by Steeds and Valdrè [57].

The electron microscopy of magnetic materials, by the so-called Lorentz method for observing magnetic domains, is also seriously limited at 100 kV, for quite different reasons. The thickness of the specimen itself is not the main difficulty, but the fact that it has to be placed well outside the magnetic field of the objective lens in order to avoid disturbing the domain structure we wish to study. It is then being imaged with very inefficient collection of the imaging beam as well as poor resolution, so that thicknesses no greater than about 0.15 μm can be adequately viewed at 100 kV. But at 500 kV films of iron, cobalt or permalloy several times this thickness can be studied, and with improved resolution. The high voltage microscope has already revealed surprising changes in domain structure with increasing thickness and on varying the angle of deposition of the evaporated film (Ferrier and Puchalska [58]).

An obvious application of high voltage microscopy is to the examination of precipitates, inclusions and grains of the order of 1 μm or more, which are liable to be lost from a foil in the drastic process of thinning required for microscopy at 100 kV. One of the first problems brought to the Cavendish 750 kV microscope was the identification of foreign particles which were causing streaks in the surface of rolled aluminium sheet. The particles were 2 to 3 μm across, but were retained in a foil of thickness suitable for penetration at 500 kV. From their shape and from the electron diffraction patterns they gave, we were able to show that they were complex silicates.

Radiation damage in metals is proving to be a fruitful problem for study by high voltage microscopy, both the type of damage produced by irradiation in a pile or with atomic beams and that caused by the electron beam itself in the microscope. It had already been predicted that a threshold voltage is required for an electron to eject an atom from a lattice by direct collision, in the so-called "knock-on" process. Vacancies and corresponding interstitial atoms are created, which then diffuse through the metal at a rate determined by the experimental conditions such as strain and temperature gradient, until they aggregate to a size that is large enough to be visible in the electron microscope. Makin [59] has now been able to confirm the threshold voltage in copper predicted by relativistic collision theory. For a displacement energy of 25 eV the threshold should be 495 keV. Above this beam voltage the cross-section for the ejection process increases rapidly, being ten times greater at 600 keV than at 500 keV in copper. The threshold energy is approximately proportional to the atomic weight of the target atom, being 166 keV for aluminium and over 1 MeV for gold or tungsten.

These predictions have now been largely confirmed by Makin in respect of aluminium and copper, but he finds the threshold energy to be very sensitive to orientation. It may vary from near 400 keV to above 500 keV for copper according to the direction the incident beam makes with the lattice. An extensive area for research is opened up by these observations, provided that the operating voltage of the microscope can be accurately adjusted over a wide range. Steeds and Valdrè [57] have begun a study of the temperature dependence of such radiation damage in lead and its removal by annealing. They report that small dislocation loops are formed in a few minutes in a strong illuminating beam at 600 kV when the specimen is at liquid helium temperature, but the damage rapidly disappears on warming to room temperature. Goringe and Valdrè [72] find considerably increased damage rates in copper at temperatures down to 10°K, and no marked annealing on warming to room temperature. The same authors have also made a preliminary study of superconducting materials by high voltage microscopy (Goringe and Valdrè [60]). Recently Ipohorski and Spring [61] have observed the creation of large loops in copper, which appear at room temperature after less than 1 min exposure to a beam of intensity about 2 A cm^{-2} and 500 kV.

The liability to such damage phenomena must be borne in mind during high voltage microscopy, especially with light elements. The exposures required to produce visible effects are much greater, however, than would be incurred in normal conditions of observation with a beam of adequate intensity for high magnification. For instance, Makin required an exposure of 15 min in a 1 A cm^{-2} beam in order to see visible damage in copper at a voltage just above threshold. But the danger of unwanted damage increases rapidly above the threshold. In absolute figures, with a beam current of 0.2 μA in a spot of 5 μm diameter on a specimen of copper, 1 atom in 400 would be displaced during a 1 min exposure at 600 kV and 1 atom in 80 at 1000 kV. Most of the displaced atoms are likely to be trapped in vacant sites, of course, so that only a small part of the damage persists and aggregates until it becomes visible. Nevertheless, the effect may be enough to complicate studies of annealing and diffusion processes (Sharp and Makin [62]). It has recently been shown by Woolhouse [63] that exposure above the threshold voltage destroys the coherence of a precipitate with the matrix lattice, in the case of cobalt precipitates in copper. Use of an image intensifier is obviously indicated for such investigations, as in the direct measurements of the mobilities of dislocations in Fe $-$ 3% Si by Imura et al. [64].

3.6. Polymers

Radiation damage of this kind will also occur when polymers and organic materials generally are being studied, in greater degree in fact because the bond energies are smaller. The vacant sites are not so mobile as in metals, however, so that the removal of carbon atoms (for instance) is not usually visible in the electron microscope, although effects such as cross-linking or simple degradation may be proved by chemical evidence. The "clearing" of embedded biological sections under observation at 100 kV is well-known, and the relative rates of removal of different embedding media have been much studied (Reimer [27]). So far no data for high voltage microscopy have been recorded, but it is likely to be a more serious problem, especially on thick sections.

Damage due to ionization, on the other hand, should be reduced as beam voltage is raised. So it should be easier to study polymers, and perhaps also living matter, in a high voltage microscope. Most polymers are so sensitive to electron damage that at 100 kV they can only be observed for very short times (seconds) in a weak beam (and so at low magnification). A detailed study at high voltages has been made on a variety of polymers by Kobayashi and Sakaoku [65], and continued by Kobayashi and Ohara [66]. They measured the electron dose needed to destroy the crystallinity of a sample, as evidenced by the diffraction pattern, at voltages up to 500 kV. The critical dose was found to be directly proportional to voltage for each of four different polymers, although their individual sensitivity to damage varied greatly. This is approximately the behaviour expected, since the energy dissipated for unit mass thickness decreases with increase in voltage, so that both ionization and temperature rise should be less. For the same reason it is possible to observe cellulose membranes, used in artificial kidney machines, more readily at high voltages. A combination of high voltage microscopy with a good image inten-sifier should enable morphological studies on polymers to be made over long periods, even if only to investigate the radiation damage process itself.

3.7. Biology and medicine

The use of the high voltage microscope in biology and medicine is less ad-vanced than in metallurgy and polymer science. The first work done on the Toulouse 1.5 MV instrument was in fact the observation of bacteria in a gas-environment cell, where they were maintained in an atmosphere of saturated water vapour. It was claimed that the bacteria, or at least some of them, sur-vived exposure to the electron beam at voltages up to 700 kV (Dupouy et al. [8]) so that living organisms had been examined for the first time by electron microscopy. Doubt was cast on the possibility of doing so, by radiation bio-logists familiar with the lethal doses found for bacteria exposed to electron beams in macroscopic experiments. Dupouy [9] now reports that he has re-peated the observations at 1 MV, with the same result. It is enough, of course, for only a few bacteria to have higher radiation resistance than the mean for growth to occur on subsequent culture. On the other hand, no successive micrographs of the same field have been published to show that given cells had developed after electron exposure, as had been demonstrated much earlier at 100 kV by von Ardenne [67] with spores which are known to be radiation resistant. Independent repetition of the Toulouse experiments is urgently needed, since an important field for high voltage microscopy would open up if it proved possible to follow the development of micro-organisms in situ, viruses as well as bacteria.

A more immediately fruitful line of research is to explore the value of high voltages for the study of thick sections of biological tissue. If sections a micron or so thick could be examined, it would greatly facilitate both the preparation and interpretation of such specimens. For 100 kV it is necessary to cut sec-tions thinner than 1000Å, and usually as thin as 300—500Å or even less. Examination of ramified structures, as in the retina of the eye, would be much easier when one thick section can yield the information at present gathered from 10 thin ones.

Several laboratories are now actively working in this direction. Hama and Porter [68] have published encouraging results from sections of a variety of tissues up to 5000Å thick, viewed at 500 kV. To assist interpretation, stereo-pairs of micrographs were taken with a specimen tilt of ± 8°. Some striking stereo-micrographs of chromosomes have similarly been obtained by Ris [69] at 1000 kV, but without embedding and sectioning. Even when the resolution is poor by the best standards of electron microscopy, it is still that much better than in light microscopy, with the added advantage of great depth of focus. On the Cavendish microscope McAlear [70] has obtained some interesting micrographs of a whole cell of acanthamoeba, containing some ingested bacteria. Clarke, Salsbury and Cosslett [71] show similar views of whole blood cells, some containing foreign particles. The more openwork the structure, the easier the interpretation, of course.

Interest in high voltage microscopy is now growing rapidly among biologists. Special techniques of operating the microscope to best advantage need to be worked out, and equally for the interpretation of the image, since the nature of the specimen and the type of details involved are quite different from those prevailing in metallurgy. In particular, radiation damage and temperature effects have to be guarded against. We have found it only too easy to melt a 3 μm section in the sort of electron beam used for metal foils. But with adequate precautions, and especially with the aid of an image intensifier, it will be possible to examine specimens of this thickness without trouble at a voltage of 600–1000 kV.

3.8. *Future developments*

There are now at least four companies manufacturing electron microscopes for voltages from 500 kV to 1 MV, some of them going down to 100 kV also. A period of intensive exploration of the uses of greater penetration can be foreseen, extending into all branches of science and technology. Out of this may come some firm evidence for an optimum voltage, perhaps higher for metals and lower for biological sections. But it is too early to say whether any such optimum exists. At the same time the French 3 MV microscope should begin to show what advantage, if any, is to be gained from going to voltages well above 1 MV. As with all new instruments, there will surely prove to be some problems which it alone can solve. What we cannot say is how far the results will justify the effort. At the least, there is every prospect of increased activity in high voltage microscopy for some years to come.

References

[1] G.Dupouy and F.Perrier, Z. angew. Phys. 27 (1969) 224.
[2] A.C.van Dorsten, W.J.Oosterkamp and J.B.Le Poole, Philips Tech. Rev. 9 (1947) 195.
[3] S.Maruse, N.J.Morito, Y.Sakaki and B.Tadano, J. Elect. Mic. 4 (1956) 5.
[4] K.Kobayashi, E.Suito and S.Shimadzu, Proc. 4th Int. Conf. Elect. Micros. 1958, Vol. 1 (Springer, Berlin, 1960) p. 165.

[5] J.H.Coupland, Proc. 3rd Int. Conf. Elect. Micros. 1954 (Royal Microscopical Society, London, 1955) p. 159.

[6] N.M.Popov, Izv. Akad. Nauk USSR 23 (1959) 436, 494.

[7] G.Dupouy and F.Perrier, J. Microscopie 1 (1962) 167.

[8] G.Dupouy, F.Perrier and L.Durrieu, C. r. hebd. Seanc. Acad. Sci. Paris 251 (1960) 2836.

[9] G.Dupouy, in: Adv. Opt. Elect. Micros., Vol. 2 (Academic Press, London, 1968) p. 167.

[10] K.C.A.Smith, K.Considine and V.E.Cosslett, Electron Microscopy 1966, Vol. 1 (Maruzen, Tokyo, 1966) p. 99.

[11] V.E.Cosslett, Contemp. Phys. 9 (1968) 333.

[12] V.E.Cosslett, Quart. Rev. Biophysics 2 (1969) 95.

[13] M.Watanabe, Y.Hinaga, M.Yamamoto, O.Nakamura, T.Someya, T.Goto, K.Konno, and T.Yanaba, J. Elect. Mic. 17 (1968) 289.

[14] W.Glaser, Grundlagen der Elektronenoptik (Springer, Vienna, 1952).

[15] G.Liebmann, Proc. Phys. Soc. London 65B (1952) 188.

[16] T.Mulvey and M.J.Wallington, J. Sci. Instr. 2 (1969) 466.

[17] W.Kamminga, J.L.Verster and J.C.Francken, Optik 28 (1969) 442.

[18] R.M.Fisher and J.S.Lally, Electron Microscopy 1968, Vol. 1 (Tipografia Poliglotta Vaticana, Rome, 1968) p. 15.

[19] M.Iwanaga, H.Ueyanaga, K.Hosoi, N.Iwasa, K.Oba and K.Shiratsuchi, J. Elect. Mic. 17 (1968) 203.

[20] S.Katagiri, M.Nishigaki and H.Todokoro, J. Elect. Mic. 17 (1968) 215.

[21] S.Katagiri, H.Kimura, S.Ozasa and K.Shiraishi, J. Elect. Mic. 18 (1969) 1.

[22] F.Lenz, Z. Naturforsch. 9a (1954) 185.

[23] R.E.Burge and G.H.Smith, Proc. Phys. Soc. 79 (1962) 673.

[24] G.H.Smith and R.E.Burge, Proc. Phys. Soc. 81 (1963) 612.

[25] G.Wentzel, Z. Physik 40 (1927) 590.

[26] W.Lippert, Naturwiss. 50 (1963) 219.

[27] L.Reimer, Elektronenmikroskopische Untersuchungs- und Praparationsmethoden (Springer, Berlin, 1967).

[28] W.Lippert and W.Friese, Proc. 5th Int. Conf. Elect. Mic., Vol. 1 (Academic Press, New York, 1962) p. AA-1.

[29] G.H.Curtis, Thesis, University of Cambridge, 1968.

[30] G.H.Curtis, V.E.Cosslett and R.P.Ferrier, Electron Microscopy 1968, Vol. 1 (Tipografia Poliglotta Vaticana, Rome, 1968) p. 61.

[31] L.Reimer and K.H.Sommer, Z. Naturforsch. 23a (1968) 1569.

[32] H.Raith, Acta Cryst. A24 (1968) 85.

[33] A.Mazel and R.Ayroles, J. Microscope 7 (1968) 793.

[34] M.J.Goringe, A.Howie and M.J.Whelan, Phil. Mag. 14 (1966) 217.

[35] A.Ichimiya, Jap. J. Appl. Phys. 7 (1968) 1425.

[36] R.Uyeda, Electron Microscopy 1968, Vol. 1 (Tipografia Poliglotta Vaticana, Rome, 1968) p. 55.

[37] D.L.Misell, Thesis, University of London, 1968.

[38] D.L.Misell and R.A.Crick, J. Physics C 2 (1969) 2290.

[39] L.Landau, J. Phys. (USSR) 8 (1944) 201.

[40] R.D.Birkhoff, Handbuch der Physik, Vol. 34 (Springer Verlag, Berlin, 1958) p. 53.

[41] G.Knop, A.Minten and B.Nellen, Z. Physik 165 (1961) 533.
[42] T.Ichinokawa, Jap. J. Appl. Phys. 7 (1968) 799.
[43] K.T.Considine, Thesis, University of Cambridge, 1969.
[44] P.B.Hirsch and C.J.Humphreys, Electron Microscopy 1968, Vol. 1 (Tipografia Poliglotta Vaticana, Rome, 1968) p. 49.
[45] V.E.Cosslett, Z. angew. Physik. 27 (1969) 138.
[46] T.Sahashi, Jap. J. Appl. Phys. 8 (1969) 305.
[47] H.Koike, Electron Microscopy 1968, Vol. 1 (Tipografia Poliglotta Vaticana, Rome, 1968) p. 65.
[48] V.E.Cosslett, Optik 25 (1967) 383.
[50] R.D.Heidenreich, Fundamentals of Transmission Electron Microscopy (Interscience, New York, 1964).
[51] M.J.Makin and J.V.Sharp, J. Mat. Sci. 3 (1968) 360.
[52] K.F.Hale and M.H.Brown, Nature 221 (1969) 1232.
[53] G.Thomas, Phil. Mag. 17 (1968) 1097.
[54] R.Uyeda and M.Nonoyama, Jap. J. Appl. Phys. 6 (1967) 557.
[55] R.Uyeda and M.Nonoyama, Jap. J. Appl. Phys. 7 (1968) 200.
[56] H.Fujita, Jap. J. Appl. Phys. 5 (1966) 729.
[57] J.Steeds and U.Valdre, Electron Microscopy 1968, Vol. 1 (Tipografia Poliglotta Vaticana, Rome, 1968) p. 43.
[58] R.P.Ferrier and I.B.Puchalska, Phys. Stat. Sol. 28 (1968) 335.
[59] M.J.Makin, Phil. Mag. 18 (1968) 637.
[60] M.J.Goringe and U.Valdre, Electron Microscopy 1968, Vol. 1 (Tipografia Poliglotta Vaticana, Rome, 1968) p. 41.
[61] M.Ipohorski and M.S.Spring (1969), unpublished results.
[62] J.V.Sharp and M.J.Makin, Electron Microscopy 1968, Vol. 1 (Tipografia Poliglotta Vaticana, Rome, 1968) p. 37.
[63] G.R.Woolhouse, Nature 220 (1968) 573.
[64] T.Imura, H.Saka and N.Yukawa, J. Phys. Soc. Japan 26 (1969) 1327.
[65] K.Kobayashi and K.Sakaoku, in: Quantitative Electron Microscopy, eds. G.F.Bahr and E.H.Zeitler (Williams and Wilkins, Baltimore, 1965) p. 359.
[66] K.Kobayashi and M.Ohara, Electron Microscopy 1966, Vol. 1 (Maruzen, Tokyo, 1966) p. 579.
[67] M.von Ardenne, Naturwiss. 29 (1941) 521.
[68] K.Hama and K.R.Porter, J. Microscopie 8 (1969) 149.
[69] H.Ris, J. Microscopie 8 (1969) 761.
[70] J.H.McAlear (1968), unpublished results.
[71] J.A.Clarke, V.E.Cosslett and A.J.Salsbury, J. Microscopy 90 (1969) 127.
[72] M.J.Goringe and U.Valdre, Radiation Effects 1 (1969) 133.

LOW ENERGY ELECTRON DIFFRACTION

P.J.ESTRUP

Departments of Physics and Chemistry, Brown University,
Providence, Rhode Island, USA

1. Introduction

In recent years there has been a rapidly growing interest in studies of solid surfaces. Much of the research is relevant to the solution of specific problems in such fields as thermionics, semiconductor electronics, film growth, corrosion and catalysis but the principal objective of many researchers is now the characterization of the fundamental properties of surfaces and a description of these on the atomic level. This approach has become possible with the development of several experimental techniques among which low energy electron diffraction, LEED, is one of the most important.

No attempt will be made in these lectures to provide a comprehensive survey of the LEED studies which have been made to date. Instead it is intended to give an introduction to the technique, to discuss the type of information we can obtain by LEED at present and to illustrate the application of the method by selected examples. However, during the past few year, various aspects of LEED have been the subject of review articles [1–6] and a bibliography on LEED and related surface phenomena has recently been prepared [7].

2. Fundamentals of LEED

2.1. *LEED technique*

In LEED experiments a monoenergetic beam of electrons is directed towards the surface of a crystal and those electrons which are elastically scattered (and diffracted) in the backward direction are observed. Typically the energy of the primary electrons is in the region $V = 10 - 300 \, eV$ and the corresponding wavelength, given by the de Broglie relation

$$\lambda = \frac{h}{p} \approx \sqrt{\frac{150}{V}} \text{ Å} ,$$

is of the order of 1 Å. At this energy both the inelastic and elastic scattering cross-sections are large; penetration without energy loss is limited to a few atomic layers and as a consequence it is only these layers which provide the elastic component of the back-scattered electrons. Compared to other diffraction methods, LEED is thus ideally suited for surface studies but the large scattering cross-sections on which the technique depends, bring about some special theoretical difficulties not encountered with X-rays, for example. Some of these difficulties are discussed in sect. 2.4.

Among the experimental requirements for successful LEED work are ultra-high vacuum ($10^{-9}-10^{-10}$ torr) and single-crystal specimens. Although these requirements represent a limitation on the materials that can be investigated, they coincide with the conditions which are imposed in most modern surface studies in order to achieve well defined and controllable systems. The experimental investigation of a given surface will usually involve (1) preparation of the sample (orientation of the single-crystal, cutting and polishing), (2) mounting in the LEED chamber and cleaning in vacuum (by heating or by ion bombardment), (3) investigations of the clean surface and (4) studies of the changes caused by a specified treatment (e.g. adsorption, surface reaction).

LEED systems of various designs are in use but fig. 1 shows schematically the main components. The crystal is mounted in a holder which preferably should permit rotation about one or more axes so that the angle of incidence of the primary electron beam can be varied. To the holder may be attached leads for ohmic heating of the sample, coils for cooling (e.g., with liquid nitrogen), connections for thermocouples, etc. Facing the sample is the electron gun which furnishes a primary electron beam with a current of a few microamperes. The diffracted electrons can be detected and measured in one of two ways: By the collector method (fig. 1a) or by the post-diffraction acceleration and display method (fig. 1b). The former method which has been developed in particular by Farnsworth [8], employs a moveable Faraday cage and gives a direct and accurate measurement of the diffracted intensity at a selected angle. With suitable electronics and automated motion of the collector an oscilloscope display of the diffraction pattern may be obtained in a matter of minutes [9]. In the alternative method [1,10], a set of concentric, hemispherical grids are used to reject the inelastic electrons and sub-

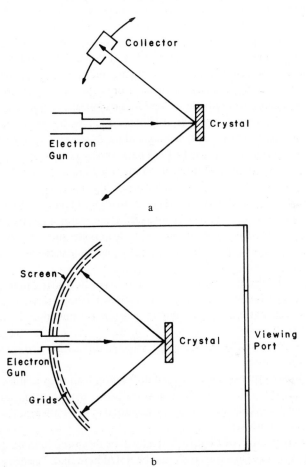

Fig. 1. Schematic of LEED chamber. a. Faraday collector system. b. Display system.

sequently to accelerate the elastic electrons to a sufficient voltage for display on a fluorescent screen. Each diffracted beam gives rise to a bright spot on the screen and the spot pattern can be observed through a viewing port. Relative measurements of the diffracted intensity are then obtained by means of a spot photometer situated outside the chamber. Although this method may give less accurate intensity data, it has the great advantage that it permits simultaneous viewing of many diffracted beams and enables one to follow rapid changes in the spot pattern. For these reasons it is at present the preferred method and it is used in all commercially available LEED systems.

2.2. LEED data

The results of a diffraction experiment may be considered a "mapping" of the diffracted intensity, I, in reciprocal space. In the case of LEED only a part of the reciprocal space can be explored because only the beams diffracted in the backward directions can be detected (and the detector arrangement will usually not allow observation of all of them) and because of the limitations on the wavelength of the primary electrons. For purposes of structure analysis it would presumably be desirable to obtain as complete a mapping as possible of the accessible region; however, as discussed below, the theoretical foundation for such an analysis is still lacking and much less extensive data are therefore taken at present. Reported LEED data usually consist of:

(a) $I(hl)$, the variation of intensity along a portion of a given Ewald sphere surface (constant wavelength, λ, and angle of incidence, ϕ_o). This information comprises a diffraction pattern and is recorded photographically in display systems. h and l are the indices of the diffraction features referred to a two-dimensional (2D) reciprocal net parallel to the crystal surface. Besides the position of the spots, their relative intensity and their shape are important quantities.

(b) $I(V)$, the variation of the intensity of a selected diffraction spot, e.g., $I(01)$, with electron energy. A curve of I versus V is sometimes called the "intensity distribution" of the beam in question (or the "pseudorocking curve" [11]).

(c) $I(T)$, the intensity variation of a selected diffraction feature with crystal temperature.

(d) $I(\theta)$, the intensity of a selected diffraction feature as a function of surface atom density. These measurements are useful in adsorption studies where θ, the adsorbate coverage, may be varied at will between, for example, zero and one monolayer.

The interpretation of the LEED data will be discussed in more detail in the following sections. However, it should be noted here that, besides yielding diffraction data, the experimental arrangement in a LEED apparatus often allows other concurrent measurements which supplement the LEED data in important ways. Among these measurements are:

(1) The energy spectrum of the inelastically scattered and secondary electrons emerging from the surface [12]. This spectrum shows characteristic energy losses due to the excitation of interband transitions and surface and bulk plasmons. In addition the spectrum contains peaks due to Auger emitted electrons which provide means for a sensitive chemical analysis of the surface species.

(2) Work function changes, which can be found for example by the retarding potential method [13] with the LEED gun as the electron source. The measurements give information about the effective dipole associated with a surface atom.

(3) Observations on the gas phase, similar to those used in conventional studies of adsorption. Examples are flash desorption measurements [14] to determine the coverage, θ, and to identify binding states; and mass-spectrometry to monitor the chemical composition. The latter method is of course essential in catalysis work.

Other techniques which can be combined directly with LEED are high energy electron diffraction (HEED), ellipsometry [15], photoemission [16], electron impact desorption [17], and field emission microscopy [15].

2.3. LEED patterns

The main features of a LEED pattern can frequently be interpreted by considering simple one or two-dimensional models of the surface and applying kinematical diffraction theory [18,19].

Fig. 2 depicts a one-dimensional (1D) periodic array of scatterers, generated by the translation vector **a**, with the primary electron beam at normal incidence ($\phi_0 = 0$). The condition for formation of a diffracted beam is that the scattered waves interfere constructively, i.e.,

$$a \sin \phi = h\lambda \tag{1}$$

where h is an integer and a is the magnitude of **a**. For a 2D array, defined by the vectors **a** and **b**, an additional condition must be satisfied:

$$b \sin \phi' = l\lambda . \tag{2}$$

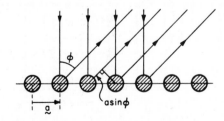

Fig. 2. Diffraction from a linear array of scattering centers. The incident beam is normal to the array.

(1) and (2) express the usual first and second Laue conditions, and together they define the directions of the diffracted beams. Conversely, from observations of the positions of the diffraction spots, **a** and **b** can be determined. In practice this is conveniently done by using the Ewald sphere construction in reciprocal space [18,19]. The reciprocal of the 2D array can be shown to consist of parallel "rods" originating in the lattice points of the reciprocal net defined by the vectors **a*** and **b***. These reciprocal translation vectors satisfy the relations:

$$\mathbf{a} \cdot \mathbf{a}^* = \mathbf{b} \cdot \mathbf{b}^* = 1 \; ; \qquad \mathbf{a}^* \cdot \mathbf{b} = \mathbf{b}^* \cdot \mathbf{a} = 0 \; ;$$

$$a^* = b/A \; ; \qquad b^* = a/A$$

where $A = |\mathbf{a} \times \mathbf{b}|$ is the area of the "unit mesh".

Fig. 3 shows a simple illustration of the Ewald sphere construction. The radius of the sphere is $1/\lambda$ and the primary beam is represented by the vector $\mathbf{K_o} = $ AO which terminates at the origin of the reciprocal net and has magnitude $1/\lambda$. The intersection of the lattice rods with the sphere defines the allowed diffracted beams, $\mathbf{K}$ (AB for example). It is seen that for this beam $1/\lambda \sin\phi = 1/a$, so that condition (1) is satisfied.

To illustrate some of the properties of LEED patterns in a simple manner we consider a (100) surface of a cubic crystal. The atoms are arranged in a square net, fig. 4a, and the corresponding LEED pattern is shown in figs. 4b and 4c. The spots have been indexed according to the values of h and l. In

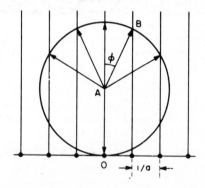

Fig. 3. Ewald sphere construction for diffraction by a two-dimensional net with mesh side a. The primary beam, AO, is normal to the surface.

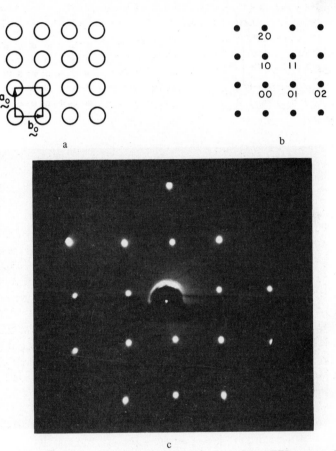

Fig. 4. a. Model of (100) face of a cubic crystal. b..Diagram of the LEED pattern. The 00 spot corresponds to the origin of the reciprocal net. c. Photograph of a LEED pattern from a W(100) surface.

practice the value of **a** will be known accurately from X-ray studies and the pattern serves as an essential reference condition in studies where the surface periodicity undergoes changes. Such changes occur frequently when foreign atoms are present but may in some system be caused also by "reconstruction" of the clean surface (sect. 3.1) or by magnetic transitions [20].

Fig. 5a shows a possible arrangement of adsorbed atoms on the surface depicted in fig. 4a. The presence of the "adatoms" means that the spacing is doubled in both directions so that the reciprocal translation vectors are halved.

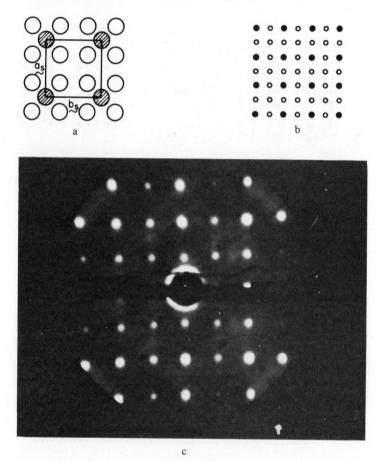

c

Fig. 5. a. Model of the (100) face with a p(2×2) superstructure due to adsorbed atoms (filled circles). b. Diagram of the LEED pattern. c. Photograph of a LEED pattern from a W(100) surface with adsorbed oxygen.

The diffraction pattern, figs. 5b and 5c, therefore shows "extra" spots in the half-order positions relative to the "normal" spots in the clean surface pattern.

The arrangement in fig. 6a differs from that of fig. 5a in that the unit mesh is non-primitive. To find the intensity associated with a given reciprocal lattice rod we examine the 2D structure factor

$$F_{hl} = \sum_j f_j \exp\left[2\pi i(hx_j + ly_j)\right]$$

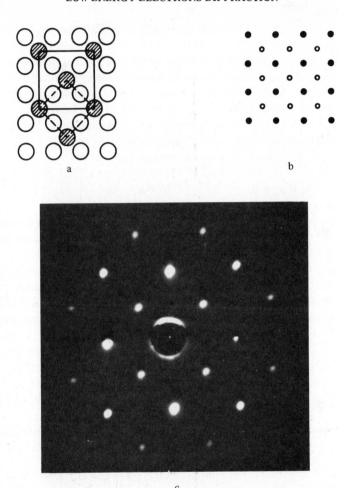

Fig. 6. a. Model of the (100) face of a cubic crystal with a c(2×2) superstructure. b. Diagram of the LEED pattern. c. Photograph of a LEED pattern from a W(100) surface with adsorbed hydrgen.

where f_j is the atomic scattering factor, (x_j, y_j) the coordinates of atom j, and the summation is over all the atoms in the unit mesh. In the present case

$$F_{hl} = f_j \{1 + \exp [2\pi i(h+l)] \}$$

which is zero except for the spots shown in fig. 6b (and 6c).

The terminology which is used to describe a surface structure is based on the simple relationship which usually exists between the substrate net and the overlayer net [21]. The structure of fig. 6a is often referred to as c(2X2), to indicate that the superstructure unit mesh is centered and has translation vectors twice those of the substrate. According to an alternative labelling, derived from the primitive unit (shown by the broken lines in fig. 6a) which has sides $\sqrt{2}a$ and is rotated 45° with respect to the substrate unit, the structure is $(\sqrt{2}\times\sqrt{2})R(45°)$. Finally, since the vectors defining the primitive unit can be expressed in terms of the substrate vectors by

$$\mathbf{a}_s = \mathbf{a}_o + \mathbf{b}_o \; ; \qquad\qquad \mathbf{b}_s = \mathbf{a}_o - \mathbf{b}_o$$

the superstructure may be designated simply by the transformation matrix [6,22] $M = \begin{bmatrix} 1 & 1 \\ 1 & -1 \end{bmatrix}$. Similarly, the (primitive) structure of fig. 5a may be defined either by writing $p(2\times2)$ or by giving the matrix $\begin{bmatrix} 2 & 0 \\ 0 & 2 \end{bmatrix}$.

In many cases a new structure can be identified simply by inspection of the pattern. It must be noted, however, that the experimental pattern often exhibits higher symmetry than the surface structure. The reason is that the cross-sectional area of the primary electron beam (≈ 1 mm^2) is large compared to the average "domain" size on the surface and that the pattern therefore may contain a superposition of diffracted beams from domains oriented along different (but crystallographically equivalent) axes of the substrate lattice. An example is given in fig. 7, in which half of the extra spots are due to domains with a (4X1) structure and the other half are due to equivalent domains rotated 90°, i.e., with a (1X4) structure.

Later sections will discuss examples of more complex LEED patterns, including some which cannot be indexed in a simple manner relative to the substrate mesh.

2.4. LEED intensities

According to the kinematical treatment, the scattered amplitude from a 2D net should be of the form [18,19]

$$A \approx \sum f_n \exp(2\pi i \mathbf{k} \cdot \mathbf{r}_n) \tag{3}$$

where $\mathbf{k} = \mathbf{K}_o - \mathbf{K}$ and the summation is over all the net vectors $\mathbf{r}_n$. The corresponding intensity, $I \approx AA^*$, becomes for an array of $N_1 \times N_2$ identical units

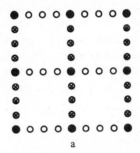

a

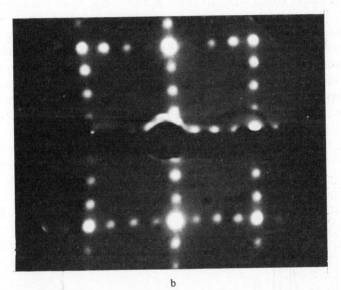

b

Fig. 7. a. Diagram of a LEED pattern due to a (4×1) superstructure. ○ and ⊗ designate extra spots from two domains rotated 90 degrees with respect to each other. b. Photograph of a LEED pattern from a W(100) surface with co-adsorbed nitrogen and carbon monoxide.

$$I \approx ff^* \frac{\sin^2 (N_1 \pi \mathbf{k} \cdot \mathbf{a})}{\sin^2 (\pi \mathbf{k} \cdot \mathbf{a})} \frac{\sin^2 (N_2 \pi \mathbf{k} \cdot \mathbf{b})}{\sin^2 (\pi \mathbf{k} \cdot \mathbf{b})}. \tag{4}$$

The diffracted beams are given by the principal maxima in I, occurring when $\mathbf{k} \cdot \mathbf{a} = h$ and $\mathbf{k} \cdot \mathbf{b} = l$. As already pointed out, this description may be adequate for a determination of the periodicity in the surface plane and it can be generalized to describe disordered 2D layers (sect. 2.6). However, since the only wavelength dependence of I enters through f, which is expected to vary slowly with energy, eq. (4) is clearly insufficient for an understanding of the strong modulation which actually is observed in $I(V)$. We can attempt to explain this behavior by including contributions from a set of N_3 layers parallel to the surface so that eq. (4) is modified by an additional factor of the form

$$\frac{\sin^2(N_3 \pi \mathbf{k} \cdot \mathbf{c})}{\sin^2(\pi \mathbf{k} \cdot \mathbf{c})}.$$

The $I(V)$ curve should then have peaks when $\mathbf{k} \cdot \mathbf{c} = n$, where n is an integer (3rd Laue condition). Fig. 8 shows data for $I(00)$ versus V at normal incidence on a $W(100)$ surface [23]. The predicted maxima, the "primary Bragg peaks", occur for $(2/\lambda)c = n$ ($c=a=3.16\text{Å}$) and the corresponding voltages (with an empirical inner potential correction) are indicated by arrows. Only a partial fit to the data is obtained and comparisons of this type show a number of phenomena which are not in agreement with the kinematical theory:

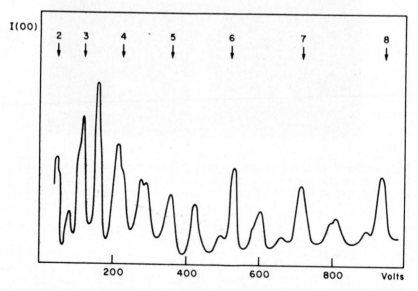

Fig. 8. $I(V)$ curve for the 00 spot from a clean $W(100)$ surface. Primary beam at close to normal incidence. The arrows indicate the positions of the primary Bragg maxima, corrected for a constant inner potential of 15 V.

(1) The $I(V)$ curves generally exhibit "secondary Bragg peaks", not predicted by the kinematical treatment.

(2) A small change in the angle of incidence may lead to abrupt changes in the intensity curve, with peaks appearing or disappearing [23].

(3) The main effect of a single layer of adsorbate on the *normal* beams is usually to attenuate the secondary Bragg peaks.

(4) "*Extra*" beams, due to a structure such as fig. 6a should show no intensity variation (except for the variations in f) but are nevertheless found to be modulated in much the same way as the normal beams [23] (see fig. 9).

As already indicated in sect. 2.1, the origin of these effects may be sought in the very strong interactions of the electrons with the solid at LEED energies. The scattering cross-sections are large and a given atom will experience not only the wave field due to the primary beam but also a scattered field

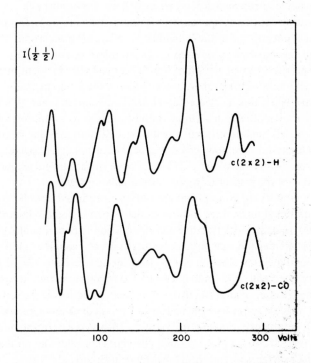

Fig. 9. $I(V)$ curves for $\frac{1}{2}\frac{1}{2}$ spots from a $W(100)$ $c(2\times2)$ structure. The upper and lower curves are from structures produced by adsorption of hydrogen and carbon monoxide, respectively.

from neighboring atoms. The latter is neglected in the kinematical treatment and to handle it properly requires the development of a dynamical theory for LEED. The problems involved herein have turned out to be highly complex and although a number of approaches have been used [24–30], none have so far been entirely successful.

One approach stresses the similarity between the diffraction problem and the band structure problem [26,28] and starts with the appropriate one-electron Schrödinger equation. The solutions inside the solid are Bloch waves and both propagating (i.e., with real wave number) and evanescent (imaginary wave number) waves must be included. In the vacuum the solution is a sum of the incident and the diffracted electron waves, and the reflection coefficients (and hence the diffracted intensities) are found by matching the wave functions at the boundary. In this description the peaks in the $I(V)$ curve can be related to the energy gaps in the band structure of the solids. The connection between this treatment and the more familiar dynamical theory [31] used at higher electron energies has recently been discussed [11].

The multiple-scattering approach [24] is conceptually different, maintaining a close connection with the individual atomic scattering events. It is assumed that the scattering properties of the atoms are known and the central problem becomes the calculation of the "effective field" incident upon an atom, i.e., the sum of the primary wave field and the field emitted by all the other atoms. When this is calculated in a self-consistent manner, the total field emitted by all the atoms can be found and from its asymptotic value, far from the crystal, the intensities of the diffracted beams may be obtained. The required summations are done layer by layer and, formally, allowance is readily made for the "selvedge" [21], i.e., those surface layers whose structure differs in some respect from that of the bulk crystal.

Various simplifying assumptions are usually introduced in order to reduce the computational difficulties and the model is then tested by determining how closely a calculated $I(V)$ curve can reproduce the experimental curve. In this manner the dependence on such factors as crystal geometry, ion core potentials and inelastic electron-electron scattering processes [30] is gradually being established and for a (model) crystal for which these factors are known, most of the features in an $I(V)$ curve can be accounted for. Unfortunately it is still not possible to reverse the analysis, i.e., to deduce an unknown surface structure from the experimental $I(V)$ curves. This is true even for clean and nearly perfect surfaces; and the problem becomes considerably more difficult for imperfect surfaces or for surfaces with an adsorbate.

However, a useful, although very approximate, description is available through the "double-diffraction" picture in which the diffracted beams are

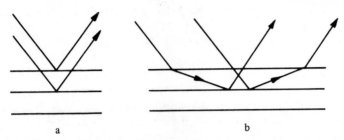

Fig. 10. a. Schematic representation of single-diffraction processes. b. Double-diffraction processes.

considered to have contributions from both single diffraction processes, depicted in fig. 10a, and double diffraction processes of the type shown in fig. 10b. This picture was originally proposed [32,33] on intuitive grounds to explain certain spot patterns but it has recently been developed systematically from the multiple-scattering approach [34] and used to explain for example the occurrence of secondary Bragg peaks in the $I(V)$ curves. In this approximation the intensity distribution for an "extra" beam, due to an adsorbate layer, is expected to be similar to that of the normal beams from a clean surface and the $I(V)$ curve should not depend very strongly on the identity of the adsorbate. Experiments [23] tend to confirm this prediction, as may be seen by comparing figs. 8 and 9. The double-diffraction picture also provides a justification for an analysis of a diffraction pattern in terms of equations such as (3) and (4).

In summary of this section it may be said that an exact theoretical analysis of LEED has not yet been provided and that experimental intensity data therefore are of limited use at present. In the absence of better procedures most experimentalists continue to rely on the kinematical treatment, as modified by the multiple-diffraction picture, and the majority of the conclusions which have been reached about surface structures have been based primarily on the LEED patterns.

2.5. Ordered surface structures

As explained in 2.3, a LEED pattern provides an image of the reciprocal net and thus serves to determine the translation vectors $\mathbf{a}_s$ and $\mathbf{b}_s$ for the surface net in terms of the substrate vectors $\mathbf{a}_o$ and $\mathbf{b}_o$. The available experimental results have shown the existence of three types of ordered surface structures: "simple" superstructures, "coincidence" structures and "incoherent"

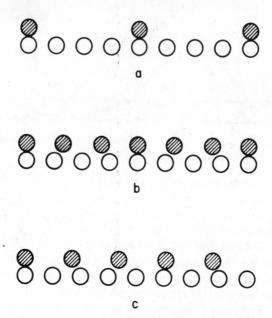

Fig. 11. One-dimensional models of: a. Simple superstructure $a_s/a_0 = 4$; b. Coincidence structure $a_s/a_0 = \frac{4}{3}$; c. Incoherent structure $a_s/a_0 = \sqrt{3}$.

structures. The distinction between these can be illustrated with the aid of 1D models, as in fig. 11, in which the substrate and the surface layer have a repeating unit of length a_0 and a_s, respectively. If $a_s/a_0 = m$ (m integer) a simple superstructure exists (fig. 11a). If $a_s/a_0 = m/n$ (m,n integers) the two nets will have a number of lattice points in common, resulting in a coincidence structure (fig. 11b). Finally, when a_s/a_0 is irrational, as in fig. 11c, no registry between the two lattices can occur and the arrangement is "incoherent" [2].

Ordered surface layers with simple superstructures are frequently seen in adsorption studies when a certain fraction of a monolayer has been deposited on the substrate. Their occurrence is to be expected from the usual model of adsorption according to which the substrate represents a regular array of sites for the foreign species. For coincidence structures [2,33,35] which generally are produced at a fairly high coverage this model must obviously be modified. It should be noted, however, that the two types of structure can give rise to the same spot pattern, as exemplified by the arrangements in figs. 11a and b. With single-diffraction only, the pattern from 11a will show extra "spots" in the positions $\frac{1}{4}, \frac{1}{2}, \frac{3}{4}$, etc., whereas 11b will give spots only at $\frac{3}{4}, \frac{3}{2}, \frac{9}{4}$, etc. However, the missing spots are produced by multiple diffraction (compare fig. 10b); thus the $\frac{1}{4}$ spot can result when diffraction by the substrate lattice (1' order beam) is followed by diffraction by the adsorbate lattice (1' order beam). In the simplest view of the double-diffraction process, the formation of the intermediate beam requires that $1/\lambda > 1/a_s = 1/4a_o$ and it should therefore be possible to distinguish between the two structures [33,36]. However, it has been pointed out that this criterion fails if evanescent waves are included as intermediate waves [35,37,38] and some other test, e.g., a coverage determination, may be necessary to resolve the ambiguity.

In the "incoherent" structures the surface atoms are not relegated to crystallographic sites so that their spacing no longer has a simple relation to the substrate lattice. The resulting spot patterns, due to single and multiple diffraction processes, can be quite complex, containing spots which cannot be indexed in a simple manner relative to the substrate reciprocal net. Such structures often occur in adsorption of metals on metals [36,39,40] where the arrangement of the adsorbate layer apparently is dominated by adatom-adatom interactions, the adatom-substrate forces playing a minor role in the ordering process.

The preceding remarks have been concerned with the relative dimensions of the unit mesh for the overlayer. Several other questions must be considered before a model of a given surface can be constructed:

(a) The identity of the scatterers. The positions of the extra spots in a LEED pattern determines the change in periodicity of the scattering potential but not the specific nature of this change. In the illustrations given so far the adatoms were considered to provide new scattering centers on an undisturbed substrate but other possibilities exist, for example the replacement of substrate atoms by adatoms to produce a "mixed" surface layer [2,8,42] or merely a distortion of the substrate lattice caused by the bonding of the foreign atoms. Where the adsorption precedes the formation of a 3D crystalline compound it is clear that, eventually, substantial relocation of the substrate atoms ("reconstruction") takes place [43,44]. In any case, conclusions regarding such processes must be based not on the LEED pattern but on supplementary data (work function changes, surface kinetics, electron impact desorption, etc.).

(b) The number of adatoms and their relative positions within the unit mesh. If coverage measurements show that there is only one atom per unit mesh, no problem exists. However, if two or more atoms are present, an arrangement must be found which is consistent with the observed intensity $I(hl) \approx |F_{hl}|^2$ (sect. 2.3). In practice this is usually done by a trial and error procedure but a systematic approach by the Patterson method has also been attempted [33]. These procedures assume that f_j is a constant, an assumption which may be invalid unless all the adatoms are identical and positioned on identical sites (since the effective value of f_j will depend on the environment).

(c) The co-ordination of the adatom site. In adsorption on, for example, a square lattice as in fig. 5a, the adatom may be bonded to one, two or four substrate atoms and a determination of which type of site is preferred cannot be made from the spot pattern. It appears, however, that in favorable cases the symmetry of the site can be deduced from observations on partially ordered structures (sect..2.6). There are also indications [41] that simple model calculations of $I(V)$ curves may help to answer this question.

2.6. Disordered structures

Ordered structures are characterized by LEED patterns with sharp spots and low background intensity. However, in experimental work it is much more common to find patterns with diffuse spots, streaks, rings, etc. which give evidence for the presence of disordered layers [45]. Some of these patterns are too complex to allow more than very qualitative conclusions about the surface but where the disordered pattern can be simply related to the corresponding ordered pattern, much valuable information can be obtained regarding the interactions at the surface. A few illustrative examples for adsorbed structures will be given and for simplicity the analysis [19] will be carried out in one dimension.

(a) Incomplete structures. One domain. Sharp superstructure spots do not occur until a sufficient number of foreign species have been adsorbed to yield the required density and it is interesting to examine the incomplete structures existing at lower coverages [23]. To discuss the gradual appearance of for example $\frac{1}{2}$ order diffraction features we consider an array generated by the vector a and made up of N_0 sites of which a fraction $\theta = N/N_0 \leqslant \frac{1}{2}$ are occupied. Letting occupied and empty sites be associated with scattering factors f and zero, respectively, eq. (3) gives:

$$I \approx AA^* = \sum_{n}^{N_0} \sum_{n'}^{N_0} f_n f_{n'}^* \exp\left[i2\pi(n-n')\,\mathbf{k}\cdot\mathbf{a}\right]$$

$$= |f|^2 \sum_{-N_0 < m < N_0} (N_0 - |m|)\, P_m \exp\left(im\delta\right) \tag{5}$$

where m is an integer and $\delta = 2\pi\mathbf{k}\cdot\mathbf{a} = 2\pi h$. P_m measures the pair correlation, giving the probablity that a given site as well as the site at a distance ma are both occupied.

An adsorption model may be chosen by specifying $P_m(\theta)$ and $I(\theta)$ can then be calculated through (5). If the superstructure grows by formation of an "island" of gradually increasing size, then $P_{2m} = \frac{1}{2}, P_{2m+1} = 0$ and evaluation of (5) gives [23]

$$I \approx \frac{\sin^2 N\delta}{\sin^2 \delta}. \tag{6}$$

A "vacancy" model may be specified by allowing occupation of only even numbered sites, i.e., $P_0 = 0, P_{2m} = 2\theta^2, P_{2m+1} = 0$, which leads to

$$I \approx N_0(\theta - 2\theta^2) + 4\theta^2 I(\theta = \tfrac{1}{2}) \tag{7}$$

where $I(\theta = \tfrac{1}{2})$ is the intensity of a beam from the completed structure. As a third illustration, random adsorption with exclusion of nearest neighbors can be shown to give [23]

$$I \approx \theta^2 \frac{\sin^2 (\tfrac{1}{2} N_0 \delta)}{\sin^2 (\tfrac{1}{2} \delta)} + N_0 \theta^2 \frac{1 - \alpha^2}{\alpha[1 + \alpha^2 + 2\alpha \cos \delta]} \tag{8}$$

with $\alpha = \theta/(1-\theta)$. The first term gives sharp peaks representing the normal "spots", the second term produces the diffuse superstructure "spots".

Expressions (6), (7) and (8) predict identical patterns for $\theta = \frac{1}{2}$ but it is seen that different models for the growth mechanism lead to different intensity and shape of the extra spots for $\theta < \frac{1}{2}$. Measurements of $I(\theta)$ therefore give information about the way the sites become occupied which in turn reflects the effective interactions between the adatoms. The models mentioned here appear to be reasonable approximations of actual physical systems [23]. However, the analytical expressions are derived for idealized systems and must be used with caution; the shape and intensity of a given spot does not uniquely define the disorder [19] and it must also be remembered that the total reflected intensity may change with adsorption.

(b) Antiphase domains. In the first example given above only one "island" is considered. It is possible, however, that several islands are formed, separated by distances smaller than the coherence width (10^2-10^3 Å) [1,6] of the electrons. If so, interference between waves from different islands will occur and when the islands are "out of step" with respect to each other, special effects in the diffraction pattern can be expected.

The general features of diffraction from such "antiphase domains" can again be discussed with the aid of a 1D model, fig. 12. The islands are separated

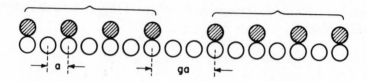

Fig. 12. One-dimensional model of an adsorbate arrangement with two domains separated by an odd number of substrate spacings.

by ga and each contains N adatoms in the half-order structure. The diffracted intensity becomes [46]

$$I \approx 4 \frac{\sin^2 N\delta}{\sin^2 \delta} \cos(N-1+g/2)\delta . \tag{9}$$

If g is even, the domains scatter in phase and the diffraction pattern is the same as from a single island (with some vacancies). However, when g is odd, the cosine term will produce a minimum for half-integral values of $h = \delta/2\pi$. These beams therefore appear to split into two with a separation depending on the relative magnitude of N and g, while the integral order beams are unaffected. If "nucleation" of the islands is random, N and g will not have fixed values and the extra spots will instead appear to be smeared out.

A similar result is obtained in the 2D case. If the size and boundaries of the domains are random, diffuse spots will appear; if the antiphase boundaries run in preferred directions, streaking will result. However, for 2D layers the normal beams may also be affected, depending on the symmetry of the adsorption site. If we consider a c(2×2) structure on a square lattice, several types of sites may be involved, e.g., sites with four-fold symmetry as shown in fig. 6a, or sites with two-fold symmetry which locate an adatom between two substrate atoms. In the former case, only the extra beams will be affected by the presence of antiphase domains; in the latter case, the separation between two domains may not correspond to a substrate net vector and broadening of some of the normal beams can occur as well. In certain systems it should therefore be possible to characterize the surface sites by studying the patterns from imperfect structures.

For more complex models of disordered layers it may be difficult to derive analytical expressions for the diffracted intensity. A useful method in these situations is the optical analogue technique [23,47] by which the LEED pat-

tern from a postulated structure can be simulated by illuminating an appropriately prepared mask with a laser beam. This technique can of course also
be used to check models of ordered structures but a direct calculation of the
structure factor may be faster in these cases.

2.7. Temperature effects

A fairly large temperature range is normally available in LEED work.
Elevated temperatures are easily produced by ohmic heating or by electron
bombardment and thermal treatment is used routinely to clean and anneal
the samples, to induce the formation of new surface structures and in general
to control the rate of surface processes. Cooling of the sample below room
temperature is technically more difficult and has so far been used in only a
few laboratories.

For a clean surface, when no structural changes are produced, the main
effect of a temperature increase on the LEED pattern is to reduce the intensity of the spots and to raise the background intensity (the "thermal-diffuse
scattering"). This phenomenon, which is due to thermal agitation of the
lattice, has been treated in the same way as in X-ray diffraction [18,19]. The
intensity of a diffracted beam is found [48] by combining the kinematical
treatment with the Debye model for lattice vibrations and in the high temperature limit

$$I(T) = I \exp(-2M) . \tag{10}$$

I is the intensity of the beam from a rigid lattice (eq. (4)). The exponential is
the Debye-Waller factor and

$$M = \frac{6h^2}{mk} \left(\frac{\cos\phi}{\lambda}\right)^2 \frac{T}{\Theta_s^2}$$

where h and k are the Planck and Boltzmann constants, m the mass of an atom
and Θ_s the effective surface Debye temperature. Eq. (10) has been found to
give a good fit to the experimenta data for a number of cubic metals and values
for Θ_s have been obtained for these. The Debye temperature is inversely proportional to the root mean square displacement of the atoms; this displacement
is expected to be relatively large for surface atoms and the fact that Θ_s consistently is found to be smaller than Θ_{bulk} (determined for example by X-ray
diffraction) is thus readily interpreted. Θ_s may depend on both the wavelength (electron penetration) [49] and the incident angle (anisotropy of the
atomic displacement) [50] of the primary beam but some representative results are listed in table 1.

Table 1
Debye temperatures.

Metal	Θ_{bulk} ($^{\circ}$K)	Θ_s ($^{\circ}$K)	Refs.
Ni(110)	390	220	[50]
Pt(100)	234	110	[49]
Ag(111)	225	155	[51]
Pb(111)	90	55	[52]
W(100)	280	183	[53]

At present, LEED results of this type are the main source of data for comparison with theoretical calculations on surface lattice dynamics [48] but there has recently been an increasing interest in quantitative studies of the thermal-diffuse scattering as well [54].

The temperature effects are important also in studies that do not attempt to investigate the lattice dynamics. As a practical matter it can be seen that since $M \propto 1/\lambda^2 \propto V$ a sharp LEED pattern cannot be expected at high voltages, even with the sample at room temperature. It has also been pointed out [55] that as a rule the theoretical calculations of an $I(V)$ curve (sect. 2.4) are done for a rigid lattice and in order to compare with experimental data, these should be corrected for the temperature effect.

Few studies have been made of $I(T)$ for surfaces with an adsorbed layer. The available experimental evidence [53] indicates that with increasing temperature the intensity of the extra spots decreases much faster than the intensity of the normal spots from the clean surface. In the case of simple overlayer structures due to light adatoms the data do not conform to eq. (10) and presumably a disordering of the surface layer, rather than adatom vibrations, is the dominating process.

3. Applications of LEED

The LEED method can be used to study metallic, covalent and ionic crystals. For a given crystal it is desirable to examine a number of surface orientations since the physical and chemical properties of the surface depend strongly on which crystal plane is exposed. The interaction of a selected surface with any foreign atoms or molecules can in turn be investigated. Thus, the total number of surface systems that may be studied by LEED is potentially very large.

In the following sections only a few specific examples will be discussed. The purpose will be to illustrate the application of LEED to problems concerning (1) clean surface studies, (2) adsorption of gases, (3) heterogeneous catalysis, (4) surface reactions (e.g., oxidation) and (5) film growth.

3.1. *Clean surfaces*

LEED studies of clean surfaces are carried out in order to correlate the structural characteristics with other physical properties (e.g., lattice dynamics, electronic and magnetic properties, surface diffusion) or as a preliminary to adsorption work. In either case a precise definition of the substrate surface is attempted, in terms of periodicity, surface morphology and imperfections, and impurities.

After appropriate preparation of the crystal, a clean surface might be expected to have the same lateral periodicity as a parallel plane in the bulk. However, an important result of LEED has been to demonstrate that this need not be the case. Superstructures are quite common on surfaces of semiconductors and have been observed on, for example, Si, Ge, GeAs, CdS, Sb and Bi [1,56]. In these covalent materials there appears to be a strong tendency to lower the surface free energy (to decrease the number of "dangling bonds") by some sort of "reconstruction". One of the best known examples is the "Si(111)-7" structure which forms on either a cleaved or a polished Si(111) surface after an anneal at about 800°C. Although it has been suggested [57] that this structure is due to a thin overlayer of Fe_5Si_3, recent Auger measurements [58] indicate that it is a property of silicon itself. The Ge(111) surface also forms several superstructures and it has recently been shown [59] that a direct correlation exists between the electronic surface states and the surface structure. There is still some uncertainty regarding the atomic positions in the various structures [60] so that full advantage of these findings has not yet been taken.

No extra spots have been seen in LEED patterns from ionic crystals, but those surfaces which might be unstable towards reconstruction, e.g., NaCl(111) [61], have not been investigated. However, from the positions of the primary Bragg maxima in the $I(V)$ curves from LiF(100) [62] and KCl(100) [63] it has been concluded that a slight dilation normal to the surface occurs in the outermost layers. This is a phenomenon which has been discussed extensively on theoretical grounds [64].

As a rule, clean surfaces of metals also show the expected lateral periodicity but there appears to be at least two exceptions, namely platinum [65] and gold [66]. The (100) faces of both of these fcc metals show a (1 × 5) superstructure and it has been proposed [66] that the tendency to reconstruction can be related to a changed effective valency of the surface atoms in these two cases.

LEED can be successfully applied to the question of surface morphology if some degree of long-range order exists. Thus, large facets [67] or regularly spaced steps [68] on a surface can be characterized from an analysis of the LEED pattern. Generally speaking, however, the pattern is not very sensitive to surface imperfections; it has been found, for example, that 0.1–0.2 mono-layer of Si atoms can be deposited on a "perfect" Si(111)-7 surface without discernible changes in the pattern [69] and that a surface requires quite large doses of bombarding ions before a substantial degradation of the beams occurs [70]. The $I(V)$ curves, on the other hand, are much more sensitive to the surface condition [71] but, as discussed in previous sections,, the interpreta-tion of these data must await further theoretical developments. The situation is very similar as regards chemical impurities but for the study of these the simple and powerful method of Auger spectroscopy (sect. 2.2) is now avail-able.

In the case of clean surfaces it can usually be assumed that the examina-tion by LEED does not alter the surface properties. It may be noted, how-ever, that surfaces of a few compound crystals have been found to be af-fected by the primary electrons [72], and that this is a fairly common pheno-menon for adsorbed layers [73].

3.2. Adsorption of gases

As previously discussed, the data which are most easily interpreted con-cern well-defined changes in a LEED pattern. Such changes frequently result from adsorption and at present the most important application of LEED is in this field.

A few studies of physical adsorption have been reported [74] and in spite of the experimental difficulties (low temperature, relatively high pressure) this promises to be a fruitful area for LEED. It appears that two-dimensional phase transitions ("gas" → "liquid" → "crystal") can be observed in the ad-layers as the density is increased, and many predictions of the detailed theories which have been developed for physisorption [75] can be tested by diffrac-tion.

Investigations of chemisorption are much more numerous and more than a hundred different systems have been studied [7]. Rather than trying to sur-vey all of these, a single representative system, namely the adsorption of hy-drogen on tungsten (100) [76], will be discussed in some detail.

As hydrogen adsorbs on W(100) at room temperature a sequence of LEED patterns is observed, the first stage consisting of the appearance of $\frac{1}{2}$ $\frac{1}{2}$ spots, i.e., the formation of a c(2×2) structure (sect. 2.3). Measurements of the coverage, θ, show that this structure is complete when the equivalent of half a monolayer of H atoms are on the surface. This result, as well as observations on the kinetics of the adsorption and of the temperature effect on $I(\frac{1}{2}\frac{1}{2})$ (sect. 2.7) suggest that no reconstruction of the substrate occurs, and the $I(V)$ curve for the same spot is in accord with the double-diffraction picture (sect. 2.6). It is concluded that the adsorbate is directly involved in the diffraction and it follows immediately that H_2 dissociates upon adsorption.

Measurements of $I(\theta)$ for the $\frac{1}{2}\frac{1}{2}$ spots show that the intensity (integrated over the spot area) increases linearly with coverage. This behavior agrees with the "island" model (sect. 2.6, eq. (6)) and since the initial collisions of gaseous hydrogen with the surface must occur at random, the result is evidence for a high mobility of H on the W(100) surface. The preference for the c(2×2) arrangement does not appear to be connected with dipole-dipole repulsions, which have been suggested as an origin for superstructures [45]; the measured work-function change indicates an effective dipole per adatom of ≈ 0.3 Debye and the total dipole interaction energy is $\ll kT$. It is possible that indirect interactions via the metallic conduction electrons are responsible [77] but an explanation involving hybridized W atom orbitals has also been attempted [78]. Additional experimental information about these interactions is obtained from the decrease of $I(\frac{1}{2}\frac{1}{2})$ with temperature [53], which is assumed to be due to a disordering of the c(2×2) structure. With the use of the Bragg-Williams treatment [79] it can be shown that $I(\frac{1}{2}\frac{1}{2}) \propto s^2$, where s is the long-range order parameter which obeys the relation $s = \tanh(s\, T_c/T)$. T_c, the critical temperature, is found to be about $500°K$ for the c(2×2) − H structure and this value is a measure of the effective interaction between the adatoms.

When the coverage exceeds half a monolayer of H atoms, the LEED pattern changes: Each $\frac{1}{2}\frac{1}{2}$ spot splits into four new spots which gradually move apart as the adsorption proceeds, finally becoming streaky before they disappear completely at saturation. The proposed model [76] for these transitions involve structures with a large unit mesh containing anitphase domains of a size depending on the adatom density. Thus, long-range interactions must again be invoked.

This example illustrates the great detail with which an adsorption system may be described. Results of this kind have shown that the available theories of chemisorption must be modified and refined to a considerable extent.

3.3. Heterogeneous catalysis

Investigations by LEED of catalysis are a natural extension of chemisorption. It is clear, of course, that the conditions under which catalytic reactions

of technical importance are carried out (e.g., high pressure, complex catalyst
structures and composition) cannot be reproduced in LEED work. However,
LEED should contribute much to an understanding of the fundamental interactions and of the influence exerted by the substrate structure.

Several LEED studies with co-adsorption of different gases have been
carried out [80–83] and it appears that the resulting adsorbed structures generally are considerably more complex than those produced by the single gases,
reflecting the interactions between the different species.With a few exceptions
[80,84], however, catalytic synthesis of polyatomic molecules from simpler
ones has not been observed in LEED systems. As would be expected on thermodynamic grounds, catalytic decomposition is found much more frequently and
many features of, for example, the decomposition of ammonia on tungsten have
been elucidated with the aid of LEED [85].

3.4. *Oxidation*

The adsorption of oxygen is discussed separately because it typifies an interaction which may lead to the formation of a stable 3D compounds, even under
LEED conditions. The reaction of oxygen with the surface may therefore be
quite complex as compared to other simple gases like H_2, N_2 and CO which
generally can be desorbed as such to reproduce the initial substrate surface.

As a specific example the interaction of oxygen with nickel will be mentioned. This system has been the subject of at least a dozen LEED investigations [86] and new phenomena are still being found [87]. The net reaction
on Ni(110), for instance, is well established [88]. Oxygen enters the substrate and forms crystalline NiO which has the (100) plane parallel to the
original Ni(110) surface. The end product is thus well defined in terms of
stoichiometry, structure and crystal orientation, implying the operation of
strong ordering forces during its growth. This is also indicated by a series of
distinct LEED patterns that are observed in the initial stages of the oxidation
[86–88]. With increasing oxygen exposure the patterns are:

$$\text{(a) Ni(110) } (1 \times 1) \rightarrow \text{(b) } (3 \times 1) \rightarrow \text{(c) } (2 \times 1)$$

$$\rightarrow \text{(d) } (3 \times 1) \rightarrow \text{(e) } (9 \times 4) \rightarrow \text{(f) NiO (3D)} .$$

Approximate coverages have been assigned to most of these structures, e.g.,
(b), (c) and (d) contain $\frac{1}{2}$, $\frac{1}{2}$ and $\frac{2}{3}$ monolayers of oxygen atoms, respectively.
At other coverages the structures are disordered but the transition (c) → (d) is
an interesting exception in that (at slightly elevated temperature) the $\frac{1}{2}$ order
spots from the (2×1) structure split into two which gradually move apart until

the $\frac{1}{3}$ order positions are reached. It appears that a uniform mixture of the two structures exists at the intermediate stages.

So far it has proven difficult to obtain unique models for all of these structures. It may be anticipated, however, that eventually LEED data will make important contributions to an atomistic foundation for macroscopic theories of oxidation [89].

3.5. Film growth

The LEED method is well suited for the study of the initial stages of film growth [90] and the dependence on substrate structure, imperfections and impurities can be explored. It has been applied especially to metal layers on a variety of substrates but we choose again a single example, namely the formation of a sodium layer on a nickel surface [40,91].

With adsorption on a Ni(111) surface the LEED pattern shows a diffuse ring when the sodium coverage is < 0.33 and the diameter of this ring is found to vary roughly as $\theta^{1/2}$. The structure which is believed to produce this pattern consists of a uniform distribution of Na atoms with an interatomic distance determined by the coverage, and this model is confirmed by a laser simulation of the diffraction pattern. As more sodium is deposited on the surface, i.e., for $\theta > 0.33$, the ring in the pattern breaks up into sets of hexagonal spots some of which move away continuously from the 00 spot with increasing Na density. The spacings in the pattern show that the Na-Na distance again is inversely proportional to $\theta^{1/2}$ but the surface structure is now incoherent.

The main features of these structures can be explained qualitatively by strong dipole-dipole repulsions between the (partially ionized) adatoms and the resulting tendency to produce optimum spacing between them. At the higher coverages this effect dominates over the preference for adsorption on specific surface sites.

A related behavior is observed in Na adsorption on the Ni (100) and Ni(110) faces. On Ni(100) a diffuse ring is again found at low coverage but at $\theta = 0.5$ a c(2×2) structure is formed, as might be expected if four-fold sites are involved in the bonding. Patterns from the Ni(110) + Na system, however, do not show rings; instead sharp streaks (in the [100] direction) are observed, as well as other diffraction features. A fairly lengthy analysis indicates that every other "trough" on this surface contains evenly distributed Na atoms with a spacing which varies inversely with θ.

Accurate measurements of the work-function changes with θ were also made and, combined with the structural information, these data should provide a sensitive test of theories for surface bonding and surface potential.

3.6. *Concluding remarks*

The main purpose of these lectures has been to give an introduction to low energy electron diffraction. An important criterion in selecting specific examples for discussion has been the extent to which they illustrate the general considerations developed in the previous sections and it has not been possible to describe many of the interesting theoretical and experimental results which have been obtained.

LEED is in a stage of rapid development but despite its present shortcomings the method has already contributed much to the study of solid surfaces. It is a measure of the value of the technique that for many systems we now know at least part of the answer to *what* happens on the surface and can begin to ask *why*.

References

[1] J.J.Lander, Progr. Solid State Chem. 2 (1965) 26.
[2] E.Bauer, in: Adsorption et Croissance Cristalline (Editions du Centre de la Recherche Scientifique, Paris, 1965).
[3] J.W.May, Ind. Eng. Chem. 57 (1965) 18.
[4] V.F.Dvoryankin and A.Yu.Mityagin, Soviet Phys.-Crystallogr. (translation) 12 (1968) 982.
[5] G.A.Somorjai, Ann. Rev. Phys. Chem. (1968) 251.
[6] E.G.McRae and P.J.Estrup, (to be published).
[7] U.S.Government Report ARL-69-0003 (prepared by A.G.Jackson, M.P.Hooker, T.W.Haas, G.J.Dooley and J.T.Grant) (January, 1969).
[8] H.E.Farnsworth, Advanc. Catalysis 14 (1963) 225.
[9] R.L.Park and H.E.Farnsworth, Rev. Sci. Instr. 35 (1964) 1592; H.E.Farnsworth, in: The Solid-Gas Interface (Marcel Dekker, Inc., New York, 1967) Ch. 13.
[10] E.J.Scheibner, L.H.Germer and C.D.Hartman, Rev. Sci. Instr. 31 (1960) 112.
[11] R.M.Stern, J.J.Perry and D.S.Boudreaux, Rev. Mod. Phys. 41 (1969) 275.
[12] L.A.Harris, J. Appl. Phys. 39 (1968) 1419; L.N.Tharp and E.J.Scheibner, J. Appl. Phys. 38 (1967) 3320; R.E.Weber and W.T. Peria, J. Appl. Phys. 38 (1967) 4355; P.W.Palmberg and T.N.Rhodin, J. Appl. Phys. 39 (1968) 2425; N.J.Taylor, Rev. Sci. Instr. 40 (1969) 792.
[13] R.V.Culver and F.C.Tompkins, Advanc. Catalysis 11 (1959) 67.
[14] G.Ehrlich, Advanc. Catalysis 15 (1964) 31.
[15] A.J.Melmed, H.P.Layer and J.Kruger, Surface Sci. 9 (1968) 476.
[16] T.A.Callcott and A.U.MacRae, Phys. Rev. 178 (1969) 966.
[17] D.Menzel and R.Gomer, J. Chem. Phys. 41 (1964) 3329, 3311. D.Menzel, Surface Sci. 14 (1969) 340.
[18] R.W.James, The Optical Principles of the Diffraction of X-rays (G.Bell and Sons., Ltd., London, 1965).

[19] A.Guinier, X-ray Diffraction (W.H.Freeman and Co., San Francisco, 1963).

[20] P.W.Palmberg, R.E.DeWames, L.A.Vredevoe and T.Wolfram, J.Appl. Phys. 40 (1969) 1158.

[21] E.A.Wood, J. Appl. Phys. 35 (1964) 1306.

[22] R.L.Park and H.H.Madden Jr., Surface Sci. 11 (1968) 188.

[23] P.J.Estrup and J.Anderson, Surface Sci. 8 (1967) 101.

[24] E.G.McRae, J. Chem. Phys. 45 (1966) 3258; Surface Sci. 7 (1967) 41; 8 (1967) 14.

[25] K.Hirabayashi and Y.Takeishi, Surface Sci. 4 (1966) 150.

[26] D.S.Boudreaux and V.Heine, Surface Sci. 8 (1967) 426.

[27] F.Hofman and H.P.Smith, Phys. Rev. Letters 19 (1967) 1472.

[28] P.M.Marcus and D.W.Jepson, Phys. Rev. Letters 20 (1967) 925.

[29] K.Kambe, Z.Naturforsch. 23a (1968) 1280.

[30] C.B.Duke and C.W.Tucker Jr., Surface Sci. 15 (1969) 231.

[31] H.Bethe, Ann. Physik 87 (1928) 55; See also the articles by A.Howie and M.M. Whelan in this volume.

[32] E.Bauer, Phys. Rev. 123 (1961) 1206.

[33] C.W.Tucker Jr., J. Appl. Phys. 35 (1964) 1897; Surface Sci. 2 (1964) 519.

[34] E.G.McRae, Surface Sci. 11 (1968) 479; 11 (1968) 492; 14 (1969) 407.

[35] E.Bauer, Surface Sci. 7 (1967) 351.

[36] N.J.Taylor, Surface Sci. 4 (1966) 161.

[37] F.Jona, R.F.Lever and J.B.Gunn, Surface Sci. 9 (1968) 468.

[38] P.W.Palmberg and T.N.Rhodin, J. Chem. Phys. 49 (1968) 147.

[39] P.J.Estrup, J.Anderson and W.E.Danforth, Surface Sci. 4 (1966) 286.

[40] R.L.Gerlach and T.N.Rhodin, Surface Sci. 10 (1968) 446.

[41] E.G.McRae (private communication).

[42] L.H.Germer, Ann. N.Y.Acad. Sci. 101 (1963) 599.

[43] P.J.Estrup and J.Anderson, 27. Ann. Phys. Electr. Conf. (M.I.T., Cambridge, 1967) p. 47.

[44] J.L.Domange and J.Oudar, Surface Sci. 11 (1968) 124.

[45] J.J.Lander, Surface Sci. 1 (1964) 125.

[46] R.L.Park, in: The Structure and Chemistry of Solid Surfaces (John Wiley and Sons, Inc., New York, 1969).

[47] W.P.Ellis and B.D.Campbell, Trans. Am. Cryst. Assoc. 4 (1968) 97.

[48] B.C.Clark, R.Herman and R.F.Wallis, Phys. Rev. 139 (1965) A860; R.F.Wallis, in: The Structure and Chemistry of Solid Surfaces (John Wiley and Sons, Inc., New York, 1969). It may be noted that for HEED a number of studies have been made of the dynamical contributions to the temperature factor. For a recent example see: J.F.Graczyk, J. Appl. Phys. 40 (1969) 3510.

[49] H.B.Lyon and G.A.Somorjai, J. Chem. Phys. 44 (1966) 3707.

[50] A.U.MacRae, Surface Sci. 2 (1964) 522.

[51] E.R.Jones, J.T.McKinney and M.B.Webb, Phys. Rev. 151 (1966) 476.

[52] R.M.Goodman, H.H.Farrell and G.A.Somorjai, J. Chem. Phys. 48 (1968) 1046.

[53] P.J.Estrup, in: The Structure and Chemistry of Solid Surfaces (John Wiley and Sons, Inc., New York, 1969).

[54] R.F.Wallis and A.A.Maradudin, Phys. Rev. 148 (1966) 962; J.T.McKinney, E.R.Jones and M.B.Webb, Phys. Rev. 160 (1967) 523; R.F.Barnes, M.G.Lagally and M.B.Webb, Phys. Rev. 171 (1968) 627.

[55] M.G.Lagally and M.B.Webb, Phys. Rev. Letters 21 (1968) 1388.

[56] F.Jona, Surface Sci. 8 (1967) 57; IBM J. Res. Develop. 9 (1965) 375.

[57] E.Bauer, Phys. Letters 26A (1968) 530.

[58] N.J.Taylor, Surface Sci. 15 (1969) 169.

[59] M.Henzler, Surface Sci. 9 (1968) 31; J. Appl. Phys. 40 (1969) 3758.

[60] J.J.Lander and J.Morrison, J. Appl. Phys. 34 (1963) 1403;
     N.R.Hansen and D.Haneman, Surface Sci. 2 (1964) 566.

[61] J.T.Kummer and J.F.Yao, Can. J. Chem. 45 (1967) 421.

[62] E.G.McRae and C.W.Caldwell, Surface Sci. 2 (1964) 509.

[63] I.Marklund and S.Anderson, Surface Sci. 5 (1966) 197.

[64] G.C.Benson and K.S.Yun, in: The Solid-Gas Interface (Marcel Dekker, Inc., New
     York, 1967) Ch. 8.

[65] L.B.Lyon and G.A.Somorjai, J. Chem. Phys. 46 (1967) 2539.

[66] P.W.Palmberg and T.N.Rhodin, J. Chem. Phys. 49 (1968) 134.

[67] C.W.Tucker, Jr., J. Appl. Phys. 38 (1967) 1968.

[68] W.P.Ellis and R.L.Schwoebel, Surface Sci. 11 (1968) 82.

[69] F.Jona, Surface Sci. 8 (1967) 478.

[70] R.L.Park, J. Appl. Phys. 37 (1966) 295;
     R.L.Jacobsen and G.K.Wehner, J. Appl. Phys. 36 (1965) 2674.

[71] H.E.Farnsworth and K.Hayek, Surface Sci. 8 (1967) 35;
     P.J.Estrup and J.Anderson, Surface Sci. 7 (1967) 255.

[72] P.W.Palmberg, C.J.Todd and T.N.Rhodin, J. Appl. Phys. 39 (1968) 4650;
     L.Fiermans and J.Vennik, Phys. Letters 25A (1967) 687;
     C.C.Chang, J. Appl. Phys. 39 (1968) 5570.

[73] P.J.Estrup and J.Anderson, Surface Sci. 9 (1968) 463.

[74] J.J.Lander, in: Fundamentals of Gas-Surface Interactions (Academic Press, New
     York, 1967) p. 25.

[75] See for example, The Solid-Gas Interface (Marcel Dekker, Inc., New York, 1967).

[76] P.J.Estrup and J.Anderson, J. Chem. Phys. 45 (1966) 2254.

[77] T.B.Grimley, J. Am. Chem. Soc. 90 (1968) 3016.

[78] P.W.Tamm and L.D.Schmidt,J. Chem. Phys. 51 (1969) 5352.

[79] W.L.Bragg and E.J.Williams, Proc. Roy. Soc. (London) A145 (1934) 699.

[80] R.L.Park and H.E.Farnsworth, J. Chem. Phys. 43 (1965) 2351.

[81] J.W.May, L.H.Germer and C.C.Chang, J. Chem. Phys. 45 (1966) 2382.

[82] P.J.Estrup and J.Anderson, J. Chem. Phys. 46 (1967) 567.

[83] G.Ertl, Surface Sci. 6 (1967) 208; 7 (1967) 309.

[84] T.Edmonds and R.C.Pitkethley, Surface Sci. 15 (1969) 137.

[85] P.J.Estrup and J.Anderson, J. Chem. Phys. 49 (1968) 523;
     J.W.May, R.J.Szostak and L.H.Germer, Surface Sci. 15 (1969) 37.

[86] L.H.Germer, J.W.May and R.J.Szostak, Surface Sci. 7 (1965) 430; and references
     listed there.

[87] J.W.May and L.H.Germer, Surface Sci. 11 (1968) 443.

[88] R.L.Park and H.E.Farnsworth, J. Appl. Phys. 35 (1964) 2220.

[89] O.Kubaschewski and B.E.Hopkins, Oxidation of Metals and Alloys (Butterworths,
     London, 1962).

[90] D.W.Pashley, Advanc. Phys. 14 (1965) 327.

[91] R.L.Gerlach and T.N.Rhodin, in: The Structure and Chemistry of Solid Surfaces
     (John Wiley and Sons, Inc., New York, 1969).

RECENT APPLICATIONS OF X-RAY TOPOGRAPHY

A. R. LANG

H.H.Wills Physics Laboratory, University of Bristol, England

1. Introduction

X-ray topography comprises a variety of X-ray diffraction techniques which record the manner and extent to which the specimen crystal departs from the ideal model of a perfect three-dimensionally periodic structure. Diffraction techniques possess the advantage of a very general applicability: important lattice defects such as dislocations reproduce the same geometry of lattice distortions independent of chemical species except within a few atomic diameters from the dislocation line itself, and the scattering by atoms in this highly distorted dislocation 'core' makes a contribution to the dislocation diffraction contrast even less significant in the case of X-rays than in the case of 100 kV electrons. Familiarity with the range of diffraction contrast phenomena exhibited by individual dislocations and other lattice imperfections as functions of X-ray wavelength, crystal scattering factor, and absorption factor enables the experimenter to assert with some confidence whether or not he is observing individual dislocations when he begins to examine X-ray topographically a crystal species not previously studied by the method. This generality of observation and interpretation is, of course, shared by transmission electron microscopy. The great difference between X-ray topography and thin-film transmission electron microscopy is the much inferior resolution of the X-ray technique. Several factors (to be enumerated below) conspire together to limit the resolution on X-ray topographic images to not better than about one micron. Against this handicap suffered by X-ray techniques one must set their capabilities for the non-destructive examination of crystals. There are two aspects to the non-destructive character of X-ray tpopography. Firstly, the X-rays will penetrate up to several millimetres in thickness of crystals containing only light elements. Thus, crystals of, say, beryllium oxide or diamond, some millimetres in diameter, may be examined whole; and in practically all studies it is safe to assume that the X-ray topographic specimen is sufficiently thick so as to be truly representative of the bulk material. Secondly, the X-ray dosage received by a crystal in the course of its topographic examination is generally several orders of magnitude less than that required to produce detectable radiation damage in sensitive crystals. It is possible to take repeated X-ray topographs of organic crystals which would quickly volatilise and decompose in the electron microscope; and in the case of that interesting crystal quartz, which manifestly suffers damage in the electron microscope, no detectable loss of X-ray diffraction contrast or change in colour have been observed after taking upwards of 40 X-ray topographs, averaging 20 hours exposure each, of one and the same specimen.

The feasibility of making repeated X-ray topographic examinations of a given specimen renders it possible to interleave such examinations between other types of experiment on the specimen, for example between mechanical deformations, or irradiation or heat treatments, or optical, electrical or magnetic measurements. Regrettably little use has been made of this capability so far, the great majority of reported X-ray topographic studies having been concerned with surveys of dislocations and other imperfections in crystals just in the 'as-grown' state. Indeed it is this straightforward application of X-ray topography that will figure most prominently among the studies mentioned in the present review. Perhaps such restriction of applications is natural while a technique is in the developing stage, yet it is now nearly twelve years since it was discovered that high-resolution X-ray topographic methods were capable of revealing individual dislocations in nearly perfect crystals! It is to be hoped that there may be a hastening in acceptance of the X-ray topographic examination as a routine, and often highly revealing, check on single crystals to be used in any experiment where the degree of lattice perfection could be a significant parameter, and that researchers who are designing experimental programs to measure changes in some property of their crystals as a consequence of laboratory-imposed conditions may be encouraged to incorporate a sequence of X-ray topographic examinations with their other experimental tests.

The X-ray topographs selected to illustrate these lectures were almost all taken by the technique of the 'projection topograph' or by its close relative (and predecessor in time) the 'section topograph'. It is appropriate therefore to devote a section (section 3) to description of the X-ray geometry of these techniques and a following section (4) to a discussion of factors which determine the quality and resolution achievable in these and other X-ray topographic arrangements. To set the techniques described in section 3 in their historical perspective, there will first be given a review of the variety of X-ray topographic techniques that have been found useful in the last few decades (section 2). Although X-ray topography can be used quite successfully with little reference to the diffraction theory which underlies the phenomena observed, familiarity with the essential theory well repays the effort of study, and is strongly recommended to all serious workers. Since theory will be well taken care of in the chapter by Professor Authier in this volume, the minimum reference to theoretical matters will be given here. When such reference does occur, the terms or concepts introduced will be found explained in most introductions to the dynamical theory of X-ray diffraction, and of these the review by Batterman and Cole [1] is strongly recommended. It should also be emphasized how frequently it is found that a comparison with the simpler theoretical analyses applicable to diffraction contrast in transmission electron microscopy facilitates the essentials of a complicated X-ray diffraction situation to be grasped. Analogies between electron microscopy and X-ray topography certainly apply in studies of fault surfaces (section 7), but with less force in the study of dislocations (section 6).

This review will conclude with an account of a recent development, X-ray moiré topography (section 10), and with a forecast of some future developments (section 11) one or more of which may possibly be realised soon.

2. Survey of topographic techniques

2.1. *Orientation contrast and extinction contrast*

X-ray topographic techniques produce an image of a surface bounding or cutting a crystal, or of the projection of a selected volume of crystal, by recording the diffracted X-ray intensity issuing from such surface or volume. The usual method of recording is by photographic emulsion and only this method will be discussed in detail in these lectures. Some other possible recording methods will be mentioned in section 11. Two factors, often largely independent and separable, determine the level of intensity reaching each point on the emulsion. The first is simply whether or not the specimen is locally oriented so that some radiation among the range of wavelengths impinging upon it can be reflected according to Bragg's law, and the intensity of such reflected rays will range from zero upwards. Its variation from point to point on the image, appropriately called *orientation contrast*, provides a measure of lattice misorientations having a sensitivity generally calculable by simple geometrical relations and controllable at will within a wide range. Clearly, insensitive experimental arrangements would result from employing either a uniform extended source of monochromatic radiation or a localised source of

white radiation. Higher sensitivity in orientation contrast would be achieved
with finely collimated characteristic radiation, and higher still with monochromatisation and achromatisation using two-crystal techniques.

The other factor determining intensity is the lattice perfection of the
crystal. Physical factors such as X-ray wavelength, specimen absorption, and
the scattering factor of the active Bragg reflection, largely determine the
range in magnitude of diffracted intensity which can lie between the two extreme cases corresponding to the "ideally perfect crystal" and to the "ideally
imperfect crystal". (The former type of crystal is well defined, the latter type
one hopes to realise in the limit of negligible primary or secondary extinction.)
Contrast arising from point-to-point variations in lattice perfection is conveniently termed *extinction contrast*. Judicious choice of diffraction geometry
(and of X-ray wavelength and specimen thickness when these parameters may
be selected by the experimenter) can make the possible range of extinction
contrast be as much as a couple of orders of magnitude in diffracted intensity
for a given volume of crystal.

Important experimental variables in the X-ray topographic arrangement include, then, the wavelength spread of the radiation, the degree of collimation
of the incident beam, and the ratio of distance from source-to-specimen to that
of specimen-to-photographic emulsion (on film or plate). How the sensitivity
to specific types of crystal imperfection depends upon these variables can be
illustrated with the following hypothetical example. Suppose the specimen
whose surface is shown in fig. 1a consists of a matrix of perfect crystal, C, in
which there are two "islands", A and B, whose lattices differ from it. The island A is imperfect compared with C, and so has a larger integrated reflection
than C, but it has negligible misorientation with respect to C. The crystal lattice in island B, on the other hand, is as perfect as that of the matrix C, but is
slightly misorientated with respect to C. (The B-C boundary would be a low-

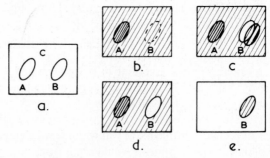

Fig. 1. Crystal surface a, and types of X-ray topograph images of it, b−e.

angle-boundary, and high-resolution topographic methods might resolve the individual dislocations in this boundary.) The specimen in fig. 1a may be regarded either as massive, and too thick for the X-rays to penetrate, or as a thin foil through which the diffracted X-rays may pass with small attenuation. In the former case only *surface reflection* topographs can be obtained, whereas in the latter one may take *transmission* topographs as well. Transmission topographs should be used whenever possible: they are generally more informative and sensitive than surface reflection topographs. The topographic image of the specimen will usually be a distorted representation of the shape of the specimen, any such distortion is neglected in the schematic topographic images in fig. 1b to e. Suppose continuous radiation is used and the X-ray plate is placed very close to the specimen. Then island A will be detected by extinction contrast, standing out by virtue of its different reflecting power (greater than that of C in the reflection case, and in the transmission case when absorption is low), whereas island B will not show any *area* contrast since one may assume that there will be wavelengths present which will enable it to satisfy Bragg's Law as fully as C does. If the distance from specimen to X-ray plate be increased, then the experimental set-up becomes sensitive to orientation contrast, and the misorientation of B can be detected by the finite linear displacement of its topographic image resulting from the different direction of the Bragg-reflected rays issuing from it compared with those from C. The topograph will then look like fig. 1c.

Now suppose that characteristic radiation is used, and the incident beam is collimated so as to have an angular range sufficiently small that when the specimen is set so that C satisfies Bragg's Law, B does not. Then the topograph will appear as in fig. 1d. Island A will show up, as before, by extinction contrast, whereas the reflection from B will be absent. An appropriate rotation of the specimen will bring B into an orientation to satisfy Bragg's Law but will then cut off the reflection from A and C (fig. 1e). This technique is thus good for detecting orientation contrast. No significant change in the intensity patterns of figs. 1d and 1e will result from a change in the distance from specimen to X-ray film, the chief consequence of such an increase would merely be an undesirable loss of resolution on the topographic image. The different response to changes in specimen-to-film distance, as just described, characteristically distinguishes continuous-radiation topographic methods from those using well-collimated characteristic radiation.

2.2. *Continuous-radiation methods*

Here (and in sects. 2.3 to 2.5) some topographic techniques will be described, chosen for their historical or practical importance, or as illustrating an

important point in diffraction geometry, but not to serve as a complete cata-
logue of all the variations in technique that have been published. A pioneer of
X-ray topography was Ramachandran [2], who was the first to set up apparatus to study extinction contrast and to realise the importance of this quantity as an indicator of lattice perfection. He worked on cleavage plates of diamond, using such plates in transmission: a good beginning in X-ray topography,
for he chose the best specimen arrangement for revealing extinction contrast,
and studied a specimen crystal highly suitable for X-ray topographic examination! Ramachandran selected reflecting planes nearly normal to the specimen
surface and he fixed angular settings of specimen and film so as to minimise
the distortion of the topographic image. He could then more easily compare
his X-ray topographs with optical pictures of the specimen. His ratio of distance of source-to-specimen to distance of specimen-to-film was about 12, so
his arrangement produced topographs with the characteristics of fig. 1b, i.e. it
was sensitive to extinction contrast but not to orientation contrast. From the
dimensions of his components Ramachandran gives one can calculate his topographic resolution to have been about 25 microns.

A useful and widely employed reflection-specimen technique with continuous radiation is that of Schulz [3], who introduced microfocus X-ray
tubes into X-ray topography. With an apparent focal spot size of, say, 3 microns by 30 microns Schulz could afford to have the distances source-to-
specimen and specimen-to-film about equal, gaining sensitivity to orientation
contrast in addition to extinction contrast and at the same time retaining as
much topographic resolution as could be successfully recorded using emulsions
no finer-grained than those in dental or light-alloy radiographic X-ray films. It
may be mentioned that, taking a little care with geometrical factors affecting
resolution, these continuous radiation methods can be quite capable of revealing individual dislocations in nearly perfect crystals. This has been done
with transmission specimens by Fujiwara et al. [4] using lightly absorbing specimens, and by Fiermans [5] with strongly absorbing ones.

The strongpoint of continuous-radiation techniques is their simplicity: the
crystal specimen does not need to be set with precision to satisfy the Bragg
condition for a particular wavelength. Also, it is often possible to receive several images of reasonable quality on one and the same film, each image being
a reflection from a different lattice plane. This group of images will contain
information on misorientation about several axes. A geometrical analysis for
interpreting images on Schulz-method films has been published by Coyle
et al. [6]. A difficulty with the method of simultaneously recording reflections from several lattice planes is that most of the images will be rather distorted, and in the cases which unavoidably occur of fairly oblique incidence

on the film, a reduction in image resolution due to the emulsion thickness will be appreciable. A more serious disadvantage of methods using continuous rather than collimated characteristic radiation is evident in all situations where the crystal texture to be studied does not consist of well-defined blocks, slightly tilted with respect to each other. When continuous lattice curvature is present, it is very difficult to assess the relative contributions of orientation contrast and extinction contrast in the mottled intensity distribution that the topograph images then exhibit.

The Schulz method has been quite widely used for inspecting lineage structures in single crystals of metals grown from the melt, a recent example of this application can be found in a study of the origin of such structures by Jaffrey and Chadwick [7].

2.3. Slit-collimated characteristic-radiation methods

The most widely used method for recording reflections from crystal surfaces is that of Barrett [8] who improved one of the arrangements discussed by Berg [9] by using a fine-grain photographic emulsion and making great effort to place the emulsion as close as possible to the specimen surface so that geometrical factors were favourable to high topographic resolution. Further improvements were made by Newkirk who, using this method, was one of the first to observe images of individual dislocations by X-ray extinction contrast [10,11]. Typically, the source-to-specimen distance would be 30 cm. If a standard crystallographic X-ray tube is employed then the apparent source size is about one millimetre square. The cross-section of the beam utilised for Bragg reflection will, close to the specimen, be also about one millimetre square, but by choosing Bragg planes inclined to the specimen surface so that the incident beam makes a relatively small grazing angle with the surface the illuminated area of specimen surface may be made to total several square millimetres. Also by using softer radiations such as CoKα and CrKα with which the diffraction angles from low-order reflections are large, the photographic plate may be set so that it is no further than a fraction of a millimetre from most parts of the specimen surface illuminated by the X-rays. When, as is then possible, the photographic plate makes a small angle with the specimen surface the topographic image forms but a slightly distorted image of the surface. An incidental advantage of soft radiations is that very thin emulsions can be used (such as those in high-resolution spectroscopic plates) without prohibitively low X-ray absorption efficiencies. With very thin emulsions it is not essential for good resolution that the diffracted X-ray beam impinges precisely perpendicularly upon the plate. With care, Newkirk's development of the Berg-Barrett technique can achieve a resolution of about one micron in images of lattice defects, quite as good as in any other, more complicated experimental arrangement. A recent description of the experimental procedure and analysis of the diffraction geometry has been given by Austerman and Newkirk [12]. Many applications of the Berg-Barrett technique have been reported over the years; a particularly fruitful one was its use by Lommel and Kronberg [13] to determine Burgers vectors of dislocations in sapphire single crystals.

When it is desired to record on one plate the Bragg reflection from a larger area of specimen surface than in Newkirk's technique (without increasing the dimensions of the apparent X-ray tube focal spot) recourse may be had to moving specimen and moving film techniques. In the arrangement of N.Wooster and W.A.Wooster [14] the whole crystal surface to be examined is illuminated by radiation diverging from a small source. The crystal and film are in fixed positions relative to each other, but are bodily rocked through a range of angles sufficient to allow all points on the specimen surface to reflect characteristic X-rays on to the film. This rocking procedure simulates the conditions of the continuous-radiation topograph, hence the method is sensitive to extinction contrast but not to orientation contrast. A technique capable of high orientation contrast was described by Merlini and Guinier [15]. The film is oriented parallel to the specimen surface so that an undistorted image of it is recorded. The film and the specimen are translated together so that an extended area of specimen surface can be scanned using a finely-collimated incident beam which gives good angular discrimination. A surface reflection technique used by Lang [16] was devised to allow the diffracted rays to fall perpendicularly on the film and at the same time to give an undistorted image of the specimen. The film is stationary and a finely collimated incident X-ray beam is used so as to provide high angular resolution. For each diffraction angle, the specimen is translated in a direction calculated so that a given length on the specimen surface produces an image of the same length on the film. Of course, if the diffraction angle is high, distortion of the image of the specimen surface will generally not be serious, just as it is generally not serious with transmission specimens and low diffraction angles. Thus the same mechanical arrangement as is used in the "projection topograph" (sect. 3.2) may be used in high-angle surface reflection topographs: specimen and plate are translated together, and the plate is normal to the diffracted beam. For a number of years, in this way surface reflection topographs have been combined with "projection topographs" and "section topographs" without much difficulty in geometrically correlating their differently shaped images; as, for example, in the studies of abraded diamonds by Frank, Lawn, Lang and Wilks [17]. Transmission specimen methods using slit-collimated characteristic radiation have much in common as regards diffraction geometry and will be discussed along with their special cases, the "projection topograph" and "section topograph", in sect. 3.

2.4. *Double-crystal methods*

The dispersionless characteristic of the "parallel" double-crystal spectrometer arrangement, combined with a photographic recording of the diffracted beam reflected from the surface of the second crystal, offers a very sensitive topographic technique for measuring lattice misorientations. The set-up is shown schematically in fig. 2. Characteristic X-rays leaving the source S are Bragg-reflected at the first crystal M and then at the specimen crystal C. As in other topographic techniques, the topographic resolution depends primarily upon how close the plate F can be placed to the reflecting surface of C (or, more strictly, upon the ratio of distance F to C to the distance C-M-S, and the smallness of the focal spot S in the direction normal to the plane of the drawing). The first crystal M is usually assumed to be perfect compared with C, so that changes in the intensity pattern on F when the angular setting of C is changed with respect to M are due to local misorientations ot imperfections in C only. This topographic technique was developed independently by Bond and Andrus [18] who applied it to studies of surfaces of natural quartz, and by Bonse and Kappler [19] who used it to detect the strain-fields of individual dislocation outcrops at the surface of germanium crystals. In principle, the effects of misorientation and of changes in interplanar spacing should be separable by rotating the specimen crystal C by 180° about the Bragg-plane normal, and repeating the sequence of topographs taken with varying angle of incidence of rays from M upon C. The sensitivity achievable with the double-crystal topograph technique has been well illustrated by the work of Bonse [20] on impurity bands in quartz and of Hart [21] on impurity bands in reputedly "perfect" silicon. Hart uses high-order reflections (such as 880) with MoKα radiation and reckons that he can detect a relative change in interplanar spacing of a few parts in 10^8.

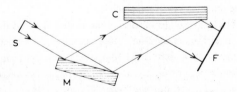

Fig. 2. Double-crystal topographic technique.

The first crystal M is often cut for asymmetric reflection, as shown in fig. 2, simply for the purpose of rendering its diffracted beam spatially wider than that incident upon it which is determined by the apparent width of S. But there is another use for asymmetric reflections: when the spatial width of the beam is increased its angular width is decreased, in the case of perfect crystals. Beams of extreme angular sharpness can be produced by successive asymmetric reflection at surfaces cut in a single block of perfect crystal [22]. In another technique, using successive symmetric reflections from the parallel sides of a channel cut in a single block [23], the pronounced "tails" of the single-crystal reflection angular profile can be effectively eliminated. Angularly narrow beams of both these types might be useful in double crystal topography for probing local misorientations and for investigating ray trajectories in lightly distorted crystals.

Illumination of the specimen crystal by radiation which itself is crystal reflected can have other topographic applications. If the value of $2\theta_B$ (twice the Bragg angle) for the reflection from the first crystal M is $90°$, then the beam incident upon C will be plane-polarised, whether M is highly perfect or not. Such plane-polarised crystal-reflected radiation was useful in a study of the periodic fading of Pendellösung fringes and the measurement of fringe spacings [24].

It is not usual to translate the specimen C in double-crystal topographic arrangements because, firstly, asymmetric reflection from M can usually provide a beam wide enough to illuminate all the area of C of interest at one setting and, secondly, if the double-crystal arrangement is being employed for the purpose of detecting misorientations and interplanar spacing changes equivalent to a fraction of a second of arc, any translation mechanism operating would have to be extremely precise so as not to wobble the specimen by an amount comparable with those small changes of angles which it is desired to measure. However, some double-crystal topographic techniques, not aiming to measure minute misorientations, have been devised [25,26] and will be described in sect. 3.2.

2.5. Methods using anomalous transmission

The phenomenon of anomalous transmission (the Borrmann effect) will be familiar to those conversant with thin-film transmission electron microscopy or with the dynamical theory of X-ray diffraction. Concomitant with anomalous transmission is the phenomenon of the progressive narrowing of the fan of energy flow within the triangle bounded by the directions of incident and diffracted rays when the product of linear absorption coefficient (μ) and crystal thickness (t) is increased, so that when μt is equal to 10 or more, the only X-rays transmitted through the crystal are those whose trajectory in the crystal makes not more than a small angle with the Bragg planes, i.e. an angle which is only a small fraction of $2\theta_B$, and which satisfy the Bragg angle more closely than those rays for which, in the non-absorbing case, the diffracted intensity would have fallen to, say, half its peak value. This narrowing of the energy-flow fan is easily observed in X-ray experiments, though, for obvious reasons of scale, is not in the electron case. Its occurrence has sufficient modifying effect in determining what diffraction geometries are permissible that techniques operating under high values of μt are worthy of separate mention. It should be emphasized, however, that there is a smooth transition from the diffraction behaviour at low values of μt to that at high values, and topographic experiments under both conditions can be performed at will using the techniques described in sect. 3.

Fig. 3 illustrates the possibilities for relative positioning of source, specimen and photographic plate when μt is large. Suppose the source S is small, and confined to the point from which is drawn the ray marked 1. Suppose also that this ray satisfies the Bragg condition precisely for the radiation and lattice planes concerned (the latter being normal to the specimen plate, as schematically indicated). Bragg-diffracted rays then travel through the crystal closely parallel to the Bragg planes until they reach the exit surface where they split into two nearly equal beams as shown, one in the direction of the incident beam, one in the direction of the diffracted beam. An imperfection, such as a dislocation, which is cut by the ray trajectory in the crystal causes some scattering of the rays satisfying the Bragg condition and consequently a deduction of intensity from the rays enjoying anomalous transmission. Thus the image of the imperfection appears as a local reduction of intensity in both the transmitted beam continuing in the direct beam direction and in the diffracted beam. Such reductions were observed in one of the first experiments showing diffraction contrast due to individual dislocations [27]. If an ex-

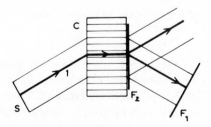

Fig. 3. Topographic techniques using anomalous transmission.

tended source is used (indicated by the full length of the line S), an image of an extended area of the specimen is recorded by the diffracted beam received on a plate placed at F_1. This arrangement was used in the topographs taken using anomalous transmission by Barth and Hosemann [28]. It suffers from the disadvantage that with a wide beam, images due to the $K\alpha_1$ and $K\alpha_2$ components overlap. This defect was obviated in the arrangement of Gerold and Meier [29] who placed their plate right in contact with the exit surface of the crystal, at F_2. Note that this latter arrangement is only feasible for quite high values of μt, for which a defect causes a reduction in intensity in *both* the directly transmitted and in the diffracted beams (which are received together on the plate at F_2 before they have become appreciably spatially separated), the contributions to diffraction contrast from both beams then reinforcing each other; and note also that only under conditions of strong anomalous transmission will rays coming from S but not being Bragg-diffracted be so stronly attenuated as to make unnecessary the insertion of a screen to prevent fogging of the plate by undiffracted continuous radiation transmitted through the specimen.

It is characteristic of topographs taken with high values of μt that only dislocations quite close to the exit surface give images with strong contrast. Provided this limitation is borne in mind, informative experiments on dislocation densities and movements in highly absorbing and relatively thick specimens can be carried out, good examples of such studies are the experiments on copper single-crystals by Baldwin, Young and their co-workers at Oak Ridge [30–35]. In conclusion one may point out that even lower values of effective absorption coefficient may be achieved in the three-beam case than in the two-beam case, in certain favourable cases of simultaneous reflection, such as 111 plus $1\bar{1}1$ in the diamond structure. The theory of this "double Borrmann effect" has now been quite fully studied [36–42]; but the effect has not yet been utilised in taking topographs of extended areas of thick crystals.

3. Transmission topographs (sections and projections)

3.1. Section topographs

The great majority of the applications of X-ray topography that will be described in the following sections were undertaken using the methods of the "section topograph" or the "projection topograph". These are also the methods of which the author has most experience. The same schematic drawing (fig. 4) serves to illustrate both techniques: in the case of section topographs the double-ended arrow (upper right) should be disregarded. The diffraction ge-

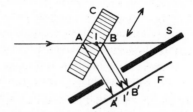

Fig. 4. Arrangements for "section topographs" and "projection topographs".

ometry of the section topograph is very simple. A narrow beam of characteristic radiation (coming from a source at some distance to the left of the diagram) cuts through the crystal C along the path AB. The angle at which the crystal is set is such that this ray is Bragg-reflected by planes parallel to those schematically indicated by the lines normal to the X-ray entrance and exit surfaces. A diffracted beam issues from the rear surface of the specimen, passes through an aperture in a screen S and is recorded as a strip of blackening of width $A'B'$ on the photographic emulsion F. When the specimen is in the form of a plate (as in the diagram), Bragg planes are chosen which lie normal, or nearly normal, to the faces of the plate. The figure shows no collimating slit: such is in fact unnecessary if the source is small, like that in a microfocus X-ray tube (apparent width about 3 microns). The width of beam cutting the crystal and being Bragg-reflected will be no wider than the source, if the crystal is nearly perfect, except for an addition corresponding to the angular spread of the perfect-crystal reflection curve plus the spread of Bragg angle due to natural wavelength spread of the radiation, both multiplied by the distance from source to specimen. The crystal, when perfect, thus acts as its own "collimator". This simple arrangement was used in early work with section topographs [43], including a study of simultaneous reflections [44]. More recently, a source with an apparent width of 100 microns has been used, about 45 cm distant from the specimen. With this wider source a slit is placed close to C in order to limit the width of the beam to about 12 microns when taking section topographs. It is the useful feature of the section topograph that it can be used to locate the position of imperfections (dislocations, inclusions, fault surfaces, etc.) within the crystal. This is done by measuring the position I' of the image produced by those rays in the diffraction contrast image of the imperfection which come from the point I where the beam AB cuts through the imperfection. It is clear that the geometric precision of determination of the location of I is largely controlled by the width of the beam

AB. It must be understood that AB is in the form of a ribbon, extended normal to the plane of the diagram to such a height as is necessary to cover the parts of the crystal of interest. The positions of inclusions may be mapped, and the shapes and inclinations of internal fault surfaces measured, by taking a series of section topographs, the specimen being translated by a known, small amount between each exposure. It cannot be too strongly emphasized how useful it is to have attached to the specimen translating mechanism an easily readable device for directly and accurately indicating the position of the specimen with respect to the X-ray beam. This indicator should be readable to at least the X-ray beam width (12 microns) and preferably to somewhat finer divisions.

If the specimen C is a plate of thickness t and the Bragg planes are normal to it, i.e. if diffraction is occurring under conditions of symmetrical transmission, then the width $A'B'$ of the section topograph is simply $2t \sin \theta_B$. If the Bragg plane makes an angle α with the normal to the surface of C, α being taken positive when measured in the same sense as the deviation of the X-rays from the direct beam into the diffracted beam direction, then the width $A'B'$ is $t \sec(\theta-\alpha) \sin 2\theta_B$. (This calculation assumes that t is so large compared with the 12 micron width of the incident beam that contributions of the latter to the width $A'B'$ may be neglected.) In careful measurements it may be necessary to consider the *vertical magnification* of the section topograph, that is magnification in the direction normal to the plane of incident and diffracted rays. If the distance source-to-specimen is a, and distance specimen to F is b, then the vertical magnification is $(b+a)/a$. It is always greater than unity, but only slightly so, by between 1 and 2 per cent with usual values of a and b. The *horizontal magnification* $\sec(\theta-\alpha) \sin 2\theta$ is generally considerably less than unity for lowest order reflections using the more penetrating (shorter wavelength) radiations, but by using asymmetric transmission and not the lowest order reflections, the horizontal magnification can often be arranged to be close to unity, which facilitates geometric interpretation of the section pattern.

From an inspection of the diffraction geometry of fig. 4 one would naively expect (at least for the case of symmetrical transmission, if the crystal is strongly absorbing) that the intensity profile across the section topograph from A' to B' would be flat-topped, i.e. rectangular, if the specimen C were quite perfect. In fact, if C is both perfect and lightly absorbing, the spatial intensity profile is very non-uniform. It was when high resolution section topographs [43] were first applied to nearly perfect silicon crystals that it became possible at last to recognise the true nature of such non-uniformities and to clearly differentiate between those that arise as a fundamental part of the diffraction process in perfect crystals, and those that arise from accidental imperfections. The overall spatial intensity profile observed with perfect and nearly perfect crystals agrees well with the predictions of dynamical theory of X-ray diffraction [45], but the manner in which thickness-dependent oscillations of intensity [46] were found to be superimposed upon the average profile could not be explained by dynamical theory as it had been developed up to 1958, and the discrepancy thus revealed stimulated the development by Kato [47,48] of the "spherical wave theory" which should properly be applied to all but a few special X-ray experiments.

For simple topographic experiments it is generally adequate to use the method of projection topographs to give an overall view of the imperfection content of the crystal, but section topographs must be used in any study which requires detailed information on the distribution of energy flow within the triangle which has apex A and base the line on the crystal exit surface between B and the ray AA'. Studies of the diffraction effects of fault surfaces naturally occurring in crystals, and more generally, of superposed, coherently reflecting crystals, have made much use of section topographs recently, and the work of Authier, Milne and Sauvage [49] well illustrates the fascinating complexity of the intensity patterns on such topographs.

Fig. 5 shows some representative section topographs, particular features in which will be referred to subsequently. Here one may just point out the regularity of the Pendellösung fringe pattern [46] in a highly perfect crystal (fig. 5a), the complexity the pattern exhibits when dislocations are introduced into a matrix of nearly perfect crystal (fig. 5b), and the effects of fault surfaces and long-range strains on Pendellösung fringe patterns (fig. 5c). Fig. 5, and the reproductions of topographs following, are positives. Thus extra blackening on these prints corresponds to extra blackening on the original X-ray plate.

3.2. Projection topographs

In the projection topograph technique the specimen crystal and the frame holding the photographic film or plate are both mounted on an accurate linear traversing mechanism that oscillates back and forth during the course of exposure so that the whole area of interest in the specimen will be scanned by the ribbon incident beam. The direction of traverse is indicated by the double-headed arrow in fig. 4. The screen S is kept stationary: it intercepts the directly transmitted beam and has a variable slot in it allowing only the desired Bragg reflection to pass through and reach the plate. The image formed on the plate will be an orthographic projection of the crystal specimen and its imperfection content. It can be regarded as a microradiograph taken with Bragg-diffracted

Fig. 5. Section topographs. a. Gently tapering wedge of perfect silicon, thickness 2.0 to 2.15 mm in upper region. Reflection 220, AgKα radiation. (Topograph courtesy of Mr. P.Aldred.) b. Aluminium, reflection 111, AgKα radiation, crystal thickness $1\frac{1}{4}$ mm. c. Quartz, reflection $30\bar{3}1$, MoKα radiation, crystal thickness 1 mm.

rays. If a dislocation is threading through the specimen then, in a section topograph, it is revealed only by the image I′ (an intense black dot, under the usual diffraction conditions of low absorption) coming from the point I where the sheet of X-rays AB cuts the dislocation. Thus, many section topographs would have to be taken in order to track the course of the dislocation through the crystal. In the projection topograph, on the other hand, the full length of the dislocation is seen. Similarly the complete outline of features such as sub-grains or domains made visible either by orientation or extinction contrast is shown clearly, and in the direct display of the extent of internal imperfections in the crystal resides the practical utility of the projection topograph method. Individual dislocations will not be seen with such intense contrast on projection topographs as they are on section topographs, but diffraction conditions can usually be chosen to make the contrast sufficient for them to stand out well above the diffracted intensity from the rest of the crystal surrounding them [50]. It is obvious, however, that with thick specimens it will not be possible to resolve individually such high densities of dislocations or, say, strain-producing precipitates as can be done in section topographs because of the superimposition of their images in the projection. This emphasizes that the projection topograph is equivalent simply to a superimposition of many section topographs; and the latter are more fundamental and interesting from the diffraction theoretical viewpoint.

When thick photographic emulsions are used, the diffracted beam must fall perpendicularly upon the emulsion. This fixes the angle between the specimen and the photographic plate, and hence the apparent angle of view of the specimen as recorded by the topograph. If the specimen is in the form of a plate of horizontal dimensions L, then the horizontal length of its image on the projection topograph is $L \cos(\theta_B + \alpha)$, α being defined as in sect. 3.1, and there is again the vertical magnification (always close to unity) of $(b+a)/a$, as in the case of the section topograph. If the nature of the experiment is such that minimising the horizontal distortion by appropriate choice of θ_B and α cannot be accomplished then it is still possible to correct quite large image distortions by a photographic rectification process in the course of making enlargements of the topographs. In principle it does not matter in which direction the specimen is traversed back and forth, provided the area of interest is covered by the incident X-rays; but in practice there are strong advantages in choosing the direction such that, for the specimen shape given, the diffracted beam oscillates laterally by the minimum amount during the back and forth traverse, for then the gap in the screen S can be made as narrow as possible within the limits of not preventing at any time the full section pattern width A'B' falling on the emulsion. In the case of plate-like specimens, this simply requires that the direction of traverse be parallel to the specimen surfaces, as shown in fig. 4.

The loss of three-dimensional information which occurs when the diffraction contrast from imperfections within the volume of the specimen is projected on to the photographic plate can be recovered by taking stereo-pairs of projection topographs. In the first method developed for doing this [50,51], a topograph of the reflection hkl and of its inverse $\bar{h}\bar{k}\bar{l}$ were compared. Chosen areas on the two topographs, suitably enlarged photographically, can be examined in a stereo-viewer. Greater sensitivity can be obtained by viewing the original topographic plates directly with twin microscopes, one plate being observed with the left eye and the other with the right eye. Sensitivities corresponding to depth differences of only a few microns in the specimen are obtainable with the latter method. An alternative, and frequently preferable method of taking stereo-pairs was developed by Haruta [52] in which the same Bragg reflection is used but the crystal is rotated about the Bragg-plane normal (i.e. **g** vector) between taking the two topographs. This is equivalent to viewing a fixed crystal from two directions, respectively above and below the mean plane of incidence. Hence, when looking at the topograph under the twin microscopes to measure depths, the plates are rotated by $90°$ about the line of sight compared with the case when the hkl and $\bar{h}\bar{k}\bar{l}$ pair of reflections is compared. Haruta's method has two important advantages. The effective stereoscopic angle can be varied at will by varying the amount of rotation about the **g**-vector, and the stereoscopic sensitivty can thereby be controlled. Adequate sensitivity can be obtained by a rotation of $2°$ to $4°$ in the case of specimens 1 to 2 mm thick, and by rotations of between $10°$ and $15°$ in cases of specimens only 100 microns thick. The second advantage of Haruta's method arises because the long-range strain fields of dislocations and other defects can appear with notably different contrast in the hkl and $\bar{h}\bar{k}\bar{l}$ reflections when the specimen is appreciably absorbing. This contrast difference, the so-called "failure of Friedel's Law" in diffraction contrast [53], is useful for determining the sense of curvature of lattice planes [54] and the sense of dislocation Burgers vectors [55,56] but confuses the stereo effect. Haruta's method is not so convenient with large plate-like specimens if more than a degree or two of rotation about the **g**-vector is needed.

Fig. 6 is a projection topograph of a large, very regular diamond octahedron. Although the crystal is about 5 mm thick, the value of μt is only about one, using MoKα radiation. Hence the diffraction contrast exhibited by the topograph is typical of conditions of low absorption: local lattice distortions are recognised by the strong increase in diffracted intensity they produce. It is not readily apparent in fig. 6 whether or not this crystal contains any dislocations. The many flecks and streaks of blackening that cover the image all come from surface damage such as scratches, and ring cracks due to percussion. The especially severe damage on the crystal edges and corners is noteworthy, this extra blackening helps to delineate the outline of the octahedral faces and shows that all parts of the crystal can contribute with equal weight to form the pattern on the projection topograph.

There exist certain variants of the projection topograph technique, known

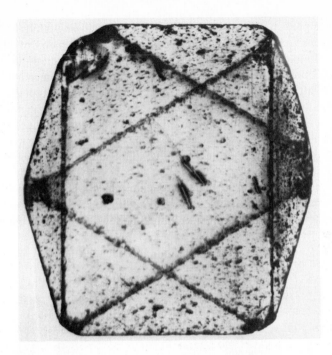

Fig. 6. Projection topograph of diamond octahedron, edge length 5 mm, 111 reflection, MoKα.

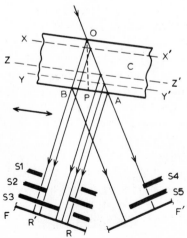

Fig. 7. Arrangements for "limited projection topographs" and "direct beam topographs".

as "limited projection topographs" [57], one of which can usefully be applied to specimens such as that shown in fig. 6. Consider the geometry of diffracted and directly transmitted rays in a parallel-faced specimen as drawn in fig. 7. Bragg reflection of the ribbon incident beam cutting the specimen in OA is occurring at lattice planes parallel to OP. In the usual projection topograph arrangement the screen (corresponding to S in fig. 4) will have its aperture set as in S_1 in fig. 7, allowing the diffracted rays issuing from the exit face of the specimen along AB to fall on the plate F along RR'. Suppose now that the two edges of the aperture in S are closed in to the position as shown by S_2. The only rays directly diffracted from the section OA which can now reach F are those originating from a volume between planes whose traces are XX' and YY', assuming, as will usually be arranged, that the direction of crystal traverse is parallel to the specimen faces. Fig. 8 is a topograph taken under these con-

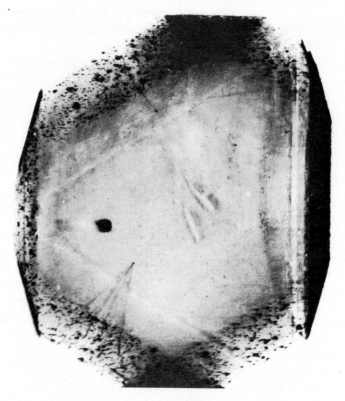

Fig. 8. Limited projection topograph showing interior of diamond of fig. 6.

ditions in order to study the interior of the crystal whose complete projection topograph was shown in fig. 6. Almost the same effect is achieved as if the damaged entrance and exit surfaces had been physically removed. The increased clarity with which defects within the interior of the diamond can now be seen is striking. One sees, for example, in the lower left quadrant of the topograph, a bundle of 4 or 5 dislocations radiating from a small inclusion. These were largely obscured by images of surface damage in fig. 6, and would only be noticed after careful inspection of the plate. Also strongly seen in fig. 8 is the image of a larger inclusion, above and to the left of the small inclusion that is the radiant for the dislocation bundle just mentioned. This larger patch of blackening, it is fair to report, was already known to be due to an internal defect since its position had already been located by stereo-topographs. The defect is a small, imperfect diamond, in roughly parallel orientation to the main crystal, and the diffraction contrast chiefly arises from strain at points of contact of the included diamond with the main diamond. This information was gained by taking a set of closely spaced section topographs cutting the inclusion and its environs.

In another type of limited projection topograph the aperture for the diffracted beam is set as S_3 in fig. 7. Now, rays diffracted from the section OA which can reach F come from the crystal surface and a small depth below it only. The chief application of this variant of technique lies in correlating lattice defects with optically visible surface features. Checking whether certain etch pits mark the outcrops of dislocations is an obvious example of such a study, and an application to diamond showed that dislocation outcrops were associated with naturally occurring pyramidal trigons [58].

One obvious application of the limited projection topograph is in reducing the confusion due to overlapping dislocation images in topographs of thick crystals which, by X-ray topographic standards, have a high dislocation density. Often a worthwhile clarification of the pattern is achieved by reducing the aperture width so that diffracted rays coming directly from just a half or a third of the length OA are recorded. If the dislocations are fairly well confined to a few not too closely spaced slip planes and if sets of active slip planes are parallel to the specimen surface, then the dislocation arrays on different slip planes can be examined one by one by suitable positioning of the aperture in S.

With nearly perfect crystals some interesting patterns can be taken with "direct beam topographs" [57] in which the photographic plate is placed at F' to receive the directly transmitted beam TT', and a screeen is placed just to prevent the ribbon incident beam reaching F' (screen position S_4), or to allow only a small fraction of the rays multiply reflected within the triangle OAB, and finally issuing from the crystal in the direct beam direction, to reach F′ (screen position S_5). The dislocation diffraction contrast obtained with the S_4 setting, when X-ray absorption is low, is complementary to that produced in the usual diffracted beam topograph. It simulates the contrast obtained in "bright-field" transmission electron microscopy.

The exposure time required for a projection topograph will be proportional to the length of specimen scanned, but it need not be very much greater than that required to take a high-resolution section topograph because the slit defining the incident beam may generally be made very much wider than the 12 micron width used for section topographs. If the X-ray tube focal spot has an apparent width of 100 microns, then the incident beam needs to be increased to at least this width in order to make use of all the characteristic radiation leaving the X-ray tube target. (A substantial widening of the incident beam cannot be allowed for limited projection topographs, for it would lead to loss of definition in the specimen of the depth limits from between which the diffracted beam is accepted.) For usual projection topographs the incident beam divergence may be increased up to any value *not* so great as to allow the $K\alpha_2$ radiation to be reflected as well as the $K\alpha_1$. This limit is easily found by calculation or experimental test.

Attempts have been made to simplify the instrumentation requirements of the projection topograph technique by eliminating the traversing mechanism and using a source and incident-beam slit sufficiently wide so that an adequate area of specimen can be irradiated while it is stationary. The geometry is shown in fig. 3; it is the "parallel-beam method" of Barth and Hosemann [28]. Its disadvantages are loss of resolution due to superimposition of α_1 and α_2 images, and a higher background than when a collimated incident beam and a relatively narrow aperture for the diffracted beam are employed. Of course, elimination of the α_2 component can always be accomplished by increasing sufficiently the distance from X-ray tube to specimen, and the stationary transmission specimen technique has been used with this distance as large as 5 metres by Layer and Deslattes [59], though this still does not eliminate the problem that with wide beams leaving the crystal, the photographic plate cannot be placed close to the crystal if the diffracted and directly transmitted rays are not to overlap. Elimination of the unwanted α_2 component and a low background intensity can be achieved if the wide incident beam is produced by reflection at a good-quality crystal monochromator, and both the parallel and anti-parallel settings of monochromator crystal and specimen crystal have been used for transmission topography by Kohra et al. [25]. Certain specimens, such as thin slices of silicon oxidised on one face, have an overall curvature, so that if it is desired to study extinction contrast due to local defects without excessive variation in intensity on the topograph image due to orientation contrast, then each part of the specimen must be given an opportunity to satisfy Bragg's Law fully during the course of exposure. Methods of accomplishing this without incurring the disadvantages of a wide beam incident upon the crystal are to rock the specimen asynchronously with its traverse back and forth, the scanning-oscillation technique used by Schwuttke [60]; and to use a divergent incident beam monochromatised by a curved crystal to illuminate the specimen which is also rocked, as has been done by Kohra and Takano [61]. The latter method has the advantage that a slit may be placed at the focus of the monochromator to allow only the α_1 component to pass through and reach the specimen as a diverging beam. Thus the topograph will not suffer from superimposition of α_1 and α_2 images even if, in order to get uniform reflection intensity the specimen must be rocked through angles greater than the difference in Bragg angles of these two radiations.

4. Influences on quality and resolution in X-ray topography

4.1. *Source size and wavelength spread*

An important factor determining the vertical resolution on X-ray topographs, i.e. in the direction perpendicular to the plane of incident and diffracted rays, is of purely geometrical nature and is easily calculated. When the distance from X-ray tube focal spot to specimen is a, the distance from specimen to photographic emulsion is b, and the apparent height of the focal spot is h as viewed from the specimen, then a point in the specimen will produce on the emulsion a line drawn out into a vertical length $h(b/a)$. The experimenter can usually make a any value he desires, so that even if he does not enjoy the use of an X-ray source with a suitable value of h, he can reduce $h(b/a)$ to a sufficiently low value, though possibly at the cost of long exposure times. For high quality topographs one should aim at preventing $h(b/a)$ being greater than one to two microns. However, it will be concluded from the discussion following that there is little purpose in trying to make it lower. It is a great convenience to have the specimen mounted on a standard goniometer head. But when this is done, or if the specimen plate has a diameter of more than one to two centimetres, it is difficult to place the photographic plate much closer to the crystal than one centimetre.

The topographic resolution in the plane of incident and diffracted rays, the horizontal resolution, depends upon the wavelength spread of the X-rays and their dispersion by the specimen, and upon the intrinsic angular range of reflection of the specimen crystal. (One could call these factors "geometrical". They do not include the spatial range of extinction contrast in the specimen: they consider only the degree to which diffracted rays issuing from a given point on the X-ray exit face of the specimen are spread out into a horizontal line on the photographic plate.) As a rough rule, one can classify X-ray topographic techniques as "low-resolution" when it is immaterial whether or not $K\alpha_1$ and $K\alpha_2$ images simultaneously appear, and "high-resolution" when such superimposition would be intolerable. The present discussion is concerned only with the latter class of technique.

The effects of wavelength spread can be calculated as follows. If $d\lambda$ be the wavelength range corresponding to the full width at half maximum intensity of the X-ray emission line profile, the corresponding range of Bragg angles (denoted by $d\theta_\lambda$) is given by

$$d\theta_\lambda = \tan \theta (d\lambda/\lambda) . \tag{1}$$

The image of a point on the crystal will be spread horizontally into a length $dx_\lambda = b \, d\theta_\lambda$ on the emulsion, the diffracted beam being assumed normal to the emulsion. Table 1 lists the Bragg angles θ, the angular spreads $d\theta_\lambda$ in seconds of arc, and the resultant values of dx_λ in microns, taking $b = 1$ cm, for a radiation of both a longer and a shorter wavelength, and for a larger and a smaller interplanar spacing, d. Topographs are not often taken of reflections having d greater than $3\frac{1}{2}$ Å or less than 1 Å.

Table 1
Resolution loss due to natural wavelength spread.

	AgKa_1			CuKa_1		
	$\lambda = 0.559$A $d\lambda = 0.28$ XU $d\lambda/\lambda = 5 \times 10^{-4}$			$\lambda = 1.540$A $d\lambda = 0.6$ XU $d\lambda/\lambda = 4 \times 10^{-4}$		
d (A)	$\theta°$	$d\theta_\lambda''$	dx_λ (μm)	$\theta°$	$d\theta_\lambda''$	dx_λ (μm)
3.5	4.6	8.2	0.4	12.7	18	0.9
1	16.2	29	1.4	50.4	99	4.8

The table contains only one significant, indeed seriously large, value of dx_λ. This shows that if Bragg angles larger than about 30° are used, which is not often the case with transmission specimens, efforts should be made to reduce b to well below 1 cm.

To estimate the possible image spreading due to intrinsic reflecting range of the crystal, it is only necessary to consider one or two cases representative of low order reflections and simple structures. It is justifiable to make the calculation for the ideally perfect crystal, since it is with crystals approaching this ideal that most interest attaches to knowing how good the topographic resolution may be. The angular range of reflection is proportional to the integrated reflection. Table 2 presents some values of angular widths, calculated for the case of symmetrical transmission and negligible absorption.

Table 2
Bragg reflection full width at half height (sec).

Crystal	Reflection	$AgK\alpha_1$	$CuK\alpha_1$
Silicon	220	1.7	5.5
Germanium	220	3.8	15

A comparison of tables 1 and 2 shows that the perfect-crystal angular range of reflection makes a much smaller contribution to horizontal spreading than does dispersion due to lack of strictly monochromatic radiation, and can generally be neglected.

Reverting to the question of elimination of the α_2 component of the $K\alpha$ doublet, it should be pointed out that the wavelength separation of the doublet components of $AgK\alpha$ is 15 times the width of the α_1 component. This emphasizes how poor would be any topographs which had images due to both components superimposed. However, there are two ways in which the worst effects of $K\alpha$ doublet superimposition can be avoided, if strict collimation or crystal monochromatisation of the incident beam is not employed. The first is to use $K\beta$ radiation, as has been illustrated by Dionne [62], though one would expect with this method to encounter occasional trouble due to a weak $K\beta_2$ image accompanying the $K\beta_1$ image. The second method has been recently described by Hosoya [63], who has had success with a technique the author tried in 1956 without very good results. This is to use ruthenium as a filter with silver $K\alpha$ radiation: the ruthenium K absorption edge falls between the $AgK\alpha_1$ and $AgK\alpha_2$ wavelengths, and so transmits the latter fairly well while heavily absorbing the former. Ruthenium metal foil in suitable thickness is not available. The author tried to make the filter with ruthenium oxide powder; Hosoya was successful with a suitably bound ruthenium metal powder.

4.2. Photographic emulsions

In optical photography, a usual approach to the problem of obtaining high resolution with photographic emulsions is to combine very small grain size with very thin emulsions. But for X-ray topography such thin emulsions would be far too inefficient in absorbing X-rays, except perhaps for the softest radiations used such as CrKα. Compared with thick emulsions, thin emulsions would also give greater statistical fluctuations in number of developed grains per unit area, a disadvantage when high optical magnification is to be performed, and they would not have as high a usable photographic density range as thicker emulsions. These disadvantages would not be offset by the reduction in scattering (optical and X-ray) and in the reduction of intercepted lengths of photoelectron tracks which thin emulsions would offer, nor by absence of the restriction necessary with thick emulsions of always ensuring that the diffracted beam impinges perpendicularly on the emulsion. The latter restriction of course becomes more severe the thicker the emulsion. If the loss of resolution due to the width of the projection of an inclined ray passing through the emulsion is not to exceed one micron, then the ray must pass within $\frac{1}{2}°$ of perpendicularity in a 100 micron thick emulsion, but only within $2°$ of perpendicularity in a 25 micron thick emulsion.

The recommended recording medium for X-ray topographic work is Ilford L4 Nuclear Emulsion. It possesses a grain size well below the topographic resolution limits set by geometrical and other factors, and it is available in thicknesses capable of ensuring high absorption efficiency for all the X-radiations likely to be used in topographic work. L4 emulsion contains a very high concentration of silver halide so that high stopping power is achieved with minimum physical thickness of emulsion. Under room temperature and humidity conditions the density of the emulsion is 3.82 g cm^{-3} and the weight fraction of halide is as high as 83%. Approximate values of the thicknesses required to absorb half the incident intensity are, for AgKα, 100 microns; for MoKα 50 microns; and for CuKα, 12 microns. In practice, emulsion 25 microns thick is used for CuKα and all softer radiations, and except when minimum exposure time is essential, 50 micron thickness is preferred to 100 micron thickness for MoKα and AgKα because of its shorter processing time and less risk of emulsion distortion.

These thick emulsions involve long processing and washing times. It is recommended to carry out the development at a constant, low temperature which is chosen for convenience to be the freezing point of the developer solution (about $-1°C$). The development time is lengthened by performing all development at this low temperature, but it ensures that the final degree of development is fairly uniform throughout the whole emulsion depth. The aim is to reduce development rate relative to diffusion rate. The latter varies little with temperature, but rate of development increases exponentially with increasing temperature. Diffusion times are proportional to the square of the emulsion thickness.

Before development, the emulsion is soaked in plain water so that it swells too allow rapid diffusion of developer into it. The developer is one volume of standard strength D19b diluted with three volumes of water. Between developing and fixing, a stop bath of 1% glacial acetic acid is used, and the fixer contains 300 g sodium hyposulphite plus 30 g sodium bisulphite per litre. The plates should be washed in cold, running, filtered water, and dried at room temperature in normal laboratory air, preferably filtered. It is essential to protect the emulsion surfaces after processing. This is done by covering them with a microscope cover glass, say 22 mm by 22 mm, secured by an inert, air-hardening, embedding medium such as "Eukitt"*. Suggested processing schedules are given in table 3.

Table 3
Processing schedule for Ilford nuclear emulsion (time in min).

Thickness (microns)	25	50	100
Soak	5	10	20
Develop	12–30	15–60	30–60
Stop bath	5	10	20
Fix	30	60	120
Wash	60	120	240

In the undeveloped L4 emulsion the grain size is about 0.14 micron. As development proceeds, the grains grow and form clumps. It has been found that, for a given X-ray exposure, within a wide range of X-ray exposures, the photographic density increases steadily as the development time increases, again within a wide range. This is an admirable characteristic of the Ilford nu-

* Supplied by E.Mertens, Bonn, Königstrasse 17a.

clear emulsions. Experience indicates that the best condition for visual study
of topographs under the microscope is when the "basic density" of the developed emulsion is about unity. By "basic density" is meant that density
present in parts of the image corresponding to perfect crystal. Under this condition the density in images of individual dislocations rises to about two. As a
consequence of the reciprocal relationship between X-ray dosage and development time for giving constant density it is possible to compensate for a poor
exposure by an extra long development, in order to bring the final density
into the preferred range. Hence the range of development times quoted in
table 3. It should be emphasized, however, that low-exposure, long-develop-
ment topographs will not be of as good quality as long-exposure, short-devel-
opment ones, for reasons explained in the following section 4.3.

Concerning resolution, one must consider the range of ionisation produced by the events following the absorption of the primary X-ray photon.
Even with such dense emulsions as L4, the ionisation spread is perhaps the
most serious limiting factor in resolution when the hardest radiation in general topographic use, AgKα, is being recorded. For CuKα and softer radiations the ionisation is restricted to a volume of diameter about one micron,
so one observes effectively one grain clump at the point of absorption. For
harder radiations, under high magnification one usually observes a short
track of grains, often with a noticeable grain clump at both ends. The occurrence of these tracks will of course diffuse the image; it imposes resolution
limits that should not be worse than $1\frac{1}{2}$ to 2 microns with MoKα and 2 to 3
microns with AgKα.

4.3. *Statistical limitations*

When topographs are examined under high magnification it often appears
that the dominating factor limiting resolution is a high "apparent granularity"
of the image. This is called "apparent" because it has little connection with
the actual size of developed grains, a very different situation compared with
that of images in the fast, coarse-grained emulsions in common X-ray crystallographic use. The average size of a single developed grain of L4 emulsion is in
fact about 0.25 micron, well below X-ray topographic resolution limits. The
apparent granularity arises from statistical variations in the number of developed grains contained below one area element of the emulsion compared
with another. Scintillation counter measurements of the intensities of diffracted beams show that even in a well exposed topograph there will be absorbed only a few photons (less than 5, say) per each square micron of emulsion surface. With photographic recording there is a fundamental obstacle to
reducing the relative importance of statistical fluctuations by increasing the

mean number of photons and that is simply that the emulsion would become too black for photographic reproduction or easy visual examination.

An assessment of the effect of statistical fluctuations in photon flux may be made by dividing the image into equal, small area elements and then establishing how small the elements may be made before a difference in blackening due to a given true difference in mean incident photon flux is masked by the fluctuations in the number of photons absorbed in each area element during the exposure. One should take into account that in interpreting an X-ray topograph the area elements into which the image is divided need not all be considered as independent. For example, one is often concerned with trying to detect an exceptional feature in a field where the mean dose varies only slowly from point to point. Two commonly occurring problems of this type are, firstly, the need to be able to assert with confidence that the diffracted intensity impinging upon a small spot is greater than on the area surrounding it: such a spot could correspond to the image of an inclusion or a precipitate in a matrix of perfect crystal. The second common problem deals with lines; the recognition of a single line on a uniform background, or the resolution of an array of lines, or of a stripe pattern due to magnetic domain structure, for example.

Consider the problem of detecting excess intensity in a spot which is a disc of diameter D microns. In the case of a small disc the best magnification to use for its detection should be not so great that the eye cannot easily integrate the intensity over the disc, while still being, of course, great enough for the eye comfortably to resolve an object the size of the disc. In the case of a large disc, the magnification can be reduced until the area over which the eye integrates corresponds to an area on the topograph image large enough to appear grainless to the eye; if this area is less than the disc area, both disc and surroundings will appear grainless and statistical fluctuations in X-rays absorbed from point to point will then not be a significant factor. In the case of a smaller disc, the eye may still be able to compare the disc with a surrounding area sufficiently large so that only the fluctuations in the number of photons absorbed in the disc have to be considered. However, to make a reasonably conservative estimate of dectability, the area of the surrounding reference density has been taken as four times the area of the disc, in a simple calculation. The photographic density may be assumed to be proportional to the number of photons absorbed per unit area. Let these be n and $n(1+h)$ photons absorbed per square micron in the surrounding area and in the disc, respectively. The criterion chosen for detectability is that the probability of there being no excess density of photons absorbed in the disc above the density in the surrounding area in a particular exposure is less than one in 10 when the true mean flux on the disc is 100 h % higher than on the surroundings. Clearly, when both D and h are small, impossibly large values of n would be required to satisfy this condition. An estimate of actual values of n needed is given in table 4.

Table 4

Number of photons required to be absorbed per square micron in surrounding area to ensure confident detection of disc, diameter D microns, in which flux if 100 h % higher than in surrounding area.

D (μm)	$h = 0.03$	0.1	0.3	1.0
1	10^4	10^3	100	(14)
2	2×10^3	196	(25)	((4))
3	10^3	92	(12)	((1.4))
10	88	((8))	((1))	((0.1))
30	(10)	((0.9))	((0.1))	((0.01))

The lowest value of h, a 3% increase in density, is near the lower limit of density differences usually detected in radiography. A flux of diffracted intensity into the disc of double that into the surrounding area, which corresponds to $h = 1$, can easily occur in the excess scattering from a localized strain centre in a matrix of perfect crystal. With usual processing conditions unit photographic density is reached with MoKα radiation when n is about 3. A density of 2, or possibly as much as 3, may be allowed for the density of images of perfect regions in topographs deliberately strongly exposed for the purpose of detecting small intensity differences, but then the density in images of imperfect regions is beyond the linear density range. Thus with MoKα the maximum value of n that can reasonably well be recorded is about 8. With the less energetic CuKα radiation a practical upper limit to n is about 25. On this basis one can decide which combinations of D and h can be confidently detected within the range of possible X-ray exposures. In table 4 a single parenthesis enclosing the value of n indicates detectability with CuKα radiation, and a double parenthesis indicates detectability by MoKα as well as CuKα. Thus $D = 2$ microns with $h = 0.3$ is a border-line case with CuKα and $D = 10$ microns and $h = 0.1$ is a border-line case with MoKα.

Practical experience seems to confirm the estimates in table 4. The analysis can be extended to the problem of the resolution of close, parallel lines. This has important practical realisations in resolving X-ray moiré fringes, and individual dislocations in dislocation arrays, and in determining whether or not the intensity profile across the image of a single dislocation line possesses a central dip. An answer to the last question helps in determining Burgers vectors. It appears that a rectangular dip 1 micron wide with 30% less than peak intensity should be detectable with CuKα.

4.4. *Photomicrography*

When care has been taken to produce a topograph approaching the limits of resolution attainable, equal care must be exercised so as not to lose this resolution in an inferior enlargement procedure. Indeed, more time and patience is often needed to produce a good micrograph from the topograph plate than to produce the topograph itself. It is most convenient to use a projection microscope and a relatively large size of recording film, 12 by 16.5 cm for example. The major problem is the large density range encountered in the average size of field it is required to photograph, and it must be remembered that the usable density range of thick nuclear emulsions greatly exceeds any optical photographic emulsion on which it is to be enlarged. In difficult cases a slightly out-of-focus enlargement of the topograph can be made on to a soft lantern plate which is inserted in the microscope illumination system so that it is projected on the topograph at just the right magnification to match the size of the X-ray image. It will then partially balance the long-range density variations in the field.

Because of the great thickness of nuclear emulsions there is no advantage in using microscope objectives with high numerical apertures since those only have a small depth of focus. Fortunately, the nuclear emulsions shrink to about 40% of their original thickness after processing. Still, not all the image will be utilised if the depth of focus is much less than 10, 20 or 40 microns for emulsions originally 25, 50 and 100 microns thick, respectively. Since good resolution is often needed over an area of diameter not less than 1 mm, wide-field objectives are generally employed. Oil immersion is not used, but, as described in 4.2, the topograph should be protected by a cover slip so as to give an optically flat surface. This avoids light-scattering from undulations of the emulsion surface due to variations in silver density and from adhering gelatine threads or other blemishes. Table 5 lists the characteristics of the microscope objectives which are used, that with numerical aperture of 0.50 being useful only on topographs taken with CuKα, CoKα or CrKα radiations. In calculating the field depth, the refractive index of the emulsion is taken as 1.4.

For photomicrography it is desirable to use a film which has a long linear range on its curve of density versus logarithm of exposure, and which has a contrast (gamma) which can be controlled over a wide range by varying the strength of developer solution and development time.

Table 5
Resolution and depth of field of microscope objectives in nuclear emulsions.

Power	N.A.	Resolution (microns)	Field depth (microns)
6.3 X	0.16	1.7	31
10 X	0.22	1.2	16
20 X	0.50	0.55	3

In a satisfactory topographic technique, it should be arranged that no contribution to the limitations of resolution from one cause greatly exceeds that from any of the rest. Then the contributions considered above, i.e. geometrical, ionisation spread, statistical fluctuations, and photomicrographic are all of about the same magnitude, for the radiation used. One can estimate the final resolution attainable, and give a guide to the maximum photomicrographic magnification it is worthwhile to attempt, as shown in table 6.

Table 6
Maximum useful magnifications and resolution limits of X-ray topographs taken with various radiations.

	Resolution limit (μm)	Maximum useful magnification
AgKα	2	150–200
MoKα	1–2	200–300
CuKα	1	400–600
CoKα, CrKα	1	600–800

5. Topographic indicators of lattice perfection

5.1. *Intensity profiles of section topographs*

Suppose a section topograph of a specimen looks life fig. 5b. No great experience in X-ray topography is demanded in order to interpret this as showing the contrast of a limited number of dislocations in an otherwise highly perfect crystal. But suppose no individual dislocation images were present, and the intensity variation across the section topograph was smooth and free from localised concentrations or deficiencies of intensity. How does one know whether the crystal is highly perfect, or highly imperfect? Of course, in the latter case a high value of the integrated reflection, and if a well-collimated incident beam is used, a perceptible broadening of the angular range of reflection, would provide evidence of imperfection. The topograph image itself, however, contains all the information that is needed to answer the question. Moreover, the intensity profile of the section can be used as a statistic, to provide a measure for those types of lattice imperfection which destroy the coherence of the X-ray waves in the energy-flow triangle without any detectable fragmentation of the lattice into a mosaic block structure. It has already been mentioned in 3.1 (p. 418) that perfect, weakly absorbing crystals give a very non-uniform intensity profile compared with the rectangular profile expected from the simple geometric considerations that suffice in the kinematic diffraction approximation. The former type of crystal always reveals itself by the "margin enhancement". The extreme rays, those which correspond to AR and BR' on fig. 7, produce much more blackening than those in the central parts of the section. This phenomenon is seen in fig. 5a and in those parts of figs. 5b and c distant from intense diffraction contrast due to local imperfections.

The margin enhancement is such a curious and unexpected phenomenon from the standpoint of kinematic diffraction theory, and indicates so directly that diffraction is occurring in a manner governed by the dynamical diffraction theory, that an elementary explanation how it arises may be justified at this point, as a demonstration of the importance of the relation between *direction* of ray trajectory in the energy-flow triangle OAB of fig. 7 and the deviation from exact satisfaction of the Bragg condition. Fig. 9 is a sketch of the dispersion surface and of the asymptotic surfaces of the wave vectors in the crystal, k_o and k_g, in the vicinity of the Brillouin zone boundary. It is convenient to take rectangular axes Ox and Oz as shown; Oz lies in the Bril-

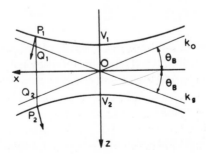

Fig. 9. Dispersion surface in vicinity of Brillouin zone boundary.

louin zone boundary and is directed downwards into the crystal, in the direction $k_o + k_g$. The hyperbolae of the dispersion surface cross the Brillouin zone boundary at V_1 and V_2. The distance $V_1 V_2$ will be called D, and in terms of familiar quantities

$$D = \frac{e^2}{mc^2} \frac{F\lambda C}{\pi V \cos\theta_B} . \tag{2}$$

F is the structure factor, V is the volume of the unit cell and C is the polarization factor ($C = 1$ for σ polarization state and $C = |\cos 2\theta|$ for π polarization state). The equations of the dispersion surfaces in the coordinates of fig. 9 are

$$z^2 = \tfrac{1}{4} D^2 + x^2 \tan^2\theta_B . \tag{3}$$

It is a fact of fundamental importance that the energy-flow vector S (Poynting vector, group-velocity vector, ray vector) of a Bloch wave corresponding to any point on the dispersion surface is normal to that point [64,65]. If Θ denotes the angle made by S with Oz (Θ must, of course, lie within the limits of $-\theta_B$ to $+\theta_B$), then it follows that

$$\tan\Theta = \frac{dz}{dx} = \frac{x \tan^2\theta_B}{z} . \tag{4}$$

It is convenient to introduce the ratio

$$p = \tan\Theta / \tan\theta_B , \tag{5}$$

so that

$$p = x \tan\theta_B / z . \tag{6}$$

Now $x \tan\theta_B$ is linearly proportional to the deviation, $\Delta\theta$, from the exact value of the Bragg angle in the crystal; but for many purposes the most convenient measure of this deviation is the *deviation parameter*, w, given by

$$w = 2x \tan\theta_B / D . \tag{7}$$

(In fig. 9, P_1 and P_2 are points for which $w = 1$; it is useful to remember that the line $P_1 P_2$ cuts the asymptotic surfaces in Q_1 and Q_2 so that $Q_1 Q_2 = V_1 V_2$.) Expressing p in terms of w gives

$$p = \frac{w}{\sqrt{1 + w^2}} \ . \tag{8}$$

which shows that for small deviations from the Bragg angle there will be a linear relation between the *position* where S reaches the base AB of the triangle OAB in fig. 7, and the *angular* deviation $\Delta\theta$; and that for large values of $|w|$, p will tend to ± 1. Thus the S vectors of waves not closely satisfying the Bragg condition will accumulate in the vicinity of the limiting rays OA and OB. If now one combines with relation (8) the expression for dependence on w of the *intensity* in the diffracted beam, which is given by dynamical theory in the symmetrical Laue case as

$$I_w = \tfrac{1}{2}I_0(1+w^2)^{-1} \tag{9}$$

for non-absorbing crystals, one finds, via the obvious transformation

$$I_p = I_w(dw/dp) \ , \tag{10}$$

the intensity profile as a function of p

$$I_p = \text{const} \ (1-p^2)^{\frac{1}{2}} \ . \tag{11}$$

If there is only a small departure from the symmetrical Laue case, such as in fig. 7, the section topograph intensity profile across the image RR' will differ very little from relation (11). Its form is that of the curve for $\mu t = 0$ on the left half of fig. 10. These curves, due to Kato [45], show also the intensity profiles in the directly transmitted beam, as would be recorded along TT'. His curves for non-zero absorption apply to X-ray reflections with which the Borrmann effect can strongly develop, such as 220 in a diamond structure, for example. They show that for such reflections the margin enhancement is rapidly attenuated with increasing thickness, and has practically disappeared by the time μt has reached the value 2.

Now another type of section topograph intensity profile can be produced by crystals which, so one would say in traditional terms, had small primary extinction but high secondary extinction. Such cases occur in practice in perfect crystals which have suffered uniform radiation damage, or in which there is a dispersion of strain-producing precipitates on a scale too fine for their individual images to be resolved on X-ray topographs. In such crystals multiple scattering occurs in the triangle AOB with loss of phase relationships between the waves concerned. The intensity profiles generated under these conditions would display a monotonic decrease in intensity from T to T′ and, in the diffracted beam, a concentration of intensity towards the centre of RR′. Generation of the latter type of profile can be visualised by considering the analogy with experiments designed to demonstrate generation of the normal distribution function, such as the quincunx of Sir Francis Galton. Since these profiles are so similar to those in Kato's curves for μt equal to a few units (except for the vestigial margin enhancement shown in Kato's curve for $\mu t = 2$) care is needed to ensure the correct interpretation when profiles of this type are observed. One must calculate not only the absorption, but also the quantity ϵ which is taken to be unity in Kato's calculations. For centrosymmetrical crystals $\epsilon = F_g''/F_0''$, where F_g'' is the imaginary part of the structure factor for the reflection g, and F_0'' is related to the normal linear absorption coefficient, μ, by

$$\mu = 2\left(\frac{e^2}{mc^2}\right)\frac{\lambda F_0''}{V}. \tag{12}$$

It will be seen then, that if the full potential of the section topograph is an indicator of lattice perfection is to be realised, the specimen thickness and wavelength should be chosen if possible to avoid a condition close to the curve $\mu t = 2$ in fig. 10, since this particular profile does not differ remarkably from that given in the kinematic approximation, or for the case of some secondary extinction and no primary extinction.

5.2. Pendellösung phenomena

The discovery of X-ray Pendellösung fringes in 1957 was valuable in demonstrating the close link between the processes of electron diffraction and X-ray diffraction in perfect crystals; Pendellosung fringes in the form of "constant-thickness" fringes in electron micrographs of wedge-shaped crystals had been adequately interpreted in terms of dynamical diffraction theory since 1953 [68,69]. For the crystallographer interested in structure analysis the significance of the X-ray discovery was that for the first time there became available a practical technique for measuring structure amplitudes *absolutely* without embarking upon precise measurements of integrated reflections with all the complications and difficulties they involve. Since its first application to absolute measurements of F for a few reflections of silicon and quartz [46], the technique has been much developed and refined, as can be judged from recent reviews by the leading workers in this field [70,71].

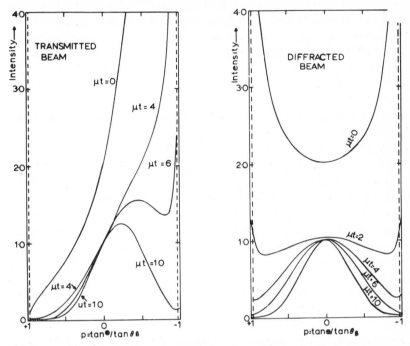

Fig. 10. Calculated spatial intensity profiles for section topographs of diffracted beam and direct beam.

For the X-ray topographer, Pendellösung fringes have a twofold usefulness. Firstly, the *visibility* of the fringes provides a statistical measure of overall lattice perfection, sensitive to lattice imperfections too small to be resolved individually on X-ray topographs, in the same way as does the "margin enhancement" discussed above in 5.1. Secondly, through the *bending* of Pendellösung fringes or a *shift* in fringe order number an extremely sensitive indicator of both local distortions (such as occur in the long-range strainfields of dislocations, for example) and of certain types of macroscopic strain in the specimen is available to the experimenter. The visibility of Pendellösung fringes will be considered first. In order to assess how far the specimen crystal falls short of being ideally perfect, it is necessary to consider two physical effects which modify fringe visibility. These are polarisation and anomalous transmission. The starting point for the discussion is the expected visibility curve for thin, non-absorbing crystals. The Pendellösung fringe spatial periodicity, as it appears on a projection topograph of a wedge-shaped crystal, is controlled by the

extinction distance, ξ_g, which, in the X-ray case, is defined as the depth periodicity of the Pendellösung oscillations, measured along the normal to the X-
ray entrance surface of the crystal. When the Bragg plane is also normal to the
X-ray entrance surface then, simply,

$$\xi_g = D^{-1} \tag{13}$$

where D is the distance $V_1 V_2$ of fig. 9 and is defined by eq. (2). For the asymmetric Laue case,

$$\xi_g = (\cos \theta_o \cos \theta_g)^{\frac{1}{2}} (D \cos \theta_B)^{-1} , \tag{14}$$

where θ_o and θ_g are the angles between the normal to the X-ray entrance surface and the direct and diffracted beams, respectively. For a crystal plate of
thickness t (or for a gently tapering wedge, at the point where the thickness is
t) the integrated reflection R as a function of t is given by

$$R = \tfrac{1}{2} \pi D d \int_0^{2\pi tD} J_0(x) \, dx . \tag{15}$$

Eq. (15) includes the simplifications that eq. (13) applies, only one polarisation mode is considered, and, as already stated, the crystal is non-absorbing.
The interplanar spacing of the Bragg reflection is d. A plot of R versus tD for
the first few oscillations is shown in fig. 11, and table 7 lists the intensities and

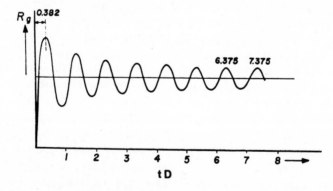

Fig. 11. Variation of integrated reflection with crystal thickness, perfect crystal, zero absorption.

Table 7

Relative intensities and specimen thicknesses for Pendellösung maxima and minima on projection topographs, zero absorption, symmetrical Laue case.

Interference order	Normalised intensity $R/\pi Dd$	Specimen thickness tD
1st max	0.735	0.382
1st min	0.334	0.878
2nd max	0.634	1.377
2nd min	0.385	1.876
3rd max	0.603	2.376
3rd min	0.406	2.876
4th max	0.586	3.376
4th min	0.419	3.876
5th max	0.576	4.376
5th min	0.428	4.876

thicknesses, the latter expressed in units of tD, at the first few extrema of intensity. After the first minimum has been passed, the Pendellösung period corresponds very closely to an increment of t by the amount D^{-1}. The amplitude of the intensity oscillations decays proportionally to $(tD)^{-\frac{1}{2}}$ about the asymptotic mean, so that the *visibility* of the fringes decays similarly.

The effect of polarisation on the visibility of fringes is easily assessed. Referring back to eq. (2) of 5.1 it will be seen that each polarisation mode has its own value of D, because of the inclusion of the polarisation factor C in the expression for D. Since the X-rays in the perpendicular and parallel polarisation states are incoherent with each other, the observed fringe pattern is the sum of the *intensities* produced by each polarisation mode. Hence it will periodically fade when the two intensity oscillations get out of step, being small at intervals of $\frac{1}{2}(2n+1)N$ fringes, where n is a positive integer or zero and N is given by

$$N = \tfrac{1}{2}(1+C)/(1-C) . \qquad (16)$$

This "beat" effect, and the complications it introduces into measurements of the Pendellösung period, has been examined theoretically and experimentally by Hart and Lang [24], Hattori, Kuriyama and Kato [72] and Hart and Milne [71]. If one is judging the perfection of a crystal by the visibility of its Pendellosung fringes, then clearly one must try and observe them at thicknesses in between the polarisation fadings, or, alternatively, use a source giving plane-polarised X-rays [24].

In absorbing crystals, the intensity oscillations on the projection topograph suffer attenuation with the normal absorption coefficient, but if the crystal exhibits anomalous transmission, that is if $\epsilon > 0$, then the *mean* intensity decays more *slowly* with increasing thickness than that expected with the normal absorption coefficient [24]. Thus the *visibility* of the Pendellösung fringes, defined in the conventional way as $(I_{max}-I_{min})/(I_{max}+I_{min})$, falls off faster than in the non-absorbing case. Thus, as in the case of "margin enhancement" on section topographs a valid comparison between observed and the ideal behaviour may require calculations involving both ϵ and μ.

On section topographs of wedges, the fringes have the characteristic "hook-shape" [46], observation of which prompted Kato to develop his "spherical-wave" theories for X-ray diffraction by perfect crystals [47]. Down the centre of the section topograph, passing through the apices of the hooks, fringes can be observed to high orders. In the non-absorbing case both the amplitude of intensity oscillation and the mean intensity fall off along this medium line at the same rate, in proportion as the width of the section pattern increases with increasing crystal thickness, so that the *visibility* of the fringes remains constant. There has been a notable improvement in the visiblity of high-order Pendellosung fringes comparing the best commercial silicon of to-day with the best available a decade ago. The improvement has nothing to do with X-ray technique: the latter has not changed at all in the period. Note the good visibility of the "hooks" at the centre of the section topograph of present-day perfect silicon shown in fig. 5a. The crystal thickness is in the range 2 to 2.15 mm over the major part of the image, with the fringe order in the range 40 to 50, the thickness being chosen to avoid a polarisation fade.

The topic of the bending of Pendellösung fringes in distorted lattices, and the change in fringe order (which is commonly in the sense as to make the crystal appear thicker than it really is) has been much studied theoretically and experimentally [73–76]; Kato's review [48] serves as a useful introduction to the subject. Suffice it to say here that it is a rare crystal that does not show some irregularity of Pendellosung fringes due to inhomogeneous strains. The distortion of fringe patterns near dislocations and fault surfaces can be remarkable, as seen in fig. 5c.

6. Studies of dislocations

6.1. *Diffraction contrast of dislocations*

Since the theory of X-ray diffraction by perfect crystals, including the theory of diffraction contrast due to lattice imperfections, comes within the scope of the lectures by Professor Authier (this volume), only a few remarks, addressed to some purely practical questions concerning the design and interpretation of X-ray topographic experiments, need be included here concerning dislocation images as they appear in X-ray topographs. One practical question the experimenter may ask is, over what specimen thickness range may clear images of individual dislocations be observed? The lower thickness limit is fairly well defined. Consider the curve shown in fig. 11. At lowest values of tD there is a linear rise in integrated reflection. This corresponds to the situation when the amplitude of the diffracted wave has not built up to more than a small fraction of that of the incident wave, even for waves which satisfy the Bragg angle precisely. Thus up to a certain thickness, the ideally perfect and the ideally imperfect crystal cannot be distinguished on the basis of integrated reflection. At these low thicknesses gross misorientations, of some minutes of arc or more, can be detected on topographs by their orientation contrast, but lattice defects such as dislocations or stacking faults do not give rise to extinction contrast (or, equivalently, in its usual sense, to diffraction contrast) until there is a significant departure of the curve of fig. 11, which corresponds to eq. (15), from the prolongation of the straight line which is tangent to it in the limit as tD tends to zero. This straight line would represent the integrated reflection of a non-absorbing, ideally imperfect crystal: an ideal which present-day experience suggests is far more difficult to realise than that of the perfect crystal! It will be seen that the integrated intensity given by the straight line is proportional to tD^2. A good deal of experience has been gained with topographs of thin crystals. Lenticular-section crystals of iron-silicon alloy which have been electrolytically polished to a feather edge, and chemically polished MgO crystals, all give a characteristically featureless "grey" appearance on topographs of areas which, for the reflection and radiation used, as too thin to give dislocation contrast. Experience suggests that dislocations first begin to stand out at thicknesses of about $\frac{1}{3}\xi_g$. This is at the upper limit of the range of minimum thicknesses for dislocation contrast suggested by Penning and Goemans [77]. As a practical guide to minimum thicknesses likely to be encountered in specimens often examined by X-ray topography, some typical extinction distances are listed in table 8.

Thus, minimum thicknesses for detecting dislocations would be 12 to 13 microns with silicon 220 reflection using $MoK\alpha$ radiation, and 2 to 3 microns with iron 110 reflection, $CoK\alpha$ radiation. Note that if topographs were taken with very weak reflections and $AgK\alpha$ radiation, slices up to a tenth or so of a millimetre thick might appear dislocation-free when they were in reality far from so!

Table 8
Representative values of extinction distance (symmetrical Laue case).

Crystal	Reflection	Radiation	ξ_g (microns)
Diamond	220	MoKα	48
Diamond	220	CuKα	27
Silicon	220	MoKα	38
Silicon	440	MoKα	60
LiF	111	MoKα	50
LiF	200	MoKα	33
a-quartz	$10\bar{1}1$	MoKα	45
a-quartz	0003	MoKα	205
a-iron	110	AgKα	13
a-iron	110	CoKα	5.7

The strongest dislocation contrast observed with all wavelengths occurs at the first Pendellösung minimum, i.e. at a thickness of 0.88 ξ_g. Thereafter, with increasing thickness there is, averaging over Pendellosung oscillation of the perfect-crystal background, a gradual decline in contrast. At high values of μt, in reflections exhibiting anomalous transmission, the dislocation contrast is reversed, and the dislocation lines appear light on a darker background. This change from "normal contrast" to "reversed contrast" was first demonstrated by taking topographs of the same area of germanium crystal, first with AgKα and then with WKα [51]. There is an awkward thickness range from μt = 2 to μt = 5 where dislocations can show both normal and reversed contrast, with often a marked change in sign of contrast (positive = excess diffracted intensity; negative = reduction of diffracted intensity) in going from the hkl reflection to its inverse, $\bar{h}\bar{k}\bar{l}$. This change in sign of contrast can be useful in determining the *sign* of dislocations [55,56]. In the approximation of isotropic elasticity, the displacement field around the dislocation contains three terms, proportional to $\mathbf{b}$, $\mathbf{l} \times \mathbf{b}$, and $\mathbf{l} \times \mathbf{b} \times \mathbf{l}$, $\mathbf{b}$ is the Burgers vector and $\mathbf{l}$ is a unit vector parallel to the dislocation line [78]. The contrast reversal between hkl and $\bar{h}\bar{k}\bar{l}$ images is most marked for dislocations with a strong edge component, and for reflections with $\mathbf{g}$ making a small angle with $\mathbf{l} \times \mathbf{b}$. In general, for easy experimental determination of Burgers vectors, the thickness range with μt equal to a few units should be avoided if possible. An example of a topograph taken under these "awkward" conditions is shown in fig. 12, but since the purpose of this topograph was to show the contrast of 90° magnetic domain walls (which it does very well; they are the dark and light stripes which slope at 45° across the

Fig. 12. Projection topograph of plate of Fe 3% Si parallel to (001), thickness about 200 microns, reflection 200, AgKα radiation, field edge length 2.5 mm.

field), and not to study dislocations, the diffuse and variable character of images of the latter is not a serious drawback.

The second practical question concerns the width of dislocation images. In the low-absorption case, the zone of strong positive contrast around a dislocation begins where appreciable "interbranch scattering" of the X-ray Bloch waves takes place, but the nature of the dislocation strainfield is such that a simple *tilt* criterion can be applied to predict dislocation widths, on the basis that the strong excess diffracted intensity comes from regions misoriented with respect to the perfect matrix by a tilt corresponding to a value of the deviation parameter of about two. This idea, employed in a very qualitative way in the earliest studies [51], developed quantitatively by Wilkens and Meier [79], and refined recently by Authier [80], works satisfactorily. Consider a pure screw dislocation: the tilt at a distance r from the core is $|\mathbf{b}|/2\pi r$. The angle corresponding to the value $w = \pm 2$ is $2dD = 2D|\mathbf{g}|^{-1}$, which is the full width at half-maximum intensity of the perfect-crystal reflection curve, in the non-absorbing case. Equating the two expressions, one obtains an estimate of the screw dislocation image width $V_s = 2r$,

$$V_s \approx (2\pi D)^{-1}\, \mathbf{g} \cdot \mathbf{b} \ . \tag{17}$$

Pure edge dislocations give widths V_E equal to about 1.75 V_s. With the help of table 8, one can make some estimates of dislocation image widths, such as: diamond, 220 reflection, MoKα, $\mathbf{g} \cdot \mathbf{b} = 2$, $V_E = 27\ \mu$m; and iron, 110 reflection, CoKα, $\mathbf{g} \cdot \mathbf{b} = 1$, $V_s = 1.1\ \mu$m. These values agree quite well with observations [56,81]. Note that in the case of iron and CoKα radiation, the dislocation image width is reduced to just about the topographic resolution limit, as determined by the factors enumerated in sect. 4. On the other extreme, when D is small, as in weak reflections, such as those given by complex structures and organic compounds, V may rise to many tens of microns [80,82,83]. In the cases when D is small, and/or $\mathbf{g} \cdot \mathbf{b}$ is equal to two or more, the dislocation images show a bimodal intensity profile. This is a general phenomenon, arising as a consequence of the form of the dislocation strain field [80]. It was observed in early topographs of silicon, and has been seen in topographs of crystals as diverse as diamond and the high-explosive cyclotrimethylenetrinitramine.

6.2. *Dislocations and crystal nuclei*

In the following paragraphs only a very few applications of X-ray topography to dislocation studies will be described. They have been selected to exemplify situations in which X-ray topographic experiments can yield information not otherwise obtainable, sometimes with unexpected results.

The first application is concerned with crystal nucleation and growth, and deals with the dislocation configurations in whole crystals. As previously mentioned, entire crystals, up to several millimetres in thickness, can have their

Fig. 13. Projection topograph of potash alum crystal, reflection 220, AgKα radiation, width of crystal about 3 mm.

content of dislocations and other lattice imperfections mapped by X-ray topography, provided they contain only elements which are lightly X-ray absorbing. A characteristically recurring configuration of dislocations in whole crystals is shown in figs. 13 and 14. Fig. 13 is a tabular octahedral crystal of potash alum [83], and fig. 14 is a tabular octahedral diamond. The projection topographs are taken so that the crystal is viewed roughly perpendicularly to the large pair of faces; this gives the clearest projection of the crystal volume. Quite similar dislocaltion configurations are found in equiaxed crystals. Both crystals show much intensification of diffracted intensity from localised surface damage such as scratches. The damage is especially severe at edges and corners. One sees that the great majority of dislocations spring from a central nucleus, and then fan out in nearly straight lines until they outcrop on the crystal faces. Only a few dislocations are nucleated elsewhere in the crystals: in the alum crystal one sees a bundle of dislocations starting at a point about

Fig. 14. Projection topograph of natural diamond, reflection 220, MoKα radiation, width
of crystal about 4 mm.

one third the way along the crystal radius in the lower left of fig. 13, and in
fig. 14 a few dislocations are nucleated at certain growth horizons in the upper
right of the image. This characteristic pattern of dislocations radiating from a
nucleus is common in the case of diamond, both natural and synthetic
[58,81,84,85], it has been observed in organic crystals, hexamethylene te-
tramine [86] and in cyclotrimethylenetrinitramine, and in rocksalt [87]. The
simplest explanation is that the crystal has commenced growth by heterogeneous nucleation, and that the dislocations have been introduced by initially
imperfect growth on a substrate. The significance of this type of dislocation
configuration, in which the great majority of dislocations originate at the crystal nucleus, and only a few at subsequent stages in the growth history, is that
while the volume of the crystal grows the total number of dislocations in the
crystal does not substantially increase. Accordingly, the perfection, as measured by the dislocation density, increases steadily as the crystal gets larger. Add
to this the tendency for the dislocations to keep together in close bundles,
running roughly normal to the crystal faces, and one perceives that in crystals
of this type one can find volumes of the order of a cubic millimetre quite dislocation-free.

There are other crystals, both natural and synthetic, in which dislocations
appear to be constantly generated during growth by the inclusion of foreign

particles. Natural quartz exhibits this phenomenon [51,88,89] and similar
patterns have been found in magnesium aluminate spinel flux-grown in the
laboratory [90]. The latter process is prone to dislocation generation by
lattice closure errors around inclusions of flux. There are crystals in which, at
a particular horizon, a catastrophic increase in amount of included foreign
matter has occurred, with a corresponding catastrophic increase in dislocation density. Such appears to be the case in coated diamond [91].

Large crystals grown from small seeds exhibit configurations comparable
to those of figs. 13 and 14. For example the pyramid caps which grow out
from seed crystals of potassium dihydrogen phosphate may contain few dislocations, since the majority of dislocations nucleated by poor epitaxy upon
the seed propagate out towards the prism faces only. On the other hand, in
the case of synthetic quartz in which practically all growth occurs normal to
a large seed plate, the dislocation density cannot be reduced by the geometric
factors which operate in the case of equiaxed crystals growing from a small
nucleus.

Finally, another dislocation generation mechanism may be menetioned.
This occurs in dendritic growth, and could possibly be a cause of configurations like figs. 13 and 14 if the initial stages of growth were dendritic due
to strong supersaturation of the surrounding medium. Excellent X-ray topographs of ice crystals by Webb and Hayes have demonstrated how dislocations can be generated by inclusions and/or lattice closure mistakes at the
deep re-entrants between spikes of dendrites [92,93]. In an equally noteworthy experiment, it has been demonstrated that if crystallisation of ice can
be so controlled as to keep the solid-melt interface flat and clsely parallel to
the basal plane, then crystals several millimetres in diameter substantially free
from dislocations may be grown [94]. The low X-ray absorption of ice makes
this crystal an excellent subject for X-ray topographic studies.

6.3. Dislocations in metals

Only three metals have been studied extensively by X-ray topography.
These are aluminium, copper and iron 3% silicon alloy. The first metal whose
interior dislocation configuration was displayed by X-ray methods was zone-
refined aluminium, single crystals of which can be grown by the strain-anneal
method. The original work of Lang and Meyrick [95] and the later studies
of Authier, Rogers and Lang [96] revealed some astonishing features. Besides the pleasant surprise that the dislocation density could be very low in
crystals with which great care had been taken to avoid plastic deformation,
the really noteworthy finding was the presence of long lines of coaxial loops.
The axes of the loops all lay exactly along the ⟨110⟩ directions and the Burgers

vectors of the dislocation loops were parallel to the loop axis. Such a line of coaxial prismatic loops is quite stable; indeed when topographs were taken in sequence showing the invasion of the crystal of mobile dislocations (such invasion occurring catastrophically under very low stress) the coaxial loops remained unmoved while the mobile dislocations enveloped them. The loop diameters ranged from the threshold of visibility, about one micron, up to about 50 microns. As many as 40 loops were counted in a single row, the overall length of the row being more than one millimetre. Another finding was that in unstrained specimens there was an extremely low dislocation density within 200 to 300 microns of the crystal surface. This was attributed to loss of dislocations during annealing of the specimen. Fig. 5b reveals this situation in a crystal $1\frac{1}{4}$ mm thick. It will be seen how the great majority of dislocations are confined in regions near the mid-plane of the specimen. Many X-ray topographic studies of aluminium crystals grown by the strain-anneal method have been made by Nøst and co-workers who have followed changes of dislocation density in controlled stressing and annealing experiments [97—100].

Authier, Rogers and Lang considered several possible origins for the rows of prismatic loops. They concluded that they were most likely to be due to the climb of long, straight screw segments into helices through the absorption of vacancies, and the subsequent interaction of the helix with itself or with a neighbouring dislocation to convert the helix into a set of coaxial loops. In this way, it is believed, the "primitive" dislocation population in the newly recrystallised material, consisting largely of long, straight screw segments, was "fossilised" by being rendered immobile through conversion into lines of coaxial loops. However, the density of those lines appears to depend upon factors other than just the heat treatment, as the experiments by Frémiot, Baudelet and Champier comparing crystals annealed in vacuum and in air have shown [101].

Quite different dislocation configurations have been found in crystals of iron 3% silicon grown from the melt and well annealed at high temperature [56]. Indeed the configurations were typical of a large class of melt-grown crystals, not only metals. The X-ray topographs can show how the number of dislocations is divided between those in low-angle boundaries and those within the volume of sub-grains. In the configurations within the latter there are many alignments indicative of movements and multiplication under stress followed by re-arrangements to reduce strain energy. The low dislocation density that can be achieved in carefully annealed crystals is illustrated by the specimen shown in fig. 12. In some sub-grains the density of dislocations is down to less than 10 lines per mm^2. Comparable low densities can be achieved by carefully annealing pure copper crystals, the X-ray topographic studies on which by Baldwin, Young and co-workers has already been mentioned [30–35]. There appears to be plenty of scope for X-ray topographic work on other metals, and it may well be easier than is generally feared to produce single crystals of sufficiently low dislocation density. In favourable circumstances, crystals of very low dislocation density can be obtained by quite simple crystal-growing arrangements, as McFarlane and Elbaum have demonstrated in their X-ray topography of gallium [102].

6.4. *Dislocations in refractory oxides and in semiconductors*

Magnesium oxide crystals give good examples of a dislocation configuration common in melt-grown crystals, that of a well-developed network of low-angle boundaries surrounding sub-grains in which local regions of low dislocation density, possibly up to a few hundred microns in diameter, may be found. It is likely that all dislocations are caused by plastic deformation due to thermal stresses in the crystal as it cools after passage of the growth front. Usually the configurations bear evidence of such a complex history of glide, climb, and sometimes polygonisation that it is difficult to reconstruct the stages in development of the configuration. The variation in dislocation density in samples taken from different regions of a large boule, and occasional evidence for anisotropy of distribution of Burgers vectors among the totality of their possible directions, together with the preponderance of dislocations of one sign (as revealed by contrast differences in hkl and $\bar{h}\bar{k}\bar{l}$ pairs) sometimes provide clues to what slip systems have been active, and the nature of the deformation that has occurred. Glide and climb at elevated temperatures may leave behind large dislocation loops. These are particularly evident in lithium fluoride [103] and they also occur in magnesium oxide [104,105]. Great climb activity may have chemical forces driving it. An extreme manifestation of extension of dislocation line length by climb was found in a magnesium oxide crystal whose dislocations were decorated by light-scattering bodies [106].

X-ray topographic studies have been carried out on crystals of corundum (Al_2O_3) grown by several methods (a) flame process (Verneuil process), (b) from vapour, (c) from flux and (d) from melt (Czochralski process). In (a) the dislocation density was around 10^6 lines cm^{-2}, needing section topographs or limited projection topographs to be taken in order to resolve individuals, and the whole crystals were irregularly warped with misorientations ranging up to about 1/10 of a degree. Vapour grown crystals were almost perfect as regards dislocation content, though strain accompanying growth layering was evident. The flux-grown crystals were very variable in quality, dislocations occurred individually or in bundles, and non-uniform incorporation of impurity gave rise

to bands of enhanced diffracting power. Czochralski grown corundum crystals
are a recent development. They show a low density of dislocations, a few
times 10^3 lines cm^{-2}, with good diffraction contrast [107]. Another interesting refractory oxide is BeO and it is also a good subject for X-ray topographic
study. Hexagonal pyramidal crystals grown from lithium molybdate flux contain a core of twinned material and an axial screw dislocation. They also show
growth bands on the X-ray topographs [108].

In the early days of X-ray topographic studies of individual dislocations,
crystals of silicon and germanium were much used in the proving of the X-ray
techniques. For example, the development of the projection topograph,
limited projection topograph, stereo techniques, and the establishment of the
visibility rules for dislocation images; and recognition of a host of interesting
diffraction phenomena, from the bimodal intensity profile for dislocations with
$\mathbf{g} \cdot \mathbf{b} \geqslant 2$, to the hkl, $\overline{hkl}$ contrast differences depending upon sign of Burgers
vector, were all performed on silicon crystals of 1957 vintage which were
quite sufficiently perfect for the purpose. At that time the problem of producing dislocation-free crystals by crucible growth was being solved, notably
through the work of Dash [109]; but was still unsolved in floating-zone grown
crystals. Thus there was some purpose in carrying out a systematic X-ray topographic study of dislocations in silicon grown by the latter method [110].
This study found the axial region of the crystal to be full of dislocation tangles
associated with the mutual intersection of active slip-planes. Evidence was obtained that the heart of the tangle consisted of one or more Lomer reactions
which produce relatively immobile dislocations. Regarding dislocation sources,
it was seen that much internal multiplication of dislocation line length during
glide had occurred by cross-slip of screw segments; but lack of stable pinning
prevented repetitive operation of sources of the Frank-Read type. (Indeed,
good topograph images of such sources can only be found in crystals very
lightly deformed within a restricted temperature range [111].)

In recent years the emphasis of X-ray topographic studies has shifted away
from pure semiconductor crystals, and, notably by Schwuttke and his colleagues, much attention has been paid to the diffraction effects of impurity
precipitation [112], to microstrains due to variable concentration of dopants
such as boron [113], and to diffusion-induced dislocations [114–118].

Finally one must briefly mention the web-dendrite twin crystals of silicon
and germanium which are not only an extremely interesting phenomenon of
crystal growth, but which also provide elegant topographs showing the dislocations and their reactions in the thin web parallel to the twin plane [119,120].

7. Studies of fault surfaces

This section will be concerned with those surfaces which may sub-divide a perfect crystal into domains by relative translations only, there being no significant change in orientation or interplanar spacing between one domain and another. The interfaces between the domains, the *fault surfaces,* are each characterised by a *fault vector* which measures the displacement of the Bravais lattice on one side of the fault surface with respect to that on the other. The condition for no significant change in orientation or interplanar spacing across the fault surface may be expressed by saying that waves whose directions lie within the angular range of Bragg reflection by one domain find themselves, after passing into an adjacent domain, to have suffered a change in deviation parameter negligibly small, $\Delta w \ll 1$. This restriction excludes fault surfaces such as low-angle boundaries and magnetic domain boundaries in the general case: we are here concerned only with the α-boundaries as defined by Gevers, van Landuyt and Amelinckx [121]. For domains separated by α-boundaries, lattice parallelism is maintained but lattice coincidence is not. The important characteristic to bear in mind concerning X-ray topographic studies of fault surfaces is that the diffraction effects, for a given fault vector, do not depend upon the structure of the transition region between one domain and another provided that the thickness of the transition region is only a small fraction of the X-ray extinction distance; and as such small fraction may be a few microns, it is very large compared with atomic dimensions. X-ray diffraction contrast measurements can give all components of the fault vector (within the standard phase ambiguity of $\pm 2\pi n$) fairly readily, because of the range of orientations and magnitudes of **g** accessible for Bragg reflection, but they cannot directly reveal the crystal structure of the transition region. This does not raise a problem in devising structures for twin boundaries in quartz and for defects in strongly-bonded structures such as the "lattice disorders" discussed by Megaw [122], when there is good evidence that only a single such defect forms the image. But in X-ray experiments a difficulty already present in transmission electron microscopy is greatly accentuated, that of uncertainty whether the contrast observed is due to a single surface or to a series of closely spaced fault surfaces not separately resolvable. However, to make a theoretical interpretation of fault-surface diffraction contrast feasible, the transition region, or set of unresolved fault-surfaces, has to be replaced by a single interface at which the standard wave-matching procedures are applied. The diffraction theory has been worked out for the X-ray case, using spherical wave theory, by Authier [123] and by Kato et al. [124], but a good start towards understanding the basic phenomena, at least as they appear on projection topographs, can be gained by reference to the simpler, plane-wave theory applicable with the electron microscope [125]. Indeed, a simple adaptation of the electron microscope theory for absorbing crystals [126,127] has been found useful in X-ray experiments to determine the *sign* as well as the *magnitude* of fault vectors at twin boundaries in quartz, using reflections which have a relatively high value of ϵ. However, for many purposes, it is adequate just to know that a fault surface whose fault vector is **f** will be invisible on an X-ray topograph when $\mathbf{g} \cdot \mathbf{f} = n$, n being zero or an integer, and the magnitude of **g** being the reciprocal of the interplanar spacing.

The characteristic stacking-fault-type fringe patterns produced by fault-surfaces were first recognised on the earliest X-ray topographs of quartz [46,51] yet after more than a decade these particular types of fault have not been fully investigated, and their origin is far from understood. Simpler to comprehend are the stacking faults that can occur in face-centred cubic crystals. Stacking faults of large extent, several square millimetres in area, were found in silicon crystals by Kohra and Yoshimatsu [128], and the vanishing conditions verified to be those expected for such faults in fcc lattices. Later Yoshimatsu observed the partial dislocations bounding such stacking faults [129]. Stacking faults of smaller size, 100 microns or less in edge length, occurring in epitaxially grown silicon, were examined X-ray topographically by Schwuttke and Sils [130]. With stacking faults whose edge lengths are of order of a few tens of microns, experimental differentiation between *area* contrast from the stacking fault and the contrast from the bounding partial dislocation *lines* requires a careful X-ray technique. It was accomplished in an investigation of such defects outcropping at the octahedral faces of an otherwise unusually perfect diamond [131]. The Burgers vectors of the bounding partials were also determined. They were normal to the stacking-fault plane, and the image strength was consistent with a Burgers vector magnitude of $\frac{1}{3}\langle 111 \rangle$. The faults observed in these X-ray studies [130,131] bear a great resemblance to those observed electron-microscopically, on a smaller scale, by Booker [132]. There could, however, be no possible electron microscope observation corresponding to that of the large tetrahedral stacking fault (edge length 115 microns) found buried in the interior of the diamond studied by Lawn, Kamiya and Lang [131].

Some fascinating diffraction phenomena associated with twin lamellae in calcite, and with their twinning dislocations, have been studied experimentally and theoretically by Authier and co-workers [133–135]. This crystal species, like quartz and others, often contains growth layers of differing impurity contents. The change in interplanar spacing at the interfaces between these layers may be sufficient to disturb diffraction conditions to the extent of producing "interbranch scattering" of the X-ray wave fields in the crystal. An interface so doing, and inclined to the X-ray entrance surface of the specimen, will produce stacking-fault-type fringes. However, it is sometimes difficult to ascertain experimentally whether one is observing a set of fault fringes from *one* fault surface, or a set of independent diffraction images marking the outcrop of a set of roughly equispaced growth layers.

Alpha quartz is one of the many crystals whose structure has a lower symmetry than that of their Bravais lattice. Twinning of the parallel-lattice type is with these a possibility; the twin law being one of the symmetry operations possessed by the lattice but not by the structure. The two common forms of twinning in quartz (Dauphiné and Brazil) are of this type. The Dauphiné twin law is a rotation of π about the *c*-axis, the Brazil twin law is a reflection in one of the $\{11\bar{2}0\}$ planes normal to the two-fold axes, which are parallel to the *a*-axes, see figs. 15 and 16. With X-rays, the enantiomorphs produced by Brazil twinning can only be distinguished when Friedel's Law is not obeyed (see sect. 9.1), but the Dauphiné twins have relatively few planes coincident which have the same structure factor modulus, $|F|$, and which would reflect with equal intensity on the X-ray topograph. Dauphiné twinning, for example, will change the very strongly reflecting major rhombohedron, r, $\{10\bar{1}1\}$, into the minor

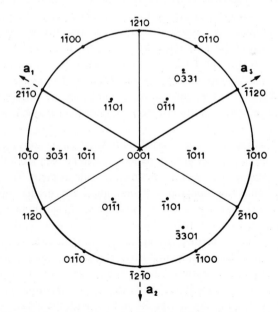

Fig. 15. Stereographic projection on basal plane of quartz.

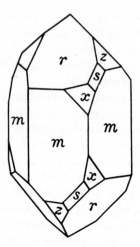

Fig. 16. Faces on a natural quartz crystal.

rhombohedron, z, $\{\bar{1}011\}$, which has a lesser value of $|F|$, by about 50%. In studies of fault-fringe contrast at twin boundaries in quartz aimed at determining the fault vector associated with the twin boundary, it must be remembered that quartz is a non-centrosymmetric structure, so that if the structure factor changes from $F \exp(i\phi)$ to $F \exp(-i\phi)$ on crossing the boundary, the total phase shift is $2\pi\mathbf{g}\cdot\mathbf{f} + 2\phi$. This point, and others connected with twin boundaries in quartz, have been previously discussed [82,88,89]. It may just be mentioned here that the fault vectors $\mathbf{f}$, and hence the twin boundary crystal structures, are a function of twin composition surface as well as of twin law.

Some fault surfaces in quartz revealed by X-ray topographs are found to coincide with boundaries of growth sectors, as can be seen from the different orientation of traces of growth layers on either side of them. The fault surfaces observed on X-ray topographs of ammonium dihydrogen phosphate by Yoshimatsu [136] may have a similar explanation. In synthetic quartz, fault surfaces giving rise to X-ray diffraction contrast form a network under growing surfaces which have formed an "impurity cell' structure. The fault surfaces lie in the boundaries of the impurity cells, outcropping at the growth surface along the grooves between the protuberances (known as "cobbles") which indicate cellular growth [137]. Examples of such impurity-cell-boundary fault surfaces are shown in figs. 24 and 25. With the aid of the extraordinary sensitivity of X-ray moiré topographs it is seen that these surfaces are not strictly α boundaries.

8. Studies of domains

Before reviewing some of the X-ray topogaphic studies of domains that have been carried out in recent years it may be relevant to question why and when the experimenter would wish to choose this technique as his observing tool. The answer is generally similar to that which would be given with respect to studies of dislocations. The X-ray topographic method is of very general application, since what are detected in the diffraction experiments are misorientations, strains, and strain-gradients; the method is non-destructive and many repeated observations on the same specimen may be made; the interior of relatively thick specimens can be investigated so that both surface domain configurations and those developed in the bulk material can be studied and compared. But once again the limited resolution of the X-ray topographic technique comes up as a barrier to work on structures on a scale below 1 to 2 microns, which is somewhat worse resolution than that obtainable with the traditional Bitter pattern (colloid) technique for ferromagnets, though it must be remembered that the latter can only show surface outcrops of domain walls, and is by no means infallible at that. And the X-ray experiments are in a completely different class compared with transmission electron microscopy (Lorentz microscopy) of thin films, but so indeed are the curious domain structures developed in such films, which bear little resemblance to those occurring in bulk specimens.

Domain walls are δ-boundaries according to the classification of Gevers, Van Landuyt and Amelinckx [121]. X-rays undergoing Bragg reflection in one domain will in general suffer a finite change of deviation parameter upon passing through a domain wall into an adjacent domain. The diffraction effects consequent upon this non-zero value of Δw, and the topographic techniques by which they can best be rendered visible, depend upon the magnitude of Δw which in turn will depend on the magnitude of the appropriate electrostriction or magnetostriction constant, besides, of course, the orientation and magnitude of the acting g-vector and the structure factor of the reflection concerned. Bearing in mind the angular range corresponding to unit values of w in the X-ray case (a few examples were given in table 2, p. 431) it will be appreciated that for ferroelectrics and antiferromagnets $\Delta w \gg 1$ in general, whereas for the ferromagnetic metals Δw will not exceed unity for strong, low-order reflections.

Now when $\Delta w \lesssim 1$, domain walls will show by extinction contrast using ordinary slit collimation of the incident beam, and the domain volumes on either side of the wall will be equally strongly reflecting (though with double-crystal techniques, such as those described in 2.4, some orientation contrast

of adjacent domains should be visible). In the case of $\Delta w \leqslant 1$ the contrast of
a wall arises from interbranch scattering, and in the case of a wall of extended
area such as a wall cutting right through the specimen from X-ray entrance to
exit surfaces, the diffraction effects are like those produced by a very low
angle boundary minus the images of the individual dislocations in the boundary. When $\Delta w \gg 1$, on the other hand, the two domains Bragg reflect as independent crystals, and it comes within the capabilities of ordinary slit collimation of the incident beam to identify different domains by orientation contrast. In cases of both small and large values of electrostriction and magnetostriction constants, extinction contrast can arise in the volume of a domain
due to distortion produced by an adjacent domain. This is common when small
domains are enclosed in larger domains with non-parallel directions of polarisation. When domain walls outcrop at crystal surfaces, stress-relieving lattice
curvature can produce strong extinction contrast, and this will be especially
evident on surface reflection topographs.

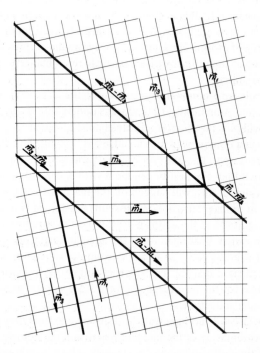

Fig. 17. Scheme of 180° and 90° walls with positive magnetostriction.

The possible situations in a multi-domain crystal, containing several directions of polarisation, m_i, are shown in fig. 17. There are two classes of boundary of interest from the diffraction point of view, walls between i and j domains whose polarisations add to zero, $m_i + m_j = 0$, and those between domains not satisfying this equation. Under usual X-ray diffraction conditions, no differentiation can be made between adjacent *domains* satisfying the above equation, nor are *walls* of the former class likely to be detectable unless the crystal structure in the wall departs sufficiently from that within the domains on either side so that the wall behaves as an α-boundary, or if there is sufficient stress in the wall structure to give rise to extinction-contrast-producing lattice curvature at its outcrops on the specimen surfaces. It is the domain walls for which $m_i - m_j$ is non-zero that can produce strong diffraction contrast and which, in reasonably perfect crystals, will appear strongly on the X-ray topographs. There are visibility rules for these walls, analogous to the visibility rules for dislocations, which make it possible for X-ray topography to be used for analysing domain structures. All the vectors m_i in a domain pattern can be determined (after choosing the *sign* of one such vector).

The material on which most X-ray topographic studies of domains have been made is iron 3% silicon alloy. Its magnetostriction constant is quite small, equal to 2.7×10^{-5}, hnece at its domain boundaries $\Delta w \leqslant 1$ in general. In this crystal, the vectors m_i lie along the cube axes. The two classes of wall consequently produced, which fig. 17 is drawn to represent, but with a vastly exaggerated magnetostriction, are called $180°$ walls and $90°$ walls, respectively. The $180°$ walls show at best very feeble diffraction contrast, observable only under specially chosen diffraction conditions. Both theory and experiment indicate a general rule for *visibility* of $90°$ walls: in the Bragg reflection g, at a boundary with $\Delta m = m_i - m_j$, the walls will be visible when

$$\Delta m \cdot g \neq 0 , \tag{18}$$

as has been shown by Polcarová and Kaczér [138] and Polcarová and Gemperlová [139]. Strictly, this rule applies to an isolated wall in an infinite crystal, but such conditions are sufficiently closely approached in specimens such as that shown in fig. 12, which is about 200 microns thick and in which the main $90°$ walls run from X-ray entrance to X-ray exit face of the specimen. These walls are spaced a few hundred microns apart, on average. In crossing a domain wall, the effective change in glancing angle $\Delta\delta$ depends upon both the change in interplanar spacing $\Delta d/d$ and the lattice rotation, $\Delta\phi$, at the boundary:

$$\Delta\delta = (\Delta d/d) \tan\theta_B + \Delta\phi . \tag{19}$$

The proportionality factor linking the diffraction-relevant change Δw with $\Delta\delta$ is, of course,

$$\Delta w = (dD)^{-1} \Delta\delta \tag{20}$$

as can be verified from fig. 9.

In the body-centred cubic structure of iron 3% silicon, ϵ is reduced below the value unity principally by the Debye-Waller factor only, so that the Borrmann effect can strongly develop in all low-order reflections. Consequently, when μt is equal to a few units, strong positive or negative contrast can develop at domain walls, depending upon the sign of Δw. This effect is noticeable in fig. 12, as are also the "black-white" contrast effects at domain corners. The contrast reversal phenomena at 90° walls have been discussed by Polcarová and Lang [140]. X-ray topographic studies of 90° walls in ironsilicon alloy single crystals under similar absorption conditions, μt equal to a few units, have been made by Schlenker, Brissonneau and Perrier [141], and under higher absorption conditions by other workers [142–144].

The ferrimagnetic crystal, yttrium iron garnet, has a very low magnetostriction constant (-2.4×10^{-6}) and it produces excellent domain wall contrast on X-ray topographs [145]. The antiferromagnet NiO has been studied X-ray topographically by several workers [146–149]. In this crystal the magnetostriction changes the interaxial angles by several minutes of arc, so that the domains can be identified both by orientation contrast and by the distortion associated with the mutual constraints between domains.

Most ferroelectrics examined by X-rays have high electrostriction constants, so that they fall in the class for which $\Delta w \gg 1$ at domain walls in the general case, and orientation contrast is observable without stringent collimation of the incident beam [150–153]. Both orientation contrast and extinction contrast contribute to the patterns obtained in surface reflection topographs of barium titanate which have been taken with the Berg-Barrett technique [154–155], since, as already mentioned, stress relief at specimen surfaces will cause strong local lattice curvatures. A characteristic of all X-ray topographic domain studies is that domain pattern changes can be followed by taking sequences of topographs. This was demonstrated in the first X-ray topographic experiments to show domain patterns in iron-silicon alloy [156]. In magnetically very soft crystals, domain pattern changes occurring undesired mid-way in the course of an X-ray topographic investigation of a particular domain structure are an experimental hazard.

9. Special techniques

9.1. *Mapping of twins and polytypes*

Crystals with the diamond structure twin according to the spinel twin law, a rotation of 180° about a three-fold axis. Let a unit vector along this axis be called **t**. Then for reflections with either **g** parallel to **t** or perpendicular to **t**, both members of the twin pair will reflect simultaneously on the topograph. For all other Bragg reflections, either one or the other member will be seen only (apart from accidental lattice coincidences). Thus with one topograph to show the whole crystal, and with two more topographs to show the shape of the twins separately, the internal twin composition surface can be traced [103]. In complicated situations, stereo-topographs and section topographs may be needed to make the spatial relations clear. Simple though this application of X-ray topography may be, it is not trivial. Twins in diamond may interpenetrate in a very complicated way. How they do so can be established only by X-ray topographs, and these may help to decide how difficult it would be to cut and polish the twinned stone. This twin-mapping technique has been applied to corundum crystals, flux-grown platelike crystals of which can show multiple twinning, the plate being divided into 30° or 60° sectors, adjacent sectors being twinned with respect to each other [157].

Parallel-lattice twins may be differentiated topographically when the common lattice plane differs in structure factor between one twin and the other. For Dauphiné twinning in quartz, the structure factor pair for the reflection $30\bar{3}1$ (very strong) and $30\bar{3}\bar{1}$ (very weak) are excellent discriminators [158]. For Brazil twinning in quartz, discrimination on topographs can be effected by making use of anomalous dispersion. This has been demonstrated with $CrK\alpha$ radiation and the $11\bar{2}1$ and $\bar{1}\bar{1}21$ reflection pair [158].

The extension of the technique to polytypes is straightforward. It has been applied to silicon carbide [159,160], and to zinc sulphide (Mardix and Lang, to be published).

9.2. *Absorption topography*

Any experimental arrangement that will produce high resolution diffraction topographs should certainly be capable of taking high resolution absorption topographs. Applying the two techniques to the same specimen can be very informative. Variation of X-ray tube target element, tube kilovoltage and filtration will generally provide the quality of X-rays to give the desired discrimination in absorption topography, but a crystal monochromatisation technique could be used if necessary, by obvious modification of one of the arrangements discussed in 2.4. To ensure a high degree of uniformity of intensity and quality of irradiation of the specimen, the addition of specimen or monochromator translating mechanism might be desirable.

Absorption topography of flux-grown corundum crystals identified flux inclusions as the cause of lattice strains and dislocation generation. In synthetic diamond, absorption topography revealed nickel-rich material in the form of globular inclusions 2 to 15 microns in diameter, and also in a very finely divided state in sheets which appeared to be the trace of the outward motion of a crystal edge during growth. The same absorbing material was present as thin films on flat crystal faces. The chemical identification was performed by comparing absorption topographs produced with crystal monochromatised radiations such as CuKα and CuKβ [85]. In the case of absorption topography of coated diamonds [91] chemical identification could not be so precise: it was concluded that the major impurity elements in the coat responsible for the absorption were either quite light, with atomic numbers up to and including titanium, or were relatively heavy, such as zirconium and heavier elements. Iron was not a significant component of diamond coat. On the other hand in amethyst quartz, the presence of iron was demonstrated by absorption topography. It was found to be preferentially distributed in major rhombohedral growth sectors, with a fine-scale variation in concentration that correlated in a remarkable way with the laminations of repeated Brazil twinning in the major rhombohedral growth sectors [161,162].

9.3. Oscillating crystals

This is a highly specialised field of application of X-ray topography which has its origins in the experiments of Fox and Carr, long ago in 1931 [163], who found an increase in integrated reflection from quartz plates which were piezoelectrically excited into oscillation. The X-ray topograph of a vibrating quartz crystal shows enhanced intensity of reflection from regions where $g \cdot u$ has a strong spatial gradient, u being the displacement due to the oscillation. Active modes, both wanted and unwanted ones, can be identified from X-ray topographs, and mode-coupling can be investigated. Such an excellent review of this work, including much material of general X-ray topographic interest, has been written recently by Spencer [164], that no more need be said upon the subject here.

9.4. Surface strains

Again an observation of many years ago forms the background to the X-ray topographic work. This is the "Fukushima effect", an enhancement of diffracted intensity coming from the boundary between abraded (i.e. surface-damaged) and etched (i.e. damage-free) areas on quartz plates [165]. This ef-

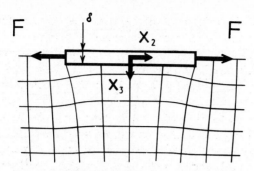

Fig. 18. Computed lattice distortion under a compressed surface layer.

fect can easily be demonstrated on X-ray topographs. It arises when the crystal is partially covered by a thin layer in a state of tension or compression. At the periphery of the layer the stress may partially relax, producing local lattice curvature. If the state of stress of the thin layer is isotropic in the plane of the layer than, at its periphery', it exerts a force **F** per unit length of periphery directed normal to the periphery and in the plane of the surface, as shown in fig. 18.

This situation has attracted interest recently through the study of semiconductor crystals which may have certain areas of their surfaces covered with oxide films or vapour-deposited layers. The sense of **F** (inwards or outwards) will depend upon the chemical nature of the layer, but in the case of abrasion patches **F** is always directed in the sense shown in fig. 18. The direction of **F** determines the relative visibility of the periphery in various Bragg reflections: in this way it can be confirmed that $|F|$ is parallel to the direction shown, and, in the isotropic case, the visibility of the periphery is zero when $\mathbf{g} \cdot \mathbf{F}$ is zero [17,166–168].

When strong anomalous transmission occurs there will be a reversal in contrast of one edge of the layer compared with the other, and also upon changing the sign of **g**. This effect enables the *sign* of **F** to be determined [17,169]. It is also possible to make reasonable estimates of the *magnitude* of **F**. This is best done under conditions of low absorption, i.e. short X-ray wavelength. The strong diffraction contrast then comes from interbranch scattering. The distance from the periphery within which strong interbranch scattering occurs can be calculated according to a tilt criterion similar to that used for estimating widths of dislocation (images (sect. 6.1), but one should include also the local lattice dilation. This leads to an expression for "effective tilt" like eq. (19). Then, for a particular reflection, one may calculate values of $\Delta\delta$ multiplied by the factor (Young's modulus/F) and plot these parameters as con-

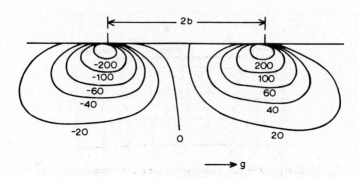

Fig. 19. Computed contours of "effective tilt", diamond, reflection 220, MoKα radiation.

tours as shown in fig. 19. One then matches the observed width of the band of blackening on the topograph with fig. 19 to select which value of this parameter best fits the experimental situation. Assuming that the critical value of $\Delta\delta$ for interbranch scattering is equivalent to one to two units change Δw (these two quantities being related by eq. (20)), the magnitude of F is then obtained.

10. X-ray moiré topography

The geometric interpretation of moiré patterns follows the same lines for X-ray, electron and light optics. When the radiation passes successively through two periodic media (1) and (2), whose reciprocal vectors are g_1 and g_2, the reciprocal vector of the moiré fringe system will be

$$G = g_1 - g_2 . \tag{21}$$

The magnitude, D, of the moiré fringe spacing is $|G|^{-1}$. Herein lies the strong interest of X-ray moiré patterns. Since large values of D can be observed (up to several mm), and on images several square centimetres in area, extremely small values of $g_1 - g_2$ may be measured. It is convenient to consider two special cases of moiré pattern, the pure "rotation" moiré pattern in which $|g_1| = |g_2|$ but in which these vectors make a small angle α with each other. In this case the moiré pattern has fringes of spacing $D = d/\alpha$ and they run parallel to the bisector of the small angle α between g_1 and g_2. The other special case is the "compression" moiré pattern, which is produced when g_1 and g_2 are parallel but there is a small difference between the corresponding spacings, d_1 and d_2

in the periodic media (1) and (2). The compression moiré pattern has its fringes parallel to the grating rulings or traces of Bragg planes in media (1) and (2), and its fringes have the spacing $D = d_1 d_2/(d_1 - d_2)$. From these expressions for D it will be seen that X-ray moiré topography is capable of measuring angles in the range of 10^{-7} to 10^{-8} radians, and relative differences of d in the same range, 10^{-7} to 10^{-8}.

There are two experimental approaches to X-ray moiré topography, the method of the X-ray interferometer, the invention of Bonse and Hart [170],

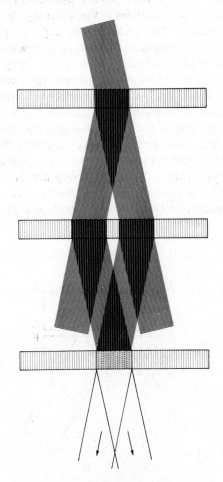

Fig. 20. The Bonse and Hart X-ray interferometer.

and the method of superposition of separate crystals of Brádler and Lang [171]. The principle of the Bonse and Hart interferometer is shown in fig. 20. It is cut from a monolithic block of perfect crystal, parts of which are milled away to leave three plates upstanding, seen in plan in the figure, and shown diffracting by symmetrical transmission a beam of X-rays incident from above the diagram. The top plate splits the X-ray beam. The middle plate functions analogously to the mirrors of a Michelson interferometer; and the lower plate diffracts the recombined beams with a partition of intensity between beams emerging down and leftwards and down and rightwards which depends upon the phase of the nodes and antinodes of the stationary wave pattern at its entrance surface relative to its own Bragg-reflecting-plane periodicity. This elegant and ingenious device has several embodiments which have been discussed by its inventors [172], and its powers have recently been demonstrated in applications to silicon, germanium and highly perfect quartz [21].

The method of superimposition of separate crystals stemmed from observations of moiré patterns produced by cracks in quartz [173], and from the strong X-ray topographic contrast exhibited by stacking faults, the latter being of interest since a moiré pattern can be regarded as that produced by a stacking fault with spatially varying fault vector. The Brádler and Lang arrangement is shown in plan in fig. 21. It is simply the X-ray analogue of the situation occurring with superimposition of simultaneously diffracting crystals in the electron microscope. However, the problem of aligning the separate crys-

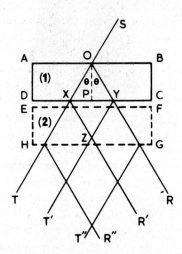

Fig. 21. Crystals superimposed to produce X-ray moiré patterns.

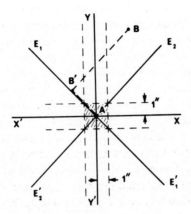

Fig. 22. Reciprocal space geometry showing crystal-aligning method.

tals so that they both simultaneously reflect X-rays, and of keeping G within the very small permissible range, is more formidable in the X-ray than in the electron case. It was solved [171] by the procedure indicated in fig. 22. This is a view in reciprocal space containing A, the tip of g_1, with g_1 normal to the drawing. The tip of g_2 is indicated by B. The problem is to bring B to coincide with A, at least within the limits of the shaded area. On the scale of this drawing the traces of intersections of the Ewald sphere with the plane of the drawing may be represented by straight lines. The trick used in bringing B to coincide with A is to rotate the crystal pair bodily about their mean g-vector. This, in the frame of reference of the crystals, would bring the Ewald sphere traces into the positions E_1E_1' or E_2E_2', say. Since the *perpendicular* distance of B from the Ewald sphere can be found from the width and intensity of the reflection profile of the Bragg reflection by the crystal pair, the two Cartesian components of G can be minimised by adjustments performed with the Ewald sphere successively in positions E_1E_1' and E_2E_2'. An example of the fringe pattern obtained by this method using perfect silicon crystals is shown in fig. 23. Excellent regularity and visibility of the fringes is evident. More interesting are experiments which exploit the capabilities of this technique to take topographs of a pair of crystals separately, then to superimpose them to produce a moire pattern. Applications to natural quartz have been described [174]; figs. 24 and 25 show an application to synthetic quartz containing dislocations and impurity-cell fault surfaces. Of course, only dislocations which outcrop on either face CD or EF (fig. 21) will produce dislocations in the moiré fringe pattern.

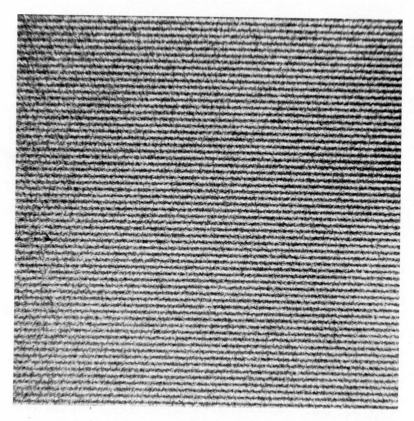

Fig. 23. Rotation moiré pattern, silicon, reflection 220, MoKα radiation, field 1 mm square.

X-ray moiré fringe patterns can also occur in cases of superimposition of nearly parallel platelet crystals of cadmium sulphide crystals grown from the vapour. These have been studied by Chikawa [175].

11. Future developments

Two impending developments may be mentioned. The first requires no new instrumention: means for its realisation are already becoming available quite

Fig. 24. Synthetic quartz with impurity-cell-wall fault fringes and dislocations. Field width 1 mm.

widely. It is concerned with the combination of X-ray topographic experiments with *high-voltage* transmission electron microscopy. An inspection of the figures for *minimum* thickness for X-ray diffraction contrast from dislocations, as given in 6.1, shows that there is no gap of significance between these and the *maximum* thicknesses at which electron diffraction contrast of individual dislocations is reasonably clear when electron microscopes operating at 0.5 MeV and above are used. The combination of X-ray topographic and high-voltage electron microscope observations on the *same* specimen should be highly informative, and one may hope that it will serve as a valuable link in relating microscopic properties with the macroscopic.

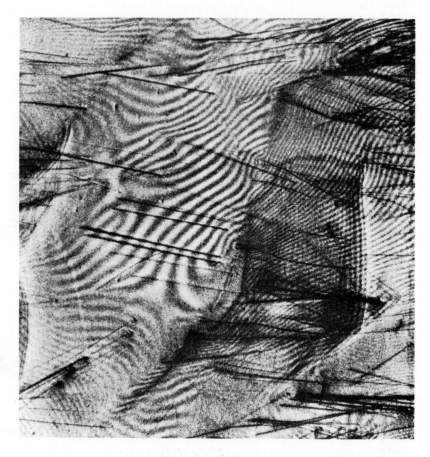

Fig. 25. Moiré pattern formed by superimposing specimen of fig. 24 upon a similar specimen.

The second impending development concerns electronic intensification of X-ray topographic images. Promising results have already been obtained by Chikawa using an X-ray sensitive Vidicon tube linked with a standard television display system [176]. The special Vidicon tube has a beryllium window and a PbO photoconductive target. An alternative approach to image intensification for X-ray topography is to couple optically a multi-stage optical image intensifier to a fine-grain X-ray phosphor or single-crystal X-ray scintillator, in an appropriate modification of a technique already successfully demonstrated in the case of Laue patterns [177]. This system has now been used in X-ray topography [178].

References

[1] B.W.Batternman and H.Cole, Rev. Mod. Phys. 36 (1964) 681.

[2] G.N.Ramachandran, Proc. Indian Acad. Sci. A 19 (1944) 280.

[3] L.G.Schulz, Trans. AIME 200 (1954) 1082.

[4] T.Fujiwara, S.Dohi and J.Sunada, Jap. J. Appl. Phys. 3 (1964) 129.

[5] L.Fiermans, Phys. Stat. Sol. 6 (1964) 169.

[6] R.A.Coyle, A.M.Marshall, J.H.Auld and N.A.McKinnon, Brit. J. Appl. Phys. 8 (1957) 79.

[7] D.Jaffrey and G.A.Chadwick, Phil. Mag. 18 (1968) 573.

[8] C.S.Barrett, Trans. AIME 161 (1945) 15.

[9] W.F.Berg, Naturwissenschaften 19 (1931) 391.

[10] J.B.Newkirk, Phys. Rev. 110 (1958) 1465.

[11] J.B.Newkirk, Trans. AIME 215 (1959) 483.

[12] S.B.Austerman and J.B.Newkirk, Advances in X-ray Analysis, Vol. 10 (Plenum Press, 1967) p. 134.

[13] J.M.Lommel and M.L.Kronberg, In: Direct Observation of Imperfections in Crystals, eds. Newkirk and Wernick (Interscience, 1962) p. 543.

[14] N.Wooster and W.A.Wooster, Nature 155 (1945) 786.

[15] A.Merlini and A.Guinier, Bull. soc. franc. mineral. crist. 80 (1957) 147.

[16] A.R.Lang, Acta Cryst. 10 (1957) 839.

[17] F.C.Frank, B.R.Lawn, A.R.Lang and E.M.Wilks, Proc. Roy. Soc. A 301 (1967) 239.

[18] W.L.Bond and J.Andrus, Amer. Mineralogist 37 (1952) 622.

[19] U.Bonse and E.Kappler, Z.Naturforsch. 13a (1958) 348.

[20] U.Bonse, Z. f. Physik 184 (1965) 71.

[21] M.Hart, Science Progress (Oxford) 56 (1968) 429.

[22] K.Kohra and S.Kikuta, Acta Cryst. A24 (1968) 200.

[23] U.Bonse and M.Hart, Appl. Phys. Letters 7 (1965) 238.

[24] M.Hart and A.R.Lang, Acta Cryst. 19 (1965) 73.

[25] K.Kohra, M.Yoshimatsu and I.Shimizu, In: Direct Observation of Imperfection in Crystals, eds. Newkirk and Wernick (Interscience, 1962) p. 461.

[26] K.Kohra and Y.Takano, Jap. J. Appl. Phys. 7 (1968) 982.

[27] G.Borrmann, W.Hartwig and H.Irmler, Z.Naturforsch. 13a (1958) 423.

[28] H.Barth and R.Hosemann, Z. Naturforsch. 13a (1958) 792.

[29] V.Gerold and F.Meier, Z. f. Physik 155 (1959) 387.

[30] M.C.Wittels, F.A.Sherrill and F.W.Young Jr., Appl. Phys. Letters 2 (1963) 127.

[31] F.W.Young Jr., F.A.Sherrill and M.C.Wittels, J. Appl. Phys. 36 (1965) 2225.

[32] F.W.Young Jr., T.O.Baldwin, A.E.Merlini and F.A.Sherrill, Advances in X-ray Analysis, Vol. 9 (Plenum Press, 1966) p. 1.

[33] A.Merlini and F.W.Young Jr., J. de Physique 27 (1966) C3-219.

[34] F.W.Young Jr. J. Phys. Chem. Solids Supplement No. 1 (1967) 789.

[35] F.W.Young Jr. and F.A.Sherrill, Can. J. of Phys. 45 (1967) 757.

[36] G.Borrmann and W.Hartwig, Z. Kristallogr. 121 (1965) 401.

[37] G.Hildebrandt, Phys. Stat. Sol. 24 (1967) 245.

[38] P.P.Ewald and Y.Heno, Acta Cryst. A24 (1968) 5.

[39] Y.Heno and P.P.Ewald, Acta Cryst. A24 (1968) 16.

[40] P.Penning, Advances in X-ray Analysis, Vol. 10 (Plenum Press, 1967) 67.

[41] P.Penning and D.Polder, Philips Research Reports 23 (1968) 1.

[42] P.Penning, Philips Research Reports 23 (1968) 12.

[43] A.R.Lang, Acta Met. 5 (1957) 358.

[44] A.R.Lang, Acta Cryst. 10 (1957) 252.

[45] N.Kato, Acta Cryst. 13 (1960) 349.

[46] N.Kato and A.R.Lang, Acta Cryst. 12 (1959) 787.

[47] N.Kato, Acta Cryst. 14 (1961) 526, 627.

[48] N.Kato, In: Crystallography and Crystal Perfection, ed. G.N.Ramachandran (Academic Press, 1963) p. 153.

[49] A.Authier, A.D.Milne and M.Sauvage, Phys. Stat. Sol. 26 (1968) 469.

[50] A.R.Lang, Acta Cryst. 12 (1959) 249.

[51] A.R.Lang, J. Appl. Phys. 30 (1959) 1748.

[52] K.Haruta, J. Appl. Phys. 36 (1965) 1789.

[53] N.Kato, Acta Cryst. 16 (1963) 276, 282.

[54] P.Penning and D.Polder, Philips Research Reports 16 (1961) 419.

[55] M.Hart, Ph. D.Thesis, Bristol (1963).

[56] A.R.Lang and M.Polcarová, Proc. Roy. Soc. A285 (1965) 297.

[57] A.R.Lang, Brit. J. Appl. Phys. 14 (1963) 904.

[58] A.R.Lang, Proc. Roy. Soc. A278 (1964) 234.

[59] H.P.Layer and R.D.Deslattes, J. Appl. Phys. 37 (1966) 3631.

[60] G.H.Schwuttke, J. Appl. Phys. 36 (1965) 2712.

[61] K.Kohra and Y.Takano, Jap. J. Appl. Phys. 7 (1968) 982.

[62] G.Dionne, J. Appl. Phys. 38 (1967) 4094.

[63] S.Hosoya, Jap. J. Appl. Phys. 7 (1968) 1.

[64] N.Kato, Acta Cryst. 11 (1958) 885.

[65] P.P.Ewald, Acta Cryst. 11 (1958) 888.

[66] R.D.Heidenreich, Phys. Rev. 62 (1942) 291.

[67] E.Kinder, Naturwissenschaft 31 (1943) 149.

[68] N.Kato, J. Phys. Soc. Japan 8 (1953) 350.

[69] H.Nierhs, Z. Phys. 138 (1954) 570.

[70] N.Kato, Acta Cryst. A25 (1969) 119.

[71] M.Hart and A.D.Milne, Acta Cryst. A25 (1969) 134.

[72] H.Hattori, H.Kuriyama and N.Kato, J. Phys. Soc., Japan 20 (1965) 1047.

[73] N.Kato, J. Phys. Soc., Japan 18 (1963) 1875.

[74] N.Kato, J. Phys. Soc., Japan 19 (1964) 67, 971.

[75] Y.Ando and N.Kato, Acta Cryst. 21 (1966) 284.

[76] M.Hart, Z. f. Phys. 189 (1966) 269.

[77] P.Penning and A.H.Goemans 18 (1968) 297.

[78] A.Howie and M.J.Whelan, Proc. Roy. Soc. A267 (1962) 206.

[79] M.Wilkens and F.Meier, Naturforsch. 18a (1963) 26.

[80] A.Authier, Advances in X-ray Analysis, Vol. 10 (Plenum Press, 1967) p. 9.

[81] F.C.Frank and A.R.Lang, In: Physical Properties of Diamond, ed. R.Berman (Clarendon Press, 1965) Ch. III, p. 69.

[82] A.R.Lang, Advances in X-ray Analysis, Vol. 10 (Plenum Press, 1967) p. 91.

[83] S.H.Emara, B.R.Lawn and A.R.Lang, Phil. Mag. 19 (1969) 7.

[84] F.C.Frank and A.R.Lang, Phil. Mag. 4 (1959) 383.

[85] Y.Kamiya and A.R.Lang, J. Appl. Phys. 36 (1965) 579.

[86] R.A.Duckett , M. Sc. Thesis, Bristol (1966).

[87] S.Ikeno, H.Maruyama and N.Kato, J. Cryst. Growth 3, 4 (1968) 683.

[88] A.R.Lang, J. Phys. Chem. Solids, Supplement No. 1 (1967) 833.

[89] A.R.Lang and V.F.Miuscov, In: Growth of Crystals, ed. N.N. Sheftal, Vol. 7 (Plenum Press, 1969).

[90] C.C.Wang and S.H.McFarlane III, J. Cryst. Growth 3, 4 (1968) 485.

[91] Y.Kamiya and A.R.Lang, Phil. Mag. 11 (1965) 347.

[92] C.E.Hayes and W.W.Webb, SCIENCE 147 (1965) 44.

[93] W.W.Webb and C.E.Hayes, Phil. Mag. 16 (1967) 909.

[94] A.Higashi, M.Oguro and A.Fukuda, J. Cryst. Growth 3, 4 (1968) 728.

[95] A.R.Lang and G.Meyrick, Phil. Mag. 4 (1959) 878.

[96] A.Authier, C.B.Rogers and A.R.Lang, Phil. Mag. 12 (1965) 547.

[97] B.Nøst, Phil. Mag. 11 (1965) 183.

[98] B.Nøst and G.Sørensen, Phil. Mag. 13 (1966) 1075.

[99] B.Nøst, G.Sørensen and E.Nes, J. Phys. Chem. Solids, Supplement No. 1 (1967) 801.

[100] B.Nøst and E.Nes, Acta Met. 17 (1969) 13.

[101] M.Fremiot, B.Baudelet and G.Champier, J. Cryst. Growth 3, 4 (1968) 711.

[102] S.H.McFarlane III and C.Elbaum, Appl. Phys. Letters 7 (1965) 43.

[103] A.R.Lang, Disc. Faraday Soc. 38 (1964) 292.

[104] V.F.Miuscov and A.R.Lang, Kristallografiya 8 (1963) 652.

[105] A.R.Lang and V.F.Miuscov, Phil. Mag. 10 (1964) 263.

[106] A.R.Lang and G.D.Miles, J. Appl. Phys. 36 (1965) 1803.

[107] C.A.May and J.S.Shah, J. Material Science 4 (1969) 179.

[108] S.B.Austerman, J.B.Newkirk and D.K.Smith, J. Appl. Phys. 36 (1965) 3815.

[109] W.C.Dash, J. Appl. Phys. 30 (1959) 459.

[110] A.E.Jenkinson and A.R.Lang, In: Direct Observation of Imperfections in Crystals, eds. Newkirk and Wernick (Interscience, 1962) p. 471.

[111] A.Authier and A.R.Lang, J. Appl. Phys. 35 (1964) 1956.

[112] G.H.Schwuttke, J. Appl. Phys. 33 (1962) 2760.

[113] G.H.Schwuttke, J. Appl. Phys. 34 (1963) 1662.

[114] G.H.Schwuttke and H.J.Queisser, J. Appl. Phys. 33 (1962) 1540.

[115] I.A.Blech, E.S.Meieran and H.Sello, Appl. Phys. Letters 7 (1965) 176.

[116] G.H.Schwuttke and H.Rupprecht, J. Appl. Phys. 37 (1966) 1167.

[117] H.Rupprecht and G.H.Schwuttke, J. Appl. Phys. 37 (1966) 2862.

[118] G.H.Schwuttke and J.M.Fairfield, J. Appl. Phys. 37 (1966) 4394.

[119] S.O'Hara, J. Appl. Phys. 35 (1964) 409.

[120] T.N.Tucker and G.H.Schwuttke, Appl. Phys. Letters 9 (1966) 219.

[121] R.Gevers, J.van Landuyt and S.Amelinckx, Phys. Stat. Sol. 11 (1965) 689.

[122] H.D.Megaw, Proc. Roy. Soc. A 259 (1960) 59.

[123] A.Authier, Phys. Stat. Sol. 27 (1968) 77.

[124] N.Kato, K.Usami and T.Katagawa, Advances in X-ray Analysis, Vol. 10 (Plenum Press, 1967) p. 46.

[125] M.J.Whelan and P.B.Hirsch, Phil. Mag. 2 (1957) 1121, 1303.

[126] H.Hashimoto, A.Howie and M.J.Whelan, Phil. Mag. 5 (1960) 967.

[127] H.Hashimoto, A.Howie and M.J.Whelan, Proc. Roy. Soc. A 269 (1962) 80.

[128] K.Kohra and M.Yoshimatsu, J. Phys. Soc. Japan 17 (1962) 1041.

[129] M.Yoshimatsu, Jap. J. Appl. Phys. 3 (1964) 94.

[130] G.H.Schwuttke and V.Sils, J. Appl. Phys. 34 (1963) 3127.

[131] B.Lawn, Y.Kamiya and A.R.Lang, Phil. Mag. 12 (1965) 177.

[132] G.R.Booker, Disc. Faraday Sco. 38 (1964) 298.

[133] M.Sauvage and A.Authier, Phys. Stat. Sol. 12 (1965) K73.

[134] M.Sauvage and A.Authier, Bull. Soc. frac. minér. crist. 88 (1965) 379.

[135] A.Authier and M.Sauvage, J. Physique 27 Suppl. 7/8 (1966) C3-137.

[136] M.Yoshimatsu, Jap. J. Appl. Phys. 5 (1966) 29.

[137] A.R.Lang and V.F.Miuscov, J. Appl. Phys. 38 (1967) 2477.

[138] M.Polcarová and J.Kaczér, Phys. Stat. Sol. 21 (1967) 635.

[139] M.Polcarová and J.Gemperlová, Phys. Stat. Sol. 32 (1969) 769.

[140] M.Polcarová and A.R.Lang, Bull. soc. franç. minér. crist. 91 (1968) 645.

[141] M.Schlenker, P.Brisonneau and J.-P.Perrier, Bull. soc. franç. minér. crist. 91 (1968) 553.

[142] B.Roessler, J.J.Kramer and M.Kuriyama, Phys. Stat. Sol. 11 (1965) 117.

[143] B.Roessler, Phys. Stat. Sol. 20 (1967) 713.

[144] M.Kuriyama and G.M.McManus, Phys. Stat. Sol. 25 (1968) 667.

[145] J.R.Patel, K.A.Jackson and J.F.Dillon Jr., J. Appl. Phys. 39 (1968) 3767.

[146] S.Saito, J. Phys. Soc. Japan 17 (1962) 1287.

[147] T.Yamada, S.Saito and Y.Shimomura, J. Phys. Soc. Japan 21 (1966) 672.

[148] I.A.Blech and E.S.Meieran, Phil. Mag. 14 (1966) 275.

[149] M.W.Vernon and F.J.Spooner, J. Materials Science 2 (1967) 415.

[150] J.Čáslavský and M.Polcarová, Czech. J. Phys. B 14 (1964) 454.

[151] A.Authier and J.F.Petroff, Comptes rendus acad. sci. Paris 258 (1964) 4238.

[152] S.Suzuki and M.Takagi, J. Phys. Soc. Japan 21 (1966) 554.

[153] A.Authier, Bull. soc. franç. minér. scrist. 91 (1968) 666.

[154] K.M.Merz, J. Appl. Phys. 31 (1960) 147.

[155] C.Bousquet, M.Lambert, A.M.Quittet and A.Guinier, Acta Cryst. 16 (1963) 989.

[156] M.Polcarová and A.R.Lang, Appl. Phys. Letters 1 (1962) 13.

[157] C.A.Wallace and E.A.D.White, J. Phys. Chem. Solids, Suppl. No. 1 (1967) 431.

[158] A.R.Lang, Appl. Phys. Letters 7 (1965) 168.

[159] W.J.Takei and M.H.Francombe, Brit. J. Appl. Phys. 18 (1967) 1589.

[160] B.J.Isherwood and C.A.Wallace, J. Appl. Cryst. 1 (1968) 145.

[161] C.Frondel, Dana's System of Mineralogy, Vol. III, Silica Minerals (Wiley, 1962) p. 171.

[162] H.H.Schlössin and A.R.Lang, Phil. Mag. 12 (1965) 283.

[163] G.W.Fox and P.H.Carr, Phys. Rev. 37 (1931) 1622.

[164] W.J.Spencer, In: Physical Acoustics, ed. W.P.Mason, vol. 5 (Academic Press, 1968) Ch. 3.

[165] E.Fukushima, Acta. Cryst. 7 (1954) 459.

[166] E.S.Meieran and I.A.Blech, J. Appl. Phys. 36 (1965) 3162.

[167] I.A.Blech and E.S.Meieran, J. Appl. Phys. 38 (1967) 2913.

[168] G.H.Schwuttke and J.K.Howard, J. Appl. Phys. 39 (1968) 1581.

[169] E.S.Meieran and I.A.Blech, Phys. Stat. Sol. 29 (1968) 653.

[170] U.Bonse and M.Hart, Appl. Phys. Letters 6 (1965) 155.

[171] I.Brádler and A.R.Lang, Acta Cryst. A24 (1968) 246.
[172] U.Bonse and M.Hart, Appl. Phys. Letters 7 (1965) 99; Z. Physik 188 (1965) 154;
          Z. Physik 190 (1966) 455; Z. Physik 194 (1966) 1; Acta Cryst. A24 (1968) 290.
[173] A.R.Lang and V.F.Miuscov, Appl. Phys. Letters 7 (1965) 214.
[174] A.R.Lang, Nature, London, 220 (1968) 652.
[175] J.-I.Chikawa, Appl. Phys. Letters 7 (1965) 193; J. Phys. Chem. Solids, Supplement
          No. 1 (1967) 817.
[176] J.-I.Chikawa, Appl. Phys. Letters 13 (1968) 387.
[177] K.Reifsnider and R.E.Green Jr., Rev. Sci. Instr. 39 (1968) 1651.
[178] A.R.Lang and K.Reifsnider, Appl. Phys. Letters 15 (1969) 258.

CONTRAST OF IMAGES IN X-RAY TOPOGRAPHY

A.AUTHIER

Introduction

The topographic technique for studying imperfections in nearly perfect crystals was developed about 10 years ago by Lang [1], Newkirk [2], Bonse [3], Borrmann [4] among others. It is now widely used throughout the world and has received a great many applications. Its principle is based mainly on the difference in the intensities of the X-rays diffracted by deformed and perfect regions of the crystal.

It is the aim of this chapter to give the theoretical basis necessary for the interpretation of the contrast of the images of defects on X-ray topographs. The first part is devoted to the theory of the diffraction of X-rays by a perfect crystal, the second one to the principles and classification of the various topographic techniques, the third one to the theory of the contrast of the images of defects.

1. Dynamical theory of X-ray diffraction

1.1. *Kinematical theory*

Two main theories have been developed to interpret the intensities of the X-rays diffracted by a crystal: the geometric, or kinematical, theory and the dynamical theory.

In the kinematical theory, it is assumed that the amplitude of the X-rays incident on all the diffracting centers of the crystal is the same, thus neglecting the amplitude diffracted by the first layers of the crystal. This leads to a very simplified calculation of the global intensity diffracted by the crystal. This assumption is based on the fact that the interaction of the photons with

matter is very weak and that the scattering amplitude of X-rays by an atom
is always small. It is however only valid for very thin crystals, for a crystal
made of a mosaic of thin crystallites or, more generally speaking, a very imperfect crystal. Its validity is impaired when the thickness of the perfect regions of the crystal excedes some limiting value: when comparing the intensity diffracted by the crystal to the theoretical value predicted by the kinematical theory, one then observes a reduction in the intensity which has been
called *extinction effect.*

When studying the diffraction by a thick perfect crystal, one has to take
into account all the interactions between the incident and diffracted waves
and the crystal. This is precisely what is done by the dynamical theory, and it
can be shown that for very thin crystals or highly deformed ones the results
of the dynamical theory tend asymptotically towards those of the kinematical
theory.

1.2. *Bases of the dynamical theory* [5]

The interaction between the incoming electromagnetic waves and matter is
mainly that with the electrons. The interaction with the protons can be neglected. We shall assume a continuous distribution of the negative charge and
that it is possible to define a dielectric susceptibility χ in every point of the
crystal. An electron in an electromagnetic field will oscillate and become an
emitting dipole. The medium becomes polarized and it is possible to show
that the corresponding dielectric susceptibility is equal to

$$\chi = -R\lambda^2\rho/\pi \tag{1}$$

R is the classical radius of the electron, ρ the electronic density and λ the X-
ray wave length.

Let us now consider a crystalline medium such as has been defined above
and bathed by an electromagnetic radiation. We shall assume the crystal to be
infinite and shall look for the propagation conditions of an electromagnetic
wave within the crystal. At each point, the values of the magnetic field and
induction, the electric field and displacement should satisfy Maxwell's equations. By combining these equations, it is possible to obtain the propagation
equation of the electromagnetic wave in the medium. Its shape is that of any
propagation equation but is more complex because electromagnetic waves are
vector waves. We shall however study here the propagation equation for a
scalar wave such as an electronic wave because it is simpler and its results are
valid for each component of the electric displacement:

$$\Delta\psi = \frac{\epsilon}{\epsilon_o}\frac{1}{c^2}\frac{\partial^2\psi}{\partial t^2} = \frac{1+\chi}{c^2}\frac{\partial^2\psi}{\partial t^2} \tag{2}$$

ϵ and ϵ_o are dielectric constants of the medium and vacuum, respectively. c is the velocity of light, χ is the dielectric susceptibility of the medium and ψ the amplitude of the wave.

Eq. (2) is a linear, homogeneous second order partial derivative equation. If we know any two particular solutions ψ_1 and ψ_2, any linear combination

$$\psi = A_1\psi_1 + A_2\psi_2 \tag{3}$$

is also a solution. Our problem is to find all possible particular solutions. Boundary conditions will show which ones are to be used and the values of A_1 and A_2.

1.3. Propagation in a medium with a continuous susceptibility

If the wave propagates in vacuum, the simplest solution is of course a plane wave

$$\psi = \psi_o \exp 2\pi i(\nu t - \mathbf{k} \cdot \mathbf{r}) \tag{4}$$

where $|\mathbf{k}| = k = \nu/c = 1/\lambda$. Either the wave length or the frequency is arbitrarily chosen.

If the wave propagates in a medium with a susceptibility χ, a possible solution is similarily

$$\psi = \psi_o \exp 2\pi i(\nu t - \mathbf{K} \cdot \mathbf{r}) \tag{4'}$$

where

$$|\mathbf{K}| = K = (\nu/c)\sqrt{1+\chi} = k\sqrt{1+\chi}. \tag{5}$$

$\sqrt{1+\chi}$ is the index of refraction of the medium. As is usual in physics, one introduces an imaginary part to the dielectric constant to take the absorption of the wave in the medium into account. This can be justified a posteriori: let us assume the wave is propagating along Oz, parallel to $\mathbf{K}$ in a non dispersive medium. If the intensity of the wave is $|\psi_o|^2$ when the wave front goes through the origin, after a path z, its intensity $|\psi|^2$ is given by

$$\frac{|\psi|^2}{|\psi_o|^2} = \exp(2\pi\chi_i kz) \tag{6}$$

assuming the imaginary part to be very small. Expression (6) is analogous to an absorption factor $\exp(-\mu z)$ where μ is the linear absorption coefficient; one deduces

$$\chi_i = -\mu/2\pi k . \tag{7}$$

The wave vector of any plane wave of frequency ν propagating in the medium has a given value, whatever the wave, its direction is arbitrary. If one of its end-points is at the origin O of the reciprocal lattice the other one lies on a sphere centered in O and with radius K.

1.4. *Propagation in a medium with a periodic susceptibility*
   In a perfect crystal without any thermal agitation nor any internal or external applied strain, the electric susceptibility is a triply periodic function of the space coordinates. It can be expanded into Fourier series

$$\chi = \sum_h \sum_k \sum_l \chi_{hkl} \exp(2\pi i h \cdot r) \tag{8}$$

h = OH reciprocal lattice vector; h, k, l are the coordinates of H. As a simplification, we shall write the expansion with only one index, h.
   Expression (1) shows that the electric susceptibility is proportional to the electron density. We have therefore

$$\chi_h = -R\lambda^2 NF_h/\pi V \tag{9}$$

where F_h is the structure factor related to reciprocal lattice point H and V the volume of the unit cell.
   According to Floquet's theorem, if the coefficient χ in eq. (2) is periodic, the solution has the same periodicity and takes the form

$$\psi = \psi_o [\exp 2\pi i(\nu t - \mathbf{K} \cdot \mathbf{r})] F \tag{10}$$

where F has the same periodicity as χ. This induces to look for a solution of the following type

$$\psi = \exp 2\pi i(\nu t - \mathbf{K_o \cdot r}) \sum_h \psi_h \exp(2\pi i \mathbf{h \cdot r}) . \tag{10'}$$

This function, called Bloch function, can also be written

$$\psi = \exp 2\pi i \nu t \sum_h \psi_h \exp(-2\pi i \mathbf{K}_h \cdot \mathbf{r}) \tag{10''}$$

with

$$\mathbf{K}_h = \mathbf{K_o} - \mathbf{h} . \tag{11}$$

A particular solution ψ of the propagation equation can thus be considered as a superposition of plane waves of which the wave vectors are related by reciprocal lattice translations. This superposition is a *wave-field*. The basic properties of the propagation of X-rays in a perfect crystal can be interpreted in terms of wave-fields. Since they were first introduced by Ewald, we shall call them *Ewald waves*.

From (11) it can be seen that a wave-field is fully defined by the knowledge of anyone of the wave vectors of the field. Let us consider a given wave-field. Whatever the vector of the field chosen as $\mathbf{K_o}$, one always obtains the same set of vectors. Its choice is therefore arbitrary. If, as we have done in this section, one assumes the crystalline medium to be infinite, there is nothing to orient the choice. In the case of a real, finite crystal, there is an obvious choice: $\mathbf{K_o}$ is the vector of the field which is closest to that of the incident wave. It is determined by the boundary conditions (sect. 1.6). For this reason, we shall call *refracted wave* that with wave vector $\mathbf{K_o}$, *reflected waves* the others. Wave vectors $\mathbf{K_o}$, $\mathbf{K}_h$ ... drawn from the reciprocal lattice points O, H ... define a point P characteristic of the wave field (fig. 1). It has been called *tie-point* by Ewald. The important result we have obtained is *that the presence in the crystal of one wave out of the field induces that of all the other waves of the field*. To all possible Ewald waves which can propagate within the crystal are related their corresponding *tie-points*. The knowledge of their locus is very useful for the study of wave-fields. This locus is a surface in reciprocal space and we shall show how it can be found.

Generally speaking, two waves only have a non negligible amplitude in the X-ray case: the refracted wave and the wave reflected on *one* set of lattice planes. There can be many more in the electron diffraction case. Far from Bragg conditions, the amplitude of one wave only is non negligible and one

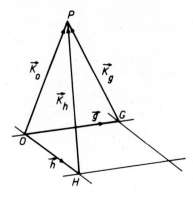

Fig. 1. Construction of the tie-point in reciprocal space.

wave only propagates through the crystal, it is the refracted wave, and the expansion reduces to

$$\psi = \psi_0 \exp 2\pi i(\nu t - \mathbf{K}_0 \cdot \mathbf{r}) .$$

A similar calculation to that which led to eq. (5) shows that

$$K_0 = k \sqrt{1 + \chi_0} \approx (1 + \chi_0/2) \, k . \tag{12}$$

The coefficients of the Fourier expansion of the electric susceptibility are very small, of the order of 10^{-5} or 10^{-6}. χ_0 is always negative and the index of refraction for X-rays, $1 + \chi_0/2$, is slightly smaller than one. The locus of point P in reciprocal space is here simply a sphere centered in O and with radius K_0. This surface is analogous to the indicatrix in optic which, in the case of an isotropic medium, is also a sphere.

When Bragg conditions are nearly fulfilled, two waves propagate through the crystal and the expansion can be written

$$\psi = \exp 2\pi i \nu t \, [\psi_0 \exp(-2\pi i \mathbf{K}_0 \cdot \mathbf{r}) + \psi_h \exp(-2\pi i \mathbf{K}_h \cdot \mathbf{r})] . \tag{13}$$

The two waves of the field are the refracted wave and the wave reflected on the set of lattice planes corresponding to the reciprocal lattice point H (OH=h).

If one puts expansions (13) and (8) in the propagation eqs. (2), one obtains a set of linear homogeneous equations in ψ_0, ψ_h. For it to admit a solution

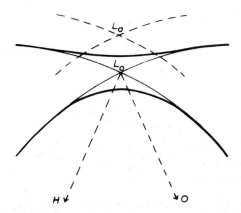

Fig. 2. Dispersion surface. La, Laue point; Lo, Lorentz point.

different from the trivial solution, its determinant should be put equal to zero. The corresponding equation is a relation between the lengths K_o and K_h of the two wave vectors of the field. It is therefore that of the locus of the tie-point P. This locus is called *dispersion surface*. It admits **OH** as revolution axis. Its intersection with a plane passing through O and H is a hyperbola of which the asymptotes are the tangents to the circles centered in O and H respectively and with radii $k(1+\chi_0/2)$ (fig. 2). The presence of the tie-point on one of these two circles corresponds to that of one wave only in the crystal; if it lies on the hyperbola *joining* the two circles, that is very near their intersection, it corresponds to the propagation of a wave field made of two waves with a non negligible amplitude. The ratio ψ_h/ψ_o of their amplitudes is obtained by solving the set of linear equations deduced from the propagation equation. The region in reciprocal space where the dispersion surface breaks away from the two spheres is very small with regard to the radius of the spheres. As mentioned above, its intersection with a plane passing through O and H is a hyperbola. Its diameter, $k\chi_h/\cos\theta$, is about 10^{-6} times the radius of the spheres. It is therefore fully justified to replace these spheres by their tangential planes. In all this region Bragg condition is practically fulfilled.

Let L_o or Lorentz point be the intersection of the two circles with radii $k(1+\chi_0/2)$. This value is equal to the wave number of a plane wave propagating alone in the crystal and it takes into account the refractive index $(1+\chi_0/2)$ of the crystal for X-rays. L_a, or Laue point, is the intersection of two circles centered in O and H and with radii equal to k. This is the wave number of a wave propagating in vacuum. L_a is the center of the Ewald sphere with radius $k = 1/\lambda$ which is used in the geometrical theory of X-ray diffraction where the refraction of X-rays by crystals is neglected. L_a is very close from one of the apices of the hyperbola. Noticing that the angle between asymptotes is 2θ, an obvious geometrical demonstration of Bragg's law can be found in triangle L_aOH

$$(OH/2 = 1/2d = L_aH \sin \theta = \sin \theta/\lambda) \, .$$

The points on the dispersion surface thus give a geometrical representation of all the solutions of the propagation equation, that is of all the wave-fields which can propagate through the crystal. Each wave field is defined by the wave vectors and the ratio of the amplitudes of its two waves.

Depending on whether the polarization of the electric displacement lies parallel or normal to the plane of the wave vectors, the dispersion surface has a slightly different position. We shall throughout neglect the effects due to polarization.

1.5. *Propagation of the energy, Borrmann effect*

We have seen above that when a plane wave is propagating through the crystal it can be represented by the end-point P of its wave vector, say $\mathbf{OP}^{\cdot}$. A second plane wave, of wave vector $\mathbf{HP}$, is necessarily associated to first one to make up a wave-field. Actually perfect plane waves never exist in the case of X-rays. An X-ray beam is always collimated and has a certain divergence. By means of a Fourier expansion, it can be resolved as a sum of continuous distribution of plane waves or *wave-packet*. If the beam propagates through a crystal, to each wave, a second wave should be associated and there is actually a packet of wave fields of wave vectors $\mathbf{OP}_x$, $\mathbf{HP}_x$ (fig. 3). Since the wave vectors $\mathbf{OP}_x$ lie very close, the corresponding waves interfere and their direction of propagation is along the normal to the locus of the end-points of the wave vectors, that is the normal to the dispersion surface. This is a very well known result in optics. It applies independently to the waves with wave vectors $\mathbf{HP}_x$, which shows that the reflected and refracted waves propagate simultaneously along the same path: the wave field has a physical reality. The propagation direction is different from that of the wave vectors and the medium behaves as a dispersive one, hence the name given to the locus of the tie-point of the wave field.

Both waves of a given field propagate along the same direction and interfere as is shown by eq. (13). This equation can also be written

$$\psi = \psi_o \exp 2\pi i(\nu t - \mathbf{K}_o \cdot \mathbf{r}) \left[1 + \frac{\psi_h}{\psi_o} \exp 2\pi i(\mathbf{OH} \cdot \mathbf{r}) \right] \qquad (14)$$

and the intensity of the wave field is equal to

$$|\psi|^2 = |\psi_o|^2 \left| 1 + \frac{\psi_h}{\psi_o} \exp 2\pi i(\mathbf{OH} \cdot \mathbf{r}) \right|^2 . \qquad (15)$$

It varies periodically in space and we have a system of stationary waves of which the nodal planes are parallel to the lattice planes and have the same spacing. This result is independent of the position of the tie-point on the dispersion surface. Far from Bragg's conditions, the ratio ψ_h/ψ_o decreases towards zero, $|\psi|^2$ tends towards $|\psi_o|^2$ and the interference effect becomes negligible. The position of the nodal planes depends on the sign of ψ_h/ψ_o only. It can be shown that this ratio takes values of opposite signs for the two branches of the dispersion surface. There are therefore two sets of stationary waves corresponding respectively to both branches. They are in opposition, the nodes of one set lying on the antinodes of the other. It is possible to show the nodes of electric field lie on lattice planes for branch 1. The absorption of the

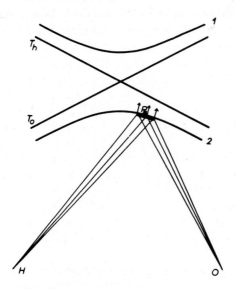

Fig. 3. Propagation direction of a wave packet.

corresponding wave fields is therefore very small. This effect has first been observed by Borrmann [6] and now bears his name. On the other hand, the antinodes lie on lattice planes for wave fields belonging to branch 2 of the dispersion surface. These wave fields are therefore highly absorbed. This effect is maximum when Bragg condition is exactly fulfilled. The intensities of both wave fields along the lattice planes are then respectively equal to

branch 1 $\psi_h = -\psi_o$ $|\psi|^2 \approx 0$

branch 2 $\psi_h = \psi_o$ $|\psi|^2 = 4|\psi_o|^2$.

After a large crystal thickness only those wave fields have a non negligible intensity which are less absorbed. Their tie-points lie in the neighbourhood of the apex of branch 1 of the dispersion surface. Their propagation direction is parallel to the lattice planes.

1.6. *Boundary conditions*

Up to now we have considered an infinite crystal and studied the properties of the wave-fields which can propagate within the crystal. We shall now study the case of a finite crystal and find out which wave-fields are actually excited by an incident wave. They are determined by the boundary conditions. The position of the tie-point is given by the condition of the continuity of the tangential component of the wave vectors (fig. 4). It applies to the wave vec-

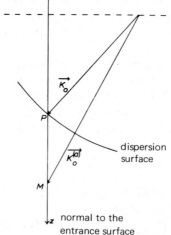

Fig. 4. Continuity of the tangential component of the wave vector.

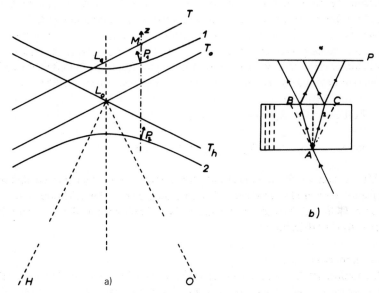

Fig. 5. Construction of the tie points excited by an incident plane wave (Laue case) .
a, reciprocal space; b, direct space.

tor $K_o^{(a)}$ of the incident wave and to that, K_o of the refracted wave. In the transmission, or Laue case (fig. 5), there is no reflected wave on the entrance surface of the crystal. In the reflection, or Bragg case (fig. 11) there is a reflected wave at the surface of the crystal. Its wave vector, $K_h^{(a)}$ and the reflected wave K_h within the crystal have same component along the surface of the crystal.

The locus of the end point M of the wave vector in vacuum is a circle centered in O and with radius $k = 1/\lambda$. It passes through the Laue point L_a (fig. 1). At the scale of the dispersion surface, it can be replaced by its tangent. The angle $\Delta\theta$ between the wave vector OM and OL_a, wave vector of that wave which would fulfill exactly Bragg conditions, is equal to

$$\Delta\theta = L_a M/k . \tag{16}$$

It is called the departure from Bragg's law. It is positive when the incidence angle is larger than Bragg's angle, θ_o.

The normal to the entrance surface, drawn from M, cuts the dispersion surface at the tie-point P_1 and P_2 characterizing the wave fields excited inside the crystal by the incident wave. If the direction of this normal lies within that angle between the asymptotes which contains the trace of the lattice planes, one is in the Laue case. The normal intersects *both* branches of the dispersion surface (fig. 5).

It is important to keep in mind that the departure from Bragg's law is defined as the angle between the wave vectors of two waves incident on the crystal. Its knowledge is not enough to determine the tie-points; the angle between the normal to the entrance surface and the lattice planes should also be known.

1.7. *Laue case*

(a) The incident beam has a very narrow divergence and is made of a small wave packet such as that of fig. 3. It excites two packets of wave fields within the crystal. To simplify the language we shall say two wave fields: a type 1 wave field less absorbed than normal absorption and a type 2 wave field which is more absorbed. Their tie-points and directions of propagation are represented on fig. 5a. They follow separate paths within the crystal giving rise to two independent beams. Each one is made of two waves: a refracted and a reflected one. When the beams reach the exit surface of the crystal, both waves are decoupled giving rise each to an independent beam outside the crystal. There are therefore four outgoing beams (fig. 5b). This result has indeed been observed experimentally with a setting described schematically on fig. 6a [7]. The four beams are shown in fig. 6b. When the incident beam is not polarized, there should actually be eight outgoing beams, four for each direction of polarization.

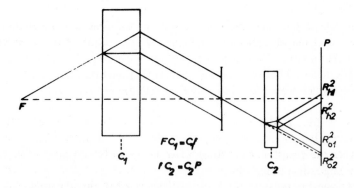

Fig. 6a. Separation of wave-fields (after [7]). Experimental set up.

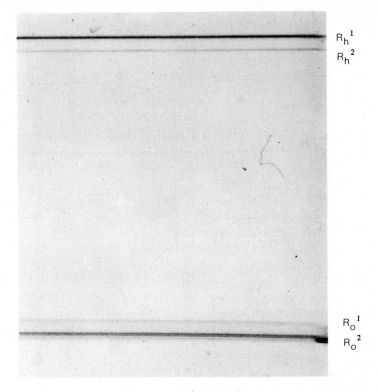

Fig. 6b. Separation of wave-fields (after [7]). R_h^1 reflected beam from type 1 wave-field, R_h^2 reflected beam from type 2 wave-field, R_0^1 refracted beam from type 1 wave-field, R_0^2 refracted beam from type 2 wave-field.

Let α_1 and α_2 be the angles between the paths of the wave fields with the lattice planes (fig. 5) and Y_1, Y_2 parameters proportional to the slopes of these paths

$$Y_1 = \mathrm{tg}\,\alpha_1 / \mathrm{tg}\,\theta \; ; \qquad Y_2 = \mathrm{tg}\,\alpha_2 / \mathrm{tg}\,\theta \, .$$

It is interesting to represent on a plot the variations of Y_1 or Y_2 with the departure from Bragg's law $\Delta\theta$ (fig. 7). When Bragg's condition is nearly fulfilled ($|\Delta\theta|$ very small), this dependence is roughly linear and that to small variations of $\Delta\theta$ correspond large differences in the path. This is readily understood since the slope of the normal to the hyperbola varies very rapidly near the apex. When the departure from Bragg's angle increases,

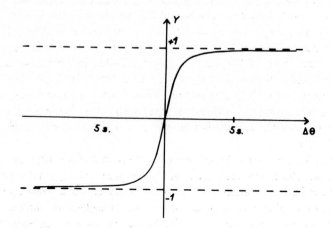

Fig. 7. Variation of the separation of wave-fields with departure from Bragg's law $\Delta\theta$.

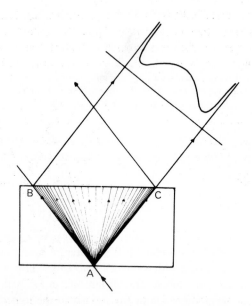

Fig. 8. Density of wave-fields in Borrmann triangle ABC.

the tie-point which moves along the hyperbola becomes close to the asymptote and the normal to the hyperbola nearly parallel to the reflected or refracted direction. To large variations of $\Delta\theta$ correspond then small differences only in the path direction. The density of paths is then very high (fig. 8), with the following experimental result: although, when the path direction lies close to either the reflected or refracted direction, the amplitude of the reflected wave is small, the intensity distribution in the reflected beam along the exit surface is than maximum. This effect, or *margin* effect, is less marked or even practically disappears for very absorbing material since only those wave fields which propagate along the lattice planes are relatively not much absorbed.

(b) The incident beam is very divergent. All points of the dispersion surface are then simultaneously excited and X-rays propagate along all possible paths. Let us describe the situation in the plane of incidence: these paths fill out a triangle ABC bordered by the incident, AB, and reflected, AC, directions respectively (fig. 9a). This triangle is called Borrmann triangle. Fig. 9b shows that along any given path AM in the triangle propagate *two* wave-fields of which the tie-points P_1, P_2 belong to *both* branches of the dispersion surface. They interfere and their intensity maxima lie on hyperbolae asymptotic to the incident and reflected direction (fig. 9a).

If the trace of the incident beam on the crystal is a straight line normal to the plane of incidence, these maxima lie on hyperbolic cylinders. For a plane parallel crystal, the exit surface will cut these cylinders along straight lines and one observes straight fringes in both the refracted and reflected beams (fig. 10).

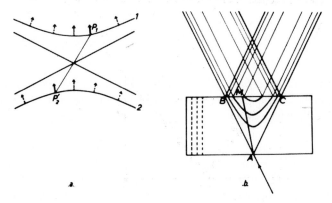

Fig. 9. Propagation of wave fields in the spherical wave case. a, reciprocal space; b, direct space.

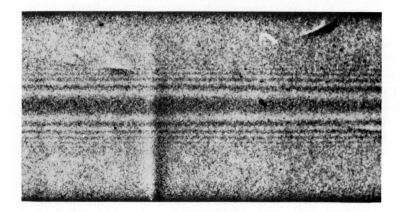

Fig. 10. Spherical wave Pendellosung fringes. Plane parallel Si crystal, 1 mm thick, 220 reflection MoKα.

Fig. 11. Spherical wave Pendellosung fringes. Wedge shaped NaNO₃ crystal, 200 reflection MoKα.

For a wedge shaped crystal, the exit surface will cut the hyperbolic cylinders along hyperbolae and one observes hyperbolic fringes (fig. 11). These fringes were first observed by Kato and Lang [8] and interpreted by Kato [9].

1.8. *Bragg case*

In Bragg case, the normal to the entrance surface lies within that angle between the two asymptotes to the dispersion surface which does not contain the trace of the lattice planes (fig. 12a). The normal to the entrance surface then cuts one branch only of the dispersion surface. For one of the two intersection points, the direction of propagation lies towards the inside of the crystal,

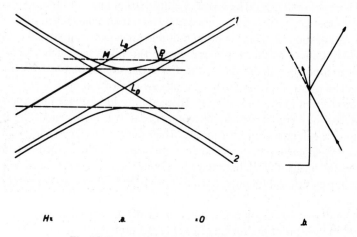

Fig. 12. Propagation of wave-fields-Bragg case.

but, for the other one, it lies towards the outside of the crystal. The only wave field excited in this case corresponds to the former: there is one beam reflected at the surface and one penetrating inside the crystal (fig. 12b). When the angle of incidence is such that the normal to the surface of the crystal passes between both branches of the dispersion surface and intersects the hyperbola at two imaginary points, there is *total reflection.*

2. Principles of X-ray topography

2.1. *Introduction*

The aim of X-ray topography is to give the distribution and nature of imperfections within a crystal such as dislocation lines, stacking faults, precipitates, long range strains, twin boundaries, ferroelectric or ferromagnetic domain walls and so on.

In studying lattice imperfections, one should distinguish between the defects themselves and the long range elastic strains they induce in the crystal. Long range strains may also be due to some external effect such as a mechanical bending or a thermal gradient.

Localized imperfections may act as independent scattering centers e.g. small angle scattering by small precipitates, thermal diffuse scattering ... On the other hand, the strains they induce will modify the diffraction of X-rays by the good crystal. This remark is most important for a good understanding of the images of defects. The image of a dislocation line, for instance, on an X-ray topograph or in electron microscopy, is not an enlargement of the "core" of the dislocation. By core we mean that inner region surrounding the line where continuous elasticity is no more valid and which has a diameter of a few ångstroms. The strains due to the dislocation are still important enough a hundred angstroms from the line in the case of electron microscopy or a few microns from it in the case of X-ray diffraction to bring about important perturbations in the diffraction by the good crystal. It is these regions, far from the core, which give rise to the images. Their dimensions are related to the diffraction phenomenon itself. The inner core is too much deformed to contribute to the image. Calculations have been made to estimate the small angle scattering by dislocation lines, but there has been no conclusive experimental evidence.

The influence of the imperfections on the diffraction phenomena is to change the widths of the rocking curves or the integrated intensity. The topographic techniques are used to reveal these changes locally so as give the distribution of imperfections with a good spatial resolution.

2.2. Influence of imperfections on the departure from Bragg's law

To every reflection of X-rays by a crystal is associated the set of lattice planes on which this reflection takes place. If a given set of planes remains invariant during the deformation, there will be no change in the X-ray reflections on this set of planes. This is the basis of the visibility rules of dislocation images on X-ray topographs. More generally speaking, the contrast of defect images depends on the variation at each point of the departure from Bragg's angle of the incident beam on the strained region.

In the most general case, the deformation can be resolved in a variation of the lattice spacing d and a rotation α of the lattice planes around a certain direction. If we call ϕ the angle between this direction and the normal to the plane of incidence, it can be shown that the variation of the departure from Bragg's law of the incident direction brought about by the deformation is equal to

$$\delta\theta = \alpha \cos\phi - \tfrac{1}{2}\alpha^2 \operatorname{tg}\theta + (\delta d/d)\operatorname{tg}\theta . \tag{17}$$

There are two important terms in the expression of $\delta\theta$: the component of the rotation normal to the plane of incidence and the dilatation. To determine separately these two terms one should use the same reflection successively with two different orientations of the plane of incidence.

It is possible to relate the value of $\delta\theta$ to the atomic displacements $\mathbf{u}$. One finds

$$\delta\theta = \frac{-1}{k\sin 2\theta}\frac{\partial(\mathbf{h}\cdot\mathbf{u})}{\partial x^h}, \tag{18}$$

x^h being a coordinate axis along the reflected direction.

It is interesting also to relate $\delta\theta$ and $\mathbf{u}$ to the local variations of the reciprocal lattice vector. When the crystal is deformed there is no more any triply periodic lattice and it is impossible to define a reciprocal lattice. It is however convenient to keep the notion of reciprocal space and to use a vector of this reciprocal space related to the set of reflecting planes (h,k,l). If the deformation is not too large, it is possible to define around any point P a small volume ΔV big enough to have a well defined lattice parameter and orientation and small enough for this orientation and this parameter to be constant within ΔV. It is then possible to imagine an perfect infinite crystal, asymptotic, so to speak, to ΔV, having the same parameter and the same orientation. One can then determine the reciprocal lattice vector $\mathbf{h}$ of this crystal and take it for the local reciprocal lattice vector of the deformed crystal. Let us calculate its value in terms of the atomic displacements $\mathbf{u}$.

The equation of the $\mathcal{N}$th plane in the stacking of direct lattice (h,k,l) planes is

$$f \equiv \mathbf{h}\cdot\mathbf{r} = \mathcal{N}. \tag{19}$$

The origin O of the position vector

$$\mathbf{r} = \text{OP}$$

is taken to be invariant during the deformation. The reciprocal lattice vector associated with the set of direct lattice planes can be defined as the gradient of f

$$\mathbf{h} = \nabla f. \tag{20}$$

After deformation, the end-point P of the position vector is displaced and the new position vector becomes

$$\text{OP}' = \mathbf{r}' = \mathbf{r} + \mathbf{u}(\mathbf{r}). \tag{21}$$

This can also be written, to the second order approximation

$$\mathbf{r} = \mathbf{r}' - \mathbf{u}(\mathbf{r}') .$$

(22)

This corresponds to neglecting $\partial u^i / \partial x^i$. Combination of eqs. (19) and (22) gives the equation of surface obtained after the deformation of the $\mathcal{N}$th lattice plane

$$f' \equiv \mathbf{h} \cdot \mathbf{r}' - \mathbf{h} \cdot \mathbf{u}(\mathbf{r}') = \mathcal{N}.$$

(23)

If we consider an infinite crystal of which the lattice planes would tangent to the surfaces

$$f' = ... \mathcal{N} - 1 , \mathcal{N}, \mathcal{N} + 1 ...$$

we can define its reciprocal lattice vector by means of (20)

$$\mathbf{h}' = \nabla f' = \mathbf{h} - \nabla(\mathbf{h} \cdot \mathbf{u}) .$$

(24)

The local variation of the reciprocal lattice vector is therefore equal to

$$\delta \mathbf{h} = \mathbf{h}' - \mathbf{h} = - \nabla(\mathbf{h} \cdot \mathbf{u})$$

and the variation (18) of the departure from Bragg's law can also be written

$$\delta \theta = \frac{\delta \mathbf{h} \cdot \mathbf{S}_h}{k \sin 2\theta}$$

$\mathbf{S}_h$ being the unit vector in the reflected direction.

2.3. *Classification of the main topographic methods*

There are several possible ways to classify the various topographic methods. One is according to the type of image obtained (with a high *spatial* resolving power – or with a high *angular* resolving power). Another one is according to the type of setting. We shall first distinguish the Bragg and Laue cases and then describe the transmission method in more detail.

(a) Reflection settings. Fig. 13 shows the principle of reflection settings. A photographic plate P is placed as near as possible of the crystal C without intersecting the direct beam *I*. When a thick nuclear emulsion is used, the plate should be normal to the reflected beam. There are two extreme experi-

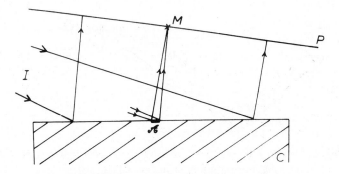

Fig. 13. Principle of Berg-Barrett topographs.

mental cases. (i) Berg-Barrett settings. The beam of X-rays is directly incident from the focus on the crystal. It is divergent and not monochromatized, but only the Kα lines are used. The divergence (of few minutes of arc) is much wider than the width of the rocking curves for perfect crystals. The dimensions of the focal spot range from that of a microfocus to values of the same order as the dimensions of the illuminated area on the crystal.

The intensity of the X-rays received at M on the photographic plate is an integrated intensity dependent on the spectral and angular distribution of the X-ray source. It has been reflected by a small area A of the crystal. It is the smaller, the closer the photographic plate from the crystal. The relative value of this intensity depends on the crystalline perfection of the surface layers in the immediate neighbourhood of A. If they are made of perfect crystal, the intensity is average, if they contain imperfections, the intensity takes very high values. The images of the deformed regions in an otherwise perfect crystal will be the points on the plate having received the maximum intensity of X-rays. The contrast depends on the degree of perfection.

On the other hand, rotations of the lattice planes or local variations of the parameter may not noticeably modify the degree of perfection: if they are very small when the crystal is perfect or when the crystal ideally imperfect. They will only be visible if they correspond to a departure from Bragg's law of the order of a few percent at least of the width of the rocking curve. This width depends on the degree of perfection and the divergence of the beam. It is usually of the order of 1 or 2 min of arc. To be visible, the misorientations should be at least of 10 or 20 sec of arc. Small strains which would not change noticeably the degree of perfection in a nearly perfect crystal would not be visible.

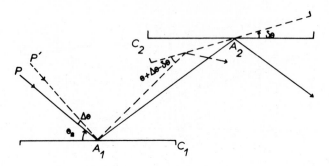

Fig. 14. Principle of double crystal topographs.

The method has a very good spatial resolving power: the width of dislocation images can be a few microns only, but is not very sensible to small strains.
The reflecting region is limited to the top superficial layers. This is interesting
when the structure which is studied is superficial or when the density of defects
in the bulk of the crystal is high. (ii) Bonse [3] or Renninger settings [10].
The beam incident on the crystal C_2 under study has first been reflected on
a crystal C_1 identical to the first one and in the parallel position (fig. 14). If
the two crystals are perfect, the width of the rocking curve is very narrow, of
the order of a few sec of arc. Let us assume that the angular setting of crystal
C_2 is such that the reflected intensity has half its maximum value. A local
misorientation of a few tenths of sec of arc of the superficial layers will induce a big change in intensity without noticeably changing the degree of perfection. There will therefore be a strong contrast on the photographic plate
with regard to the average intensity. What is more, the sign of the misorientation will be given by that of the contrast of the image on the topograph
which will thus represent a map of small strains at the surface of the crystal.

(b) Transmission settings. Let us consider an X-ray beam incident on a
crsytal at the Laue setting (fig. 15). As we have seen in the first chapter, it
gives rise to a reflected and a refracted beam which have undergone interference effects within the crystal and a direct beam which contains all the
rays with a departure from Bragg's law too high to give rise to a reflection. It
undergoes simply the normal photoelectric absorption.

There are two main types of transmission topography: Lang's method, corresponding to small values of μt, where μ is the absorption coefficient and t
the thickness of the sample; and anomalous transmission methods, corresponding to high values of μt. Actually, it is better to consider values of μt between
2 and 4 and to extrapolate to the two extreme cases. It is also more convenient

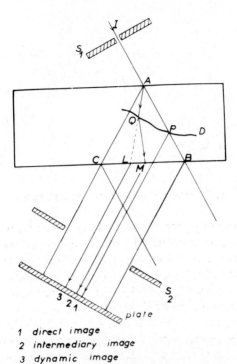

1 direct image
2 intermediary image
3 dynamic image

Fig. 15. Principle of transmission topographs.

to study first what happens when the crystal is immobile, the X-ray beam comes from a point focus, and is limited by a fine slit (section topographs); and then to study the influence of a translation applied to the crystal (traverse topographs) or that of a long focus in the high μt range (parallel beam method).

Fig. 15 depicts the well-known experimental setup for section topographs. The influence of a dislocation can be described schematically as being three-fold [11].

1. The dislocation cuts the direct beam. The region around the dislocation line reflects intensity from this direct beam, giving rise to the *direct* image.

2. The dislocation line cutting the paths of wave-fields propagating within the Borrmann fan **ABC** casts a shadow, giving rise to the *dynamic* image.

3. The wave-fields intercepted by the dislocation line decouple into their incident and reflected wave components which, on reentering good crystal, excite new wave-fields. These give rise to a third type of image, the *interme-diary* image. This is equivalent to interbranch scattering, or transfer of energy

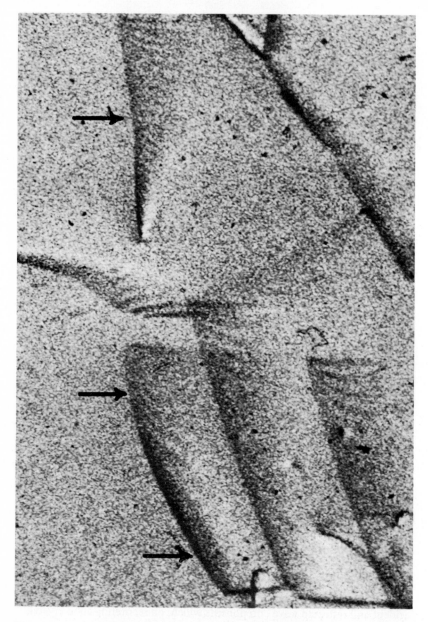

Fig. 16. Traverse topograph of dislocation in silicon. $2\bar{2}0$ reflection, crystal face [111], thickness 0.8 mm, MoKα radiation (after [11]).

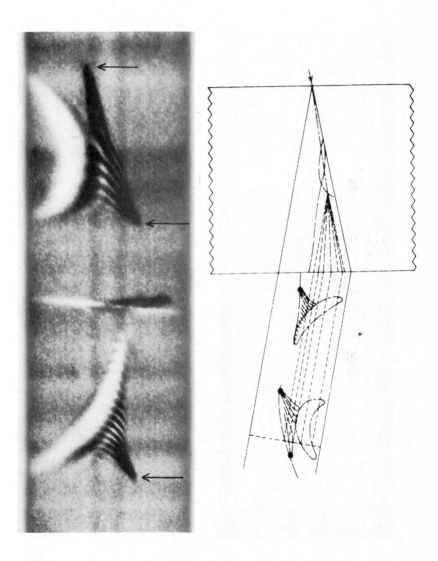

Fig. 17a. Section topographs of the same crystal as in fig. 16 (after [11]) 2$\bar{2}$0 reflection.

Fig. 18a. Schematical explanation of the image formation in fig. 17a.

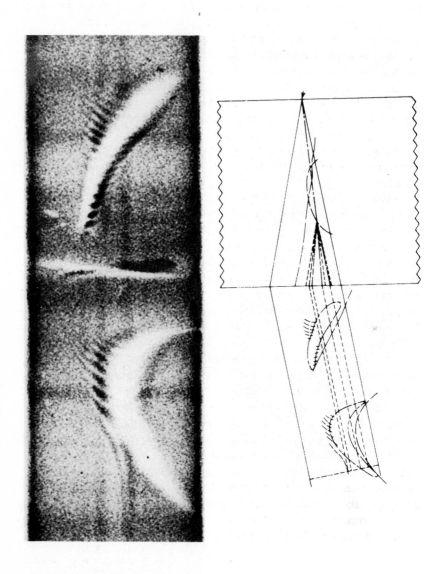

Fig. 17b. Section topographs of the same
crystal as in fig. 16 (after [11]) $\overline{2}20$ reflection.

Fig. 18b. Schematical explanation of the
image formation in fig. 17b.

from one branch to the other. As the path of the wave-fields incident on the dislocation line becomes closer to that of the direct beam (when Q moves into P), the intermediary image gradually merges into the direct image.

Figs. 16, 17 and 18 give examples of the three types of image. Fig. 16 is a traverse topograph of silicon (0.8 mm thick, reflection $2\bar{2}0$ MoK$_a$). One sees the thin black direct images, the white diffuse dynamic images, and, in between, the fringes in the shadow of the dislocation images. Fig. 17 is a section topograph of the same region. The direct image here is a black point, the dynamic image a thick white line, and the intermediary image a series of black fringes. Fig. 18 is a schematic drawing showing the formation of the images. The top part of the drawing is a projection on the incidence plane, the lower part a projection on the photographic plate placed normal to the reflected direction.

(i) Lang type topography. When μt is of the order of 1 or less, the total absorption of the direct beam is small and direct images have a strong contrast. On a *section* topograph, the direct image is that of the intersection of the dislocation line with the direct beam. To obtain an image of all the defects within the crystal, Lang has suggested to traverse both photographic plate and crystal. During this translation dynamic and intermediary images become blurred and are not very contrasted, direct images form projection of the defects in the reflected direction. They are the interesting features of the Lang-type topographs or *projection* topographs.

(ii) Anomalous transmission topography. When μt is very large, higher than 10 or 20, the direct beam is completely absorbed out and direct images are not visible at all. Type 2 wave-fields are also completely absorbed out. Type 1 wave-fields are only weakly absorbed for waves with a very small departure from Bragg's law: their paths are practically parallel to the lattice planes. Under these conditions, only dynamic images are visible as well as intermediary images for the portion near the surfaces of the crystal.

Direct images lead to a very good spatial resolution. Dynamic images have a poor spatial resolution but good angular resolution on section topographs for small values of μt. For high values of μt and a traverse topograph or a topograph taken with a long focus (parallel beam method), dynamic images have a reasonably good spatial resolution, the better the closer the dislocation lies from the exit surface of the crystal.

3. Contrast of dislocation images

3.1. *Direct images*
3.1.1. Theoretical considerations

A small angular fraction only of the beam incident on the crystal is near enough the Bragg angle to give rise to wave-fields propagating within the Borrmann fan ABC (fig. 15). The major part propagates along AB, undergoing normal attenuation. It is made of "rays" with a large departure from Bragg's law with regard to the perfect crystal, i.e., a Fourier analysis of the direct beam AB would show that its plane-wave components with a departure from Bragg's law less than once or twice the width of the rocking curve for the perfect crystal have very low intensity.

There is of course no abrupt transition between the "fan" and the direct beam. A possible definition might be that a wave-field belongs to the direct beam if the intensity ratio $|R_h^2|$ of its reflected and incident components is less than 1 to 5%. We shall see that as far as the gross interpretation of the contrast of direct images is concerned, this definition is satisfactory.

The direct beam, thus defined, is very intense in low absorbing material. When it enters a deformed region, it will satisfy the Bragg condition for this deformed region provided the effective misorientation is larger than once or twice the width of the rocking curve for the perfect crystal and less than the total divergence of the direct beam. This last limitation is unimportant in the case of a dislocation line for which the misorientation is bigger the closer one is to the core. It is the first limitation which leads to an explanation of the width and the contrast of the images. If the divergence of the direct beam were not bigger than the width of the rocking curve, there would be no direct image.

Fig. 19a gives equal effective misorientation curves around an edge dislocation line parallel to the crystal face with a Burgers vector parallel to the crystal face.

From what we have seen above, it is the region inside these curves, drawn for an effective misorientation equal to x times the width of the rocking curve ($x \approx 1$ or 2), which reflects the direct beam and contributes to the formation of the direct image. Because of the divergence of the direct beam, it is reasonable to assume that the intensity reflected by these regions is an integrated intensity and that the direct image is an integrated image. This is true in all cases for a traverse topograph. Since these regions reflect as "mosaic crystals" imbedded in an X-ray beam, the integrated intensity on the photographic plate is proportional to the volume of the mosaic crystal crossed by the reflected beam. Fig. 19b shows the profile we should expect for the direct image of an edge

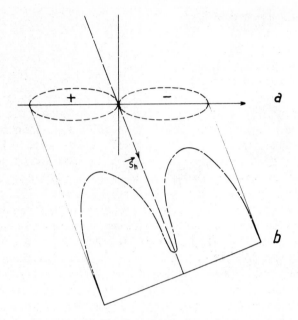

Fig. 19. Principle of the formation of direct images. (a) equal effective misorientations around a dislocation line. (b) corresponding intensity distribution in the reflected direction.

dislocation with Burgers vector parallel to the crystal faces. The direct image should thus have a double contrast on traverse as well as on section topographs.

It can be shown that the distance L_1 between the two maxima is equal to the maximum distance from the dislocation core for which the effective misorientation is equal to $x\delta$ where δ is the width of the reflecting range for the perfect crystal.

It is given by

$$\delta = \frac{2|C|}{\sin 2\theta} \sqrt{\frac{\gamma_0}{\gamma_h}} \chi_h \chi_{\bar{h}}$$

$C = 1$ or $\cos 2\theta$, depending on the polarisation direction. χ_h is given by eq. (9).

The width δ and the resolving power of the Lang method increase with increasing wavelength.

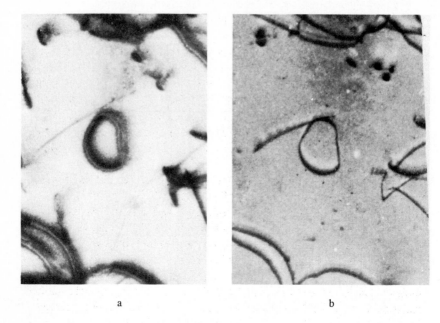

a   b

Fig. 20. Traverse topograph of a dislocation loop in silicon-MoKα; thickness 500 μm
(after [11]).

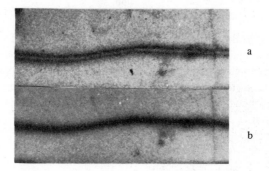

a

b

Fig. 21. Traverse topograph of a dislocation line in mica-MoKα; thickness 100 μm
(after [28]). (a) 400, (b) 200.

3.1.2. Experimental evidence

(i) Qualitative study of the double contrast. The contrast of direct images is
usually simple, but is sometimes double as has been noted by Authier and
Petroff [12] and by Lang [13]. We shall show that when the width δ is small

enough, L_1 becomes larger, and the two parts of the image can be separated and the double contrast appears. The value of δ may be decreased by using either a shorter wavelength or a different reflection. The latter case is illustrated by fig. 20 in the case of silicon (double contrast for 333, $\delta = 2.6 \times 10^{-6}$); single contrast for 111, $\delta = 14 \times 10^{-6}$, MoK$\alpha$ radiation and by fig. 21 in the case of mica (double contrast for 400, $\delta = 2.26 \times 10^{-6}$; single contrast for 200, $\delta = 3.63 \times 10^{-6}$). In both cases, the Burgers vector is parallel to the crystal face and has the same indices ($1/2\ [1\bar{1}0]$). For practical purposes, it may be noted that in silicon the $\{111\}$ topographs have the highest resolving power.

Fig. 22 compares a section and a traverse pattern of two dislocations in mica, showing the double contrast (reflection 060, $\delta = 4.8 \times 10^{-6}$).

(ii) Sign of misorientations. The two regions giving rise to the two sides of the image correspond to misorientations of opposite sign, as fig. 19 shows. It is possible to check this with a technique first used by Chikawa [14].

The experiment was performed by Petroff on a dislocation in triglycine sulfate. He used a straight portion running parallel to the crystal faces. It is shown between two arrows on fig. 23, which is a 200 topograph with MoKα radiation ($\delta = 3 \times 10^{-6}$). Three rocking curves were then carefully recorded for three different positions of the crystal in front of a slit $10\,\mu \times 25\,\mu$, such that the incident beam would hit one after the other the two maxima of the dislocation image, $55\,\mu$ apart, and a dislocation-free region. The angular position of the peak was accurately determined for each rocking curve by taking

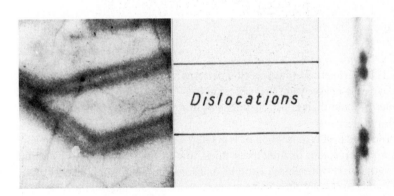

Fig. 22. Traverse and section topographs in mica-MoKα-060 thickness $100\,\mu$m (after [11]).

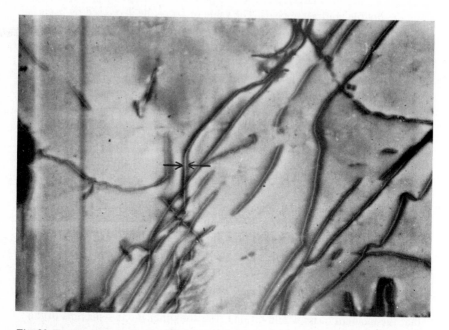

Fig. 23. Traverse topograph of triglycine sulfate-200-MoKα-thickness 300 μm (after [11]).

the middle point of successive chords. Petroff was thus able to show that the effective misorientation is of opposite sign for each maximum and equal to $\pm 5 \times 10^{-6}$ rad, which is what one expects from the effective strain field 30 μ away from the dislocation core.

3.2. Dynamic images

3.2.1. Experimental study: section patterns (simple images)

Dynamic images were first observed in silicon by Borrmann, Hartwig and Irmler [4] and their contrast studied by Borrmann [15], Authier [16] and Ishii [17].

They are best visible when μt is greater than 1 or 2, that is, either in a highly absorbing crystal or in a relatively thick, low-absorbing material. They usually present a black-white-black contrast and sometimes subsidiary fringes which are visible in fig. 24. Their contrast is the same in hkl and $\bar{h}\bar{k}\bar{l}$ reflections, as can be seen in figs. 17a and 17b. When they correspond to dislocations lying close to the surface of the crystal, their contrast is black-white; it is reversed in the direct-beam section topograph and in the $\bar{h}\bar{k}\bar{l}$ reflections. This effect may easily be explained by Penning and Polder theory [18].

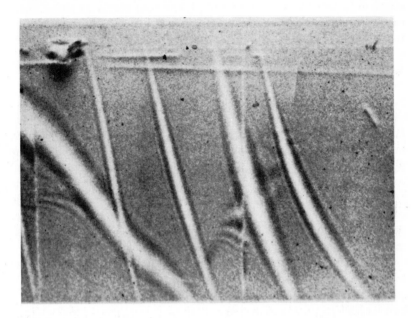

Fig. 24. Section topograph of silicon-220-AgKα-thickness 4 mm (after [11]).

As is shown schematically in figs. 15 and 18, dynamic images may be considered as shadows cast by the dislocation along the path of the wave-fields incident at each point. Knowing both the direct and dynamic images, it is possible to reconstruct the position of the dislocation line within the crystal without using a stereopair.

The width of the dynamical images may be considered as having a triple origin.

1. The width $2L_1$ of the region surrounding the dislocation line and within which the effective misorientation is a fraction of the width of the rocking curve. This width is evaluated in the same way as the direct image, but is much larger of course.

2. The divergence of the wave-fields intercepted by this width $2L_1$. It is largest when point Q of fig. 15 lies in the middle of the fan or near the entrance surface. It can be seen in fig. 24 that the image is narrower near both sides of the section and it broadens considerably when the dislocation is near the entrance surface.

3. Fraunhofer diffraction. The influence of the dislocation line may be considered as that of a linear screen. Fresnel and Fraunhofer diffraction

effects are magnified by the crystal which acts as an angular amplifier: the angular spread in path directions is much bigger than that of the wave vectors.

3.2.2. Experimental study: traverse patterns and parallel beam method (integrated images)

When crystal and photographic plate are traversed or a long focus line is used, the dynamic image becomes diffuse, since in this case the shadow is cast in all directions within the 2θ-fan drawn from Q. In low-absorbing, relatively thick crystals, it is not very visible and does not decrease the visibility of the direct images. On the contrary, for high-absorbing material, the direction of energy flow is close to that of the reflécting planes (Borrmann effect) and the image is not broad. However, its angular divergence is seldom smaller than a degree, except for extremely high values of μt, and it is only when the dislocation lies less than a few tenths of a millimeter from the exit surface that the resolving power may be compared to that of the direct images in Lang's method. These methods are nevertheless very useful and the only possible ones for high values of μt. They have been used with great success by many authors: for example, Meier with germanium [19], Hart with indium antimonide [20] and Young with copper [21].

3.2.3. Theoretical study

Two origins may be attributed to the dynamical images.

1. Curvature of wave-fields propagating in the lightly distorted region away from the dislocation line. The paths of the X-rays near a dislocation line have been thus calculated by Kambe [22] using Penning and Polder theory.

2. Creation of new wave-fields due to the decoupling of the wave-fields incident on the more distorted regions nearer the dislocation (interbranch scattering). These new wave-fields take up intensity from the incident wave-fields and propagate in a different direction, giving rise to the intermediary image discussed in the next section. In the high μt case, when the only propagation direction is practically that of the reflecting planes, the incident wave-fields correspond to branch 1 of the dispersion surface, the newly created wave-fields, to branch 2 and are absorbed out. In both cases, the result is depletion of intensity in the direction of the incident wave-fields.

It is possible to calculate the contrast of dislocation image by solving with a computer the generalized equations such as those given by S.Takagi. Fig. 25 shows the theoretical result corresponding to the dislocation image on the section topograph of fig. 17a [24]. There is very good agreement between theory and experiment.

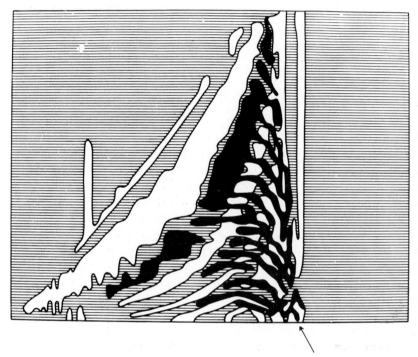

Fig. 25. Calculated dislocation image profile on a section topograph (after [24]). (Compare with fig. 17a.)

3.3. Intermediary image

When a wave field propagating in a crystal reaches a slightly deformed region, its path will be deviated and its tie-point moves along the branch of the dispersion surface it belongs to. This has been accounted for by Penning and Polder. When the wave field reaches a region with a very strong strain gradient new processes will take place: there will be diffraction (in the optical sense) and it has been shown by F.Balibar that this leads necessarily to interbranch scattering [25], that is the incoming wave field will excite new wave fields belonging to the other branch of the dispersion surface. The paths of these new wave fields are along QM on fig. 15. At M there are interferences between these wave fields and normal wave fields having traveled along AM and which did not meet the dislocation line. It is those intereferences which give rise to the fringes in the intermediary image.

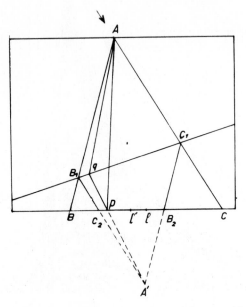

Fig. 26. Paths of wave-fields in a crystal containing a stacking fault.

3.4. *Contrast of stacking faults* [26]

When a wave field reaches a planar defect such as a stacking fault, a twin boundary, a gap, a growth band or, generally speaking, any discontinuity in the crystalline lattice, it will decouple into its two components, the reflected and the refracted wave. Upon entering the good crystal on the other side of the planar defect each wave will excite two wave fields, exactly as any wave travelling in vacuum and incident on a crystal. Fig. 26 shows the path qp of the new wave fields excited at the planar defect $B_1 C_1$.

These new wave fields are at the origin of two types of interference patterns:

(a) if the incident wave is a spherical wave, the whole dispersion surface is excited and along the path Aq in the first half of the crystal propagate two wave fields of which the tie-points are the end points of a diameter of the dispersion surface. Both these wave fields will excite a new wave field travelling along qp. They will interfere giving rise to Pendellösung fringes described in ch. 1. Fig. 26 shows that the paths of the new wave fields are limited to the triangle $B_1, A'C_1$. They are represented on fig. 27 (thin lines). It will be noticed that they are asymptotic to the sides $A'B_1$ and $A'C_1$ of the triangle.

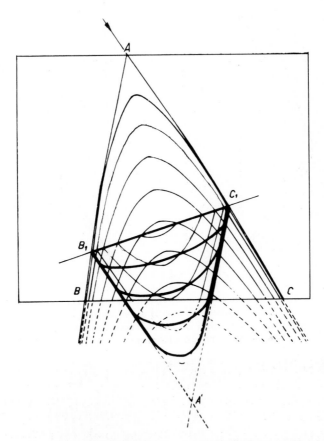

Fig. 27. Formation of interference fringes in a crystal containing a stacking fault.

(b) At any point p of the exit surface arrive both new wave fields such as Aqp and wave fields whose path have not been deviated upon crossing the fault. These two types of wave fields also interfere giving rise to interference fringes which are represented by thick lines on fig. 27. They have *twice* the period of the first type of fringes.

If the fault makes an angle with the surface of the crystal, the region containing the fringes take an hour glass shape as is shown in fig. 28.

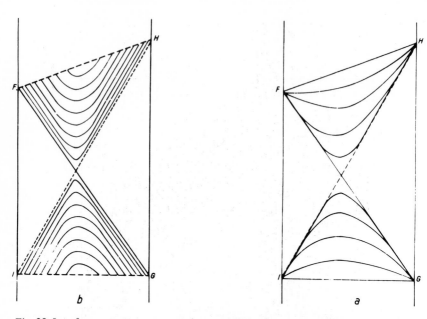

Fig. 28. Interference patterns on a section topograph of a crystal containing a stacking fault (after [26]). a. Interference between wave fields which have suffered interbranch scattering. b. Interference between wave fields which have, and have not, suffered interbranch scattering.

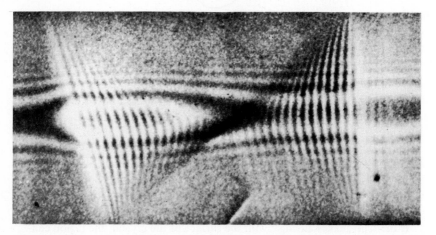

Fig. 29. Section pattern of a dolomite crystal with a stacking fault, 100, MoKα, thickness 1 mm (after [27]). (Compare with pattern on fig. 28a.)

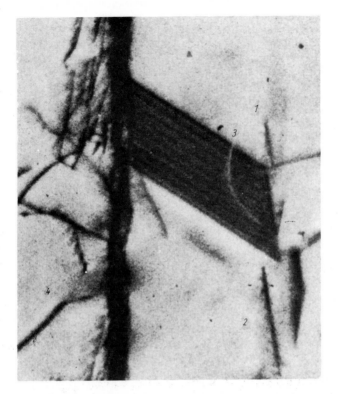

Fig. 30. Traverse topograph of a silicon crystal with a stacking fault (after [26]) 111 reflection - MoKα.

For a crystal with an average value of μt, both systems of fringes are simultaneously present, but for relatively high values of μt only the second system is visible (fig. 28a). An example is given in fig. 29 in the case of a growth band in dolomite [27]. On a traverse pattern one will observe equal thickness fringes as is shown in fig. 30 in the case of a stacking fault in silicon.

References

[1] A.R.Lang, J. Appl. Phys. 29 (1958) 597.
[2] J.B.Newkirk, Trans AIME 215 (1959) 483.
[3] U.Bonse and E.Kappler, Z. Naturforsch. 13a (1958) 348.

[4] G.Borrmann, W.Hartwij and H.Irmler, Z. Naturforsch. 13a (1958) 423.

[5] M.v. Laue, Röntgen Strahl Interferenzen, Frankfurt, 1960.

[6] G.Borrmann, Z. Physik 127 (1950) 297.

[7] A.Authier, Bull. Soc. Fr. Minér. Crist. 84 (1961) 51.

[8] N.Kato and A.R.Lang, Acta Cryst. 12 (1959) 787.

[9] N.Kato, Acta Cryst. 14 (1961) 526, 627.

[10] M.Renninger, Phys. Letters 1 (1962) 104, 106.

[11] A.Authier, Advances in X-ray Analysis, Vol. 9 (Plenum Press, N.Y., 1967) p. 9.

[12] A.Authier and J.F.Petroff, Comptes Rendus 258 (1964) 4238.

[13] A.R.Lang, Z. Naturforsch. 20a (1965) 636.

[14] J.I.Chikawa, Appl. Phys. Letters 4 (1964) 154.

[15] G.Borrmann, Physik. Bl. 15 (1959) 508.

[16] A.Authier, Bull. Soc. Fr. Minér. Crist. 84 (1961) 115.

[17] Z.Ishii, J. Phys. Soc. Japan 17 (1962) 838.

[18] P.Penning and D.Polder, Philips Res. Repts. 16 (1961) 419.

[19] F.Meier, Z. Physik 168 (1962) 10, 29.

[20] M.Hart, Ph. Thesis Bristol University, 1963.

[21] F.Young, Advances in X-ray analysis, Vol. 9 (Plenum Press, N.Y., 1965) p. 1.

[22] K.Kambe, Z. Naturforsch. 189 (1963) 1010.

[23] S.Takagi, Acta Cryst. 15 (1962) 1311.

[24] F.Balibar and A.Authier, Phys. Stat. Sol. 21 (1967) 413.

[25] F.Balibar, Acta Cryst. A24 (1968) 666.

[26] A.Authier, Phys. Stat. Sol. 27 (1968) 77.

[27] A.Zarka, Bull. Soc. Fr. Minér. Crist. 92 (1969) 160.

[28] C.Willaime and A.Authier, Bull. Soc. Fr. Minér. Crist. 89 (1966) 279.

ADVANCES IN X-RAY AND NEUTRON DIFFRACTION TECHNIQUES

A.GUINIER

1. General review of the experimental methods for the determination of atomic structures

1.1. *Introduction*

The different chapters of this book are devoted to various methods able to furnish informations on the atomic structure of matter at an atomic scale. Generally speaking, all these methods are based upon some interaction of matter with radiations of different kinds.

The necessary condition is that the resolving power of any of these devices be sufficient to allow the localization of the individual atoms. A general rule in optics is that the limiting value of the resolving power (i.e. the shortest distance between two points which can be distinguished) is of the order of the wave-length of the radiation used. Every atom having a diameter of the order of 1 Å, that implies that one must use radiations of a wave-length of 1 Å or shorter.

1.2. *Classification of methods*

We can now classify the possible methods of observation by making a list of radiations within this range of wave-lengths.

(1) Among the electromagnetic radiations, we find *X-rays* and fortunately the desired wave-lengths (0.1−1 Å) correspond to radiations which are both easy to produce, easy to detect and have a suitable interaction with matter. X-rays of longer wave-length (10 to 100 Å) are so easily absorbed in the matter that they cannot reach the sample to be studied and X-rays of shorter wave-length (0.01 to 0.1 Å) require the use of cumbersome and expensive high-tension generators.

(2) Besides these electromagnetic radiations, we have at our disposal the radiations associated to beams of various particles, the wave-length of which is given by the de Broglie formula

$$\lambda = \frac{h}{mv} \qquad \text{or} \qquad \lambda = \frac{h}{\sqrt{2m}\,\sqrt{E}} \tag{1}$$

E being the kinetic energy of the particule of mass m. Numerically, for electrons, with E expressed in electron-volts ($E=eV$) and λ in Ångstroms (Å)

$$\lambda = 12.5/\sqrt{V}.$$

So for electrons, the 1 Å wave-length corresponds to electrons accelerated by a tension of a few hundred volts. Such electrons are stopped by one or two atomic layers: thus they can only be used for the observation of the structures of *surfaces* (LEED methods, p. 377). With an increasing acceleration tension, the electrons are able to pass through layers of 100 to 1000 Å which allows the observation of a three dimensional structure. The wave-length of such electrons is of the order of 0.1 Å; it is well known that technically the production and the detection of 10 to 100 kV electrons do not encounter special difficulties. In fact, electrons are now the agents of the most effective means for the observation of atomic structures (p. 529).

(3) For heavy particles, the same wave-length is obtained, according to formula (1) when the particles have much lower energy. For instance in a neutron beam of 1 Å wave-length, the neutron has a velocity of 4000 m/sec and an energy of 0.08 eV. This is the energy of particles in thermal equilibrium at a temperature of 600°K. Neutrons have a special interest for the study of atomic structures because their interaction with the atoms is of a quite different nature from the interaction of atoms with photons or charged particles. Thus the neutrons "see" different aspects of the atoms. Furthermore the absorption of neutrons in matter is very low. Thus an entire specimen of very large size may be observed (a few centimeters instead of a fraction of millimeters for X-rays, or a fraction of microns for electrons). Of course, the use of neutrons cannot be general in every Solid State Physics laboratory, since it is restricted to the laboratories attached to the few big research reactors in operation in the world.

(4) Some charged heavy particles are also utilized but protons have a serious inconvenience; they produce serious damages in the matter under examination and so the observed structure may not be the primitive one. But helium ions are used in a very interesting instrument (field-ion microscope).

1.3. *Image formation and diffraction techniques*

The value of the wave-length of the radiation gives an unavoidable limitation of the resolving power but the physical properties of the radiation must make possible the realisation of a practical device able to approach as far as possible the theoretical limit.

The most obvious method is the formation of an image, as in an optical instrument, with a magnification high enough to show distinctly the details which can be separated. But with some of the radiations which enter the category of the "possible" radiations, no image forming device may be realised. Thus X-rays propagate in straight line and can be deviated neither by reflection nor by refraction at the interface of two material mediums. So, the rays issued from a point source cannot be focused in a point image and — at least up to now — no X-ray microscope is available. In fact, reflection of X-rays indeed occurs on a plane surface, but only if the angle of incidence is lower than a few minutes and the attempts to construct an X-ray microscope with an interesting resolving power have not been successful. The situation is the same for the neutrons.

On the other hand, the trajectory of a charged particle may be altered by the forces exerted by electrical or magnetic fields. Combination of such fields may lead to an image-forming system and so microscopes, even with a very high magnification, are possible. These instruments (electron microscopes and ion-microscopes) are now essential tools for Solid State physicists.

The formation of images is not the only way to collect informations about the structure of an object. There is a second possibility, much more general since it is applicable for all kinds of radiations, the phenomena of diffraction. The object is bathed in a coherent plane wave; the different atoms receiving this primary radiation become sources of scattered radiation; the total diffracted radiation results from the interferences between the ensemble of the coherent secondary sources. The repartition of the diffracted radiation in the different directions of space depends upon the nature of the interaction of the atoms and the primary beam and on the arrangement of the atoms in the object. Thus the knowledge of the diffracted radiation gives information on the atomic structure of the object and, even in some cases, that is sufficient to build a model of the structure; but this is possible only because the wave-length of the primary beam is short enough, the concept of the resolving power used in the case of image being also valid for the diffraction phenomena. But in the general case, the information contained in the diffraction data do not allow to give an unambiguous structural model. Nevertheless diffraction is in the present state of the technique the most direct approach to this model.

In conclusion, table 1 gives the summary of this rapid review.

Table 1

Nature of radiations.		Methods of observation	
Particle	wave-length		
X-ray photons	1A		diffraction
electrons	⎧ high energy	microscopy	diffraction
	⎨		
	⎩ low energy		diffraction
neutrons	1–10A	microscopy	diffraction
ions		microscopy	

2. X-ray diffraction (kinematical theory)

2.1. *The two aspects of the diffraction theories*

The scattering due to the individual atoms being provoked by the incident beam, the energy of the scattered radiation is substracted from the incident energy. The characteristics of the diffraction phenomena depend on the value of the ratio of these two energies. If the scattered energy is very small relative to the incident energy, one can admit that the wave-field after diffraction is simply the addition of the incident unperturbed wave plus the scattered radiation. That is called in quantum mechanics the Born approximation and for diffraction the "kinematical" case. This approximation is generally valid for X-rays but there are some exceptions, rare but very interesting: when the diffracting body is a large and perfect crystal, i.e. when the atoms, in volumes of the order of $[10 \text{ to } 100 \, \mu\text{m}]^3$ are located at the nodes of one single lattice, the intensities of the diffracted beam and of the incident beam become comparable. Another theory of diffraction – called dynamical – is then valid: the diffraction phenomena are profoundly altered (p. 35). In electron diffraction, the cases where the dynamical theory has to be applied are much more frequent. In this chapter, only the kinematical theory will be treated.

2.2. *Elementary aspects of the diffraction of X-rays by crystals*

The most important and also the more generally. known case is that of the diffraction of X-rays by crystals: we shall give here only a short survey of the elementary facts. A complete development of the diffraction theory at an elementary level can be found in the following references:

C.S.Barrett and T.B.Massalsky, Structure of Metals, 3rd ed. (McGraw Hill, 1967).

B.D.Cullity, Elements of X-ray Diffraction (Addison-Wesley, 1956).

We consider a crystalline lattice with a unit cell defined by a set of three vectors $\mathbf{a}, \mathbf{b}, \mathbf{c}$. All the nodes of this lattice may be distributed on series of identical planes, parallel to each other and separated by a uniform spacing. There exists an infinity of families of *reticular planes*: each of them are defined by a set of 3 integers, the Miller indices (hkl), which determine: (i) the orientation of the planes in relation to the axes of the unit cell and (ii) the interreticular spacing. For instance in a cubic lattice of parameter a, the (hkl) planes are parallel to the plane HKL, $H K$ and L being situated on the axes of the cubic cell respectively at the distances from origin O

$$OH = a/h , \qquad OK = a/k , \qquad OL = a/l$$

and they have a spacing

$$d_{hkl} = \frac{a}{\sqrt{k^2 + k^2 + l^2}} .$$

The crystal being irradiated by a plane wave of wave-length λ, the resultant of the waves scattered by the atoms located at the nodes of a three dimensional lattice is in general reduced to exactly zero, as a result of the regularity of the positions of the atoms, *except* for special directions of the incident wave. The primary beam must make with one of the reticular planes (hkl), an angle of incidence θ, such that

$$\lambda = 2 d_{hkl} \sin \theta .$$

Then, a diffracted beam is produced in the direction of the beam reflected on this (hkl) plane. That is the Bragg Law.

Every crystal is made of a motive identically repeated around each lattice node. The Bragg conditions for the X-ray reflection are independent of the nature of the motive. Conversely, from the knowledge of the directions of reflections for a given incident beam, the orientation and the spacing of the various families of reticular planes may be found and thus the *lattice of the crystal is determined*. The intensity of a given diffracted beam produced by the (hkl) planes is proportional to the square of the amplitude diffracted by the motive for this particular incidence, which is called the "structure factor" for this reflection F_{hkl}. Of course this set of numbers is determined by the atomic structure of the motive in the cell. It is the central problem of the X-ray crystallography to deduce the positions of the atoms in the cell from the measured F_{hkl}'s. There is no general automatic solution: that is, as it was

said in the introduction, the essential difference between the ensemble of the
diffraction data and a true "image" of the structure. Nevertheless, in many
cases, a solution can be found and considerable progress has been made since
the structure of crystals with motives comprising several thousand of atoms
have now been established without ambiguity. These problems of structure
determination are very important but they are mainly essential for crystal
chemistry and therefore we shall not discuss them anyfurther.

In Solid State Physics, the crystals which are studied have generally a
simple and very well known structure. X-ray diffraction is used to solve
other problems which often require the knowledge of a more refined theory.
Thus we shall insist here on some features of the general theory of diffraction
and describe the mathematical methods with which the Solid State physicists
now should be familiar because they simplify considerably the interpretation
of X-ray data and broaden their range of application.

2.3. General theory of X-ray diffraction

In classical electromagnetism, one calculates the amplitude scattered by an
isolated electron put in vibration by action of an incident wave. Diffraction
is the result of the interference between the waves emitted by all the electrons
of the diffracting body.

Let us consider, first of all, an object consisting of just two electrons, one
of which is at the origin O and the other at the extremity M of the vector $\mathbf{x}$
(fig. 1). Let there be an incident beam Γ_0 parallel and monochromatic rays
characterized by the unit vector $\mathbf{S}_0$ and wave-length λ. The scattered wave Γ

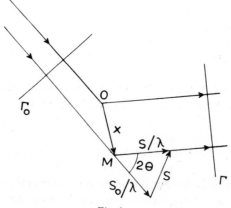

Fig. 1.

is observed in the direction **S**. A formula which plays a fundamental role in the theory of diffraction gives the phase shift between waves issuing from O and M. The difference in path length between the wave-planes Γ and Γ_o is

$$\Delta = (S - S_o) \cdot x \,.$$

Thus the phase difference is

$$\phi = \frac{2\pi\Delta}{\lambda} = 2\pi \left(\frac{S - S_o}{\lambda} \right) \cdot x \equiv 2\pi s \cdot x \,.$$

The amplitude of the resultant wave (Γ) is the sum of the amplitudes emitted by O and M with the phase difference ϕ.

The first consequence of this formula is that diffraction phenomena for a given group of electrons, no matter how complicated the distribution, depend only upon the vector $s \equiv (S - S_o)/\lambda$. Two diffraction experiments, if S, S_o and λ all differ but correspond to the same vector s, will give the same result. The vector s has the direction of the bisector of S and S_o and its length is

$$s = (2 \sin \theta)/\lambda$$

where θ is half the scattering angle (fig. 1).

If the object contains n electrons in the positions $x_1, x_2 \ldots x_n$, the scattered amplitude, taking as unity the amplitude scattered by one electron, is found by a simple summation to be

$$A(s) = \sum_{j=1}^{n} \exp\left(-2\pi i s \cdot x_j\right) \,.$$

For an object defined by the electron density $\rho(x)$, the volume element d^3x at the extremity of the vector x contains $\rho(x) d^3x$ electrons, and the scattered amplitude will be

$$A(s) = \int \rho(x) \exp\left(-2\pi i s \cdot x\right) d^3x \,. \tag{2}$$

Let us consider a diffracting body defined by an ensemble of N atoms located at $x_1, x_2 \ldots x_n$. Except for the valence electrons the influence for diffraction of which is very small, $\rho(x)$ is only different from zero in the electron cloud of one of the N atoms. Then if $\rho_n(x-x_n)$ is the density of the electron cloud of the nth atom whose center is situated at x_n,

$$\rho(x) = \sum_i^N \rho_n(x-x_n) .$$

The integral (2) can thus be written as a sum

$$A(s) = \int \sum_1^N \rho_n(x-x_n) \exp(-2\pi i s \cdot x) \, d^3x$$

$$= \sum_1^N \exp(-2\pi i s \cdot x_n) \int \rho_n(x-x_n)$$

$$\times \exp(-2\pi i s \cdot (x-x_n)) \, d^3x$$

$$= \sum_1^N f_n(s) \exp(-2\pi i s \cdot x_n) .$$

$f_n(s)$ is called the scattering factor of the nth atom. In fact, the scattering factor depends only on the modulus s of the vector s. It represents the number of isolated free electrons which give the same scattering as the atom for a particular value of s. It is equal to the atomic number for small s, i.e. for small diffraction angles. It decreases when s increases; the integral defining f_n shows that the decrease is due to the spreading of electrons in the volume of the atom.

The formula (2) shows that the diffracted amplitude is the Fourier transform of the electronic density.

This is the *fundamental result* of the diffraction theory which is thus considerably simplified by the systematic use of the mathematical properties of the Fourier transformations*.

To illustrate this point we shall, in the following paragraphs, deduce the main features of the diffraction of X-rays by crystals by means of Fourier theory.

* The results of the Fourier theory which are necessary for the physicist using X-ray diffraction are given in: A.Guinier, X-ray diffraction (Freeman, 1962) appendix A.

2.4. *Atomic structure determination by X-ray diffraction*

The three dimensional map of the electronic density in the unit cell is the most complete description of the structure: the knowledge of the repartition of the electron density $\rho(\mathbf{x})$ contains the precise location of the atoms in a unit cell.

According to (2), $\rho(\mathbf{x})$ is given by a Fourier transform of the diffracted amplitude

$$\rho(\mathbf{x}) = \int A(\mathbf{s}) \exp(2i\pi\mathbf{s}\cdot\mathbf{x}) \, d^3s \,. \tag{3}$$

Compared with formula (2), the sign of the exponent is changed and (3) is extended to the whole $\mathbf{s}$ space called *reciprocal space* as the integral (2) was extended to the whole $\mathbf{x}$ space, called crystalline or direct space.

What is possible to measure, for a given crystal is not the amplitude $A(\mathbf{s})$ but the *intensity* $I(\mathbf{s})$ of the diffracted beam as a function of $\mathbf{s} = (\mathbf{S}-\mathbf{S_0})/\lambda$. Therefore (3) is not directly usable with the available diffraction data, but may be transformed.

$$I(\mathbf{s}) = |A(\mathbf{s})|^2 = A(\mathbf{s}) \cdot A^*(\mathbf{s}) \,. \tag{4}$$

The Fourier transform of $I(\mathbf{s})$ is the faltung product of the Fourier transform of $A(\mathbf{s})$, i.e. $\rho(\mathbf{x})$ and $A^*(\mathbf{s})$, i.e. $\rho(-\mathbf{x})^{\ddagger}$. Therefore

$$I(\mathbf{s}) = \int P(\mathbf{x}) \exp(-2\pi i\mathbf{s}\cdot\mathbf{x}) \, d^3x$$

with

$$P(\mathbf{x}) = \rho(\mathbf{x}) * \rho(-\mathbf{x}) = \int \rho(\mathbf{u}) \cdot \rho(\mathbf{u}-\mathbf{x}) \, d^3u \,.$$

This integral is extended to the whole direct space and is called "Patterson function". It represents the average in the diffracting body of the product of the electronic densities at two points separated by the vector $\mathbf{x}$. For instance if the atoms were punctual, $P(\mathbf{x})$ would be zero unless $\mathbf{x}$ is one of the interatomic vector. In a single crystal with one atom per unit cell, the Patterson function reproduces the crystalline lattice. But in a complex crystal, it is the superposition of N lattices, N being the number of atoms in unit cell trans-

---

$\ddagger$ A.Guinier, X-ray diffraction, p. 360.

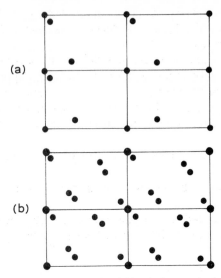

Fig. 2. Two-dimensional crystal containing 3 identical atoms in the unit cell, a crystal structure, b Patterson function.

lated by the interatomic vectors between the atoms of the motive in the unit cell (fig. 2).

The exact Patterson function requires the knowledge of the diffracted intensities in the whole reciprocal space. In fact, since $s = 2 \sin \theta/\lambda$, for a fixed wave-length, only the sphere of radius $2/\lambda$ may be experimentally explored in the reciprocal space. The inaccuracy due to this limitation corresponds to a limitation of the resolving power which is better with short wave-lengths (as for optical images).

It is *not straight forward* to deduce the atomic structure of a crystal from its Patterson function which contains all the available informations from diffraction. This is the major problem of the crystal structure determination. We shall not treat here this purely crystallographic question (H.Lipson and W.Cochran, The Crystalline State, Vol. 3 (Bell and Sons, London, 1953)). But we shall find in any problem the same fundamental difficulty due to the fact that only the amplitude of the diffracted wave is known but that its phase is lost. That is equivalent to say that X-ray diffraction does not give us a complete "image".

2.5. Reciprocal space of a crystal

Our aim is to determine the Fourier transform $A(\mathbf{s})$ (in the reciprocal space) of the electronic density $\rho(\mathbf{x})$ of the crystal with the aid of the general results of Fourier theory.

(a) Let us consider first the ensemble of the nodes of a crystalline lattice built on 3 fundamental vectors $\mathbf{a}, \mathbf{b}, \mathbf{c}$. We use the following property: its Fourier transform is another periodical lattice, called reciprocal lattice (r.l.). The importance of the reciprocal lattice in crystallography is a consequence of that relation with the crystal lattice. The properties of r.l. which we shall utilize are

1. the basic vectors of r.l. are $\mathbf{a}^{\times}, \mathbf{b}^{\times}, \mathbf{c}^{\times}$ defined by the relations

$$\mathbf{a} \cdot \mathbf{a}^{\times} = 1 \qquad \mathbf{b} \cdot \mathbf{a}^{\times} = 0 \qquad \mathbf{c} \cdot \mathbf{a}^{\times} = 0 \qquad \text{etc.}$$

2. If two vectors are defined, the one in the direct lattice $\mathbf{x} = X\mathbf{a} + Y\mathbf{b} + Z\mathbf{c}$ and the other in r.l. $\mathbf{s} = h\mathbf{a}^{\times} + k\mathbf{b}^{\times} + l\mathbf{c}^{\times}$ their scalar product is

$$\mathbf{s} \cdot \mathbf{x} = hX + kY + lZ .$$

Simple examples: the r.l. of a cubic lattice of parameter a is a cubic lattice of parameter $1/a$. The r.l. of a hexagonal lattice $(\mathbf{ac})$ is an hexagonal lattice of parameters $(1/2a \sqrt{3}), 1/c)$; the axis $\mathbf{c}^{\times}$ is parallel to $\mathbf{c}$. The axes $\mathbf{a}^{\times}$ make the angle $30°$ with $\mathbf{a}$. The correspondence between the two lattices (crystalline and reciprocal) is mathematically expressed in the following way. A point is represented by a three dimensional delta-function $\delta(\mathbf{x}-\mathbf{x}_n)$ and the ensemble of the nodes by the sum $g(\mathbf{x}) = \Sigma\ \delta(\mathbf{x}-\mathbf{x}_n)$ where $\mathbf{x}_n$ stands for $\mathbf{x}_{n_1 n_2 n_3} = n_1\ \mathbf{a} + n_2\ \mathbf{b} + n_3\mathbf{c}$, the integers $n_1 n_2 n_3$ taking every value positive or negative. The transform of $g(\mathbf{x})$ is

$$G(\mathbf{s}) = \frac{1}{V_c} \sum \delta(\mathbf{s}-\mathbf{s}_n)$$

where $\mathbf{s}_n$ is any r.l. vector $\mathbf{s}_n = h\mathbf{a}^{\times} + k\mathbf{b}^{\times} + l\mathbf{c}^{\times}$; V_c is the volume of the unit cell of the crystalline lattice. Therefore, the amplitude diffracted by the crystal proportional to $G(\mathbf{s})$ is zero unless the vector $\mathbf{s}$ is equipollent to a lattice vector of the r.l. This is the Bragg Law. The r.l. vector $\mathbf{s}^{\times}_{hkl} = h\mathbf{a}^{\times} + k\mathbf{b}^{\times} + l\mathbf{c}^{\times}$ is normal to the reticular plane of the crystal lattice (hkl) and the length of $r^{\times}_{hkl}$ is equal to $1/d_{hkl}$. Thus

$$s = \frac{2 \sin \theta}{\lambda} = \frac{1}{d_{hkl}}$$

or

$$\lambda = 2 d_{hkl} \sin \theta .$$

(b) We suppose now that the unit cell is filled with atoms producing an electronic density $\rho(\mathbf{x})$ in this cell. $\rho(\mathbf{x})$ is zero outside the unit cell, this cell being identically repeated around each node of the crystal lattice. That is expressed by a faltung of the density within one cell $\rho(\mathbf{x})$ by the crystal lattice $g(\mathbf{x})$. Thus the density in the whole crystal is written as

$$\rho'(\mathbf{x}) = \rho(\mathbf{x}) * g(\mathbf{x}) .$$

Now because of the faltung theorem, the diffracted amplitude which is the Fourier transform of $\rho'(\mathbf{x})$ is the simple product of the Fourier transform of $g(\mathbf{x})$ (or the r.l.) by $F(\mathbf{s})$, the Fourier transform of $\rho(\mathbf{x})$

$$A(\mathbf{s}) = F(\mathbf{s}) \cdot G(\mathbf{s}) = \frac{F(\mathbf{s})}{V_c} \sum \delta(\mathbf{s}-\mathbf{s}_n) .$$

We thus find the two well-known features of X-ray diffraction by crystals: (i) the location of the reflection of a crystal depends only on the crystal lattice, because $A(\mathbf{s})$ is zero if $\mathbf{s} \neq \mathbf{s}_n$ (ii) the amplitude of the reflection hkl is affected by the coefficient F_{hkl}, the *structure factor* which depends on the content of the cell

$$F_{hkl} = F(h\mathbf{a}^\times + k\mathbf{b}^\times + l\mathbf{c}^\times) = \int_{V_c} \rho(aX+bY+cZ)$$

$$\times \exp -2\pi i(hX+kY+cZ) \, dv_x .$$

The intensity of the reflection (hkl) is proportional to $|F_{hkl}|^2$.

The measurement of the relative intensities of the various reflections gives the value of the modules of the Fourier transform of $\rho(\mathbf{x})$ at regularly spaced points of the reciprocal space. This set of values (sometimes many thousands for large cell crystals) constitutes the data from which the determination of $\rho(\mathbf{x})$ is sought.

2.6. *Reciprocal space of a crystal of limited size*

Let us proceed a step further. In fact the crystal examined is always limited and sometimes very small. Previously, we had considered an infinite lattice, but now the diffracting body is a finite volume or *grain*. We write the density of the diffracting body as

$$\rho(x) = g(\mathbf{x}) \cdot \sigma(\mathbf{x}) . \tag{5}$$

$g(\mathbf{x})$ represents the unlimited lattice and $\sigma(\mathbf{x})$ the "form function" which is equal to 1 inside the grain and 0 outside.

Again we use the faltung theorem for calculating the transform of $\rho(\mathbf{x})$.

We know the transform of the first term of the product, $G(\mathbf{s})$, and we shall call $\Sigma(\mathbf{s})$ the transform of the second term $\sigma(\mathbf{x})$:

$$\Sigma(\mathbf{s}) = \int \sigma(\mathbf{x}) \exp(-2\pi i \mathbf{s} \cdot \mathbf{x}) \, d^3\mathbf{x} . \tag{6}$$

$\Sigma(\mathbf{s})$ has the following properties: it is a centrosymmetric function about the origin. It is maximum for $s = 0$. Further, $\Sigma(0) = V$, V being the volume of the diffracting crystal. (Recall $\sigma(\mathbf{x})$ is a step function of magnitude unity or zero.) Also, inverting eq. (6), we see that

$$\sigma(\mathbf{x}) = \int \Sigma(\mathbf{s}) \exp(2\pi i \mathbf{s} \cdot \mathbf{x}) \, d^3\mathbf{s} . \tag{7}$$

Setting $x = 0$ in eq. (7), we obtain

$$\Sigma(\mathbf{s}) \, d^3\mathbf{s} = 1 .$$

Since the integral of $\Sigma(\mathbf{s})$ over all $\mathbf{s}$ space is unity, and it achieves a value V for $s = 0$, it is clear that it can be appreciable in magnitude over a volume of s space only of the order $1/V$, or can have a linear extent of only $V^{-1/3} = D^{-1}$, where D is a linear dimension of the diffracting crystal.

The transform of $\rho(\mathbf{x})$ is, according to the faltung theorem

$$A(\mathbf{s}) = \int G(\mathbf{u}) \, \Sigma(\mathbf{s} - \mathbf{u}) \, d^3\mathbf{u} = 1/V_c$$

$$\times \int \sum_{o}^{\infty} \delta(\mathbf{u} - \mathbf{s_m}) \, \Sigma(\mathbf{s} - \mathbf{u}) \, d^3\mathbf{u} .$$

Consider one of the Dirac delta functions constituting $G(\mathbf{u})$: $\delta(\mathbf{u}-\mathbf{s}_j)$. (This is a normalized function equal to zero for all values of u different from $\mathbf{s}_j$.) The resulting integral gives

$$\int \delta(\mathbf{u}-\mathbf{s}_j)\,\Sigma(\mathbf{s}-\mathbf{u})\,\mathrm{d}^3\mathbf{u} = \Sigma(\mathbf{s}-\mathbf{s}_j)\ .$$

Each of the δ functions corresponding to a node of the reciprocal lattice gives a similar contribution $\Sigma(\mathbf{s}-\mathbf{s}_i)$. In all, the series of functions referred to each node of the reciprocal lattice constitutes the desired function

$$A(\mathbf{s}) = \frac{1}{V_c} \sum_i \Sigma(\mathbf{s}-\mathbf{s}_i)\ .$$

Now we have seen that each function was confined about the origin to distances of the order of D^{-1}. If, therefore, the crystal is not too small, say $D \approx 1000\,\text{Å}$, the domain which surrounds the node will have a linear dimension of the order of $1/1000$ that of the unit cell of the reciprocal lattice; therefore, there will be essentially no overlapping of one function $\Sigma(\mathbf{s}-\mathbf{s}_i)$ and the complex conjugate of any other $\Sigma(\mathbf{s}-\mathbf{s}_j)$, if $j \neq i$, so that the square of the modulus of the scattered amplitude reduces to a sum of squares over all reciprocal lattice points,

$$I(\mathbf{s}) = |A(\mathbf{s})|^2 = 1/V_c^2 \sum_j |\Sigma(\mathbf{s}-\mathbf{s}_j)|^2 \tag{8}$$

all cross terms vanishing to a very good approximation because of this orthogonality.

If the vector $\mathbf{s}$ coincides exactly with a reciprocal lattice vector $\mathbf{s}_j$ (recall $\Sigma(0) = V$), the scattering power $I(\mathbf{s})$ becomes (V^2/V_c^2), V/V_c is the number of unit cells in the crystal. That is, all unit cells scatter coherently.

Thus, when the diffracting crystal is small, the *r.l. nodes are replaced by domains which surround the nodes*: that means that the diffracted intensity is no more concentrated in one direction but in a solid angle around this direction. The smaller the crystal the broader the angular domain of diffraction. On the photographic diagram, the tiny Bragg spots are replaced by diffuse spots, the width of which is inversely proportional to the size of the crystal.

With usual X-ray wave-length, it is experimentally possible by measurement of the broadening of reflection spots for isolated crystals, or Debye-Scherrer lines for power, to determine the size of submicroscopic crystals in the range of 10 to 500 Å.

2.7. *Small angle scattering*

The formula (8) shows that every r.l. node is broadened by the size effect, thus in particular the node 000. That corresponds to a scattering surrounding the incident beam: this is the "small angle scattering". For a small crystal, SAS gives the same information as the observation of any r.l. node. But the applications of SAS are much more general: (i) For a powder, every grain whatever its orientation, contributes to SAS. Thus, the SAS spot is much more intense than a broadened DS line. It gives an average value of the transform of the form factor of the grains. In fact SAS leads to a well defined geometrical parameter, the *radius of gyration R* of the grains ($MR^2 = I$, M being the mass of the particle and I its moment of inertia relative to the center of mass); (ii) The SAS depends only on the shape and size of the grain but not on its atomic structure. Suppose that its density ρ_o is uniform: the grain is described by $\rho_o \sigma(\mathbf{x})$, $\sigma(\mathbf{x})$ being the form factor. The diffracted amplitude is $\rho_o \Sigma(\mathbf{s})$ and the intensity $\rho_o^2 |\Sigma(\mathbf{s})|^2$. This is exactly the same formula as for the crystal. The result can be generalised to amorphous solids, liquids, etc.

To sum up, SAS is characteristic of the heterogeneity of electronic density and gives information about the size of this heterogeneity (but the method is practical only in the range of 10 to 1000Å for experimental reasons).

When the grain is very anisotropic, its shape is easy to find through the SAS. As an example, let us calculate the reciprocal lattice for a cubic crystal having the shape of a parallelepiped with sides $N_a\mathbf{a}, N_b\mathbf{b}, N_c\mathbf{c}$ ($a=b=c$). Let us call x_a, x_b, x_c the projections of the vector $\mathbf{x}$ on the crystal axes. The form function $\sigma(\mathbf{x})$ is equal to unity in the volume where, simultaneously,

$$|x_a| < N_a a/2 , \quad |x_b| < N_b a/2 , \quad |x_c| < N_c a/2 .$$

To calculate the Fourier transform,

$$\Sigma(\mathbf{s}) = \int \sigma(\mathbf{x}) \exp(-2\pi i \mathbf{s} \cdot \mathbf{x}) \, dv_x ,$$

we define **s** by its projections s_a, s_b, s_c on the axes of the reciprocal lattice

$$\Sigma(s) = \int_{\text{crystal}} \exp\left(-2\pi i(s_a x_a + s_b x_b + s_c x_c)\right) dv_x$$

$$= \int_{-N_a a/2}^{+N_a a/2} \exp\left(-2\pi i s_a x_a\right) dx_a \int_{-N_b a/2}^{+N_b a/2} \exp\left(-2\pi i s_b x_b\right) dx_b$$

$$\int_{-N_c a/2}^{+N_c a/2} \exp\left(-2\pi i s_c x_c\right) dx_c \, .$$

This gives

$$|\Sigma(s)|^2 = \frac{\sin^2(N_a s_a a)}{\pi^2 s_a^2} \frac{\sin^2(N_b s_b a)}{\pi^2 s_b^2} \frac{\sin^2(N_c s_c a)}{\pi^2 s_c^2}$$

and

$$I(s) = \frac{1}{V V_c} |\Sigma(s)|^2$$

$$= \frac{1}{N_a N_b N_c} \frac{\sin^2(\pi N_a s_a a)}{(\pi s_a a)^2} \frac{\sin^2(N_b s_b a)}{(\pi s_b a)^2} \frac{\sin^2(N_c s_c a)}{(\pi s_c a)^2} \, . \tag{9}$$

Eq. (9) is obtained by neglecting all the terms of the rigorous eq. (8) except that which is related to the nearest node. The exact calculation (8) leads to a formula similar to (9) but containing in the denominator $(\sin(\pi s_a a))^2$ instead of $(\pi s_a a)^2$, and so on. For not too small crystals the results are practically equivalent, because each one of the factors of the product appearing in eq. (9) is nearly zero for $s_i > 1/N_i a$. However, because of the function $\sin^2 \Phi / \Phi^2$ we can expect weak secondary maxima. These have been observed experimentally with very thin crystals obtained by evaporation: the spacing of the secondary maxima gives the thickness of the crystals.

If the crystals have the form of thin plates of large area (N_a small, N_b and N_c large), the reflection domain, according to eq. (9) is elongated like a needle of length $1/N_a a$ and is perpendicular to the plane of the crystal. Inversely, if the crystals are needle shaped (N_a large, N_b and N_c small), the reflection domain has the form of a plate which is perpendicular to the axis of the needle and whose diameter is of the order of $1/N_b a$. The reciprocity existing between the functions and their Fourier transforms is illustrated in fig. 3.

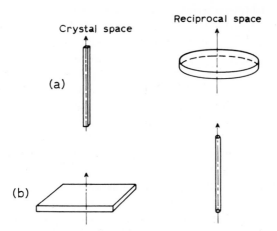

Fig. 3. The reflection domain for a small crystal having the form of a needle, at a, and of a small plate, at b.

2.8. *Reciprocal space of an imperfect crystal*

In real crystals, the atoms are not rigourously located on a periodic lattice and the defects play a prominent role for determining many properties of the solid. It is thus very important to detect the crystalline defects and to observe their structure at an atomic scale. It is in fact a very difficult experimental problem. Any of the possible methods are sensitive only to some peculiar kinds of defects. In this chapter we shall show the possibilities of X-ray diffraction. The limiting condition is that the number of atoms, anomalous either by their nature or their position, represent a not too small proportion of the total number of atoms (at least a few %). We suppose that the real crystal may be described by a deformation of the regular crystal, small enough to allow a one to one correspondence between any atom and one site of the ideal lattice. Thus the real crystal is represented by the ensemble of the nodes of a regular lattice; the nth node being affected by the scattering factor f_n. In the perfect crystal, f_n was independent from the number of the node. If different atoms A, B ... are mixed on one lattice (substitution disorder), f_n is either f_A or f_B etc. If the homologous atoms are all similar, but are displaced from the node, by a vector Δx_n, it is equivalent to an atom located at the node but having a complex scattering factor $f \exp(-2i\pi s \cdot \Delta x_n)$; of course substitution and displacement disorders may be simultaneous.

We have then, for evaluating the diffracted amplitude, to calculate the Fourier transform of a geometrically regular lattice the nodes of which are affected by variable coefficients f_n. Let us recall that in the case of a crystal in which the atoms are distributed in the unit cell ($\rho(x)$ is different from zero outside the nodes of the crystalline.lattice), there corresponds a r.l. whose nodes have variable coefficients, (namely the structure factors F_{hkl}). Conversely, because of the perfect reciprocity of the Fourier transformation, a lattice of points with variable coefficients corresponds to a transform which has the same periods as the reciprocal lattice and which can have non-zero values in the unit cell outside the nodes.

It is possible to foresee in a very general way the effects of perturbations in the crystal lattice on the diffraction pattern. An imperfect crystal produces diffracted radiation which is not well localized, as is that produced by a perfect crystal. There are still strong diffractions according to the Bragg law for the average ideal lattice, but in other directions the wavelets emitted by the individual atoms do not cancel perfectly by interference because cancellation is the direct consequence of the perfect periodicity of the diffracting medium.

The diffraction can be appreciable in directions close to those of the perfect average crystal and then, experimentally, the diffraction lines or spots are broadened. We have already seen an example of this in our study of small crystals, but irregularities in large crystals can have similar effects.

The diffracted intensity can also be appreciable in all directions, even in directions remote from those of diffraction by the average perfect crystal. This effect is called diffuse scattering, the term diffraction being reversed for the lines or spots which can be either sharp or broad, but whose positions are given by the Bragg Law. In general, diffuse scattering is very weak compared to the normal diffractions.

In the case of the perfect crystal, the intensity is entirely concentrated at the nodes of the r.l. For the imperfect crystal, a fraction of this intensity is removed from the nodes and distributed in the unit cell. Diffuse scattering therefore produces a decrease of the intensity of the Bragg reflections.

We shall use the following theorem[‡]: the intensity of the diffuse scattering is the Fourier transform of the pattern formed by the nodes of the average crystal lattice: the coefficient Φ_m affected to the node defined by the lattice vector x_m (m for m_1, m_2, m_3) is the difference between the average of the product $F_n F_{n+m}^x$ of the structure factors of two unit cells separated by the vector x_m and the squared average $|\overline{F}_n|^2$. Thus the observed scattering depends not only on the magnitude of the deviation from the average cell but on the *correlation* between these disorders.

[‡] See the demonstration in: A.Guinier, X-ray diffraction (Freeman, 1963) p. 164.

(a) When there is no correlation between the perturbations existing in the unit cells even when they are neighbours, only ϕ_0 is different from zero, thus ϕ_m is represented by a delta function $\delta(\mathbf{x})$, whose transform is a *constant*.

(b) If there exists a strong correlation between the perturbation in the various unit cells, i.e. if the coefficients ϕ_m decrease slowly with m, the scattered intensity is concentrated around the nodes of the reciprocal lattice. This is the case where we simply have a broadening of the nodes or of the lines in powder patterns.

It is obvious that all the intermediate cases are possible where we have at the same time broad diffraction spots and diffuse scattering which is more or less intense and more or less modulated.

The influence of the correlation is especially striking for *planar* or *linear* disorders. In the first, the lattice planes of a certain family (π) preserve their accurate periodicity and remain parallel between themselves, but they are no more arranged periodically. The amplitude diffracted by a single plane (π) is concentrated on the rows of r.l. normal to (π). In the regular crystal, inter-ferences between the planes cancel any intensity except at the r.l. nodes, but in the disordered crystal, this cancellation is not total and scattering is ob-servable along the rows and outside these rows, the diffracted intensity is zero as for a single plane (fig. 4).

For linear disorder, the periodicity is preserved in only one direction (D) and the scattering is concentrated on the family of reticular planes of the r.l. normal to (D). This second case is the inverse of the first, because of the reciprocity of Fourier transforms.

We shall now discuss two examples of studies of imperfect crystals for which X-ray diffraction gives better results than any other method.

(a) *Measurement of short range order parameters*. A binary solid solution has a geometrically perfect lattice but the crystal is non periodic because the homologous nodes are occupied by different atoms A or B. It becomes a per-fect crystal only if A and B are rigorously ordered. The Long Range Order produces new nodes in the reciprocal space (superlattice reflections). In the opposite extreme case, A and B atoms are distributed at random and in the intermediate cases, there exists a certain correlation between the nature of the atoms located at neighbouring sites. These correlations are defined by Short Range Order parameters corresponding to the different lattice vectors but only the short ones intervene.

The substitution disorder produces a diffuse scattering from the measure-ment of which the values of SRO parameters may be deduced. Experimentally, the scattering is characterised by broad and diffuse maxima located in r.l. at the positions, where the superlattice nodes would appear if the lattice were completely ordered.

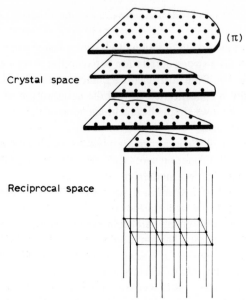

Fig. 4. Planar disorder. The planes (π) are identical and parallel, but arranged irregularly.
Scattering in reciprocal space is then limited to the rows normal to (π).

According to the general theory, we have calculated the coefficient ϕ_m corresponding to the lattice vector x_m

$$\phi_m = \langle (F_n - \overline{F})(F^*_{n+m} - \overline{F^*}) \rangle$$

F_n being F_A or F_B. The SRO parameter for x_m, α_m, is proportional to ϕ_m which defines the degree of correlation between the two sites. It can be shown[‡] that:

$$\phi_m = C_A C_B (F_A - F_B)^2 \, \alpha_m \, ,$$

where C_A and C_B are the atomic concentrations; $\alpha_m = 0$ (for $m \neq 0$) if the disorder is total, and reaches its maximum value for perfect order. Its statistical definition is

$$\alpha_m = 1 - \frac{n_{BA}}{C_A} \, .$$

[‡] A.Guinier, X-ray diffraction, p. 264; B.E.Warren, X-ray diffraction (Addison Wesley, 1961).

n_{BA} is the proportion of the pairs of atoms, in which a B atom is at the origin and A at the extremity.

The α_m may be calculated by a Fourier transform of the repartition of the diffuse scattering in the reciprocal space. This implies very long measurements but Warren and his school have shown on numerous examples (especially Au Cu alloys) the accuracy which can be obtained. X-rays are an essential tool for determining the details of the structure of a solid solution.

Generally, when in a system there is no ordered state, it is considered that the solid solution is random. If the disorder is perfect, that means that there is *no* correlation between the occupation of any couple of sites in the lattice: all the α_m are equal to zero, except α_o which is equal to 1. The direct space is thus constituted by a single point at the origin affected by the coefficient $\phi_o = C_A C_B (f_A - f_B)^2$. The Fourier transformation gives a diffuse scattering which is uniform in the reciprocal space and equal to $C_A C_B (f_A - f_B)^2$. This is called the "Laue monotonic scattering". But this result supposes that none of the atoms are displaced from the nodes of a periodic lattice. The correction for such distorsions may be not negligible.

Any difference found experimentally with this result proves that the solid solution is not completely random. For instance it has been shown that in dilute Al-Zn solid solution, the Zn atoms are not randomly dispersed, but that they have a tendency to cluster with an average of 2 atoms per cluster.

(b) *Displacement disorder in the perovskite KNbO$_3$.* The phase transformations of perovskites have been extensively studied since they are linked to the ferroelectric properties: but in addition to these changes between normal crystal structures, it has been recently shown that the crystal exhibits a special kind of lattice imperfection which should also play an important role in the ferroelectricity. The phenomena are especially intense and easy to study in the case of KNbO$_3$; we shall here discuss this example, and show how a model for the irregular structure can be deduced from experiment.

KNbO$_3$ is rhomboedric at low temperatures and with increasing temperature becomes successively orthorhombic, tetragonal and finally cubic (fig. 5).

In every form except the first and less symmetrical, a strong scattering is observed. The first task is to localize the scattering in the reciprocal space. In this case, one finds that it is concentrated in the three $|h\ 0\ 0|$ planes for the cubic form, $|h\ 0\ 0|$ and $|0\ h\ 0|$ for the tetragonal, $|0\ h\ 0|$ for the orthorhombic. Generally it was admitted that the perovskite was a normal crystal having a cubic cell in the high symmetry form and that this cell is distorted when the symmetry is lowered. In fact the existence of a scattering proves that the perovskite is not rigorously periodic: in other words the unit cells, except in the rhomboedral form, are not identical. Because the effect does not depend on the purity of the crystal, the disorder must be due to atomic displacements.

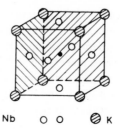

● Nb   O O   ⊘ K

Fig. 5. Unit cell of the cubic form of KNbO$_3$.

The hypotheses which have proved to be successful are: (i) the main-cause of disorder is the displacement of the Nb atom out of the center of the ideal perovskite cell, and (ii) that this atom is pushed in one of 8 equivalent sites on the four [111] axes passing by the center of the cell. If in every cell the direction of the displacement is the same, the crystal is perfect and its symmetry is rhomboedral: this is what happens at low temperature. For the other phases the direction of displacement varies from cell to cell between 2, 4 or 8 axes respectively in the orthorhombic, tetragonal and cubic forms.

The general theory shows that the repartition of the intensity of scattering depends on the nature of correlation of the disorder between cells. From the localization of the scattering in r.l. planes, one deduces immediately that the correlation must be extended at large distances along axes ⟨0 0 h⟩ in the crystal. For simplicity sake, we shall now consider only the orthorhombic phase.

Let us consider a crystal of N_1, N_2, N_3 cells along the three pseudo-cubic axes. The scattering being visible only on the |0 k 0| r.l. planes, the crystal must be constituted by perfectly periodical |0 k 0| rows, the period being **b** along this axis, but there rows are not all identical and that is the origin of the disorder in the structure.

There is one half of the |0 k 0| rows of cells with a displacement Δx, $+\Delta y$, Δz and the other half with a displacement Δx, $-\Delta y$, Δz (positions 1 and 2, fig. 6).

In the x, z plane, the projection of all the rows are identical and thus there is no cause of disorder: but the square is distorted into a losange by the $(\Delta x, \Delta z)$ displacement of the Nb atoms. The average cell is thus orthorhombic.

The rows are arranged at the nodes of a perfectly periodic two dimensional lattice of $N_1 \times N_3$ cells and the two kinds of rows (up and down) are distributed at random.

The scattering produced by the disorder described above is easy to calculate.

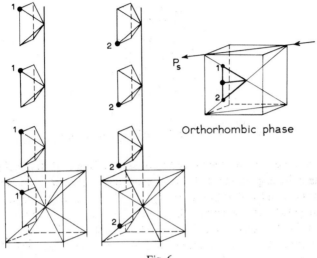

Orthorhombic phase

Fig. 6.

We take into account only the Nb atoms, this simplification being justified by the relatively small scattering factor of 0 and K. The structure factor of a cell "up" is: $f \exp(2\pi i s \cdot \Delta y)$ and $f \exp(-2\pi i s \cdot \Delta y)$ for a cell "down". The amplitudes for the two kinds of rows are

$$F_1 = f \sum_{n=0}^{n=N_2} \exp(2\pi i s \cdot n b) \exp(2\pi i s \cdot \Delta y)$$

$$F_2 = f \sum_{n=0}^{n=N_2} \exp(2\pi i s \cdot n b) \exp(-2\pi i s \cdot \Delta y) .$$

The irregular mixture of the two kinds of rows at the nodes of the two-dimensional lattice in the xz planes gives rise to a "Laue monotonic scattering" equal to $N_1 N_3 C_1 C_2 (F_1 - F_2)^2$. Here $C_1 = C_2 = \frac{1}{2}$. Thus

$$I(s) = \frac{1}{4} N_1 N_3 f^2 \left| \sum \exp\left(2\pi i s \cdot n b\right) \right|^2 \, 4 \sin^2\left(2\pi s \cdot \Delta y\right)$$

$$= N_1 N_3 f^2 \, \frac{\sin^2 \pi N_2 s \cdot b}{\sin^2 \pi s \cdot b} \, \sin^2 \pi s \cdot \Delta y \, .$$

This formula explains the main features of the observed scattering. (1) If N_2 is very large, the function $\sin^2 N_2 \pi s \cdot b / \sin^2 \pi s \cdot b$ is different from zero, only if $s \cdot b$ = integer the scattering is thus localized in the family of reticular planes of the r.l. (0 k 0). (2) If N_2 is not very large, the width of the planar domain of scattering increases, and N_2 may be determined by its broadening. Experimentally, N_2 is found of the order of 10 to 20. (3) Δy is parallel to b and s_y very nearly equal to hb, thus $s \cdot \Delta y = hb\Delta y$. The intensity in one plane of scattering is determined by the factor $\sin^2 (2\pi h b \Delta y)$. It is zero in the plane passing through the origin and grows with increasing h. That is just what is observed. The fact that there is no scattering at the center is characteristic of a displacement disorder. It is *not* zero if there is a substitution disorder alone or superposed to the displacement disorder. (4) We have supposed that the mutual arrangement of the rows "up" and "down" was random. Therefore the intensity is uniform in the plane (0 k 0). If it was not the case, that would mean that there exists a kind of more or less definite order between the rows "up" and "down", either a segregation in bundles of the two types or inversely a tendency to alternation.

This example shows all the informations that a simple qualitative experiment brings on the structural defects of a crystal. No other method than X-rays is able to give this kind of results so easily. It is interesting to note that these disorder phenomena were not known until some years ago, although perovskites, and especially $BaTiO_3$, have been the subject of extensive studies. That shows that the technique of X-ray scattering is not yet used as it should be.

However it must be pointed out that the scattering, characteristic of the disorder in crystals, is generally weak and requires much more elaborate techniques than the conventional X-ray methods (rotating crystal, etc.).

Especially the counter diffractometer which constitutes the standard equipment of most of X-ray laboratories is not well adapted if used alone to this kind of work. The repartition of scattering may be so complicated that a preliminary photographic diagram is often necessary and also the filtered radiation of the usual diffractometer must be replaced by a monochromatic one.

Finally, one must not forget that the scattering data, even if they are complete and accurate, are not equivalent to an "image". Their interpretation may be not unique and sometimes one can only verify if a proposed model of imperfection is or is not compatible with the experiment.

3. Neutron diffraction

The associated wavelength of a neutron of velocity v is according to the De Broglie formula

$$\lambda(\text{Å}) = 4/v_{(km/s)} \, .$$

The neutrons are not accelerated. One simply uses their thermal agitation: from the moderator of the reactor a fine beam is selected by two apertures. This beam is polychromatic; it contains neutrons of different velocities, the repartition of which depends on the temperature of the source. When it is near the room temperature, the predominent wave lengths are of the order of 2Å, which is nearly equal to the wave length of the X-rays used in crystallography. Therefore the diffraction phenomena with neutrons are expected to be very similar to those given by X-rays. The theory of diffraction is the same and the various techniques of X-ray diffraction are transposed with neutrons. Why then use neutrons in addition to X-rays? This is the question we shall now answer in evaluating the advantages but also the disadvantages of neutrons.

3.1.

The sources of neutrons give a continuous spectrum (neutrons of various velocities) whereas a X-ray tube emits the strong characteristic radiation with a well defined and isolated wave-length. This fact greatly facilitates most of the diffraction experiments: a monochromator is only used to eliminate the weak continuous background. But with neutrons a narrow band is cut by the necessary monochromator from the continuous spectrum, but this band is always much broader than the X-ray characteristic radiations and furthermore is never very intense.

The monochromatic flux which is practically obtained in the best conditions from a reactor of average power is of the order of 10^6 n/cm^2/s, whereas in the monochromatic beam of an ordinary X-ray tube,, the number of photons is of the order of 10^{10}. Fortunately, this inferiority of the neutrons may be partly compensated because the absorption of neutrons in most of the substances is very small. Therefore the volume of the specimen for a neutron experiment may be 10^3 thicker than for an X-ray experiment: the volume of the diffracting sample may be very much increased, and so the intensity of the diffracted beam.

3.2.

The experiments with neutrons require a reactor of course, large diffracto-meters, heaving shieldings for protection, the counting time for measuring the neutron flux with a reasonable accuracy is long because of the weak intensity of the neutrons sources. Thus these experiments are complicated and very costly.

Nevertheless, neutrons are used by solid state physicists more and more fre-quently, because neutrons give informations which no other diffraction method can give. That is due to the modes of interaction between neutrons and atoms.

3.3. *Interaction between neutrons and atoms*

There are two processes which we shall describe successively (i) the neu-trons is scattered by the *nucleus* of the atoms and (ii) because the neutron has a magnetic moment, it interacts with the atoms having a *magnetic mo-ment*. In opposition, X-rays are scattered only by the *electrons* of the atoms.

3.3.1. Nuclear scattering

Consider a beam of monoenergetic (or monochromatic) neutrons travelling along the Z axis with a velocity v.

The corresponding wave is represented by the equation

$$\psi = \exp(2\pi i K z) \qquad \text{with} \qquad K = \frac{1}{\lambda} = \frac{mv}{h}.$$

The density of neutrons is $\psi\psi^*$, i.e. 1, and the flux of neutrons traversing the area per unit time is equal to v. A nucleus receiving this wave produces a scattered spherical wave coherent with the incident wave, which we can write

$$\psi' = -\frac{b}{r} \exp(2\pi i K r)$$

b defining the scattered amplitude is called the *scattering length*. It depends on the interaction potential between the neutron and the nucleus: but this po-tential is not theoretically calculable. Nevertheless, something is known: the domain of interaction is very small, of the order of the nucleus diameter, 10^{-13} cm and as this range of interaction is very much smaller than the wave length, the nucleus scatters like a point: consequently, we can predict that the amplitude of scattering is uniform in the reciprocal space (the Fourier transform of a δ-function is a constant). In fact, it is verified that the scattering length does not depend neither on the angle nor on the neutron wavelength. The density of scattered neutrons at a distance r is $\psi'\psi'^x = |b|^2/r^2$, the flux of scattered neutron is $(b^2/r^2)v$ per unit area and the total number of scattered neutrons is $4\pi|b|^2v$, since b is constant in any direction. As the incoming flux of neutrons is equal to v, the cross-section for scattering is $4\pi b^2$; the differential cross-section $d\sigma/d\omega$ is equal to $|b|^2$. For X-rays, the differential cross section $d\sigma/d\omega$ for one atom is equal to $\frac{1}{2}f^2r_e^2(1+\cos^2 2\theta)$, r_e is the classical radius of electrons (2.8×10^{-13} cm) and f the atomic scattering factor. Thus b plays for neutrons the role of f for X-rays.

The experimental measurement of b for the different atoms leads to the following conclusions: (1) b is real, (with some exceptions) positive for most atoms (that corresponds to a phase change of π in the process of scattering), and negative for only 5 atoms, among them H; there is then no phase change). (2) The absolute value of b is of the order of 10^{-12} cm. It varies *irregularly* across the periodic table without any obvious correlation with the atomic number or the rank of the column. It varies from -0.38×10^{-12} for H to 1.3×10^{-12} for Hg.

This is a major difference with X-rays for which the scattering factor increases proportionally to Z. The consequence is that with X-rays: (i) it is practically impossible to distinguish atoms of consecutive Z. For instance $(f_{Cu}/f_{Zn})^2 = 0.96$. (ii) it is practically impossible to measure the diffraction due to a light atom in a crystal in which the other atoms are heavy. For instance, oxygen in UO_2; the proton does *not* scatter X-rays. Thus it is not possible to localize hydrogen atoms in organic molecules etc.

On the other hand, with neutrons neighbouring atoms *may* have different scattering length $(b_{Cu}/b_{Zn})^2 = 1.7$; the ratio of b for a hydrogen atom and another is suitable for good measurements (the ratio (b_H/b_U) is about 5).

Thus one sees that the neutron diffraction may give results which it is impossible to get with X-rays and it is one of the cause of the importance of neutron diffraction.

3.3.2. Incoherent scattering

A complication which does not exist in X-ray diffraction occurs with neutron. When we have attributed *one* scattering length to a given nucleus, it was correct only for nuclei with zero-spin. When the nucleus has a nuclear spin I and interacts with the neutron (spin $\frac{1}{2}$), the transitory complex constituted by the neutron absorbed in the nucleus may have two spins $I + \frac{1}{2}$ or

$I - \frac{1}{2}$. The atoms affected by the scattering lengths b_+ or b_- are mixed in complete disorder at the nodes of the crystal lattice in proportion w_+ and w_-, (these numbers are theoretically calculable). The diffraction by such a disordered solid solution is a problem which we have discussed for X-rays: (1) the diffraction figure is that of a perfectly periodic crystal with a single fictitious atom the scattering length of which would be the average scattering length. (2) in addition there is a background of uniform scattering in any direction. It is equivalent to say that the atoms emit a "coherent" scattering giving rise to intereferences with a coherent scattering length $b = (w_+b_+ + w_-b_-)$, and in addition an "incoherent" scattering which gives no interference, the total intensity of which is the sum of the incoherent intensity of each atom. According to the Laue formula valid for solid solutions, the cross-section for incoherent scattering is: $4\pi w_+ w_- (b_+ - b_-)^2$. It may be important because b_+ may be very different from b_-. For instance, for hydrogen b_+ and b_- are equal to $+1.04 \times 10^{-12}$ and -4.7×10^{-12}, w_+ and w_- are $\frac{3}{4}$ and $\frac{1}{4}$. Thus the average scattering length is much smaller than b_+ or b_- (-0.38); the incoherent cross-section is 78.5 barn (or 10^{-24} cm^2), whereas the coherent cross-section is only 1.8 barn.

There is another cause of incoherent scattering when an atomic species is really a mixture of different *isotopes*, because these isotopes may have very different scattering lengths. Thus an "element" is really an alloy of isotopes and this mixture of different atoms at the nodes of a lattice produces also a "Laue scattering"; one can say that this atom (with isotopes) emits an incoherent scattering. If the isotopes 1, 2, 3 ... have the concentration $c_1 c_2$ ... and respectively the scattering lengths $b_1 b_2$ ... the incoherent scattering correspond to a cross-section given by the Laue formula $4\pi[(c_1 b_1^2 + c_2 b_2^2 ...) - (c_1 b_1 + c_2 b_2 + ...)^2]$.

In spite of the relatively large value of the incoherent scattering in some cases, it is generally not very troublesome in the study of the diffraction of crystals. Consider a crystal of N atoms: when the conditions of a Bragg reflection are fulfilled the cross-section for the maximum of the reflection is $N^2 b_{coh}^2$ whereas the background of incoherent scattering has an intensity $N b_{incoh}^2$. Therefore even for a powder of microcrystals, the diffraction lines appear very clearly above a weak constant background. However, in the study of the crystalline imperfections by means of the diffuse scattering outside the Bragg reflections this diffuse scattering may be of the same order or weaker than the incoherent scattering. These conditions are very variable with the nature of atoms. Before planning this kind of experiments, it is necessary to evaluate the intensity of the unavoidable incoherent scattering. The ideal atom which does not give any incoherent scattering is formed by one single isotope without nuclear spin.

3.3.3. Magnetic scattering

The neutron has a magnetic moment ($\gamma = 1.9$ nuclear Bohr magneton) and thus has an interaction with the magnetic field of an atom possessing a magnetic moment. This interaction is the origin of a scattering of the neutron. The magnetically scattered wavelets issued from the different atoms may interfere and the resulting diffraction gives informations about the mutual arrangement of the magnetic moments as interferences of the wave scattered by the nucleus give informations on the *atomic* structures. Neutron diffraction through the magnetic scattering has very important and specific applications for the study of magnetic materials.

The magnetic interaction and hence the magnetic scattering cross-section may be calculated from the electronic state of the atoms. We shall give here only the main conclusions. For simplicity sake, we shall consider only atoms in s state (without orbital moment).

The scattered amplitude is defined by two parameters, its magnitude or scattering length *and* the phase change due to scattering, therefore the amplitude is generally represented by a vector. Let us consider the scattering vector $\mathbf{K}$ ($K = 2 \sin \theta / \lambda$) parallel to the bissectrice of the direction of incident and scattered neutrons, and the plane (π) normal to $\mathbf{K}$ passing by the atom O.

The atomic spin S makes an angle α with $\mathbf{K}$. (1) The magnitude of the amplitude is equal to

$$b_{cm} = 0.539 \times 10^{-12} \, S \sin \alpha f(K) . \tag{10}$$

(2) The phase is given by the angle between the projection Sq of S and an arbitrary direction in (π) chosen as origin. The vector representing the amplitude is then

$$\mathbf{b} = 0.539 \times 10^{-12} \, S \sin \alpha f(K) \mathbf{q} . \tag{11}$$

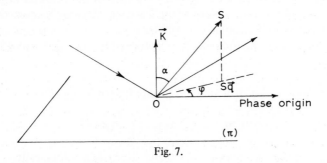

Fig. 7.

Let us now interpret these results. As S is of the order of unity, the first point is that the magnetic scattering has an intensity comparable to that of the nuclear scattering.

In opposition to the nuclear scattering, the magnetic scattering is a function of the scattering angle, because the responsible electrons are spread in the volume of the atom: $f(K)$ is a form factor representing the Fourier transform of the density of the electrons carrying the spin of the atom: it is equal to unity for $K = 0$ and decreases with K like a scattering factor for X-rays. However the two form factors are not identical for the same atom, because all the electrons scatter X-rays but only the outer d or f electrons intervene in the magnetic moment (consequently the form factor for neutron decreases more rapidly than for X-rays).

The neutrons of the incident beam can be seen as the addition of two beams having their spin directions parallel and antiparallel to any arbitrary direction. If the number of the two species are equal, the beam is called unpolarised and in this case, the nuclear and magnetic scatterings are *incoherent*: that is to say, the total intensity is simply the sum of the intensities of the two scatterings. For a single direction of spin, there is no more simple addition of the intensities. The amplitude of the magnetic scattering is different for neutrons of opposite spins. It happens that in the reflection by a magnetized crystal, the nuclear and magnetic scatterings cancel each other almost exactly for one spin direction. Thus in this special case the reflected beam is totally polarized.

3.3.4. Diffraction by crystals containing magnetic atoms

Now we shall study the magnetic scattering produced by an assembly of atoms with a magnetic moment. The results of the interferences between the magnetically scattered wavelets depend on the magnetic order.

(1) Paramagnetic crystals. The moments ($\mu = 2S\mu_B$) of the atoms at the nodes of the crystal lattice are completely disoriented and therefore according to the formula (11), the phases of the scattered waves are random without any correlation even between near neighbours. According to a general theorem in diffraction theory, the total intensity diffracted by N atoms is equal to $N \langle b^2 \rangle$.

$$\langle b^2 \rangle_{cm2} = 0.29 \times 10^{-24} \langle S^2 \rangle \langle \sin \alpha^2 \rangle f^2(K)$$

$$= 0.29 \times 10^{-24} S(S+1) \tfrac{2}{3} f^2(K) .$$

The scattering is maximum for $K = 0$ and decreases monotonically with increasing K. It is superimposed to the nuclear diffraction and the nuclear incoherent scattering. If these contributions can be substracted, one can measure the form factor $f(K)$ and, thus, the distribution of the magnetic electrons in the atom.

(2) Ferro- and antiferro magnetic crystals. There is a long range order between the atomic moments. The phases of the magnetic scattering by all the atoms are well defined and interferences produce a crystalline diffraction. In a ferromagnetic crystal, all the spins are parallel and the scattering factors are identical within a ferromagnetic domain. The magnetic diffraction is simply superimposed upon the nuclear diffraction at the same location in reciprocal space.

In a antiferromagnetic crystal, the atoms alternate with opposite spin directions. The neutrons differentiate the two series of atoms, because the phases of the scattered waves are opposite. The crystal is equivalent to an ordered alloy and magnetic reflections appear as superlattice reflections. The analysis of the diffraction diagram shows the repartition of the spins in the cell. Because the angle α between the moment and the scattering vector intervenes (formula (11) and fig. 7), it is possible to find the direction of the spins in relation to the crystal axes.

3.4.4. Inelastic scattering

The scattering is inelastic when the energy of the scattered particle (photon or neutron) is different from that of the incident one. In the case of a crystal, the difference of energy may be furnished or absorbed by the lattice vibrations. The thermal agitation of the atoms produces an inelastic diffuse scattering: the difference of the energy of the particles before and after the scattering represents one photon (or sometimes 2, 3 ...). The quantum for the elastic waves in a crystal is of the order of 0.01 eV. Therefore this difference is completely invisible for X-ray photons ($h\nu \cong 10000$ eV), but it is quite important for thermal neutrons (0.05 eV for 1 Å wave length). The change of momentum is considerable and may be measured. So neutrons are an unique tool for the study of the phonons in a crystal.

The two equations of inelastic scattering are written as the conservation of energy and the conservation of momentum. Let us consider an elastic wave of wave vector $\mathbf{q}$ ($q = 1/\Lambda$, normal to wave planes). If $\mathbf{S}$ and $\mathbf{S}'$ are the wave vectors corresponding to the momentum ($mv=h/\lambda$) of the incident and scattered neutrons, the equation for conservation of momentum is

$$\mathbf{S} - (\mathbf{S}'+\mathbf{q}) = \mathbf{r}_{hkl}^{\times} \tag{12}$$

because in the lattice the balance of the momenta after and before the collision may be either 0 or any vector of the reciprocal lattice.

The difference of energy is equal to one quantum $\hbar\omega$:

$$\frac{h^2}{2m}(S^2 - S'^2) = \hbar\omega .\tag{13}$$

Experimentally S is known, S' may be determined by measuring the wave length of scattered neutron (by a crystalline reflection) or the velocity of the neutron (chopper). Geometrically from the direction of S, S' and the orientation of the crystal, q is determined. Eq. (13) gives then the frequency of the vibration as a function of the wave vector q. This is the dispersion curve which is simply a linear dependence for very low frequencies (elastic vibrations).

The results of the neutron method are more complete than X-ray scattering. Unfortunately, these experiments are long and difficult chiefly because, in spite of the weakness of the scattering, it is necessary to determine the wave length of the scattered radiation.

SCANNING ELECTRON MICROSCOPY
The Instrument

G.R.BOOKER

1. Introduction

The scanning electron microscope (SEM) is a valuable addition to the range of microscopes already available. Its resolution is intermediate between that of the optical microscope (OM) and the transmission electron microscope (TEM). It can be used to examine solid specimens, reveals surface topographical features in a strikingly three-dimensional manner, and has a large depth of focus. As a result, the SEM is being successfully used for surface topographical studies in a wide range of materials investigations.

However, the SEM is not just a superior type of OM. Many other modes of operation can be used which provide considerable additional information about both surface and bulk properties of the specimen. In particular, information can be obtained relating to chemical elements, magnetic and electric fields, voltage distributions, resistivity variations, electrical recombination centres, defect structures, light-emitting properties etc. A better description of the SEM would probably be a versatile, high-performance electron probe instrument for the examination of materials.

It is remarkable that although the present-day commercial SEM is a completely sophisticated instrument and is having a major impact in almost all fields of materials science, its full potentialities are still to be exploited. Rapid advances are being made on both the instrumental and applications sides. Of special importance are the improvement in resolution resulting from the use of high-intensity electron sources, and the crystallographic orientation effects arising from electron channelling behaviour.

The SEM can now perform many functions not possible by any other instrument, and during the next few years further advances will be made. There is no doubt that the SEM will increasingly challenge the TEM, even on those fronts where the TEM was thought to be completely impregnable.

2. Historical

The initial work on the scanning electron microscope (SEM) took place in Germany during the 1930s, suggestions being put forward by Stintzing [1] and Knoll [2], and the first instrument being built by von Ardenne [3]. The SEM was developed further in the USA in 1942 by Zworykin et al. [4], who obtained a resolution of 500Å for solid specimens. Work on the SEM was commenced in France in 1946, this leading to studies of cathodoluminescence in crystals by Davoine et al. [5]. The modern development of the instrument has been almost entirely due to work which was started in Cambridge, England in 1948 by Oatley [6] and which has been expanded since 1959 by Nixon [7]. Oatley and his colleagues made notable instrumental improvements, especially to the electron collection system, and obtained a better understanding of the resulting image contrasts. Nixon and his colleagues constructed several SEMs, one of which exhibited a resolution of 100Å for solid specimens. Following from this work at Cambridge, Stewart developed the first commercial SEM, the Cambridge Scientific Instruments Limited "Stereoscan". Several other commercial instruments have now become available.

Review articles on the SEM have been published by Oatley et al. [6] and Nixon [7], bibliographies complied by Wells [8] and Johnson [9], and a book written by Thornton [10].

3. Principle of the instrument

The principle of the SEM as used in its most common mode, the emissive mode, is illustrated schematically in fig. 1. Electrons from a filament (F) are accelerated by a voltage commonly in the range 5 to 30 kV and directed down the centre of an electron optical column usually consisting of three magnetic lenses (L_1, L_2 and L_3). These lenses cause the electrons to be formed into a fine electron beam, and focus it onto the surface of a solid specimen (S). Scanning coils (SC), generally placed between lenses 2 and 3, cause the electron spot to be scanned across the specimen surface in the form of a square raster, similar to that of the raster on a commercial television screen. The currents passing through the scanning coils are also made to pass through the corresponding deflection coils of a cathode ray tube (CRT), so as to produce a

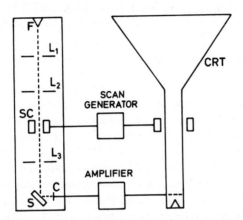

Fig. 1. Diagram illustrating the principle of the SEM.

similar but larger raster on the viewing screen. The electron beam incident on
the specimen surface causes the emission of secondary electrons. These electrons strike a collector (C), and the resulting current is amplified and used to
modulate the brightness of the CRT. The times associated with the emission
and collection of the secondary electrons are negligibly small compared with
the times associated with the scanning of the incident electron beam across
the specimen surface. Hence, there is a one-to-one correspondence between
the number of secondary electrons collected from any particular point on the
specimen surface and the brightness of the analogous point on the CRT screen.
Consequently, an image of the surface is progressively built up on the screen.
The factors that give rise to variations in the number of collected secondary
electrons, and so produce contrast in the image, will be described later.

It should be noted that the SEM has no imaging lenses in the true sense of
the word. The image magnification is determined solely by the ratio of the
sizes of the rasters on the CRT screen and the specimen surface. In order to
increase the magnification, it is only necessary to reduce the currents in the
SEM scanning coils. For example, if the image on the CRT screen is 10 cm
across, magnifications of 100X, 1000X and 10 000X are obtained by using
scanned specimen areas 1 mm, 0.1 mm and 0.01 mm across respectively. One
consequence of this is that high magnifications are easy to obtain with the
SEM, while very low magnifications are difficult. Thus, for a magnification of
10X it would be necessary to scan a specimen area approximately 10 mm
across, and this presents difficulties because of the large deflection angles required, i.e. the electron beam may strike lens pole-pieces, apertures etc. at the
extremes of its scan, the scan linearity may not be maintained etc.

It is worthwhile emphasising at this point the completely different principle of the SEM compared with most other microscopes. Because there are no imaging lenses, *any* signal that arises from the action of the incident electron beam, e.g. reflected electrons, transmitted electrons, emitted light etc. can be used to give an image on the CRT screen. It is only necessary for the signal to be collected sufficiently rapidly, and converted if necessary into an electric current. It also follows that several such signals can be dealt with at the same time, and hence several different types of information can be displayed on adjacent CRTs simultaneously, all from identical areas of the specimen.

Another major difference is that each particular point in the image is recorded sequentially in time. In other words, a complete image is not seen until the whole raster has been scanned. This has practical disadvantages in that focussing and recording tend to be more tedious, special electronic amplifiers may be required etc. Nevertheless, it also has important advantages in that the signal is in a convenient form to be "operated on" in a variety of ways, thereby enabling considerably more information to be extracted. Such operations include electronic signal processing, energy analysis, wavelength separation etc., and all of these operations can be applied to each point of the image in turn and the resulting information appropriately displayed. Such procedures are not usually possible with other types of microscope because all points in the image are recorded simultaneously.

4. Modes of operation

There are several different modes of operation of the SEM, each corresponding to the collection of a different type of signal arising from the incident primary electron beam. The main modes can be listed as follows

                    emissive
                    reflective
                    absorptive
                    transmission
                    beam-induced conductivity
                    cathodoluminescent
                    X-ray

For the emissive mode, the secondary electrons emitted from the specimen are collected. These electrons have energies in the range approximately 0 to 30 eV, and come from material within approximately 50Å of the specimen surface. This mode is the most common way of operating the SEM. It is especially suitable for obtaining information concerning the surface regions of the specimen.

For the reflective mode, the primary electrons back-scattered from the specimen are collected. These electrons have an energy range, the energy of the majority being close to that of the incident primary electron beam, and they come from material within a few microns of the specimen surface. This mode provides information which is more characteristic of the bulk material.

For the absorptive mode, an electrical lead is attached to the specimen and the current that flows through the lead to earth is used as the signal. Any local increase in the number of secondary emitted electrons or primary reflected electrons causes a corresponding local decrease in the absorbed current. Consequently, absorptive mode images are complementary in contrast to emissive and reflective mode images.

For the transmission mode, those electrons that completely penetrate thin specimens are collected. These electrons have a wide energy range, the energies depending on the nature and thickness of the specimen. This mode often enables thicker specimens to be examined and higher contrasts to be obtained than is possible using the more conventional transmission electron microscope method.

For the beam-induced conductivity mode, electrical leads are attached to a portion of the specimen, a voltage is applied, and the current flowing through the leads is used as the signal. The action of the primary electron beam incident on the specimen surface is to produce additional electrical carriers within the specimen. These carriers cause local changes in specimen conductivity, and hence give differences in current flowing through the leads. This mode is especially suitable for examining resistivity variations, junction field-regions etc. in semiconductor specimens.

For the cathodoluminescent mode, the light that is emitted from the specimen is collected and used as the signal. Either the light is used as it arises, or particular wavelengths are selected with the aid of a monochromator. This mode is valuable for studying phosphors, light-emitting semiconductor materials etc.

For the X-ray mode, the X-rays that are emitted are collected and used as the signal. Either the X-rays are used as they arise (non-dispersive), or particular wavelengths are selected (dispersive) with the aid of a crystal spectrometer or pulse-height analyser. This mode is the basis of the X-ray probe micro-analyser.

5. Resolution limitations

The best resolution that can be obtained for any particular mode of operation depends on a number of factors which may be listed as follows

    A electron spot size
    B spreading effects in specimen
    C signal/noise ratio
    D stray fields
    E mechanical vibrations

The resolution cannot be smaller than the size of the electron spot incident on the specimen surface. Any detail finer than this will be lost because the signal collected is at all times an average over the complete spot size. The minimum spot size that can be obtained depends on the electron accelerating voltage, aberrations of the electron lenses etc.

When the electron beam strikes the specimen surface, the electrons are scattered as they penetrate into the specimen. Consequently, the effective spot size is greater than the incident spot size because of spreading effects in the specimen. The extent of the spreading depends on the electron accelerating voltage, type of specimen, mode of operation etc.

When a signal is collected to form an image, it can only give useful information if the signal level is sufficiently above the noise level. The signal depends on the electron accelerating voltage, total current in the electron spot, type of specimen, mode of operation etc., while the noise depends on the type of specimen, mode of operation, collector used etc. In order to detect the signal, it is often necessary to increase the signal/noise ratio. In many instances, the only practical way of doing this is to increase the current in the electron spot, which usually means an increase in the electron spot size and hence a loss in resolution.

Stray electric and magnetic fields arising from either inside or outside the SEM can distort the final electron spot and change its motion across the specimen surface, thereby lowering the quality of the resulting image. Mechanical vibrations can have similar effects. These factors are not usually important at the 500 Å resolution level, but are of the utmost importance at the 50 Å level. However, because they are not basic limitations, they are ignored in the remainder of this lecture. Nevertheless, it is emphasised that the most stringent precautions may be necessary to deal with these effects if the highest resolutions are required.

An approximate guide to the manner in which the factors listed above limit the resolution for the various modes of operation is as follows. Consider a typical commercial SEM using an average specimen and operating at an electron accelerating voltage of 20 kV.

For the transmission mode, when suitable thin specimens are used, little if any spreading takes place in the specimen. Consequently, the resolution on collecting the transmitted electrons is limited only by mechanisms A and C above. Typical resolutions are in the range 50 to 100 Å.

For the emissive mode, the situation is more complicated. The emitted secondary electrons arise in two ways, either directly by the incident high-energy electrons as they enter the specimen, or indirectly by the back-scattered high-energy electrons, X-rays etc. as they leave the specimen. The former are subject to relatively small spreading effects, while the latter are subject to large spreading effects. For specimens with fine structure, the tendency is for the former electrons to produce contrast which reveals the fine structure, and the latter electrons to produce a general background contrast. This is fortunate because it means that to a first approximation the resolution is determined only by the former electrons. However, the situation is not as favourable as for the transmission mode, and the resolution is limited by mechanism C. Typical resolutions are in the range 100 to 300 Å.

For the reflective mode, the back-scattered electrons are subject to pronounced spreading effects, and the resolution is limited by mechanism B. Typical resolutions are in the range 500 to 2000 Å.

For the absorptive mode, no electron collector is used, the large amount of noise-free amplification generally associated with such collectors is not available, and so additional conventional amplification is required. The latter usually introduces appreciable noise, and so the resolution is limited by mechanism C. Typical resolutions are in the range 0.1 to 1.0 μm.

For the beam-induced conductivity, cathodoluminescence and X-ray modes, the signals are generated by the high-energy electrons within the complete volume of the specimen penetrated. In addition, the signals for the cathodoluminescence and X-ray modes are small, especially if specific wavelengths are selected. The resolutions for all of these modes tend to be limited by mechanisms B and C. Typical resolutions are in the range 0.3 to 1.0 μm.

The effect on the factors A, B and C of changing the electron accelerating voltage V is as follows. In general, increasing V makes factors A and C more favourable for good resolution (see later), and factor B less favourable. For example, increasing V makes the emissive mode resolution better. In a particular instance, resolution values of 1100, 500, 300 and 200 Å were experimentally obtained for 1, 3, 10 and 30 kV respectively. Conversely, increasing V makes the reflective mode resolution poorer.

In order to obtain the resolutions given above, the optimum conditions

should be used appropriate to the particular mode of operation. To understand how these conditions are determined, further information concerning
the electron optical system is required.

6. Electron lenses

The function of the electron lenses is to focus a fine electron beam onto
the specimen surface. The important parameters associated with such a focussed beam are the electron spot size d, the electron beam divergence α and
the total current in the electron spot I. Different values of these parameters are
required for different operating conditions, and these can be obtained by
suitable choice of the currents in the lenses etc.

A schematic diagram illustrating the electron ray paths for a three-lens system is shown in fig. 2. It corresponds to no deflection of the beam by the scanning coils, and the relative widths of the electron beams etc. are considerably
exaggerated for the purpose of clarity. All three lenses give real and demagnified images. The usual procedure with such a system is to select the currents
in lenses 1 and 2 to give a particular condition, and then to adjust the current
in lens 3 to focus the image from lens 2 onto the specimen surface. If lens 3 is

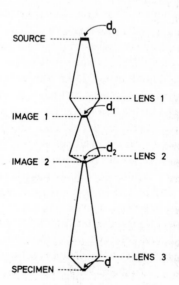

Fig. 2. Electron ray paths for a three-lens system.

not correctly focussed, the spot size at the specimen surface is larger, and the resolution is poorer. Hence, the exact focus is obtained by adjusting the current in lens 3 until the final image on the CRT screen shows maximum detail. The process is analogous to the focussing of an electron micrograph in the TEM by using an imaging lens (objective), although in the case of the SEM the focussing is performed by using an illuminating lens (condenser).

In fig. 2, the effective size of the electron source has been denoted by d_0, the size of the two intermediate images by d_1 and d_2, and the size of the final image by d. If the magnifications of lenses 1, 2 and 3 are M_1, M_2 and M_3 respectively, (M_1, M_2 and M_3 all less than 1), then the resulting spot size at the specimen is given by $d = M_1 M_2 M_3 d_0$, if lens aberrations are assumed for the moment to be negligible. The spot size calculated in this manner is often termed the Gaussian spot size. The advantage of using three lenses, rather than two, is the greater flexibility and larger overall demagnification that is possible. The values of M_1 and M_2 are determined by the currents C_1 and C_2 in lenses 1 and 2 respectively, and the value of M_3 mainly by the working distance L of lens 3, i.e. the distance from the centre of the lens to the specimen. For any particular SEM, graphs are usually supplied by the manufacturer showing the relationships between C_1, C_2, L and d, and in particular what combinations of C_1, C_2 and L will give any required value of d. These are usually based on a heated tungsten hair-pin filament with an effective electron source size of approximately 50 μm. Clearly, as C_1 and C_2 progressively increase, d progressively decreases.

Inspection of fig. 2 shows that all of the electrons that leave lens 1 to form the image between lens 1 and 2 do not enter lens 2. The number accepted is approximately proportional to $(\alpha_2/\alpha_1)^2$, where α_2 and α_1 are the cone angles subtended by this image at lenses 2 and 1 respectively (fig. 3). Because all of the lenses are demagnifying, $\alpha_2 < \alpha_1$, and so many of the electrons do not continue down the column but are lost to the side. Consideration shows that as C_1 is increased, the resulting image moves closer to lens 1, α_1 increases while α_2 remains substantially unchanged, and so the number of electrons lost increases. A similar behaviour occurs to the image between lenses 2 and 3 when C_2 is increased. The overall result is that as C_1 and C_2 progressively increase, I progressively decreases.

It is standard practice to incorporate a number of apertures in the electron optical column. The main function of most of these apertures is to prevent electrons which are lost from the electron beam as described above from striking pole-pieces etc. and causing them to become contaminated. Such apertures are usually termed spray apertures. However, the most important aperture in the electron optical column is generally located within the centre of lens 3,

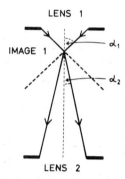

Fig. 3. Details of electron ray paths for one of the intermediate images.

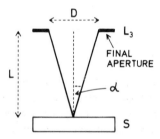

Fig. 4. Diagram showing relationship between beam divergence α, final aperture diameter D, and working distance L.

and is used to control the divergence of the final electron beam at the specimen surface (fig. 4). If this aperture is of diameter D and the working distance is L, then the beam divergence is given by $\alpha = D/2L$. The apertures used in practice are commonly 200, 100 or 50 μm in diameter, and the range of beam divergences these cover are indicated in fig. 5. If D is changed, I also changes (I proportional α^2 proportional D^2), but on the simple geometrical argument used here d remains the same. In practice, d may also change because of the aberrations of the lenses. However, this is only important for very small final spot sizes, and is discussed later.

For many purposes it is advantageous to know the absolute value of I. For any particular electron optical system, the brightness B, defined as the electron current per unit area per unit solid angle, is given by

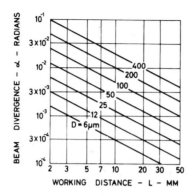

Fig. 5. Graphs showing relationships between a, D and L.

$$B = \frac{I}{\pi(d/2)^2\pi\alpha^2} = 0.4\,\frac{I}{d^2\alpha^2} \tag{1}$$

and is constant for successive images in the system, irrespective of lens currents, aperture sizes etc. Consequently, once d and α have been fixed as described above, I can be calculated so long as B is known.

Justification for B being constant for successive images can be seen from the following. First, consider the electrons immediately on either side of an image in such a system, as in fig. 3. Clearly, d is constant, and as was described above, $I \propto \alpha^2$. Second, consider the electrons which leave an image in such a system, enter a lens, and are focussed to form a further image. Clearly, I is constant, and consideration shows that $d \propto 1/\alpha$. The combination of these two relationships is then equivalent to eq. (1). In this treatment, d is the Gaussian spot size because lens aberrations have not been taken into account. The value of B in any particular instance is determined by the type of electron source and the operating conditions used.

The maximum current that can be imaged into a focussed electron spot from a thermionic cathode has been calculated by Langmuir [11] to be

$$j = j_0 eV\alpha^2/kT \tag{2}$$

where j is maximum current density in the spot, j_0 is current density at the cathode surface, V is voltage between the cathode and image point, α is beam divergence at image point, T is cathode temperature in $^\circ$K, e is electronic charge and k is Boltzmann's constant.

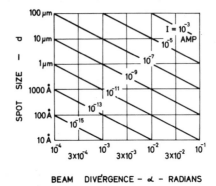

Fig. 6. Graphs showing relationships between electron spot size d, beam divergence a and current in spot I for a system with brightness $B = 4 \times 10^4$ A cm^{-2} sr^{-1}.

This can be rearranged for our purpose to give

$$B = j/\alpha^2 = (e/k)(j_0/T)V \tag{3}$$

showing that the maximum brightness depends on both the manner in which the filament is operated (the term j_0/T), and the SEM electron accelerating voltage (the term V). As an example, consider a tungsten hair-pin filament and take $j_0 = 1$ A cm^{-2}, $T = 2800°$K and $V = 20$ kV. Calculation then gives $B = 10^5$ A cm^{-2} sr^{-1}. Such a high brightness is not usually achieved in practice with tungsten hair-pin filaments, and so a value of 4×10^4 A cm^{-2} sr^{-1} will be taken as being more typical of standard operating conditions.

The relationship between I, d and α is shown in fig. 6 for $B = 4 \times 10^4$ A cm^{-2} sr^{-1}. From this figure it can be seen, for example, that if a value α of 3×10^{-3} radians were being used, then spot sizes d of 1 μm, 1000 Å and 100 Å would correspond to spot currents I of 10^{-8}, 10^{-10} and 10^{-12} A respectively.

7. Minimum obtainable spot size

When small final electron spot sizes are required, the aberrations of the lenses need to be considered. Because all of the lenses are demagnifying, it is the final lens that is most important. Each point of the image which is located between lenses 2 and 3 is not imaged as a point on the   specimen surface but as a disc of confusion. Different aberrations give discs of different sizes, each depending on the beam divergence α at the specimen. It is common practice to consider each aberration separately.

(a) For spherical aberration, the disc has a size

$$d_s = C_s \alpha^3 \tag{4}$$

where C_s is the spherical aberration coefficient.

(b) For chromatic aborration.

$$d_c = C_c(\delta V/V)\alpha \tag{5}$$

where C_c is the chromatic aberration coefficient and δV is the spread of voltage in the electron beam of nominal voltage V. The term δV arises because of the fluctuations in the high voltage supply, the thermal energy spread associated with the heated filament etc.

(c) For astigmatism

$$d_a = (\delta z)\alpha \tag{6}$$

where δz is the distance between the two line foci arising because of the astigmatism.

(d) Finally, there is the fundamental diffraction limitation, which gives

$$d_d = 1.22\,\lambda/\alpha \tag{7}$$

where λ is the electron wavelength given approximately by $\lambda = (150/V)^{\frac{1}{2}}$ if λ is in Å and V is in volts.

The size of the disc of confusion resulting from the superimposition of these different effects is d_{aber} where

$$d_{aber}^2 = d_s^2 + d_c^2 + d_a^2 + d_d^2 \tag{8}$$

$$= C_s^2\alpha^6 + C_c^2(\delta V/V)^2\alpha^2 + (\delta z)^2\alpha^2 + (1.22\,\lambda)^2\,1/\alpha^2 . \tag{9}$$

This equation shows that there is an optimum value for α which gives a minimum value of d_{aber}. Clearly, C_s and C_c should be as small as possible, favouring magnetic rather than electrostatic lenses. In practice, C_s and C_c increase with the focal length of the lens, favouring operation at short working distances. It is partly for this reason that the scanning coils are placed between lenses 2 and 3, rather than between lens 3 and the specimen. Values of C_s and

C_c for the final lens of an SEM operating at a working distance of 10 mm are typically 20 mm and 8 mm respectively. If the residual astigmatism in the final lens is carefully corrected with the astigmator provided for this purpose, the term $(\delta z)^2\alpha^2$ can then usually be neglected. It should also be noted that C_s, C_c and λ all depend on the voltage V, and so the optimum divergence α and the minimum value of d_{aber} also depend on V.

When the calculations are performed for an SEM with a well-designed final lens operated under good conditions, it is found that the optimum value for α is typically 3×10^{-3} radians and the corresponding value of d_{aber} is typically 50Å. This means that for a system with such a final lens, the minimum possible final spot size that can be obtained irrespective of the amount of overall demagnification used is approximately 50Å.

If the three lenses are adjusted to give a final Gaussian spot size of d_g, i.e. ignoring lens aberrations, then the resulting spot size taking into account aberrations is d_{total} where

$$d_{total}^2 = d_g^2 + d_{aber}^2 . \tag{10}$$

Hence, for the final lens considered above, the effect of the final lens aberrations can be neglected so long as the lens currents are set to give values of $d_g > 200$ or 300Å. This holds providing of course that the astigmatism remains carefully corrected, and that α remains close to 3×10^{-3} radians so that d_{aber} remains close to 50Å.

In the above treatment, a number of assumptions were made. For example, in practice the current densities in the electron spots are not uniformly distributed, the intensity decreasing at the spot edges. Nevertheless, the treatment allows the important principles to be illustrated, and the equations give quantitative values that are reasonably close to those that occur in practice.

8. Scanning coils

The electron beam is scanned across the specimen surface by using two sets of coils at right angles to one another, one set giving the line scan and the other set the frame scan. If the line scan time is t_1 and the frame scan time is t_f, then the number of lines in the raster is given by $N = t_f/t_1$. Most SEMs provide a wide choice of scan times, e.g. $t_1 = 0.001, 0.002, 0.004, 0.01, 0.02, 0.04,$ 0.1, 0.2 and 0.4 sec and $t_f = 0.1, 0.2, 0.4, 1, 2, 4, 10, 20, 40, 100, 200, 400$ and 1000 sec.

The electron ray paths for a system using two such sets of coils are given in

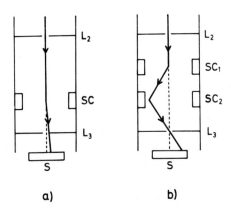

Fig. 7. Electron ray paths illustrating scanning arrangements using (a) single deflection, and (b) double deflection.

fig. 7a. The line scan coils only are shown for the purpose of clarity. The single lines indicating the electron ray paths in fig. 7a correspond to the cones of electrons shown on an exaggerated lateral scale in fig. 2. It can be seen that the maximum area which can be scanned on the specimen surface is limited because of the presence of the pole-pieces, aperture etc. in lens 3.

The procedure generally adopted to overcome this difficulty is to use a double scanning system as shown in fig. 7b. The first set of coils causes a deflection in one sense, while the second set further down the column causes a larger deflection in the opposite sense. The line scan coils only are shown in fig. 7b. The system is adjusted so that the combined scanning actions cause the electron beam to pivot about a point located in the centre of lens 3. As a result, the maximum scanned area on the specimen surface is considerably increased.

9. Interactions between electron lenses and scanning coils

In the treatment given above, the actions of the electron lenses and scanning coils were considered independently. In practice, the action of one system can affect the other. For example, if the current in lens 3 is changed to a different value, the amount of rotation of the electrons by lens 3 changes, and so the orientation of the scanned raster on the specimen surface changes. Consequently, the final image on the CRT screen may be slightly rotated. Conversely, if the electron beam is focussed on the surface of a tilted specimen in the central region of the scanned raster, the electron beam may not be focussed on the specimen surface at the edges of the scanned raster. Consequently, the final image on the CRT screen may be slightly out of focus at the edges.

10. Noise considerations

It was shown above that there was a limit to the smallest spot size that could be obtained because of the final lens aberrations. There is also a limit to the smallest spot size that can be used because of noise considerations. This noise can arise in several ways. First, there is the noise associated with the electron beam incident on the specimen surface, usually called "shot" noise. The beam consists of individual electrons, and their arrival at the specimen surface is subject to statistical fluctuations. If the total current in the spot decreases, the statistical fluctuations increase, and so the noise increases. This noise is a fundamental effect and is a basic limitation to the operation of the SEM. Second, there is additional noise associated with the events occurring within the specimen, e.g. additional statistical fluctuations characteristic of the secondary electron emission process. Third, there is additional noise associated with the signal collection and amplification system. Extremely efficient systems are now available for dealing with the emitted and reflected electrons, and so the noise arising from this third cause will for the present treatment be neglected.

The amount of noise that can be tolerated depends on the amount of contrast in the image that is to be detected. This is illustrated by the diagrams of fig. 8, which show the signal intensity as a function of distance across an

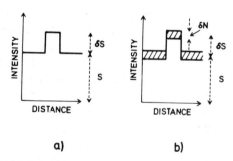

a)   b)

Fig. 8. Diagrams showing signal intensity traces (a) without noise, and (b) with noise.

image. In fig. 8a, the general signal level is S, and a particular feature has a signal level $S + \delta S$. The contrast for this feature is defined as $C = \delta S/S$. No noise is present. In fig. 8b, precisely the same signal is shown but an amount of noise δN is superimposed on the signal. Clearly, as δN increases, the feature will become less distinct and eventually will not be detected. The criterion often adopted for the detection of such a feature is that

$$\delta S > 5\, \delta N. \tag{11}$$

Let us first consider the noise arising from the incident electron beam. If the total number of electrons striking a particular point in the specimen surface is n, the statistical fluctuation associated with this number is $n^{1/2}$. The criterion then becomes:

$$\delta S/S > 5\, \delta N/S \tag{12}$$

i.e.

$$C > 5\, n^{1/2}/n \tag{13}$$

i.e.

$$n > 25\,(1/C)^2. \tag{14}$$

It is now necessary to consider the noise arising from within the specimen. The empirical procedure suggested by Oatley et al. [6] is adopted, namely, to increase the factor 5 in the above equations to 10. The criterion then becomes

$$n > 100\,(1/C)^2. \tag{15}$$

The minimum number of electrons necessary to reveal various levels of contrast in the resulting image have been calculated from eq. (15) and are given in table 1. It may be noted that if the contrast to be detected decreases by 10X, the number of electrons required increases by 100X.

It is common practice to use 10^3 lines per frame in the scanned raster. The line spacing on a typical micrograph (10 cm across) is then approximately equal to the smallest distance that the eye can readily detect (0.01 cm). If the number of lines used were less than this, the individual lines would be seen on the final micrograph and the picture would be of poor quality. If the number were greater than this, no advantage would result. In a similar manner, it is common practice to consider that there are 10^3 picture points per line in the scanned raster. Hence, there are 10^6 picture points for frame, and each of these

Table 1

Contrast C%	Electrons per picture point n
100	10^2
30	10^3
10	10^4
3	10^5
1	10^6
0.3	10^7
0.1	10^8

points has to be considered separately if information is not to be lost in the image.

As a result, the minimum number of electrons required to detect a particular contrast level given in table 1 needs to be applied to each picture point in the scanned raster. For example, a contrast of 10% requires 10^4 electrons per picture point, or 10^{10} electrons per frame. Now 10^{10} electrons is approximately 10^{-9} A/1 sec, 10^{-10} A/10 sec, etc. Consequently, for each particular contrast level to be detected, a definite minimum number of electrons is required, and these can be obtained by using various combinations of total currents in the electron spot I and frame scan times t_f. These relationships are shown in fig. 9. It is emphasised that the data in this figure relate to a fundamental limitation of the SEM imaging process, and do not depend on the particular SEM used, the conditions of operation etc.

11. Minimum usable spot size

The small final spot sizes that can be obtained at the specimen surface may not always, therefore, be usable in practice because the corresponding small total current in the spot is insufficient to reveal the contrast in the image against the background noise. The amount of current required to detect such contrast is generally termed the threshold current. Rearrangement of eq. (1) gives

$$d_{th} = \left(\frac{0.4\,I_{th}}{B}\right)^{\frac{1}{2}} \frac{1}{\alpha} \tag{16}$$

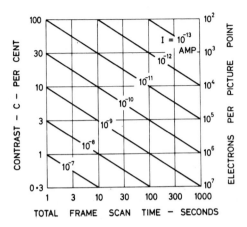

Fig. 9. Graphs showing relationships between image contrast C, current in spot I and frame scan time t_f.

showing that the spot size d_{th} to give a spot current I_{th} depends on both the brightness B and the beam divergence α. Hence, the minimum spot size that can be used is obtained by combining eqs. (8) and (9) with eq. (16) to give

$$d^2 = d_s^2 + d_c^2 + d_a^2 + d_d^2 + d_{th}^2 \tag{17}$$

$$= C_s^2 \alpha^6 + C_c^2 (\delta V/V)^2 \alpha^2 + (\delta z)^2 \alpha^2 + (1.22\,\lambda)^2 (1/\alpha)^2$$

$$+ 0.4\, I_{th}/B\, (1/\alpha)^2 . \tag{18}$$

A convenient way of expressing these separate effects diagrammatically is given in fig. 10, following a procedure used previously by Everhart [12]. The size of the particular disc of confusion d is plotted as ordinate against the beam divergence α as abscissa. The line shown as d_s represents the spherical aberration limitation for a lens with C_s = 20 mm, and the line d_c represents the chromatic aberration limitation for a lens with C_c = 8 mm, δV = 2 V and V = 20 kV. For both of these aberrations, d increases as α increases. The line d_d represents the fundamental diffraction limitation for V = 20 kV (λ=0.086Å). For this aberration, d decreases as α increases. The spot size resulting from the superimposition of these separate aberrations is shown by the dark line marked I_{th} = 0. The minimum of this curve occurs at α = 4 × 10^{-3} radians and corresponds to d = 40Å.

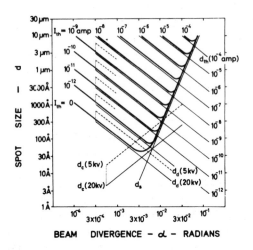

Fig. 10. Graphs illustrating the factors that limit the final spot size d for a typical commercial SEM with a brightness $B = 4 \times 10^4$ A cm^{-2} sr^{-1}.

The lines shown as d_{th} represent the noise limitation for a system with brightness $B = 4 \times 10^4$ A cm^{-2} sr^{-1}, and correspond to threshold currents $I_{th} = 10^{-12}$, 10^{-11}, 10^{-10} A etc. The resulting spot sizes taking account of the noise limitations are shown approximately by the dark lines marked 10^{-12}, 10^{-11}, 10^{-10} A etc. The minimum values for $I_{th} = 10^{-12}$, 10^{-11}, 10^{-10}, 10^{-9} and 10^{-8} A occur at $\alpha = 6 \times 10^{-3}$, 8×10^{-3}, 1.0×10^{-2}, 1.5×10^{-2}, 2.0×10^{-2} radians etc. and correspond to $d = 70, 200, 400, 900, 2300$ Å etc. respectively. The marked increase in spot size that is necessary if appreciable current in the spot is required is clearly demonstrated.

In order to illustrate the above, suppose a value of $I_{th} = 10^{-9}$ A is required, and the optimum conditions of $\alpha = 1.5 \times 10^{-2}$ radians and $d = 900$ Å are to be used. The procedure to be followed in practice is to select the final aperture size D and working distance L to give $\alpha = 1.5 \times 10^{-2}$ radians (fig. 5), and then to select the lens currents C_1 and C_2, in conjunction with the value of L, to give a Gaussian spot size $d_g = 900$ Å (manufacturer's graphs).

The continuous lines in fig. 10, and the quantitative values given above, all correspond to a beam accelerating voltage $V = 20$ kV. An indication of how the situation is changed if V decreases can be obtained as follows. In fig. 10 the line for d_s (eq. (4)) does not change (neglecting any variation of C_s with V). The line for d_c (eq. (5)) changes because of the term $(\delta V/V)$, its new position for $V = 5$ kV being shown dashed (neglecting any variation of C_c with

V). The line for d_d (eq. (7)) changes because of the term $\lambda(\propto 1/V^{1/2})$, its new position for $V = 5$ kV being shown dashed. The lines for d_{th} (eq. (16)) change because of the term $1/B^{1/2}(\propto 1/V^{1/2})$, their new positions for $V = 5$ kV being shown dashed. It can be seen that the effect of decreasing V is to increase d, and sometimes to change the optimum value of α. It might be mentioned with regard to fig. 10 that the line for d_{th} and $I = 10^{-13}$ A coincides with the line for d_d. This is entirely fortuitous and arises because of the particular value of brightness used, namely, $B = 4 \times 10^4$ A cm^{-2} sr^{-1} for $V = 20$ kV.

The contribution due to astigmatism is not included in fig. 10. The lines for d_a (eq. (6)) have the same dependence on α as the lines for d_c, and so are parallel to the d_c lines. Consideration shows that the two d_a lines for $\delta z = 0.8$ and 3.2 μm coincide with the two d_c lines for $V = 20$ and 5 kV respectively, indicating the extent to which the astigmatism needs to be corrected so as not to have a detrimental effect on the minimum spot size.

The minimum usable spot sizes shown in fig. 10 and discussed above can be equated approximately to the best resolution obtainable for those modes of operation where mechanisms A and C (sect. 5) only are limiting, i.e. the transmission and emissive modes. This is not the case when spreading effects are important and mechanism B is limiting, e.g. the reflective mode.

12. Maximum useful magnification

The maximum useful magnification M for a micrograph is given by

$$M = R/r \tag{19}$$

where R is the minimum distance resolved by the eye, and r is the resolution referred to the specimen.

The quantity R is usually taken as 0.01 cm, and the relationship expressed by eq. (19) is shown in fig. 11 as line X. This value of R is perhaps on the low side and is appropriate for negatives if some further enlargement is to be made. A more suitable value of R for average prints is 0.03 cm, and for enlargements for display purposes is 0.10 cm. The analogous relationships for these values of R are shown in fig. 11 as lines Y and Z respectively.

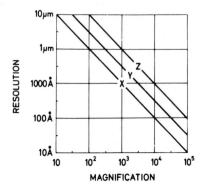

Fig. 11. Graphs showing maximum useful magnification as a function of resolution.

13. Magnification and spot size

It is common practice to operate the SEM with 1000 lines per frame. This number is based on what occurs at the CRT screen. In particular, the line spacing on the screen is then equal to R of eq.(19) (image 10 cm across, line spacing 0.01 cm). It then follows that the line spacing on the specimen is equal to r of eq. (19). It is now necessary to discuss how the combination of line spacing r and electron spot size d affect the resolution in the final micrograph.

If $d > r$, consecutive lines on the specimen overlap, and the resolution corresponds to d rather than r. This is the case when the magnification is set too high for the conditions. Conversely, if $d < r$, there are gaps between consecutive lines on the specimen, information is lost and misleading results can be obtained. This is the case when the magnification is set too low for the conditions. Clearly, the optimum setting is when $d = r$.

In practice, operators do not usually work with $d > r$, but frequently work with $d < r$. For example, suppose a magnification of 1000X is to be used. The best resolution that can be revealed is then 1000Å (fig. 11, line X), and so this is the optimum spot size. If $d \gg r$, e.g. 1 μm, the micrograph would show considerable "empty" magnification, and the operator would immediately alter the conditions. However, if $d \ll r$, e.g. 100Å, a micrograph would be obtained and the operator might not realise that it would have been advantageous to alter the conditions. The information in the micrograph could be misleading. In addition, because the spot size is smaller than is necessary, the current in the spot is smaller, and the noise larger. Consequently, recording is slower, micrographs are inferior etc. Moreover, no genuine improvement in resolution is possible beyond that appropriate to the magnification setting which was used, namely, 1000Å corresponding to 1000X.

14. Depth of focus

The depth of focus F at the surface of a specimen when it is examined with a microscope, i.e. the range of distance measured parallel to the optical axis for which the image still appears in focus, is given by

$$F = d/\tan \alpha \tag{20}$$

where d is the resolution being used and α is the beam divergence. For the SEM, α is small and so

$$F = d/\alpha . \tag{21}$$

The relationship expressed in eq. (21) is illustrated in fig. 12 with lines corresponding to $\alpha = 10^{-1}$, 10^{-2}, 10^{-3} and 10^{-4} radians. The ratio R_F of the depth of focus to the lateral resolution is given by

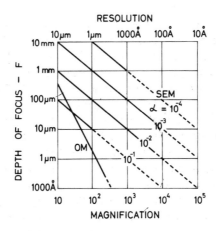

Fig. 12. Graphs showing relationships between depth of focus F, resolution d and beam divergence a.

$$R_F = F/d = 1/\alpha .\tag{22}$$

This equation shows that if, for example, $\alpha = 3 \times 10^{-3}$ radians, then $R_F = 300$ for all magnifications.

For an optical microscope, the resolution d is given by

$$d = \lambda/(\text{N.A}) = \lambda/\mu \sin \alpha \tag{23}$$

where λ is the wavelength of the light, N.A. is the numerical aperture of the lens, μ is the refractive index of the medium between the specimens and lens, and α is the beam divergence.

The depth of focus is given by combining eqs. (20) and (23). The line for a typical optical microscope with $\lambda = 5000\,\text{Å}$ and $\mu = 1$ is also shown in fig. 12. It can be seen that for low magnifications, $R_F > 1$, but for high magnifications, $R_F < 1$, a behaviour markedly different from that of the SEM.

Comparison of the performance of the SEM and OM with regard to depth of focus for similar resolutions, and hence similar magnifications, shows the following if α is taken as 3×10^{-3} radians for the SEM. For a resolution of $5\,\mu\text{m}$, $F_{SEM}/F_{OM} = 30$, while for a resolution of $0.5\,\mu\text{m}$, $F_{SEM}/F_{OM} = 1000$. The much greater depth of focus of the SEM, especially at the limit of resolution of the OM, is clearly demonstrated.

It is pointed out that the lines of fig. 12, corresponding to different values of α, are deduced directly from eq. (21). It does not follow that an SEM can be operated with these values of α, or that these values of resolution can be obtained with an SEM. It is for this reason that some of the lines in fig. 12 are shown dashed.

It is sometimes advantageous to know the depth of focus for an SEM in terms of the total current in the spot I rather than the beam divergence α. This can be obtained by combining eq. (21) with eq. (1) to give

$$F = (B/0.4\,I)^{1/2}\, d^2 .\tag{24}$$

The relationship expressed in eq. (24) is illustrated in fig. 13 for $B = 4 \times 10^4$ A cm^{-2} sr^{-1} and various values of I. Once again, it does not follow that the resolution shown can be obtained for the particular values of I given, and so some of the lines are shown dashed. In addition, it is assumed that the resolution is equal to the spot size.

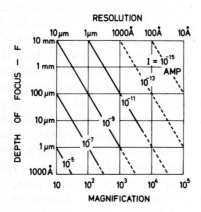

Fig. 13. Graphs showing relationship between depth of focus F, resolution d and current in spot I for a brightness $B = 4 \times 10^4$ A cm^{-2} sr^{-1}.

15. Selection of operating conditions

In order to illustrate the topics discussed above, two examples are given as follows.

Case 1. Suppose it is required to obtain micrographs at a magnification of 100X. From fig. 11, line X, this magnification means that a resolution of 1 μm only is required, and so a spot size of 1 μm should be used. The simplest manner to proceed in order to decide on conditions is to draw a line in fig. 10 parallel to the α axis corresponding to a value of $d = 1$ μm, and to note where it intersects the dark lines corresponding to the various values of I. It can then be seen that $I = 10^{-6}$ A for $\alpha = 3 \times 10^{-2}$ radians, $I > 10^{-7}$ A for $\alpha = 10^{-2}$ to 3×10^{-2} radians, $I > 10^{-8}$ A for $\alpha = 3 \times 10^{-3}$ to 3×10^{-2} radians etc. As the value of I that can be accepted decreases, so the range of values of α that can be used to provide it increases. From fig. 9, $I = 10^{-6}$, 10^{-7} and 10^{-8} A all give excellent combinations of recording times and contrast levels.

This example illustrates the favourable situation where considerable current in the spot is available, and so a wide range of possible conditions can be used. A final choice of $I = 10^{-9}$ A and $\alpha = 10^{-3}$ radians might be made to take advantage of the extremely large depth of focus of 1 mm that then results (fig. 12). Micrographs could be recorded in 1 sec to give contrast down to the 10% level, and 10 sec down to the 3% level (fig. 9).

Case 2. Suppose it is required to obtain micrographs at a magnification of 3000X. From fig. 11, line X, a resolution of 300 Å is required. A line is drawn in fig. 10 parallel to the α axis corresponding to a value of d = 300 Å. It can be seen that $I = 10^{-10}$ A for $\alpha = 10^{-2}$ radians, $I > 10^{-11}$ A for $\alpha = 3 \times 10^{-3}$ to 10^{-2} radians, $I > 10^{-12}$ A for $\alpha = 10^{-3}$ to 10^{-2} radians. From fig. 9, $I = 10^{-10}$ A enables a reasonable combination of recording times and contrast levels to be attained, but $I = 10^{-11}$ and 10^{-12} A are restricting.

This example illustrates the less favourable situation where little current in the spot is available, and some difficulty is beginning to be experienced in selecting conditions to give the required information. A final compromise of $I = 10^{-11}$ A and $\alpha = 3 \times 10^{-3}$ radians might be made. This gives a depth of focus of 10 μm (fig. 12), and micrographs could be recorded in 10 sec to give contrast down to the 30% level, and 100 sec down to the 10% level (fig. 9). Images observed on the screen using a frame scan time of 1 sec would exhibit considerable noise.

It may be mentioned that all of the above magnifications have been taken from fig. 11, line X, and are appropriate for the recording of negatives. If average prints are required, then the magnifications should be taken from fig. 11, line Y. The treatment is then precisely the same except that the magnification values are increased by 3X. Moreover, all of the data refer to an SEM with the final lens aberration constants used for fig. 10, V = 20 kV and $B = 4 \times 10^4$ A cm^{-2} sr^{-1}.

16. Practical considerations

Because all three lenses in the electron optical column demagnify, and as a result only a small fraction of the electrons that leave, for example, lens 1 are accepted by lens 2, the problems of lens alignment are not critical. Consequently, it is often possible to pre-align all three lenses. Alignment controls are provided for the filament so that it can be adjusted to give maximum brightness. Final apertures covering a range of sizes are located within lens 3 and can be rapidly interchanged. The particular final aperture being used can be mechanically centred so that no lateral movement of the image occurs during focussing. An astigmator is incorporated to correct the residual astigmatism associated with lens 3 and the final aperture. Specimen chambers are large and can accommodate numerous collectors, ancillary equipment etc. Specimen stages provide x, y and z lateral movements, and tilt and rotation controls, so that all degrees of freedom are possible. Specimens are usually mounted on stubs and inserted directly into the stage. For insulating specimens, it may initially be necessary to evaporate a thin (100 to 300Å) layer of aluminium or carbon onto the specimen surface in order to prevent charging effects occurring during subsequent examination.

The microscope column is evacuated in most instances using conventional oil diffusion pumps, the pressure in the specimen chamber during operation commonly being 10^{-4} torr. The hydrocarbon vapours present in the system cause contamination to build up on the specimen surface when it is scanned by the electron beam. The effect is insignificant at low magnifications when the scanned raster is spread over a large specimen area, but can be troublesome at high magnifications when the scanned raster is concentrated in a small specimen area. The problem of contamination can be reduced by incorporating cold traps etc., or eliminated by using ion pumps.

The image is displayed on a CRT with a long persistence screen for viewing purposes. Two such CRTs are often positioned close to one another so that images obtained by two different modes of operation can be simultaneously observed. Either of these images can be switched to another CRT with a high resolution screen for photographic recording purposes, and the recording is performed using conventional cameras, film etc.

17. Detectors

For the emissive and reflective modes, the electrons leaving the specimen surface have to be collected to provide the signal for the final image. These electron currents are small and so efficient collectors capable of considerable amplification are required. The ideal electron collector should possess a linear response, large band-width, high gain and low noise. The band-width required is typically 10 Hz to 1 MHz. The lower limit arises so that coarse intensity variations can be followed during photographic recording (1 picture point per line, and 0.1 sec line scan time), and the higher limit so that fine intensity variations can be followed during visual display (10^3 picture points per line, and 10^{-3} sec line scan time).

By far the most efficient electron collector used for the SEM to date is the scintillator/light-pipe/photo-multiplier system of Everhart and Thornley [13] illustrated in fig. 14. The specimen is usually inclined at an angle such as 45° to the incident electron beam, and the collector is placed to the side so as to face the inclined specimen surface. The collector consists of a Faraday cage with a metal mesh at the front. For the emissive mode, +250 V is applied between the mesh and specimen so that the low-energy secondary electrons leaving the specimen bend around and enter the cage, the effective solid angle

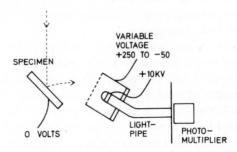

Fig. 14. Diagram illustrating scintillator/light-pipe/photo-multiplier collector system.

of collection thereby being large. High-energy reflected electrons also enter the cage. However, the latter electrons leaving the specimen travel in straight lines, and so the solid angle of collection is small. Under the above conditions and with the usual geometrical arrangement, approximately 90% of the total signal collected is due to the secondary electrons, and so the resulting image is generally taken as the emissive mode image. For the reflective mode, −50 V is applied between the mesh and specimen. The signal is then entirely due to the reflected electrons because the secondary electrons are prevented from entering the cage.

After the electrons have passed through the mesh, irrespective of whether they were initially secondary or reflected electrons, they are accelerated so as to strike a scintillator screen attached to the end of a light-pipe. The acceleration is obtained by applying +10 kV between a thin (500 Å) layer of aluminium deposited on the scintillator screen, and the mesh. All of these electrons on striking the screen produce photons, and the resulting light signal passes along the light-pipe and is incident on a photo-multiplier located immediately outside the specimen chamber. The output current from the photo-multiplier is taken and used to modulate the intensity of the CRT. This system has an output that is proportional to the initial electron signal over a wide range of signal strength, has an extremely large band-width, can give gains of up to 10^6, and contributes virtually no noise. It is also convenient to use because it can readily be moved around in the specimen chamber, and the Faraday cage can be placed close to the specimen surface without interfering with the scanning incident electron beam.

Solid state detectors have been used as electron collectors for the SEM, especially silicon surface barrier diodes. The junction depletion region for such diodes usually extends several microns below the surface, further than the electron penetration distance for the incident high-energy electrons. Reflected electrons from the specimen striking the detector create electron/hole pairs, e.g. approximately 6000 pairs for 20 kV electrons, and most of these are recorded by the detector. On the other hand, secondary electrons from the specimen make an insignificant contribution, e.g. approximately 3 pairs for 10 V electrons. Consequently, these detectors effectively record only the reflected electrons. Although the overall performance of these collectors is inferior to the scintillator/light-pipe/photo-multiplier system, they can sometimes be used with advantage when resolution is not a major factor, e.g. in certain semiconductor applications. A further type of electron detector is the channel electron multiplier. However, these have not yet been extensively used for the SEM.

For the transmission mode, the electron collector is placed directly beneath the specimen. All of the electron detectors described above could be used. However, if the high resolutions of which this mode is capable are required, then the scintillator/light-pipe/photo-multiplier system is most suitable.

For the cathodoluminescent mode, the standard detector used is a light-pipe/photo-multiplier system. The arrangement is similar to that of fig. 14 except that no metal mesh or scintillator screen is present, and no voltages are applied. Care should be taken with this mode to ensure that spurious signals do not arise from reflected electrons, X-rays etc. striking the light-pipe and creating photons, even though no scintillator screen is present.

For the X-ray mode, the collectors used are the same as for the X-ray probe micro-analyser. These range from simple non-dispersive counters located near to the specimen, to complex X-ray spectrometer systems contained in separate compartments built onto the side of the SEM specimen chamber.

18. Image contrast

18.1. Contrast mechanisms

There are a large number of mechanisms that give image contrast when specimens are examined in the SEM. If the modes of operation involving only electrons are considered, then contrast can be obtained if differences occur in any of the following

> surface topography
> atomic number
> surface magnetic fields
> surface electric fields
> surface potential

specimen conductivity
crystallographic orientation

18.2. *Surface topography*

Contrast arising from differences in surface topography can be understood
from the following. Suppose that a specimen with a flat surface is being examined in the SEM using a collector system similar to that of fig. 14. If the specimen is tilted so that the angle θ between the incident beam and the normal
to the specimen surface progressively increases from $0°$ to, say, $80°$, then experiment shows that the signal collected for both the emissive and reflective
modes progressively increases. There are two reasons for this.

First, as θ increases, the number of both secondary emitted electrons and
reflected electrons that leave the specimen surface increases. This is due to
various electron path lengths within the specimen changing. For reflected electrons, the situation is illustrated in fig. 15. As θ increases, the mean distance
R that the incident electron beam penetrates into the specimen measured
along the beam direction remains the same, but the electrons are on the average nearer to the specimen surface. Hence, the number of reflected electrons
that leave the surface increases. For secondary emitted electrons, the outermost 50Å only of the specimen needs to be considered. As θ increases, the
number of emitted secondary electrons arising from the incident electron

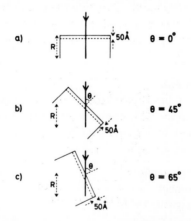

Fig. 15. Diagram illustrating electron ray paths within specimen as tilting occurs.

beam on entering the specimen increases because the path lengths of the incident electrons within the 50Å layer increases (fig. 15). In addition, as θ increases, the number of emitted secondary electrons arising from the reflected electrons on leaving the specimen increases because the number of reflected electrons increases. Hence, the total number of secondary emitted electrons increases.

Second, as θ increases, the fraction of both the secondary emitted electrons and reflected electrons that are collected increases. This arises because the electrons leaving the specimen surface possess angular distributions. For example, if the incident electron beam is normal to the specimen surface, then the number of emitted secondary electrons is approximately proportional to cosine ϕ, where ϕ is the angle between the direction considered and the surface normal. Because of this distribution, tilting of the specimen towards the collector causes the direction of the intensity maximum to move towards the collector, and so the fraction of the emitted secondary electrons that are collected increases.

In order to determine how the signal collected varies with θ, it is necessary to form the "product" of the two effects described above. The magnitude of the combined effect depends on the particular specimen, collector geometry, mode of operation etc. An experimental curve obtained using the emissive mode for a silicon specimen is shown in fig. 16. It can be seen that at $\theta = 45°$, a change in θ of $1°$ causes a change in the signal collected of approximately 2%.

Suppose now that a specimen with a faceted surface is being examined in the SEM. In particular, consider a 45° tilted specimen which has two symmetrical facets making angles of 20° with the specimen surface, as in fig. 17. For the general surface A, $\theta = 45°$, while for the two facets B and C, $\theta = 25°$ and 65° respectively. Hence, in the resulting image, facet B is darker than the

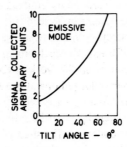

Fig. 16. Experimental results showing how the number of secondary electrons collected depends on the specimen tilt.

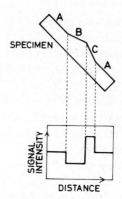

Fig. 17. Diagram illustrating how surface topography contrast arises.

general background, while facet C is brighter. If the data of fig. 16 are used, and the signal intensity for A is taken as 1.0, then the signal intensities for B and C are approximately 0.6 and 1.6 respectively. Because of these differences in intensity, the image appears to be "shadowed" and exhibits a strikingly three-dimensional form. The contrast is such as would be seen if the operator looked down onto the specimen from the position of the electron source, and a light was shone onto the specimen surface from the position of the electron collector. A micrograph of small growth pyramids on a flat substrate surface illustrating this three-dimensional effect is given in fig. 18.

Surface topography contrast occurs, therefore, for both the emissive and reflective modes of operation. However, the emissive mode is nearly always preferred in practice for the following reasons. First, the resolution is better (sect. 5). Second, if a collector such as that of fig. 14 is used, the signal is much larger. Third, because the secondary emitted electrons follow curved paths to the collector, image detail can be seen for specimen areas not in the direct line of sight of the collector, and so structure is revealed in cracks etc. A good illustration of the differences in such emissive and reflective mode images is given in fig. 19, taken from the work of Kimoto and Hashimoto [14]. Three metal meshes are shown mounted one above the other. In the emissive image (fig. 19a), all three meshes are clearly seen. In the reflective image (fig. 19b) the lower mesh is not visible because the reflected electrons leaving the lower mesh cannot "see" the collector. The shadows on the middle mesh arise for the same reason, but in this case it is the bars of the upper mesh that are in the way.

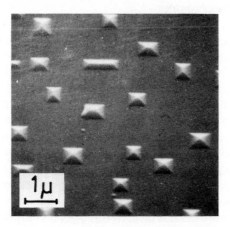

Fig. 18. Growth centres on (100) silicon substrate. Scanning electron micrograph using emissive mode. Specimen tilted 45°.

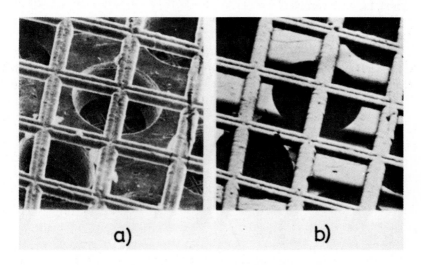

Fig. 19. Three metal meshes. Scanning electron micrographs using (a) emissive and (b) reflective modes. Work of Kimoto and Hashimoto [14].

18.3. *Atomic number contrast*

Contrast can arise from specimens if they contain material with differences in atomic number Z. The effect is due mainly to the behaviour of the reflected electrons. Experiment shows that the fraction of the number of incident electrons that are reflected, known as the back-scattering coefficient η, is relatively independent of the incident electron beam accelerating voltage in the range 10 to 40 kV, but progressively increases with Z. The relationship between η and Z for 30 kV electrons is given in fig. 20 using data obtained by Bishop [15]. It can be seen that for $Z = 20$, a change in Z of 1 causes a change in η of approximately 5%. Hence, if the reflective mode is used, because the signal intensity is proportional to η, relatively strong contrast changes occur due to differences in Z. The relationship between the number of emitted secondary electrons and Z is similar, but the magnitude of the effect is smaller. Hence, if the emissive mode is used, relatively weak contrast changes occur due to differences in Z. An illustration of atomic number contrast for the emissive and reflective modes is given in fig. 21, taken from the work of Kimoto and Hashimoto [14]. The micrographs show an Al − 2% Mn alloy containing tungsten carbide.

18.4. *Surface magnetic and electric fields*

If magnetic fields occur close to the specimen surface in small local areas, e.g. where magnetic domain walls meet the surface, then the secondary emitted electrons from these areas will undergo small deflections as they leave the sur-

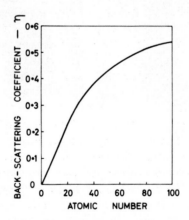

Fig. 20. Experimental results showing how the number of reflected electrons depends on the atomic number of the material. Work of Bishop [15].

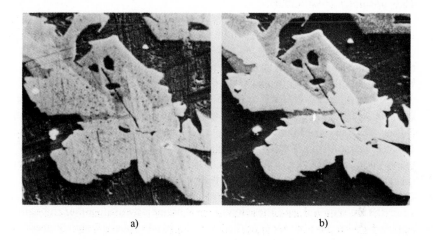

a) b)

Fig. 21. An Al − 2% Mn alloy containing tungsten carbide. Scanning electron micrographs using (a) emissive and (b) reflective modes. Work of Kimoto and Hashimoto [14].

face, and so the angular distribution curve will be slightly tilted. Hence, if the emissive mode is used, these magnetic field areas will be revealed in the image by differences in contrast. The magnitude of the effect depends on both the field strengths, and the sensitivity of the collector in detecting small changes in the angular distribution. The latter can often be improved by placing apertures, slits etc. at suitable places in front of the collector. On the other hand, if the reflective mode is used, the reflected electrons are insignificantly deflected by the magnetic fields, and so little if any contrast effects occur. Examples of magnetic contrast are given on p. 601.

Surface electric fields produce analogous contrast effects.

18.5. Surface potential

If areas of the specimen surface are at different potentials, e.g. when semiconductor electrical devices are examined under biased conditions, contrast differences can occur for the following reason. For the emissive mode, the signal collected depends on the voltage between the collector mesh and the specimen. If different specimen areas are at different voltages, different signals are collected from the different areas, and different contrasts result. To a first approximation, specimen areas at lower voltages give larger collected signals, and so in the image are brighter. Examples of such voltage contrast are given on p. 603. For the reflective mode, the collected signals are not similarly affected, and so little if any voltage contrast effects occur.

18.6. *Specimen conductivity*

Contrast can arise using the beam-induced conductivity (BIC) mode of operation for several reasons, depending on the particular experimental arrangement used, type of specimen etc. The principle of the BIC mode in its most common form is to attach electrical leads to the specimen, apply a voltage V, scan the specimen surface with the incident electron beam, and use the resulting current I as the signal to give the image. It is mostly used for the investigation of semiconductor specimens. The effect of the incident beam is to produce large numbers of electron/hole pairs in the specimen, and these carriers move under the action of the electric field E produced in the specimen by the application of the voltage V. If the carriers are removed from the specimen before they can recombine, the current I changes, and contrast occurs in the image. For significant differences to be detected, large field strengths are required, and these have been obtained by using either the fields associated with p-n junctions, or the fields that occur on applying voltages across thin specimens. Contrast differences can be obtained which provide information concerning the extent of the field regions, the presence of local recombination centres etc. Examples of BIC contrast are given on p. 603.

18.7. *Crystallographic orientation*

When thin foils of crystalline material are examined in either the TEM or SEM, contrast can occur in the image because of anomalous absorption effects associated with Bragg reflections. Similar effects have only recently been observed when solid specimens are examined in the SEM [16,17]. The effects are weak, but can nevertheless be detected. This result is extremely important because it means that crystallographic information can be obtained from solid specimens using the SEM, enabling a wide range of applications to be performed which were not previously possible. Because of its importance, pp. 613–653 are devoted to this topic, and it is not discussed further here.

19. Additional features

19.1. *Image foreshortening*

When specimens are tilted in the SEM, a foreshortening of the image occurs in a direction perpendicular to the tilt axis. If the tilt axis is parallel to the line scan direction on the specimen, as is usually approximately the case, then this foreshortening can be precisely annulled if required by using separate magnification controls for the line- and frame-scan coils, and appropriately adjusting the currents in each set of coils.

19.2. *Stereo-microscopy*

The large depth of focus of the SEM makes it eminently suitable for stereo-microscopy. The standard procedure is to record pairs of micrographs with the specimen slightly either tilted or rotated between the exposures. In order to obtain the best results, it may be necessary to make small corrections before recording the second image, e.g. to annul the additional foreshortening caused by the tilting.

19.3. *Y-modulation*

It is standard practice, when quantitative measurements of signal intensities are required, to make a single line trace across the image, and to apply the signal to the Y-plates of a separate CRT synchronously scanned. In this way, a plot of signal intensity against distance is obtained.

This Y-modulation technique can be used to display complete SEM images covering the full scanned raster [18], thereby providing a useful alternative to the more conventional intensity-modulated image. The number of lines per frame is chosen to suit the particular requirement, type of specimen etc., values between 50 and 1000 commonly being used. The main advantages of the technique are that it can provide considerable quantitative information on a single micrograph, and can produce strikingly three-dimensional images. Micrographs illustrating intensity- and Y-modulated images are given in fig. 22.

19.4. *Signal processing*

An important advantage of the SEM arises because the signal collected is a continuously varying function of time. Consequently, electronic processing can be performed on the signal before it is used to produce the image, and so considerable additional information made available. Some of the processing techniques are as follows.

First, the contrast can be increased overall by backing-off the DC level and increasing the amplification. For example, consider the case where a particular feature has $\delta S = 3$ against a background level of $S = 100$ (fig. 8). The contrast is $C = 3\%$. Suppose that the DC level is reduced to $S = 20$, and the amplification is increased $5\times$. The general signal level is now approximately the same, but the contrast is 15%. It may be mentioned that the noise δN is increased in the same proportion as the feature δS, and so the fundamental noise limitation discussed in sect. 10 cannot be overcome in this way.

Second, the contrast can be changed in a variable manner by taking the nth root ($n=2,3,4$ etc.) of the signal, and increasing the amplification. This variable γ control increases weak contrast in low signal regions, and decreases strong contrast in high signal regions.

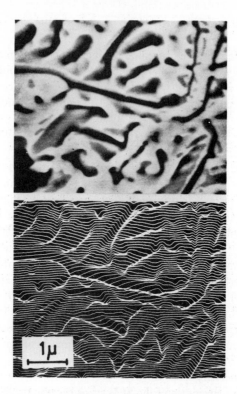

Fig. 22. Si-Au alloy. Scanning electron micrographs using (a) intensity modulation and (b) *Y*-modulation.

Third, contrast can be increased and features sharpened by differentiating the signal with respect to time. This can be performed using simple resistance-capacitance circuits with suitable time constants.

All of the above processing techniques are in day to day use on SEMs. Other more complex techniques are continually being developed for particular applications.

19.5. *Beam-chopping*

It is sometimes advantageous to use a pulsed incident electron beam, rather than a continuous beam. The electron pulses are generally obtained by placing a slit and an additional scan coil in the upper portion of the electron optical column, and applying appropriate currents to the coil. The beam then either proceeds down the column, or is deflected and lost on striking the edge of the slit. Square-wave pulses with adjustable on/off periods can readily be generated. Frequencies in the range 50 Hz to 10 MHz have been used.

The main applications of this beam-chopping technique to-date have been either with regard to improving the signal/noise ratio, or for stroboscopic observations. For the former, although beam-chopping means a lower average signal intensity at the specimen surface, tuned amplifiers, phase sensitive detectors etc. can be used. Hence, for investigations in which appreciable noise is introduced in either the specimen or collector system, a significant improvement in the signal/noise ratio is possible. It should be noted that this procedure cannot be used to overcome the fundamental noise limitation discussed in sec. 10.

For stroboscopic observations, the beam-chopping frequency is set equal to the frequency of the particular process being studied, e.g. the frequency of a vibrating reed. The incident electron beam is made to trace out the standard scanned raster, and the on period is adjusted to correspond to, say, the first 10% of each cycle. Consequently, the signals collected to form the image only arise when the reed is in one particular position. The result is that although some resolution is lost, an image of the reed occurs corresponding to the one position. Images corresponding to other positions can be obtained by altering the timing of the on period, i.e. by altering the phase.

19.6. *Contrast separation*

It is often advantageous to be able to separate the various contrasts that occur in SEM images. Surface topography and atomic number contrast have been separated by using two symmetrical collectors, one on either side of the specimen. To a first approximation, if a feature gives signals arising from the surface topography mechanism, then the two signals are different, while if they arise from the atomic number mechanism, then they are the same. Consequently, images formed by subtracting the two signals show mainly topography contrast, while images formed by adding the two signals show mainly atomic number contrast.

Voltage contrast has been separated from a combination of surface topography and atomic number contrast [19] by a beam-chopping technique. The voltage is applied to the, say, semiconductor electrical device during the even number pulses, but not during the odd number pulses. Signals corresponding to each set of pulses are separately extracted electronically, and subtracted. The resulting image shows only the voltage contrast.

These methods have the advantage that the separation is performed before the image is displayed, and so the separate image contrasts can be seen directly on the CRT screen during the examination.

19.7. *Energy analysis*

When the emissive and reflective modes of operation are being used, the electrons collected in both instances cover a range of electron energies. It is sometimes advantageous to place an energy analyser between the specimen and the collector so that the signal corresponds to only a narrow range of electron energies. This has been successfully performed for both secondary and reflected electrons. The main applications of such energy analysis are as follows.

First, if the signal intensity is plotted as a function of energy, the shape of the curve, positions of peaks etc., allow information to be deduced regarding the specimen, e.g. the identity of the material, the potential of the surface etc. Second, the manner in which the image contrast changes when electrons of different energies are collected provides information about contrast mechanisms. Third, if only the high energy electrons which have lost no energy (elastically scattered electrons) are used to form the image, spreading effects in the specimen are almost completely eliminated, and high resolution images can be obtained.

19.8. *Tape recording of images*

SEM images can be recorded using magnetic tape etc. instead of conventional photographic methods. This procedure has the advantage that the images can later by played back after being operated on, e.g. subjected to a whole range of signal processing techniques. The resulting images can be observed on a CRT screen, and photographed when considered satisfactory.

19.9. *Beam programming*

The principle of using on and off periods for the incident electron beam, as in beam-chopping experiments, can be extended. In particular, the beam can be programmed so as to trace out on the specimen surface intricate figures on an extremely fine scale. Such procedures can be used with advantage for high-resolution etching studies, semiconductor device fabrication etc.

19.10. *Stages*

A wide variety of stages can be constructed so that specimens can be heated, cooled, elongated, compressed, twisted, fatigued, fractured, coated, sublimed, ion-bombarded, chemically reacted, electrically stressed, magnetised etc. Observations may be made either at intervals or continuously.

20. Brighter electron sources

A problem continually encountered with the SEM is the need to detect a signal against a background noise. For example, the resolution of the instrument in its most common mode of operation, the emissive mode, is limited by the noise in the incident electron beam.

These noise problems can be made less restricting if brighter electron sources are used. For example, if the brightness were increased 100X, then the current in the spot I could be increased 100X for the same spot size d and beam divergence α (eq. (1)), and hence the noise decreased 10X (sect. 10). However, if high resolution is required, this procedure would not be used, as can be seen from the following

The curves of fig. 10 apply to a brightness $B = 4 \times 10^4$ A cm^{-2} sr^{-1}, and show how the resolution is limited by I. For example, if $I = 10^{-10}$ A is required for contrast reasons, i.e. to overcome the signal/noise limitation, then the best resolution is 400Å. However, if $B = 4 \times 10^5, 4 \times 10^6$ or 4×10^7 A cm^{-2} sr^{-1}, then the treatment is precisely the same except that the new 10^{-10} A curves take the places in fig. 10 of the $I = 10^{-11}, 10^{-12}$ and 10^{-13} A curves respectively. The corresponding best resolutions are, therefore, 200, 70 and 40Å respectively.

If the noise limitation can be overcome by using brighter electron sources, and if the effects due to chromatic aberration, astigmatism, stray fields etc. can be made insignificantly small, the only terms left in eq. (18) are those due to spherical aberration and diffraction. Differentiation then shows that the minimum value of the electron spot size d is $1.6 \ C_s^{\frac{1}{4}}\lambda^{\frac{3}{4}}$ and occurs when the beam divergence α is $0.8 \ C_s^{-\frac{1}{4}}\lambda^{\frac{1}{4}}$. For a standard commercial instrument with $C_s = 20$ mm and $\lambda = 0.086$Å (V=20 kV), the minimum spot size is 30Å. If C_s could be reduced to 1 mm by using a specially designed lens, then the minimum spot size would be 14Å for $\lambda = 0.086$Å (20 kV) and 11Å for $\lambda = 0.060$Å (40 kV). These values give an indication of the ultimate point-to-point resolution of the SEM, provided that spreading effects are unimportant. It follows that these resolutions are likely to be attained for the transmission mode, but probably not for the emissive mode.

Brighter electron sources have been used on experimental instruments, but are not yet available on commercial instruments. Pointed tungsten filaments and pointed lanthanum hexaboride filaments heated by conventional means can be incorporated into standard SEMs, and give brightnesses in the range 10^5 to 10^6 A cm^{-2} sr^{-1}. Similar pointed filaments can be used to produce electrons by cold field-emission if a vacuum of approximately 10^{-10} torr is maintained in the filament region, and give brightnesses of better than 10^8 A

cm^{-2} sr^{-1}. A further advantage of pointed filaments is that the effective size of the electron source is smaller than for conventional tungsten hair-pin filaments. Typical sizes for hair-pin filaments are 50 μm, for heated pointed filaments 1 to 10 μm, and for cold field-emission pointed filaments 100 to 1000Å. Consequently, less demagnification is required to give the final spot size.

Broers [20] has used heated lanthanum hexaboride filaments and obtained a resolution of 50Å for solid specimens with the emissive mode. Crewe [21] has used cold field-emission tungsten filaments and obtained a resolution of 30Å for thin foils using the transmission mode and energy analysis. Only one lens was required to produce the final small electron spot. Crewe [21] has also been able to resolve lattice planes with approximately 5Å spacing, but this is apparently a diffraction effect [22] and not a genuine point-to-point resolution.

21. Future trends

The important future trends in SEM instrumentation are likely to include brighter electron sources, contamination-free systems, signal processing, energy analysis, and modifications so that numerous experiments, especially dynamic, can be performed directly in the SEM.

References

[1] H.Stintzing, German patent No. 485 (1929) 155.
[2] M.Knoll, Z. Techn. Phys. 11 (1935) 467.
[3] M.von Ardenne, Z. Techn. Phys. 19 (1938) 407.
[4] V.K.Zworykin, J.Hillier and R.L.Snyder, Astm. Bull. No. 117 (1942) 15.
[5] F.Davoine, P.Pinard and M.Martineau, J. Phys. Rad. 21 (1960) 121.
[6] C.W.Oatley, W.C.Nixon and R.F.W.Pease, Advances in Electronics and Electron Physics, Vol. 21 (Academic Press, New York, 1965) p. 181.
[7] W.C.Nixon, Scanning Electron Microscopy Symposium (11T Research Institute, Chicago, 1968) p. 55.
[8] O.C.Wells, Bibliography on the Scanning Electron Microscope, IBM Research Report RC (1968) 2158.
[9] V.Johnson, Bibliography on the Scanning Electron Microscope, Scanning Electron Microscopy Symposium (11T Research Institute, Chicago, 1969) p. 485.
[10] P.R.Thornton, Scanning Electron Microscopy (Chapman and Hall, 1968).
[11] D.B.Langmuir, Proc. IRE 25 (1937) 977.
[12] T.E.Everhart, reported in ref. [10] (1968) p. 38.

[13] T.E.Everhart and R.F.M.Thornley, J. Sci. Instr. 37 (1960) 246.

[14] S.Kimoto and H.Hashimoto, Scanning Electron Microscopy Symposium (11T Research Institute, Chicago, 1968) p. 65.

[15] H.E.Bishop, reported in ref. [10] (1966) p. 88.

[16] D.G.Coates, Phil. Mag. 6 (1967) 1179.

[17] G.R.Booker, A.M.B.Shaw, M.J.Whelan and P.B.Hirsch, Phil. Mag. 6 (1967) 1185.

[18] T.E.Everhart, Proc. IEEE (Letters) 54 (1966) 1480.

[19] C.W.Oatley, J. Sci. Instr. (1969) (in press).

[20] A.N.Broers and E.K.Brandis, Scanning Electron Microscopy Symposium (11T Research Institute, Chicago, 1969) p. 15.

[21] A.V.Crewe, Scanning Electron Microscopy Symposium (11T Research Institute, Chicago, 1969) p. 11.

[22] P.B.Hirsch (1969) private communication.

SCANNING ELECTRON MICROSCOPY
Applications

G.R.BOOKER

1. Introduction

The applications of the scanning electron microscope (SEM) can be conveniently divided into three categories. First, there are conventional applications in which the emissive mode is used for topographical studies. Second, there are nonconventional applications in which various modes are used to obtain specialised information. Third, there are dynamic experiments performed in the SEM, e.g. the direct observation of specimens as they are deformed.

2. Conventional applications

The SEM is valuable for surface topographical studies because (a) solid specimens can be examined, often without any preparation treatment, (b) a wide range of magnification can be used, e.g. with commercial instruments 20X to 20 000X, (c) a large depth of focus is available, and (d) strikingly three-dimensional images can be obtained, especially on tilting the specimen. Some examples of conventional applications taken from the fields of crystal growth, fracture failure, ingot solidification and plastic deformation are as follows.

Epitaxial growth of silicon onto a (111) silicon substrate on which liquid gold droplets were present (1) is shown in fig. 1. The specimen was tilted through an angle $\theta = 80°$ (p. 582, fig. 15), and the emissive mode was used. The silicon has grown faster via the gold droplets by the vapour-liquid-solid mechanism of Wagner and Ellis [2] than on the substrate in between the droplets. As a result, a massive silicon growth has formed beneath each gold droplet. The SEM examination revealed new information about both the massive growths and the regions in between [1].

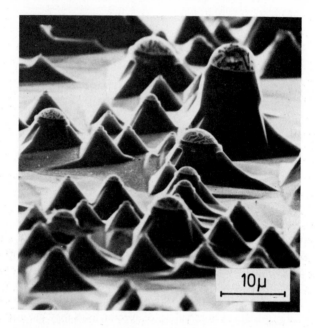

Fig. 1. Epitaxial silicon layer grown on (111) silicon substrate. Massive growths occur under gold-silicon droplets. Emissive mode. Specimen tilted 80° [1].

Fig. 2. Fracture surface of carbon fibre reinforced resin. Emissive mode. Specimen tilted 45°. (Work of Sharp and Reynolds [3].)

A fibre-reinforced resin that has been fractured [3] is shown in fig. 2. The specimen was tilted through approximately 45°, and the emissive mode was used. The fibres are carbon and approximately 8 μm in diameter. The SEM examination showed how the fractures had occurred, and enabled the effects of fibre coatings, heat-treatments etc. to be followed [3].

A transverse section through an Al-12%Si ingot which was unidirectionally frozen at 1 mm/hr [4] is shown in fig. 3. The specimen was tilted through 45°, and the emissive mode was used. The specimen was deeply etched to remove the aluminium matrix near the surface, thereby exposing the silicon platelets formed during solidification. The SEM examination enabled detailed information to be obtained concerning the morphology of the platelets, habit planes, twinned regions etc. [4]. This method for investigating eutectic structures has the advantage over extraction replicas that the relative orientation of the platelets is correctly preserved.

The specimens shown in figs. 1 to 3 are ideal subjects for surface topographical investigations using the SEM because they possess marked variations in surface slope, and hence exhibit strong contrast. They can be examined initially at low magnification and the observations correlated with previous optical microscope (OM) results. The magnification can then be increased so that additional structural information is obtained. The specimens can be tilted so that three-dimensional configurations are observed. Stereo-micrographs can

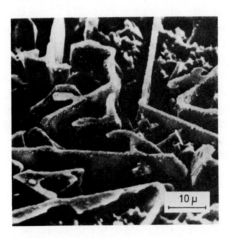

Fig. 3. Deeply etched Al-12%Si eutectic structure showing silicon platelets. Emissive mode. Specimen tilted 45°. (Work of Day and Hellawell [4].)

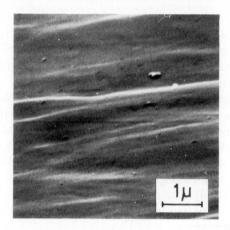

Fig. 4. Wavy slip-lines on the surface of a single crystal niobium specimen pulled in tension. Emissive mode. Specimen titlted 60°. (Work of Bowen [5].)

be recorded so that more detailed three-dimensional studies, and quantitative measurements, can be made.

Wavy slip-lines on the surface of a deformed niobium single crystal [5] are shown in fig. 4. The specimen was tilted through 60°, and the emissive mode was used. Owing to the high lateral resolution of the SEM, details of step branching etc. can be seen which are not revealed by the OM. However, the steps comprising the slip lines are shallowly inclined to the specimen surface, and so they exhibit weak contrast. In order to improve the contrast, tilting of such specimens is usually required. This has the additional effect of causing the relative orientation of the lines on the surface to be distorted in the image unless a suitable magnification corrector is used (p. 588, sect. 19.1). It is worthwhile pointing out that much of the improvement in contrast for such specimens that occurs on tilting arises because the total signal collected increases, and so the signal/noise ratio increases. Consequently, the D.C. signal level can be reduced and the contrast increased (p. 589, sect. 19.4).

3. Non-conventional applications

3.1. *General*

There are many non-conventional applications of the SEM in which spe-

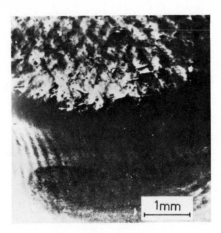

Fig. 5. Single crystal cobalt specimen showing magnetic domain structures. Emissive mode. (Work of Joy and Jakubovics [6].)

cialised information is obtained from specimens. This information may relate to either the surface of the specimen or the interior. Some examples of such applications are as follows.

3.2. *Magnetic domains*

A cylindrical single-crystal cobalt specimen [6] is shown in fig. 5. The specimen possesses uniaxial anisotropy: the magnetisation direction is parallel to [0001], the axis of the cylinder. The micrograph shows the main domain walls. These intersect the curved sides of the cylinder as straight lines (fig. 5, bottom) and intersect one end of the cylinder as wavy lines (fig. 5, top).

The method [6] for obtaining this micrograph was to use the emissive mode with a small aperture in front of the Faraday cage of the electron collector (p. 580, fig. 14). The contrast arises [6] because the emitted secondary electrons are deflected by the external magnetic fields associated with the domain structure. It is considered that the number of electrons *emitted* from the different areas is approximately constant, while the number *collected* varies.

Recent work on cobalt [7] and iron [8] has shown that similar but much weaker contrast can be obtained by using the absorptive mode, i.e. by collecting the specimen current electrons. A micrograph of a polycrystalline cobalt specimen obtained in this way [7] is shown in fig. 6. Because the specimen current is complementary to the secondary emitted electron current and primary reflected electron current, this observation suggests that the number of

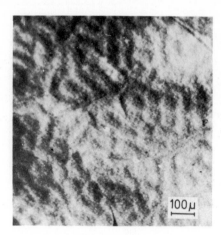

Fig. 6. Polycrystalline cobalt specimen showing magnetic domain structures. Absorptive
mode (specimen current). (Work of Joy, Jakubovics and Schulson [7]).

electrons *emitted* from the different areas varies slightly. The full explanation
for this behaviour is not yet clear. Nevertheless, the result is important because it means that magnetic domains can be revealed with the SEM without
any modifications to the instrument.

These methods for revealing magnetic domain structures possess the advantage that no magnetic particles need to be deposited on the specimen surface, as in the Bitter pattern technique. Consequently, changes in the positions
of the walls or the strengths of the fields, as caused by applying external magnetic fields, heating the specimen etc., can be continuously followed.

3.3. *Voltage distribution*

A shallow-diffused silicon transistor [9] is shown in fig. 7. The specimen
has been cleaved so that both the cross-section through the transistor (fig. 7,
bottom), and the upper surface of the transistor (fig. 7, top), can be seen. The
emissive mode was used, and the specimen was electrically biased. The specimen
was tilted so that the normal to the cleaved surface made an angle $\theta = 60°$ with
the incident electron beam. The emitter, base and collector regions of the
transistor are clearly delineated in the cleaved area because of the voltage contrast that is present. This contrast arises mainly because the different areas of
the specimen are at different voltages with respect to the Faraday cage of the
electron collector, and so the number of electrons collected from the different
areas is different (p. 587, sect. 18.5).

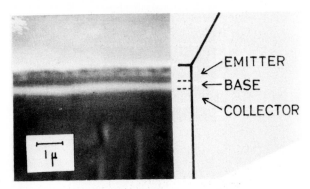

EMITTER

BASE

COLLECTOR

Fig. 7. Cleaved shallow-diffused silicon transistor showing positions of p-n junctions.
Emissive mode [9].

Voltage contrast is extremely valuable when examining semiconductor devices in the SEM. In general, little or no specimen preparation treatment is
required. Sufficient voltage bias can often be obtained from the charging effects of the SEM electron beam, and so no electrical leads need to be attached
to the specimen. The true electrical junction is revealed. In the example described above (fig. 7), measurement shows that the transistor base region
width is approximately 6000Å, after allowing for the specimen tilt. This
value is more accurate than could be obtained by conventional angle-lapping
and staining techniques because the latter do not usually delineate the precise electrical junction.

The voltage contrast method has been applied with considerable success to
the investigation of irregularities in junction geometry, shorts across junctions,
discontinuities in electrical leads etc.

3.4. Junction field regions

Three micrographs showing a section through a semiconductor junction
diode [10] are given in fig. 8. The junction is perpendicular to the specimen
surface. Electrical leads were attached, a reverse-bias voltage V applied to the
junction, and the beam-induced conductivity (BIC) mode used, i.e. the junction current was taken as the signal for the SEM image. The bright zone in
the micrographs corresponds to the electrical field region of the junction.
Figs. 8a, b and c were recorded with $V = 0$, 35 and 460 V respectively. The
micrographs show that there is a narrow residual electric field region when
no bias is applied, and that the field region increases in width as the bias increases.

The contrast arises because the incident SEM electron beam scanning across

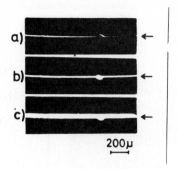

Fig. 8. Cross-section through junction diode. Beam-induced conductivity mode. (Work of Thornton [10].)

the specimen surface creates large numbers of electron/hole pairs within the specimen. In the regions away from the junction, the electrons and holes recombine without contributing to the junction current, and so these regions are dark. In the field region of the junction, the electrons and holes contribute to the junction current, and so this region is bright.

This BIC method for investigating junction field regions in semiconductor specimens is especially suitable for studying junction break-down behaviour, and in particular the role played by processing faults etc. on device failure [11].

3.5. Electrical recombination centres

A diffused silicon diode [12] is shown in fig. 9. The junction is parallel to, and approximately 3 μm below, the specimen surface. The junction was reverse-biased, and the BIC mode used as described in section 3.4. The contrast arises because many electrons and holes are formed in the junction field region and contribute to the junction current. If the material in the immediate neighbourhood of the junction were completely homogeneous, the image would be uniformly bright. The irregular dark lines that can be seen in fig. 9 running along crystallographic directions are regions of reduced junction current. They correspond to defects which are present in the junction region and act as electrical recombination centres. This BIC method is valuable for investigating the electrical behaviour of defects associated with p-n junctions.

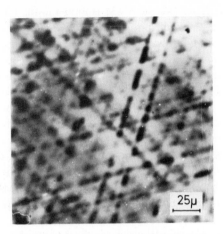

Fig. 9. Diffused silicon specimen with p-n junction approximately 3 microns below surface. Irregular dark lines are electrical recombination centres associated with crystallographic defects. Beam-induced conductivity mode [12].

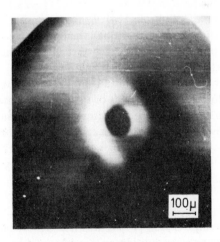

Fig. 10. Melt-grown silicon specimen with central hole after jet thinning. Bright zone indicates electrical carrier collection region. Beam-induced conductivity mode [13].

A melt-grown silicon specimen [13] is shown in fig. 10. The specimen has been chemically jet thinned from both sides so that a central hole is present, and the material on going away from the edge of the hole progressively increases in thickness. No p-n junctions are present in the specimen. Electrical leads were attached to the two opposite sides of the specimen, a voltage V applied, and the BIC mode used. Although the precise mechanism is not yet clear, the voltage V causes a strong electric field to occur within the specimen in the thin regions near the central hole. As a result, the electrical carriers formed within this region contribute to the current in the leads, and so a bright zone forms in the image around the central hole. If any electrical recombination centres had been present in this specimen, they would have appeared as dark regions within the bright zone. This BIC method is valuable for investigating the electrical behaviour of defects when p-n junctions are not present.

Suitably performed experiments using these methods can give information concerning carrier recombination distances, minority carrier lifetimes, trapping cross-sections etc.

3.6. Resistivity variations

A method has been developed by Munakata [14] for determining resistivity variations in semiconductor specimens using the SEM. It is well-known that when a semiconductor bar is irradiated with light, a voltage is developed at the ends of the bar if the resistance is not uniform [15]. A similar effect occurs if the bar is irradiated with electrons [14]. In the latter case, if the electron beam is incident at a particular point on the bar, then the voltage δV developed between the ends is proportional to the rate of change of resistance $d\rho/dx$ along the bar at that particular point.

The SEM electron beam was scanned along the length of the bar, and the voltage which occurred across the ends of the bar was measured [14]. This voltage was amplified and integrated electronically, the resulting signal showing how the resistivity varied along the length of the bar. The method has been improved [16] by using a pulsed-beam, and the theory refined. Good agreement between the SEM results, and measurements made by more conventional procedures, was obtained.

3.7. Cathodoluminescence

A zinc selenide single crystal [17] is shown in fig. 11. The crystal has a hexagonal structure, but contains in addition a number of fine lamellae with cubic structure. The incident SEM electron beam scanning the surface of the specimen gives rise to radiative recombination processes within the crystal, and

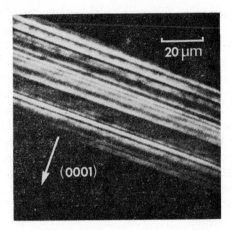

Fig. 11. Single-crystal zinc selenide specimen with lamellar structures. Cathodoluminescent mode. Light of wavelength 4480Å only collected. (Work of Williams and Yoffe [17].)

hence the emission of light. The wavelength of the light depends on the band
structure of the material. For the zinc selenide crystal of the present work,
transitions associated with bound excitons give strong intensity peaks at
4400Å for the hexagonal structure, and at 4480Å for the cubic structure [17].
The micrograph of fig. 11 was obtained by using a monochromator to select
emitted light of wavelength 4480Å only, and then converting the light into a
suitable electrical signal with a photo-multiplier, amplifier etc. The lamellae
all appear bright against a dark background, showing conclusively that they
consist of the cubic zinc selenide phase. When the monochromator was set to
4400Å, the background appeared bright and the lamellae dark, showing that
the general matrix consists of the hexagonal zinc selenide phase.

The use of a monochromator to select definite wavelengths to obtain SEM
cathodoluminescent micrographs is an extremely valuable technique for studying radiative processes in crystals. It enables particular energy transitions to
be related to specific areas of the crystals, and with relatively good resolution.

4. Dynamical experiments

4.1. *General*

The SEM is especially suitable for dynamical experiments performed directly in the instrument. Specimen chambers are generally relatively large and so a

variety of additional stages, collectors etc. can readily be incorporated. If the highest resolution is not required, the final lens can be operated at a long working distance, allowing more scope in stage design. Solid specimens can be examined and so a wide range of mechanical experiments can be performed. The depth of focus is large, and so focusing is not critical.

Some of the experiments performed in the SEM are analogous to experiments carried out in other instruments, e.g. the transmission electron microscope (TEM). These include heating, cooling, deposition, evaporation etc. Other experiments performed in the SEM could probably not be carried out in any other instrument. These include mechanical deformation of solid specimens, stroboscopic observation of oscillating systems etc. Some of these latter type of experiments are now briefly described.

4.2. Probe manipulation

A titanium carbide stylus sliding across the surface of a gold specimen [18] is shown in fig. 12. The stylus has a fine point and is just making contact with the surface. The motion of the stylus in this particular instance is to cut from the surface a chip approximately 1000 Å thick.

This micrograph is an example of a range of work performed at the Cavendish Laboratory, Cambridge, involving the manipulation of fine probes in the SEM [18,19]. Much of the work relates to the use of such probes to study surface wear, abrasion, cutting, indentation etc., and how it is influenced by the

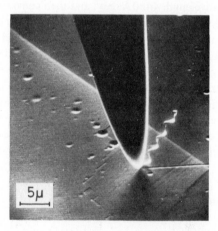

Fig. 12. A titanium carbide stylus being moved across the surface of a gold specimen. Emissive mode. (Work of Gane and Bowden [18].)

Fig. 13. Slip-lines on the surface of a Cu-13% Al single crystal deformed 25% in tension. Emissive mode. Specimen tilted 45°. (Work of Dingley [20].)

applied load, speed of application, presence of surface contaminating layers etc. Other work concerns the use of such probes for assessment purposes, e.g. to determine the detailed shapes of micro-hardness indentations, micro-craters formed by laser pulses etc.

4.3. Tensile deformation

A Cu-13%Al single crystal pulled in tension [20] is shown in fig. 13. The micrograph corresponds to a specimen extension of 25%, and is one of a series of such photographs taken as the specimen was progressively deformed in a specially constructed straining stage. The specimen is held by two symmetrical cross-heads that are made to move in opposite directions by a motor drive. As a result, the centre portion of the specimen remains approximately stationary during deformation, and can be continuously examined using the SEM emissive mode. The specimen surface is tilted at 45° with respect to the SEM electron beam in order to increase the contrast from the slip-lines.

The use of this stage has enabled the deformation to be continuously followed [20]. Initially straight primary slip-lines occurred, and these were followed by faint secondary slip-lines. Both systems then developed, the latter slip-lines becoming extremely wavy as they crossed the former, and eventually developing kinks. Cross-slip was frequently observed. The smallest steps detected were estimated to be a few tens of Burgers vectors high.

For the micrograph of fig. 13, the tensile axis runs from left to right. The primary slip-lines run from bottom left to top right, and the secondary slip-lines from top left to bottom right. The extremely fine lines running from left to right are an electronic recording fault, and not a surface feature.

4.4. *Stroboscopic observations*

A metal-oxide-semiconductor transistor ladder micro-circuit [21] is shown in fig. 14. A 5 V peak-to-peak MHz sine wave has been applied to the bottom-right bonded metal electrode. The micrograph is one of a stroboscopic series which shows how the voltage distribution on the surface of the micro-circuit varies during the course of an individual cycle of the applied voltage [21]. In order to obtain these micrographs, the incident SEM electron beam was chopped (p. 590, sect. 19.5) at the same frequency as the voltage applied to the micro-circuit, the beam only being on during the same small portion of each cycle. The emissive mode was used and so voltage contrast occurred in the image. The result of using this technique is that the voltage distribution is

Fig. 14. Semiconductor micro-circuit with 5 V since wave signal applied at 7 MHz. Strobo-scopic micrograph showing surface voltage distribution for one particular phase of the cycle. Emissive mode. (Work of Plows and Nixon [21].)

"frozen" in the image for the particular phase of the cycle corresponding to the period for which the beam is on. The voltage distribution for other periods of the cycle can be observed by altering the phase. The investigation [21] revealed that appreciable voltages were induced in neighbouring portions of the micro-circuit (fig. 14) due to the rapidly changing applied voltage, whereas such voltages would have been completely absent if the applied voltage had been DC.

The stroboscopic technique for the direct observation of oscillating systems in the SEM has also been applied to mechanical problems, e.g. the motion of vibrating metal contacts [22].

References

[1] J.D.Filby, S.Nielsen, G.J.Rich, G.R.Booker and J.M.Larcher, Phil. Mag. 16 (1967) 561.
[2] R.S.Wagner and W.C.Ellis, Trans. Metall. Soc. AIME 233 (1965) 1053.
[3] J.V.Sharp and W.N.Reynolds (private communication) (1968).
[4] M.G.Day and A.Hellawell, Proc. Roy. Soc. A., 305 (1968) 473.
[5] K.Bowen (private communication) (1967).
[6] D.C.Joy and J.P.Jakubovics, Phil. Mag. 17 (1968) 61.
[7] D.C.Joy, J.P.Jakubovics and E.M.Schulson (private communication).
[8] J.Philibert and R.Tixier (submitted for publication).
[9] J.M.Titchmarsh (unpublished results) (1968).
[10] P.R.Thornton, Cambridge Scientific Instruments Ltd., England (1966) Scientific Leaflet No. 178 B6, Sheet C.
[11] I.G.Davies, K.A.Hughes, D.V.Sulway and P.R.Thornton, Solid State Electronics 9 (1966) 275.
[12] A.M.B.Shaw, Ph. D. Thesis, University of Cambridge (1969).
[13] A.M.B.Shaw and G.R.Booker, Scanning Electron Microscope Symposium (11T Research Institute, Chicago, 1969) p. 459.
[14] C.Munakata, J. Appl. Phys., Japan 4 (1965) 815.
[15] J.Tauc, Photo and Thermoelectric Effects in Semiconductors (Pergamon Press, 1962) Ch. 3.
[16] C.Munakata, Microelectronics and Reliability 6 (1967) 27.
[17] P.M.Williams and A.D.Yoffe, Nature 221 (1969) 952.
[18] N.Gane and F.P.Bowden, J. Appl. Phys. 39 (1968) 1432.
[19] T.J.Baston and F.P.Bowden, Nature 218 (1968) 150.
[20] D.J.Dingley (private communication) (1969).
[21] G.S.Plows and W.C.Nixon, J. Scient. Instr. 1 (1968) 595.
[22] J.R.Banbury and W.C.Nixon (private communication) (1969).

SCANNING ELECTRON MICROSCOPY
Electron channelling effects

G.R.BOOKER

1. Introduction

It has been known for several years that when thin foils of crystalline material are examined with either the transmission electron microscope (TEM) or the scanning electron microscope (SEM), contrast can arise in the image because of anomalous absorption effects associated with Bragg reflections [1,2]. It was only recently that similar, although much weaker, effects were observed when the SEM is used to examine solid specimens [3,4]. The latter result is extremely important because it means that crystallography has been introduced into the field of scanning electron microscopy, where it was previously almost completely absent.

Since the first observation of such effects for the SEM and solid specimens [3], considerable work has been performed on the conditions necessary to observe the effects, the mechanisms whereby the effects arise, and the applications of such effects to materials problems. As a result of this work, many of the procedures which have been used for several years with the TEM to examine thin foils are rapidly becoming available with the SEM to examine solid specimens.

In order to describe how these anomalous absorption effects arise with the SEM and solid specimens, it is convenient to start with the case of the TEM and thin foils. This is also the way in which the subject developed historically.

2. Historical

It is well-known that when high-energy electrons are incident on single-crystal material in the neighbourhood of a Bragg reflection, and only one

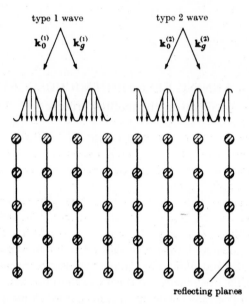

Fig. 1. Diagram illustrating the behaviour of Bloch waves 1 and 2 in a crystal set at the
Bragg position (ref. [1]).

strong diffracted beam is excited, the electrons inside the crystal can be described by the superposition of two Bloch waves. For a detailed description
of such waves, and of previous work see ref. [1]. The type 1 wave has nodes
located at the positions of the atoms of the reflecting planes, while the
type 2 wave has nodes located at the positions in between the atoms (fig. 1).
The absorption coefficient for the transmission of the type 2 wave through
the crystal is greater than the corresponding absorption coefficient for the
type 1 wave. This is because on average the various processes giving rise to
the absorption are located nearer to the centres of the atoms than to the
regions in between. When the crystal is set at the precise Bragg position, the
type 1 and type 2 waves are equally excited. When the crystal is set slightly
off the Bragg position in one sense ($s<0$), the type 2 wave is preferentially
excited, while when set in the opposite sense ($s>0$), the type 1 wave is preferentially excited. Consequently, when high-energy electrons are incident on
a crystal, the overall absorption is not symmetrical on either side of a Bragg
reflection, but is greater in the region for $s < 0$ than for $s > 0$. This result is
well-known in transmission electron microscopy. For example, it explains the

image contrasts associated with Bragg reflections when bent foils are examined in the TEM. In particular, such bend contours are dark on one side ($s < 0$) of the precise Bragg position, and bright on the other side ($s > 0$).

Because of the foregoing, Hirsch et al. [5] predicted in 1962 that the intensity of X-rays emitted from thin foils due to the incidence of high-energy electrons should be orientation-dependent in the neighbourhood of Bragg reflections. The argument used was that the absorption process for producing such X-rays should occur nearer to the centres of the atoms than to the regions in between. Hence X-ray production should be associated more with the type 2 wave than the type 1 wave, and so more with the $s < 0$ regions of Bragg reflections than the $s > 0$ regions. This meant in practice that if thin foils were examined in the TEM, the dark regions of bend contours should give enhanced X-ray emission.

This prediction for thin foils was verified in 1962 by Duncumb [2], who used a combined transmission electron microscope (TEM) and X-ray probe micro-analyser (XRPM) to examine a single-crystal gold foil 200Å thick. He observed that bend contours, which were dark in transmission electron micrographs, appeared bright in scanning X-ray micrographs. His results also showed that the same dark bend contours appeared bright in scanning electron micrographs, i.e. an analogous orientation-dependent effect occurred for thin foils and emitted electrons.

These observations [2] suggested to Duncumb et al. [6] that if similar effects occurred for solid specimens, then a whole range of interesting possibilities existed. Perhaps the most exciting was that SEM examinations of solid specimens might reveal dislocations emerging at the specimen surface because of the local bending of lattice planes [6]. On the other hand, of considerable practical importance was the possibility that significant errors might arise when XRPMs are used to make quantitative chemical analyses of solid specimens because no account of crystallographic orientation is then taken [6]. Because of these considerations, two projects were initiated at Cambridge as follows.

Hall [7] in 1964–65 examined thin foils of nickel and germanium in a modified TEM, and measured the X-ray emission as a function of distance across bend contours. He found that the ratio R of maximum to minimum intensity of emitted X-rays for individual contours decreased with increasing foil thickness, typical values ranging from 1.8 to 1.2 on going from a thickness of 1000 to 4000Å. Extrapolation of the results to solid specimens gave a value of R between 1.00 and 1.03, indicating that any X-ray orientation effects for solid specimens would be extremely small.

Shaw and Booker [8] in 1965–66 examined gold and platinum thin foils in a standard TEM and then in a Stereoscan SEM*. They observed that the SEM contrast from bend contours decreased as the foil thickness increased, e.g. on going from 200 to 800Å for gold foils, and that the SEM contrast differences on either side of twin boundaries could be reversed by tilting the specimen. They were not successful in detecting genuine orientation-dependent contrast from dislocations in the foils, or subsequently in solid specimens. As is shown later (sect. 13), this lack of success was because standard SEMs do not as yet possess sufficient sensitivity for this purpose.

Coates [3] at the Royal Radar Establishment, Malvern, in 1967 examined single-crystal semiconductor solid specimens with a Stereoscan SEM and noted weak bands of contrast, similar to Kikuchi bands in electron diffraction patterns, crossing the micrograph image when certain non-standard operating conditions were used. The bands moved when the specimen was tilted or rotated. He deduced that the bands were related to the crystallography of the specimen, and demonstrated how such bands could be used to determine the crystallographic orientation of specimens.

The origin of the bands and patterns observed by Coates [3] was explained qualitatively by Booker et al. [4] in 1967 in terms of the anomalous absorption effects described above. The latter workers recorded numerous patterns from semiconductor and metal solid specimens, experimentally verified that the bands possessed the predicted angular width 2θ (where θ is the corresponding Bragg angle), and found that the ratio R of maximum to minimum intensity of emitted electrons for individual bands was in the range 1.02 to 1.08.

It may be mentioned that in all of the work on the SEM electron orientation effect referred to above, contrasts were observed for high-order, as well as for low-order, reflections. Moreover, the contrast occurred when using either the emissive or reflective modes, i.e. on collecting either the primary reflected electrons or the secondary emitted electrons.

Several attempts have subsequently been made to detect the analogous X-ray orientation effect for solid specimens. Coates [9] examining silicon and Shaw and Booker [10] examining germanium did not observe an effect. Bramman and Yates [11] examining polycrystalline uranium dioxide, nickel and stainless steel observed an effect with R in the range 1.01 to 1.02. Schulson et al. [12] examining single-crystal silicon observed an effect with R equal to 1.01. The latter workers also detected a photon-orientation effect by collecting the light emitted from a cadmium sulphide crystal due to the excitation of cathodoluminescence by the incident SEM electron beam.

---

* Kind collaboration of Mr. A.D.G.Stewart and Cambridge Scientific Instruments Limited, Cambridge.

By far the most important result of the above work is the electron orientation effect, and the patterns that can be obtained because of this effect from solid specimens using the SEM. The manner in which these patterns arise is described in the next section, starting with the similar patterns that occur when thin foils are examined in the TEM.

3. Nature of patterns

A transmission electron micrograph of a bent metal foil [13] is shown in fig. 2. The foil is extremely thin, and the absorption of the incident electrons is small. The dark lines are bend contours and are located where Bragg reflections occur in the foil. The lines form in pairs where the lattice planes bend in opposite senses, and correspond to reflections $+g$ and $-g$. For this particular micrograph, four pairs of such lines are present corresponding to $2\bar{2}0$ and $\bar{2}20$, 220 and $\bar{2}\bar{2}0$, 200 and $\bar{2}00$, and 020 and $0\bar{2}0$ reflections. The symmetrical position where the pairs of lines intersect one another corresponds to the [001] pole, i.e. where the incident electron beam is parallel to the [001] direction in the foil.

A transmission electron micrograph of another bent foil [14] is shown in fig. 3. The foil is of moderate thickness, and the absorption of the incident electrons is appreciable. The general appearance of the micrograph is similar to that of fig. 2. However, each pair of lines is replaced by a continuous dark band, and immediately outside the dark band are narrow bright bands. The reason for this is indicated in fig. 4a. The incident electrons experience higher absorption on the absorption on the $s < 0$ sides of the Bragg reflections, than on the $s > 0$ sides (sect. 2). Consequently, the bend contours at A and B appear dark on the sides facing towards one another, and bright on the sides facing away from one another. As the foil becomes thicker and the amount of absorption greater, the dark regions join and form a continuous dark band. For this particular micrograph, the three main bands correspond to $2\bar{2}0$ and $\bar{2}20$, $20\bar{2}$ and $\bar{2}02$, and $02\bar{2}$ and $0\bar{2}2$ reflections. The symmetrical position corresponds to the [111] pole.

The important points regarding these patterns are as follows. The patterns occur when *micrographs* are recorded. The patterns are irregular because the bending of the foils occurs in an irregular manner. Tilting of the specimen causes the patterns to move laterally across the surface of the specimen. High-order reflections are also present. The contrasts arise because of local differences in the scattering behaviour of the electrons within the foil. It is only necessary to scatter the incident electrons through an angle of, say, $0.5°$ to

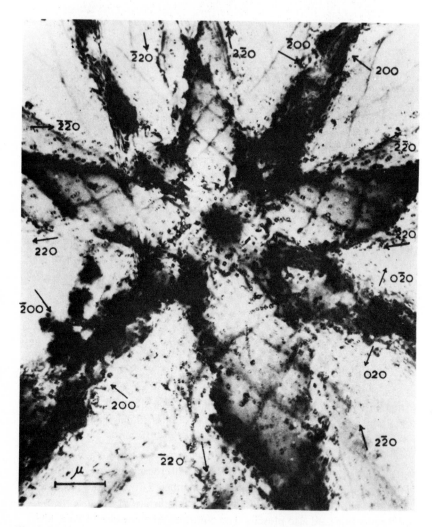

Fig. 2. Extinction or bend contours in a thin Cu-Co single-crystal foil. Transmission electron micrograph. (Work of Ashby [13].)

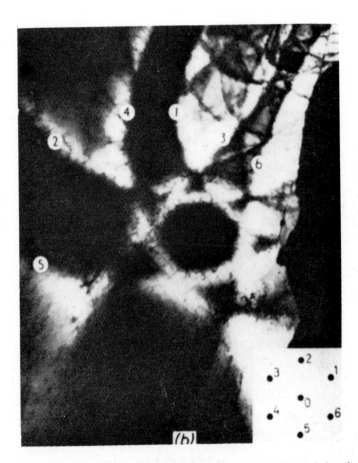

Fig. 3. Extinction or bend controus in a thin Cu single-crystal foil. Transmission electron micrograph. (Work of Steeds [14].)

produce contrast because the electrons then strike the contrast aperture of the electron microscope, and so are lost from the image (termed "absorption" in transmission electron microscopy).

A scanning electron micrograph of a single-crystal (100) gallium arsenide solid specimen is shown in fig. 5. The micrograph was recorded at low magnification with the specimen untilted and using the emissive mode. Surface topo-

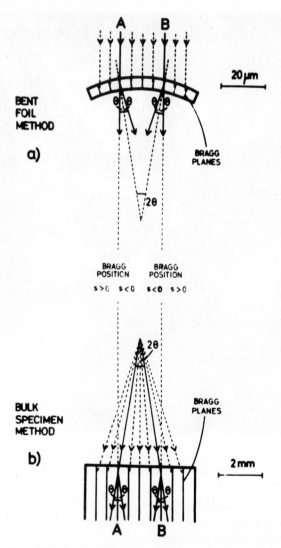

Fig. 4. Diagram showing Bragg positions for (a) a bent single-crystal foil using the transmission electron microscope (TEM), and (b) a solid single-crystal specimen using the scanning electron microscope (SEM) [4].

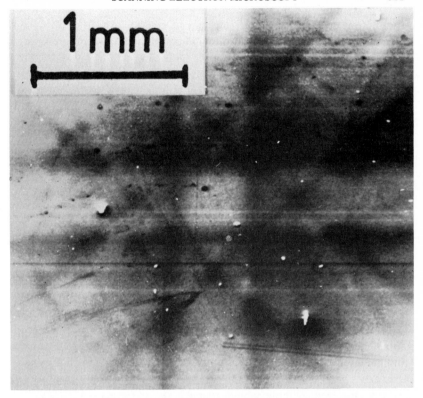

Fig. 5. An electron channelling pattern (ECP) obtained using the SEM, emissive mode, and a (100) solid GaAs specimen. Note the surface topographical features and the bands of contrast.

graphy structure can be seen, and also weak bands of contrast crossing the field of view in a regular manner. These bands are of the type first observed by Coates [3]. The bands are bright with narrow dark edges. If the reflective mode had been used, the contrast would have been similar, while if the absorptive mode (specimen current) had been used, the contrast would have been reversed, i.e. the bands would be dark with narrow bright edges.

The origin of such patterns can be explained qualitatively by reference to fig. 4b. When the SEM is used at low magnifications, e.g. 20X, the area on the specimen scanned by the electron beam is large, e.g. 4 mm across, and so the angle the electron beam makes with the specimen surface changes appreciably, e.g. ± 7°. This is large compared with the Bragg angle θ for low-order reflections and typical SEM accelerating voltages (table 1). Consequently, Bragg re-

Table 1
Calculated Bragg angles θ for silicon for different electron accelerating voltages.

Reflection	Lattice spacing (Å)	θ^0			
		30 (kV)	20 (kV)	10 (kV)	5 (kV)
111	3.14	0.63	0.79	1.11	1.58
220	1.92	1.03	1.28	1.82	2.58
311	1.64	1.22	1.50	2.13	3.03
400	1.36	1.48	1.82	2.58	3.66
331	1.25	1.60	1.98	2.81	3.98
422	1.11	1.81	2.22	3.16	4.48

flections occur at positions such as A and B, and bands of contrast arise in the image. For the particular micrograph of fig. 5, the four main bands correspond to 022 and 0$\bar{2}\bar{2}$, 02$\bar{2}$ and 0$\bar{2}$2, 040 and 0$\bar{4}$0, and 004 and 00$\bar{4}$ reflections. The symmetrical position corresponds to the [100] pole.

The main points regarding these patterns are as follows. They again occur in *micrographs*. They are precisely regular because the scanning action of the electron beam across the specimen surface is precisely regular. They move on tilting the specimen, and high-order reflections are also present. The contrast again arises because of local differences in scattering behaviour, although the processes involved are more complicated, e.g. the scattering angles for reflected electrons are $> 90°$, and secondary electrons need to be considered. Nevertheless, the general similarity between the contrast of the bands in figs. 3 and 5 (in this instance complementary contrast) is striking.

4. Origin of contrast

4.1. *Reflective mode*

Consider the SEM patterns obtained on using the reflective mode. A simple explanation of the contrast that occurs in these patterns is as follows. The scattering processes giving rise to the reflected electrons are located nearer to the centres of the atoms than to the positions in between (Rutherford scattering), and so the number of such electrons is greater for the $s < 0$ regions than the $s > 0$ regions, i.e., the ratio of maximum to minimum intensity $R_p > 1$. Consequently, bright bands with dark edges should occur, as are observed.

A more realistic treatment takes into account the progressive change in behaviour with the depth of penetration.of the incident electrons into the specimen. Thus, for the first few 100Å, the majority of the incident electrons are still travelling in their original directions, the mechanism described above closely applies, and R_p for the associated reflected electrons is probably quite large, say, 2.0. As the incident electrons penetrate further, many are multiply scattered and no longer retain their original directions. When such electrons are back-scattered and leave the specimen, they tend to provide a general background to the patterns, and so R_p decreases. As further penetration occurs, the majority of the electrons become diffusely scattered, the associated reflected electrons mostly contribute to the background, and so R_p again decreases. For solid specimens, it is difficult to predict the value of R_p, which will in any case depend on the particular specimen, electron accelerating voltage, set of crystallographic planes etc. Nevertheless, it is reasonable to expect values slightly > 1.

On the above model, R_p increases as the specimen thickness decreases, as is observed. However, it should be mentioned that although R_p increases, the total signal decreases because the total volume from which the signal comes decreases. The maximum theoretical values of R_p may not, therefore, be realised in practice because of noise limitations. From the model it follows that high values of R_p should be obtained with solid specimens if most of the inelastically scattered electrons were removed by some form of energy analyser, but this experiment does not yet seem to have been performed. The model also predicts that because the pattern contrast arises mainly from the incident electrons during their travel through the first few 100Å of the speciment, i.e. when they have lost little energy, the Bragg angles which are important in determining the width of the bands (fig. 14b) are those corresponding to the accelerating voltage of the *incident* electrons, as is observed.

4.2. Emissive mode

Consider the SEM patterns obtained on using the emissive mode. Most of the secondary emitted electrons arise from the outermost approximately 50Å of the specimen, and are generated by two main processes, namely, by the incident electrons on entering the specimen, and the reflected electrons on leaving. Although the details are not clear, it seems likely that most of the secondary electrons will in fact arise by the latter process. If this is so, then the value of R_s (the corresponding ratio for the secondary electrons) should be similar to R_p, and show a similar dependence on specimen thickness. Thus, the emissive and reflective mode patterns in any particular instance should be much the same. Experiment shows that such patterns are usually similar, and that R_s is generally slightly less than R_p.

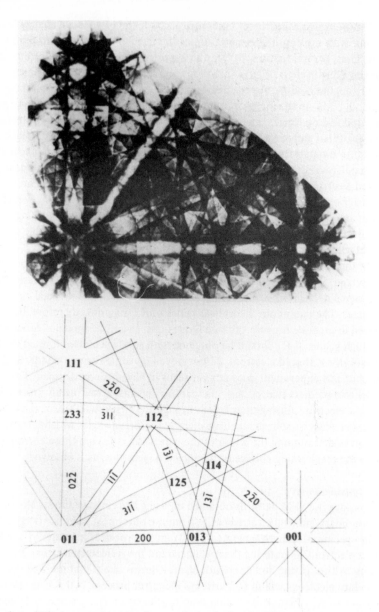

Fig. 6. An ECP stereographic triangle map obtained using the SEM, reflective mode, and a solid Cu single-crystal specimen. The map was made by joining together several ECPs with different specimen tilts [15].

4.3. Term for patterns

The term electron channelling pattern (ECP) is frequently used to cover all of the various types of SEM pattern. This term arises because of the initial behaviour of the incident primary electrons on penetrating the specimen. In particular, in the $s < 0$ region, the incident electrons experience high absorption, i.e. do not channel well into the specimen, and the number of reflected primary electrons and emitted secondary electrons is high. In the $s > 0$ regions, the opposite situation occurs. Consequently, the contrast variations in the patterns can be considered as indications of the initial channelling behaviour of the incident electrons. For example, in fig. 5, the bright bands occur where channelling is difficult, and the dark edges where channelling is easy. The analogy is not precise, but the term electron channelling pattern does give some indication of the physical processes occurring.

4.4. Relationship to Kikuchi patterns

ECPs are often confused with genuine Kikuchi electron diffraction patterns. The main reasons for this are that (a) Kikuchi patterns would be expected to form when high-energy electrons are incident on a crystalline specimen surface, and (b) the intensity variations in the two types of pattern are so closely similar. The latter is especially the case when no topographical features can be seen in the ECPs, as for example in fig. 7.

In spite of these factors, ECPs formed in the SEM are not Kikuchi patterns, at least in the hitherto accepted sense of the meaning of the term Kikuchi pattern. The error is equivalent to saying that the transmission electron micrograph of fig. 3 is a Kikuchi electron diffraction pattern, and few people would be prepared to do this even though the bands etc. in the micrograph can be crystallographically indexed. The relationship between the two types of pattern can be seen from the following.

Suppose the SEM electron beam is incident on a specimen surface at approximately 90° (untilted specimen), and the beam is stationary. The angular distribution of the reflected electrons will not be entirely "smooth". If a photographic film were placed above the specimen, a genuine back-reflection Kikuchi electron diffraction pattern would be recorded. If an electron detector is used to collect the reflected electrons, as when recording ECPs, the pattern blurs out because the detector records the *total* number of reflected electrons leaving the specimen at any particular time, regardless of the emergence angle. In practice, an angular range only is accepted and this depends on the detector and geometry used. Nevertheless, it may be almost as large as a solid angle of 2π. The signal recorded can be regarded, therefore, as an in-

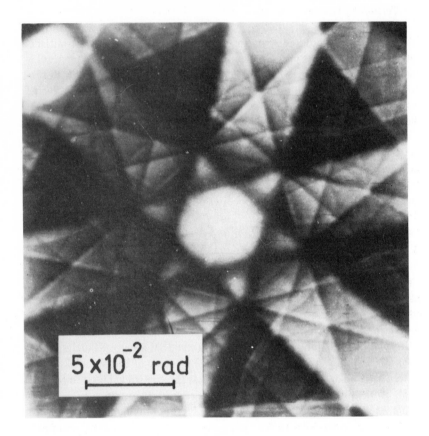

Fig. 7. An ECP obtained using the SEM, reflective mode, and a solid Si single-crystal specimen. The electron beam parameters were adjusted to give a high angular pattern resolution [12].

stantaneous mean intensity for a large portion of the complete Kikuchi pattern, and almost all of this signal corresponds to a general background level. The contrast in ECPs occurs because this background level rises and falls as the angle changes that the incident electron beam makes with the specimen surface, or rather with the crystallographic planes. Little if any trace of a genuine Kikuchi pattern remains.

The question still arises as to why the contrast variations in ECPs should so closely resemble those in Kikuchi patterns. The reason for this can be seen from the following. Suppose that a point source of electrons is positioned just below the surface of a specimen, and a photographic film is placed parallel to, and at some distance above, the surface of the specimen, so that a genuine Kikuchi pattern may be recorded. The intensity of the electrons striking the film is given by $I = f(\phi)$, where ϕ is the angle between the specimen normal and the direction of the electrons leaving the specimen, and f is the Kikuchi electron diffraction pattern intensity distribution function.

Suppose now that the point source of electrons is transferred to a particular point in the photographic film, and the electrons are allowed to strike the specimen. The intensity of the electrons which reach the interior of the specimen is, according to the theory of reciprocity, i.e. reversibility of ray paths, again given by $I = f(\phi)$, where ϕ is the same angle and f is the same function. This means that if the point source is moved to different points on the film so that ϕ varies, then the current reaching the interior of the specimen undergoes intensity variations precisely analogous to those that occur in genuine Kikuchi patterns. It follows directly from this that the contrast in ECPs using the absorptive (specimen current) mode should be precisely analogous to the contrast in genuine Kikuchi patterns, as is observed. It also follows because of the general nature of SEM images that the contrast in FCPs using the reflective and emissive modes should be complementary to that of genuine Kikuchi patterns, as is observed.

5. Properties of patterns

Because ECPs depend on the crystallography of the specimen, they have the following properties

(1) Lateral movement of the specimen causes the surface topographical features in the image to move, but not the bands of contrast.

(2) Tilt or rotation of the specimen causes the bands to move as if rigidly fixed to the specimen, as with Kikuchi bands in transmission electron diffraction patterns.

(3) A change in magnification of the topographical micrograph due to changing the current in the scanning coils (the standard procedure for changing magnification) causes the same change in the magnification of the bands. For example, doubling the micrograph magnification is brought about by halving the total amplitude of the electron beam scan, and this clearly also doubles the band magnification.

(4) A change in the magnification of the topographical micrograph due to

raising or lowering the specimen in the SEM does not affect the magnification of the bands. This is because although such movements change the total amplitude of the electron beam scan on the specimen surface, the fraction of the amplitude representing a band in the pattern is precisely the same.

(5) The angular width of any band is 2θ, where θ is the corresponding Bragg angle and depends on the particular specimen, electron accelerating voltage and crystallographic planes.

(6) A change in the electron accelerating voltage causes a change in the band widths. This occurs because the Bragg angle θ changes as the voltage V changes (table 1). The Bragg angle is given by $2d \sin \theta = \lambda$, and so to a first approximation $\theta \propto \lambda \propto 1/V^{1/2}$. Hence, a decrease in voltage causes an increase in band width.

It may be mentioned in regard to the latter point that the angular distance between crystallographic poles does not depend on the accelerating voltage. Consequently, when the voltage is changed, all the lines associated with any one particular pole move either towards or away from the other poles, and these movements can be appreciable for high-order lines. Lines which are inclined to one another can intersect at markedly different points. For these reasons, it can be extremely misleading to try and index the lines in the ECPs obtained at, say, 20 kV by comparing them with lines in Kikuchi transmission electron diffraction patterns obtained at, say, 100 kV, as is frequently done.

6. Indexing of patterns

When ECPs are obtained, a frequent requirement is to be able to recognise the pattern because this then allows the crystallographic orientation of the specimen to be determined. If the pattern contains a low-index pole, as in fig. 5, it is a simple matter. On the other hand, if the pattern contains only, say, the edge of one band and a few lines, then it is more difficult. Clearly, recognition is easier the more bands, lines etc. that are present in the pattern, favouring low magnifications (25X) and high electron accelerating voltages (30 kV). Several procedures can be used.

First, the required ECP can be recorded, and then the viewing screen observed while the specimen is slowly tilted. The pattern slowly moves across the screen, and soon low-order bands leading to recognisable poles are seen. The angular distances of the original ECP from these poles can then be determined by either recording a series of ECPs, or noting the mounts of tilt used.

Second, the ECP can be recorded and later compared with a complete ECP map covering the whole of the standard stereographic triangle. Such maps can be constructed by recording numerous ECPs as the specimen is progressively tilted in various directions, and the patterns joined together. Such a map is shown in fig. 6 [15] for an electron accelerating voltage of 20 kV. In this way, the position of the pattern within the stereographic triangle can be directly located.

Third, in some instances it may not be possible or desirable to tilt the specimen from the initial setting, and the pattern may not be sufficiently characteristic to assign with certainty to a particular position in the stereographic triangle map. Additional information can then be obtained by making use of the relationship between the Bragg angle and the electron accelerating voltage. Thus, without moving the specimen etc., ECPs are recorded for two or three different voltages, and the movements of the band edges, lines etc. noted. If for any particular line an angular movement $\Delta\theta$ occurs for a change in electron wavelength of $\Delta\lambda$, then to a first approximation $2d\,\Delta\theta = \Delta\lambda$. Hence if $\Delta\theta$ is measured, and $\Delta\lambda$ is obtained from either calculation or calibration, d can be deduced and the indices of the line obtained. This method has been used by Schulson [16] and shown to be reliable for low-order reflections. The additional information then obtained enables the pattern to be more definitely located within the stereogrpahic triangle map.

7. Pattern quality

7.1. Electron beam parameters

There are three important parameters associated with ECPs. First, there s the topographical micrograph resolution, and this is determined mainly by he incident electron spot size d. Second, there is the angular pattern resolution, and this is determined mainly by the electron beam divergence α. Thus, he best angular resolution would occur for a parallel electron beam. Any inite divergence α of the beam causes a blurring of the lines in the pattern by corresponding amount. Third, there is the amount of contrast C in the pattern. In order to reveal this contrast against the background noise, the electron beam current I has to exceed a certain minimum value. (The angular resolution of the pattern is strictly determined by the complete range of angles in the incident electron beam, i.e. 2α rather than α (p. 562, fig. 4), and this should be taken into consideration if any accurate quantitative work is performed.)

Hence, the three important parameters for ECPs depend on the three main parameters associated with the electron beam incident on the specimen surface, namely, d, α and I. The patterns will, therefore, depend markedly on

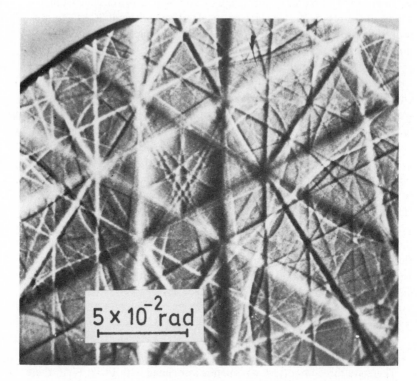

Fig. 8. As fig. 7, but with the collected signal differentiated [12].

the beam conditions used. Moreover, for any particular electron optical system, the values of d, α and I are related to the brightness B of the electron source (p. 593) by the equation

$$B = 0.4 \, I/d^2\alpha^2 \tag{1}$$

and only two of these parameters can be independently chosen. This will, therefore, impose a restriction on the patterns that can be obtained.

Suppose a specimen is being examined which gives ECPs with 3% of contrast, and that the only noise of significance is the shot noise associated with the incident electron beam. If in order to view the pattern on the SEM screen a frame scan time of 1 sec is used, then a current I of 10^{-8} A is required (p. 571, fig. 9). If the SEM has a bright ness B of 4×10^4 A cm^{-2} ster^{-1}, then a current of

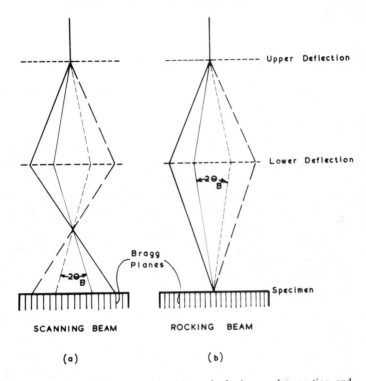

Upper Deflection

Lower Deflection

$2\theta_B$

Bragg
Planes

Specimen

$2\theta_B$

SCANNING BEAM   ROCKING   BEAM

(a)   (b)

Fig. 9. SEM scanning-coil ray diagrams showing (a) standard micrograph operation, and (b) selected-area ECP operation [19].

10^{-8} A can only be obtained by certain combinations of d and α (p. 564, fig. 6), e.g. 30 μm and 10^{-4} radians, 3 μm and 10^{-3} radians, 0.3 μm and 10^{-2} radians etc. This means that it is not possible to obtain simultaneously good topographical micrograph resolution, and good angular pattern resolution. If there is a need to reveal lines with less contrast than the main bands, or it is not required to work on the limit of noise, or if the electron gun is not operating at its maximum efficiency, the situation will be less favourable than indicated above.

The ECP of fig. 5 was recorded under conditions corresponding approximately to a micrograph resolution of 1 μm and a pattern resolution of 10^{-2} radians. The micrograph resolution was determined from higher magnification micrographs, while the pattern resolution was estimated knowing the main bands to be of width 4 $\times$ 10^{-2} radians (2θ for GaAs, 20 kV and 220 planes). An ECP recorded under quite different conditions [12] is shown in fig. 7. The pattern resolution is high, 2×10^{-4} radians, while the micrograph resolution is extremely poor, no surface structure being detected. What this means in practice is that on going from the pattern of fig. 5 to the pattern of fig. 7, the beam divergence α has been decreased so as to make the beam more parallel, and in order to maintain sufficient current I in the electron spot, the spot size d has had to be increased. Patterns such as fig. 5 can be immediately obtained with the standard Stereoscan SEM by using currents in lenses 1 and 2 that are slightly lower than usual. Patterns such as fig. 7 require markedly lower currents, and these can be obtained with the aid of simple lens current attenuators. A detailed description of the optimum lens settings in order to obtain the various combinations of d, α and I suitable for ECPs using the Stereoscan SEM has been given by Schulson and van Essen [17].

7.2. Condition of specimen

EPCs can only arise from specimens which are crystalline because an essential requirement is the anomalous absorption effect. No such patterns can be obtained from amorphous materials. It would be expected, therefore, that as the crystallographic perfection of the specimen decreased, e.g. due to progressive tensile deformation, the quality of the ECPs would decrease, and this is observed in practice. However, a relatively large amount of deformation, e.g. 20% elongation, is generally necessary before the pattern can no longer be detected. From this aspect, ECPs may possess an advantage over the analogous X-ray technique, namely, that of Kossel lines, for which it seems specimens of relatively high crystalline perfection are usually required.

The quality of ECPs also depends on the specimen surface preparation treatment. For example, the presence of amorphous surface films, such as oxide, may cause the incident high-energy electrons to be scattered over a range of directions before reaching the underlying crystalline material. This gives the equivalent of a large incident beam divergence α, and hence a poor quality pattern. Residual mechanical surface damage can have a similar effect. The decrease in pattern quality due to such surface irregularities is generally more pronounced when using the emissive mode than the reflective mode. If quantitative measurements are to be made, e.g. if values of R_p and R_s for various specimens are to be compared, care may be necessary in the surface preparation treatments.

7.3. Signal processing

Additional information present in ECPs can often be revealed by signal processing. The most common procedure used is to differentiate the signal [18], as has been done in fig. 8 [12]. Such a procedure evens out intensity differences which are present on a coarse scale, and both sharpens and increases the contrast of fine lines. For example, in fig. 8 the high-order systematic reflections associated with the 220 bands can be seen out as far as 10, 10, 0, and the symmetrical array of high-order lines within the [111] pole is clearly revealed. However, caution is necessary in the interpretation of differentiated patterns because any pattern lines parallel to the scan direction are lost, and bands, lines etc. running across the scan direction tend to exhibit asymmetrical contrasts. For example, for all three 220 bands in fig. 8, the high-order systematic reflections are all dark on one side of the band, and are all bright on the other side, markedly different from their symmetrical appearance in fig. 7.

7.4. Basic limitations

The fact that good micrograph and pattern resolutions cannot be obtained simultaneously for ECPs is a limitation of the present technique. The numerical values given above for d and α may be a little pessimistic because they correspond to the observation of patterns on the screen with a frame scan time of 1 sec. An improvement would result by recording the patterns with longer frame scan times, but this would not dramatically change the situation.

There seem to be two main possibilities for improvements. First, an increase in the amount of contrast that can be obtained from ECPs (*before* signal processing) would be valuable. For example, if the contrast C were increased 10X, the electron current I could be decreased 100X, and either d or α decreased 10X. Such an increase in contrast could undoubtedly be obtained simply by using thin, rather than solid, specimens, but this would of course restrict the range of application of the method. Such an increase could probably be obtained from solid specimens by using energy analysis and collecting only the elastically reflected electrons.

Second, an increase in the brightness B of the SEM electron source would be extremely valuable. For example, an increase of B from 10^4 to 10^8 A cm^{-2} sr^{-1} would enable either d or α to be decreased 100X. With present specimens and detectors, micrograph and pattern resolutions of, say, 300Å and 10^{-3} radians respectively could then be obtained simultaneously. This kind of performance should be possible with cold field-emission electron sources.

7.5. *Conditions to obtain ECPs*

It may perhaps seem surprising that ECPs were not observed by SEM users many years ago. The reason for this is that a number of conditions have to be simultaneously satisfied, and several are rather non-standard. These conditions may be summarised as follows

(1) large single-crystal specimen ($>$ 3 mm across)

(2) high crystalline perfection at surface

(3) low magnification ($<$ 50X)

(4) high current in spot ($> 10^{-8}$ A)

(5) low beam divergence ($< 10^{-2}$ radians)

(6) large spot size ($>$ 1 μm)

(7) high contrast setting.

The large spot size is necessary only in so far as it is not otherwise possible to obtain a small beam divergence. The high contrast setting is a further consequence of the small amount of contrast present in ECPs. Thus, even if the noise has been reduced to a negligible level by increasing the current in the spot, a small amount of contrast, e.g. 5% corresponding to I_{max}/I_{min} = 1.05, is still difficult to detect. The usual procedure adopted is to increase the contrast by signal processing, and in particular by subtracting a certain amount from the DC signal level, and increasing the gain (p. 589, sect. 19.4).

An important practical advantage of ECPs is that they can be observed directly on the SEM viewing screen. As a result, conditions can be progressively changed and the effect on pattern quality systematically determined. In this way high quality patterns can be obtained before any photographic recordings need be made. This factor has undoubtedly played a major role in advancing the ECP technique so rapidly during the last two years.

8. Selected-area patterns

In the standard procedure for obtaining ECPs, it is necessary to operate the SEM at low magnifications in order to obtain sufficiently large variations in the angle of incidence (fig. 4b). This means that single-crystal specimens a few mm across are required to obtain the patterns. Clearly, it would be advantageous if the patterns could be obtained from much smaller areas, and Coates [3] suggested that this might be achieved by using a stationary electron beam and rocking the specimen.

The alternative procedure of keeping the specimen stationary and rocking the electron beam has been developed at Oxford by van Essen and Schulson [19]. This rocking was achieved by using a standard Stereoscan SEM and attenuating the currents in the lower scan coils of the double-deflection system. As a result, the electron beam no longer rocked about a point within the third lens (fig. 9a), but about a point on the specimen surface (fig. 9b). Consequently, the electron beam underwent a complete line and frame scan in angular motion, and the collected signal corresponded to a complete ECP. In order that the scanning motion of the electron beam was not obstructed by the aperture in lens 3 (p. 562, fig. 4), the three-position aperture holder of the Stereoscan was modified so that a "straight-through" position was available for this mode of operation. A scanning electron micrograph of a polycrystalline copper specimen with grains a few 100 μm across is shown in fig. 10, together with ECPs obtained by this method from the three grains marked 1, 2 and 3 [19].

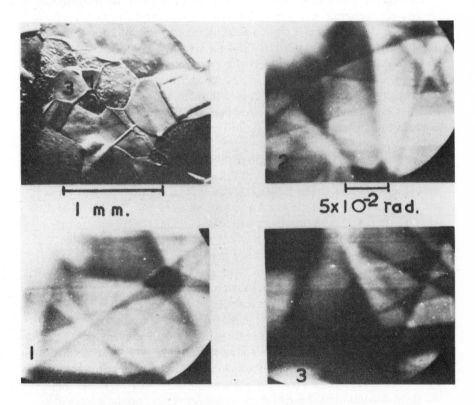

Fig. 10. A scanning electron micrograph of a polycrystalline copper specimen, together with ECPs from the grains marked 1, 2 and 3 using the selected-area method of fig. 9b [19].

Such selected-area ECPs exhibit the full amount of crystallographic information of standard ECPs. However, they are not micrographs and show no topographical detail because the electron beam is not scanned across the specimen surface as in standard ECPs. The beam divergence α again determines the angular pattern resolution, while the main role of the spot size d is in determining the size of the area from which the pattern comes. These patterns do not possess a topographical micrograph resolution.

The selected-area ECP method is undoubtedly one of the most important developments in materials examination techniques of recent years. Crystallographic information from known small areas of solid specimens can be directly displayed almost instantaneously on a viewing screen. The method will become progressively more valuable as the minimum size of the area from which the patterns arise is made progressively smaller. There are two main limitations in reducing the area.

First, if the spot size d is set to a particular value when the electron beam is stationary, this size is unfortunately not maintained when the beam scans the complete angular raster. A larger effective size occurs because of the electron optical aberrations of the scanning coils etc. If the total scanned angle is reduced in order to decrease the effect of the aberrations, then the resulting ECP corresponds to an extremely small portion of the stereographic triangle and recognition becomes difficult. Consequently, a compromise has to be made.

Second, the limitations associated with the electron source brightness described in sect. 7.1 above for standard ECPs apply equally well to selected-area ECPs. However, the limitations are more restricting in the latter case because it is no longer possible to accept a large value of spot size d in order to obtain a small value of beam divergence α, as was done for example to obtain fig. 7. If the SEM has a brightness B of 4×10^4 A cm^{-2} sr^{-1}, and a spot current I of 10^{-7} A is used to overcome noise, then possible combinations of d and α are 10 μm and 10^{-3} radians, 1 μm and 10^{-2} radians etc. (p. 564, fig. 6). Consequently, a compromise again has to be made.

In practice, the effects of electron optical aberrations can be reduced by applying suitable "corrections" to the scanning coil circuits of existing SEM electron optical systems. Alternatively, new electron optical systems can be designed for the rocking beam mode of operation, and the aberrations made small in the first instance. The limitations due to electron source brightness can of course be made less restricting by using brighter sources. For example, for the case considered above, and for an angular pattern resolution of 10^{-3} radians, brightness of 4×10^4, 4×10^6 and 4×10^8 A cm^{-2} sr^{-1} would correspond to stationary spot sizes of 10, 1 and 0.1 μm respectively.

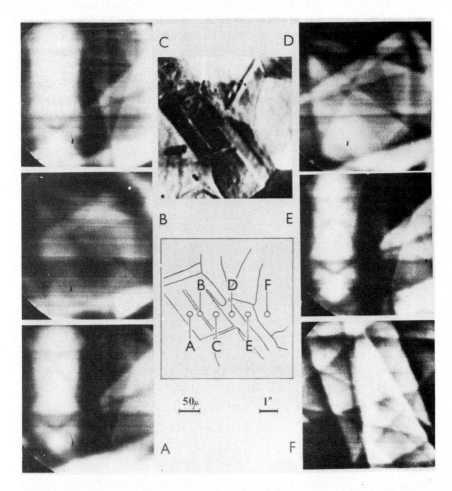

Fig. 11. A scanning electron micrograph of a polycrystalline copper specimen with individual grains containing twins, together with selected-area ECPs from the six areas 10 μm across indicated [20].

A recent set of selected-area ECPs obtained at Oxford is given in fig. 11 [20]. The specimen is polycrystalline copper and the individual grains contain twin lamellae. A scanning electron micrograph is shown at the top-centre, and redrawn for clarity immediately beneath. Selected-area ECPs obtained from six areas A to F of the specimen by a slight variation of the method illustrated in fig. 9b are also shown. Each ECP comes from an area 10 μm (or slightly less) across, has an angular resolution of approximately 3×10^{-3} radians, and corresponds to a total scanned angle of approximately $\pm 4°$. Patterns B and D are the same and arise from two different twin lamellae within grain 1. Pattern F arises from grain 2.

Present indications are that patterns of reasonably good quality will shortly be obtained from specimen areas only a few microns across using SEMs with conventional electron sources and from still smaller areas when SEMs with high-intensity electron sources are available.

9. Determination of crystallographic orientation

9.1. Standard ECPs

One of the most important applications of standard ECPs is to the determination of the crystallographic orientation of single-crystal solid specimens. For flat specimens, the specimen is set with its surface perpendicular to the stationary electron beam, and an ECP then obtained. The centre point in the ECP corresponds to the direction of the stationary electron beam, i.e. to the normal to the specimen surface. The crystallographic direction corresponding to this point in the ECP can be determined as described in sect. 6 above, e.g. by locating its position in the stereographic triangle map. Hence, the crystallographic orientation of the specimen surface is determined. For facets etc. on specimens, the specimen is tilted until the facet surface is perpendicular to the stationary beam, and an ECP then obtained. The analysis gives the crystallographic orientation of the facet surface.

The accuracy of such determinations generally depends on the accuracy with which the surface of the flat specimen etc. can be aligned perpendicular to the stationary electron beam. If the goniometer holder used in the SEM stage is initially precisely aligned with the stationary electron beam, then it depends on the accuracy with which the specimen be inserted into the holder. As a result, the overall accuracy is typically $1°$.

When a single-crystal specimen contains a boundary across which there is a small crystallographic misorientation, the amount of the misorientation can readily be determined as follows. The specimen is positioned with the boundary in the field of view, and an ECP recorded in the usual manner. Such an ECP obtained from a silicon specimen with a boundary along AA is shown in fig. 12 [12]. The patterns on either side of the boundary are the same, but are displaced with respect to one another. Measurement of the displacements for two non-parallel bands completely determines the misorientation. The accuracy

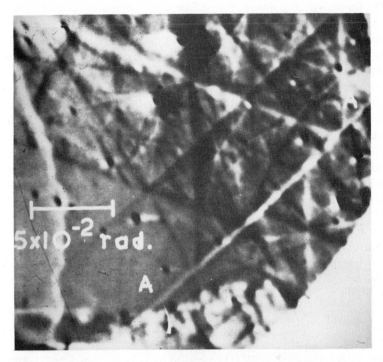

Fig. 12. A standard ECP from a silicon single-crystal specimen containing an abrupt misorientation boundary at AA. Note the displacements of the pattern on crossing the boundary [12].

for such determinations depends on the quality of the patterns and the accuracy with which the displacements can be measured, and is typically 0.1°.

When a specimen contains large grains, each of which is a differently oriented single crystal, and the standard ECP mode is used, each grain exhibits its own extremely small pattern. If the grains are randomly oriented, the patterns are generally too small to recognise, and so little quantitative information can be obtained. However, if the grains are only slightly misoriented, particular bands, lines etc. in the patterns can often be seen to cross many grains, undergoing small displacements at the various boundaries. Analysis of such patterns can then provide information concerning the crystallographic texture of the specimens.

When a specimen containing small grains is similarly examined, each grain exhibits a relatively uniform contrast that varies from grain to grain. The con-

trast for individual grains can be considered as corresponding to particular
points in the stereographic triangle map. No quantitative crystallographic information can be obtained from such ECPs. Nevertheless, the technique is
extremely useful because it enables differences in crystallographic orientation
to be immediately detected. Because there is no longer any need to use a small
beam divergence α, a relatively small spot size can be used, and relatively high
magnification micrographs obtained. An example of such a micrograph is
shown in fig. 13 [20] for a polycrystalline copper specimen. Twin lamellae in
individual grains are clearly revealed. This technique is known as grain orientation contrast, and is generally more pronounced with the reflective, than
emissive, mode. The contrast can be obtained without the need of etching the
surface to show up the positions of the individual grain boundaries, and this
may be advantageous for some investigations.

Fig. 13. Contrast differences arising from crystallographic orientation differences. Scanning electron micrograph, reflective mode, polycrystalline Cu specimen [20].

9.2. Selected-area ECPs

The crystallographic orientation of solid specimens can also be determined using selected-area ECPs. The procedure for obtaining the crystallographic orientation from such ECPs is precisely as described in sect. 9.1. The selected-area method has the advantage that the orientation of individual grains can be separately determined, and this provides a more satisfactory way of investigating crystallographic textures. A convenient procedure is to mark the positions of the orientations for the various grains directly on the stereographic triangle map, so that particular groupings etc. can be immediately seen.

Crystallographic orientations of solid specimens can at present be determined by this method for areas down to $10\,\mu m$. This enables a great deal of useful information to be rapidly and conveniently obtained regarding a variety of physical processes, e.g. crystal growth, deformation, recrystallisation, martinsitic transformations etc. The field of application will considerably increase as the minimum size of area from which the patterns can be obtained is made smaller.

10. Determination of unit cell size

The positions of the bands, lines etc. in ECPs depend on the Bragg relationship $2d \sin \theta = \lambda$. If θ is obtained for a particular set of crystallographic planes from measurements on the ECPs and the geometry of the scanning system, and the value of λ is known for the electron accelerating voltage used,, then the spacing of the planes d, and hence the unit cell size for the material of the specimen, can be calculated. Unfortunately, the errors involved in making an absolute determination in this way are rather large. A better procedure is to use a comparison method as follows.

The specimen of interest is mounted on the specimen holder, and alongside it is placed a suitable standard specimen. ECPs are recorded consecutively from the two specimens. The patterns should be of high angular resolution for the best accuracy. Measurements are made on the individual ECPs of the distances between suitably identified high-order lines, or between such lines and particular crystallographic poles. In this way, values of θ_1 and θ_2 are determined corresponding to planes with spacings d_1 and d_2 in the "unknown" and standard specimen respectively. These values are then related by the equation

$$\frac{\sin \theta_1}{\sin \theta_2} = \frac{d_2}{d_1}.$$

(2)

If d_2 is known, d_1 can be calculated, and hence also the unit cell size.

The use of a comparison method eliminates the need to know the electron wavelength λ, and reduces the error in relating the distances on the ECPs into angles. The main errors remaining are due to possible non-linearity of the line and frame scans, pattern distortion from specimen tilting, and slight uncertainty as to where the precise Bragg positions are located with regard to the lines in the patterns. Nevertheless, under favourable circumstances, an accuracy in determining unit cell sizes of approximately 1% can be obtained.

This method may prove to be valuable in conjunction with selected-area ECPs. Thus, if small crystalline particles of an unknown phase are present in a crystalline matrix of a known phase, then it should be possible to identify the particles from a determination of their unit cell size, at least if some idea of the possible included phases is known. In this case, the matrix would be used as the "standard", and the particles as the "unknown". Such an examination should also enable the habit planes of the particles, the crystallographic orientation relationships between the particles and matrix etc., to be determined.

11. Assessment of crystalline perfection

Information concerning the crystalline perfection of specimens can be obtained from ECPs (sect. 7.2) because the pattern quality deteriorates as the crystalline perfection decreases.

ECPs obtained from a Cu − 10 at % Al single-crystal specimen deformed in compression are shown in fig. 14 [12]. Bands and lines can be seen in both patterns, but the definition is poorer for the 20% compression than the 10% compression. Faint bands could still be detected after 40% compression, but no lines were visible. Such a series of ECPs can be used as a standard to assess qualitatively the amounts of deformation undergone by other similar specimens.

ECPs obtained from a silicon single-crystal specimen which had been irradiated with 3×10^{15} cm^{-2} 80 kV neon ions are shown in fig. 15 [21]. The effect of the irradiation is to transform the crystalline silicon in the neighbourhood of the specimen surface into amorphous silicon. In order to investigate the manner in which the crystalline perfection varied with the distance from the surface, uniform layers of silicon were progressively stripped from the surface using the standard anodic oxidation HF method, and ECPs recorded after each stripping. It can be seen from fig. 15 that the material progressively recovers its crystallinity in the depth range 1450 to 2500Å. The pat-

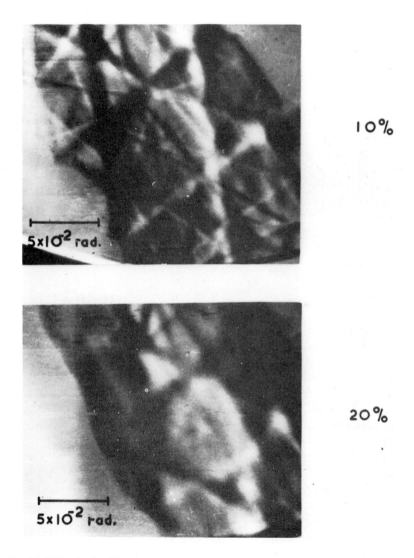

Fig. 14. ECPs obtained from a Cu − 10 at % Al single-crystal specimen after (a) 10% and (b) 20% compression [12].

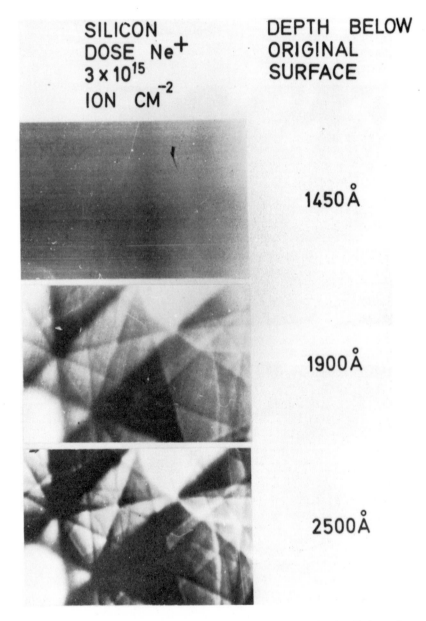

Fig. 15. ECPs obtained from a Si single-crystal specimen after neon ion irradiation and stripping layers (a) 1450 Å, (b) 1900 Å and (c) 2500 Å thick from the surface [21].

tern corresponding to the latter depth was indistinguishable from patterns from similar unirradiated material.

The qualitative interpretation of such ECPs is relatively striaghtforward for an investigation such as that of fig. 14 because for each specimen the deformation is relatively uniform, at least on a macro-scale. It is perhaps more difficult for invesitations such as that of fig. 15 because the amount of damage varies with depth in the material, and each pattern arises from a finite depth in the material. Nevertheless, useful qualitative information can still be obtained, and it may later be possible to make the method more quantitative when the detailed theory of the mechanism of formation of ECPs (sec. 14) is further advanced.

12. Detection of magnetic fields

ECPs can be used to obtain information concerning the presence of demagnetising fields which are present outside the surface of solid ferromagnetic specimens [22]. The fields cause the incident electron beam to be slightly deflected from its initial direction just before entering the specimen. Thus, electrons that would have been at the precise Bragg position arrive slightly off the Bragg position, and vice-versa. As a result, the ECPs exhibit small local distortions.

ECPs obtained from a single-crystal cobalt specimen containing magnetic domains are shown in fig. 16 [22]. The pattern of fig. 16a was obtained using a 1000 μm spot size, large compared with the domain size, and so an average pattern resulted. On the other hand, fig. 16b was obtained using a 10 μm spot size, small compared with the domain size, and so a specific pattern resulted. The distorted nature of the latter pattern is clearly apparent. It is in principle possible from a comparison of such patterns to deduce the strengths, distribution etc., of the demagnetising fields associated with the domains. The method should also be applicable to specimens which have associated surface electric fields.

13. Detection of crystallographic defects

When crystallographic defects emerge at the surface of specimens, the lattice planes are locally bent due to surface relaxation. A similar behaviour can arise when small precipitate particles etc. are located near the specimen surface.

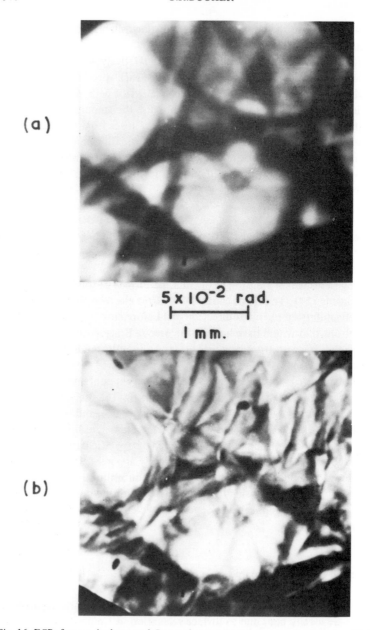

Fig. 16. ECPs from a single-crystal Co specimen containing magnetic domains. Distortion in (b) is due to effect of demagnetising fields outside specimen [22].

It was realised as long ago as 1962 [6] that such bending night enable dislocations etc. to be directly revealed when solid specimens were examined with the SEM. The argument used was that the bending would slightly change the electron absorption in the neighbourhood of Bragg reflections, and that this might provide detectable contrast if, for example, the reflected electrons were collected. Experiments of this kind performed in 1965–1966 [8] were unsuccessful in revealing such contrast.

The amount of lattice plane bending that occurs when dislocations emerge at a specimen surface is known from elasticity theory. If the planes in the immediate vicinity of the specimen surface only are considered, the bending is generally a maximum at the dislocation core, and progressively decreases as the distance from the core increases. Typical values might be 10^{-3} radians at a distance of $300\,\text{Å}$, 10^{-4} radians at $3000\,\text{Å}$ etc. The bending also decreases as the distance below the specimen surface increases but this may not be a serious disadvantage because the main contrast associated with ECPs arises from the first few $100\,\text{Å}$ of the specimen.

In order to detect a dislocation using this method, it would be necessary to obtain simultaneously, for example, a micrograph resolution of $300\,\text{Å}$ and a pattern resolution of 10^{-3} radians. The amount of contrast that the dislocation would then give with the specimen set at a Bragg position would be typically 1%, and the current in the spot I necessary to detect such contrast would be typically 10^{-7} A for a frame scan time of 1 sec (Ch. 00, fig. 9). Consequently, the electron beam parameters d, α and I required would be $300\,\text{Å}$, 10^{-3} radians and 10^{-7} A. These correspond to a brightness B of 4×10^9 A cm^{-2} sr^{-1} (eq. (1) above), which may be compared with the brightness B of a typical tungsten hair-pin filament operating at 20 kV of 4×10^4 A cm^{-2} sr^{-1}. This explains why dislocations were not observed with solid specimens using present day commercial instruments, i.e. sufficient electron source brightness was not available.

It is likely that dislocations etc. could be detected without the need for quite such high brightness by increasing the frame scan time and recording photographically, or by a variety of other procedures, e.g. using thin specimens, energy analysis, high-order Bragg reflections, signal differentiation etc. However, the ultimate aim will be the direct observation of dislocations in solid specimens without such procedures, and this should be possible using cold field emission electron sources. The applications of such a technique would be considerable. For example, dislocations in solid specimens could be directly observed, their Burgers vectors determined by using different Bragg reflections and analysing the resulting contrasts, and their motion, interactions etc. caused by heating, straining etc. directly followed.

14. Theoretical treatment of ECPs

It would clearly be extremely valueable if a quantitative theory were available which described the mechanism of formation of ECPs. Such a theory could be applied initially to perfect crystals to test its validity, and subsequently to imperfect crystals to obtain information regarding the contrast to be expected from dislocations etc.

The main difficulty with any such theory is how to treat those electrons which, after penetrating an appreciable distance into the specimen, become multiply, and eventually diffusely, scattered. Hirsch and Humphreys [23] have overcome this difficulty by calculating the total number of reflected electrons as a function of the angle of incidence of the primary electron beam for *thin* specimens. It was considered that the effect of increasing the specimen thickness would be to increase the number of randomly reflected electrons, and that this would simply decrease the magnitude of the contrast without appreciably changing its general form. They treated the problem theoretically by extending the approach used previously by Hall and Hirsch [24] to calculate the manner in which electrons were scattered by thin specimens in the forward direction, of importance in transmission electron micro-

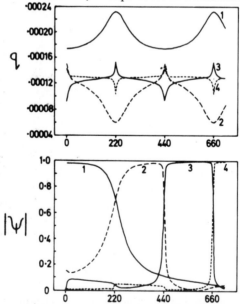

Fig. 17. Calculated profiles for ECPs showing (a) scattering cross-sections for reflected electrons, and (b) excitation of various Bloch waves [23].

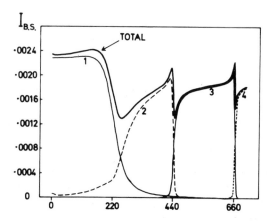

Fig. 18. Calculated profiles for ECPs showing number of reflected electrons for various Bloch waves [23].

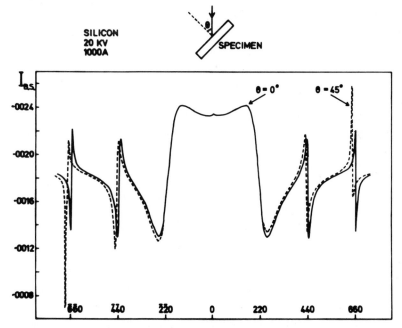

Fig. 19. Calculated profiles for ECPs showing number of reflected electrons when specimen normal is inclined at 0° and 45° to the incident electron beam. Note asymmetry for 45° profile [23].

scopy. Some preliminary results obtained by Hirsch and Humphreys [23] using this method for a silicon specimen 1000Å thick, and 20 kV incident primary electrons, are shown in figs. 17 to 19. Computed profiles are given which correspond to the angle of incidence being progressively varied from the central 000 position through the 220, 440 and 660 Bragg positions.

Fig. 17b shows the variation in the excitation ψ of each of the Bloch waves 1 to 4. The excitation is a measure of the amount of electron current flowing through the crystal associated with each wave, Fig. 17a shows the corresponding variation of the effective scattering cross-section q for reflected electrons for each Bloch wave.

From these profiles it can be seen that the excitation of Bloch waves 1 and 2 are equal at the exact 220 Bragg position, Bloch wave 1 is excited more on going from this position towards the central 000 position ($s < 0$), and Bloch wave 2 is excited more on going from this position towards the 440 Bragg position ($s > 0$). Moreover, the scattering cross-section for reflected electrons is greater for Bloch wave 1, whose nodes are located at the positions of the atoms, than for Bloch wave 2, whose nodes are located at the positions in between the atoms. It may be recalled that these were the factors which were used previously in a qualitative manner (sects. 2 and 4) to predict an anomalous absorption effect for reflected electrons. Figs. 17a and b show that analogous relationships also occur for Bloch waves 2 and 3, and 3 and 4. (It is pointed out that the description given here with regard to Bloch waves 1 and 2 is precisely *opposite* to that which was given in sects. 2 and 4. The reason for this is Hirsch and Humphreys [23] have allocated numbers to the Bloch waves in a manner which they consider to be more logical than that conventionally used. One result of this is that the numbers for Bloch waves 1 and 2 have been interchanged.)

In order to obtain the number of reflected or back-scattered electrons I_{BS}, it is necessary to form the product of ψ and q for each Bloch wave, and then to add the individual contributions. The corresponding profiles are given in fig. 18. The profile for the total number of reflected electrons has been re-drawn as the continuous line in fig. 19, where it covers the complete angular range from $\overline{660}$ to 660.

This calculated profile needs to be compared with the corresponding experimental result, namely, a line trace drawn perpendicular to a 220 band across an ECP such as that of fig. 7. The central pole region should be avoided, and all lines crossing the trace at angles other than $90°$ ignored. The calculated profile shows that the contrast is symmetrical about the central 000 position. A relatively uniformly bright central band occurs, immediately bordered by narrower darker bands. The 220 Bragg position is not clearly defined, but lies approximately at the edge of the bright band. A line occurs at the 440 Bragg position that changes abruptly from bright to dark on going in the direction away from the central 000 position. A similar, but narrower, line occurs at the 660 Bragg position. All of these features can be seen in the ECP of fig. 7. In addition, the calculated profile gives a contrast value for the central band of approximately 90% ($R_p = I_{max}/I_{min} = 1.90$), entirely plausible for a silicon specimen 1000 Å thick.

Hirsch and Humphreys [23] have also applied the theory to the same specimen with the crystallographic planes similarly oriented with respect to the

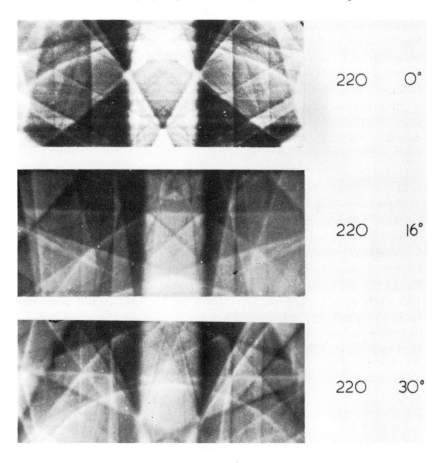

Fig. 20. ECPs showing effect of tilting specimen 0°, 16° and 30°. Note asymmetry in ECP for 30° tilt [15].

electron beam, but with the specimen surface inclined as in the diagram at the top of fig. 19. The effect of the tilted surface is to cause the profiles for the excitation ψ of the various Bloch waves of fig. 17b to be moved small distances relative to one another parallel to the abscissa axis. These movements occur in the *same* direction on opposite sides of the central position, and so produce an asymmetry in the contrast. The calculated profile for a tilt of $45°$ is shown as the discontinuous line in fig. 19. The 440, 660 etc. lines on the "uphill" side are brighter than usual, while the $\overline{4}40$, $\overline{6}60$ etc. lines on the "downhill" side are darker. This effect is observed experimentally [25] and is illustrated in fig. 20 [15], where the specimen has been progressively tilted from 0 to $30°$. The 440 and 660 type lines on the left correspond to the "uphill" side and become brighter, while the 440 and 660 type lines on the right correspond to the "downhill" side and become darker. It is emphasised that this is a genuine ECP contrast effect, and is not an asymmetry produced by signal differentiation, as in fig. 8.

The initial success of this theoretical treatment of ECPs is encouraging, and it is hoped that the theory will soon be further developed so that it can be applied to imperfect crystals.

Acknowledgments

The author would like to thank the numerous people who have helped in a variety of ways with regard to the preparation of these lectures. These include useful discussions and suggestions, the supplying of illustrations, and permission to quote both published and unpublished results. The author would like to mention in particular Professor P.B.Hirsch, F.R.S., Dr. M.J.Whelan, Dr. C.J. Humphreys, Dr. J.P.Jakubovics, Dr. E.M.Schulson, Mr. A.M.B.Shaw, Mr. J.M. Titchmarsh, Mr. C.G.van Essen, Mr. D.C.Joy and Mr. S.M.Davidson of the University of Oxford. The author would also like to point out that much of the first of his three articles is based on the excellent review article published in 1965 by Professor C.W.Oatley, F.R.S., and his colleagues (p. 594, ref. [6]).

References

[1] P.B.Hirsch, A.Howie, R.B.Nicholson, D.W.Pashley and M.J.Whelan, Electron Microscopy of Thin Crystals (London, Butterworths, 1965).
[2] P.Duncumb, Phil. Mag. 7 (1962) 2101.
[3] D.G.Coates, Phil. Mag. 16 (1967) 1179.
[4] G.R.Booker, A.M.B.Shaw, M.J.Whelan and P.B.Hirsch, Phil. Mag. 16 (1967) 1185.

[5] P.B.Hirsch, A.Howie and M.J.Whelan, Phil. Mag. 7 (1962) 2095.

[6] P.Duncumb, P.B.Hirsch, A.Howie and M.J.Whelan (1962), private communication.

[7] C.R.Hall, Proc. Roy. Soc. A295 (1966) 140.

[8] A.M.B.Shaw and G.R.Booker (1965–1966) unpublished work.

[9] D.G.Coates, Scanning Electron Microscopy Symposium (11T Research Institute, Chicago, 1969) p. 29.

[10] A.M.B.Shaw and G.R.Booker (1967) unpublished work.

[11] J.I.Bramman and G.Yates, Phil. Mag. 17 (1968) 195.

[12] E.M.Schulson, C.G.van Essen and D.C.Joy, Scanning Electron Microscopy Symposium (11T Research Institute, Chicago, 1969) p. 47.

[13] M.F.Ashby (1962) unpublished work.

[14] J.Steeds (1964) unpublished work.

[15] C.G.van Essen (1969) unpublished work.

[16] E.M.Schulson, J. Sci. Instr. 2 (1969) 361.

[17] E.M.Schulson and C.G.van Essen, J. Sci. Instr. 2 (1969) 247.

[18] A.M.B.Shaw, G.R.Booker and D.G.Coates, J. Sci. Instr. 2 (1969) 243.

[19] C.G.van Essen and E.M.Schulson, J. Mat. Science 4 (1969) 336.

[20] C.G.van Essen, E.M.Schulson and R.H.Donaghay (1969) unpublished work.

[21] S.M.Davidson and G.R.Booker (1969) unpublished work.

[22] D.C.Joy, E.M.Schulson, J.P.Jakubovics and C.G.van Essen, Phil. Mag. 20 (1969) 843.

[23] P.B.Hirsch and C.J.Humphreys (1969) unpublished work.

[24] C.R.Hall and P.B.Hirsch, Proc. Roy. Soc. A286 (1965) 158.

[25] E.D.Wolf and T.E.Everhart, Scanning Electron Microscope Symposium (11T Research Institute, Chicago, 1969) p. 43.

MIRROR ELECTRON MICROSCOPY
THEORY AND APPLICATIONS

A.B.BOK

1. Introduction

From the birth of electron optics (about 1920) till the late 1950's most efforts in the field of electron optics were concentrated on the theory, the design and development of the nowadays widely available transmission electron microscope. A guaranteed point resolution of less than 0.5·nm is considered normal for high quality instruments.

Since the transmission electron microscope provides information about the internal structure of an electron transparent specimen, this technique does not allow for the direct investigation of surfaces of solids. Two useful alternatives are either putting both the illuminating and imaging system at a glancing angle with the surface to be examined (reflection electron microscopy) or the application of the replica technique. The indirect observation of a surface by means of a replica permits a resolving power up to 5 nm.

The increasing interest in direct observation of surfaces of solids or investigation of surface phenomena has resulted during the last 15 years in the development of the following types of electron microscopes:

(1) Scanning electron microscope;
(2) Emission electron microscope;
(3) Reflection electron microscope;
(4) Mirror electron microscope.

Before going in more detail concerning the mirror electron microscope a brief description of the other types of microscopes is presented.

1.1. *Scanning electron microscope* [1]

In a scanning electron microscope a primary electron beam, emitted from a heated tungsten filament, is focused into a fine electron probe on the specimen and made to scan on a raster — similar to television techniques — on the surface by a deflection system. Electrons liberated from the specimen by the focused primary beam are detected by a photomultiplier tube with a scintillator mounted on top. The photomultiplier output signal is used to modulate the brightness of the electron beam in a cathode-ray tube, which is scanned in synchronism with the electron probe. The resolution — being of the order of 20 nm in favourable operating conditions — depends upon the diameter of the electron probe, the accelerating voltage, the detector system and the type of specimen.

1.2. *Emission electron microscope*

In an emission electron microscope the specimen acts as a self-illuminating object. Electrons are liberated from the specimen by either heating of the specimen (secondary emission) or quantum irradiation of the specimen (photo emission). The image is usually formed by a combination of two or three electron lenses. The obtainable resolution — mainly determined by the energy spread of the emitted electrons and the strength of the electrostatic field at the specimen surface — amounts to about 20 nm. In the case of thermionic and photo emission the image contrast is mainly dominated by the local work function of the specimen surface. Since the successful application of photo emission, by means of ultra-violet radiation, this type of microscope has become of great importance.

1.3. *Reflection electron microscope*

Reflection electron microscopy is rarely nowadays. The first experiments (Ruska [2]) did not show very promising results until von Borries et al. [3] suggested that the large energy spread of the scattered electrons could be reduced by having the illuminating and imaging system at a glancing angle with the specimen. The remaining energy spread still requires a small aperture in order to minimize the dominating chromatic aberrations. Since the reflected electrons are scattered over a wide angle, a small angular aperture of the accepted beam has to be selected. This gives an image barely bright enough to be focused at the necessary magnification.

1.4. *Mirror electron microscope*

Contrary to the techniques mentioned above the specimen is neither struck by electrons nor emits electrons. An accelerated electron beam enters the retarding field of an electrostatic mirror. Application to the mirror electrode of a potential, which is slightly more negative than the accelerating voltage, causes the electrons to be reflected from an equipotential plane closely in front of the mirror electrode, which is in this technique the specimen surface. The electron trajectories near the point of reversal, in front of the specimen, are highly sensitive to deviations from flatness of the reflecting equipotential plane. These deviations are either caused by electrostatic or topographic perturbations at the physical specimen surface.

The possibility of converting on a microscopic scale electrostatic and, to a certain amount, magnetic potential distributions into a directly observable image has given access to new information in phenomena such as diffusion of metals, contact potentials, surface conductivity and magnetic properties. The first experimental results of Hottenroth [4] and the calculations of Recknagel et al. [5,6] clearly revealed the feasibility of mirror electron microscopy. Hottenroth showed that the manner of formation of non-focused images of the mirror electrode closely resembles that of the light optical "Schlieren" method. Following his experiments the research in this field was mainly directed towards the application of this technique for visual observation of surface phenomena. Numerous articles, especially by Mayer [7–10] and Spivak et al. [11–14] are published about different kinds of applications with this type of microscope.

Little attention has been paid to optimizing the imaging technique of the mirror electrode. It was Le Poole [15] who, in 1964, pointed out that the attainable resolving power for this type of microscope could be improved considerably by forming a focused image of the mirror electrode onto the fluorescent screen. Also it became evident that mirror electron microscopes with rotationally symmetric lenses require a separation of the illuminating and reflected beam in order to obtain a focused image of the specimen with sufficient field of view. In instruments with rotationally symmetric lenses and without beam separation [16–18] the specimen is illuminated through a central hole in the final screen. The field of view, which disappears entirely when the mirror electrode is exactly conjugated to the final screen, can only be increased by a defocusing. The formation of contrast in a microscope with focused images is achievable in a way similar to the transmission electron microscope by having an aperture in the objective lens. To avoid a new limitation of the field of view and to have at the same time normal incidence of the illuminating beam this aperture must be in the back focal plane of the objective lens. Simultaneous focusing of the specimen and a sufficiently large field of view can be obtained by the separation of the illuminating and reflected beam with a magnetic prism or the use of magnetic quadrupoles.

Concerning this latter method a scanning mirror electron microscope with magnetic quadrupoles has been designed and constructed [19]. Although beam separation with a magnetic prism has been applied earlier by several experimenters [20–23], it was never used (except for the instrument of Schwartze [23]) in combination with a contrast aperture in the back focal plane of the objective lens. The absence of this aperture means that for in focus images the contrast disappears. Here defocusing provides the necessary image contrast.

From geometrical considerations it follows that for an imaging mirror microscope special attention has to be paid to the condenser system. Seen from the objective aperture the electron source must appear as large as the required field of view. This leads to the conclusion that all mirror electron images, obtained so far, except for some pictures made by Schwartze [23], are point projection, out of focus, images.

When a point projection image of the mirror electrode is to be made, an electron probe is formed in front of the specimen. The electrons then reflect from a paraboloid of revolution which is the envelope of all parabolic electron trajectories in the retarding field. Contrary to this, in a microscope with focused images and an objective aperture in the back focal plane, all electrons reflect from a flat equipotential plane normal to the z-axis.

The effect of the reflecting paraboloid in defocused instruments is clearly observable from most of the photographic results published.

Where electrons strike the specimen surface local negatively charged spots occur. Negative spots give rise to black "bubbles" in the final image. For positively charged spots, caused for instance by a positive ion bombardment on areas where the electrons do not reach the specimen surface, white "stars" emerge on the final screen [24].

When, in a mirror projection microscope, the electrons with the highest energy in the Maxwellian distribution and incident close to the axis are allowed to strike the specimen, the central region on the final screen shows mainly black bubbles. The more off axis electrons reverse their direction before reaching the specimen surface and give mainly white stars for the outer regions.(fig. 1). On the other hand, the occurrence of some stars in the central region and bubbles in the outer regions is comprehensible owing to the fact that, apart from local charges, the topography of the surface also gives rise to similar effects. In focus images show hardly any black bubbles and white stars. Near the focusing condition, where the contrast reverses, the bubbles change into stars and vice versa (figs. 2a and b).

2. Contrast formation in a mirror electron microscope with focused images

2.1. Principle

When a mono-energetic and axially parallel beam of electrons enters a homo-

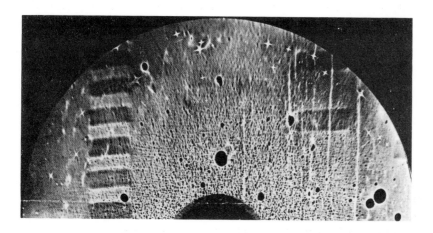

Fig. 1. Mirror projection image of a magnetic recording pattern made by Mayer L.

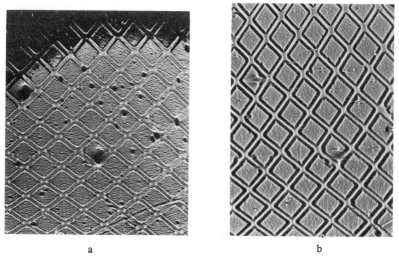

a   b

Fig. 2. Gold squares, about 20 nm thick, vacuum deposited through a 750 mesh grid on a layer of gold. Magnification 330X. (a) Slightly under focus. (b) Slightly over focus.

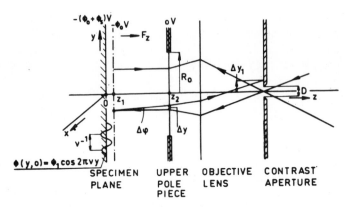

Fig. 3. Retarding field with perturbed specimen and characteristic quantities.

geneous electrostatic retarding field, reflection occurs against a flat equipotential plane normal to the z-axis (fig. 3) and all electrons return along the same trajectories.

Owing to local deviations from flatness of the reflecting equipotential plane, the electrons which approach these perturbations receive a tangential impulse. These electrons describe a different trajectory after reversal and intersect the aperture plane at a height Δy_1, which depends on the perturbation present. When Δy_1 exceeds $D/2$, the radius of the contrast forming aperture, the electrons impinge on the aperture and are removed from the reflected electron beam. The formation of contrast in a mirror electron microscope resembles the technique (an aperture in the back focal plane of the objective) applied in transmission electron microscopes or the optical "Schlieren" technique. The separation of the tangentially modulated electron pencils from the unperturbed pencils allows for visual observation of perturbations in the reflecting equipotential plane, in terms of current density modulations in the final image. The origin of these perturbations can be twofold, topography of an equipotential specimen surface or electrostatic disturbances on a flat specimen surface. In practice, mostly a combination of both is encountered.

The current density modulations in the final image do not provide direct information about the type of perturbation present at the specimen. Perturbations at the specimen of magnetic origin, in comparison with electrostatic and topographic perturbations, hardly affect an axially parallel beam of electrons.

2.2. *Calculations*

The purpose of the calculations given in sections 2.3 and 2.4 – restricted to electrostatic and topographic contrast – is to find the dependence of the lateral shift Δy_1 or the related angular deflection $\Delta\varphi_1$ of a reflected electron pencil on the specimen perturbation.

All sections assume a mono-energetic ($e\phi_0$) and axially parallel beam of electrons in the homogeneous retarding field.

In fig. 3 the specimen coincides with the xoz-plane. The electrostatic retarding potential ($\phi_0 + \phi_s$), a superposition of the accelerating voltage ϕ_0 and an additional voltage ϕ_s is considered homogeneous and unaffected by the bore in the upper pole piece. This is valid provided that z_2 is at least three times the bore radius R_0. This assumption permits the separation of the divergent lens action of the upper pole piece from the contrast formation mechanism near the specimen. Apart from lens defects the divergent lens action does not affect the contrast formation. It only requires a slightly higher excitation of the objective lens to maintain the parallel incidence into the mirror field. The behaviour of electrons in the retarding field can be described either classically by the equations of motion (1a and b) or wave mechanically by the time independent Schrödinger eq. (2).

Classically

y-direction

$$-e\,\frac{\partial\phi(y,z)}{\partial y} = -e\,\frac{\partial\phi(y,z)}{\partial y} = m\,\frac{d^2 y}{dt^2} \tag{1a}$$

z-direction

$$-e\,\frac{\partial\phi(y,z)}{\partial z} = -eF_z - e\,\frac{\partial\phi(y,z)}{\partial z} = m\,\frac{d^2 z}{dt^2} \tag{1b}$$

Wave mechanically

$$-\frac{\hbar^2}{2m}\left(\frac{\partial^2 u}{\partial y^2} + \frac{\partial^2 u}{\partial z^2}\right) + (V-E)u = 0 \tag{2}$$

where

$$\Phi(y,z) = \phi_0 + \phi_S + \phi(y,z) \tag{3}$$

e is elementary charge, m is electron rest mass, $\Phi(y,z)$ is the perturbation potential, F_z is the strength of the retarding field. For 30 kV across a gap of

3.5 × 10⁻³ m, $F_z = 8.57 \times 10^6$ V/m.

$\hbar = h/2\pi$, h is Planck constant, $u = u(y,z)$ the wave function, V is $V(z)$ the potential energy in the retarding field, E is the kinetic energy of the incident beam.

For all calculations following it is assumed that $\phi_s \ll \phi_0$. Two models A and B, sections 2.3 and 2.4, are based on the equations of motion (1a, b), whereas model C (not described in the lecture notes) uses the Schrödinger equation (2). It would be obvious to describe the formation of contrast in a way comparable with the modulation transfer functions in the light optics. The non-linear character of eqs. (1a and b), however, does not allow for such a description because no linearity exist in the case of sufficient contrast between the perturbation amplitude at the specimen and the tangentially modulated electron pencils. Since it is wished to provide an analytical description of the contrast mechanism, preferably in a way resembling the modulation transfer functions, eqs. (1a and b) are linearized by the assumption

$$\frac{\partial\phi(y,z)}{\partial z} \ll F_z \qquad \text{(model A)}.$$

This causes a sinusoidal specimen to produce a sinusoidal modulation. Contrary to the approximated model A, model B provides information about the solution of the exact eqs. (1a and b). The calculations for this model were both performed on a digital computer and an analog computer. These calculations provide the Δy value and the corresponding coordinates of the point of reversal for different heights of incidence. The omitted index 1 for Δy and $\Delta \varphi$ indicates that these values are measured in the plane $z = z_2$, the upper pole piece of the objective lens.

A comparison of the results obtained with model A and B is shown to lead for certain values of the local slope of the reflecting plane to a matching of both models. This means that the non-linear model B shows a linear behaviour.

As $\phi(y,z)$ fullfils the Lapalce equation $\Delta\phi(y,z) = 0$ a sinusoidal perturbation potential $\phi(y,0) = \phi_1 \cos 2\pi n\nu y$ causes a potential $\phi(y,z) = \phi_1 \cos 2\pi n\nu y \cdot \exp(-2\pi n\nu z)$, where ν is the spatial specimen frequency and ϕ_1 the perturbation amplitude.

Since the assumption

$$\frac{\partial\phi(y,z)}{\partial z} \ll F_z$$

involves simultaneously moderate values $\partial\phi(y,z)/\partial y$, it can be expected prior to the calculations following that model A and B match only for specimens

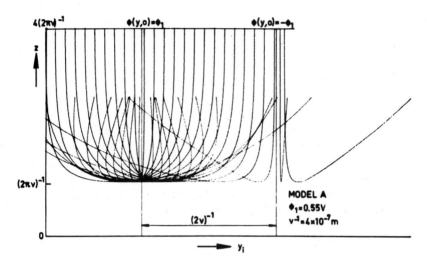

Fig. 4a. Electron trajectories according to model A.

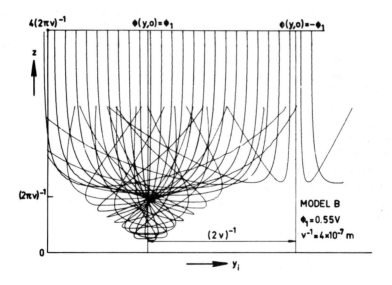

Fig. 4b. Electron trajectories according to model B.

slightly perturbed (small values of $\phi_1 v$). Specimens with more contrast are not accessible to a simple analytical description. In that case numerical calculations should provide information. Figs. 4a and b, both made on an analog computer, demonstrate the effect of the assumption

$$\frac{\partial \phi(y,z)}{\partial z} \ll F_z$$

on the electron trajectories near a sinusoidal perturbed specimen. In model A all electrons reflect from a flat equipotential plane whereas in model B $\partial \phi(y,z)/\partial z$ leads to a variable depth of penetration into the retarding field. It is clear from figs. 4a and b that for the values of v and ϕ_1 used ($\phi_1 v = 1.37 \times 10^6$ V/m), model A acts only as a first order approximation for model B. Apart from eqs. (1a and b) a second non-linear effect in the formation of contrast is introduced by the filtering of tangentially modulated electron pencils from the reflected beam with a circular contrast aperture.

Since this effect is independent from the sign of the lateral deflection, the modulated current density distribution in the final image shows the double frequency of a sinusoidal perturbation. This double rectifying effect can be avoided by using a knife edge as aperture or in case of two dimensional perturbed specimens two perpendicular perturbed edges.

In order to avoid, in this stage, the choice between the non-linearly filtering circular aperture and the linearly operating edge aperture, the lateral displacement Δy and the angular deflection $\Delta \varphi$ are both plotted against the spatial perturbation frequency and amplitude.

2.2. Model A

(a) Electrostatic contrast.

The simplified equations of motion are

$$-e \frac{\partial \Phi(y,z)}{\partial y} = m \frac{d^2 y}{dt^2} \qquad (4a)$$

$$-eF_z = m \frac{d^2 z}{dt^2} \qquad (4b)$$

where

$$\Phi(y,z) = \phi_0 + \phi_s + \phi(y,z) ; \qquad \phi_s = \phi_{SC} + \phi_{SV} . \qquad (4c)$$

Superimposed on the retarding potential ϕ_o is a "specimen" voltage ϕ_s. This additional negative voltage prevents electron from striking the specimen near positively charged perturbations. ϕ_s, which is the sum of ϕ_{SC}, the contact potential between the specimen material and the tungsten filament in the electron gun, and ϕ_{SV} a variable voltage, determines the distance z_1 of the reflecting equipotential plane in front of the specimen surface. If ϕ_{SC} is corrected for then

$$z_1 = \frac{\phi_{SV}}{F_z} \ll z_2 .$$

In this linearized model it is useful to represent an electrostatic (or topographic) perturbation $\phi(y,0)$ along the y-axis as a Fourier series (or integral).

$$\phi(y,0) = \sum_{n=1}^{\infty} \phi_n \cos 2\pi n v y . \tag{5}$$

The omitted term with $n = 0$, an additional voltage on top of the specimen potential, is defined as ϕ_{SA}.

In these calculations no incident electrons are allowed to reach the physical specimen surface, because the electron scattering effects which would occur, destroy the validity of the results obtained. Experiments revealed, that for a specimen biased slightly positive (some tenth of volts) with respect to the accelerating voltage ϕ_o, the image contrast deteriorated considerably due to the electron scattering phenomena at the specimen surface.

The lateral impulse Δmv_y given an electron travelling towards and from the specimen amounts to

$$\Delta mv_y = -2 \int_{z_1}^{z_1} e \frac{\partial \phi(y,z)}{\partial y} dt \approx -2 \int_{0}^{\infty} e \frac{\partial \phi(y,z)}{\partial y} dt . \tag{6}$$

Inserting eqs. (4c) and (5) into (6) and neglecting the lateral displacement during reversal, which is permissible for small values of Δmv_y, it follows that

$$\Delta m v_y = e \sum_{n=1}^{\infty} [\phi_n 2\pi n v \cdot \exp(-2\pi n v z_1);$$

$$\sin 2\pi n v y] \, 2 \int_{0}^{\infty} \exp[-2\pi n v (z - z_1)] \, dt$$

or

$$\Delta m v_y \left(\frac{4\pi^3 me}{F_z}\right)^{\frac{1}{2}} \sum_{n=1}^{\infty} [\phi_n (nv)^{\frac{1}{2}} \sin 2\pi n v y \quad \exp(-2\pi n v z_1)] \quad (7)$$

ϕ_{SV} has been introduced by writing $(z - z_1)$ instead of z.

If y_i represents the height of incidence above the z-axis and y_r the corresponding height for the reflected electrons, both measured in the plane $z = z_2$, then

$$y_r - y_i = \Delta y \Big|_{z=z_2} = v_y t$$

and

$$\Delta y \Big|_{z=z_2} = \frac{2\pi}{F_z} (2 z_2 v)^{\frac{1}{2}} \sum_{n=1}^{\infty} [\phi_n n^{\frac{1}{2}} \sin 2\pi n v y \cdot \exp(-2\pi n v z_1)] \; . \quad (8)$$

After interaction with the specimen the reflected electrons follow parabolic trajectories in the retarding field, owing to the lateral momentum received.

The corresponding angular deflection $\Delta\varphi$ is

$$\Delta\varphi = \Delta y / 2 z_2 \; . \quad (9)$$

For $n = 1$, Δy and $\Delta\varphi$ are determined as a function of ϕ_1 and v, the spatial frequency of a sinusoidal perturbation at the specimen surface.

$$\Delta y \Big|_{z=z_2} = \Delta y_v = \frac{2\pi}{F_z} (2z_2 v)^{\frac{1}{2}} \phi_1 \sin 2\pi v y \cdot \exp\left(-2\pi v \frac{\phi_1}{\phi_0} z_2 v\right)$$

$$\cdot \exp\left(-2\pi \frac{\phi_{SA}}{\phi_0} z_2 v\right). \tag{10}$$

The index v in Δy_v and $\Delta \varphi_v$ refers to electrostatic contrast in $z = z_2$.

$$z_1 = \frac{\phi_1 + \phi_{SA}}{\phi_0} z_2$$

(with ϕ_{SC} corrected for) has a minimum value ϕ_1/F_z which prevents electrons in case of electrostatic contrast from striking the specimen near positively charged perturbations.

The difference $\phi_{SV} - \phi_1 = \phi_{SA}$ corresponds to an additional voltage for adjusting the reflecting equipotential plane away from the perturbed specimen surface.

In fig. 5 the maximum values of Δy_v and $\Delta \varphi_v$, following from eq. (10), are plotted against v with ϕ_1 as curve parameter. For all curves presented it is assumed that $\sin 2\pi v y = 1$, $\phi_{SC} = \phi_{SA} = 0$.

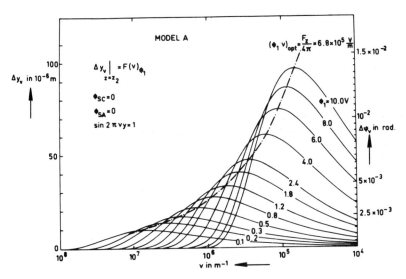

Fig. 5. Modulation functions Δy_v and $\Delta \varphi_v$ plotted against v (model A).

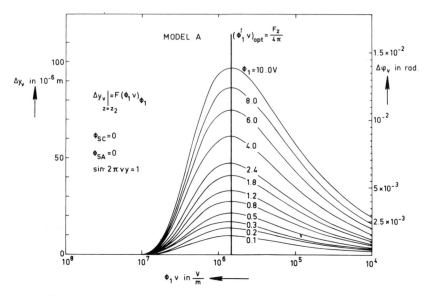

Fig. 6. Modulations functions Δy_v and $\Delta\varphi_\mathrm{v}$ plotted against $\phi_1\nu$ (model A).

Since the local "slope" $\phi_1\nu$ of the perturbations in the reflecting equipotential plane plays the main role in this contrast mechanism, Δy_v is also plotted against $\phi_1\nu$ (fig. 6).

The maxima of the plotted Δy_v and $\Delta\varphi_\mathrm{v}$ values for each curve $F(\phi_1\nu)_{\phi_1}$ coincide with the straight line $(\phi_1\nu)_\mathrm{opt}/F_z = 8 \times 10^{-2}$ or in the microscope designed $(\phi_1\nu)_\mathrm{opt} = F_z/4\pi = 6.8 \times 10^5$ V/m.

(b) Topographic contrast.

Provided that $\partial d(y,z)/\partial y \ll 1$ the topographic "displacement" Δy_t is found by substituting in eq. (8).

$$\phi_n = d_n F_z \text{ and } z_1 = \phi_\mathrm{SA}/F_z . \tag{11}$$

These relations are only applicable for small perturbations with moderate curvatures $(\partial^2 d(y,z)/\partial y^2 \ll 1)$ because then the z component of the field strength near the specimen equals F_z.

d_n represents the amplitude of the composing harmonics in the specimen topography.

$$d(y,0) = \sum_{n=1}^{\infty} d_n \cos 2\pi n\nu y . \tag{12}$$

Contrary to electrostatic contrast all topographic perturbations coincide with one equipotential plane. This causes that the minimum required bias for electrostatic contrast (for $n=1$ is $z_1 = \phi_1/F_z$) can be omitted for topographic contrast. If $\phi_{SA} = 0$ and $n = 1$ all electrons reach exactly the "topographic specimen" and

$$\Delta y_t \Big|_{z=z_2} = 2\pi (2z_2\nu)^{\frac{1}{2}} d_1 \sin 2\pi\nu y .\qquad (13)$$

A similar plot as fig. 5 represents the maximum values of Δy_t as a function of ν and d_1 with $\sin 2\pi\nu y = 1$, $\phi_{SA} = 0$ and $\phi_{SC} = 0$ (fig. 7).

(c) Conclusions and remarks for model A.

Conclusions. (i) An electrostatic or topographic cosine perturbation at the specimen surface gives a sine modulation on the angle of the reversing electron pencils. For electrostatic contrast the specimen should be at least biased with an additional negative voltage, equal to the positive amplitude of the perturbation signal. This prevents electrons from reaching the specimen surface.

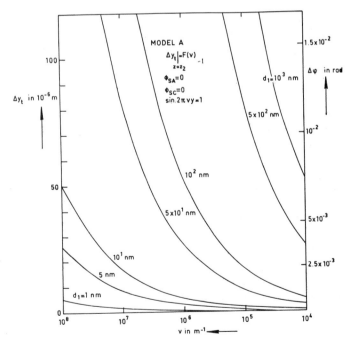

Fig. 7. Modulation functions Δy_t and $\Delta\varphi_t$ plotted against ν (model A).

(ii) It follows directly from the linear character of the eqs. (4a and b) that the modulation effect of an arbitrary periodic perturbation, either electrostatic or topographic, can be calculated by summing the separate modulation effects of the composing harmonics.

(iii) For topographic contrast with $\partial d(y,0)/\partial y \ll 1$ and $\partial^2 d(y,0)/\partial y^2 \ll 1$ a linear relation exists between the perturbation amplitude and the modulation effect (Δy_t or $\Delta \varphi_t$) on the angle of the reversing electron pencils. A similar linear relation is valid for electrostatic contrast provided that $2\pi \phi_1 \nu \ll F_z$.

(iv) A discrimination between topographic and electrostatic contrast is possible in principle, because for topography the modulation function is independent of the position on the specimen. For electrostatic contrast it varies from place to place owing to the additional damping factor.

(v) The fact that $\phi_1 \nu$ possesses a constant value corresponding to the maxima of the plotted Δy_v or $\Delta \varphi_v$ values (figs. 5 and 6) means that once ϕ_1 is given, the optimum ν value for maximum electrostatic contrast follows immediately. The conclusions stated above involve the assumptions:

(i)   the illuminating beam in the retarding field is parallel to the z-axis;

(ii) $\dfrac{\partial \phi(y,z)}{\partial z} \ll F_z$;

(iii) $\dfrac{\partial d(y,0)}{\partial y} \ll 1$ and $\dfrac{\partial^2 d(y,0)}{\partial y^2} \ll 1$ for topographic contrast;

(iv)   electrons do not reach the specimen surface;

(v)   the illuminating beam is mono-energetic ($e\phi_o$).

2.4. Model B (solution of the exact equations of motion (1a and b))

Electrostatic contrast calculations with a digital computer. By means of a digital computer plots, similar to figs. 5 and 6 for the maximum values of Δy_v and $\Delta \varphi_v$ depending on ν and ϕ_1 as curve parameter, are presented in fig. 8. The condition $\sin 2\pi \nu y = 1$ of model A is not tenable for model B because it does not coincide with the maximum values of Δy_v and $\Delta \varphi_v$. For comparison the curves of model A (dashed lines) and model B (full lines) are both pictured in fig. 8.

Conclusion (fig. 8). For small values of Δy_v and $\Delta \varphi_v$, corresponding to a low contrast, both groups of curves match accurately as expected. Comparison of the curves $\Delta y_v = F(\phi_1 \nu)\phi_1$ of model A (fig. 6) with those of model B leads to matching within 2% of A and B provided that

$$\phi_1 \nu / F_z < 1.2 \times 10^{-2} \quad \text{and} \quad \phi_1 \nu / F_z > 6 \times 10^{-1} .$$

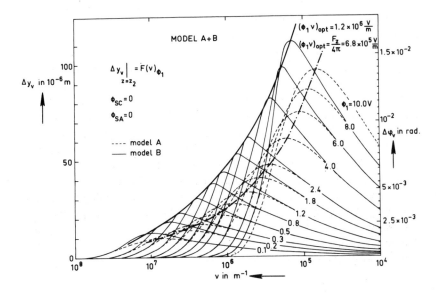

Fig. 8. Modulation functions Δy_V and $\Delta \varphi_V$ plotted against ν (models A and B).

3. Description of a mirror electron microscope designed for focused images

3.1. *Description*

Summary. Apart from the requirement of separated axes for the illuminating and imaging system, a continuously variable magnification of 250 ... 4000 X at the final fluorescent screen was desired. On the basis of fig. 9 the instrument will be described by following the accelerated electron beam in the illuminating system towards the specimen surface (mirror electrode) and after reflection towards the final fluorescent screen.

3.2. *The illuminating system*

When a magnetic prism is applied, it is favourable to minimize the deflection angle with regard to errors caused by the deflection field. These effects are proportional to the second and higher powers of the angle of deflection.

In order to create sufficient clearance for the miniaturized illuminating system, the angle between this system and the vertical main axis is fixed at 30°. The main axis represents the centreline of the specimen and the projector lens. The deflection angle of the magnetic prism is further reduced to

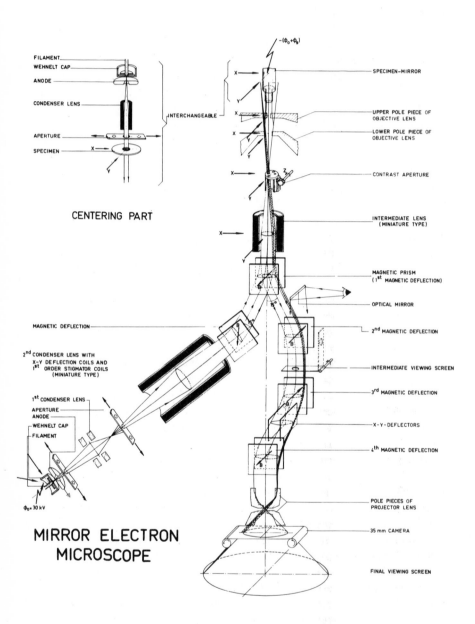

Fig. 9. Mirror electron microscope.

15° by mounting on top of the second condenser lens an additional deflector, which matches the axis of the illuminating system with the proper direction of incidence for the prism. A 30 kV electron beam is produced by a conventional triode electron gun. The first condenser lens with iron pole pieces demagnifies the electron source 10 ... 40 X. The second condenser lens, a miniature magnetic lens without iron circuit, images the demagnified electron source through the injector-deflector prism and intermediate lens into the contrast aperture.

An adjustable holder for three apertures is mounted between the first and second condenser lens in order to obtain a fixed angular aperture of the illuminating electron beam.

Each deflector (the injector-deflector, the prism and the later discussed additional "bridge-deflectors") consists of pairs of circular air coils. The inner sides of the coils are covered with thin sheets of transformer iron. The resulting magnetic field is quite homogeneous and has an almost rectangular boundary.

Experiments revealed that, for electron beams with a diameter nearly equal to the separation of the iron sheets, the image distortion still remains within admissible limits.

The second condenser lens is provided with additional pairs of x- and y-deflectors for centring the lens and two quadrupoles for correcting astigmatism. Iron tubing screens the illuminating system against stray magnetic fields. Near the second condenser lens the iron tubing is connected with a rectangular iron plate, covering a hole in the vertical main column housing.

Care has been taken to separate the magnetic fluxes in the main column. Especially, interaction of magnetic fluxes generated in different parts of the instrument gives rise to problems in the centring of the electron optics. In order to minimize this coupling effect, additional concentric iron cylinders are used near the joining of the illuminating system and the main column, and around the intermediate lens.

3.3. *Imaging system*

The imaging system consists of the objective lens with contrast aperture and the intermediate lens. The combination of objective, intermediate and projector lens allows a continuously variable magnification of 250 ... 4000 X at the final fluorescent screen.

The imaging system and the prism form a group of electron optical components which are passed both by the illuminating and the reflected beam. This feature sets high requirements of the centring accuracy of both lenses. The axes of both lenses should coincide perfectly with the main axis of the vertical column, because each residual inclination or decentring produces a

transverse magnetic field which acts as a prism. In order to make the, in practice always inclined and decentred, lens axes coincident with the main axis,
these lenses are centred by combining current reversing with pole piece centring,
as proposed by Haine.

Limitation of the field of view can be avoided by positioning the contrast
aperture in the back focal plane of the combination objective and electrostatic lens. The negative lens action of the upper objective lens pole piece,
which forms the earthed boundary of the retarding field, necessitates a slightly
higher excitation of the objective lens to assure normal incidence onto the
mirror plane. Since for changes in the magnification the objective lens excitation has to be varied, the contrast aperture is, apart from the x- and y-
centring, also adjustable along the main axis (z-direction). To each setting of
the objective lens current there corresponds an optimum z-position of the contrast aperture providing maximum field of view.

Both the objective and the intermediate lens are provided with two crossed
quadrupoles for correcting astigmatism.

3.4. *The deflection bridge and the projector lens with camera*

In previous mirror electron microscopes, equipped with a magnetic prism,
the reflected electron beam (after passing the magnetic prism) is observed by
a skew projection system.

In this microscope the reflected beam, after passing the prism, is made to
coincide again with the main axis by means of three additional deflectors. The
magnetic prism with the three following deflectors form the deflection bridge
(fig. 9).

The advantage of making the reflected beam again coincident with the main
axis are:

(i) The effective deflection of the bridge is zero. Therefore this system
shows an achromatic behaviour for high voltage fluctuations. In addition,
when the deflectors of the bridge are energized in series, correction against
fluctuations in the series current is established. Without this compensation
the required current stability for the prism amounts to a few parts per million.
The use of the deflection bridge lowers the stability required for achieving
identical quality in the final image at least by two orders of magnitude.

(ii) Except for the illuminating system, the main column can be erected
vertically, which makes it easier to achieve the high requirements for mechanical stability.

(iii) A considerable facilitation for the alignment of the electron beam
through the microscope is achieved.

Thanks to the insensitivity of the deflection bridge for variations of the series current over a wide range a current setting can been selected for which the astigmatism, which is a by-product of the deflection fields and results in different magnifications in perpendicular directions, is minimized.

4. Results and applications

4.1. Results

Since interpretation of mirror microscope images is rather complicated, only test specimens are selected which possess a known composition and topography. Most of the pictures presented in this chapter are therefore vacuum deposited layers onto accurately polished glass disks. A first conductive layer makes the glass surface coincident with an equipotential plane, whereas additional layers, mostly evaporated through a grid of known dimensions, provide a regular pattern. The advantage of using a regular pattern is found in the easy determination of image distortion and magnification. Although in principle discrimination between electrostatic and topographic contrast is possible (conclusion 4 sect. 2.3 (c)), no clear practical evidence is found yet in the images obtained. Due to the high sensitivity for slight differences in height, the possibility of preparing a specimen with purely electrostatic contrast appears to be rather doubtful. In view of this difficulty it was decided to concentrate primarily most of our efforts on the focused imaging of specimens with topographic contrast. The photographic results presented are only meant to demonstrate the remarkable improvement in image quality of the focused mirror microscope in comparison with the results from mirror projection microscopes. The author is aware that this series of photographs only provides a limited outlook at the large, but hardly explored, field of possible applications. The achieved improvement in image quality and resolving power of this type of mirror electron microscope, the main purpose of this instrument, makes it worthwhile to initiate a more systematic research for widening the scope of useful applications.

(a) Figs. 10a, b, c and d. This group of figures represents a through focal series of a topographic specimen, consisting of a polished glass disk covered with a layer of gold. On top of it a layer of gold has been vacuum deposited through a 750 mesh grid (a period of 33 μm). The magnification amounts to about 2000X. The thickness of the second layer is (10±2) nm. The arrows mark again the same characteristic spot at the specimen in the various figures. For the in focus image (fig. 10b) "structures" are observed smaller than 50 nm while a point resolution of 80 ... 100 nm has been achieved. Fig. 10d is iden-

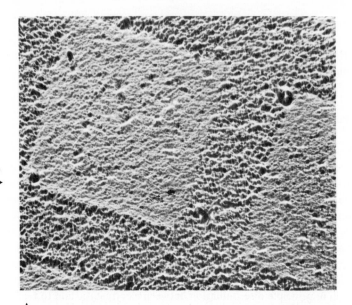

↑ Fig. 10a. Under focus (distance off focus −5 μm). 2000X.

↑ Fig. 10b. In focus. Magnification 2000X.

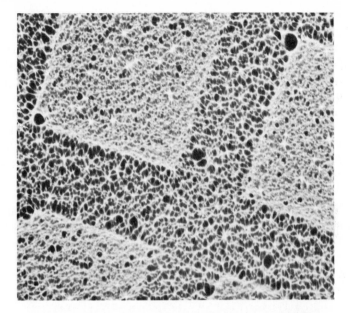

Fig. 10c. Over focus (distance off focus +5 μm). 2000X.

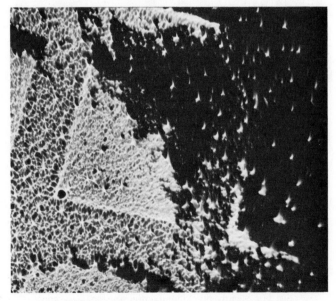

Fig. 10d. Same condition as fig. 10c with tilted illumination.

tical to fig. 10c except for the slight tilt of the illuminating beam. The increase
in contrast for fig. 10d is tremendous. A step of 10 nm in height already casts
large shadows. Similar results, although with less contrast, are achieved for
steps of (5±2) nm. In the dark field region of fig. 10d only electrons reflected
near elevated spots and local charges at the specimen pass the contrast aperture, which then partially acts as a knife edge. A comparison of fig. 10b and
10c learns that the increase of contrast for an out of focus image (fig. 10c)
occurs at the expense of resolving power. Contrary to the more out of focus
images in mirror projection microscopes this series of figures is equally sharp
across the entire final screen (about the size of the figures presented here).
The diameter of the contrast aperture used was $D = 100\,\mu$m.

(b) Figs. 11a, b and c. These figures demonstrate the effect of an increasing tilt of the illuminating beam. Accurate positioning of the contrast aperture
in the back focal plane of the combination objective and electrostatic lens
gives a knife edge filtering for the entire illuminated area at the specimen. The
specimen pictured is the same as in figs. 10. The magnification is 800X. The
inclined incidence of the illuminating beam causes a narrowing of the bars

Fig. 11a. Slightly tilted illumination. Magnification 800X.

Fig. 11b. Tilted illumination (same specimen area as fig. 11a). 800✕.

Fig. 11c. Grazing incidence of the illuminating beam (same specimen area as figs. 11a and b). 800✕.

(actual width about 8 μm) between the squares. The increasing concave mirror action of the bars for tilted illumination provides sharp line foci in the final image.

4.2. *Applications*

The applications mentioned in brief hereafter are not meant to provide the reader with a complete survey about all possibilities of the mirror electron microscope. It only presents a number of applications which might be of interest to physicists investigating surface phenomena at a microscopic scale.

1. The investigation of semi-conductor electronics (micro-circuits). Apart from the surface topography, electric properties as potential distributions across resistors, condensers, etc. and current flow in separate components can be observed. Especially the visualization of the dynamic behaviour of micro-circuits allows for determination of interruptions and breakdowns in the circuitry [26–30].

2. The investigation of surface conductivity, diffusion of metals [31] and ferro-electric domain patterns [32,33].

The movement of electric charges across surfaces, having a poor surface conductivity, can be studied dynamically. Measuring the propagation velocity of electric charges provides information about the surface conductivity [34]. The storage of charges on photo-sensitive layers (image intensifiers) can be visualized at a high magnification.

When the mirror electrode is replaced by a photo-sensitive layer, an image intensifier with a high resolving power could perhaps be realized. Changes in the local work function, resulting from diffusion of metals or doping effects, lead to current density modulations in the final image.

3. The investigation of thin films. The high sensitivity for topography and local charges offers the possibility to test the quality of evaporated layers. Contaminations and impurities can be easily detected.

4. The dynamic observation of magnetic domain patterns [35,36], for instance the imaging of patterns recorded on magnetic tape [37,38] and magnetic stray fields on grain boundaries [39]. Some experimenters have successfully reported on observations of ferro-magnetic phenomena [20].

5. The investigation of the local work function, as already performed in the emission electron microscope. In addition to the mirror images, secondary emission images are obtainable by bombarding the specimen with low energy electrons (in the order of tens of electron volts). This feature provides the possibility to obtain two different types of images from the same specimen area. A stable 100 V source on top of the accelerating voltage is under construction.

In how far low energy electron diffraction (LEED) is possible in this instrument remains to be seen.

6. An improvement of the vacuum near the mirror electrode and a rough filtering of the illuminating beam yield interesting perspectives for investigation of physi- and chemi-sorption phenomena. Contrast will be obtained in this case by changes in the local work function resulting from adsorption.

References

[1] M.Z.Knoll, Techn. Phys. 16 (1935) 767.
[2] E.Z.Ruska, Phys. 83 (1933) 492.
[3] B.von Borries and S.Z.Jansen, Verein. Dtsch. Ingen. 85 (1941) 207.
[4] G.Hottenroth, Ann. Phys., Paris, 30 (1937) 689.
[5] A.Recknagel and W.Henneberg, Techn. Phys. 16 (1935) 621.
[6] A.Recknagel, Z. f. Phys. 104 (1936) 381.
[7] L.Mayer, J. Appl. Phys. 28 (1957) 259.
[8] L.Mayer, J. Appl. Phys. 28 (1957) 975.
[9] L.Mayer, J. Appl. Phys. 30 (1959) 2525.
[10] L.Mayer, J. Appl. Phys. 31 (1960) 346.
[11] G.V.Spivak et al., Dokl. Akad. Nauk SSSR 105 (1955) 965.
[12] G.V.Spivak et al., Kristallografiya 4 (1959) 123.
[13] G.V.Spivak et al., Ivz. Akad. Nauk SSSR 23 (1959) 729.
[14] G.V.Spivak et al., Ivz. Akad. Nauk SSSR 26 (1962) 1332.
[15] J.B.Le Poole, Discussions on the Conf. non-conventional electron microscopy (Cambridge, 1964).
[16] H.Bethge et al., Exp. Techn. der Phys. 8 (1960) 49.
[17] G.Forst and B.Wende, Z. angew. Phys. 17 (1964) 479.
[18] M.E.Barnett and W.C.Nixon, J. Sci. Instr. 44 (1967) 893.
[19] A.B.Bok, J.Kramer and J.B.Le Poole, 3rd Eur. Conf. on electron microscopy (Praag, 1964) A9.
[20] R.Orthuber, Z. angew. Phys. 1 (1948) 79.
[21] G.Bartz et al., Radex-Rundschau (1956) 163.
[22] H.Höpp, Thesis (Berlin, 1960).
[23] W.Schwartze, Optik 25 (1967) 260.
[24] F.Lenz and E.Krimmel, Z. f. Phys. 175 (1963) 235.
[25] F.H.Plomp and J.B.Le Poole, 3rd Eur. Conf. on electron microscopy (Prague) 9 (1964) A10.
[26] E.Igras, Bull. Acad. Polon. Sci. Ser. Phys. 9 (1961) 403.
[27] E.Igras and T.Warminski, Phys. Stat. Sol. 9 (1965) 79.
[28] E.Igras and T.Warminski, Phys. Stat. Sol. 13 (1966) 169.
[29] K.N.Maffit and C.R.Deeter, Symp. the mirror electron microscope for semiconductors (1966) 9.
[30] R.D.Ivanov and M.G.Abalmazova, Sov. Phys.-Tech. Phys. 12 (1968) 982.
[31] E.Igras and T.Warminski, Phys. Stat. Sol. 20 (1967) K5.
[32] E.Igras et al., Sov. Phys. Cryst. 4 (1959) 111.

[33] G.V.Spivak et al., Sov. Phys. Cryst. 4 (1959) 115.
[34] L.Mayer, J. Appl. Phys. 28 (1957) 259.
[35] G.V.Spivak et al., Dokl. Akad. Nauk USSR 105 (1955) 706.
[36] L.Mayer, J. Appl. Phys. 30 (1959) 252S.
[37] L.Mayer, J. Appl. Phys. 29 (1958) 658.
[38] G.V.Spivak et al., Bull. Acad. Sci. USSR Phys. Ser. 28 (1963) 1210.
[39] L.Mayer, J. Appl. Phys. 30 (1959) 1101.
[40] G.V.Spivak et al., Dokl. Akad. Nauk USSR 105 (1955) 965.

SURFACE STUDIES BY FIELD EMISSION

Erwin W.MÜLLER

Department of Physics, The Pennsylvania State University,
University Park, Pa. 16802 USA

1. Introduction

The study of field emission of electrons from a metal surface is attractive
because its results lead to an interpretation in terms of the atomistic and electronic structure of the surface. The experimental technique based on the field
emission microscope (FEM) permits handling the specimen of well established
cleanliness in a temperature range from near zero to near the melting point,
and provides detailed information on topographic, electronic and other surface properties in their dependence on crystallographic orientation. The FEM
is a powerful tool for the investigation of adsorption and surface migration. In
a modification of the FEM permitting high resolution measurements of the
total energy distribution (TED) of the emitted electrons, energy levels of adsorbed atoms and molecules can now be observed.

2. The field emission current

The Sommerfeld free electron model of a metal at $0°K$ sees the electrons
held inside the metal by a potential barrier of height ϕ, the work function,
above the Fermi level. With a high external field applied, the barrier assumes
a triangular shape comparable in width with the de Broglie wavelength of the
electrons near the Fermi level. Now the exponential decay of the wave function within the barrier is not complete before the electron emerges into the
vacuum where the potential sinks below the Fermi level. Fowler and Nord-
heim (FN) have calculated the transparency of the barrier, including the refinement of rounding off the triangular shape by the image force potential of
the electron [1]. Using the Fermi-Dirac statistics for the electron energy dis-

tribution at T°K, and the WKB method for calculating the transmission probability, the current density of field emission at a field F is [2,3]

$$J = \frac{e^2 F^2}{8\pi h\phi\; t^2(y)} \exp \frac{-4(2m\phi^3)^{\frac{1}{2}}}{3\hbar e F} v(y) \frac{\pi kT/d}{\sin(\pi kT/d)}, \tag{1}$$

where

$$d = \frac{\hbar e F}{2(2m\phi)^{\frac{1}{2}}\; t(y)} \tag{2}$$

and where $t(y)$ and $v(y)$ are slowly varying elliptical functions of $y = (e^3 F)^{\frac{1}{2}}/\phi$, the ratio of the potential hump reduction by the Schottky effect to the work function. These functions have been tabulated by Good and Müller [2].

Because of the WKB approximation, eq. (1) is valid in the temperature and field region where $kT < d$. Since temperature effects below about 600°K are small, one can simplify eq. (1) for $T = 0°$K, and with numbers for the constants inserted, one obtains the FN-equation of the current density

$$J = \frac{1.54 \times 10^{-6} F^2}{\phi\; t^2(y)} \exp\left[-6.83 \times 10^7 \phi^{\frac{3}{2}} v(y)/F\right] \; A/cm^2, \tag{3}$$

and for the band width parameter

$$d \cong \frac{0.98 \times 10^{-8} F}{\phi^{\frac{1}{2}}}, \tag{4}$$

where the applied field F is measured in V/cm and the work function ϕ in eV.

The free electron approximation based on Fermi-Dirac statistics is justified by Harrison's [4] investigation of the effect of the density of states on tunneling from transition metals. Band structure effects should be negligible in the total current, as the emission is sampled from the Fermi level to about 0.5 eV below only.

Stratton [5] investigated field emission of electrons originating from an arbitrary band structure by assuming that the tangential components P_y and P_z of the electron quasimomentum are conserved in the transmission process. As a result, the energy in the x direction is no more equal to $P_x^2/2m$. Band structure effects are negligible unless the maximum lateral energy component $E_m = (P_y^2 + P_z^2)/2m$ is smaller than d.

Field emission from metal crystals with an arbitrary electron distribution has also been treated by Itskovich [6], who finds close agreement with the free electron model if the Fermi surface is intersected by an axis perpendicular to the emitting crystal plane. If there is no such intersection, conservation of the tangential quasimomentum of the electrons results in a larger effective work function, compared to the work function measured by thermionics or photo electric emission.

The validity of the FN-equation for metals such as tungsten has been checked repeatedly with ever increasing accuracy [2,7,8]. The simplest test is through an FN plot of the log of current density versus the reciprocal field which should be close to a straight line. The slope of the FN plot is essentially proportional to $\phi^{\frac{3}{2}}$. Actual measurements give indeed reasonable work functions, not only for clean metals, but also for adsorbates which produce a positive or negative dipole layer at the surface.

3. The energy distribution

The most critical test of an emission theory is the energy distribution of the electrons. The first retarding potential tube with spherical symmetry [9] already demonstrated that the electrons essentially come from below the Fermi level, and a distribution width of less than 0.5 eV also seemed to fulfill the expectation. Young [3] realized that the spherical retarding potential analyzer, if properly designed, measures the total energy distribution rather than the normal distribution used for the derivation of the FN-theory in a linear model. He derived the total energy distribution to be

$$P(E)dE = \frac{4\pi md}{h^3} \exp \frac{-4(2m\phi^3)^{\frac{1}{2}}}{3heF} v(y) - \frac{\phi}{d} \frac{\exp(E/d)}{\exp[(E-\phi)/kT]+1} dE . \quad (5)$$

Experimental verifications with a tube design by Young and Müller [10] and a further improved device by van Oostrum [8], the latter reaching a resolution of 0.01 eV, demonstrated satisfactorily all the features expected from the FN-model. At liquid helium temperature the onset of the distribution curve at the Fermi level is sharp within the resolution. In fact, according to Young and Kuyatt [11], the onset is the best means of evaluating the energy resolution of the device. The half width of the distribution is found to be proportional to the field and to the inverse square root of the work function, as expected from eq. (2). The tail of the Fermi-Dirac distribution above the Fermi level is strongly temperature dependent because of the increased transparency of the barrier at higher energy levels. In agreement with Harrison's calculation

no energy band effects are seen in the total energy distribution. Van Oostrum's
slightly wider energy distribution can be explained by a refinement in the image
force potential as introduced by Cutler and Nagy [12].

The total energy distribution was measured for a number of different
crystal planes as they were accessible in the experimental tubes, and the entire
range was found to be featureless, indicating no band effects, as expected. It
was therefore quite surprising when Swanson and Crouser [13], measuring for
the first time the distribution from the (001) plane of tungsten, obtained a
pronounced hump about 0.4 eV below the Fermi level. They later also found
a small deviations in the TED of (001) molybdenum [14]. This must be a
band effect. Gadzuk [15] suggested its origin from a tight binding d-band,
while Nagy and Cutler [16], using the Stratton theory, were able to correlate
the anomaly with a small lens shaped feature in energy surfaces of tungsten
0.4 eV below the Fermi energy.

4. Field emission microscopy

The bulk of our experience with field emission is based on the field emission microscope [2]. In this device the field emitter in the form of a fine
needle tip is placed opposite a fluorescent screen at anode potential. Field
emitted electrons radially project the nearly hemispherical surface of the tip
onto the screen. The emission pattern visually displays the field emission current density of the various crystallographic planes, giving at least qualitative
information on the relative work functions of clean crystal surfaces as well as
their changes by adsorption. While these basic features had been realized immediately with the inception of the instrument more than 30 years ago [17],
the systems studied at that time, tungsten, molybdenum, copper, nickel and
the adsorption of oxygen and barium, today still are the objects of increasingly
refined experimentation and interpretation. The sensitivity of the field emission microscope towards changes in work function makes it possible to detect
the adsorption of a small fraction of a monoatomic layer [18], but the lateral
resolution is limited to much less than truly atomic dimensions. The resolution
is determined [2,19] by both the lateral velocity component of the Fermi-
Dirac electrons, and by a diffraction limit due to the de Broglie wavelength or
the Heisenberg uncertainty principle, whichever way one wishes to look at it.
In practice, spots 25 Å apart on the emitter tip can be seen separated.

The smooth surface of the emitter tip is essential for the proper operation
of the radial projection principle. Usually it is achieved when the specimen
assumes a shape of minimum free surface energy during the annealing process

performed for cleaning and outgassing the emitter. The annealing end from consists of atomically flat low index planes, connected by rounded regions that are revealed by field ion microscopy to be atomically rough, if not amorphous. This tip preparation method fails particularly with the non-refractory metals when impurities, such as oxides, are not evaporated or dissociated at the highest permissible annealing temperature. In this case the use of low temperature field desorption and field evaporation is more practical [20,21]. It produces surfaces of a cleanliness limited only by the bulk concentration of impurities in the specimen material. Using an alternating voltage with properly chosen, different amplitudes in the positive and negative directions, controlled field desorption is performed in the positive half phase, while the electron image is viewed in the negative phase. Clean patterns of iron tips were thus obtained for the first time [22]. It should be noted that neither the annealing nor the desorption endform are exactly hemispherical, and they differ from each other as well.

The measurement of work functions in different crystallographic planes is one of the more useful applications of field emission microscopy. In order to get qualitative data it is not sufficient to take photometric intensities from the visual display of the electron image because of the exceedingly large contrast between various emitting regions. The problem was overcome with the introduction of the probe hole technique [9,23]. The local current density is measured in a Faraday cage placed beyond a small probe hole in the screen, onto which the desired crystallographic region is projected by either turning the emitter tip or by magnetically deflecting the image. Early data by Müller of the work function of various crystal planes of tungsten [24], all based on the $\frac{3}{2}$ power slope of the FN plot, have been confirmed by more recent investigations. The most striking result was an unexpectedly high value of $\phi = 6.0$ eV for the (011) plane. An uncertainty remained due to the unknown local field strengths caused by the flattening of the (001) plane and the thermal roughing of other planes during the tip annealing process. The experiments were resumed, when field-ion microscope techniques and particularly the effect of field evaporation permitted more finely detailed observations and the formation of atomically smooth and ideally perfect net planes [25]. Comparison with the total emission, 8 to 9 orders of magnitude larger than the current through the probe hole in the (011) region of the pattern, gave again a work function near 6 eV. It was further realized in this investigation that the uncertainty in the field/voltage factor β could be eliminated by measuring another quantity of the emission through the probe hole that depends on F and ϕ in a different way than the $\phi^{\frac{3}{2}}/F$ relation of eq. (1). Thereby a second equation is obtained for solving for the two unknowns F and ϕ. For instance, the half-width of total energy distribution according to eq. (4) depends on $F/\phi^{\frac{1}{2}}$. Instead of this the relative temperature dependence $[J(T_2)-J(T_1)]/J$ can be used as it depends upon $(T_2^2-T_1^2)\phi/F^2$ according to eq. (1). The results may be affected by a possible anomalous distribution width attributable to band structure, or by a temperature dependence of the work function.

In the straightforward method of comparing the slopes of FN characteristics measured for various crystal orientations in order to get relative work functions an important detail is pointed out by van Oostrum [8]; Because of the widely varying local tip radius, and particularly at the large flat of the (011) plane on a thermally smoothed tungsten tip, the magnification of the field emission microscope is not uniform. On the (011) plane the area covered by the probe hole is more than a hundred times larger than on the more evenly curved regions, and the true current densities are that much smaller than is apparent from the direct measurement.

If regions of different work functions lie side by side on the emitter tip, there exists a local patch field which Young and Clark [26] showed to be quite significant. If there is a potential difference V_o between a disc of radius R and a surrounding infinite plane, the patch field at the center of the disc $F_o = V_o/R$. On a field-emission tip a typical (011) plane with a radius of 25 to 50Å and an assumed work function of 6 eV, surrounded by a thermally disordered region with a work function of 4.5 eV, would have a patch field of from 6 to 3 MV/cm. This is additive to a typical emission field of 40 MV/cm, and thus not at all negligible but rather leads to a correction of ϕ_{011} to about 7.0 eV. At the other, more extended low work function regions the effect of the patch field is not significant.

The determination of absolute work functions from the FN slope requires the knowledge of the effective field, while only the applied voltage is accurately known. When the combination of the FN slope and the energy distribution is used for an absolute determination of ϕ and F, the limited energy resolution becomes a problem. Young and Clark bypass this difficulty by calculating the slope S of the integrated total energy distribution measured as a current $i(E)$ in a retarding potential analyzer, using eq. (5) and obtain

$$S_E = d[\log(i_o-i(E))]/dE = \frac{0.434 \times 2(2m\phi)^{\frac{1}{2}} t(y)}{\hbar eF}. \tag{6}$$

Here i_o is the maximum collected current. Combining this with the slope S of the FN equation gives the work function

$$\phi = -\frac{3}{2} \frac{S \, t(y)}{S_E \, s(y) \, V} \, \text{eV} \, . \tag{7}$$

In a recent paper Young and Clark [27] use this formula to interpret measurements for a (011) plane of 50Å diameter and perfected by field evaporation, for which they obtain ϕ = 7.1 eV without a patch field correction. After enlarging this plane to several times the original size by a heat treatment in the presence of a field [25], the uncorrected work function changes to 8.78 eV. Taking into account the patch field complicates the "absolute" method of determining ϕ and F, and the accuracy is disappointing even when iteration is employed for assigning proper values of F_0, $s(y)$, $t(y)$ and β.

We have dwelt for some length on the discussion of the work function of the (011) plane of tungsten because it illustrates the limit of our knowledge on such a basic quantity of the simplest plane of the thermionically best known metal. Work function data with two or three significant figures, often found in the literature for a number of metals with much more poorly defined surface conditions must therefore be considered with reservations.

Another useful subject of field emission microscopy of clean metals is surface selfdiffusion. Müller [28] followed the gradual blunting of the tip by annealing, or the re-establishment of the endform of tungsten emitters whose surface had been brought out of equilibrium by either vapor depositing a few atomic layers of the same metal or by deforming the tip at higher temperature with the application of an electric field. Measurements of rates at various temperatures were used in an Arrhenius plot to derive activation energies of surface migration. Tip blunting required 4.6 eV activation energy, while movement of possibly single atoms over a barrier of 1.2 eV on the (011) plane could be seen down to 830°K.

A higher degree of accuracy seemed to be obtainable by following the collapse of faintly visible net plane rings around low index planes while the tip is annealed. Tip deformation by the field stress is completely eliminated when the observation field is applied in the form of microsecond pulses with a low duty cycle [29]. The activation energy of surface migration as well as the diffusivity constant have been measured for W, Re, Ir and Rh by this pulse technique, but it has become doubtful that the free surface energy can be reliably derived from the field which needs to be applied for stopping the rings to collapse [30]. Closely connected with the observation of surface migration is the study of nucleation of crystallites of vapor deposited metals, which is recognized by the formation of bright spots in regions where the thickness of the deposit is large enough to build up crystallites. A detailed discussion of this technique has been given by Gretz [31].

The range of lower melting point metals accessible to field emission microscopy has been greatly extended by Melmed [32] . Epitaxial crystals of various metals are grown in situ by vapor deposition on a tungsten field emission tip, and the nucleation process can be followed in crystallographic detail by varying the substrate temperature and deposition rate. With copper, "large" crystals whose surface area is comparable to the emitting area of the tungsten tip are grown at temperatures above $625°K$ and up to at least $1050°K$, giving very regular field emission patterns characteristic of the deposit metal. Activation energies of surface migration under the influence of the applied field, Q_F, are measured by the buildup rate of sharp edges, and zero-field activation energies, Q_o, are obtained by measuring the rates of annealing the previously buildup tips in the absence of a field, observing the pattern only at frozen-in states. Q_F is found to be 11.8 kcal/mole for Cu, 7.5 kcal/mole for Pb, and 19.1 kcal/mole for Pd, all at about 30 to 35 MV/cm. The activation energies, Q_o, for the same metals are found to be larger by 1.2 kcal/mole, 0.8 kcal/mole and 2.4 kcal/mole for Cu, Pb, and Pd, respectively. Similar differences appear with Ni and Pt [33] .

Surface diffusion of adsorbed species can be followed by direct observation when sharp diffusion edges or large changes in work function occur. Beginning with the spreading of barium deposited on one side of the tip the method of deriving surface migration activation energies of such films [18] has been applied to many adsorption systems. Instead of sideways shadowing, the required sharp edge of the film can also be produced by partial field desorption [34] of an originally homogenously spreadout adsorbate. If the deposit has a too large vapor pressure at the ambient temperature, the entire FEM can be immersed in a cryogenic bath. This method was originated by Müller and Wiegmann [23] for the study of adsorption of water vapor, and has been brought to perfection by Gomer [35] when he used liquid helium cooling for observing the detailed mechanism of film mobility of hydrogen, oxygen, carbon monoxide and various noble gases on tungsten and metal. In a series of skillful experiments Ehrlich [36] has added to the large body of information on adsorbed noble gases, carbon monoxide and nitrogen by using a more convenient cold-finger microscope tube with concentric dewars, a device originally designed by Müller for a field ion microscope. Ehrlich [37] has given a lucid report on the adsorption studies by field emission microscopy and attempts to correlate the results with those of the macroscopic flash filament technique. The latter method has been extended by Kohrt and Gomer [38] to flashing the adsorbed layer of CO from a heated single crystal tungsten ribbon and using a field emitter only as a detector of the amount of desorbing gas.

In his thorough investigation of the validity of the FN theory van Oostrum [8] used a probe hole retarding potential tube to obtain FN plots of various crystal planes of tungsten when they are covered by adsorbed nitrogen. Changes in the overall pre-exponential term of the FN equation upon adsorption have been known to occur, but van Oostrum's single plane data show for the first time the different behavior of the individual planes. Obviously the decrease of work function with a simultaneous large reduction of the pre-exponential term indicates the need of a modification of the tunneling mechanism in the surface barrier.

5. Resonance tunneling

In spite of the experimental advances in field emission microscopy during the past decade the interpretation has essentially been based on the forty years old FN theory which actually applies to a clean metal surface only. Some minor modifications were considered including improvements in the image force potential and the effect of atomic polarization of adsorbates [39,40]. It was therefore timely when in 1967 Duke and Alfiereff [41] undertook the development of a new model for field emission from a metal through both metallic and neutral adsorbates. Although the exactly solvable one-dimensional pseudopotential model consists only of a simple delta function outside the metal with an inserted square well to represent the adsorbate (fig. 1), the results are quite remarkable. Metallic adsorbates may produce a large resonance enhancement R, a factor of several thousand in the transmission probability for electrons connected with a reduction of the slope of the FN plot. These resonances also produce a shoulder in the energy distribution for weak and moderate fields, and dominate the distribution curve at high fields. Strongly bound neutral adsorbates, which have their atomic bound state below the metal's conduction band, reduce the transmission probability, but details of the pseudopotential applicable in a special case will still have to be determined, perhaps by precision energy distribution measurements.

These changes in the emission are derived from wave-mechanical interference effects caused by the presence of discrete atomic levels outside the metal surface. They cannot be considered in terms of work function changes by dipole layers, except perhaps in the case of a dielectric surface film model proposed by van Oostrum [8] for neutral adsorbates.

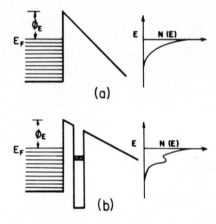

Fig. 1. Surface barrier and total energy distribution for a clean metal (a), and for a metal
with an absorbate causing resonance tunneling (b).

6. Total energy distribution spectroscopy

In their theory of resonance tunneling Duke and Alfiereff suggest that the
most sensitive test of the new concept would be the changes in the total energy
distribution. Peaks in this distribution will reflect the virtual atomic states of
the adsorbate, promising a kind of spectroscopy of the levels near the surface.
While the original treatment of the pseudopotentials of the system might not
be too realistic, Gadzuk [15] has recently arrived at a very detailed analysis
by using a combination of Oppenheimer's perturbation theory [42], rearrangement collision theory [43] and the WKB approximation for tunneling [44]. If
one defines the resonance enhancement factor $R(E)$ as the ratio of the tunneling probability at energy level E of the barrier with the adsorbate to the probability for a clean surface, this factor can be used for correlating the details of
the total energy distribution with the features of the electronic interaction between the adsorbate atom and the metal surface.

As early as 1935 Gurney [45] has proposed a quantum-mechanical picture
of the change of a sharp energy level in an atom to a broad band of width Γ
when the atom interacts with the metal (fig. 2). Concomitant with the lifetime
broadening of the state is a shift ΔE of the center of the band. The derivation
of these parameters has been the aim of several theoretical studies [46,47], as

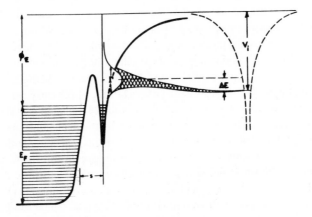

Fig. 2. The ground level of an atom approaching the surface to an adsorbed state broadens to a width Γ and shifts by ΔE. Adapted from ref. [15].

this information is needed for the calculation of the effective charge on the adsorbate atom, its dipole moment, and its binding energy. It is thus a worthwhile endeavor to measure Γ and ΔE directly from experimental TED data.

A general interpretation of the details of the TED in terms of atomic energy levels of the adsorbate is dependent upon a proper elimination of the nonresonant enhancement due to the potential well of the adsorbate. The latter contribution in effect shifts and deforms the TED peaks asymmetrically in a still quite uncertain way. Plummer and Young [48] have numerically calculated what the TED will look like with an adsorbate having an atomic band 0.4 eV below the Fermi level, assuming band widths Γ between 0.28 and 0.72 eV. The hump in the distribution disappears at $\Gamma > 0.7$ eV, and this explains why no peaks in the TED should be expected for adsorbed alkali metals whose s-bands will be wider than 1 eV. However, even if the center of the band is one eV above or below the Fermi surface, it can still affect the logarithmic shape of the TED or its half width. Narrow states can be expected when either the adsorbate is farther removed from the surface, thereby decreasing the lifetime broadening, or when higher angular momentum states like d-bands are present within the narrow energy range accessible to TED. Clark and Young [49] find that a strontium atom on an oxygen covered tungsten emitter caused a current density increase accompanied by an increase in the log slope of TED, which must be due to a wide band above the Fermi level. By studying the log slope of

TED of zirconium and of x-nitrogen adsorbed on tungsten planes of different
work functions the atomic band of the adsorbate can be roughly localized [50].

New TED measurements were made by Plummer and Young [48], using a
precisely constructed retarding potential tube and recording directly the TED
by ac-modulating the tip voltage and recording the ac component in the collector current. The experimental resonance enhancement factor is obtained by
comparing the measured adsorbate TED with that of the clean substance.

The single adatom through which the resonance emission is measured occu-
pies only a small fraction of the area covered by the probe hole, so that the experimental enhancement factor is much smaller than the one predicted by the
theory. This uncertainty is not serious as the sought for information on the
TED shape is still preserved in the resonance peaks. The most promising data
have been taken by Plummer and Young for barium on tungsten (fig. 3a, b).
On various crystal planes three resonance peaks appear which can be assigned
to atomic levels of the adsorbate. A free barium atom has a $6s^2$ ground state
5.2 eV below the vacuum level (ionization potential). The lowest excited
states are a triplet ^3D 6s 5d state between -4.02 and -4.09 eV and a singlet
^1D 6s 5d state at -3.80 eV. The $6s^2$ ground states will be strongly broadened
and shifted upon adsorption, while the 6s 5d levels may not be affected too
much (fig. 4). This is exactly seen in the resonance enhancement factors derived from the TED of low work function substrate planes. On regions with

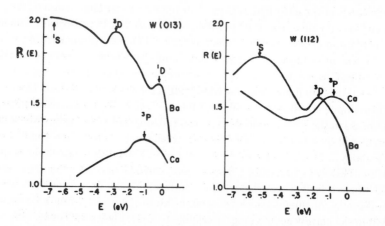

Fig. 3. Experimental resonance enhancement factor $R(E)$ in the total energy distribution
upon adsorption of Ba and Ca on the (013) plane of tungsten (a) and on the (112) plane
(b). From ref. [48].

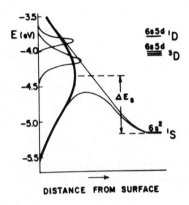

Fig. 4. Shift of the three lowest energy levels of Ba by adsorption on tungsten. From ref. [48].

higher work functions the sharp d levels disappear as they shift above the Fermi level, leaving only the broadened $6s^2$ atomic level recognizable. Finer details about the dependence of the shift upon local field strength and the adsorption site, which determines the distance of the adatom from the surface, are being discussed by the investigators.

The atomic levels in adsorbed strontium and calcium are not so favorably located with respect to the Fermi surface to fall into the narrow region of the accessible TED band, but some general resonance effects of the ground states can still be seen.

The general interpretation of anomalous shapes of TED in the emission through adsorbates in terms of atomic energy levels cannot be done by resonance effects alone. Particularly in large adsorbed molecules the tunneling electrons may be scattered inelastically be exciting a vibrational level of frequency ν. Instead of tunneling near the Fermi level, the electrons appear at a level lower by the amount $h\nu$ (fig. 5). This energy loss as seen in a displaced new peak of the TED can be directly correlated to an optically known frequency of the adsorbate. Swanson and Crouser [51] have measured TED of field emission through phthalocyanine (fig. 6) and carbon monoxide (fig. 7) both adsorbed on molybdenum. Several new peaks appear up to 1 eV below the one of the clean surface, way below the ordinary band width accessible to TED.

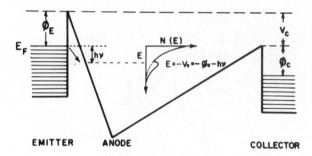

Fig. 5. Energy loss due to vibrational exictation of an adsorbate, as seen in the total energy distribution. From ref. [51].

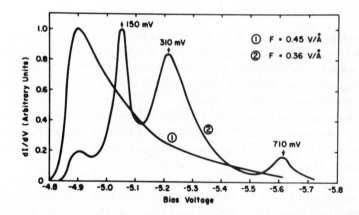

Fig. 6. TED of a clean molybdenum surface at a field of 0.45 V/Å, and of adsorbed phthalocyanine at 0.36 V/Å according to Swanson and Crouser.

The new peaks are particularly pronounced with phthalocyanine where some of them are also found to be strongly field dependent. Both features are due to the large size of the molecule, some sections of which are farther removed from the metal surface.

The peaks, obviously replaying the shape of the primary Fermi level peak

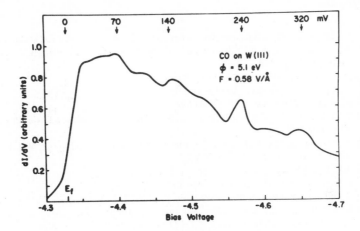

Fig. 7. TED of the (111) plane tungsten with adsorbed CO. Ref. [52].

of the clean metal, are located between 130 and 950 meV, six of them in close coincidence with infrared optical levels. On (011) of tungsten a peak was also found 950 meV above the Fermi level, which indicates an Auger excited state.

The TED peaks of CO on tungsten again indicate inelastic scattering due to excitation of molecular levels. The small size of the molecule causes the absence of field shifts. Major peaks are located at 70, 140, 240 and 320 meV below the Fermi level, and these agree with low energy electron scattering data obtained by Probst [52] and approximately with the first vibrational level of the free molecule at 270 meV.

From the above results it is evident that the interpretation of the fine structure of field emission TED is a difficult task. Three different effects may be superimposed, the band structure of the substrate, resonance tunneling, and vibrational excitation, but as in some cases these three effects can be separated, the method is certainly capable of giving new and detailed information on the electronic features of adsorption on metals.

The author wishes to express his appreciation to Drs. L.Crouser, J.W.Gadzuk, E.W.Plummer, L.W.Swanson and R.D.Young for their permission to use some of their unpublished results.

References

[1] R.H.Fowler and L.Nordheim, Proc. Roy. Soc. (London) Ser. A 119 (1928) 173.

[2] R.H.Good Jr. and E.W.Müller, Handbuch der Physik, Vol. 21 (Springer Verlag, Berlin, 1956) p. 179.

[3] R.D.Young, Phys. Rev. 113 (1959) 110.

[4] W.Harrison, Phys. Rev. 129 (1963) 2503.

[5] R.Stratton, Phys. Rev. 135 (1964) 794.

[6] F.I.Itskovich, Zh. Eksperim, Teor. Fiz. 50 (1966) 1425, transl. in Soviet Phys. JETP 23 (1966) 945.

[7] W.P.Dyke and W.W.Dolan, Adv. in: Electronics and Electron Physics, Vol. 8 (Academic Press, New York, 1956) p. 89.

[8] A.G.J.van Oostrum, Diss. Univ. of Amsterdam (1965).

[9] E.W.Müller, Zeit. Physik 120 (1943) 261.

[10] R.D.Young and E.W.Müller, Phys. Rev. 113 (1959) 115.

[11] R.D.Young and C.E.Kuyatt, Rev. Sci. Instr. 39 (1968) 1477.

[12] P.H.Cutler and D.Nagy, Surface Sci. 3 (1965) 71.

[13] L.W.Swanson and L.C.Crouser, Phys. Rev. Letters 16 (1966) 389.

[14] L.W.Swanson and L.C.Crouser, Phys. Rev. Letters 19 (1967) 1179.

[15] J.W.Gadzuk, Phys. Rev. 182 (1969) 416.

[16] D.Nagy and P.H.Cutler, Phys. Rev. 186 (1969) 651.

[17] E.W.Müller, Zeit. Physik 106 (1937) 541.

[18] E.W.Müller, Zeit. Physik 108 (1938) 668.

[19] E.W.Müller, Zeit. Physik 120 (1943) 270

[20] E.W.Müller, Zeit. Elektrochem. 59 (1955) 372.

[21] E.W.Müller, Phys. Rev. 102 (1956) 618.

[22] E.C.Cooper and E.W.Müller, Rev. Sci. Instr. 29 (1958) 309.

[23] E.W.Müller, Ergebn. Exakten Natwiss. 27 (1953) 290.

[24] E.W.Müller, J. Appl. Phys. 26 (1955) 732.

[25] R.D.Young and E.W.Müller, J. Appl. Phys. 33 (1962) 91.

[26] R.D.Young and H.E.Clark, Phys. Rev. Letters 17 (1966) 351.

[27] R.D.Young and H.E.Clark, Appl. Phys. Letters 9 (1966) 265.

[28] E.W.Müller, Zeit. Physik 126 (1949) 642.

[29] J.P.Barbour, F.M.Charbonnier, W.W.Dolan, W.P.Dyke, E.E.Martin and J.K.Trolan, Phys. Rev. 117 (1960) 1452.

[30] P.C.Bettler and G.Barnes, Surface Sci. 10 (1968) 165.

[31] R.E.Gretz, in: High Temperature-High Resolution Metallography, eds. H.I.Aaronson and G.A.Ansell (Gordon and Breach, New York, 1965).

[32] A.J.Melmed, J. Appl. Phys. 36 (1965) 3585.

[33] A.J.Melmed, J. Appl. Phys. 38 (1967) 1885.

[34] E.W.Müller, Naturwissenschaften 29 (1941) 533.

[35] R.Gomer, Field Emission and Field Ionization (Harvard University Press, Cambridge, Mass., 1961).

[36] G.Ehrlich and F.G.Hudda, J. Chem. Phys. 35 (1961) 1421.

[37] G.Ehrlich, Ann. Rev. Phys. Chem. 17 (1966) 295.

[38] C.Kohrt and R.Gomer, J. Chem. Phys. 48 (1968) 3338.

[39] L.Schmidt and R.Gomer, J. Chem. Phys. 42 (1965) 3573.

[40] A.Bell and L.Swanson, Surface Sci. 10 (1968) 255.

[41] C.B.Duke and M.E.Alferieff, J. Chem. Phys. 46 (1967) 923.

[42] J.R.Oppenheimer, Phys. Rev. 31 (1928) 67.

[43] T.Y.Wu and T.Ohmura, Quantum Theory of Scattering (Prentice Hall, Englewood Clifts, N.J., 1962).

[44] E.Merzbacher, Quantum Mechanics (John Wiley and Sons, New York, 1961).

[45] R.W.Gurney, Phys. Rev. 47 (1935) 479.

[46] L.Schmidt and R.Gomer, J. Chem. Phys. 45 (1966) 1605.

[47] J.W.Gadzuk, Surface Sci. 6 (1967) 133.

[48] E.W.Plummer and R.D.Young, Phys. Rev. (March 1970).

[49] H.E.Clark and R.D.Young, Surface Sci. 12 (1968) 385.

[50] E.W.Plummer, J.W.Gadzuk and R.D.Young, Solid State Comm. 7 (1969) 487.

[51] L.Swanson and L.Crouser, Progress Report, Contract NAS-1516, November 1968.

[52] F.Probst, J. Vac. Sci. Techn. 4 (1966) 53.

PRINCIPLES OF FIELD ION MICROSCOPY

Erwin W.MÜLLER

Department of Physics, The Pennsylvania State University,
University Park, Pa. 16802, USA

1. Introduction

When the resolution of the point projection microscope was realized to be limited by the image spot size due to the lateral velocity component of the emitted particle and their de Broglie wavelength [1], it was clear that the FEM could never be improved to resolve atomic spacings. With electron emission from a degenerate Fermi gas both limiting factors are large and cannot be controlled. However, if the imaging could be done with positive ions originating from the specimen surface, the lateral energy component, equivalent to kT of the emitter, could be reduced at will by cooling, and the de Broglie wavelength of the ions is negligibly small. In order to make a field ion microscope work at a resolution down to atomic spacings, two basic problems must be solved: (1) Ions cannot be emitted from a specimen surface after being supplied by a mechanism similar to electron transport. Thus a new effect, field ionization of an externally supplied gas [2] had to be invoked. (2) The poor resolution of the FEM covers the quite amorphous structure of the first surface layer existing on the annealing end form on all but the low index planes. In order to make the radial projection principle work down to atomic dimensions, a superior surface polishing procedure was needed: Another new effect was conveniently discovered, field evaporation [3].

Switching from electron emission to ion emission in order to gain a factor of ten in resolution requires a ten fold increase of the applied field, between 200 and 600 million volts/cm, to a range that was experimentally totally inaccessible before.

2. Field ionization

The image gas is admitted to the microscope tube at a pressure of a few millitorrs, so that the ions originating at the tip can travel to the phosphor screen without being scattered by collisions. This condition severely limits the available image brightness, as in a steady state no more ions can flow away from the tip than are supplied to the tip by gas kinetic motion. Fortunately, due to the presence of the high field around the tip, the gas supply is some 10 to 100 fold enhanced [2] with respect to the ordinary gas kinetic arrival rate at pressure p as a result of the attraction of polarized gas molecules, having a polarizability α. The rate, calculated for an idealized spherical emitter [4] , is

$$Z = \frac{p}{(2\pi MkT)^{\frac{1}{2}}} \left(\frac{\pi\alpha F^2}{2kT}\right)^{\frac{1}{2}} . \tag{1}$$

A small mass M, a low gas temperature T, and a high field F all increase the supply. However, there is a new problem: Dipole attraction makes the image gas molecules impinge at the tip surface with a kinetic energy $\frac{1}{2}\alpha F^2$, equivalent to 0.15 eV at the typical operational condition of the FIM. While this small energy does usually not inflict any bombardment damage, it may have another effect: If the gas molecule is ionized after bouncing off the surface, a large fraction of the impact energy may appear in a lateral velocity component, thereby wrecking the resolution. Fortunately, the probability of field ionization as a tunnel effect depends upon the length of time the gas particle spends in the narrow ionization zone at the surface. A fast transversing gas molecule will rarely be ionized, but will rather be reflected from the surface. If its energy loss in this collision is greater than kT_{gas}, usually a few percent of its total energy ($\frac{3}{2}kT + \frac{1}{2}\alpha F^2$), it remains trapped in the field near the tip and returns to it in a series of hops of decreasing height until it is fully accommodated to the tip temerature [5] . Now its velocity is small, and it will be ionized when it passes through a region of high local field above a protruding surface atom. Repelled from the positive tip, the ion travels to the screen with little lateral velocity. The angular width of the ion bean coming from one surface atom may be as narrow as a few minutes of arc for a 1000 Å tip radius, thus giving sharp images on the screen 10 cm away (fig. 1). Fairly independent of tip radius one average image spot carries some 10^5 ions/sec, or a current of the order of 10^{-14} A. Up to 10^5 individual atom spots are seen on a tip of 1000 Å radius, as only one-fifth to one-tenth of all the surface atoms protrude enough to cause ionization.

Fig. 1. A platinum tip of approximately 1500 Å radius imaged with helium at 28000 V.

Field ionization occurs when an electron of the ground state of the image gas tunnels into the surface where the local field is sufficiently high. In the metal all states below the Fermi level are occupied, so field ionization is possible only beyond a critical distance $x_c = (I-\phi)/F$ where the ground level is above the Fermi level [6]. A surprise was the narrowness of the energy distribution of the ions as obtained by retarding potential analysis [7]. The zone of high ionization probability is located closely above a protruding surface atom, about 4 Å away from the electronic mirror surface, and in a disc only 0.2 Å thick, that is one tenth of the diameter of the helium atom. This is quite unexpected and cannot be derived from a calculation of tunneling probability using the WKB approximation. The sharp localization looks more like a hard collision. Indeed, Boudreaux and Cutler [8] have successfully applied re-arrangement collision theory to arrive at such a narrow energy distribution width of the emitted ions, but their results are given for the simplification of a hydrogen atom in front of a plane surface.

Primarily, field ionization is determined by the local field strength, enhanced by the various degree of protrusion of the imaged surface atom. This is measured quantitatively by Moore's computer model [9] which considers all surface atoms to be imaged whose centers are located within a spherical shell of thickness between 5 and 20% of the lattice parameter. A plot of atom dots computed for an fcc or a bcc lattice resembles quite well a field ion pattern, except that any chemical specificity is absent. In reality, there is a great difference in the appearance of various bcc metals such as W, Mo, Ta, Nb and Fe due to variations in regional brightness and emphasis of relative brightness at individual atom sites [10]. Such differences are somewhat less pronounced on patterns of fcc metals such as Ir, Pt, Pd, Ni, Co, Au and Cu, and on hcp metals such as Re, Ru, Hf, Zr, Co and Be. In comparing these micrographs we have to abstract from imperfect imaging of some metals due to their low lattice strength, which often makes them difficult to handle.

The required chemical specificity in the field ionization effect can be introduced by a closer consideration of the electronic interaction between the image gas and the surface atom. In the view of quantum mechanics the electronic transition probability P is given by the overlap of the wave function ψ_a of the image gas atom with the wavefunction ψ_s of the surface atom

$$P = \frac{4\pi^2}{h} N(E_s) |\langle \psi_s | V | \psi_a \rangle|^2 , \qquad (2)$$

where h is Planck's constant, $N(E_s)$ the density of surface states, and V the interaction potential [8]. These parameters are not yet explicitly available for the conditions of our experiments, and we can only make some guesses about the significance of the redistribution of electronic surface charge due to the crystallographic features of the surface and due to the surface polarization by the applied field. Gauss' law relates the two-dimensional surface charge density with the strength of the external field, and field penetration into the depth of the surface needs to be taken into account to obtain the effective surface field at the location of the ionizing image gas atom. Certainly, the local effective field is no more proportional to the externally applied voltage.

The concept of field ionization by overlapping of the wave functions of the surface atom and the image gas atom is supported by the consideration of directional orbitals extending from the surface atom. The idea of metal surface atoms projecting localized bonds has recently been increasingly applied to the interpretation of chemisorption and catalysis effects. In this view surface atoms have orbitals partially or fully occupied by electrons that emerge in spatial directions corresponding to those of the bonds to nearest and second nearest neighbors in the bulk lattice [11,12]. Adsorption is caused by the overlap of these dangling orbitals with atomic orbitals of the adsorbate. It is now proposed to see the process of field ionization in a similar way. The ioni-

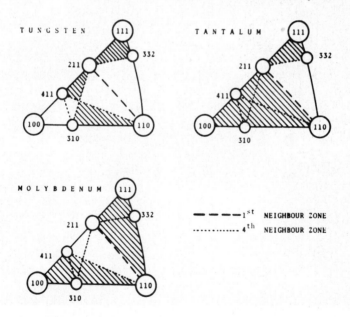

Fig. 2. Broken bonds map of the crystallographic triangle, adapted from ref. [14], and regions of greater brightness in patterns of W, Ta and Mo.

zation probabuity as expressed by the matrix elements of the wave functions and the interaction potential can now be looked at in greater detail by identifying effects of orbital direction [13]. These are primarily seen in the distribution of regional brightness of field ion patterns.

There are abrupt changes of brightness across certain zones even within one net plane edge where the degree of protrusion, as measured in Moore's thin shell model, does not vary. What does change, however, is the direction and number of nearest, next nearest and so on dangling bonds or, in other words, empty or partially occupied orbitals extending into space. These change abruptly as we cross contain zones whose axis is parallel to the bond vector. Purely phenomenologically Moore and Brandon [14] have recently mapped geometrical zones across which the number of internal bonds changes for the bcc and fcc lattices. If we compare these plots (fig. 2) with micrographs of W, Ta and Mo (fig. 3). It is evident that indeed some, but not all the 1st and 4th neighbor zones affect the regional brightness. The chemical specificity

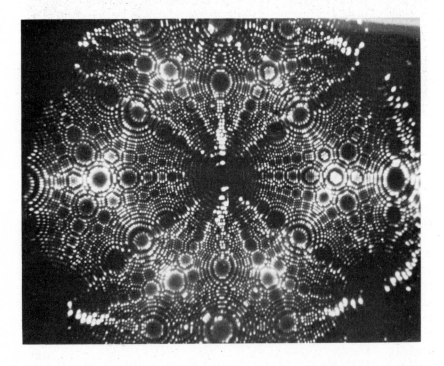

Fig. 3a. Helium field ion micrograph of W (011 in center).

Fig. 3b. Helium field ion micrograph of Ta in equal position (011 in center).

within one lattice type, particularly pronounced in the lower coordinated bcc lattice, must enter by the different degree of occupation of the conjugated orbitals extended away from the surface, and also by their hybridization.

The most direct indication of the effect of extended orbitals on field ionization probability is a feature at the vicinals of the basal plane of the hcp lattice. First found on rhenium [15] (fig. 4) and subsequently seen on cobalt [16], ruthenium [17], beryllium [18] and hafnium [19] is an alternation in visibility of the 60° sectors of the stacked (0001) net planes. By comparison with the threefold symmetry around the (111) poles of Pt one can conclude that the effect is due to the AB AB AB stacking of close packed planes in the hcp lattice. It must be the single nearest neighbor bond t_{2g} orbital with a large component normal to the surface that contributes most to the ionization, while the two sideways extending t_{2g} orbitals at the alternate (0001) plane edges are ineffective for field ionization.

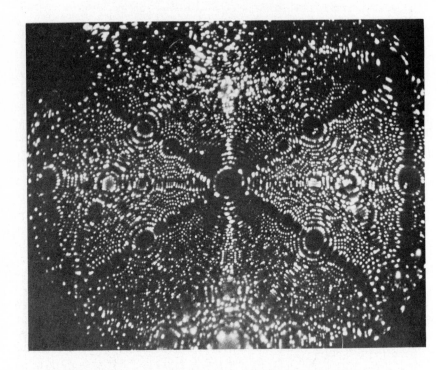

Fig. 3c. Helium field ion micrograph of Mo in equal position (011 in center).

One of the more conspicuous details of many field ion patterns are the rows of bright atom spots that decorate certain zones, notably the [100]-zone on tungsten, the [110] zone on platinum and iridium, and the [$2\bar{1}\bar{1}0$] zone of rhenium (fig. 4). These are single atoms adjacent to the net plane edge in a metastable position [20] where they obtain their extra binding energy required to withstand field evaporation in spite of their exposed location by the effect of field penetration and a subsequently strong polarization bonding $\frac{1}{2}\alpha F^2$. Viewed closely these decoration spots on hcp rhenium appear round when leaning on an invisible edge, and winged when they are attached to a strongly ionizing lattice step. As a comparison with a lattice model reveals, the winged decoration atoms at the latter sites have two, somewhat sideways directed t_{2g} orbitals extending, while the round decoration spots at the invisible edge have only one dangling t_{2g}, nearest neighbor orbital.

Fig. 4a. Basal plane region of rhenium with alternating brightnesses of A and B layers, and zone decorations.

Similarly, one can also see sideways satellites on the [100] zone decoration atoms on tungsten, due to the same nearest neighbor dangling bonds. Thus the field ionization probability reflects the spatially extended orbitals quite directly.

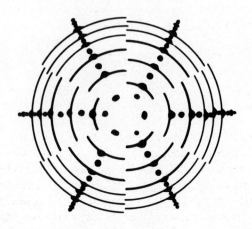

Fig. 4b. Schematic of brightness distribution around 0001 pole of rhenium.

3. Field evaporation

The surface atoms of any metal can be evaporated, in the form of positive ions, by the application of an electric field of sufficient magnitude. In field ion microscopy this effect is applied routinely in order to prepare the perfectly smooth surface of the specimen from a roughly etched tip [21]. The field evaporation polishing process is self regulating in that by applying a gradually increasing voltage the critical evaporation field is first reached at the sharp protrusions, and eventually removes surface atoms all over the tip cap when the field evaporation endform is reached. The image force theory of field evaporation as developed by Müller [3], refined by Gomer and Swanson [22], and more recently by Brandon [23] suggests that the metal ion is held to the surface until the field is large enough to reduce to essentially zero the potential barrier Q due to the image force attraction. To remove an n-fold charged ion from the surface, the required energy is the sum of the vaporization energy of the neutral atom, Λ, and the nth ionization energy I_n. When the n electrons are returned to the metal of work function ϕ, the energy $n\phi$ is gained. An additional binding term is due to polarization, $\frac{1}{2}\alpha F^2$, where α actually denotes the not well known difference of polarizability of the surface atom and the ion, $(\alpha_a - \alpha_i)$. The reduction of the image force bond by the applied field, the Schottky hump, is $(n^3 e^3 F)^{\frac{1}{2}}$. Thus, for $T = 0$, field evaporation occurs without activation at a field

$$F_o = n^{-3} e^{-3} (\Lambda + I_n - n\phi + \tfrac{1}{2} \alpha F^2)^2 . \tag{3}$$

As the energy terms amount to several eV, the evaporation field at the cryogenic temperatures usually applied in field ion microscopy is not much lower than F_o.

For a given metal the expected evaporation field F_o is a minimum for certain integer charges n, presumably either 1 or 2. Higher charges are conceivable and are indeed experimentally established by the atom-probe FIM [24], but cannot be predicted because of the unavailability of accurate data for the higher ionization potentials of most metals. Table 1 gives a list of the expected data adapted from Brandon [23] and a comparison with experimental results. The latter are essentially all based on Müller and Young's field calibration [25] obtained by taking the FN plot of field emission from the same tip, and are uncertain by about ± 10%. Nakamura [26] applied recently the same method to a number of metals, and other experimental data are simply estimates from the observed onset of field evaporation with respect to the imaging voltage needed with different gases. Here it is tacitly assumed that the ionization field for each gas is independent of the tip metal, which is not certain for the overlapping orbital model of field ionization.

The magnitude of the evaporation field with respect to the ionization field is one major factor which determines the applicability of field ion microscopy for a given metal. Obviously, stable images can only be obtained when the imaging field is lower than the evaporation field. As seen from table 1, only the highly refractory metals evaporate above 400 MV/cm, as required for helium ion imaging. By sacrificing in resolution, some metals can be imaged with neon [27,28] at fields down to 330 MV/cm, while hydrogen is the most useful gas when the admissible fields are in the 200 MV/cm range.

In the practice of field ion microscopy the onset of evaporation is not the only problem with the less refractory metals. All too often the mechanical stress $F^2/8\pi$ of the field, amounting to 1 ton/mm^2 at 475 MV/cm, proves to be destructive when the specimen yields to the shear component of the stress due to the inhomogenous field distribution over the tip cap and the shank. It was noticed early [21] that the presence of hydrogen may greatly reduce the evaporation field of the less refractory metals, and this effect can be profitably applied to prepare the final shape of specimens made of easily yielding metals under much lower stress conditions. Mass spectrometric analysis [29] of the

Table 1
Calculated and experimental evaporation fields.

Metal	F^+ (V/Å)	F^{++} (V/Å)	$F_{observed}$ (V/Å)
Be		3.84	3.40
B	6.48		
Al	1.61		2.20
Si		3.17	3.00
Ti		2.33	2.50
V		2.50	3.00
Cr		2.64	3.00
Fe		3.18	3.60
Co		3.49	3.70
Ni		3.30	3.60
Cu	3.08		3.00
Zn	2.87		3.20
Ge		2.73	
Zr		2.84	3.50
Nb		3.48	4.00
Mo		4.52	4.50
Ru		3.66	4.50
Rh		4.07	4.50
Pd	3.63		
Ag	2.31		
Sn	2.24		
Ta		4.60	4.90
W		5.50	5.70
Re		4.34	5.00
Os		4.82	
Ir		5.03	5.10
Pt		4.42	4.75
Au	4.02		3.50

field evaporation products under the operational conditions of the FIM reveals the formation of metal hydride ions which have lower binding energy than the pure metal atoms.

4. Surface charge redistribution

Hydrogen also has a surprising effect on the field ionization of helium. Normally the field required for the ionization of helium is 450 MV/cm, but when a small quantity of hydrogen is added a very bright and well resolved helium ion image is obtained [30] at only 300 MV/cm. This seems to be effective with several metals [31] and is of practical use as it allows imaging of metals with a low cohesion energy at a much reduced field stress. Niobium [10], iron [30], cobalt [16], nickel [30] and even gold [32] have given well structured images previously unattainable. The explanation for this surprising effect is a transfer of electronic charge from the protruding metal atom to an adjacently adsorbed hydrogen atom forming a hydride like bond [33]. Only on those crystallographic regions where the interstices can accommodate the negative hydride ion of 1.3 Å radius is field ionization effectively promoted. The local charge density in the metal atoms, and by Gauss' law the field above those atoms, is now at 300 MV/cm externally applied field as large as it would be at 450 MV/cm without the hydrogen.

Redistribution of surface charge, although to a lesser degree, must also be the reason for the anomalous imaging of the constituents of alloys. In ordered alloys, such as Pt-Co or Pt_3-Co the location of one atomic species with respect to the other is known from the superlattice structure. The interpretation of the net plane configuration of these alloys is only possible by assuming that under the conditions of the applied field the Pt surface atoms carry a higher positive charge than the Co atoms. As a result, the latter remain invisible [34]. Quite complex situations exist in the case of chemisorption of electro-negative gases. Most of the adsorbate disappears from the surface when the field is applied after adsorption without field has been allowed to take place. With carbon monoxide, nitrogen and oxygen admitted, a number of bright atom spots remain at the fully applied imaging field which have been variously interpreted as representing the adsorbate molecules or atoms [35], or metal atoms displaced to a more protuberant position [36], with the adsorbate already removed by field desorption. A more likely explanation might be that the bright spots represent highly positive charged metal atoms, possibly displaced, which have an invisible electronegative adsorbate attached, into which they have drained some of their electronic charge [37].

In the above discussion of the field ionization process we have involved various mechanisms such as simple linear tunneling into the metal, the directional orbital overlapping of wave functions, and the concept of local field enhancement by surface charge rearrangement. Actually all of these processes are closely related, and it is nothing but our inability to express the wavefunctions of the surface states in a unified way that forces us to use the various schemes that are most suitable for the description of particular situations.

References

[1] E.W.Müller, Z. Physik 120 (1943) 270.
[2] E.W.Müller, Z. Physik 131 (1951) 136.
[3] E.W.Müller, Phys. Rev. 102 (1956) 618.
[4] M.J.Southon, Ph. D. Thesis, Cambridge University (1963).
[5] E.W.Müller, J. Appl. Phys. 27 (1956) 474.
[6] M.G.Inghram and R.Gomer, Zeit. Naturforsch. 10a (1955) 863.
[7] T.T.Tsong and E.W.Müller, J. Chem. Phys. 41 (1964) 3279.
[8] D.S.Boudreaux and P.H.Cutler, Surface Sci. 5 (1966) 230.
[9] A.J.W.Moore, J. Phys. Chem. Solids 23 (1962) 907.
[10] E.W.Müller, Science 149 (1965) 591.
[11] J.B.Goodenough, Magnetism and the Chemical Bond (Interscience, New York, 1963).
[12] G.C.Bond, Discuss. Faraday Soc. 41 (1966) 200.
[13] Z.Knor and E.W.Müller, Surface Sci. 10 (1968) 21.
[14] A.J.W.Moore and D.G.Brandon, Phil. Mag. 17 (1968) 679.
[15] E.W.Müller, Proc. Third European Regional Conference on Electron Microscopy, Prague, 1964, Vol. 1, p. 161.
[16] O.Nishikawa and E.W.Müller, J. Appl. Phys. 38 (1967) 3159.
[17] A.J.Melmed and R.Klein, J. Less Common Metals 10 (1966) 225.
[18] J.A.Panitz, MS. Thesis, Pennsylvania State University (1966).
[19] T.Reisner and E.W.Müller, to be published in: Surface Sci. (1970).
[20] E.W.Müller, Surface Sci. 2 (1964) 484.
[21] E.W.Müller, in: Advances in Electronics and Electron Physics, Vol. 13 (Academic Press, New York, 1960) p. 83.
[22] R.Gomer and L.Swanson, J. Chem. Phys. 39 (1963) 2813.
[23] D.G.Brandon, Surface Sci. 3 (1965) 1.
[24] E.W.Müller, J.A.Panitz and S.B.McLane, Rev. Sci. Instr. 39 (1968) 83.
[25] E.W.Müller and R.D.Young, J. Appl. Phys. 32 (1961) 2425.
[26] S.Nakamura, J. Electron Microscopy (Japan) 15 (1966) 279.
[27] E.W.Müller, Ann. d. Physik 20 (1957) 315.
[28] O.Nishikawa and E.W.Müller, J. Appl. Phys. 35 (1964) 2806.
[29] D.F.Barofsky and E.W.Müller, Surface Sci. 10 (1968) 177.
[30] E.W.Müller, S.Nakamura, O.Nishikawa and S.B.McLane, J. Appl. Phys. 36 (1965) 2496.
[31] O.Nishikawa and E.W.Müller, Surface Sci. 12 (1968) 247.
[32] D.G.Ast and D.M.Seidman, Appl. Phys. Letters 13 (1968) 348.
[33] E.W.Müller, Surface Sci. 8 (1967) 462.
[34] T.T.Tsong and E.W.Müller, Appl. Phys. Letters 9 (1966) 7; J. Appl. Phys. 38 (1967) 545; J. Appl. Phys. 38 (1967) 3531.
[35] G.Ehrlich, Discuss. Faraday Soc. 41 (1966) 7.

[36] W.M.H.Sachtler and A.A.Holscher, Discuss. Faraday Soc. 41 (1966) 29.
[37] E.W.Müller, Quarterly Reviews (Chem. Soc., London) 23 (1969) 177.

APPLICATION OF FIELD ION MICROSCOPY

Erwin W.MÜLLER

Department of Physics, The Pennsylvania State University,
University Park, Pa. 16802, USA

1. Introduction

The field ion microscope (FIM) is basically a device for surface studies. While the capability of imaging the surface in atomic details alone would make it a useful tool for materials research, its utility is greatly enhanced by the possibility of dissecting a specimen atom by atom and layer by layer using controlled field evaporation. Thus, at least in principle, each atom in a bulk specimen can be recorded as the new surface is gradually moved through the original volume of the tip. In the following we will review briefly two applications to surface physics, and in more detail discuss the techniques and results in metallurgical investigations.

2. Surface binding and migration

In 1957 it was demonstrated [1] that experimentation with single atoms is feasible for instance by planting individual tungsten atoms onto the atomically perfect surface of a field evaporated tungsten tip, and mapping their evaporation fields in order to obtain the binding energy on a single net plane. It was also suggested to follow the surface migration of those adatoms during intermittant annealings. No new techniques were required when ten years later these experiments were actually carried out with the necessary fine greained data taking and a detailed discussion. The migration of an atom over its own lattice represents one of the most fundamental surface effects, as the diffusing particle probes the potential variations above the surface. Only the FIM gives the assurance that a well defined path is taken, and these measurements thus can provide the basis for the more complex processes of evaporation, condensation, and crystal growth. The most comprehensive experiments and interpretations were made by Ehrlich and his co-workers [2,3]. The diffusion coefficient is calculated from the probability of displacement by a random walk, $x^2 = 2Dt$, and complications due to the limited size of the net plane are taken into account. It is striking that the activation energy for surface migration of a tungsten atom on various planes increases in the order of $(112) < (123) < (011)$, in strong disagreement with the sequence $(011) < (112) \approx (123) < (103) < (111)$ calculated from a pairwise interaction theory [4]. Since two-body interaction is successful in the treatment of bulk properties, the deviation indicates an important effect of a rearrangement of the electronic surface structure.

To the same conclusion came Plummer and Rhodin [5] in their thorough investigation of binding energies of adatoms. Their experimental data are particularly useful as their extend through a series of atoms of the sixth period, Hf, Ta, W, Re, Os, Ir, Pt and Au on the four low index planes of tungsten and also include some data on Mo, Rh and Pd of the fifth period of the table of the elements. The authors use Pauling's [6] concept of a split of the d-bands into one band of diffuse, bonding wavefunctions, and another band representing localized, antibonding wavefunctions. They find the normalized bonding energy of the atoms with respect to tungsten to be an integral multiple of a bond by one d-electron, assuming 6 d-bonds for tungsten. The bonding number is thus seen as a surface valency, however, in some cases a change of the ground state of the atom's electronic configuration has to be assumed, and this change depends upon the substrate crystal plane. These concepts of surface binding look very promising, but of course there are still some problems in determining the relative field strengths of various crystal planes of the tungsten field evaporation end form, and the possibility that the presence of the image gas might have a larger effect than expected. Another remaining problem is the uncertainty of the charge of the field evaporated adatom, which probably will be available soon with the application of the atom-probe FIM [7]. As it is not known which charge an adatom assumes at the surface just before field evaporation, the evaporation fields cannot be expected to be proportional to the measured evaporation voltages, so that a great uncertainty remains in the interpretation of Plummer and Rhodin's data.

3. Lattice defects

3.1. *Vacancies*

The FIM is still the only instrument that shows point defects directly and can thus reach beyond the range of transmission electron microscopy. In principle individual vacancies, interstitials and impurity atoms can be seen in their locations, and their density and their spatial distribution throughout the bulk can be determined by controlled field evaporation [8,9].

The first determination of the vacancy concentration in a Pt tip quenched from near the melting point gave a satisfactory result [10]. By controlled field evaporation 72 successive (012) layers were inspected, containing a total of 8500 atoms and 5 vacancies. In a frozen-in equilibrium, the vacancy concentration should be

$$c = e^{-E_f/kT} , \tag{1}$$

where E_f is the energy of formation and T the specimen temperature before quenching. The above data give a reasonable formation energy of 1.15 eV. This result, however, became questionable when Speicher et al. [11] found much higher vacancy concentrations, up to 2%, in long field evaporation sequences on the (012) plane of well annealed platinum. This suggests that their vacancies are artifacts possibly due to random field evaporation, a point of view supported by Fortes and Ralph [12], when they found no significant difference in vacancy counts in annealed iridium and in iridium specimens that had been neutron irradiated with 10^{14} to 10^{17} nvt, the defect concentration being about 2×10^{-4} when counted on the (011) plane, and five times higher on higher index planes. As the binding energy of an atom inside a high index plane is not much higher than at the edge, field evaporation from the edge only is not assured. An accurate calculation of the small difference in binding energy is presently not possible because of the limitation of the pairwise binding concept and the uncertainty of the magnitude of the contribution of the polarization in the field.

In a recent resumption of vacancy counting Chun [13] found again concentrations as high as 1.08% in annealed platinum. However, when the image gas was removed for each field evaporation step, a quite tedious procedure, the vacancy concentration in annealed Pt was 19 among 17 258 counted atoms, that is 1.1×10^{-3}. This is still in the range of what would be expected from quenched material, but it definitely shows that the artifacts are due to the image gas or its contaminants. This interpretation is supported by the observation of ample artifact vacancies (fig. 1) when 1% hydrogen is admitted to the image gas [14,15], and by the atom-probe results which show the frequent field evaporation of metal atoms in the form of metal-hydride ions [16], even when hydrogen is present in the 10^{-8} torr range only. Since hydrogen is a constituent of the residual gas in almost any FIM design, it is evident that special precautions must be taken before a successful vacancy count can be performed.

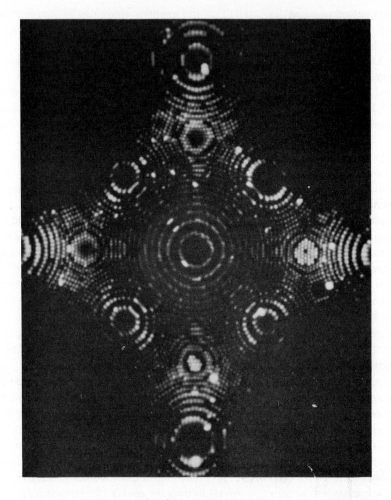

Fig. 1. Artifact vacancies on the {012}planes of iridium due to preferred field evaporation
in the presence of hydrogen.

By field evaporating in vacuum, and using an active getter, it should be possible
to obtain reliable data.

One of the practical problems is the large number of micrographs that
must be taken and carefully inspected. Attardo and Galligan [17], in observing neutron irradiated tungsten specimens, checked 8×10^5 atomic sites, so

that concentrations below 10^{-5} could be observed. Although the atom-probe FIM also indicates the occurrence of tungsten hydride molecular ions as field evaporation products, Attardo and Galligan did not observe unusually high vacancy concentrations. What they did obtain was in agreement with a formation energy of 3.3 eV.

3.2. Interstitials

While the problem with vacancies is their possible origin as artifacts, in the case of interstitials it is the imaging mechanism that poses an equally difficult question. Irradiation experiments [8] leave little doubt that interstitials can be seen as extra bright spots superimposed to the normal FIM pattern. Interstitials can be generated in situ when the tip is held at liquid hydrogen temperature and is then bombarded with α-particles or with other positive ions or neutrals of sufficient energy [18,19]. In these bombardment experiments the surface acts as a sink for mobile interstitials or for focussing collision sequences, so that the number of interstitials visible in the surface is a good fraction of all defects generated in the entire tip volume. Subsequent isothermal or isochronal annealing of the tip makes more interstitials appear at the surface, so that a direct indication of the nature of the lattice defect mobile in certain stages is obtained. In tungsten, the arrival rate at the surface is large in the 80 to 90°K range, while some subsurface interstitials already come out at 21°K. Similar results were recently found by Petroff and Washburn [20] who bombarded iridium tips at 5°K with 10 MeV protons from the Berkeley 88″ cyclotron. Stage I recovery by annealing between 14°K and 40°K resulted in a 60% decrease of the interstitial concentration.

By the presently used methods it is not possible to discriminate between self-interstitials and impurities. Both appear as randomly distributed bright spots. An unknown impurity was observed in rhodium [8]. It could not be identified as oxygen as the concentration was found to be independent of pre-annealing of the tip wire material in either ultra high vacuum or in air. Definite oxygen interstitials can be obtained by in-situ annealing of tantalum tips [21] at temperatures above 600°K, where rapid diffusion is taking place. The activation energy for diffusion is 1.1 eV. By 120 hr in-situ annealing at a temperature as low as 360°K one can associate 15% of the impurity atoms to form di-interstitials, indicating the attractive force between two interstitials. In tantalum single oxygen interstitials are not seen in the (011) to (031) region, while they show up clearly in the (011)–(121)–(111) triangle (fig. 2). This may indicate the location of the interstitial between two atoms at a cube edge.

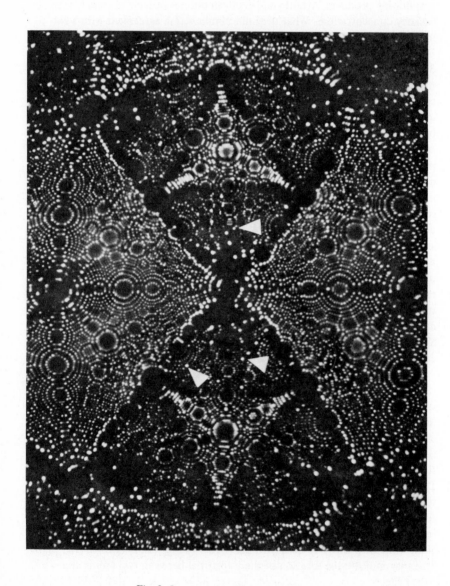

Fig. 2. Oxygen interstitials in tantalum.

The imaging mechanism of interstitials is still a matter of conjecture. Originally it was thought [8] that the interstitial in a location immediately underneath the surface would bulge out the regular lattice array to relax the strain. However, this would affect several of the top atoms and should produce an oblong image spot on a net plane with a definite row structure such as (112) on tungsten. Instead, a self interstitial as well as an impurity always appears as a round spot, indicating an effect upon only one surface atom. As we are now inclined to see enhanced local field ionization caused by an electronic charge rearrangement which not necessarily requires a geometrical protrusion, it apprears more likely that the atom above the intersitial assumes a higher positive charge, or empties an extending orbital, when it has to supply a bonding electron to the extra atom below. This mechanism should be particularly effective when the impurity interstitial has an electronegative character.

3.3. Dislocations

The most important crystal defects are dislocations, as they are the cause of the low critical shear stress of metals. The easy motion of dislocations through the lattice may remove these defects from the small volume of the FIM specimen through the stress $F^2/8\pi$ excerted by the field. Moreover, since the imaged area is of the order of 10^{-10} cm^2 only, the probability of finding a dislocation is not very great anyway in annealed materials with a typical dislocation density of 10^8/cm^2. When specimens with a high dislocation density are used, such as coldworked metals, there are considerable interactions between the dislocations to form networks that remain stable under the field stress. This outward directed stress, amounting to 1 ton/mm^2 at 475 MV/cm is by no means hydrostatic. Rather large shear components are developed as the field distribution over the tip is very anisotropic. As a result of these complications, the dislocations seen in the FIM often have a rather complex structure, or develop one when the dislocation line is followed into the depth of the specimen by continued field evaporation. The geometrical conditions given by the intersection of a dislocation with the surface of an FIM tip have been analyzed by Ranganathan [22]. The dislocation line is described by a vector N, the Burgers vector of the dislocation is b, and the net plane normal is the vector g of length $1/d_{hkl}$, where d is the net plane spacing. Ranganathan considers two cases defined by the dot products of the vectors:

$$N \cdot g \neq 0 , \qquad g \cdot b = 0 \qquad (2)$$

and

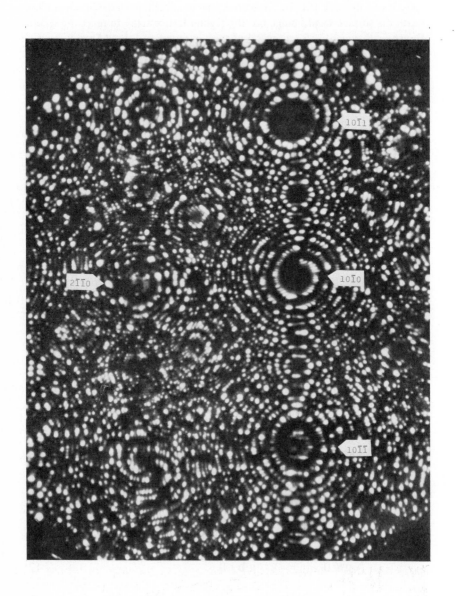

Fig. 3. Spirals due to dislocations in hcp hafnium.

$$N \cdot g \neq 0 , \qquad g \cdot b \neq 0 \qquad\qquad (3)$$

In both cases the first condition excludes a dislocation lying in the plane. The condition $g \cdot b = 0$ makes the Burgers vector lying in the plane and the net planes would close in themselves, making the dislocation nearly invisible. If $g \cdot b \neq 0$, the net plane edges will not form closed rings but rather appear as spirals. These are single leaved for $g \cdot b = 1$, double leaved for $g \cdot b = 2$, and so on. Sanwald et al. [23] have applied computer simulation to display such structures, and corresponding single and double spirals are indeed found quite often in real micrographs (fig. 3). It should be noted that the occurence of a spiral structure does not imply a screw character of the dislocation.

The information on single dislocations obtained so far from field ion microscopy does not go beyond of what can be deduced from transmission electron microscopy; in fact the latter's larger specimen size causes fewer dislocations to slip out of the specimen before they can be detected. The definite advantage of atomic resolution field ion microscopy is the more detailed display of the many complex sessile and crossover structures that result from interactions of dislocations. This difficult subject has not yet been studied in detail. The hope that the core structure of the dislocation may be accessible to field ion microscopical inspection is somewhat frustrated by the occurrence of preferred field evaporation in the critical area due to the reduced coordination of the atoms. Field evaporation may produce an "etch pit" of a few atom spacings diameter, and the ensuing contrast conditions are difficult to interprete at the present time.

3.4. Stacking faults

A perfect dislocation can dissociate into partial dislocations separated by stacking faults in order to lower the energy of the system. Transmission electron microscopy has been very successful in showing stacking faults [24], but as the fault width may be narrower than the about 100 Å width of a dislocation interference fringe, the field ion microscopical observation has its place here as well. Ranganathan [22] has discussed the geometrical aspects of stacking faults and the contrast that may appear in an FIM pattern. So far, however, actual observations, particularly in bcc metals have been scanty, and a method for deriving the stacking fault energy is yet to be developed. Ryan and Suiter [25] have interpreted a crossover structure in tungsten as being due to stacking faults. More frequently, dissociated dislocations separated by a few atomic layers, and also wide stacking faults have been seen in fcc metals [26]. Particularly clear are the observations of Nishikawa and Müller [27] on

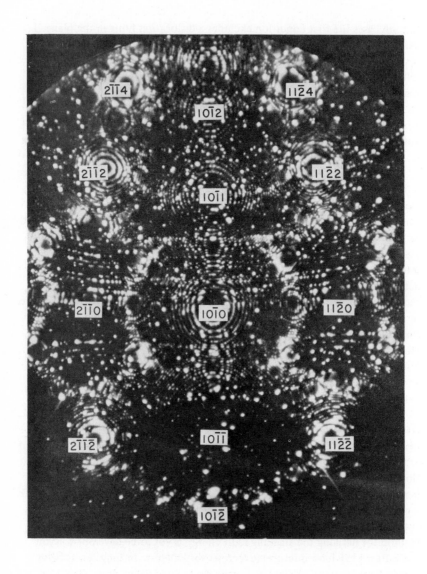

Fig. 4. Stacking faults in hcp cobalt.

the fcc and hcp phases of cobalt. While the stacking fault density in the fcc crystal is so small that only a few faults appear in the limited field of view, the density in the hcp phase is very high and varying in different sections of the image (fig. 4).

A complex planar defect of a still unknown configuration causes the appearance of bright image streaks to which particular attention was given by Brandon and Ralph [28] in their study of tungsten-rhenium alloys. In the opinion of the present author these streaks are artifacts, produced inadvertedly by coldworking the tip during an inappropriate electropolishing procedure, and grossly distorted in the imaging process due to crossover of the ion's trajectories.

3.5. Grain boundaries

In well annealed tip materials the grains are too large for making it probable for a grain boundary to appear within the small field of view. Preferential chemical attack during tip etching and a good chance of rupturing the tip by the field stress contribute further to the lack of good examples of what may be called in this context intrinsic grain boundaries. However, the occurrence of two or more crystallites in the field of view can be forced by a proper coldworking and annealing procedure. From field ion micrographs the relative misorientation of the two crystals is obtained with an accuracy of ± 2 degrees. For low-angle boundaries the dislocation model as reviewed and rigorously treated by Amelinckx and Dekeyser [29] is confirmed with the interpretation of field ion micrographs by Ranganathan [22], although the analysis of the component dislocations from the small sections of interlocked and interleaved spirals is usually not possible. Coherent twin boundaries with the (111) twin plane have been observed in iridium [30], and a non coherent twin with good atomic matching has been analyzed by Hren [31].

The particular value of high resolution field ion microscopy in grain boundary studies lies in the demonstration of a very close atomic fit of the two crystals even in the case of high-angle boundaries as predicted earlier [29]. Usually a narrow dark band of one atomic spacing width, showing alternating straight sections and jogs, represents the boundary (fig. 5). Brandon et al. [32] have worked out a new model for a high angle boundary by demonstrating that two crystallites, related by an angular rotation about an axis, have certain common sites that are located on a lattice of larger cell dimensions, called the coincidence site lattice. An arbitrary grain boundary will follow this lattice by forming a special boundary, and will then be accommodated by a stepped structure in order to maximize the surface area of the special boundary of lowest energy. Ranganathan [33] has worked out the possible combinations for the cubic system of axis-angle pairs and the corresponding coincidence lattices.

Fig. 5. Grain boundary in tungsten, going parallel to the [011] tip axis and matching a
(100) plane of the left crystal with a (334) plane of the right crystal.

The study of physical properties of grain boundaries with the help of the FIM is still in its early stages. Piling up of dislocations, segregation of impurities, diffusion along grain boundaries, and their effect on radiation damage density have all been observed in an exploratory manner but need more attention to details. The same is true for phase boundaries in systems with precipitates as observed with nickel-beryllium and with iron-carbon alloys [34].

Within the frame of this brief review we cannot dwell at any length with the considerable amount of work that has been spent on the experimentation with ordered alloys and their domain boundaries. The interpretation given by Southworth and Ralph [35], based on the preferred field evaporation of cobalt, as well as by Tsong and Müller [36], based on the invisibility of cobalt, is still controversial.

4. Special field ion microscopical techniques

With the achievement of a broad, if still incomplete understanding of the problems of imaging various lattice defects it may now be appropriate to recount a number of special techniques that are useful or promising in materials research.

The opportunities offered by field ion microscopy in radiation damage studies beyond the investigation of point defects already mentioned are most promising in the elucidation of vacancy clusters which are still below the reach of transmission microscopy. The most attractive technique is in-situ irradiation with slow ions, representing the effect of cathode sputtering [8], with medium energy neutral helium atoms obtained by charge exchange in the image gas [19], and with high energy alpha-particles [18] or protons from an accelerator [20]. Neutron irradiation [22a,37] as well as fission fragment bombardment [38] cannot very well be performed in-situ, and are therefore subject to a considerable loss of information due to defect annealing at room temperature. Nevertheless, the large clusters of defects which are of interest in engineering materials are profitably observed.

The controlled introduction of lattice defects by mechanical deformation can be achieved by various in-situ experiments. When the tip is subjected to the field stress at elevated temperature, crystallographically distinct region begin to glide and slip bands appear. These defects should be confined to the surface if they were caused by simple glide of dislocations to the surface. Actually, subsequent field evaporation reveals a quite complex defect pattern reaching deep into the interior of the specimen [26]. The field stress may be applied cyclically by superimposing a half wave ac component over the dc image voltage. The gradual development with time of fatigue cracks can thus be observed [26]. FIM tips may also be subjected to mechanical deformation by touching them in-situ with a known force by a contact plate made of various hard or soft materials [39,40]. Thereby the typical lattice deformations responsible for the behavior of contacts, for the elementary process of dry friction, and coldwelding become accessible. Large thermal stresses can be imposed on a specimen by heating the tip with a focussed, Q-spoiled laser beam [34,41]. Within a few nanoseconds the tip can be heated to near its melting point, and the self quenching by heat conduction through the tip shank after termination of the laser pulse is almost as fast. Thus a large activation energy is provided, while the short duration of the heat pulse prevents the diffusion of the defects to a large distance.

5. The atom-probe FIM

Image interpretation is often limited by the inability of identifying the chemical nature of an individual image spot or of a selected region. The size or brightness is no indication of the identity, as even on a pure, single metal specimen the image spots cover a wide range, making it impossible to unambiguously recognize single foreign atoms or constituents of an alloy by their appearance. The new atom-probe FIM [42,43], which combines a conventional FIM with a mass spectrometer of single particle sensitivity, might well provide the answer to many open questions in field ion microscopy, and, being the most sensitive microanalytical tool that can be imagined, might open significant avenues of analytical research in metallurgy at the atomic level.

The new device (fig. 6) consists of an FIM in which the tip can be moved to point the image of one atom or a small part of the surface onto a probe hole in the screen. Behind the probe hole follows the mass spectrometer section, most conveniently a time-of-flight system consisting of a one to two meter long drift tube, an electron multiplier detector capable of signaling a single ion impact event, and an oscilloscope for recording the time-of-flight. When the operator has selected an atom spot of interest, he superimposes a 2 to 20 nanosecond high voltage pulse over the dc image voltage in order to field evaporate the target atom, together with some others. The selected atom, in the form of a multiply charged ion, travels through the probe hole and the drift tube over a path of length l for the measurement of the flight time t. As the kinetic energy of the particle equals its charge ne times the sum of the applied voltages, the identifying mass-to-charge ratio m/n can be calculated:

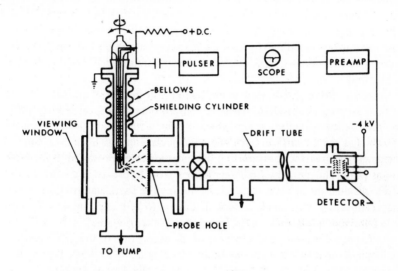

Fig. 6. Atom-probe FIM.

$$\frac{m}{n} = \frac{2e}{l^2} (V_{dc} + V_{pulse}) \, t^2 \, .$$

(4)

With our present system we obtain a mass resolution of ± 0.2 amu in the middle of the mass range. This accuracy is possible in spite of difficulties of measuring the exact pulse voltage at the tip, which is not equal to the applied pulse because of a reflection in the unterminated pulse transmission line, and of possible time delays in the triggering of the oscilloscope, by calibrating [44] the instrument with multiply charged ions from single isotope metals pulsed in ultra high vacuum.

The use of the atom-probe is still in its early stages. After it had been introduced by the present author [42], a slightly modified instrument has been built by Brenner and McKinney [45], and another very simple system without the provision of tip motion has been devised by Southon and Turner [46]. The first significant result is the occurrence of three and even fourfold charged ions as field evaporation products of tungsten, tantalum, rhenium and molybdenum, and of triply and doubly charged ions of iridium, platinum and iron. The cause for the unexpectedly high charges is not yet understood as the lack of data for the higher ionization potentials of the refractory metals as well as the complicated electronic conditions at the surface prevents the application of a simple theory. Partial tunneling of the ions [47] may be involved. The very high charges appear more abundantly when extremely high evaporation rates are enforced by large pulses. We have evaporated 10 atomic layers within one nanosecond, which equals an evaporation rate of 3 meters of metal per second.

Another, although not quite unexpected result in view of our earlier analysis of field evaporation products by more conventional mass spectrometry [48], is the occurrence of molecular ions when oxygen, water vapor, or hydrogen are adsorbed at the tip surface. Such metal-molecular ions originate even from seemingly clean surfaces, supporting the long suspected notion of "invisible" atoms [49]. The metal hydride ions formed from hydrogen as a constituent of the residual gas of most vacuum systems require particular attention when mass calibrations with single isotope metals are to be made, and may also affect data obtained in quantitative field evaporation experiments.

Unexpected was also the discovery of the adsorption of the image gases helium and neon [49,50] at temperatures as high as $78°K$. While the van der Waals adsorption energy of these noble gases on metals is of the order of 0.015 to 0.030 eV only, the electric field causes the adsorption with the polarization energy $\alpha F^2/2$, which at normal image conditions is 10 times the van der Waals binding energy and is sufficient to cover the FIM tip with a monolayer of a noble gas adsorbate. These atoms are invisible as they carry little positive charge, are mobile, and constantly interchange with newly impinging image gas atoms. Their effect on field evaporation is not negligible. They cannot be field desorbed without the simultaneous field evaporation of an adjacent metal atom. Often the two remain together as a molecular ion, at least for the time needed to travel through the acceleration region near the tip, so that they can be identified as molecule ions such as $RhHe^{++}$, $RhHe_2^{++}$, $RhHeH^{++}$, $RhHeH_2^{++}$ and similar ones with tungsten.

These results, of great interest for the consideration of surface processes, but also indicating the complicated situation at field ion emitters in the presence of the image gas, do not seriously affect the utility of the instrument as a research tool for the atom by atom analysis of surfaces. The nature of adsorbates, the existence of invisible constituents of the surface, the distribution of solutes and the composition of precipitates in alloys are just some of the problems that can now be solved with the application of the atom-probe FIM.

References

[1] E.W.Müller, Z. Elektrochem. 61 (1957) 43.
[2] G.Ehrlich and F.G.Hudda, J. Chem. Phys. 44 (1966) 1050.
[3] G.Ehrlich and C.F.Kirk, J. Chem. Phys. 48 (1968) 1465.
[4] M.Drechsler, Z.Elektrochem. 58 (1954) 327.
[5] E.W.Plummer and T.N.Rhodin, J. Chem. Phys. 49 (1968) 3479.
[6] L.Pauling, Phys. Rev. 54 (1938) 899.
[7] E.W.Müller, J.A.Panitz and S.B.McLane, Rev. Sci. Instr. 39 (1968) 83.
[8] E.W.Müller, in: Advances in Electronics and Electron Physics, Vol. 13 (Academic Press, New York, 1960) p. 83.
[9] E.W.Müller, in: Vacancies and Interstitials in Metals, eds. A.Seeger, D.Schumacher, W.Schilling and J.Diehl (North-Holland, Amsterdam, 1969).
[10] E.W.Müller, Z. Physik. 156 (1959) 399.
[11] C.A.Speicher, W.T.Pimbley, M.J.Attardo, G.M.Galligan and S.S.Brenner, Phys. Letters 23 (1966) 194.
[12] M.A.Forbes and B.Ralph, Phil. Mag. 14 (1966) 189.
[13] U.H.Chun and E.W.Müller, to be published.
[14] E.W.Müller, Science 149 (1965) 591.
[15] O.Nishikawa and E.W.Müller, Surface Sci. 12 (1968) 247.
[16] E.W.Müller, S.B.McLane and J.A.Panitz, Surface Sci. 17 (1969) 430.
[17] M.J.Attardo and G.M.Galligan, Phys. Stat. Sol. 16 (1966) 449.
[18] E.W.Müller, in: Proc. Fourth Intern. Symp. on the Reactivity of Solids, eds. J.H. de Boer et al. (Elsevier Publishing Co., Amsterdam, 1960) p. 682.
[19] M.K.Sinha and E.W.Müller, J. Appl. Phys. 35 (1964) 1256.
[20] P.Petroff and J.Washburn, Intern. Conf. on Vacancies and Interstitials in Metals, Kernforschungsanlage Jülich, Germany, Sept. 1968, Vol. II, 485.
[21] S.Nakamura and E.W.Müller, J. Appl. Phys. 36 (1965) 3634.
[22] S.Ranganathan, J. Appl. Phys. 37 (1966) 4346; also in Field Ion Microscopy, eds. J.J.Hren and S.Ranganathan (Plenum Press, New York, 1968).
[23] R.C.Sanwald, S.Ranganathan and J.J.Hren, Appl. Phys. Letters 9 (1966) 393.
[24] G.Thomas, Transmission Electron Microscopy of Metals (John Wiley and Sons, New York, 1962).
[25] H.F.Ryan and J.Suiter, J. Less Common Metals 9 (1965) 258.
[26] E.W.Müller, in: Proc. Fourth Intern. Conf. Electron Micrsocopy, Berlin, 1958, Vol. 1 (Springer, Berlin, 1960) p. 820.
[27] O.Nishikawa and E.W.Müller, J. Appl. Phys. 38 (1967) 3159.
[28] D.G.Brandon and B.Ralph, Phil. Mag. 8 (1963) 919.
[29] S.Amelinckx and W.Dekeyser, Solid State Physics 8 (1959) 325.
[30] K.D.Rendulic and E.W.Müller, J. Appl. Phys. 37 (1966) 2593.
[31] J.J.Hren, Acta Met. 13 (1965) 479.
[32] D.G.Brandon, B.Ralph, S.Ranganathan and M.Wald, Acta Met. 12 (1969) 813.
[33] S.Ranganathan, Acta Cryst. 21 (1966) 197.
[34] E.W.Müller and T.T.Tsong, Field Ion Microscopy, Principles and Applications (American Elsevier, New York, 1969).
[35] H.N.Southworth and B.Ralph, Phil. Mag. 14 (1966) 383.
[36] T.T.Tsong and E.W.Müller, Appl. Phys. Letters 9 (1966) 7; J. Appl. Phys. 38 (1967) 545, 3531.

[37] M.J.Attardo and J.M.Galligan, Phys. Rev. 161 (1967) 558.

[38] K.M.Bowkett, L.T.Chadderton, H.Norden and B.Ralph, Phil. Mag. 15 (1967) 415.

[39] E.W.Müller and O.Nishikawa, in: Adhesion and Cold Welding of Materials in Space Environment, STP No. 431, ASTM (1968) p. 67.

[40] O.Nishikawa and E.W.Müller, IEEE-Transactions PMP-5 (1969) 38.

[41] E.W.Müller, S.B.McLane and O.Nishikawa, 6th Int. Congr. Electron Microscopy, Kyoto, Japan, Vol. 1 (1966) 235.

[42] E.W.Müller and J.A.Panitz, 14th Field Emission Symposium, National Bureau of Standards, Washington, D.C., June 1967.

[43] E.W.Müller, J.A.Panitz and S.B.McLane, Rev. Sci. Instr. 39 (1968) 83.

[44] J.A.Panitz, S.B.McLane and E.W.Müller, Rev. Sci. Instr. 40 (1969) 1321.

[45] S.S.Brenner and J.T.McKinney, Appl. Phys. Letters 13 (1968) 29.

[46] M.J.Southon and P.J.Turner, private communication.

[47] T.T.Tsong, Surface Sci. 10 (1968) 102.

[48] D.F.Barofsky and E.W.Müller, J. of Mass Spectrometry and Ion Physics 2 (1969) 125.

[49] E.W.Müller, Centenary Lecture, Chem. Soc. London, Quarterly Reviews 23 No. 2 (1969) 177.

[50] E.W.Müller, S.B.McLane and J.A.Panitz, Surface Sci. 17 (1969) 430.

SUBJECT INDEX